Working in Memphis: The Production of Faience At Roman Period Kom Helul

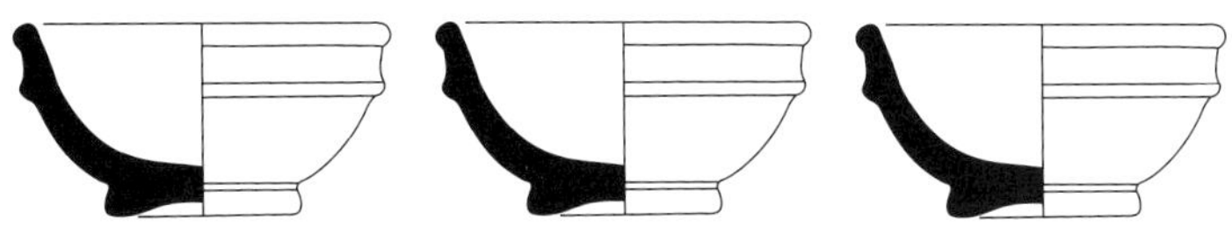

Paul T. Nicholson

With Contributions by
Peter French, Rowena Hart, Panagiota Manti,
Marie-Dominique Nenna, Hendrikje Nouwens and Ross Thomas

Illustrations by
Tessa Baber, Alexandra Blakemore, Ian Dennis, Kirsty Harding, Joanne Hodges, Anne Jenner,
Howard Mason, Emily Stewart, Frances Taylor and Laura Woodham

Photographs by
Janice Coyle, Paul T. Nicholson and Anna Stagg

Film by
Gerald Mee

Excavation Memoir 105
Egypt Exploration Society
2013

ISBN 978-0-85698-210-1

SOLD AT THE OFFICES OF THE EGYPT EXPLORATION SOCIETY
3 Doughty Mews, London WC1N 2PG

A catalogue entry for this book is available from the British Library

ISBN 978-0-85698-210-1

Front Cover: Saggar IM-144 with faience vessel fragment F-96. Background view of the Memphis ruin field looking East from the E.E.S. Workroom.
Rear Cover: Faience head of Serapis F-1616

Set in Adobe InDesign CS4 by Ian Dennis and Kirsty Harding (Cardiff University)

Printed in Great Britain by Short Run Press Ltd., Exeter.

For My Mother
Doris Nicholson

Contents

Section I

Section II

List of maps, figures, plates and tables

List of Maps

List of Figures

List of Plates

3.8 The blocked access opening [235] in the west wall of the kiln looking east from the access pit. The blocking [330] comprises the bases of broken Type 12 saggars.

3.9 Photo-composite of the kiln and its access pit. The step down into the pit is at far left, the blocked kiln entrance at centre and the southern retaining wall at right.

3.10 Trench HAC3 looking east down the slope of saggar fragments [244] onto the kiln [040]. The deposit has not been fully excavated.

3.11 Trench HAC3 looking south over slag deposit [239] and saggars [214].

3.12 Trench HAC3 looking south. The wings either side of the stoke-hole are visible at bottom right and mid-right.

3.13 Trench HAC3 looking north over the southern wing of the stoke-hole. The arrow indicates the position of deposit [186] which yielded a mid-late 4th Century B.C. coin. The wall to the right of the arrow is thought to predate the kiln.

3.14 The lowest part of the interior of the kiln looking west. The thick deposit of slag [208] can be seen running to within c.0.5m of the opening [235] which was still closed by the saggar bases at this time. The wood is part of the safety shoring installed within the structure.

3.15 Trench HAD1 looking south. The trench [030] [031] running approximately north-south and visible above the blackboard is believed to be from Petrie's work at the site. The burned brick platform of the building is clearly visible.

3.16 Trench HAD2 looking south. Damage caused by the construction of *zeriba* enclosures is apparent.

3.17 Trench HAD3 looking south.

4.1 The kiln excavated by Petrie in 1908. It is thought that this shows the interior of the structure and is only partially excavated. No scale or orientation are given.

4.2 The lowermost opening of the kiln at HAC3 blocked by re-used saggar bases which have been cemented into place with mud. This access opening was probably partly blocked during firings and so served as a vent. After the kiln had cooled it would be fully opened so that ash and slag could be removed. The lowermost vent is visible above the blocked opening.

4.3 Looking north over the kiln at HAC3 during excavation. The projections on the north wall are clearly visible above the head and to the right of supervisor R. Hart.

4.4 Reconstruction of the chequer used in the HAC3 kiln showing how the actual kiln tower may have been somewhat larger than the preserved footprint of the structure. Top row: the kiln ground plan as excavated with a simple chequer added. Middle row: the chequer expanded beyond the limit of the brickwork. Bottom row: showing (L) part of the tower wall added and (R) one row of three saggars inside it.

4.5 A pottery kiln at Fustat, Cairo. The lower of the two domed structures is covering the pit in which both firing and cleaning out take place, the uppermost is the tower structure into which the stacked vessels are placed for firing. Photographed in 1998 at the workshop of Ahmed Abu Hassan.

4.6 A pottery kiln at Fustat, Cairo (the same one as in Plate 4.5) showing the domed tower structure into which the pots are placed for firing, via the entrance door. No saggars are used in this industry. Photographed in 1998 at the workshop of Ahmed Abu Hassan.

4.7 Looking into the HAC3 kiln showing part of the extensive slag unit [208] which adhered to the walls of the kiln. The timbers at left and right are part of the suspended shoring placed in the kiln to allow it to be excavated in safety.

4.8 A piece of the slag (V-21) from the HAC3 kiln preserving the impressions of halfa grass. Between the impressions small drips of vitreous slag are visible, emphasising how fluid it was in firing.

4.9 (A) Slag (V-22) preserving the impression of woven matting. (B) Detail of the weave.

4.10 Detail of the fibrous texture left by the silica skeletons of halfa grass in the slag (V-31).

5.1 The saggar maker's workshop at the Gladstone Pottery Museum, Stoke-on-Trent (formerly the Gladstone Pottery). In the background is the saggar maker's bench, a metal frame runs around the back and sides of it. In this exhibit a saggar drum and two finished saggars stand within the frame. A circular frame used for making saggar bases leans against the leg of the bench. The wheelie is in the foreground and has the perforated metal plate (shord) used to lift saggars, on top of it. A completed saggar stands on the plate.

5.2 Mr. Fred Boulton using the 'grafter' to flatten down individual strips of side-marl into the frame. It would then be beaten using the mau'. Photographed at the Burgess and Leigh factory, Middleport 1964.

5.3 Mr. Fred Boulton using the wooden mau' to flatten bottom-marl into a circular metal frame used for making the saggar base. The mau' is also used to flatten side-marl. Photographed at the Burgess and Leigh factory, Middleport 1964.

5.4 Mr. Fred Boulton using a wooden straight edge – 'rule' – and blade to cut strips of side-marl to the appropriate width ready to be rolled onto a wooden drum. Photographed at the Burgess and Leigh factory, Middleport 1964.

5.5 Mr. Fred Boulton rolling a strip of side-marl onto a wooden drum. Photographed at the Burgess and Leigh factory, Middleport 1964.

5.6 Mr. Fred Boulton has placed the drum covered in side-marl onto a ready knocked bottom on the wheelie. The hand-hole in the top of the drum is clearly visible. Photographed at the Burgess and Leigh factory, Middleport 1964.

5.7 Mr. Fred Boulton using a topping stick to finish the rim of the saggar. The vessel is still on the wheelie. Photographed at the Burgess and Leigh factory, Middleport 1964.

List of Tables

Colour Plates (Following index)

ACKNOWLEDGEMENTS

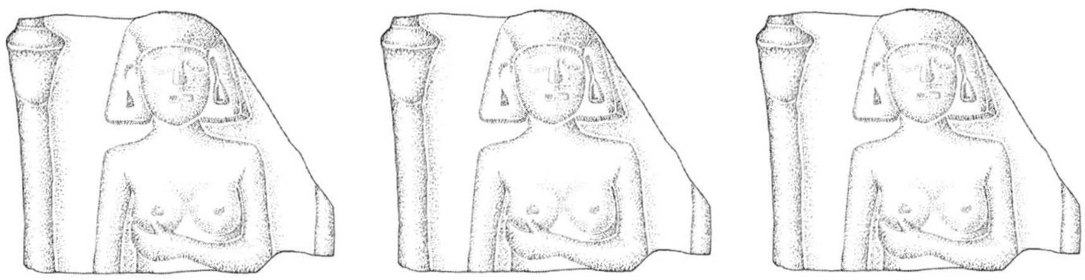

The Memphis Faience Project has been made possible thanks to the generous collaboration of our colleagues in the Egyptian *Supreme Council for Antiquities*, and I am grateful to the Permanent Committee of that body for their continued support of the work. The inspectors provided by the S.C.A. have been helpful to us throughout the project and their contributions are individually acknowledged below.

The excavation and study of the material has been carried out with the co-operation of the *Egypt Exploration Society*, and in particular Dr. David Jeffreys who has worked for the Society at Memphis for many years. I am grateful to him for suggesting that the Memphis project be co-directed, with the Kom Helul work being conducted by me and the survey and excavation of the Saqqara escarpment by him. This arrangement also allowed me to use the Saqqara house, made available to the E.E.S. through the generosity of the S.C.A.

The staff at the Saqqara house, Gabr el-Khourougi, Ali Hussein and Youssef Gabriel became legendary for their length of service to the E.E.S. and each new generation of scholars came to rely on their services, and tribute must be paid to them here. They were the last link between the current projects and those run by Professor W.B. Emery (1903-1971) on behalf of the Society. Sadly, Youssef died just before the scheduled retirement of the staff in summer 2007, and Gabr shortly afterwards. They are much missed. Whilst the archaeology itself is enough to bring scholars to Memphis and Saqqara year after year, the contribution of the staff at the Saqqara house surely had its part to play, and the tradition of Gabr, Ali and Youssef is continued by their successors, relatives of Ali Hussein.

Salah Hassibullah has acted as the representative of the mission in many matters relating to the daily running of the excavation, and I am indebted to him for his help and patience in dealing with financial matters, and my sometimes faltering Arabic. Our transport to and from Mit Rahina has, as ever, been provided by Demerdash whose friendly and efficient work has come to be relied upon by all of us.

Dr. Rawya Ismail and Faten Abd el-Halim Saleh acted as the *Egypt Exploration Society*'s representatives in Cairo during the duration of the project, and I am indebted to both of them for the courtesy and efficiency in submitting applications to work to the S.C.A. and relaying information on the progress of these to me at regular intervals.

The project would not have been possible without the generous support of the *British Academy* (grants listed below), *Wainwright Fund*, *Seven Pillars of Wisdom Trust* and *Thames Valley Ancient Egypt Society* all of whom provided funding for the excavation.

I am grateful to all those local people who took part in the excavation over the years, they have been a pleasure to work with and our debt to them is evident in the following pages. The excavation supervisors are acknowledged below, but special mention must be made of several individuals who have contributed to the project over most or all of its duration. Ms. Rowena Hart supervised Trench HAC3 from its beginning and also conducted the geophysical survey which was responsible for the positioning of the trench. She further acted as research assistant on a *Leverhulme* funded project dealing with the work carried out by Petrie at Amarna and Memphis and relating his work to the new excavation. During this time she prepared many of the site plans as well as writing the database for the project. My indebtedness to her work will be obvious.

Hendrikje Nouwens acted as finds registrar throughout the whole project. This has been no mean feat, and without her organisation and efficiency the task would have been a very great deal more difficult. She has also undertaken numerous other tasks on behalf of the project and been involved in many aspects of its day to day running and has acted as assistant-director on several occasions. Amongst these other tasks has been regular assistance with the collating and organising of materials ready for publication, and the cross-checking of databases. Her long term involvement in the project has been a great asset.

Finally, Peter French and Janine Bourriau were kind enough to take on the enormous task of processing the domestic pottery from the site, and did so on top of their other commitments. It has been a great pleasure to work with them again, not least since I began my work at Memphis as an assistant to Janine in 1985.

To all those who have taken part in the project for a season or for part of a season, I am also indebted. Without their contributions the work would not have been possible and life at the Saqqara house would have been less enjoyable.

2000 Excavation.
August 27th – October 3rd, 2000.
Inspector: Mr. Zaky Awad
Dr. Sally-Ann Ashton (Pottery)
Ms. Amy Goldsmith (Supervisor)
Ms. Joanne Hodges (Illustrator)
Mr. Andrew Holbrook (Conservator)
Ms. Hendrikje Nouwens (Registrar)
Dr. Paul T. Nicholson (Director)
Funding: *British Academy* (Grant SG-30317), *Seven Pillars of Wisdom Trust*, *Thames Valley Ancient Egypt Society*

2001 Excavation.
August 10th – September 22nd, 2001.
Inspector: Mr. Zaky Awad
Ms. Janine Bourriau (Pottery)
Mr. Peter French (Pottery)
Ms. Jennifer Harden (Finds Assistant)
Ms. Rowena Hart (Geophysical Survey and Site Supervisor)
Ms. Joanne Hodges (Illustrator)
Dr. Paul T. Nicholson (Director)
Ms. Hendrikje Nouwens (Registrar)
Ms. Katinka Stentoft (Site Supervisor)
Ms. Leslie Weber (Conservator)
Funding: *British Academy* (Grant SG-31928), *Wainwright Fund, Thames Valley Ancient Egypt Society*

2002 Excavation.
August 8th – September 16th, 2002.
Inspector: Mr. Mohammed Mohammed Youssef
Mr. Thomas Brindle (Assistant Site Supervisor)
Mr. Peter French (Pottery Specialist)
Ms. Rowena Hart (Site Supervisor)
Ms. Joanne Hodges (Illustrator)
Ms. Cara Jones (Site Assistant)
Dr. Marie-Dominique Nenna (Faience)
Dr. Paul T. Nicholson (Director)
Ms. Hendrikje Nouwens (Registrar)
Anna Stagg (Photographer)
Ms. Nicole Stahl (Conservator)
Funding: *British Academy* (Grant: SG-34156), *Seven Pillars of Wisdom Trust, Wainwright Fund*

2005 Excavation.
August 9th – September 19th, 2009.
Inspector: Mr. Mostafa Hassan Abdel Rahman.
Ms. Alexandra Blakemore (Illustrator)
Ms. Janine Bourriau (Pottery)
Ms. Janice Coyle (Photographer)
Mr. Peter French (Pottery)
Ms. Rowena Hart (Site Supervisor)
Ms. Cara Jones (Assistant Site Supervisor)
Dr. Paul T. Nicholson (Director)
Ms. Hendrikje Nouwens (Registrar)
Ms. Konstantina Tsatsouli (Conservator)
Funding: Year 1 of *British Academy* Larger Research Grant (LRG-39343)

2006 Study Season.
July 22nd – August 31st, 2006.
Inspector: Mr. Abd El-Hamid Mohammed Mahmoud
Ms. Janine Bourriau (Pottery)
Mr. Peter French (Pottery)
Ms. Anne Jenner (Illustrator)
Dr. Marie-Dominique Nenna (Faience)
Dr. Paul T. Nicholson (Director)
Ms. Hendrikje Nouwens (Registrar)
Ms. Frances Taylor (Illustrator)
Funding: Year 2 of *British Academy* Larger Research Grant (LRG-39343)

2007 Study Season.
July 27th – September 8th, 2007.
Inspector: Mr. Shaaban Ahmed Mohamed
Ms. Janine Bourriau (Pottery)
Mr. Peter French (Pottery)
Dr. Salima Ikram (Faunal Remains)
Dr. Paul T. Nicholson (Director)
Ms. Hendrikje Nouwens (Registrar)
Ms. Laura Woodham (Illustrator)
Funding: *E.E.S.*

2008 Study Season.
September 12th – September 25th, 2008.
Inspector: Mr. Shaaban Ahmed Mohamed
Paul T. Nicholson (Director)
Ms. Hendrikje Nouwens (Registrar)
Ms. Emily Stewart (Illustrator)
Funding: Ms. Stewart was funded by grants from the *School of History and Archaeology, Cardiff University* and the *Society for Economic History*. Dr. Nicholson and Ms. Nouwens were self funded.

Beyond the excavation itself, I am grateful to a number of individuals and institutions for their help. Barabara Adams, Rosalind Janssen, Stephen Quirke and Sally MacDonald have all provided access to the collection at the Petrie

Museum, University College London. Professor Rosalie David kindly arranged similar access at the Manchester Museum. Sarah L. Hodgkinson of the Arts and Heritage Resource Centre at Rochdale Museum kindly provide access to Petrie's Memphis material and allowed me to photograph it.

For several years I was able to work at the *Metropolitan Museum of Art* in New York, and so examine at first hand many key pieces of early glass and faience. This work was facilitated by Dr. Dorothea Arnold and I am indebted to her and her colleagues, particularly Dr. Susan Allen, Dr. Marsha Hill and Dr. Christine Lilyquist, for the help and hospitality I received there. Dr. Florence Friedman of the Rhode Island School of Design generously invited me to work on her *Gifts of the Nile* project which was of great help in my study of faience.

The work on saggar making was largely conducted in Stoke-on-Trent and I am grateful to the *Stoke Sentinel* for carrying a piece on my request for information on saggar making in their issue of October 7th, 2009 and putting it on their website. Amongst those who came forward with help were Mr. Baggott, Mr. Berks, Mr. Boardman, Mr. Boulton, Mr. Glover and Mrs. Fiona Purcell to all of whom I am indebted. Mr. Gerald Mee was kind enough not only to provide me with a copy of his excellent film *Mau'ing the Saggar* (1981) but to let me hear the several hours of audio tape prepared for the sound track but not used in their entirety. Mr. Gordon Simcock generously loaned several books on the ceramic industry which have proved very useful. Mr. Boulton showed a series of pictures of his father at work which had been taken by Mr. Donald Morris. Mr. Morris kindly provided high resolution scans of some his photographs of saggar maker Fred Boulton at the *Burgess and Leigh* potbank, Middleport in 1964 and has allowed their reproduction here. I am also grateful to the Gladstone Pottery Museum for allowing me to reproduce Plate 5.1 and 5.17.

Duncan Ayscough of the Ceramics section of the Cardiff School of Art and Design kindly discussed the reconstruction of the kiln with me and was generous enough to lend me several important texts on the subject of kilns and their firing. Joe Finch, an expert on kiln design and independent potter was kind enough to discuss aspects of the functioning of the kiln.

The 4th Century B.C. coins were examined by Dr. Andrew Meadows, Curator of Greek coins at the British Museum and I am indebted to him for his assistance. Dr. Donald Bailey kindly commented on the pottery lamps from the excavation. Dr. Ross Thomas of the British Museum provided many of the parallels for the figurines section of the catalogue and co-authored the text for that section of the book. Dr. Virginia Webb made helpful suggestions regarding some of the amulets and their moulds.

I am indebted to all those who have authored or co-authored chapters for this volume or provided appendices for it. I am particularly grateful to Dr. Marie-Dominique Nenna for her hospitality and hard work in Lyon which permitted us to prepare Chapter 7 reconstructing faience technology.

The bulk of the writing and editing of this volume was made possible by the *School of History, Archaeology and Religion* at Cardiff who kindly granted me study leave from the end of January until the end of August 2012. I am grateful to Niall Sharples, Head of the Archaeology Section and Professor Terry Threadgold, Head of School, for granting this leave. My teaching during this period was covered by Dr. Clive Broadhurst and I am particularly grateful to him for taking on this task at short notice. Dr. Panagiota Manti was kind enough to discuss aspects of furnaces with me and to assist in the identification of furnace related materials. She also commented on several sections of the text.

The typesetting and page layout for the book along with numerous other tasks relating to the illustrations was carried out by Kirsty Harding and Ian Dennis of the *School of History, Archaeology and Religion* at Cardiff and I am indebted to them for their hard work and good humour. Some of the post-excavation drawings were made and digitized for publication by Tessa Baber who also assisted with identifying images for the catalogue.

The staff of the Arts and Social Studies Library, in particular Helen D'Artillac Brill, have been of great help in obtaining Inter-library-loan requests for me. For references to relevant publications I am indebted to Dr. Roberta Tomber, Professor W.H. Manning, Professor Michael Mackensen, Dr. Robert Morkot, Professor Dominic Rathbone, Dr. Nicholas Reeves and Professor Nick Syred.

I must express my gratitude to my partner Ms. Cerian Whitehurst for dealing with numerous telephone queries from the field, and for preparing spreadsheets for the expedition accounts as well as making amendments to aspects of the finds database. She has made it possible to export the data from Microsoft Access® into Microsoft Word® with the minimum of reformatting. Her help in the U.K. has been invaluable. The academic and copy editing was kindly undertaken by Dr. Ian Shaw to whom I am grateful for his patience and helpful comments.

This book is dedicated to my mother with thanks for all her help and support over many years.

Section I

Kom Helul and its Kilns

Chapter I

Kom Helul, Memphis, its Archaeological Context and Early Work

P.T. Nicholson

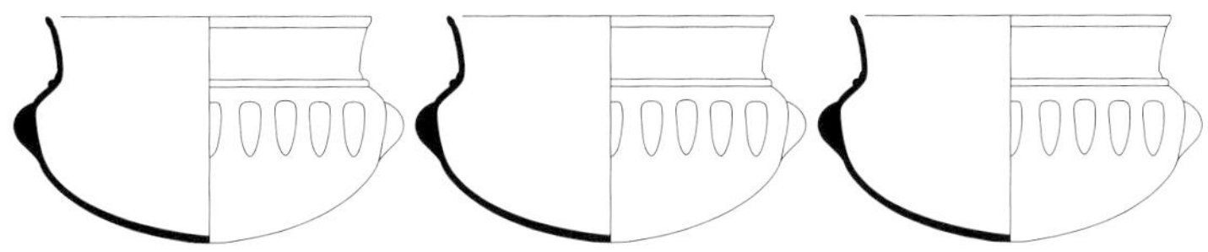

Introduction

For over a century accounts of the making of faience in Ptolemaic and Roman Egypt have been based on work undertaken by W.M. Flinders Petrie (1853-1942) during two seasons of excavation at Kom Helul, Memphis in 1908 and 1910 (Petrie 1909a, 1911a). Petrie was pioneering in his attitude toward the study of the small objects of daily life which were often overlooked by his contemporaries. Perhaps even more significant was his attitude toward recreating the technologies used to produce these common items. His work at the faience production site of Kom Helul and at the faience and glass workshops of Tell el-Amarna (Petrie 1894) are excellent examples of his approach.

The Petrie approach to reconstructing industrial processes was to excavate, sometimes at several different sites at a particular location, collect together all those pieces of industrial debris which seemed to offer clues to the process under investigation and to arrange them into a logical order. The order was often influenced by his knowledge of industrial processes of his own day or by his reading of early treatises on the crafts concerned. From the perspective of the early 21st Century his approach has several flaws. Frequently Petrie did not record the locations of the individual sites within the location at which he worked (Amarna and Kom Helul are examples of this) nor which finds came from which of these sites. As a result, material from a range of locations was studied together on the assumption that it was all contemporary, or nearly so, and that it all belonged to the same industrial process.

With hindsight we now know that Egyptian craftsmen often worked in close proximity and that the detritus of their, sometimes related, industries became mixed. Similarly, that an industry might be located in the same general area over several generations, so that the debris collected might reflect technological changes over time rather than be part of a linear process. This is not to decry Petrie's work. Were his accounts fanciful or ridiculous they would long ago have been discarded. In fact, the problem from a contemporary perspective is that they are carefully put together and offer plausible accounts of the making of the items he studied. It is this plausibility combined with (until recently) a general lack of interest in Egyptian crafts and industries which has ensured that Petrie's accounts have stood for so long.

Like most archaeologists and Egyptologists the writer has a great respect for Petrie's work, and it is that work which has inspired the research reported on here. Since the early 20th Century a great deal more excavation, typology and laboratory analysis of Egyptian vitreous materials has taken place and this has raised questions over some of Petrie's interpretations. Recent work has demonstrated that whilst he was correct in his view that by the time of Pharaoh Akhenaten (1352-1336 B.C.) the Egyptians could make glass from its raw materials, many of the details of his reconstruction are erroneous (Nicholson 2007). Petrie's views on the making of glass, and of faience, at Amarna were in part influenced by a preliminary visit to Memphis and the writer was interested to examine the industrial evidence at both sites.

At Kom Helul, Memphis, Petrie excavated a number of kilns for faience production. However, his reconstruction of them as semi-subterranean towers on whose base stood piles of cylindrical pottery containers (saggars) holding the faience seemed questionable. The lack of any perforated floor would mean that the fuel, which he believed was straw, would have to be thrown between them – a difficult operation which would leave the saggars part-buried in ash at the end of each firing.

The work reported on here draws on Petrie's published works, collections of material from Kom Helul, particularly those held at the Petrie Museum, University College London, and on field and laboratory studies which have taken place in the century or so since his reports were published. This information has been used to help to inform the excavation of a kiln site at Kom Helul and a number of associated trenches.

The approach taken in interpreting the material has similarities with that taken by Petrie in that the range of material is studied in order to reconstruct the steps in the production process. The difference is that the material from the new work is closely provenanced and can draw on more refined typologies for the faience (e.g. Nenna and Seif el-Din 2000) and pottery (Appendix 2) as well as on numerous laboratory studies (e.g. Kaczmarczyk and Hedges 1983, Tite and Shortland 2008). This combination has allowed the writer and his colleagues to develop what would now be thought of as Petrie's 'forensic' approach and in so doing resolve some of the questions raised by his work.

The following chapters attempt to present the evidence for a reconstruction of the kiln excavated, for the making and use of saggars and kiln furniture and of the faience found at the site, before attempting to give a general overview of the stages of the faience production process, now generally termed the *châine opératoire* (Lemmonier 1993). The text moves from the particular and detailed to the general and in so doing offers a significantly different picture of faience production at ancient Memphis than that provided by Petrie over a century ago.

Kom Helul

The site of Kom Helul (Plate 1.1) lies at the southern end of the Memphis ruin field, where it adjoins Kom Qala'a immediately to its north (Jeffreys 1985: 19 and Maps 4 and 7). Petrie's map (1909a: Pl.I, here Map 1.1) shows an area identified as Kom Qalama lying between Kom Helul[1] and Kom Qala'a, but this name now seems to have been subsumed within Kom Qala'a. It is approximately 600 metres to the south-east of the present Memphis Museum Garden. Kom Helul is centred around N.29° 50' 38, E.31° 15' 25 (Map 1.2).

A small settlement of sedentary Bedouin has been established at Kom Helul, and is today known as Ezbet al-'Arab (Jeffreys 1985: 19). This village begins at the

Plate 1.1 View of Kom Helul looking south over the mounds. The mounds conceal the remains of the kilns and are comprised, in part, of kiln debris. (Photo: P.T. Nicholson).

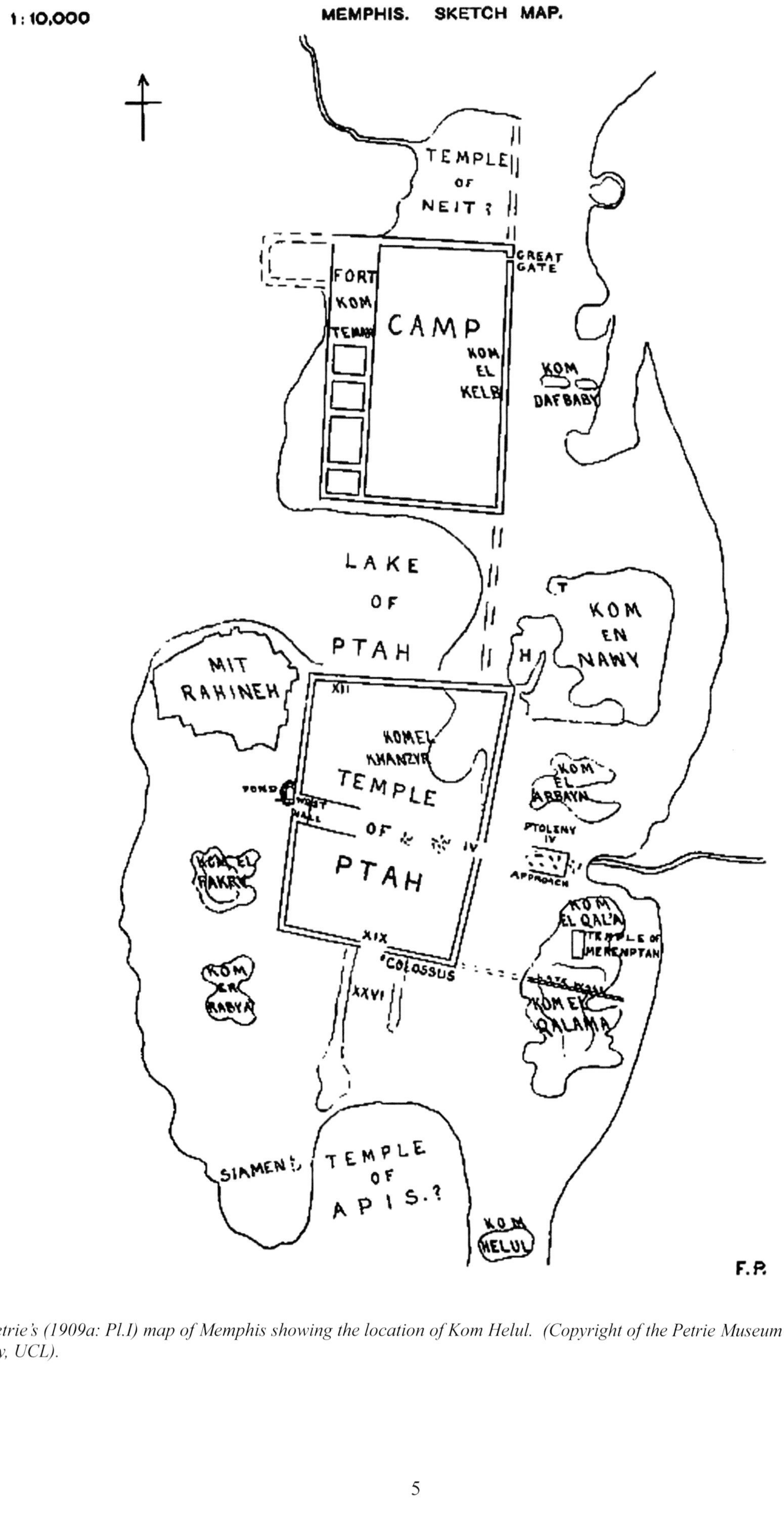

Map 1.1 Petrie's (1909a: Pl.I) map of Memphis showing the location of Kom Helul. (Copyright of the Petrie Museum of Egyptian Archaeology, UCL).

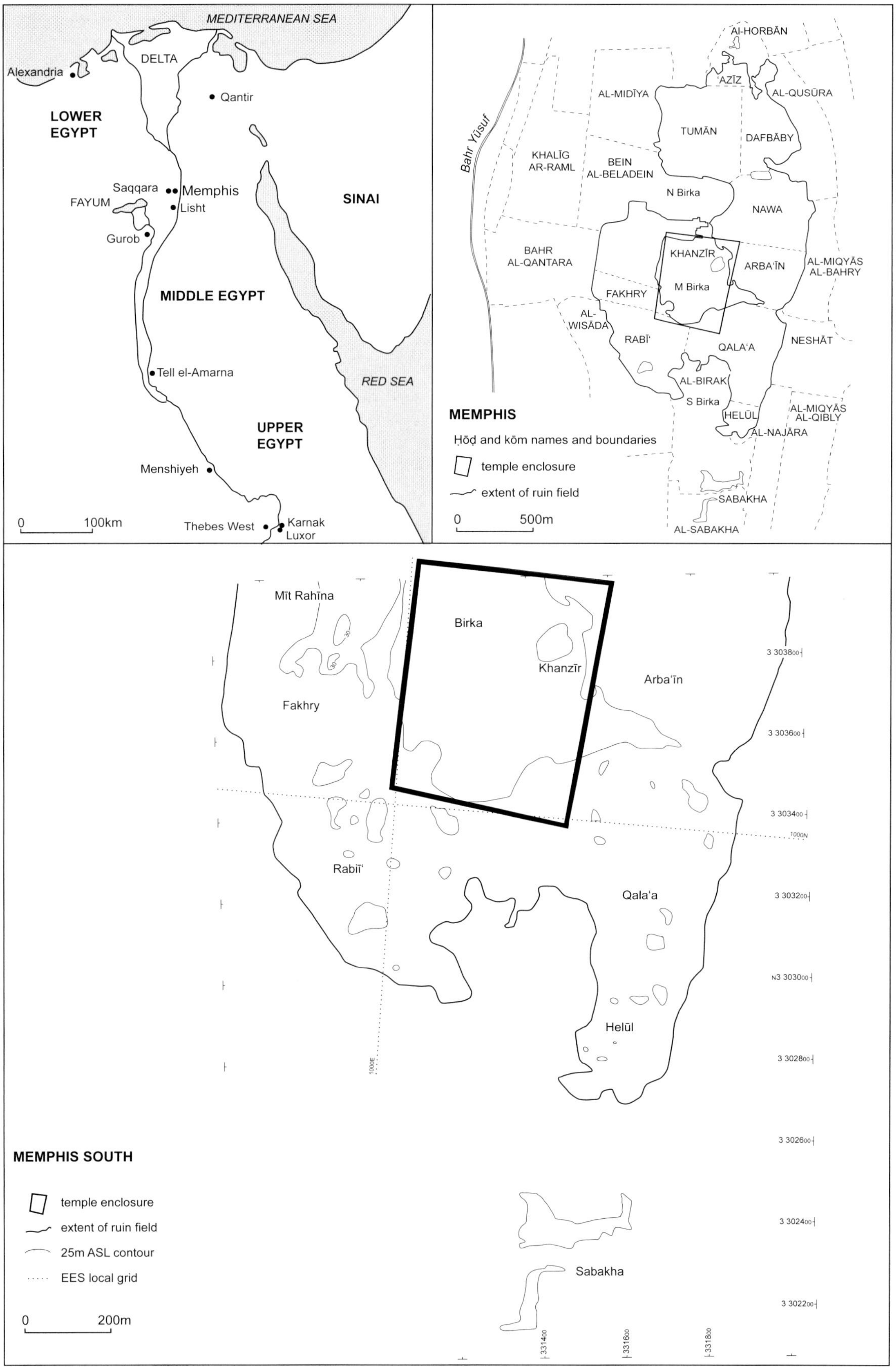

Map 1.2 Map showing the location of Memphis (inset top left) and the location of Kom Helul at the southern end of the Memphis ruin field. (Adapted from Jeffreys 1985 maps 4 and 7).

southern boundary of the former military camp which encompasses Kom Qala'a and extends almost as far north as the University of Pennsylvania Expedition House, which is now used for storage and as offices by the S.C.A. Ezbet al'Arab is a settlement of recent times, and was not present when Petrie first investigated the area in the 1880s. Petrie's own excavation house, dating from January 1908,[2] is believed to be the mudbrick building which abuts the Museum Garden enclosure on its south-eastern corner. The present workroom of the E.E.S. Memphis Project is located a few metres to the east of this, abutting the south-western corner of the Pennsylvania house.

Apart from the abandoned military camp on its northern edge and the village of Ezbet al-'Arab, Kom Helul probably looks today much as it did in Petrie's time, a series of low mounds and hollows covered with hardy grasses and camel thorn (Plate 1.1). Probably as a result of the establishment of the village it has been used as a dumping ground for rubbish, but not to any great extent. Metal items had to be cleared in advance of the geophysical survey (Appendix 1) but the volume of rubbish otherwise posed no problems.

Research History

The site of Kom Helul is first recorded as El-goum haloul on Mariette's map (Mariette 1882,[3] see also Jeffreys 1985: 19 and 2010: 186 fig. 42)[4] and features under its more familiar name on Petrie's Plate I of *Memphis I* (Petrie 1909a: Plate 1, see Map 1.1 here). That it was always a forgotten corner of the ruin field, as it still remains, is indicated by Petrie's statement (1911a: 34) that no roadways were found in the area of his excavations and that as a result he felt it unnecessary to give a detailed plan (below).

Despite its apparent lowly status the site was to play an important role in the history of technological research in Egypt, not only in terms of the manufacture of faience at Memphis but also at Tell el-Amarna.

Petrie and the 'Plunderer'

Petrie seems to have first visited the site of Kom Helul in around 1886. This date is based on his statement that "About twenty-five years ago, while examining the mounds of Memphis, I noticed the site of the kilns for glazed pottery by Kom Helul, at the south end of the ruins" (Petrie 1911a: 34).[5] At that time he did not have permission to excavate at Memphis, possibly because of his poor relationship with Eugene Grébaut (1846-1915), the then head of the *Egyptian Antiquities Service*, and so his interest had to be confined to examining surface finds. These evidently made such an impression on him that "So soon as Memphis was in my hands I began excavation there..." (Petrie 1911a: 34).

What Petrie appears to have seen were the remains of what he describes as "blue glazed pottery" (1909a: 14), by which he means faience of the Ptolemaic and/or Roman periods. Along with these were the remains of the cylindrical pottery vessels in which the faience was fired. These vessels, which are here referred to as 'saggars', were sometimes glazed on their interior. On the basis of these finds Petrie formed the view that faience was glazed by first making the object and then applying a glaze to it, and that the glazed objects were then fired in saggars. This view was to have a profound influence on his interpretation of the finds he made at Amarna (Petrie 1894; Nicholson 2007).

However, Petrie's first visit to Kom Helul unintentionally led to the site being damaged in the period between 1886 and his return, to carry out excavations, in 1908. In *Historical Studies I* he says that he had mentioned his discovery of the faience factory mounds "to a friend; and that unhappily resulted in the site being plundered by another person who had no interest in the technical questions to be studied, and who merely looked for specimens which have not yet been published" (Petrie 1911a: 34).

The identity of Petrie's friend and of the plunderer, effectively the first person to 'excavate' at the site, has long been a mystery. There appear to be no published records of excavations at Kom Helul in the period, but it has recently been possible to throw some light on the matter and the individuals concerned.

Dr. Nicholas Reeves, formerly of the Myers Museum at Eton College, kindly drew my attention to the fact that some of the Roman period faience vessels in the collection had been acquired by Captain William Joseph Myers (1858-1899) around the time of the desecration of the site, and suggested that Myers might be a candidate for Petrie's "plunderer."[6]

Myers served as an officer in the British Army until his death during the Boer War in October 1899. During his service he fought in the Zulu Wars and was part of the Nile expedition stationed in Egypt from 1882 to 1887 (Dawson, Uphill and Bierbrier 1995: 305; Spurr 1999). During this time he formed a significant collection of antiquities, and it was during this same period that the site at Kom Helul seems to have been looted.

Through Dr. Reeves I was able to obtain copies of Myers' diaries, and it seems that in April 1896 he purchased several faience items from Giovanni Dattari (d.1923) (Dawson, Uphill and Bierbrier 1995: 116), a Cairo dealer. He afterwards showed these pieces to "the Brugschs" - Émile Brugsch (1842-1930) and his family - whom Myers had met several times on visits to Egypt. Brugsch was at this time Keeper of the Cairo Museums (Dawson, Uphill and Bierbrier 1995: 66) and seems to have been a friend and advisor to Myers in making his collection. Nothing in the diaries suggests that Brugsch saw anything untoward in the pieces of faience purchased and one must assume they were believed to have been legitimately acquired.

These pieces cannot, of course, be linked with certainty to Kom Helul, but some of the vessels[7] (Plate 1.2) have pooled glaze on the interior, suggesting that they were rejects. Amongst the other pieces in the Eton collection are fine two handled vases, one of which bears an exhibition date of 1897 (Plates 1.3 and 1.4) as well as featuring in the Exhibition Catalogue of the *Burlington Fine Arts Club* two years earlier (Burlington Fine Arts Club 1895). This certainly suggests that in the period 1894 -1897, during which he made three trips to Egypt (Spurr 1999: 3), Myers was actively collecting faience, as well as other antiquities. The fact that his collection included pieces which seem to be wasters, as well as finer pieces, may indicate that they came from different sources, the more complete fine examples perhaps having come from tombs. It is possible that the person supplying the pieces had mixed the complete examples with wasters from Kom Helul, where he perhaps had permission to dig, in order to give them a false provenance. It is even possible that some of these fine pieces were recovered from Kom Helul, if that is indeed the source of Myers' faience. It should be noted however, that Petrie (1911a: 36) claims that "at Kom Helul..the wasters are all of the coarser wares" and that the fine piece he illustrates (1911a: Pl. XIII) is reconstructed from other Memphite fragments. However, Nenna (Chapter 6) notes that while her decorated vessel type T19.3 may not have been made in the area of the most recent excavations at Memphis, it is likely to be a Memphite product and this is the form of one of Myers' pieces now in the Eton collection.[8]

The dates of Myers' visits to Egypt and the record in his diary of a faience purchase in 1896 (there may well have been others), as well as the inclusion of wasters of a type known from Kom Helul in the Eton collection all point to Myers' connection to the site. One wonders if he might be the friend to whom Petrie mentioned the site and who then inadvertently gave the information to someone who damaged it – and perhaps who subsequently sold pieces to him. It is unlikely that Myers himself was responsible for the looting, but Dattari or one of his contacts might have been. That Petrie does not mention Myers by name might have been out of respect for him, his having been killed at the Battle of Ladysmith on October 30th 1899, less than a decade before Petrie began his work at the site.

Petrie's Excavations at Kom Helul

In 1908 Petrie returned to Memphis, this time with permission to excavate. The expedition began in January of that year[9] with excavation being undertaken from the end of that month and lasting till the first week of May[10] (Petrie 1909b: 1). The workmen were directed by G.A. Wainwright[11] (1879-1964) and a single kiln was unearthed. After falling from use this had subsequently been used as a dump for wasters from other kilns; this Petrie "carefully verified, by working for some time myself, that the wasters had been moved out from the kiln where they were baked" (Petrie 1909a: 14). The exact process by which this verification was achieved is not made clear. No plan of the kiln was produced, but a photograph was taken and reproduced as Plate XLIX of *Memphis I* (Petrie 1909a; here Plate 4.1). The view is reproduced without a scale, and is said to show the interior of the kiln. The accompanying report is very brief and no plan of the kiln is given, nor its relationship to other features of the site.

In February 1910[12] Petrie returned to Memphis. This year he was accompanied by J.P. Bushe-Fox[13] (1880-1954,

Plate 1.2 Vessel ECM586 from the collection acquired by Captain William Joseph Myers (1858-1899). It is likely that this and other vessels in the collection came from the looting of the Kom Helul site by a third party. Pooled glaze is visible on the interior. (Photo: P.T. Nicholson. Reproduced courtesy of the Myers Museum, Eton College).

Plate 1.3 Vessel ECM570 from the Myer's collection. The vessel bears a date of 1897 on the label on the base. (Photo: P.T. Nicholson. Reproduced courtesy of the Myers Museum, Eton College).

Plate 1.4 Vessel ECM570 from the Myer's collection showing the exhibition label of 1897. (Photo: P.T. Nicholson. Reproduced courtesy of the Myers Museum, Eton College).

Times 1954: 11) who was keen to work on the Roman period at Memphis. Wainwright remained at Meydum during the 1910 season (Petrie 1910: 1).

Petrie (1910: 1; 1911a: 34) states that "we cleared over the whole site of the kilns" though the work reported in the present volume shows that this was not so. Although the introduction to *Meydum and Memphis (III)* speaks of Bushe-Fox's work on the "pottery kilns" (Petrie 1910: 1), the work is not reported in that volume but in *Historical Studies I* (1911a). Apparently both volumes were completed during the Autumn of 1910 (Petrie 1931: 218) but published in succeeding years. Sadly Petrie did not think fit to include more on the kiln excavation in the 1910 volume, and Bushe-Fox seems to have written nothing on it himself.

As in the 1908 season no plan of Kom Helul was made to show the location of the kilns, and it is not completely clear how many were excavated. Petrie (1911a: 34) states that "The kilns all lie square with one another; six of them are within space of 60 to 70 feet, but as no roadways were found, it is hardly of use to give the plan here, in addition to the dimensions. The forms are all square with vertical sides." We therefore know that 6 kilns were excavated, but whether that number includes the one dug in 1908 or not is uncertain. One might reasonably suppose that it does not, since its approximate dimensions do not correspond with the more detailed ones published in 1911 (below).

It is worth noting also that Petrie carried out work at Kom Qalama (now regarded as the southern part of Kom Qala'a, within the former military camp – above). He notes that the clay cones from that site are smaller, and in his view earlier, than those from Kom Helul (Petrie 1911a: 35). This view cannot, however, be confirmed (Nicholson 2002a: 93-4, also Ashton 2003: 42). It may be from Kom Qalama that his evidence for the making of Egyptian blue is derived though this is not clearly stated in the 1911 paper and individual finds in the Petrie Museum at University College London are not marked with one or other location.[14] This may also be the site of "a factory north-east of the glazing kilns" (Petrie 1910: 44) where pottery was being manufactured.

As well as working at Kom Qalama, immediately north of Helul, Petrie also seems to have worked south of where the *Memphis Faience Project* located a kiln (HAC3 – Chapters 3 and 4). He speaks of having found "a great burnt house south of the pottery kilns" (Petrie 1910: 44). Here he found a false door of Ptolemaic date (sent to the Rochdale Museum, Plate 1.5)[15] and bronze corners and hinges etc. (Plate 1.6). The building was denuded and only the "raised basement, and the flight of stone steps for access to the house itself remained" (1910:44). It is tempting to identify this structure with the large building excavated during the first seasons (2000 and 2001) of the present project and described in Chapter 3.

The 1910 season appears to have been the last during which any archaeological excavation at Kom Helul was undertaken prior to that reported on here. In the early 1980s the area was surveyed by David Jeffreys as part of the *Egypt Exploration Society*'s *Survey of Memphis* (Jeffreys 1985) and was first shown to the writer by Dr. Jeffreys around 1986. The construction of a military camp immediately north of Kom Helul has caused some damage to Kom Qalama/ Qala'a but its extent cannot yet be judged. It is intended that a larger project can be carried out in this area in the future.

New excavation work was begun by the writer on behalf of the E.E.S. in 2000 and the project continued until 2008.

Petrie's Industrial Evidence and Reconstuction

Petrie produced no location map, plans or elevations of the kilns and published only one photograph (Petrie 1909a: Pl. XLIX, here Plate 4.1). He does, however, make valuable observations on his findings.

The first point to note is that he refers to the kilns as "pottery kilns" and the material from them as "blue glazed pottery" (1909a: 14). This designation may be significant for two reasons. Petrie was well aware of what faience looked like, he had excavated workshops for it at Amarna (Petrie 1894), though he seems always to have preferred to refer to it as "glazed ware", and this may be one of the reasons for his describing it as if it were pottery at Memphis. The other reason may be that the vessel forms of this time have much in common with clay-ceramics and some use may have been made of the potter's wheel (see Chapter 7). Recent work by Vandiver (1998: 123) has suggested that between 5 and 25% clay may have been added to the faience mixture at this time, again strengthening the link with clay ceramic production.

The kiln found in the 1908 season is said to be "six feet square and eight feet deep" (Petrie 1909a: 14). The excavation revealed no opening at the bottom, only a hole more than halfway up on the west side and about two feet wide. This, he believed, was intended to let air into the upper part of the kiln.

As well as the kiln he found cylindrical pottery vessels "10 inches wide and 7½ inches high" (1909a:14) which were the containers ("supports" in Petrie's terms) for the glazed pottery. They were of "coarse brown and yellow pottery, fusing to a dirty yellow green" (1909a: 14). Petrie is clear that they stood mouth upward, which might appear obvious, but as he goes on to say "such jars were placed mouth downwards in the time of the XVIIIth dynasty" (1909a: 14-15), a statement he bases on his work at Amarna. In fact it has now been shown that his interpretation of the Amarna evidence was mistaken on this point (Nicholson 2007: 115) and that the cylinders served a wholly different purpose there than at Memphis.

Plate 1.5, The false door stele found by Petrie at the "great burnt house" (1910: 44). Traces of burned brick are visible on areas of the face. H.56.5cm. W.36.2cm. (Courtesy of Rochdale Museum No. T11852).

Plate 1.6 Copper alloy door bolt from the "great burnt house" (Petrie 1910: 44). L:7.7cm. (Courtesy of Manchester Museum. No.4796).

Within these cylindrical vessels – saggars - the faience vessels were stacked "face down one over the other, supported apart by four cones of pottery between each. Such cones were about half an inch high in Ptolemaic times, but varied up to an inch high in Roman use" (Petrie 1909a: 15). The stacking of vessels within the saggar will be discussed more fully in Chapters 4 and 5, suffice it to say that Petrie's view seems only partially correct here, and the dating of the cones according to size is uncertain.

The report on the 1910 season (Petrie 1911a) is more full and gives dimensions (Table 1.1) and other information for the kilns as follows (1911a: 34).

Inexplicably, Petrie chose to give the dimensions of the kilns in inches rather than in feet and inches or yards. As a result they seem to have been passed over by scholars as almost unworthy of note. However, when converted to metres (Table 1.2) the enormous scale of these structures becomes apparent:

Table 1.1: Petrie's (1911a) kiln dimensions in inches

Kiln	i	ii	iii	iv	v	vi
Out N-S	145	(walls 18 to 21 inches)				
Out E-W	155					
In N-S	83	50	42	--	57	46
In E-W	79	69	52	50	66	42
Depth now	121	133	133	146	187	60
Draught hole	W	?	?	?	W	N

Particularly striking is the great surviving depth of these structures, 4.75m in the case of kiln v. Petrie regarded the structures as being semi-subterranean: "The draught hole, or stoke-hole...was more than half way up in i, 34 inches from the top in v, and about half-way up in vi. It is 19 inches wide in I, 10 inches in v, 17 inches in vi, where it has been subsequently blocked up so as to leave only a hole 7 inches wide and 5 high" (Petrie 1911a: 35). The walls are noted as deeply burned but "are not generally slagged below the hole, and never down the bottom; above the stoke-hole the slag is thick upon the sides." This point, and Petrie's interpretation of the holes, will be discussed in Chapter 4.

Table 1.2: Petrie's (1911a) kiln dimensions converted into metres

Kiln	i	ii	iii	iv	v	vi
Out N-S	3.70	(walls 0.46 to 0.54 metres)				
Out E-W	3.94					
In N-S	2.11	1.27	1.65	--	1.45	1.17
In E-W	2.00	1.75	1.32	1.27	1.68	1.07
Depth now	3.07	3.38	3.38	3.71	4.75	1.52
Draught hole	W	?	?	?	W	N

(Metric figures are rounded to the nearest cm.)

The kilns apparently bore no trace of a perforated floor on which to support the saggars. Petrie believed that this was because the saggars stood in tall piles and that the fuel was thrown and burnt between them. This he thought might account for the positioning of the stoke-hole part way up the kiln wall. The fuel used to fire the vessels he believed to be straw, as he had found carbonised straw amongst the slag which had run down and covered it (Petrie 1911a: 35). Both of these conclusions are discussed further in Chapter 4.

The saggars found varied in size. Two unused examples measured "8 and 8½ inches wide, 5½ and 6 inches high. The largest sizes among the fragments of used saggars are 30 inches across and 8 high, another 19 inches across" (Petrie 1911a: 35). Only the small examples seem to have been included in the Petrie Collection.[16] Petrie's observation that the height remained almost constant whatever the diameter is an interesting one, and was felt to represent the maximum height to which the contents could be stacked without slumping under their own weight at glazing temperature. Petrie evidently believed that he could distinguish several fabrics within the faience material, presumably according to its coarseness (1911a: 34).

Petrie could not fail to notice the coloured glaze on some of the saggar vessels and believed that the undersides had become glazed because the vessels had cracked and the glaze had run underneath (1911a: 35). That this is not the case will be demonstrated in Chapter 5. The vessels within the saggars were supported on conical clay stands as noted above. Clay was also used to lute the saggars together in the stack and Petrie found what he believed to be "the waste ends of the strips, which were then accidentally fired in the kiln" (1911a: 35). An alternative interpretation for some of these waste ends is offered in discussing saggars in Chapter 5.

A variety of items that were interpreted as "potter's waste" (1911a: 35) were also identified, including possible tools and moulds. He seems to have distinguished between moulds made of clay, including items such as a shabti[17] (1911a: Pl XX no.241) and those made of plaster for lamps etc. However, as he goes on to make clear, lamps could be made of faience ("glazed ware") as well as clay, hence the material from which a mould was made did not determine the material to be used in it.

Petrie is clear that the wares almost all belong to the 1st century B.C. (Petrie 1911a: 36). The dates of the material found in the recent work are discussed by Nenna in Chapter 6.

The question of the making of Egyptian blue, which Petrie believed was used for the glaze at Memphis, is also discussed. Whilst he interpreted some of his Amarna finds in the light of his field survey at Memphis, he now used his Amarna experience to reconstruct the making of blue pigment at Memphis (1911a: 35). The frit colour was made up into balls or pills in two size ranges 0.03m (1.2 inches) and 0.008m (0.3 inches) diameter, the latter being more common. These were then placed in ovoid jars 0.5-0.61m (20-24 inches) long and 0.25-0.30m (10-12 inches) in diameter with a flat base and a mouth some 0.09 (3½ inches) wide. The mouth was sealed with a pad of clay and set mouth down on the base of another jar onto which it was luted with clay. The jars were themselves lined with a thick coating of blue frit to prevent the blue being discoloured by the iron which was naturally present in the clay. The whole would then be roasted for some considerable time.

Rationale for the new work

The work reported on in this volume grew from a desire to better understand Petrie's findings at Tell el-Amarna where the writer was working on an industrial site where glass and faience were being produced, possibly along with frit (Nicholson 2007). It was increasingly clear that Petrie's (1894) interpretation of the Amarna industrial evidence was coloured by his observations at Memphis. It was also clear that in his understandable hurry to publish his finds he sometimes changed his mind or misremembered information and reinterpreted his earlier statements without being explicit about that fact.

It was hoped that excavation at Kom Helul might place some of Petrie's Memphis finds into a more secure archaeological context, and throw new light on his interpretation not only of the Amarna finds but more especially of those from Memphis.

There were particular areas which seemed to need explanation at Memphis. For example, why did the kilns have no perforated floors? Could straw really have served as the fuel for such large structures given that straw is rapidly burned and, on modern analogy, might be expensive? Could the vessels have been stacked in the way that Petrie suggested and on separator cones whose size varied by date?

The question of the Egyptian blue industry was also worthy of investigation. Did it go on alongside the making of faience at Kom Helul or was it practiced at some little distance? Could the practioners have been the same people as those who produced the faience or are these distinct but related industries? What could be learned about the operation of the industry at Kom Helul?

As the writer's work at Amarna site O45.1 came to an end he was in a position to better understand that material on the basis of Petrie's work at Memphis, but the work also raised the possibility of investigating the organisation of the later Memphite industry in relation to its earlier counterpart at Amarna. What is sometimes forgotten is that Petrie was a pioneer in the study of early technology. He was reconstructing as much as possible from what he saw on the ground and from what he knew of industry in his own time. Like any Victorian scholar he would have been well aware of industrial developments and their summaries in works such as those of Muspratt (1860) (see Nicholson 2006) and used this knowledge, perhaps not always fully understood, in his interpretations. As a pioneer, Petrie was painting his outlines of technology with a broad brush. The detailed history of the particular technologies and the changes in their organisation over time were left for those who followed him to complete. The writer has been fortunate enough to be amongst those followers who have the opportunity to fill in some of the outlines and to adjust them in places. This book summarises an attempt to interpret the industry at Memphis, and to see how faience was produced in Roman times. First, however, a short introduction to the origins of faience and its development in pre-Roman times must be provided.

Postscript to the new work

At some time during the Egyptian Revolution of 2011 the workroom of the *Egypt Exploration Society* was burned and looted the adjoining storage magazine of the S.C.A. looted. The destruction took place some time between January 25th and June 4th, 2011 when Dr. Mark Lehner photographed the building. The matter was reported to the E.E.S. and field directors on June 7th by Ana Tavares.[18] All of the finds recovered from the excavations reported here were stolen so that this remains the only record of them. Fortunately, all of the material had been recorded although better photographs and drawings of some were intended and cannot now be undertaken. With the permission of the antiquities inspectors, casts had been taken of a few of the objects and these are currently held by the writer.

Endnotes

1 Petrie is inconsistent in his spelling of the name. It appears as Kom Helul on his map (Petrie 1909a: Pl.I) but as Kom Hellul in his text (1909a: 14 etc.).

2 This building was constructed by Mr. Ward and Herr Schuler and begun before Petrie arrived at the site "but German ideas did not fit with Egyptian conditions, and there was hardly a habitable room by the 27th when I moved there" (Petrie 1931: 210). This is in marked contrast to the house he built for himself at Amarna, which was finished in about a day (Petrie 1894: 1).

3 The text was actually published by Gaston Maspero using Mariette's manuscript after the latter's death. Maspero is not mentioned in all editions. I am grateful to David Jeffreys for providing this information.

4 Modified from the original.

5 Petrie (1909a: 14) locates the kilns "to the south end of Memphis beyond the Kom Hellul". However, his 1911 statement that they are "by Kom Helul" suggests that the area was somewhat ill defined. The fact that he includes Kom Helul on his map (1909a: Pl. I) may suggest that the kilns were actually at Kom Helul.

6 I am indebted to Dr. Reeves for this information and for making the Myers diaries available to me.

7 Myers Museum, Eton ECM586.

8 Myers Museum, Eton ECM570.

9 The date is uncertain, he gives both January 1st 1908 (Petrie 1931: 210) and January 3rd 1908 (Petrie 1909b: 1) as the date when construction of the excavation house was begun. Petrie himself arrived on January 26th 1908.

10 Petrie himself left at the end of April, and was already in London by May 5th 1908. However, Howard Carter (1874-1939) joined the project for its last three weeks (Petrie 1931: 210). As a veteran of Petrie's work on industrial sites at Amarna his presence at Memphis is of particular interest.

11 Gerald Avery Wainwright (1879-1964) worked with Petrie as an assistant and student from 1907 until 1912 before working for Sir Henry Wellcome (1853-1936) and others as well as becoming an antiquities inspector for Middle Egypt. His estate established the *Wainwright Fellowship*, and the *Wainwright Fund* from which part of the excavation reported on in this volume was funded (Dawson, Uphill and Bierbrier 1995: 429).

12 The exact date is again uncertain and is given as February 6th (Petrie 1931: 216) and February 10th (Petrie 1909b: 1).

13 Jocelyn Plunket Bushe-Fox (1880-1954) is not well known in Egyptological circles. He was in Egypt recovering from consumption when he met with and began working for Petrie. After his return to Britain he established himself as an authority in Roman archaeology, particularly at Richborough, and became noted for his close attention to typology and study of coarse pottery. In 1931 he was buried alive whilst working at Colchester, after which his health suffered and his archaeological fieldwork was somewhat curtailed. His obituary appears in the *Times* for October 19th, 1954 (Times 1954: 11).

14 I am indebted to Dr. Steven Quirke, Dr. Sally MacDonald, Dr. Rosalind Janssen, Dr. Margaret Serpico and the late Dr. Barbara Adams for making material in the Petrie Collection available to me, and for sharing their knowledge on Petrie's work with me.

15 Rochdale Museum T:11852. I am indebted to Ms. Sarah Hodgkinson for permitting me to see this piece.

16 Notably UC33565 (Petrie 1911a: Pl.XIX no.239) which is a complete example. There are also fragments with glaze such as UC47378 and UC36458.

17 UC47629 (note that the catalogue cross reference to 1911a: Pl.XX no. 24 should read 241).

18 Joint Field Director of *Ancient Egypt Research Associates*, Giza, who were at the time planning a field-school jointly with the E.E.S. for S.C.A. inspectors at Memphis and planning to use the workroom there. The field school subsequently took place and at the time of writing repairs to the building are pending.

Chapter 2
Pre-Roman Faience

P.T. Nicholson

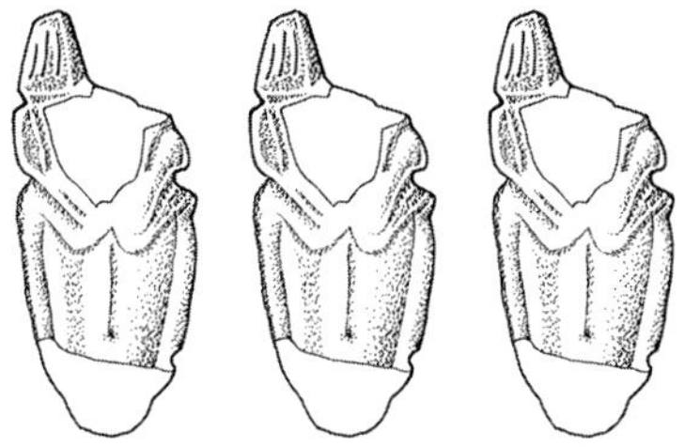

Introduction

Chapter 1 has outlined Petrie's interest in the production of faience and his work at the Ptolemaic/Roman (332 B.C. – A.D. 395) site at Kom Helul which is the focus of this volume. His work at the New Kingdom (1550-1069 B.C.) site of Tell el-Amarna has also been mentioned but these sites represent but two points in the long history of the production of faience and related vitreous materials in Egypt. In order to appreciate the significance of the changes which take place in faience production under the Ptolemies and Romans it is necessary to understand what the material is and how the craft might have been organised. This is not as simple as one might wish because, contrary to Drenkahn's (1995: 336) view that all crafts are known from artistic representations, there is no uncontentious scene of faience manufacture. The only candidate is a very uncertain scene from the tomb of Ibi (TT36) belonging to the reign of Psamtek I (664-610 B.C.) (Davies 1902). There is sometimes archaeological evidence for workshops but often it is not sufficient to make generalisations about craft relationships.

In examining the background to the organisation of faience production and the chronology of the introduction or prominence of particular techniques it rapidly becomes apparent that although a great deal of work has been undertaken on the material (see for example Wulff *et al.* 1968; Kiefer and Alibert 1971; Tite *et al.* 1983; Kaczmarczyk and Hedges 1983, Vandiver 1983 and recent summaries in Tite and Shortland 2008) there are significant gaps in our knowledge of it. Little work has been done on the relationship which is proposed here between faience and stone, especially in terms of how the earliest glazing techniques relate to one another. This is, in part, because of a lack of well dated material which is available for scientific analysis. The same difficulty holds true of faience from many other periods, including that of the Ptolemaic and Roman eras which have often been lumped together as 'Graeco-Roman' with little attempt to differentiate and date particular forms. This latter difficulty has recently been overcome by the provision of better corpora such as that provided by Nenna and Seif el-Din (2000).

Where there are well dated finds for any given period they frequently cannot be related to known and excavated workshops which means that less is known of their methods of production than is desirable. This makes the work carried out by Petrie at Memphis and Amarna all the more remarkable in that he attempted to link forms produced at the workshops to methods of manufacture. This linking of well dated forms to technologies has often been lacking and researchers have scientifically analysed material without sufficient grasp of factory evidence or the necessity of using closely dated samples. This is now beginning to change and a more holistic approach is being taken to the material, though there is still a long way to go before a wholly convincing history of faience and its technology can be put together. The summary given in this chapter is not intended to be exhaustive but rather to draw attention to what is known about the organisation of the craft so that developments in the era covered by this volume can be seen in context.

Faience

The term 'faience' is a contentious one (Peltenburg 1987: 5-6). Its origins lie with the early travellers to Egypt who tried to find a term to link the bright, usually blue or green, glazed material they found with a more widely familiar material (Nicholson 1993: 9). Because these glaze colours reminded them of tin glazed earthenware from Faenza in Italy, which had come to be known as 'faience' or 'fayence' in much of Europe this was the term adopted.[1] More recently, the qualifier 'Egyptian' has sometimes been added to the term but it is nonetheless one which many scholars dislike. Petrie himself (1909c: 107) preferred the term "glazed ware" but like most of the alternatives such as 'glazed composition', used at the British Museum, it did not find wide usage and Lucas (1962: 156 ff) chose to retain the term "faience" and to use "glazed ware" as an over-arching heading for all glazed materials. The Egyptians themselves referred to the material as *tjehenet*[2] or more rarely *khesbed*,[3] the latter referring more properly to lapis lazuli (Aufrère 1991: 465). However, the term *tjehenet* was unknown to the early travellers and hence they provided a substitute. With the term 'faience' so well established in the literature and forming part of the history of Egyptology, there seems little point in trying to replace it and so it is the term which is used here.

Discussion of what this material should, or should not, be called has tended to overshadow consideration of what it actually is. Whilst its colours may have triggered early comparison with tin-glazed earthenware, the material is not a kind of pottery. Faience is a non-clay ceramic and this is a very significant aspect of the material; it is not made of clay and it does not behave like clay (even *if* a small amount *may* occasionally be added). Instead of being a plastic material which is easily deformed into new shapes and which will then retain those shapes whilst drying, faience paste is thixotropic. It tends to tear as it is deformed and even when shaped it can quickly lose some of that shape which makes it difficult to mould or incise sharp relief into – not for nothing do Egyptologists refer to some shabti figurines as 'jelly baby shabtis'.[4] The fact that faience is not clay-based is fundamental to understanding how it is integrated into the canon of Egyptian crafts and to appreciating its significance in the history of technology.

The significance of the material and its separation from pottery is nowhere better summarised than by Vandiver and Kingery (1987a: 19ff) who called it "the first high-tech ceramic" by which they mean "contrived compositions made of novel, specially prepared materials manipulated with imaginative manufacturing methods to achieve new or improved properties not obtainable by traditional ceramic practices" (Vandiver and Kingery 1987a: 19). As Spencer and Schofield (1997: 104) note in discussing the glazing of faience, the "first glazes on clay based ceramics did not appear until the Late Bronze Age, in around 1600 B.C." and therefore well after the glazing of stone and faience. The "technology [of faience] appears to be related to methods for working soft stone and to have evolved independently of clay based pottery" (ibid). This definition immediately makes it clear that this is not the preserve of the potter and the archaeological evidence for its ancestry tends to confirm this.

The Origins of Faience

The earliest developments of faience are not well recorded but it seems likely that it developed from the practice of glazing quartz and steatite (Beck 1934) during the Predynastic period probably as early as the 6th millennium B.C. Although there are three main methods of glazing faience (for summary see Vandiver 1983, here Fig. 2.1) it is often forgotten that this earliest glazing of stone was by application – the applying of the glaze to the surface of the stone object.

The means by which the application glazing was achieved has not been adequately studied, most researchers having concentrated instead on the glazing of faience. It might have been achieved by coating the object in a soda-lime-silica paste coloured with copper oxide or it may have been achieved by a reaction between the object and the glazing ingredients. This latter method is still practiced today in the Luxor area of Egypt where replica scarab amulets, carved in steatite, are glazed by burying them in a mixture of charcoal, calcined salinated bone and copper scale and then heating them (Friedman and Leveque 1998).

The objects themselves were, of course, shaped. This process meant that the steatite or quartz had to be carved or abraded in some way to give the desired form before it was coated in glaze. Carving hard stones such as quartz is not an easy or straightforward process and every piece would be unique. The same individuality is true of the carving of the softer steatite. It is perhaps not surprising therefore to find that ways of overcoming the difficulty of making uniformly similar items are developed very early; the desire to shape more easily and more uniformly may be the origin of faience.

Rather than taking a hard (or soft) stone and carving it away to make a shape, the earliest faience workers adopted the idea of taking a powdered stone – crushed quartz or quartz sand – mixing it with water, soda and lime and making it into a paste. The paste could be shaped with the fingers and then, as it dried, finer detail could be achieved by cutting away some of the excess or by allowing the piece to dry and abrading the surface away. The object could then be glazed. This development of shaping a soft, malleable, material is also a Predynastic one and – though it has not been well researched – it seems to happen shortly after, and in tandem with, the glazing of stones from the 6th millennium B.C. (Peltenburg 1971: 6, Moorey 1994: 68 for a summary see Nicholson 2012). In discussing the relationship between glass and faience Peltenburg (1987: 20) notes that "faience workers formed their glazes essentially in a cold state" (the same is true of the body) whilst glass was formed hot. This use of a 'cold' technology may favour the view that faience has a close link to stone manufacture.

What is evident from this examination of the earliest faience is that its origins lie in the shaping and glazing of stones rather than in the shaping and glazing of clays. Glazes, indeed, are unrelated to pottery production at this time – whilst pale steatite and brilliant white quartz, or its powder, would give a dazzling substrate to the blue coloured

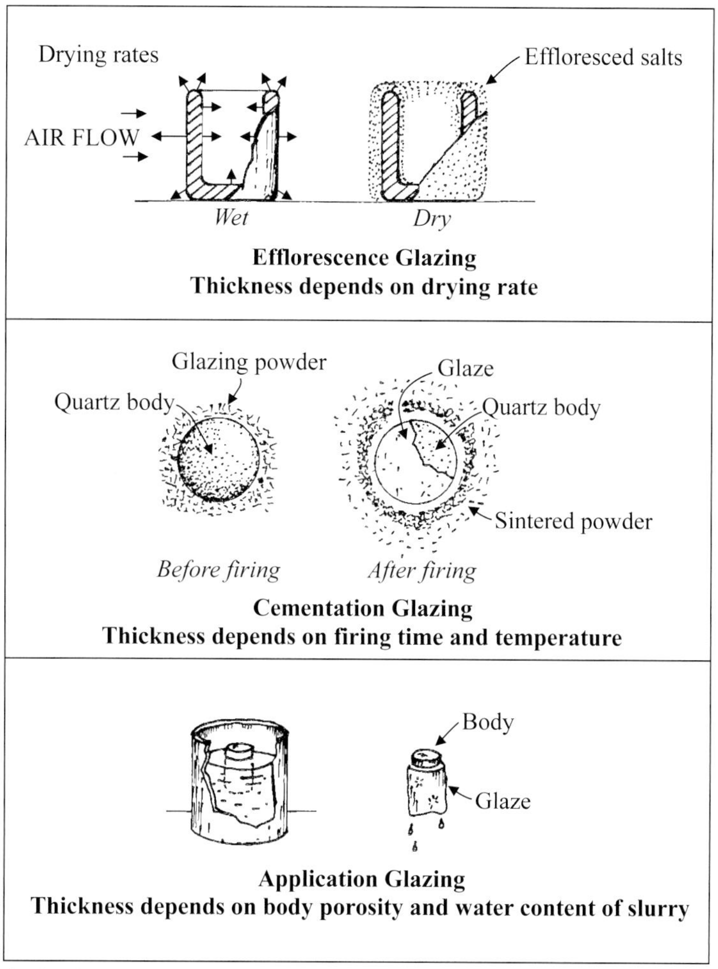

Figure 2.1. The three main methods of glazing faience. (Adapted from Vandiver 1983: Fig. 23).

glaze which was highly desired by the Egyptians as an imitation of turquoise (Hermann 1968), itself representing the brilliance of the sky (Hart 1986: 76). The iron rich clays which represent the main source for Nile Valley pottery tend to give a murky effect when glazed.

Although many questions remain about the methods of glazing employed by the earliest faience workers and the process of shaping faience it is evident that this was a time of experimentation and it is unlikely that there was any single recipe or glazing method in use. It is equally clear that these experiments went on beyond the sphere of the potter.

By the Early Dynastic period (3100-2686 B.C.) faience is already an established craft and is used in the manufacture of small figurines, beads, amulets and other decorative items. It had come to serve as an acceptable substitute for turquoise and lapis-lazuli, though the fact that throughout the pharaonic era it is a material suitable for inclusion in the burials of even the highest individuals indicates that it should not be seen as merely a cheap substitute (see Patch 1998: 33).

The prominence of the material is well demonstrated by its use in the mass production of some 36,000 blue-green tiles for the galleries beneath the Step Pyramid of king Djoser (2667-2648 B.C.) at Saqqara (Vandiver and Kingery 1987a: 24). This feat would have been hugely time consuming had it been attempted in glazed stone and it could not have been satifactorily achieved in pottery. The employment of a medium which could be made to resemble turquoise and yet was more easily available and more easily shaped clearly demonstrates that there was already a mastery of this high-tech ceramic. Perhaps even more significant is the way in which these tiles were glazed.

The Djoser tiles are glazed by the self-glazing technique known as 'efflorescence' (Vandiver 1983: A-31-33) in which all of the ingredients of the faience, including those of its glaze, are mixed together into a paste and allowed to dry. The alkali salts which may be derived from plant ash or from the mineral soda natron migrate to the surface of the object to form an effloresced scum or bloom. In firing this "melts to fuse with the fine quartz, copper oxide and lime and gradually to dissolve the surfaces of the quartz particles" (Vandiver 1983: A32). Because the material is thoroughly mixed, the firing also results in the formation of a significant glassy phase in the matrix, forming interparticle or interstitial glass and making the material more durable than it might otherwise be.

The efflorescence technique seems to be particularly prominent from the Early Dynastic into the First Intermediate Period (2181-2055 B.C.) (see Vandiver and Kingery 1987a: 26; Nicholson and Peltenburg 2000: 188). What should be remembered is that the glazing of stones does not cease with the development of faience, though it becomes less prominent. This has implications for where faience craftsmen might be located in terms of the organisation of crafts. The obvious place is surely with the stone workers who have now extended their range into the production of artificial stones.

Faience of the Middle and New Kingdom

Evidence for the manufacture of faience increases significantly with the re-unification of Egypt under the rulers of the Middle Kingdom (2055-1650 B.C.) following the disunity of the First Intermediate Period (2181-2055 B.C.). In terms of faience production this new stability seems to be marked by a period of experimentation during which cementation and application glazing methods are firmly attested alongside efflorescence. While it is likely that application was developed for faience in the Predynastic (see above) cementation is not certainly attested at that time and it is only now that the three main techniques are evident.

The cementation technique is also regarded as a self glazing method. The method was first discovered by Wulff *et al.* (1968) still being practiced in Iran and Kiefer and Allibert (1971) proposed that it was indeed used in ancient times. In this method the object is shaped and dried before being buried in a container filled with a powder, which, when heated, reacts with the surface of the object to glaze it (Vandiver 1983: A33ff). The alkalis can come from either the dry faience body or from the surrounding powder which comprises lime, ash, silica, charcoal and colourant (Wulff *et al.*1968). So far as the writer is aware this is a technique unknown in traditional clay-based ceramics.

It is from the Middle Kingdom that the earliest evidence for the organisation of the craft of faience manufacture comes. Archaeological work conducted at the site of Lisht in the 1920s is not well published but there is evidence to suggest that it was a production site. The features of the site need to be reassessed and re-dated, but there is no doubt about the burial from shaft 879 from which comes the coffin of one Debeni whose title was 'overseer of faience workers'[5] (Bourriau 1991: 13; 1996: 110-111). There is no link in this title to anything to do with pottery, nor is there any direct link to the making or glazing of stone objects, however, the term *tjehenet,* meaning 'brilliant' or 'dazzling', is usually applied to turquoise, suggesting that the origins of faience working may indeed lie in the production of stone items.

The technique of application glazing (Vandiver 1983: A27ff) has already been discussed above. Suffice it to say that the glaze can be added to the dried faience object either by applying it as a powder or coating it onto the object as a slurry by brushing or even by dipping the object. Application is the means by which most pottery is glazed today and was the method familiar to Petrie from Victorian factory production of ceramics.

Given that he was familiar with the principles of application glazing and that he believed that he had seen examples of it on faience from Kom Helul when he walked over the site in the 1880s (Petrie 1911a: 34) it is not surprising that when excavating at the New Kingdom (1550-1069 B.C.) site of Tell el-Amarna in 1891-2 (Petrie 1894) he assumed that all the faience he found was glazed by application. In fact, most of it is actually glazed by efflorescence (Nicholson 2007). What he did correctly note, however, were the great quantity of fired clay moulds used to make faience objects. In just the same way as with the tiles of the Step Pyramid the faience paste allowed the replication, effectively the mass-production, of virtually identical pieces.[6] The combination of moulding with efflorescence meant that the pieces were relatively strong and so could be used for making finger rings and earrings as well as a whole range of other products, such as inlays, for which increased mechanical strength was not so necessary.

Petrie's work at Amarna also provides the first clear glimpse of how faience production relates to other crafts of the time. He notes that he and Howard Carter (1874-1939) found "the sites of three or four glass factories, and two large glazing works" (Petrie 1894: 25) and, although he is not explicit on the matter, it seems that finds of faience and glass were occurring in the same locations, in other words that the new craft of glass manufacture was going on alongside that of faience making. This is not the place to discuss the coming of glass to Egypt, and specifically to Amarna, as the subject has already been extensively covered (for example Oppenheim 1973, Nicholson 2007). The same is true for discussion of the relationship of glass to existing crafts; suffice it to say that Nicholson (2012) has argued that the earliest glass seems to be treated as though it were a type of stone. That both glass and faience might be treated as types of stone is unsurprising given the origins of the material suggested here.

Work by the writer (Nicholson 2007) showed that at Amarna site O45.1 there was evidence for the making of glass and the production of faience in the same or adjoining work areas. There was also evidence of pottery production. Might this mean that by the time of Amarna, faience making was being integrated into clay-based ceramic production? The writer believes that this is not the case and that what was being shared at the site was a common purpose in the use of pyrotechnology and perhaps also cobalt used for colouring glass and sometimes faience and for painting pottery.[7] Clay would have been needed to produce the moulds for making faience and also the cylindrical crucibles used in glass production so this grouping together of high temperature industries into a small 'industrial estate' was probably a matter of convenience and some shared expertise rather than the subsuming of faience and glass production under the banner of pottery manufacture.

It is worth noting that from site O45.1 there are kilns or furnaces. These are of two broad types: a very substantially built circular type which is believed by Nicholson (2007) to be for glass and a smaller, lightly constructed type of circular or ovoid form which is well known for pottery manufacture.[8] However, given that faience is being made at the site and would not have required temperatures significantly different to those used for pottery production it is proposed that faience kilns of the New Kingdom might be uniform in design with those used for pottery. In this sense there is a link to conventional ceramic production but it need not be an organisational one.

That such links with pottery are not part of New Kingdom thought is implied by the existence of a 19th Dynasty (c.1295 B.C.) funerary stele, itself made of faience, of one Rekhamun[9] (see Friedman 1998: 156). This bears the inscription "the Osiris [i.e. deceased and thus united with Osiris] maker of [or worker in] faience for [the god] Amun, Rekhamun"[10] (Friedman 1998: 250). Unlike the earlier Debeni inscription, this one refers to faience as *khesbed* – the term for lapis lazuli, again emphasising the origins of the material in stone. An argument might be made that here faience is being used to produce the stele of someone who actually worked in lapis lazuli because that material was too expensive for a craftsman, though it seems to the writer more likely that the material is that used by the craftsman (Nicholson 2012: 16). A second faience stele of similar date[11] is for a man called Kar who was a servant of Amun while a third[12] belongs to Amenemheb and his wife. Amenemheb was an overseer of the artisans of Ptah, creator god of Memphis, and was probably responsible for overseeing makers of faience and hence chose this artificial stone as something suitable for his prominent rank. Though stelae are known in a variety of materials they are most commonly produced in stone, so these examples might be considered to be in an artificial stone (see Nicholson 2012: 16).

Also of the 19th Dynasty is the funerary papyrus of Qn-hr[13] (Bellion 1987: 320, 397; Marucci 1891) who, like Debeni, has the title 'overseer of faience makers.'[14] The word used for faience is again that for lapis lazuli but by this time it is already in common use for faience (above).

Third Intermediate and Late Periods

The Third Intermediate Period (1069-747 B.C.) and Late Period (747-332 B.C.) may be the time at which the organisation of the faience industry begins to diverge from its proposed roots in stone glazing. These are periods of increasing foreign influence in Egypt and faience may be being exported from Egypt to the wider Mediterranean as well as from there into Egypt. Efflorescence and application glazing are the predominant techniques used at this time.

Vandiver (1983: A124) suggests that there may be evidence of the wheel throwing of faience from the New Kingdom onward and Nicholson and Peltenburg (2000: 185) took the same view. However, the writer is yet to see definite examples of free thrown[15] faience and this is clearly an area where further research is needed. It may be a trait which develops after c.1069 B.C. but without more detailed study this cannot be said with certainty.

Kaczmarczyk and Hedges (1983: 265) also suggest that the increasing influence of the Greeks in Egypt from the 26th Dynasty (747-656 B.C.) and particularly their settlement at Naukratis may bring their pottery making traditions to Egypt and have an affect on faience production. In particular they suggest (1983: 269) that black faience is deliberately produced under oxygen deficient (reducing) conditions, a technique very familiar to Attic potters. However, the Egyptian potters too were familiar with the reduction technique and had used it since Predynastic times. That it had not been applied to faience may once again reinforce the view that it was a craft completely separate from the potting industry. The appearance of black faience made by reduction replaces a much older tradition of creating black faience through the use of manganese and breaks "a technical tradition that endured for over 2000 years" (Kaczmarczyk and Hedges 1983: 269) perhaps inspired by a link between potting and faience production in the Greek world which had now been imported to Egypt.

Lead is found in higher concentrations at this time than in the New Kingdom (Kaczmarczyk and Hedges 1983: 267) but not at the levels found in Roman period lead-glazed pottery and the link may have more to do with the use of high-lead bronze scrap in colouring the glaze than with experiments by potters. Naukratis faience sometimes contained copper from "unusual" (Kaczmarczyk and Hedges 1983: 272) non-Egyptian sources too, making the link between metal scrap and colourants. Kaczmarczyk and Hedges (1983: 266) comment on the high quality of much of the 26th Dynasty faience and on the characteristic soft apple green shade which was particularly prominent. This was often matte rather than highly glazed, though the faience workers were quite capable of producing very highly glazed pieces in greens and blues if required.

Conclusions

The evidence both archaeological and linguistic seems to support the view that traditional Egyptian faience manufacturing came from the desire first to glaze stones and then to manufacture those stones artificially. The material was a truly high-tech development and seems to have taken place separately from developments in clay based ceramics.

The link with stone technology seems to be preserved, at least in the terms used for the craft, through the New Kingdom when the earliest glass too seems to follow patterns of stoneworking (Nicholson 2012). Whilst pottery production and faience making are found in the same industrial quarters there is no good evidence to suggest that they were linked organisationally and some evidence to imply that they were not.

From the Third Intermediate Period, and more especially from the Late Period there are hints at change. Faience is now a widely made product of the Mediterranean and its place of origin can be difficult to determine stylistically. Greek settlements in Egypt, such as Naukratis, included faience manufacture amongst their repertoire of crafts and it may be that in setting up such workshops the Greeks imported working practices from their homeland. Such practices might have included organisational links between pottery and faience production or the close proximity of the two in those settlements in Egypt where they were prominent might have fostered new developments. Whatever the case, there does seem to be more evidence for the use of potting techniques in this later faience. With this in mind one might wonder whether the technological stage was set for more radical changes under the Ptolemies and Romans. These developments will be discussed in Chapter 7.

The site of Kom Helul offers an opportunity to examine whether there were such significant changes in organisation and technology of the industry, and that has been a major purpose of the excavation reported on in chapter 3, the results of which are discussed in chapters 4 to 8.

Endnotes

1 Ironically the original tin-glazed wares dating from the 16th Century onwards are now usually referred to as 'maiolica' or 'majolica' (see Thornton 1997).

2 *ṯḥnt.*

3 *ḫsbḏ.*

4 Shabtis or ushabtis are servant figurines frequently included in burials from the 12th Dynasty onwards (though a case can be made for earlier figures being 'shabtis' (Stewart 1995: 14). For a detailed typology see Schneider (1977). The term 'jelly baby shabti' is widely used by Egyptologists to refer to poorly detailed and mass produced shabtis particularly those from the Third Intermediate Period (1069-747 B.C.) though the term is not properly defined and not generally used in the literature.

5 *Imy-r ṯḥntyw Dbh n=*i.

6 That two pieces from the same mould might not actually be identical is the result of the deformation of the thixotropic paste after removal from the mould.

7 Though it is by no means certain that blue-painted pottery was produced at Amarna site O45.1.

8 The type is first recorded at Amarna by Borchardt (1932) but was mistakenly believed to be a bread-oven.

9 National Museums of Scotland A.1956.153.

10 *Wsir, irw ḫsbḏ n Imn, Rḫ-Imn.*

11 National Museums of Scotland A.1956.152.

12 Rijksmuseum van Oudheden, Leiden AD 37.

13 Also known as Qennou. Papyrus Vatican 64.

14 *Imy-r-irw-ḫsbḏ.*

15 That is faience thrown on the wheel without the use of a mould.

Chapter 3
The Excavation

R. Hart and P.T. Nicholson

Introduction

This chapter summarises the excavations undertaken at Kom Helul. The structural account which forms the basis of this chapter follows the format employed by the *Glamorgan Gwent Archaeological Trust* in conformity to the standards of *Management of Archaeological Projects* (English Heritage 1991).

Archaeological context (or unit) numbers are indicated by square brackets. A list of contexts is given at the end of this chapter. The / symbol is used to denote contexts which are 'equal', that is contexts which have been given different numbers (usually in different seasons) but are the same context of archaeological stratigraphy. In order to avoid cluttering the text, not all of these 'equal' numbers are given in the text but are to be found in the context list.

The Excavation

It was decided to excavate in several distinct areas, each chosen for a different reason and to attempt to answer specific questions. The areas open in particular years are as follows:

2000 Excavation Season
HAC1 (Supervisor: Amy Goldsmith)
HAC2 (Supervisor: Amy Goldsmith)
HAD1 (Supervisor: Amy Goldsmith)

2001 Excavation Season
HAC3 (Supervisor: Rowena Hart)
HAD1 (Supervisor: Katinka Stentoft)
HAD2 (Supervisor: Katinka Stentoft)
HAD3 (Supervisor: Katinka Stentoft)

2002 Excavation Season
HAC3 (Supervisors: Rowena Hart, Assistant: Thomas Brindle)

2005 Excavation Season
HAC3 (Supervisor: Rowena Hart, Assistant: Cara Jones)

2006, 2007 and 2008 Study Seasons
No excavation undertaken

The location of the trenches is shown on Figure A1.4 of Appendix 1.

Trench HAC1

The first area, HAC trench 1, was located immediately to the west of the homes of the settled Bedouin who now live at Kom Helul, and immediately south of the wire fence surrounding a former military area now returned to the care of the S.C.A. (Figs. 3.1-3.3, Plates 3.1-3.2). The site of the trench slopes from east to west and, like much of the area, has been used as an unofficial rubbish dump in the past, though it was largely clear of debris when the excavation began.

The reason for choosing this particular part of Kom Helul for excavation was that it incorporated significant geophysical anomalies when surveyed by Mr. Ian Mathieson as part of his work on the S.C.A. approved *Royal Museums of Scotland* project at Memphis/Saqqara. His survey in this area was limited, but he identified a number of places with high magnetic readings which might suggest the location of kilns or furnaces. The area also appeared to be relatively undisturbed and incorporated both high and low ground which, it was hoped, were indicative of sub-surface structures.

A trench measuring 5.0m north-south by 10.0m east-west was laid out and excavated. As elsewhere at Kom Helul the high water table would have prevented complete excavation but since it was quickly apparent that the trench did not

Plate 3.1. Trench HAC1 looking toward the south-west. The figures in the middle distance are at Trench HAC2. (Photo: P.T. Nicholson).

Plate 3.2. Trench HAC1 looking north-east. The large wall [008] is clearly visible at the centre. The trench measures 5.0 x 10.0m. (Photo P.T. Nicholson).

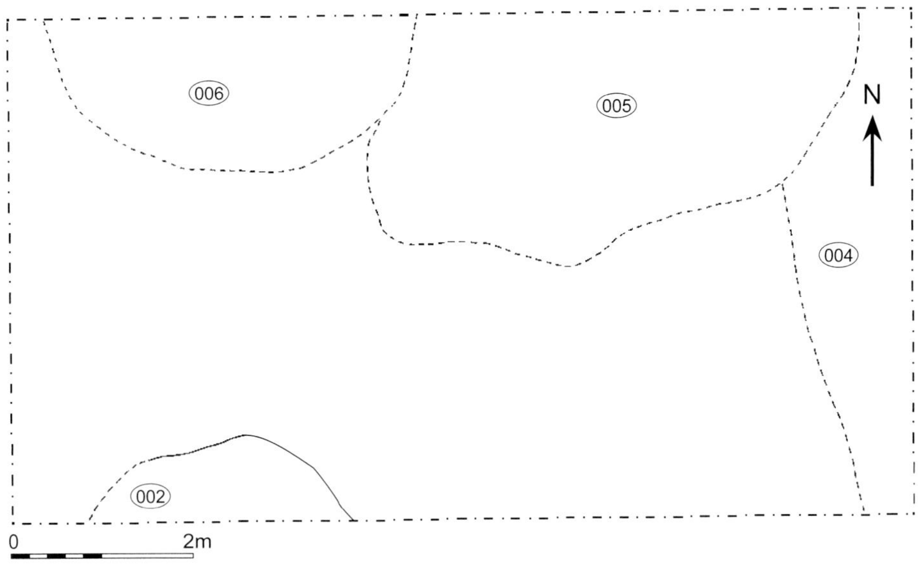

Figure 3.1. Trench HAC1 after removal of the uppermost contexts. (Plan: A. Goldsmith and R. Hart).

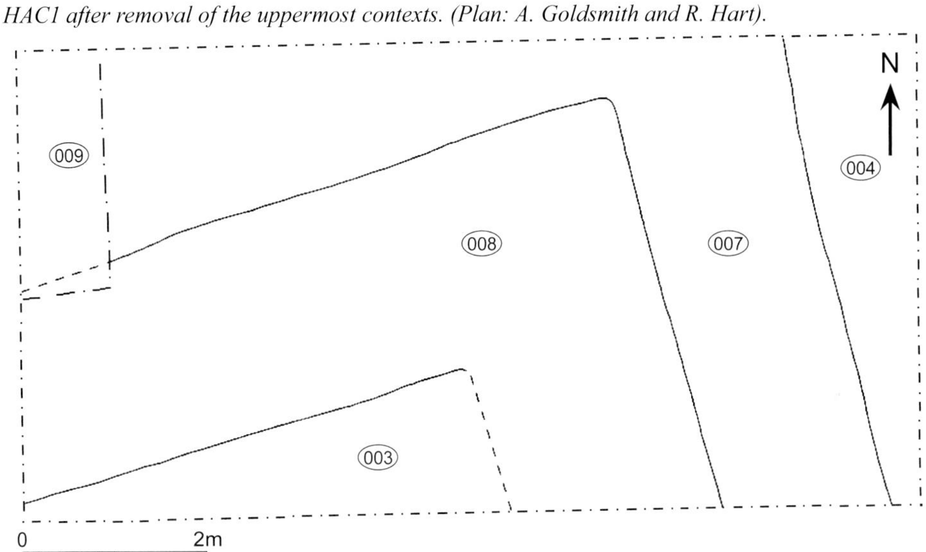

Figure 3.2. Trench HAC1 showing the location of the substantial mudbrick wall [008]. As no industrial features were present in this trench it was not further excavated. (Plan: A. Goldsmith and R. Hart).

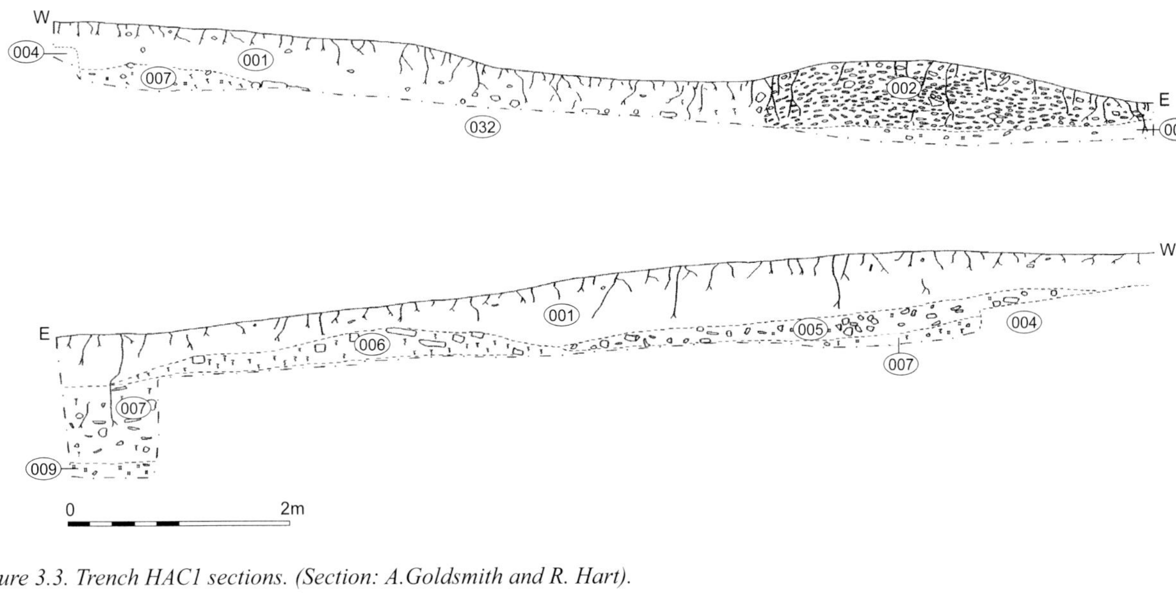

Figure 3.3. Trench HAC1 sections. (Section: A.Goldsmith and R. Hart).

contain industrial remains it was decided that excavation here would be minimal.

The lowest context reached was [008] a very substantial wall built of unfired mudbricks. This ran roughly north-east to south-west across the trench, with a right-angled corner turning to the south-east, giving the wall an L-shape within the trench. The wall was approximately 2.0m wide.

The foundation of the wall [008] was not reached and clearly goes deeper than context [009], a mid-brown silty deposit which was excavated in a sondage of 0.90m width at the north-west corner of the trench and extended from the wall to the northern limit of excavation. The area was chosen as a sondage because drill corings made by Dr. David Jeffreys included fragments of fired brick but it seems that these were simply residual material left in the area and are now known to be common over Kom Helul as a whole. Context [009] was overlain by context [007], a mid-brown sandy silt layer which abutted the wall [008] on its north and east. The deposit included charcoal flecks and fragments of fired mudbrick.

Above [007] on the north side of the wall was a semi-circular deposit [006] measuring 4.10m east-west along the edge of the excavation by 1.50m north-south and comprising a mid-brown to orange sandy layer with fragments, and occasionally whole, fired and unfired mudbricks, all in very degraded condition. Immediately east of this deposit was a mid-brown to grey sandy layer [005] measuring 5.0m east-west along the edge of the trench by 2.40m north-south and containing fragments of fired bricks as well as small fragments of limestone and charcoal flecks. [005] overlies [007] and in part deposit [004] (described below).

To the south of wall [008] is a dark brown sandy-silt layer [003]. Since [008] continues below the level of [003] this latter deposit has evidently built up against the wall. It occupies the whole area to the south of the wall. Overlying the western part of [003] is [002] a mid brown-grey sandy deposit with a high concentration of domestic pottery. At its north the deposit slightly overlies the southern edge of wall [008].

At the extreme eastern end of the trench and running north-south is context [004]. This is a much degraded mudbrick wall or bank. The bricks are very degraded but include some fired bricks. The surface context across the whole trench is [001] a mid-brown-grey sandy silt with heavy root disturbance and patches of modern burning.

Interpretive Summary

The main feature in trench HAC1 is wall [008] whose size and construction suggests that it may have been a major boundary wall. Its surviving height and extent are not known but it is possible that it may have enclosed part of the industrial area at some time.

Context [002] is a dump of pottery and runs onto the top of the surviving wall [008] suggesting that the ground level at the time of the dumping was already close to the level of the wall top, which in turn suggests that the wall had been sleighted at this time or that the ground level had gradually risen so that the height above ground was not great.

Wall [004] runs along the line of the modern trackway on the western edge of Kom Helul village and could not be further excavated without disturbing traffic. It may be a boundary wall or it may represent the piling together of re-used bricks to make a trackway in relatively recent times.

No significant *in situ* industrial remains were found in the trench and the area of high magnetic intensity detected by Mr. Ian Mathieson's survey appears to have been a small concentration of burned bricks lying to the west of wall [008], and does not represent an actual structure. Exploratory borings made by Dr. David Jeffreys in the western area of the trench confirmed that no furnace was present.

Once it had become clear that the relatively sparse industrial remains found in trench HAC1 were secondary, that is the result of the dumping of furnace debris, it was decided not to excavate the trench to a deeper level. This was so that the lower, earlier deposits, which were not of relevance to the present work would remain undisturbed for future archaeological exploration.

The trench was back-filled at the end of the season in order to further protect it.

Trench HAC2

Trench HAC2 was chosen as being likely to include a great deal of industrial debris, as well as offering the possibility that it might include one of the furnaces examined by Petrie. It formed one of several squarish hollows on the east side of a series of mounds of debris which make up the western limit of the site (see Plate 3.1). Trial borings by Dr. David Jeffreys again suggested the presence of burned pottery or brick in the area, but it was suspected that this might simply be the remains of coarse pottery. This proved to be the case when excavation began.

Unusually it was not possible to differentiate a surface context from the material beneath, other than the fact that it supported vegetation (Fig. 3.4). The whole trench was therefore given context [010] and recorded as a mid-dark brown-grey sandy silt with abundant finds of saggar fragments and glaze as well as some charcoal.

It was obvious from the surface indications that a large amount of debris would be found in the 5.0m square excavation here, and consequently after cleaning the top few centimeters across the square it was decided to restrict the work. An examination of the north-western corner of the

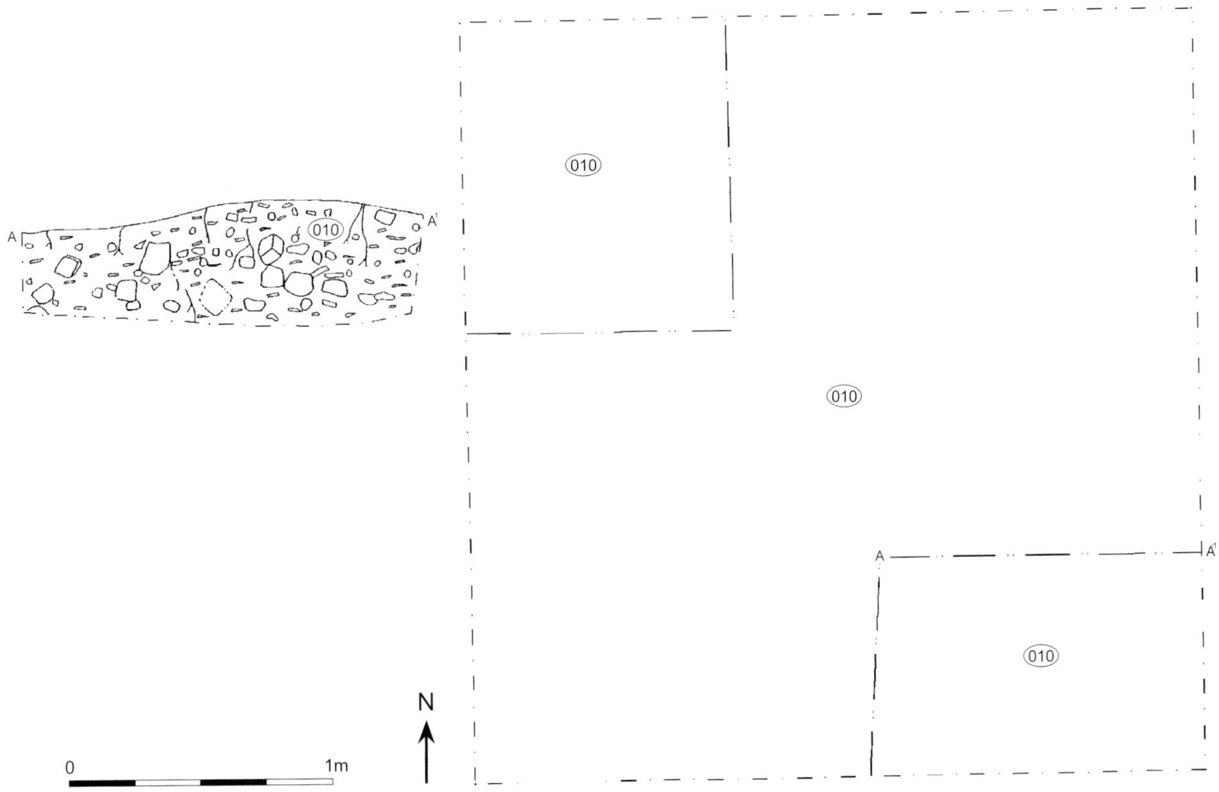

Figure 3.4. Trench HAC2. This trench was a single context dump largely comprising broken saggars of Type 3. The section A-A1 is shown at left. (Plan: A. Goldsmith and R. Hart).

square yielded an enormous quantity of industrial ceramic debris, vitrified furnace lining and misfired faience. It was also quickly apparent that no structure existed at this corner.

Work was therefore concentrated in a 1.0 by 2.0m area at the south-east corner of the square. At this corner the modern topography suggested a slight mound which it was believed might overlie the wall of a furnace. Once again, a very large quantity of industrial ceramic, vitrified kiln lining and misfired faience was removed. This too was clearly dumping of material in the area and despite excavation to a depth of some 0.75m no sign of structures was evident.

Interpretive Summary

It is clear that all of the material excavated was from a dump deposit. All was collected and examined and was almost exclusively industrial in nature. Much of this industrial ceramic had glaze adhering to it, the result of having served as containers ('saggars') for the making of faience. Other sherds were entirely unglazed. All of this material was carefully examined and weighed. A large amount was then selected as a sample for permanent curation and the rest, once recorded, was re-buried at the site. All of the vitrified material ('slag') was examined and weighed as was all of the very coarse industrial ceramic. As always all of the misfired faience was kept.

It became apparent as excavation at HAC3 progressed that the dump at HAC2 probably came from a separate kiln whose purpose was glaze ('glost') firing and which represents a separate stage in the production of faience.

Trench HAC3

This trench was located on the basis of the geophysical survey (Appendix 1) which showed the likely presence of a kiln in the area. The original 5.0 by 5.0m trench was located such that the anomaly was almost central to the excavated area. The trench was extended to the west by 2.0m in 2002 and a further 2.0m to the west was added in the 2005 season in order to completely excavate the western access to the firing pit. The overall trench was therefore 5.0m north-south by 9.0m east-west. The overall plan of the trench is shown as Figure 3.5.

The basal deposit [316] encountered in this area was a grey-brown silty clay. This is unlikely to be natural alluvium of the area as this is more deeply buried than could have been reached by the excavation. Overlying [316] was a mid-brown silty sand deposit [339] which might represent part of the naturally undulating topography. Into this [339] a cut [333] was made. The cut was rectangular in plan measuring approximately 4.1m east-west by 1.9m north-south. The maximum depth of the cut was approximately 3.75m.

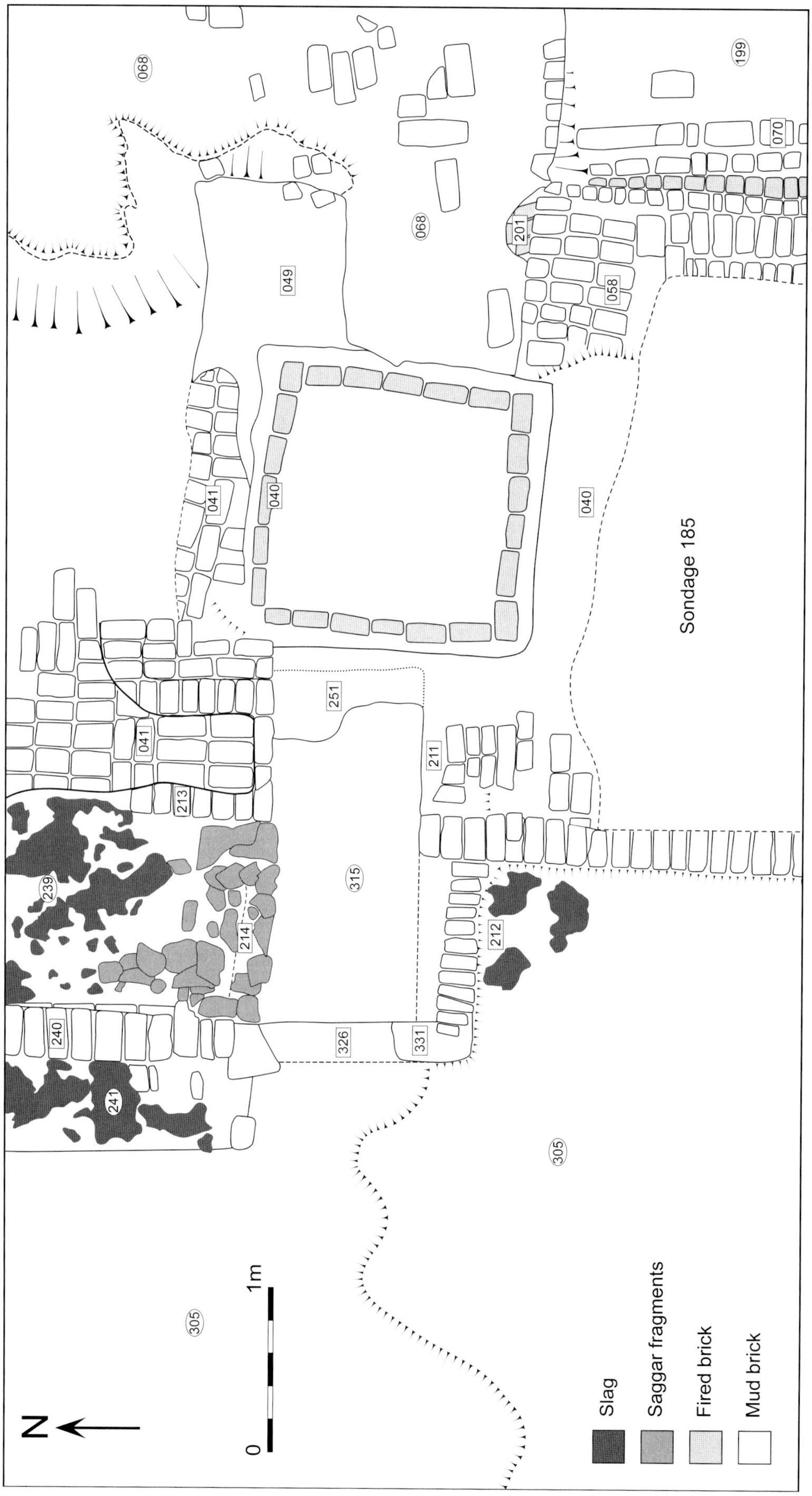

Figure 3.5. Trench HAC3 overview. (Plan: R. Hart).

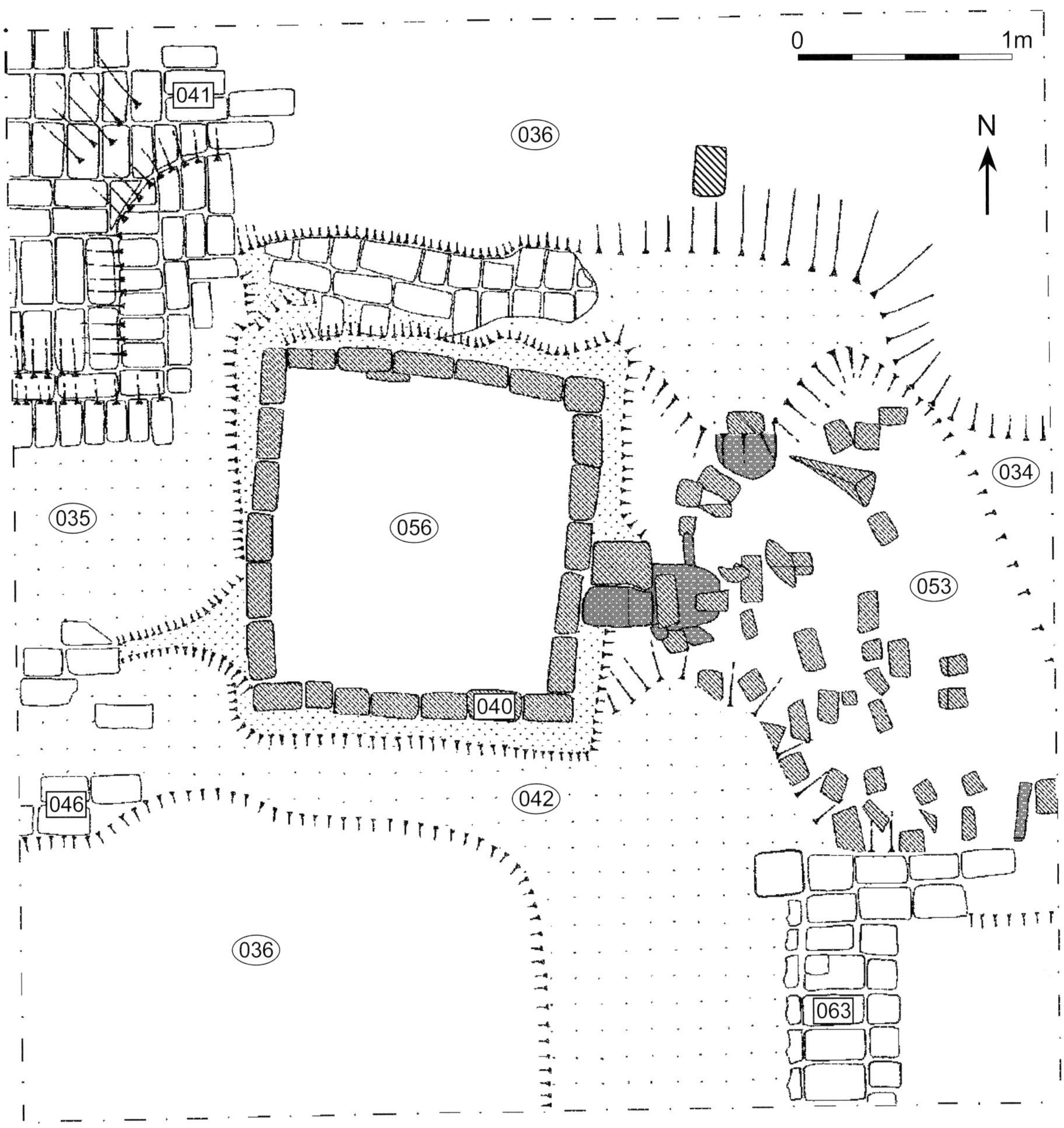

Figure 3.6. Trench HAC3 at an early stage of excavation in 2001 showing the kiln [040] with debris [053] in front of the area which revealed the stoke-hole. (See also Fig. 3.11). (Plan: T. Brindle and R. Hart).

A further cut [334] was made to the west of [333] with a maximum depth of 1.2m where it met wall [326] and then sloped upward toward the west to the ground surface over a distance of 1.8m. (see Fig. 4.1).

Cut [333] contained a brick structure [040] which was roughly square in plan measuring 1.6m along its northern wall, 1.54m along its southern wall, 1.6m along the eastern Wall and 1.7m along the western Wall (exterior measurements – Fig. 3.6, Plates 3.3 - 3.5). The maximum depths recorded for each elevation were north 3.28m, south 3.63m, east 3.7m and west 3.7m. The last of these could be recorded on the western exterior as well as the interior of the structure whilst the rest could only be measured on the interior.

All four walls were constructed from mudbricks with bonding mud mortar. Where visible the brickwork was seen to be laid in alternate courses of headers and stretchers. The brickwork had become fired after construction as was evident from the firing of the mortar as well as the bricks. Over large areas of the interior the elevations were vitrified, often thickly, which obscured some of the brickwork. Toward the bottom of the structure the vitrified ('slag') layers merged to form a thick expanse [208] which extended to within 0.23m of the west wall.

Built into the structure of the east wall was an arched vent [335] (Fig. 3.7, Plate 3.6). This measured 0.35m in height by 0.24m in width and was constructed of mudbrick laid end-on (i.e. as headers). It was located 0.50m below the

Plate 3.3. Trench HAC3 looking north over the kiln [040] at an early stage of the excavation. (Photo: P.T. Nicholson).

Plate 3.4. Trench HAC3 looking west over the kiln [040] at an early stage of the excavation. The sondage inserted by the S.C.A. inspector is visible on the left. (Photo: P.T. Nicholson).

Plate 3.5. Trench HAC3 looking west over the kiln [040] at an early stage of the excavation. (Photo: P.T. Nicholson).

Plate 3.6. Trench HAC3 looking south-west. The stoke-hole [335] is clearly visible at right (see Fig.3.7) and is flanked by mudbrick walls. (Photo: P.T. Nicholson).

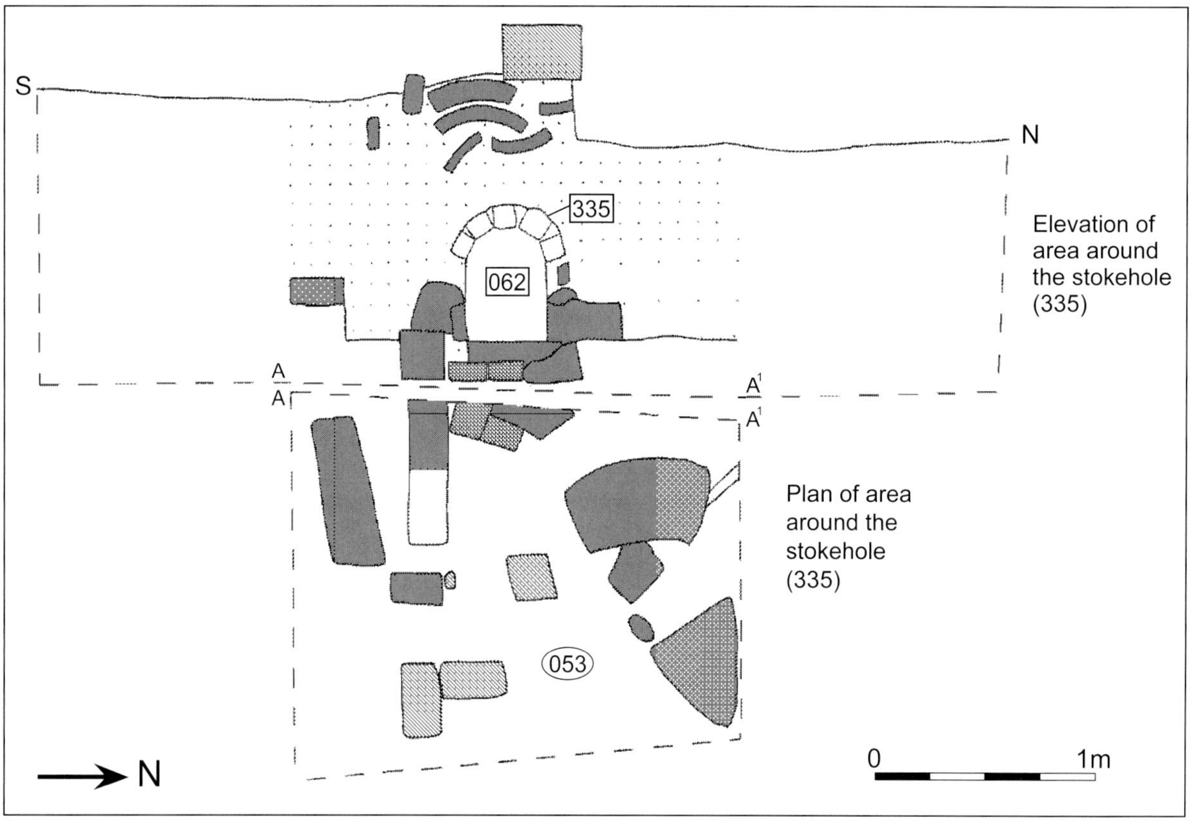

Figure 3.7. Looking west at the stoke-hole [335] area of HAC3 with a plan of the debris [053] in front of it. The deposit [062] still filled the upper part of the kiln at this time. (Plan: T. Brindle and R. Hart).

surviving upper course of brickwork of the structure [040]. The fill of the vent comprised fired mudbricks, as well as industrial and domestic pottery fragments [062]. Outside the vent on the east side the basal deposits are, from east to west, [068], [205] and [206] with [229] abutting the brickwork of the south-eastern part of the platform [041/058]. Deposit [068] was a reddish sand whose colour was largely derived from the erosion of fired bricks and included a large quantity of burnt material notably bricks and charcoal (Fig. 3.8). It sloped gently from the eastern edge of the section toward the vent hole but stopped short of the kiln structure by some 0.50m. It also had domestic and industrial pottery as well as a coin (N-8). Within deposit [068] were some five mudbricks [223] which might represent a surface or may be tumble from the kiln. Deposit [205], to the west of [068], was a dark humic layer with some domestic pottery and burnt brick. It was roughly rectanguar measuring c.1.0m in length and 0.6m in width. west of [205] and abutting the exterior of the kiln was a deposit [206] measuring 0.55m north-south by 0.2m east-west and comprising burnt brick and small fragments of industrial pottery. Deposit [229] abuts the north edge of brick platform [058] and is bounded on its north by deposits [205] and [206]. The deposit [229] is predominantly white, probably from lime. Two large fired mudbricks [202 and 203] initially thought to be structural buttressing were given individual numbers but subsequently proved not to be structural. These sat on top of deposit [229].

Overlying [205], [206] and [229] was deposit [053A] which consisted of fragmented mudpack and brick fragments as well as a large quantity of industrial pottery. Overlying the western part of [068] was a grayish sandy deposit [067] containing fired mudbrick, domestic and industrial pottery. This was in turn overlain by deposit [065] which was a loose grey sandy deposit containing both fired and unfired brick tumble as well as industrial and domestic pottery. [053A] and [065] were overlain by the more extensive red deposit [053], comprising burned brick tumble and industrial pottery. [053] measured approximately 1.1m east-west by 0.8m north-south.

The west wall of the kiln [040] preserves three openings all of them centrally aligned (Fig. 4.2, Plate 3.7). The uppermost of these is another arched vent [336] measuring 0.20m in height and 0.19m in width. It is located 0.80m beneath the uppermost course of brickwork. This is not visible on the exterior because an area of brickwork [251] runs across it. The vent contained a very fine grey, ashy, fill [054] with sherds of pottery and fragments of slag mixed among it. The second opening on the west wall [337] also comprised an arched vent measuring 0.25m in height and 0.21m in width. It is located 1.68m from the uppermost course of brickwork (this is 0.68m beneath the sill of the upper vent). The vent was filled by [059/254] which was similar in composition to [054]. However, this vent was

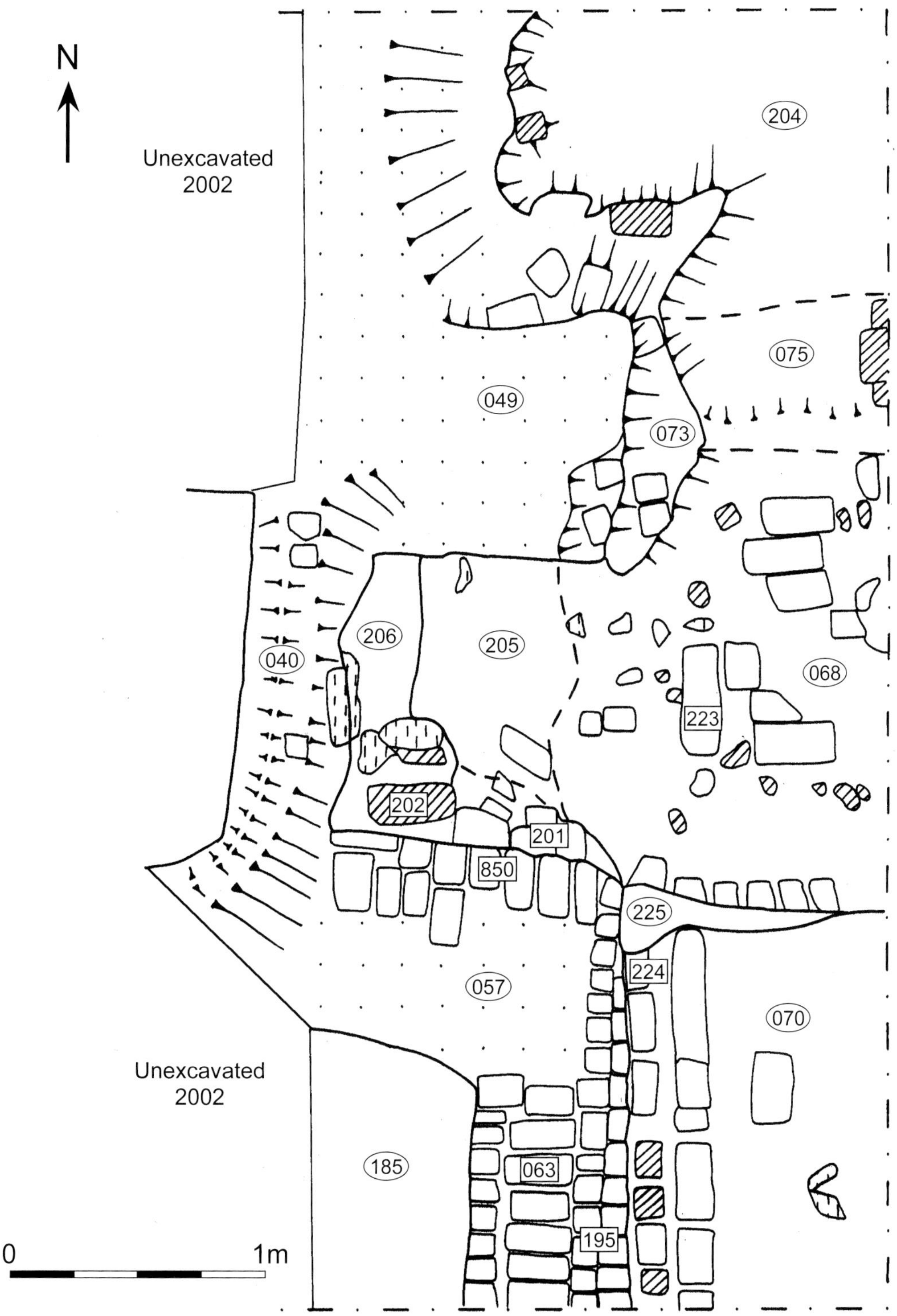

Figure 3.8. The eastern part of trench HAC3 showing the brickwork which forms part of the H-shape around the kiln [063] and [049] on either side of the stoke-hole. The sondage made at the request of our S.C.A. inspector is visible as [185]. (Plan: T. Brindle and R. Hart).

blocked on the exterior by a single brick and a fragment of saggar both of which were firmly wedged in place and were removed during excavation.

The lowest opening [235/338] was considerably larger than the rest (Fig. 4.2). It comprised an arched 'doorway' whose opening measured 1.5m in height and 0.5m in width. The arch itself was well constructed and comprised three courses of arched brickwork the uppermost course of which forms the sill of the vent above [337]. The uppermost point of the opening of [338] was 2.25m below the uppermost course of the surviving brickwork and extended to the deepest point in the excavation (3.75m). This access hole was blocked with the re-used bases of large saggars [330] (Plates 3.8 and

Plate 3.7. Interior view of the west wall of the kiln. The upper vent is [336] and the lower [337]. The upper vent is blocked on the exterior and has a brick wedged into it. The lowermost access opening [235/338] is not yet visible. (Photo: P.T. Nicholson).

3.9). On the inside of the kiln and abutting these saggar bases three distinct fills could be recognised. The lowest of these deposits [253/220 probably equivalent of 311] had an average depth of 0.51m and comprised ash overlain by deposit [237] which had a depth 0.84m and contained saggar fragments, fired brick fragments and a large quantity of kiln furniture. The uppermost deposit in the access hole was a fine grey-brown sandy deposit [236/332] which had an average depth of 0.15m. The uppermost 0.07m of the access hole had no fill.

Abutting the western face of structure [040] the sloping cut [334] is reinforced by a series of parallel walls (Plate 3.9). The foundations for these walls seem to have been laid on top of a natural grey-brown silty-clay deposit [316], the depth of which is not known as it could not be fully excavated. The northern series of walls (Fig. 4.1) comprised a deposit of slag [317] resting on deposit [316] on top of which stood mudbrick wall [242]. This has a maximum height of 2.96m and maximum width east-west of 0.95m. Sealing [242] was a mud pack [252] with a maximum depth of 0.2m. Context [252] was sealed by the brick platform [041]. Also sat on deposit [316] was a foundation of mudbrick [319] which was three courses in height (here 0.28m) and which abutted the large slag lump [317] which is likely to have acted as part of the foundation. On top of foundation [319] was a wall made up of saggar fragments [214]. This wall had a maximum height of 3.55m and maximum width of 1.18m east-west.

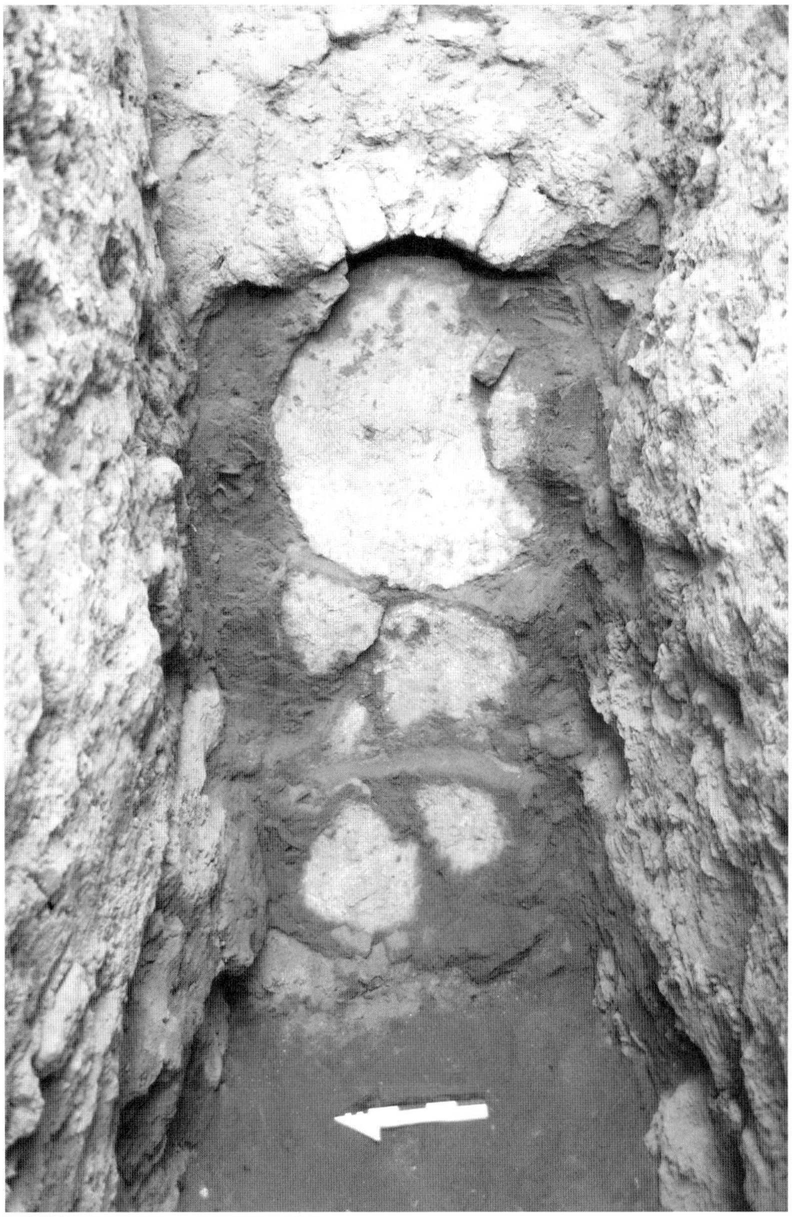

Plate 3.8. The blocked access opening [235/338] in the west wall of the kiln looking east from the access pit. The blocking [330] comprises the bases of broken Type 12 saggars. The scale bar is 0.25m. (Photo: P.T. Nicholson).

The southern series of walls comprised a slag deposit [318] overlying [316] and on top of which stood mudbrick wall [211] which had a maximum height of 3.06m. On top of this wall sat a patch of mudpack [193] which was approximately square in plan measuring 0.3m x 0.35m. Adhering to the face of [211] were two similar sandy deposits [228] and [230]. Also adhering to the face of [211] was an area of compacted mud [232] which was removed to reveal the extent of the wall. The packed mud [232] measured 0.7m in length by 0.4m in width. On its west this wall [211] abutted a complex of walls whose lowermost part comprised mudbrick wall [320] and which stood on top of [316]. This mudbrick structure [320] was 3 courses in height (c.0.28m) and is equivalent to [319] on the north side. [320] is 0.80m wide. Overlying [320] was a wall of unfired mudbrick mixed with fired (and therefore re-used) brick [321]. The width of this wall is 0.80m.

On top of [321] was a section of wall built with fragments of saggar vessels [322]. This wall remained to a height of approximately 0.20m. Originally this wall probably continued to roughly the same height as [211] (i.e. 3.06m). However, it appeared that the saggars had collapsed onto the slope forming deposit [244] (Plate 3.10) and revealing mudbrick wall [323] behind it with additional mudbrick wall [212/324] on top of this. Wall [323] was excavated to a height of 2.45m but probably continued downward behind [322/325] and perhaps also behind [321]. After discussion with the S.C.A. representative it was decided that all walls in this complex should be left *in situ*.

Plate 3.9. Photo-composite of the kiln and its access pit. The step down into the pit is at far left, the blocked kiln access opening at centre and the southern retaining wall at right. (Composite: J. Coyle).

Plate 3.10. Trench HAC3 looking east down the slope of saggar fragments [244] onto the kiln [040]. The deposit has not been fully excavated. (Photo: P.T. Nicholson).

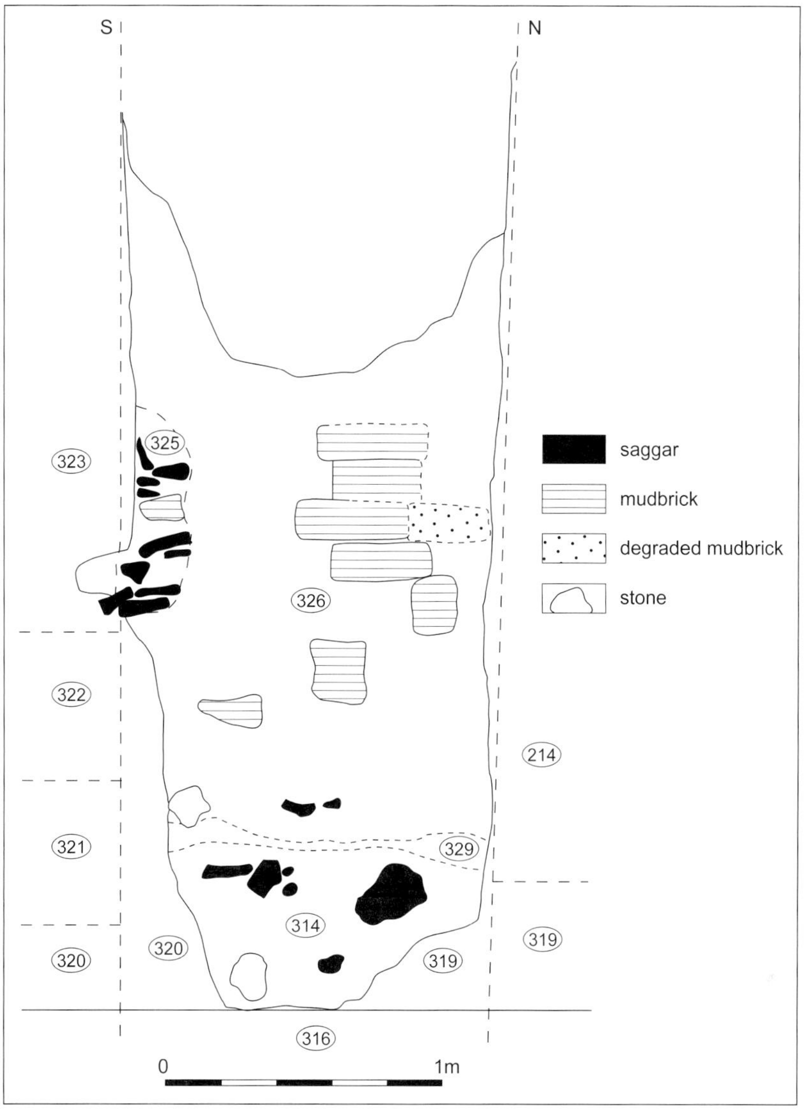

Figure 3.9. Looking west onto the step in the access trench in front of the main opening in the kiln at HAC3 (see Fig. 4.1). The contexts to north and south are shown beyond the vertical dotted lines. (Elevation: R. Hart).

Perpendicular to these east-west walls on the western side of structure [040], at a distance of 2.08m from the west face of the structure, was a retaining wall [326] (Fig. 3.9). This wall was constructed of mudbrick some 12 courses high (1.28m) and was constructed on top of the thin deposit [329], a dark humic layer with a maximum depth of 0.12m which sealed deposit [314]. [326] marks the western extent of cut [333] and its top marks the start of the slope of [334]. Overlying wall [326] was a small mudbrick wall [331] aligned north-south. This was 0.5m long and 0.25m wide and made up of three courses.

Although it cannot be proven, it is likely that the wall numbered [240] is in fact the northerly continuation of [326] but is only visible in its uppermost courses. Beyond [326], wall [240] measures 1.5m north-south with a maximum width of 0.40m. This area separates two deposits of slag [241] on its west and [239] (Fig. 3.10, Plate 3.11) on its east. Deposit [241] measured 1.3m x 0.58m and [239] measured 1.1m x 1.2m. The northern extent of both of these deposits, as of wall [240] is unknown as they continue beyond the extent of the excavation. Contexts [239], [240], [241] were overlain by a dark brown sandy deposit [231] which measured 2.3m east-west by 1.3m north-south. This was itself overlain by a light brown sandy deposit which contained some modern rubbish and slag as well as large pieces of domestic pottery. This deposit had the same dimensions as [234]. Deposit [231] was overlain by the surface context in the area [074/33/233/300].

Deposit [239] was bounded on its south by saggar wall [214] and on its east by [213] a small mudbrick wall to the west of the kiln. To the east of wall [213] a platform survives to varying degrees of preservation which include well preserved areas [041] to the north of the kiln structure and [058], [043], [063], [198] and [201] (with [225] possibly forming part of its foundation) to the south-east of the kiln where individual mudbricks can clearly be seen. The rest

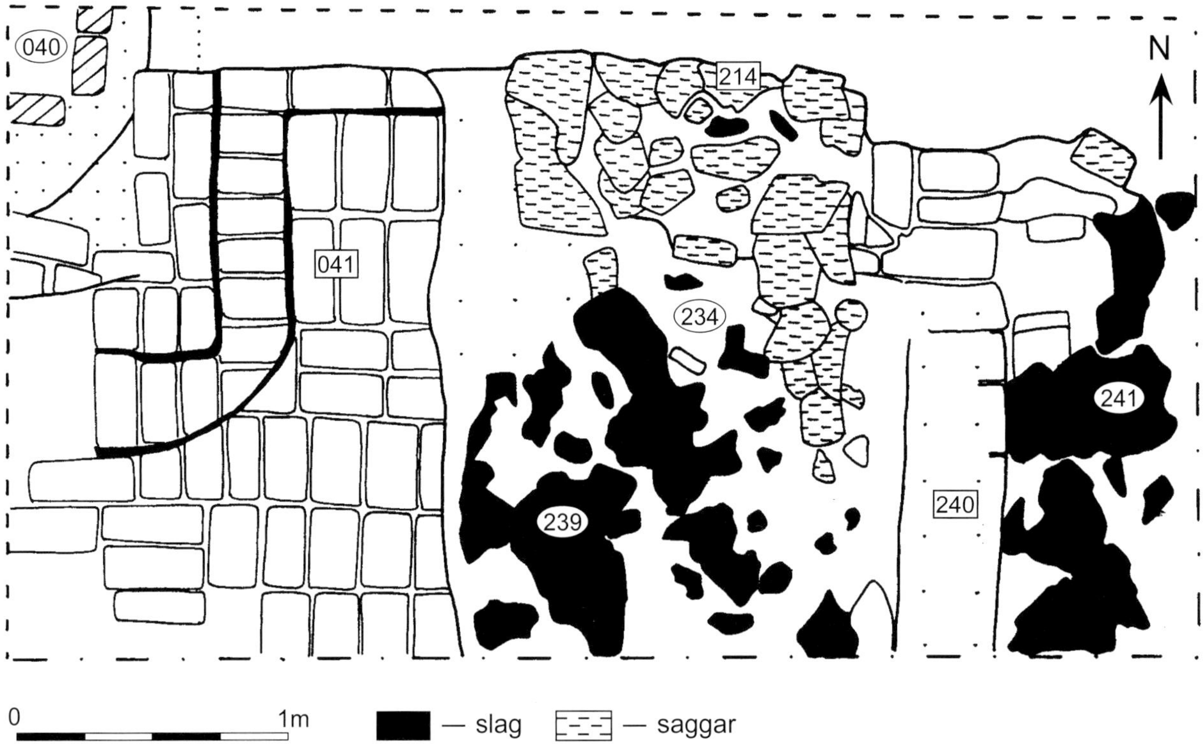

Figure 3.10. The north-western part of trench HAC3. The kiln [040] is visible at top left along with the brickwork of [041] forming part of the kiln surround. Areas of broken saggars [214] and dumped slag [239] and [241] are visible. (Plan: C. Jones and R. Hart).

Plate 3.11. Trench HAC3 looking south over slag deposit [239] and saggars [214]. Scale by north arrow is 0.5m that to the west is 1m. (Photo: P.T. Nicholson).

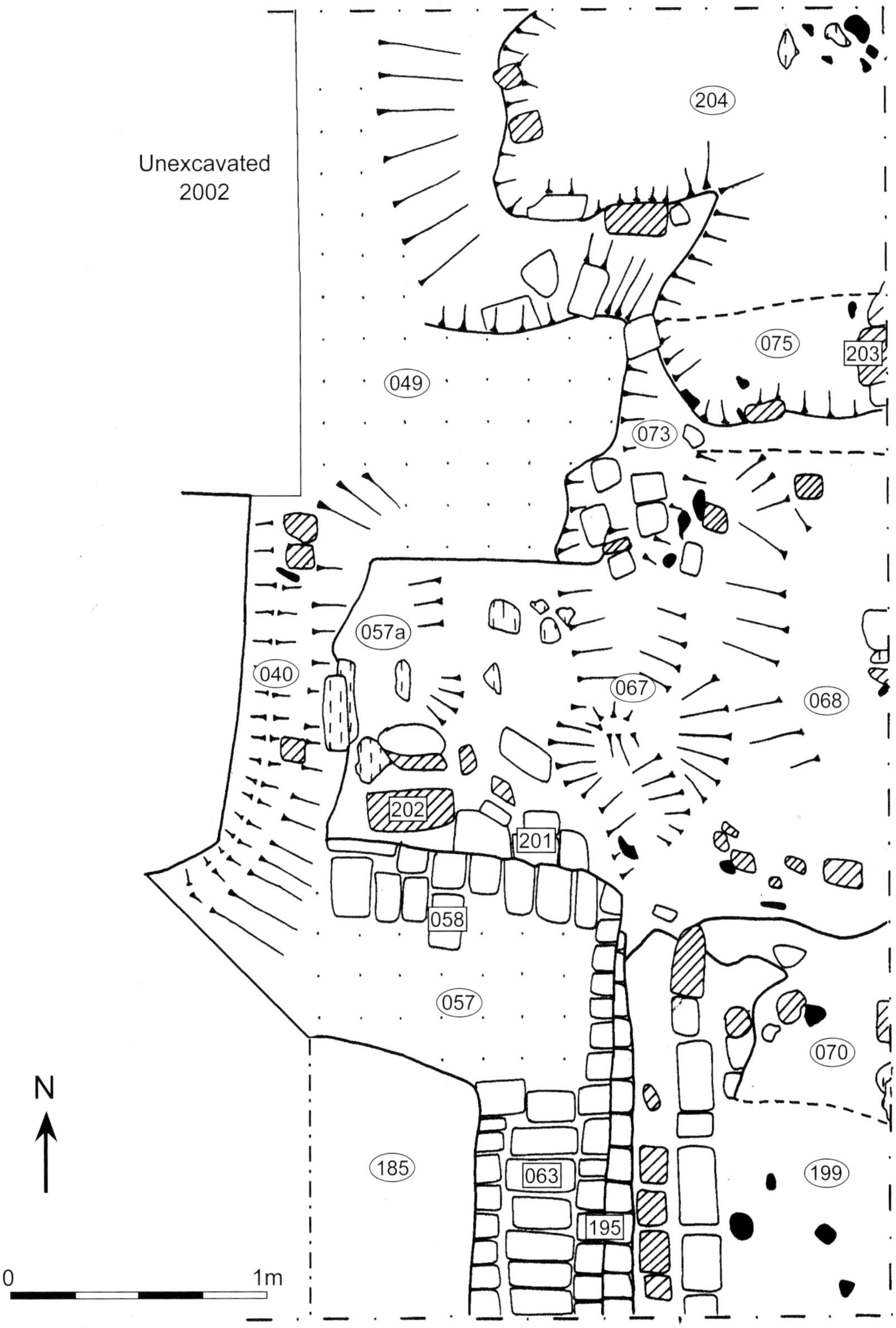

Figure 3.11. The eastern end of trench HAC3 . (Plan: T. Brindle and R. Hart).

Plate 3.12. Trench HAC3 looking south. The wings either side of the stoke-hole are visible at bottom right and mid-right. (Photo: P.T. Nicholson).

of the area of the platform is covered by a layer of very decayed mudbrick where individual bricks cannot readily be identified [042] and [049]. On the west [041] has mudbricks [227] sitting on top of it, probably collapse. To the east of [042] and [049] was a small deposit of decayed mudbrick [075] which also contained faience and pottery. To the north-east of platform area [049] was a rectangular deposit of decayed mudbrick [204]. The deposit measured 1.3m east-west and 1.1m north south.

Amongst the decayed mudbricks of [042] two distinct areas [045/046] of identifiable bricks, including fired bricks, were discernible. Overlying [042] in the northernmost 1.0m strip of the trench was a deposit of dark brown organic-rich sand [037/039]. The organic material is thought to be decayed wood, although this has not been examined by a specialist. Also overlying [042] in the east of the trench was a light brown-grey sandy deposit [036] which included large charcoal fragments. Into [042] to the west of the kiln structure was an oval shaped cut [044] measuring 0.44m in its long axis by 0.3m on the shorter axis. Its lower fill [243] was a loose grey sand which overlain by [060] comprised a loose, brown, sandy fill, this itself overlain by the uppermost trench deposit [033]. Although excavated in succeeding years it is likely that [060] and [243] are actually the same deposit. Deposit [033] also overlay [036] and [037/039]. Deposit [033] contained a small irregular patch of dark grey-brown deposit [035].

The platform structure seems to step upward toward the kiln structure, this is most notable on the north-west side [041] (Fig. 3.6) although it is likely that this stepped arrangement continued, perhaps all along the northern side of the kiln to allow for the local topography in that area.

The depth of the platform was tested by a sondage [185] inserted by our inspector and proven to be at least 0.4m in depth (Fig. 3.11). This sondage [185] measured 2.4m east-west and a maximum of 1.4m north-south. The basal deposit of the sondage was [048] a friable grey sandy deposit.

The eastern wall of structure [040] was accessed by an open area (0.80m wide north-south) bounded on its south by an east-west projection of the brick platform [057/063/198] and on its north by an east-west projection of [049] (Fig. 3.11, Plates 3.6 and 3.12). These projections of the brick platform extend c.1.4m to the east of structure [040], thus making the open area between the projections 0.80 x 1.4m. The lowest course (as excavated) [198] of the platform on its eastern face to the south of the vent projects 0.10m beyond the courses above. The projection of this lowest brickwork is also visible on the north face [201] where it projects 0.2m over a distance of 0.3m. Overlying [057/063/198] were seven mudbricks aligned roughly east-west [061] and initially thought to be a wall. However, these were not bonded to one another or to the platform [057/063/198]. They were removed to reveal the actual north-east corner

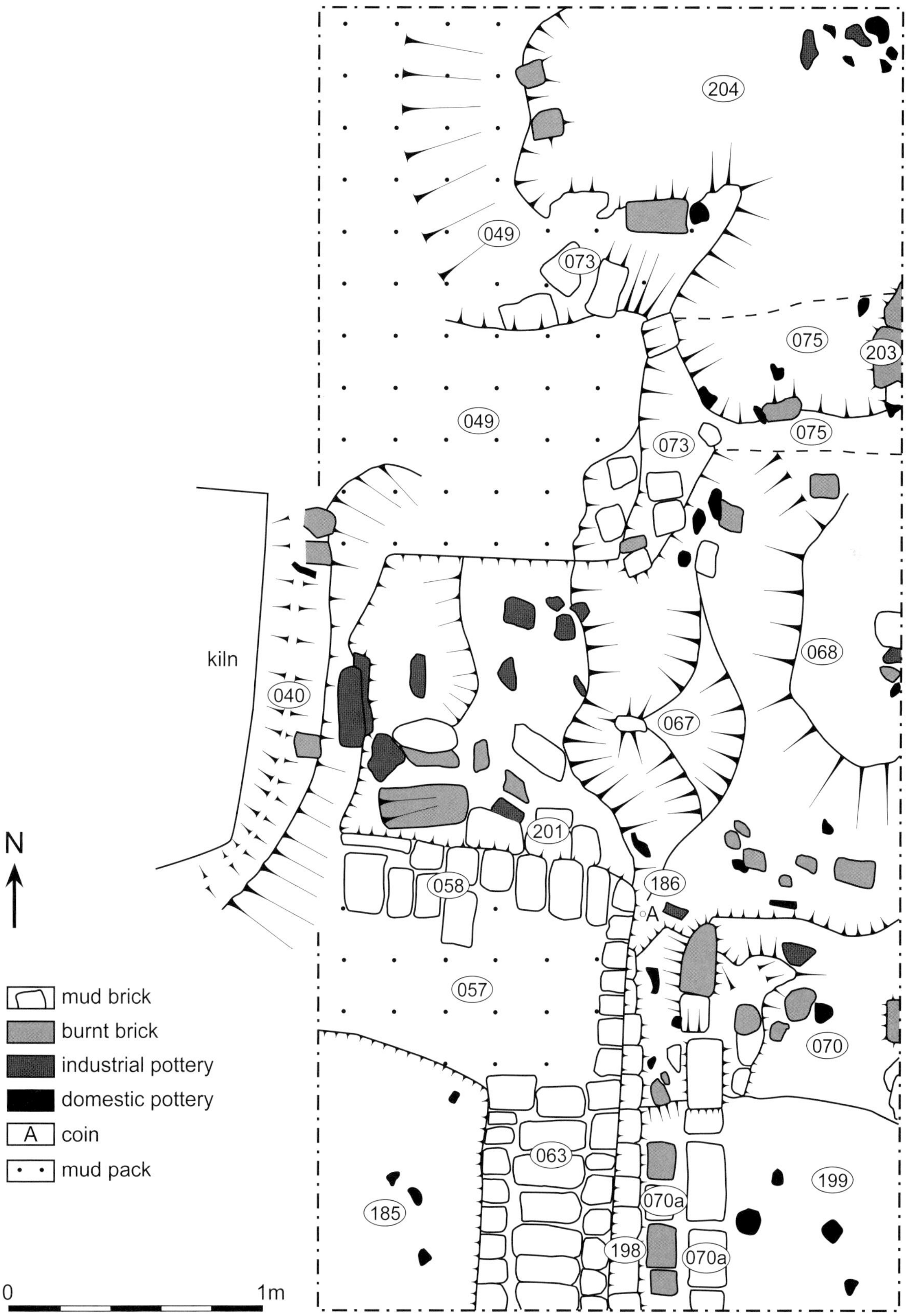

Figure 3.12. The eastern end of trench HAC3 . 'A' marks the findspot of coin N-5 from unit [186]. (Plan: T. Brindle and R. Hart).

Plate 3.13. Trench HAC3 looking north over the southern wing of the stoke-hole. The arrow indicates the position of deposit [186] which yielded a mid-late 4th Century B.C. coin (N-5). The wall to the right of the arrow is thought to predate the kiln. The large scale bar measures 1.0m. (Photo: P.T. Nicholson).

of the platform. An similar deposit of tumbled fired bricks [047] was revealed in the north-east corner of the trench.

Immediately to the east of brick platform [044/063/198] was a probable decayed brick surface [223]. The relationship between [225] amd [223] and wall [070A] which ran parallel to the brick platform (north-south) could not be ascertained because the wall was not removed during excavation (Fig. 3.12). Wall [070A] might have been built on top of this surface [225] and [223] or might predate it. The mudbrick wall comprised of two stretcher courses of brick giving it an overall width of c.0.24m and a length of 0.80m. It has a maximum height of three courses, c.0.3m and minimum of one course c.0.1m measured from surface [225] and [223]. This difference in height probably represents partial destruction of the wall. Wall [070A] was separated from brick platform [063] and lower courses [198] by rubble deposit [192/200] which had a maximum width of 0.10m. Following excavation of deposit [192/200] a further three mudbricks were exposed [224]. These may be a northern extension of [070A].

To the east of the northern part of [070A] is a deposit [186] comprised of mudbrick fragments, domestic pottery and a coin (N-5) this is overlain by brick tumble [070] which also contained pottery, charcoal and plaster (Plate 3.13). Overlying [070] were the contents of a vessel [071] fine and grey brown in colour and with plant or fabric remains within it. Overlying this was deposit [069] a light brown sandy deposit which also contained fragments of brick.

Plate 3.14. The lowest part of the interior of the kiln looking west. The thick deposit of slag [208] can be seen running to within c.0.5m of the opening [235] which was still closed by the saggar bases at this time. The wood is part of the safety shoring installed within the structure. The scale bar represents 0.2m. (Photo: P.T. Nicholson).

Kiln Fills

Within structure [040] are a number of deposits relating to both its use and abandonment. The basal deposit within the kiln is a compact brown clay [247] which was overlain by a smaller deposit of yellow clay [248] measuring 0.15m by 0.28m (Plate 3.14). Clay [248] was overlain by [226/221], natural clay which has become reddened from heating. It measured a maximum of 0.05m in thickness and is likely to have covered the whole base of the kiln although it was visible only in the western part of the kiln, the eastern being covered by dense slag. At the same level as clay [247] and at the extreme west of the kiln interior, running north-south and exactly aligned on the western wall and protruding into the kiln by 0.10m was an area of reddened clay, probably much deteriorated brick [246].

Overlying [226/221] was a deposit of charcoal [222] again visible only in the western half of the kiln. This was overlain by [220/311] a deposit of fine grey, fibrous, ash. Overlying [220] was a series of alternating ash and slag deposits. All of the slag was numbered [208] since it was difficult to differentiate individual deposits. The ash within the kiln was given individual numbers[1] but is essentially the same as [220] includes plant macrofossils.

Overlying the uppermost ash deposit were two deposits [184] and [076]. [184] consisted of fired brick fragments, kiln furniture and domestic pottery and was found in the centre of the kiln structure it was circular in shape with a diameter of 0.75m. The second deposit was [076] which was less red than [184] and surrounded it on all sides, abutting the kiln walls. With the exception of the slag, which adhered to the walls of [040], context [184/196/197] was the largest deposit, in terms of its volume, within the kiln. Sealing this deposit was context [077] which is similar in character to [184] and varied only due its higher concentration of fired bricks. The deposit forms a semi-circle with its straight edge, of 0.8m, formed by the west wall of the kiln.

The deposit overlying [077] is [072] which is a light brown sandy deposit which contained both domestic and industrial pottery (including some saggar fragments) and also fragments of kiln furniture. Above [072] was a red sandy deposit [066] which contained fired mudbrick, domestic and industrial pottery, kiln furniture and a significant quantity of unworked quartz and which filled the kiln structure. Context [056] which was on top of [066] was of similar character, it was overlain by a small semi-circular shaped deposit [055] comprising small angular fragments of granite, alabaster and other stones. The straight side of the semi-circle was defined by the north wall of [040].

Overlying [055] was deposit [052] over half of whose volume was comprised of broken brick tumble. It also included slag, faience and saggar fragments. This was in turn overlain by [051], about half of whose volume comprised industrial remains, stone fragments and some domestic pottery as well as faience. [050], which was above [051] contained less fired brick as well as faience, shell and domestic pottery.

Context [038] is the uppermost deposit in the kiln. It was an orange-red colour and of sandy texture with fragments of fired bricks mixed amongst it. It was sealed by deposit [034] which represents the uppermost surface in this part of the site.

Access Pit Fills

The access pit is the east-west running trench which is defined on its east by the large arched opening [235] of [040] and on its north and south by the mudbrick and saggar walls. Its easternmost end steps up toward a series of less well defined deposits (see below).

The basal deposit here was a grey-brown, compacted clay [316]. Overlying this were two deposits [315] at the east end and [314] at the western end. [315] was a reddish brown clay whilst [314] was similar but included fragments of fired brick and ash. Above [315] was an ash deposit [311] situated directly in front of the stoke-hole. It had a maximum depth of 0.20m and this was found immediately outside the blocked access hole. In the deposit were a number of unfired objects, possibly bats or jar stoppers.

Deposits [314] and [312] were reddish brown clay deposits with fragments of fired mudbrick and kiln furniture. [312] included an area of compacted clay [313]. On top of [311] and [312] was a large deposit [309] consisting of mainly domestic pottery with a few saggar fragments, pieces of kiln furniture and slag fragments as well as amphora fragments, including the large amphora [310] (Fig. 3.13).

The succeeding deposit [244/307/303] was comprised of saggar fragments which probably derive from a collapse of the upper part of the saggar wall [322]. Above [244] on its western side was a thin, loose, sandy deposit [215] with occasional pieces of domestic pottery and faience (Fig. 3.14). Above [244] on its eastern side and thus closest to the kiln was deposit [245] a similar deposit including industrial ceramic. These were sealed by a large deposit of domestic pottery [189], many of the pots semi-complete as well as a large granite block (T-36). [189] contained a small slag deposit [216] and a compacted lens of grey sand [218]. Two compacted grey, sandy and pottery rich deposits were found adhered to walls [214] and [211] ([207] and [219] respectively. These are likely to be compacted areas of [189]. A deposit [188] similar to [189] was found to the south of wall [212]. Context [188] overlaid a slag deposit [250] which was probably the equivalent of the area of slag dumping [239] and [241] on the north of the stoking pit. Context [188] contained generally smaller sherds of pottery than [189] in a fine sandy matrix. Both [189] and [188] were sealed by the uppermost deposit in the western area [074] which was a grey sandy deposit including domestic pottery, slag and some bone fragments. Near the kiln [189] was overlain by a red sandy deposit [238] which contained frequent small sherds of domestic pottery. In this area [238] is overlain by the suface context [074].

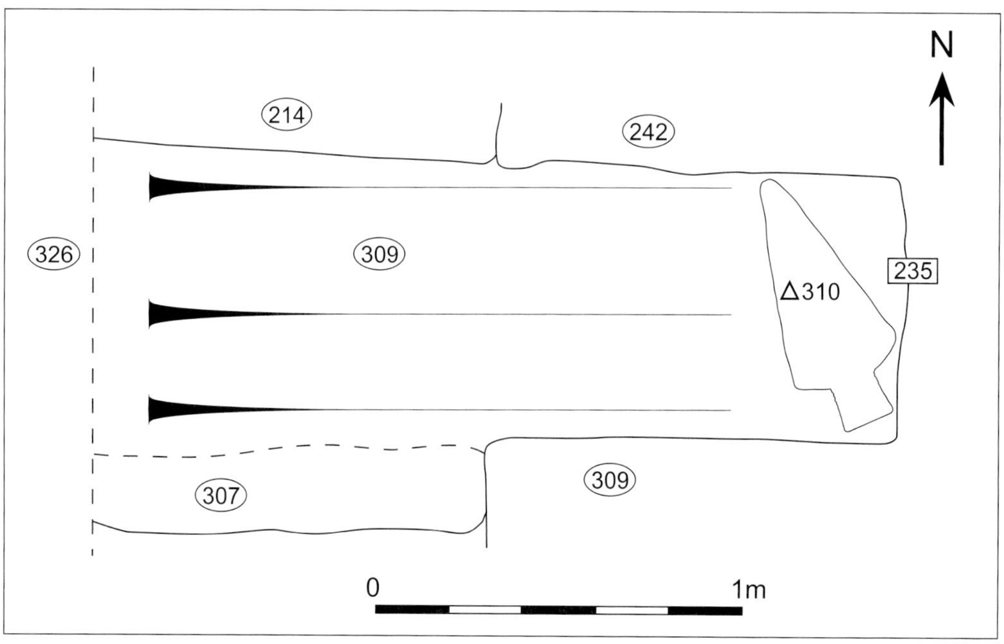

Figure 3.13. The slope of the access pit to the kiln in course of excavation. The 2nd - 3rd Century amphora [310] lies immediately in front of the west side of the kiln. (Plan: C. Jones and R. Hart).

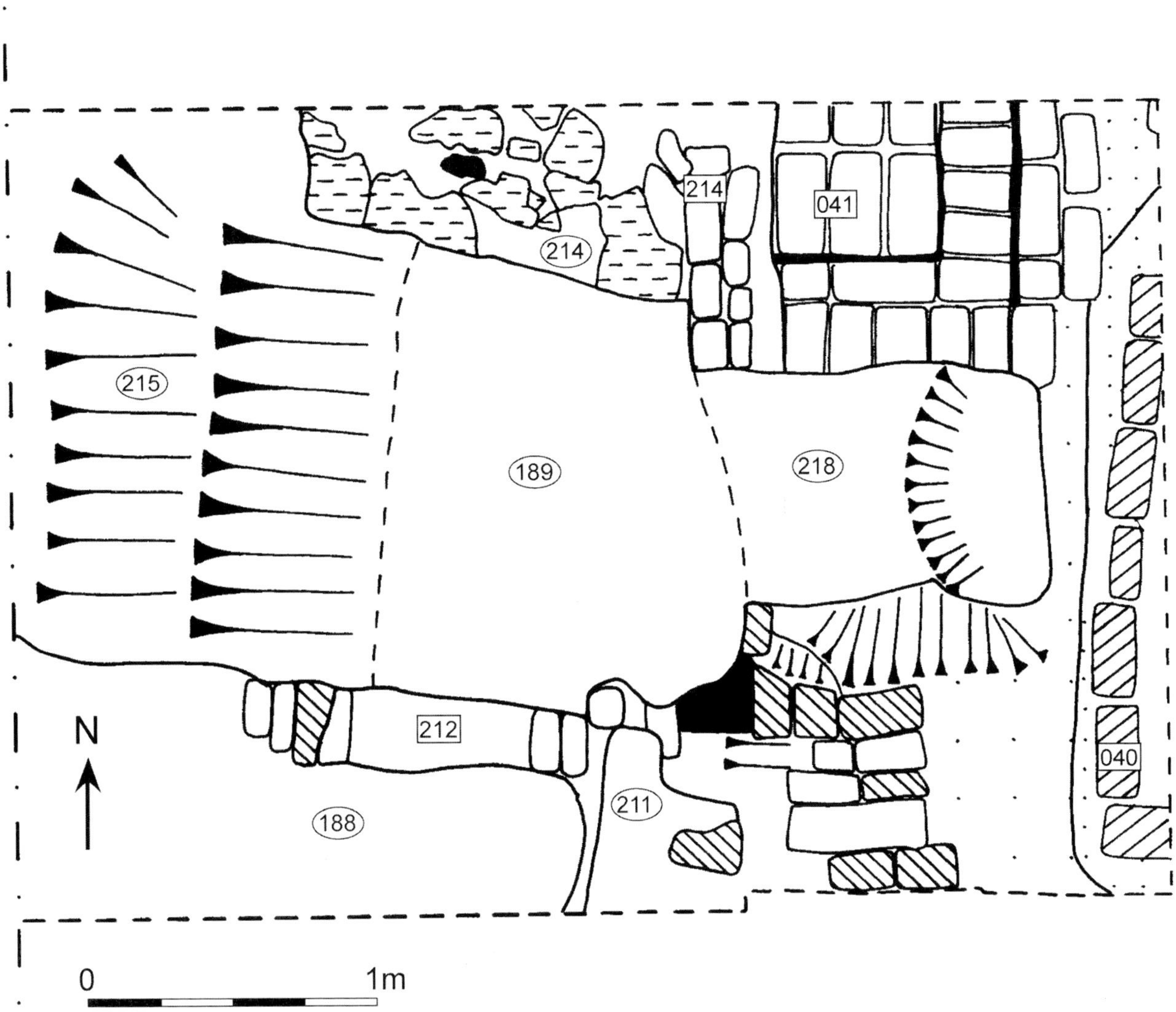

Figure 3.14. The access pit of the kiln [040] showing the deposit [189] from which came much of the domestic pottery at the western end of trench HAC3 . (Plan: R. Hart).

The basal deposit encountered in the western (extended 2005) part of the trench was [306] a light-grey brown sandy deposit which measured a maximum of 1.25m wide by 1.6m in length. Overlying [306] to the north was a mud-pack surface [305] which extended beyond the limit of excavation to the north and west. To the south [306] was overlain by a similar mud-pack surface [302] whose extent is unknown as it was overlain by deposit [308] which was not fully excavated due to time constraints. Deposit [308] contained a large quantity of slag, fired unfired mudbrick and industrial ceramic. This deposit was similar to deposit [301] which overlaid it and all other deposits in this extension area. Overlying [301] was the surface deposit [300/33].

Interpretive Summary

It is unlikely that the kiln [040] was the first structure on the HAC3 site. Finds of coins[2] dating to the mid-late 4th Century B.C. in the south-east corner of the site beside the rather damaged wall [070A] suggest that the kiln may have been constructed on a site where there had been previous structures – perhaps a previous kiln. The fact that slag such as [317] was incorporated into the lowest part of the mudbrick wall [242] which was probably built at the same time as the kiln certainly suggests that there had been earlier kilns in the area, possibly on exactly this site. Such a phenomenon would not be unusual since kilns would regularly need to be rebuilt, not least because of the problem of slagging caused by the fuel (see Chapter 4). The kiln itself was dug into the ground but surrounded by an H-shaped platform of unfired brickwork [041] on top of which the kiln superstructure would have stood and which would have given access to the superstructure.

On the west side of the kiln the mudbrick walls [242] and [211], which were probably constructed at the same time as the kiln or very shortly thereafter, were soon supplemented by saggar walls [214] and [322], the latter of which eventually collapsed to form a slope of broken saggars [244].

When the kiln went out of use, probably sometime in the 1st Century A.D. the main access hole [235] on the west side was left completely blocked by the cemented wall of saggar bases [330] and rubbish was gradually thrown into the stoking pit including an almost complete amphora [310] of 2nd/3rd Century date. The saggars of [244] probably collapsed around this time and the deposit of well preserved domestic pottery [189], also of the 2nd/3rd Century, was thrown in on top of them, as was a very large granite block.[3] That the block did not fall further down the slope indicates that the deepest part of the pit had already filled with rubbish and the collapsed saggars by around the time [189] with its granite block were deposited.

By the end of its life the kiln itself had become choked with slag [208] such that deposits of collapsed brickwork built up on top of the slag and ash of the kiln and probably filled it quite rapidly. What became of the superstructure can only be speculated upon but it is likely that if the faience industry continued much beyond the demise of this kiln the bricks of the firing chamber would have been taken away for re-use. If industry in this area had ceased then the bricks may still have been pilfered for use in domestic structures. The kiln would soon have been reduced to the level of the perforated floor (chequer) of which only traces of the springers remained at the time of its discovery. Some of the brick tumble from the robbing/collapse of the superstructure is probably represented by contexts such as [061] and [047].

Trench HAD1

Trench HAD1 is located on the far south of Kom Helul and is separated from the other two sites by a small irrigation canal. Here are a series of orange coloured mounds with very few traces of industrial activity visible on the surface, apart from the presence of a few fired bricks, some apparently *in situ*.

Trial borings by Dr. David Jeffreys, and geophysical survey by Mr. Ian Mathieson both suggested that this area had experienced considerable burning such as might be expected from a kiln or furnace. Furthermore, the remains of a fired brick structure were visible out-cropping at the surface of the site. In the first season of work this was chosen as the focus for excavation in the hope that the structure might be the remains of a furnace, and furthermore that it might be a furnace which had not previously been examined. That being so it might offer a great deal of information which might supplement the work of Petrie.

The excavation here was begun in the 2000 season by Ms. Amy Goldsmith, whose 5.0 x 5.0m trench exposed the

Plate 3.15. Trench HAD1 looking south. The trench [030] [031] running approximately north-south and visible above the blackboard is believed to be from Petrie's work at the site. The burned brick platform of the building is clearly visible. Scale bar measures 0.5m. (Photo: P.T. Nicholson).

Figure 3.15. Trench HAD1 showing the extensive mudbrick platform which had been fired during a conflagration. A trench [030] [031], thought to be part of Petrie's work, is located on the north side at the centre. (Plan: A. Goldsmith and K. Stentoft).

burned brickwork of a substantial structure. In 2001 Ms Katinka Stentoft continued the excavation of the site. Prior to her beginning work a geophysical survey by Ms. Rowena Hart (Appendix 1) had shown that the brickwork exposed in 2000 belonged to a structure larger than a kiln. As a result Ms. Stentoft was able to complete the excavation of HAD1 and undertake two more trial trenches (HAD2 and HAD3) in the hope of learning more about the nature of the burned structure (Plate 3.15).

HAD1 comprised a 5.0 x 5.0m square. Although during the course of the excavation some 40 contexts were assigned to this square the archaeology is much simpler than such a quantity might suggest and can readily be reduced to the making of a structure and subsequent damage to it.

The basal contexts here are [021], [022] and [023] brown sandy deposits. On top of these contexts were laid a series of layers of mudbrick [013, 014, 020, 024/091, 025, 026,

027/085/086/094/095/098,099] making up a brick platform. Where complete the bricks measured 0.40 x 0.20 x 0.10m. Mortar layers between some of the brick layers were also numbered [088, 090, 093, 097, 100] (Fig. 3.15).

A deep east-west trench [011] is located on the north side of the brick platform extending from the edge of the brickwork to the northern limit of the excavated area. At the western end this trench is filled by deposits [021] and [016] and at the east by contexts [022], [019] and [018]. It is likely that the lowest deposits reached [022] and [021] are the same but they are separated from one another by a further trench which has been cut in two phases.

This trench runs approximately north-south with its southern end, cut [030], cutting into the brickwork of the platform [027/099] at its unfired edge and extending into the fired part of the same context. The trench was then cut deeper at its northern end [031] to give it a stepped profile.

The basal context forming the bottom of cut [030] was numbered [023] and the trench at this southern end infilled with deposits [029], [014], [028] and [027] whilst cut [031] was filled by deposits [017] and [015] with [012] sealing these and extending well beyond the limits of the cut and forming the surface context for the trench.

To the south of the preserved area of the platform was an area of decayed fired brick [082] and orange sand [083].

The surface contexts in this trench were [081] and [084].

At the close of the excavation HAD1, like the other excavation trenches, was back-filled in order to protect the structures.

Interpretive Summary

When first encountered it was thought that the fired brick platform might be the floor of a furnace whose superstructure was now lost. The heavy burning of the brickwork clearly accounted for Mr. Ian Mathieson's high geophysical readings and for the results of the coring. Ms. Katinka Stentoft observed that the mortar between the bricks was fired, suggesting that the bricks had become fired *in situ*. The north face of the edge of the structure is unburned, perhaps suggesting that the fire which reddened the bricks to the south was in some way contained at this point. These features supported the initial hypothesis that this structure might be the remains of a kiln.

The availability of geophysical results in 2001, however, made it clear that the burned area was much larger than the excavation of 2000 suggested and that the brickwork formed part of a large platform. Trenches HAD2 and HAD3 were dug to confirm this view (below).

There were virtually no finds from trench HAD1 and in the hope of determining its date and function, as well as elucidating its construction, a sondage was made through some of the brickwork. The aim of this investigation was to find dating evidence between the levels of brickwork, but none was found. On the south side of the trench were two areas which lack brickwork. These may have be parts of casemates, but this could not been investigated without extending the trench to the south, and time did not permit this.

On the basis of the geophysical evidence and excavated results Dr. David Jeffreys suggested that the structure may represent a platform of the type sometimes said to be for constructing peripteral temple buildings, but from our excavation there is nothing to suggest what may have stood on the brick platform. We can only conclude that this is part of a large brick platform with casemates which was subjected to fierce burning at some time in the past.

Petrie (1910: 44) talks about "a great burnt house south of the pottery kilns" from which came a false door, bronze fittings etc. It also had a flight of stone steps and had been subject to "an immense conflagration". It is suggested here that the platform in HAD1 is in fact Petrie's "great burned house", but rather than being an actual house it was in fact a temple building as Jeffreys suggested on the basis of the geophysical survey. Such an interpretation would explain the presence of a false door stela, bronze fittings (Plates 1.5 and 1.6) and stone steps. Examination of the stela showed that it still retained small quantities of burned mudbrick adhering to it and whilst it was not possible to check this scientifically the colour appears consistent with the brickwork from HAD1. The lack of other finds from this trench might also be explained by the likelihood that this building had already been excavated by Petrie.

The east-west trench [011] probably belongs to the construction phase of the platform and facilitated the laying of bricks on its south side. It may have been partially refilled at the end of the construction. This trench was subsequently bisected by trench [030] which encountered the brickwork, this trench was then made deeper at its northern end as trench [031]. The purpose of these trenches is uncertain but it may be suggested that they relate to Petrie's excavations.

Although the S.C.A. permit the construction of *zeriba* structures for the drying of dates on the site these ephemeral millet-stalk structures generally have very shallow, and usually narrow, foundations. They are usually little more than the width of a *turyeh* (hoe) blade and no more than 0.20m deep whereas these trenches are up to 1.0m deep from the original ground surface. This might suggest that trenching by Petrie's men encountered bricks at the southern end of [030] and that the trench was made deeper

Plate 3.16. Trench HAD2 looking south. Damage caused by the construction of zeriba *enclosures is apparent. Foreground scale bar is 0.5m, that in the background 2.0m. (Photo: P.T. Nicholson).*

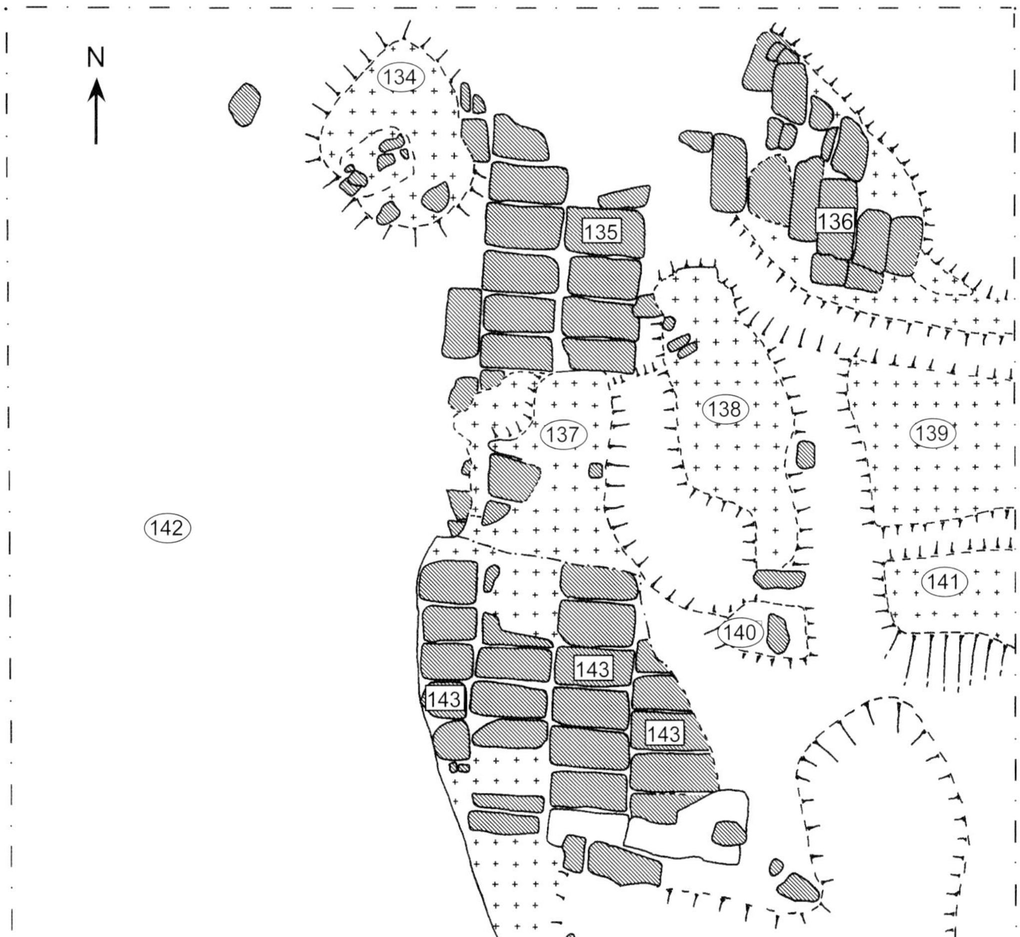

Figure 3.16. Trench HAD2, part of the same building as HAD1 with extensive damage caused by the building of enclosures. Context [133] underlies [142] at the south end of the trench. (Plan: K. Stentoft).

at the north as [031] in search of a floor. At this point it may have been realized that the workers were outside the building and attention then moved to the brick platform itself, leaving little trace – other than a paucity of finds – in the archaeological record.

The decayed brick [082] and orange sand [083] probably represent areas where the fired brick has been robbed for re-use.

Trench HAD2

This was also a 5.0 x 5.0m trench, situated due west of HAD1, and intended to locate the corner of the structure shown in the geophysical survey (Plate 3.16).

The stratigraphy was very shallow in this trench as over most of trench HAD1. The basal deposit excavated [133] was a stamped or trampled clay surface.

The archaeology comprised the remains of laid, fired mudbrick [135], [136] and [143] surrounded by and in places overlain by mudbrick rubble [134] [137], [138], [139], [140] and [141]. The bricks had been laid at approximately the level of the trampled surface though they survive to its north and are confined to the eastern side of the trench, the western part being occupied by a layer of red-orange sand [142]. Overlying the bricks on the eastern side was a red-orange sand and rubble deposit [132] (Fig. 3.16).

The whole trench was overlain by surface context [131].

Interpretive Summary

The fired brickwork in this trench, again in several layers, is the same as encountered in trench HAD1. However, the brickwork was much damaged by the modern practice of building date drying enclosures (*zeriba*) across the area. This practice accounts for the numerous narrow and shallow trenches which have damaged the brickwork. As in trench HAD1 there were virtually no finds from the trench.

Trench HAD3

This was a 2.5 x 2.5m trench located between HAD1 and HAD2 and to the south of them. It was clear from the geophysical survey that this was part of the same structure as that in trenches HAD1 and HAD2 (Fig. 3.17, Plate 3.17).

Here unfired mudbricks were located [183] apparently forming the corner of a casemate. Beyond the visible structure was an area of unfired mudbrick rubble [182]. The presence of unfired mudbrick suggests that at least part of the interior of the structure had not been burned.

The whole trench was overlain by surface context [181].

Interpretive Summary

This is clearly part of the same building as HAD1 and HAD2, as confirmed by the geophysical survey. The fact that the bricks are unfired suggests that they were in an area protected from the heat from the conflagration which destroyed the building.

Plate 3.17. Trench HAD3 looking south. (Photo: P.T. Nicholson).

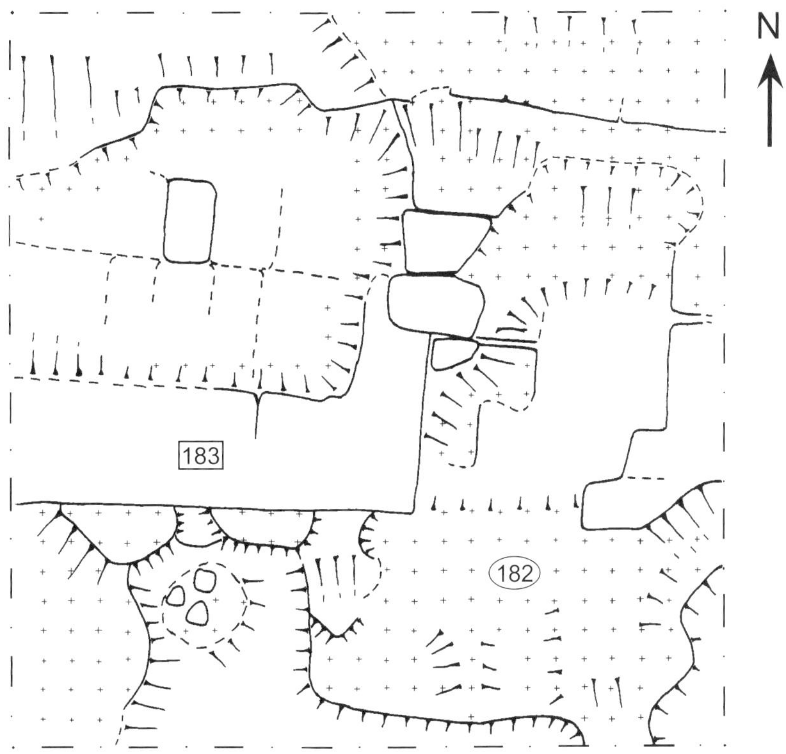

Figure 3.17. Trench HAD3. This is a small trench over part of the same building as HAD1 and HAD2 and showing extensive damage. (Plan: K. Stentoft).

Endnotes

1 [078/079/080/187/190/191/194/195/209/210/217/222].

2 2002-N-0129 N-5 and 2002-N-0387 N-8. Dating kindly provided by Dr. Andrew Meadows.

3 T-36.

Memphis
Context List

Context.	Character
	HAC 01
001	Surface context
002	Deposit
003	Deposit
004	Unfired mudbrick wall
005	Deposit
006	Deposit
007	Deposit
008	Unfired mudbrick wall = 032
009	Deposit
032	Wall = 008
	HAC 02
010	Deposit
(011-030)	(HAD 01)
	HAC 03
033	Surface Deposit =74= 300
034	Surface Deposit over kiln
035	Deposit
036	Deposit
037	Deposit = 037
038	Deposit including fired brick tumble in kiln
039	Deposit = 039
040	Kiln structure
041	Mudbrick platform
042	Mud pack equivalent to 049
043	Mudbrick collapse
044	Cut
045	Mixed mudbrick
046	Mixed mudbrick
047	Fired brick tumble
048	Basal Deposit in sondage
049	Mud pack equivalent 42
050	Deposit in kiln
051	Deposit in kiln
052	Deposit in kiln
053	Deposit
053A	Deposit
054	Deposit in kiln west kiln vent
055	Deposit in kiln comprising angular stone fragments
056	Deposit in kiln
057	Mudbrick platform
058	Mudbrick platform
059	Fill of western lower vent hole of kiln = 254
060	Deposit
061	Mudbrick
062	Fill of vent on eastern wall of kiln
063	Mudbrick platform
064	Not Assigned
065	Deposit
066	Deposit in kiln
067	Deposit
068	Deposit
069	Deposit
070	Brick Tumble

Context.	Character
070A	Wall
071	Vessel contents
072	Deposit in kiln
073	Mudbrick
074	Surface context from western area 2002 = 33=300
075	Decayed mudbrick
076	Deposit in kiln
077	Deposit in kiln
078	Ashy deposit in kiln = 080
079	Ashy deposit in kiln = 080
080	Ashy deposit in kiln = 078 = 079
(081-183)	**(HAD 01 and HAD 03)**
184	Fired brick rubble deposit in kiln =196 =199
185	SCA Sondage through brickwork
186	Deposit = 196 =197
187	Ashy deposit in kiln =080
188	Deposit
189	Deposit of domestic pottery
190	Ashy deposit in kiln = 080
191	Ashy deposit in kiln = 080
192	Rubble fill = 200
193	Mud pack
194	Ashy deposit in kiln = 080
195	Ashy deposit in kiln = 080
196	Deposit in kiln = 184 = 197
197	Deposit in kiln = 184 =196
198	Mudbrick platform, (lower courses beneath 063)
199	Floor
200	Rubble fill = 192
201	Mudbrick platform (projecting bricks)
202	Fired brick
203	Fired brick
204	Decayed mudbrick
205	Deposit
206	Deposit
207	Mud pack
208	Slag in kiln
209	Ashy deposit in kiln = 080
210	Ashy deposit in kiln = 080
211	Wall = 324
212	Mudbrick wall
213	Mudbrick wall
214	Wall of saggars (north)
215	Deposit
216	Slag deposit
217	Ashy deposit in kiln = 080
218	Deposit
219	Mud pack
220	Ashy deposit in kiln (probably equivalent of 311 outside kiln). =253
221	Deposit in kiln = 226
222	Ashy deposit in kiln
223	Brick deposit
224	Mudbrick
225	Mudbrick (platform?)
226	Deposit in kiln = 221
227	Mudbrick
228	Deposit
229	Deposit

Context.	Character
230	Deposit
231	Deposit
232	Mud pack
233	Surface context in south west extension of trench = 074
234	Deposit
235	Access hole in west wall of kiln = 338
236	Deposit. Uppermost context in 235 western access hole = 332 (probably equivalent o 077)
237	Deposit. Middle context in 235 western access hole
238	Deposit
239	Slag
240	Mudbrick wall
241	Slag
242	Wall
243	Deposit
244	Deposit of saggars = 303
245	Deposit
246	Fired brick/reddened clay
247	Basal deposit in kiln
248	Clay Deposit
249	Mud pack
250	Deposit
251	Brick ledge (over upper west vent 336)
252	Mud pack
253	Lowermost context in access hole = 220
254	Fill of lower west vent hole = 059
(255-299)	Not Assigned
300	Surface context over western extension of trench =74=300
301	Deposit
302	Deposit

Context.	Character
303	Deposit
304	Deposit =244 = 307
305	Mud pack
306	Deposit.
307	Deposit =303 =244
308	Slag
309	Deposit
310	Amphora situated in 309
311	Deposit (equivalent of 220 on inside of kiln).
312	Deposit
313	Feature in 312
314	Deposit
315	Deposit
316	Lowermost Deposit of stoking pit.
317	Slag as foundation of wall 242
318	Slag as foundation of wall 211
319	Mudbrick structure
320	Mudbrick wall
321	Wall of mixed bricks
322	Saggar wall (south) = 325
323	Mudbrick wall
324	Wall = 212
325	Saggar wall (south) = 322
326	Mudbrick wall - step
327	Deleted
328	Deleted
329	Deposit
330	Blocking of kiln access hole with saggar bases
331	Wall

Context.	Character
332	Deposit. Upper fill in 235 western access hole = 236 (probably equivalent o 0770
333	Cut
334	Cut
335	Eastern stoke-hole
336	Upper Vent on west wall
337	Lower Vent on west wall
338	Access hole on west wall = 235
339	Deposit
	HAD 01
011	Cut
012	Surface Deposit
013	Fired mudbrick = 085 =086
014	Fired mudbrick = 027
015	Fired mudbrick
016	Deposit
017	Deposit
018	Deposit
019	Mudbrick
020	Fired mudbrick = 089
021	Basal deposit
022	Basal deposit
023	Basal deposit
024	Fired mudbrick = 091
025	Fired mudbrick
026	Fired mudbrick
027	Fired Mudbrick = 014 = 099
028	Deposit = 096
029	Deposit
030	Cut

Context.	Character
031	Cut
032	Wall
(033-080)	(HAC 03)
081	Surface context
082	Fired mudbrick as south of platform
083	Sand deposit at south of platform
084	Surface context in south west quadrant
085	Fired mudbrick = 013
086	Fired mudbrick = 013
087	Deposit
088	Mortar
089	Fired mudbrick = 020
090	Mortar
091	Fired mudbrick = 024
092	Unfired mudbrick = 027 = 099
093	Deposit
094	Unfired mudbrick = 027 = 099
095	Wall
096	Deposit = 028
097	Mortar
098	Fired mudbrick
099	Mudbrick = 027
100	Mortar
	HAD 02
131	Surface context
132	Deposit
133	Basal deposit
134	Mudbrick rubble
135	Fired mudbrick

Context.	Character
136	Fired mudbrick
137	Mudbrick rubble
138	Mudbrick rubble
139	Mudbrick rubble
140	Mudbrick rubble
141	Mudbrick rubble
142	Deposit
143	Fired brick
(144-180)	Not Assigned
	HAD 03
181	Surface context
182	Unfired mudbrick rubble
183	Unfired mudbrick surface/wall

Chapter 4
The Kiln

P.T. Nicholson

Introduction

The kilns at Memphis are well known from Petrie's work (Petrie 1909a, 1911a) and it might be argued that the excavation of another example serves little purpose. However, Petrie's account of the kilns he excavated is unclear and the manner in which he believed them to have operated raises several questions, not least in terms of the lack of flooring and the type of fuel. The new research aimed to provide a better understanding of the kiln structures and so to set Petrie's findings in a more secure context.

In passing it should be noted that the term 'furnace' is sometimes used for structures used to fire faience. Either term is acceptable but the term kiln is used here.

Petrie's work

The 1908 season of excavation at Kom Helul led to the excavation of a single kiln. No plan of it exists though it was photographed (Petrie 1909a Plate XLIX reproduced here as Plate 4.1, see also Chapter 1). The 1910 season led to the excavation of either five, or more likely six[1] further kilns. Once again Petrie did not produce plans of these structures nor do there seem to be any further photographs so that only the dimensions and orientations are available for study.

The structure excavated in 1908 was said to be "six feet square and eight feet deep" (1.82m square by 2.43m deep) (Petrie 1909a: 14) whilst those dug in 1910 were almost all deeper as shown in Table 4.1.

Table 4.1. Petrie's (1911a) kiln dimensions converted into metres and with draught hole data added[*]

Kiln	i	ii	iii	iv	v	vi
Out N-S	3.70	(walls 0.46 to 0.54 metres)				
Out E-W	3.94					
In N-S	2.11	1.27	1.65	--	1.45	1.17
In E-W	2.00	1.75	1.32	1.27	1.68	1.07
Depth now	3.07	3.38	3.38	3.71	4.75	1.52
Draught hole	W	?	?	?	W	N
Hole size	0.49	?	?	?	0.25	0.43
Height	>1.53[**]	?	?	?	0.86†	0.76‡

(Metric figures are rounded to the nearest cm.)

[*] For figures in inches see Chapter 1, Table 1.1.
[**] "more than half way up" (Petrie 1911a: 34).
[†] "34 inches from the top" (Petrie 1911a: 34.)
[‡] "about halfway up" (Petrie 1911a: 34).

Unfortunately it is not made clear whether the "six feet square" (1.82m) (Petrie 1909a: 14) was an internal or external measurement, though comparison with the 1910 examples suggests that it may be an internal measurement.

The photograph (1909a: Plate XLIX, here Plate 4.1) is helpful in checking Petrie's description. He states that "no hole was traced in the lower part, but more than halfway up there was an arched opening to the west, about two feet wide. This could not be for out-draught as it faces the usual wind; and therefore it seems that the air was admitted to the upper part of the kiln" (Petrie 1909a: 14). The published image is cropped and has no scale on it, but it seems to show most of the width of the kiln. If one takes the "two feet" (0.61m) width of the hole to be correct then three times the width of that hole should give the "six feet" (1.82m) of the kiln.

However, this scaling up on the photograph does not correlate with Petrie's measurements. It can be seen that at the left and right of the photograph there are distinct ledges in the profile. If one measures *between* these ledges then the kiln would be about three times as wide as the opening, however, the ledges do not appear to be built, but rather to be compacted ash and rubble. Had they been part of the masonry then it is likely that Petrie would have seen them as supports for a perforated floor and he is very clear that such did not exist (Petrie 1911a: 35) indeed he states that the kilns "are all square, with vertical sides" (Petrie 1911a: 34). Admittedly, he is here speaking of the kilns found in 1910 but there is no indication that they were different to that found in 1908. It can therefore reasonably be assumed that the ledges visible in the photograph are uncleared debris, perhaps left by Wainwright to show the stratigraphic section, and that the six feet is measured between them.

If one takes the opening as two feet wide and measures right across the image from the vertical wall, visible on the left, the interior width is more like 12 feet (3.65m) wide. This would be larger than any of the interior dimensions which are recorded for the 1910 season (Kilns i-vi). It is very unlikely that Petrie would have made an error of a factor of two even if he were working only from rough notes. One must therefore assume that he either took the width between the ledges and then failed to correct it when (if?) they were removed or that he mis-recorded the width of the opening.

If one compares the openings on Petrie's kilns with those on the kiln excavated at HAC3 and reported on in this volume there are some interesting differences. Petrie states that the opening in his 1908 kiln is two feet wide and that it was located "more than halfway up...to the west" (1909a: 14). An opening of this size (0.61m) is substantial, and is larger than the lowermost opening on HAC3 which

INSIDE OF KILN, WITH WASTERS. ROMAN.

Plate 4.1. The kiln excavated by Petrie in 1908. It is thought that this shows the interior of the structure and is only partially excavated. No scale or orientation are given. (Petrie 1909a:Plate XLIX. Copyright of the Petrie Museum of Archaeology, UCL).

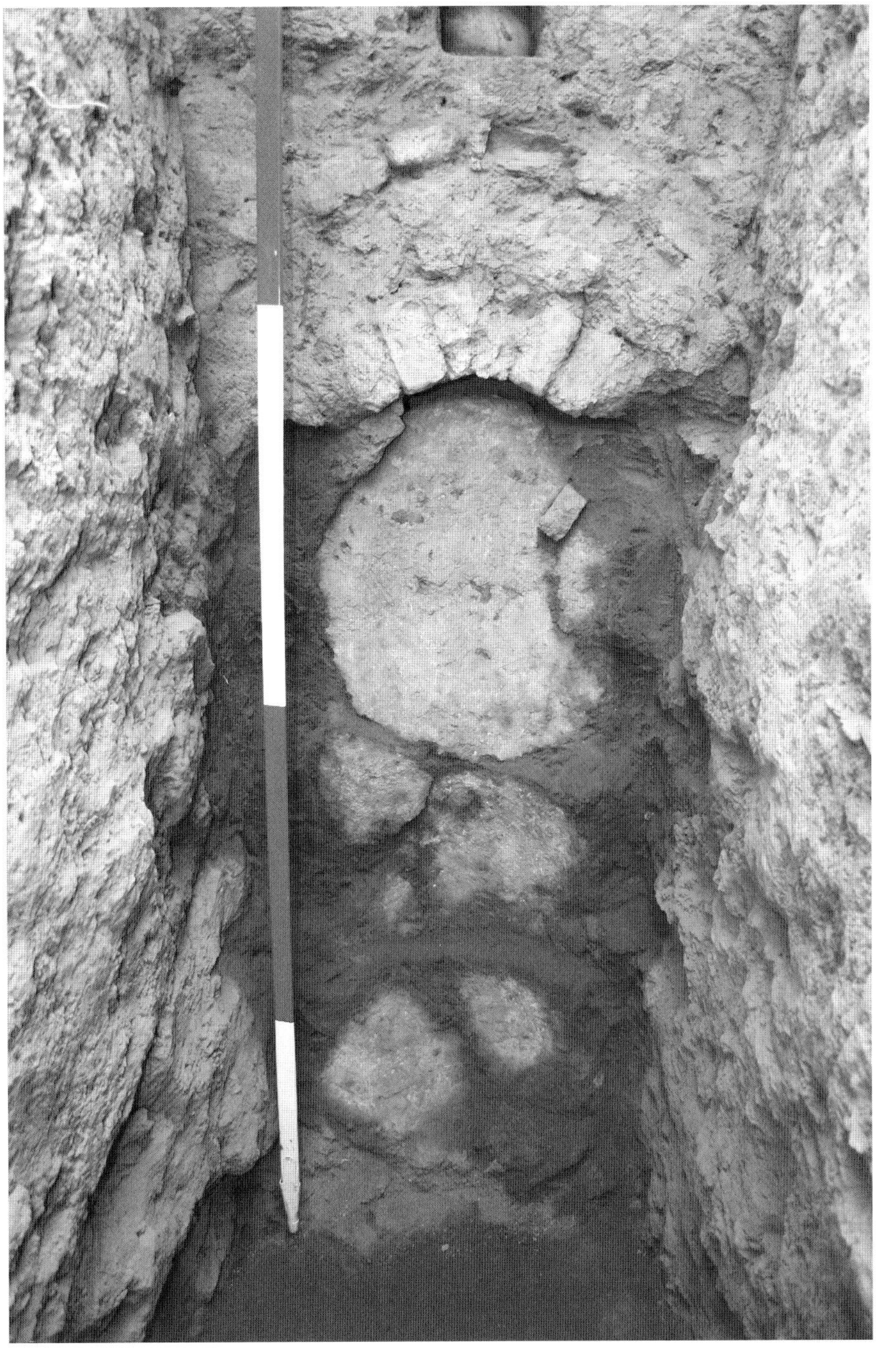

Plate 4.2. The lowermost opening of the kiln at HAC3 blocked by re-used saggar bases which have been cemented into place with mud. This access opening was probably partly blocked during firings and so served as a vent. After the kiln had cooled it would be fully opened so that ash and slag could be removed. The lowermost vent is visible above the blocked opening. North is to the left. (Photo: P.T. Nicholson).

measures some 0.49m (19.29") in width. It is also much larger than the those recorded in 1910 which are described as "19 inches wide in i, 10 inches in v, 17 inches in vi, where it has been subsequently blocked up so as to leave only a hole 7 inches wide and 5 high" (Petrie 1911a: 35).

Whilst it is not possible to say how typical the kiln from HAC3 is, one can use some of its measurements as a guide. The uppermost vent on the west side measures 0.18m wide by 0.2m high (c.7" x 7.8") and the lower one (located immediately above the large access opening) measures 0.12m wide by 0.21m high (4.7" x 8.3"). The stoke-hole on the east side is 0.24m wide by 0.34m high (c.9.4" x 13.4"). The large opening at the bottom of the kiln on the west, which probably served as both a vent and cleaning hole, has a maximum height of 1.5m and a width of 0.49m.

All of the vent openings described by Petrie are therefore somewhat larger than those found on kiln HAC3. Unfortunately he only gives the height of the vent in vi where it has been blocked up. The rest have no indication of height. The width of the vents in i and in vi in particular are substantial and the same is true of the 1908 structure. How might these be interpreted?

In the view of the writer the "draught-hole, or stoke-hole" (Petrie 1911a: 35) on kilns i and vi is indeed a stoke-hole. The reason that they appear so high in the profile may be explicable by referring to the kiln in HAC3 which also has its stoke-hole high in the profile though on the east side.

There is, however, another possible explanation, particularly relevant to kiln vi whose surviving depth suggests that it had been severely truncated. Kiln HAC3 had its lowest, vent/access hole blocked at the end of firing using the bases of broken saggars cemented into place (Plate 4.2). It is likely that the lowest of these were put in place before firing began, so partially blocking the large opening. This would have the effect of allowing some air into the kiln as well as helping to retain heat whilst allowing ash to build up against the temporary wall. The wall would be removed when it was necessary to rake out the accumulated ash before a further firing. However, because Petrie evidently excavated his kilns only from the inside, he may not have realised that any blockings he encountered were temporary, whether they were made of brick or of saggars. From the inside the blockings would have appeared permanent. His actual openings, therefore, have (at least in kilns i and vi) a width consistent with a stoke-hole but *appear* high up the wall. This may be because only the open, upper part, of the opening was recognised as a "draught-hole, or "stoke-hole" by Petrie. Some support for this view comes from careful examination of the photograph (Plate 4.1) in which the upper part of the opening is cleared and has presumably been seen to meet earth beyond (outside) the kiln whilst below this open part are what may be either secondary mud bricks or compacted ash and debris built up against a blocking. This is very similar to the appearance of HAC3 during excavation.

It is therefore likely that Petrie's apparently large "draught-hole or stoke-hole" (1911a:35) on his kiln vi and quite possibly kiln i, actually represent the upper part of a vent/access hole as on the west side of HAC3. The location of the "draught hole" on the west side of his kiln i makes this all the more likely.

This is not to say that there were no small vents allowing air inlet like those found on HAC3 which has two on the west side, though they are higher up the profile than any opening recorded by Petrie (see Figure 4.1). It is possible that similar vents were missed by Petrie, Wainwright and Bushe-Fox, especially if sections were left unexcavated as the photograph seems to imply. They may also have become covered in slag and could therefore have been missed by the excavators. It is worth noting that Kingery (1997: 16) locates the air vent *beneath,* and on the same side as, the stoke-hole of his hypothetical kiln.[2] The writer has not seen such an arrangement on any kiln from modern or ancient Egypt and Blackman (1927: 302) comments only that the kilns of her time closely resemble those of the ancient Egyptians. No vent is noted. The only exception known to the writer is one of the pottery kilns from Buto which has a pipe running from ground level to the area below the stoke-hole (Hartung *et al.* 2003; Ballet 2004: 18).

It is difficult to know whether any of the kilns dug by Petrie were eventually excavated to their full depth across their whole profile or only down one or two walls. It would be easy to miss vents if excavation was only partial or if the brickwork were not thoroughly cleaned once excavated. The confined space in the kilns makes them very difficult to excavate and dust and dirt from excavation continually re-adheres to the walls obscuring features. Unless great care was taken to re-clean the walls features might easily be missed.

It is apparent from Petrie's descriptions, and from the photograph, that the kilns were literally 'dug out' as "a pit" (Petrie 1909a: 14) rather than also being excavated around so that the external features of the kiln were revealed. For this reason there is no mention of access pits and the assumption seems to be made by Petrie that what he believed to be stoke-holes, about half way up the walls, were originally at the level of the ground outside the kiln.

Petrie (1911a: 35) commented on the lack of any perforated floor and this matter will be addressed later, but for the moment it is sufficient to have established that the structures excavated by him in 1908 and 1910 are essentially uniform with HAC3. Unfortunately, what cannot be established is what kinds of saggars he found with which kilns. His finds are linked only to the site[3] rather than to specific structures within it.

Kiln HAC3

The excavation of Kiln HAC3 was carried out very differently to the excavation of Petrie's kilns. A large surface was exposed and excavation work carried out inside the kiln and around it simultaneously so that the operation of the structure as a whole could better be understood.

The trench measured 5.0m north-south by 7.0m east-west having been expanded to the west from the original 5.0m square so that the extent of the firing pit on the west side could be properly investigated. The kiln itself is located at the centre of the trench and the uppermost courses of the structure measure approximately 1.60m square. It is oriented almost exactly east-west with two vents and a large vent/access hole on the west side and a stoke-hole on the east.

The kiln [040] as it survives today does not represent the earliest activity at HAC3. This is clear from the ephemeral

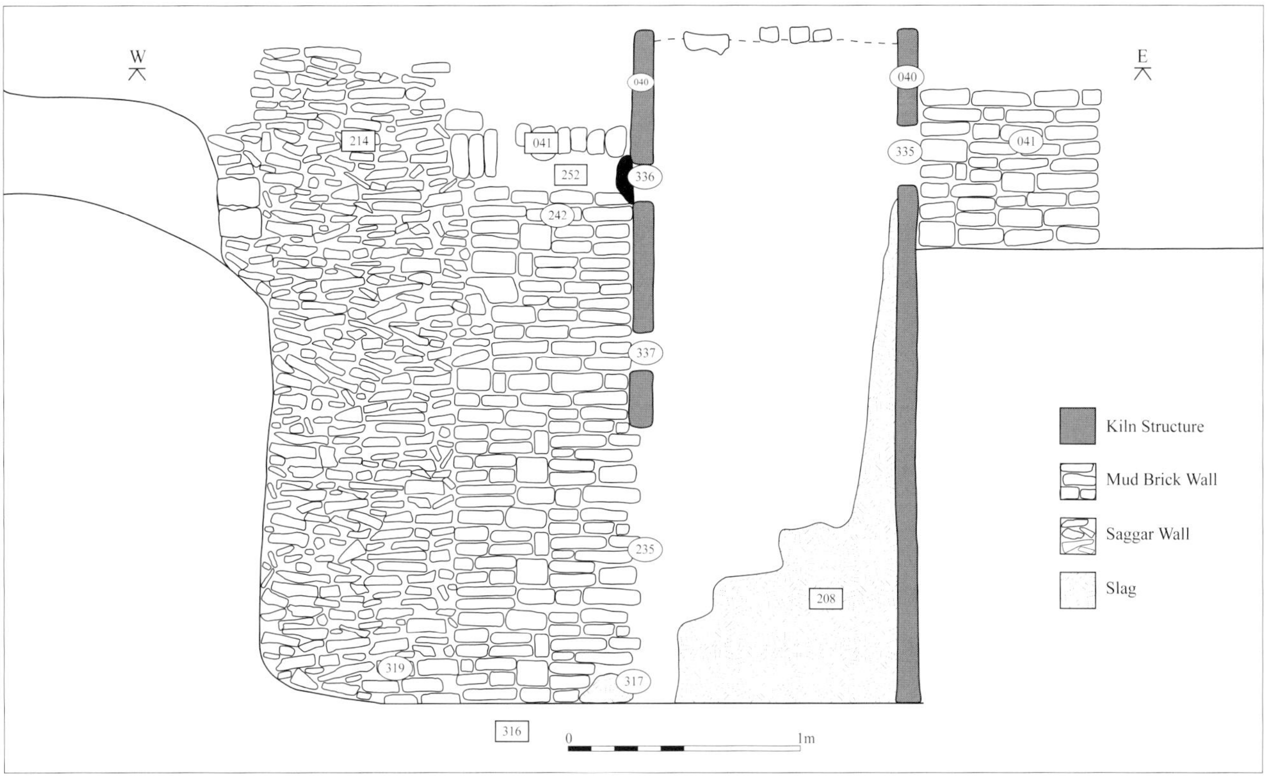

Figure 4.1. East-west section of the HAC3 kiln showing the openings in the structure. The stoke-hole is at [335] and on the opposite wall are vents [336] and [337]. The access doorway is [235]. (Drawing: Tessa Baber).

Plate 4.3. Looking north over the kiln at HAC3 during excavation. The projections on the north wall are clearly visible above the head and to the right of supervisor R. Hart. (Photo: P.T. Nicholson).

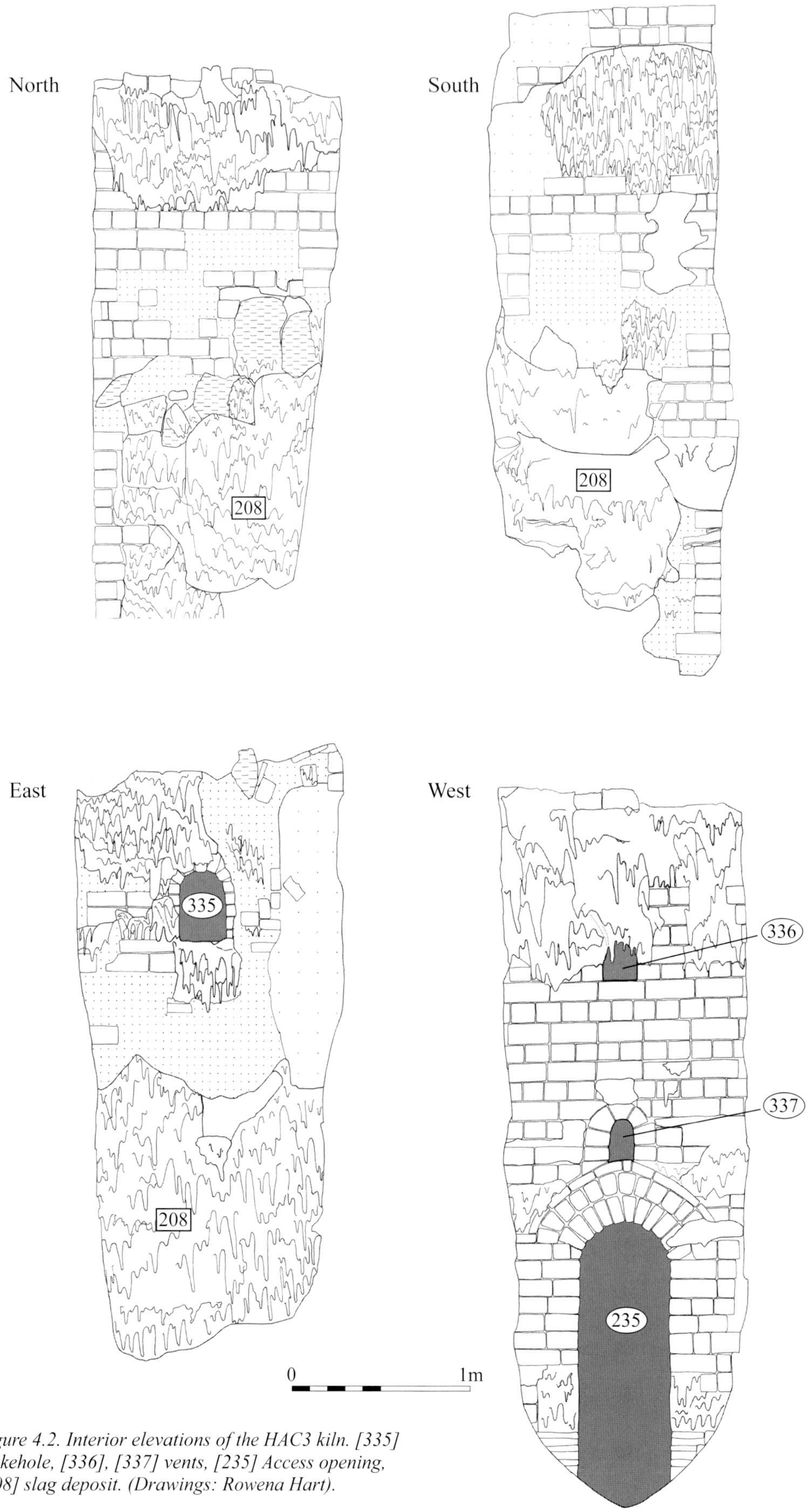

Figure 4.2. Interior elevations of the HAC3 kiln. [335] Stokehole, [336], [337] vents, [235] Access opening, [208] slag deposit. (Drawings: Rowena Hart).

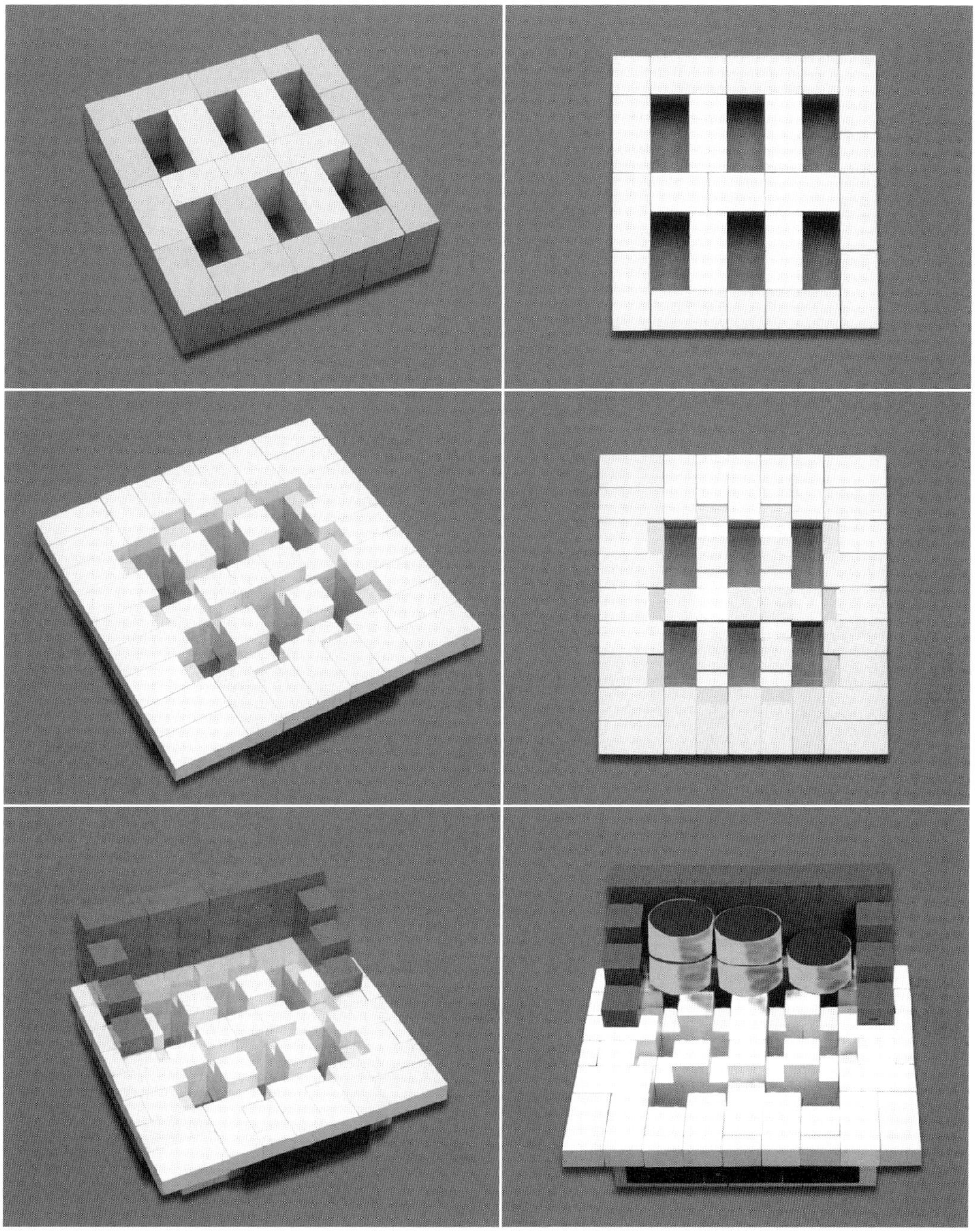

Plate 4.4. Reconstruction of the chequer used in the HAC3 kiln showing how the actual kiln tower may have been somewhat larger than the preserved footprint of the structure. Top row: the kiln ground plan as excavated with a simple chequer added. Middle row: the chequer expanded beyond the limit of the brickwork. Bottom row: showing (L) part of the tower wall added and (R) one row of three saggars inside it . (Reconstruction and photos: P.T. Nicholson).

remains of structures in the south-east corner of the trench (see Chapter 2). Furthermore, it is likely that the kiln is not the first evidence of industrial activity at this site, or at least close by it, since a large lump of 'slag' [317] is built into the lowermost course of the retaining wall of the firing pit on its north side where it abuts the kiln (See Fig. 4.1). Such a lump of slag can only have come from a pre-existing kiln, either demolished in order to build this one or from a similar kiln nearby.

The kiln has been constructed by digging a deep pit into the existing ground surface and then building a roughly square tower structure within it (Fig. 4.2). The tower forms the kiln proper and is built of alluvial mudbricks laid in alternating header and stretcher courses.[4] According to Olsen (1983: 26) this method of construction is "the most common method of construction using dense firebrick" and though firebrick is not used here it is notable that the technique clearly has a long ancestry in kiln building. The bricks were then fired *in situ*. This is confirmed by the fact that the brickwork inside the kiln is reddish orange but grades to unfired grey toward the exterior. It is likely that at the original ground level the footprint of the kiln was somewhat larger than what now survives but that this has been eroded or robbed away (below).

Around this tower-like kiln structure a revetment in a distorted, overturned, H-shape was created (see Fig. 3.5). This was built down the slope on the north and more shallowly at the south. Its purpose seems to have been to provide both insulation and support for the kiln as well as to give a level working platform around it at, or just above, ground level.

On the west side of the kiln the face of the structure was left exposed and made up the eastern end of a deep trench about 1.0m wide and 1.5m long. This pit gave access to the large opening at the base of the kiln which would be used for cleaning it out between firings and which, partly blocked, served as a vent during firings. The north and south walls of the pit were made from mud brick and the remains of broken saggars. These very large pieces of saggar were carefully laid like thin bricks or Roman tiles to make up the walls.

It is significant that the saggar fragments used to build up the walls of the access pit are from the large, coarse saggars which are referred to here as 'Type 12' (see Fig. 4.1 context [242]). It is unlikely that these fragments were brought from any great distance which makes it likely that these were the type of saggars being used at HAC3. Assuming that the wall needed to be revetted from the outset the first fragments to be used would have been those lying around from the previous kiln on the site, but if the firing pit wall was not initially revetted then the saggars must have come from breakages during the life of the excavated kiln.

Because the revetment walls appear to be built in two phases (units [242] [214] and [211] [320]) it is tempting to see the first phase, that which immediately abuts the kiln, as having been built at the same time. The second phase, which extends the revetment wall to the west, was constructed as further waste saggar fragments accumulated during the use of the kiln.

That these large Type 12 saggars were indeed in daily use in this kiln may be confirmed by the fact that it is bases of this type which were cemented together to make up the blocking of the kiln at the end of its final firing. It is likely that a temporary blocking was already built during this last firing (as it would have been on all previous ones), forming a wall against which ash would build up and which would protect the legs of the workmen from the heat but which could be removed if it was necessary to rake out ash. At the end of the firing, in order to retain heat in the kiln and to allow it to cool slowly, the stoke-hole was then completely blocked (Plate 4.1). Since the kiln was abandoned after that last firing the vent/access hole was never unblocked for re-use and the structure was allowed to decay.

Entry to the access pit was via the slope on the west side. There was a drop down into the bottom of the pit which could have been lessened by using loose bricks or rubbish to form a temporary step.

It is clear then, that by clearing only the inside of the kilns Petrie missed the full extent of the openings and that he believed ground level to have been about half way up the large opening which he identified as a stoke-hole. This appears to be a misunderstanding, quite literally, on two levels. As has been demonstrated, the ground level for those cleaning the kiln was at the bottom of the vent/access, which it is suggested (above) he did not recognise. This ground level is up to a metre below the part of the opening which he saw. However, this was an artificial ground level, the floor of an access pit, the overall level – at HAC3 at least – being over 2.0m above this point.

This misunderstanding of the ground level led Petrie to misinterpret the kiln and its functioning. He assumed that saggars stood in stacks at the bottom of the kiln and that fuel was thrown in between them. He could find no evidence of a perforated floor above the level of the stoke-hole. The writer has always been puzzled by this reconstruction since it would be difficult to get the fuel to the rear of the stacks of saggars and so to heat them efficiently. The saggars would also have to be dug out of the ash at the end of the firing which would be an awkward and clumsy operation. Nonetheless initial examination of kiln HAC3 seemed to support Petrie's view – at least in so far as there was no obvious perforated floor.

Against Petrie's view, however, was the fact that at the bottom of HAC3 was a substantial build-up of rock-hard 'slag' (see Chapter 3 and Figure 4.1). Since no saggars were trapped in the slag it was initially assumed that it had built up over the life of the structure and that new surfaces had been made above it by compacting the ash around the slag to make a new level surface whenever necessary.

This initial view is, however, erroneous. Examination of the uppermost surviving course of brickwork, and of the 'H' shaped revetment around the kiln, made it clear that, contrary to Petrie's view, most parts of the structures he excavated had not stood above ground. What remained of Petrie's kilns, as at HAC3, was simply the subterranean part of the structure and comprised only the firebox.[5] The uppermost brickwork of HAC3 showed eroded traces of bricks protruding into the interior of the kiln at approximately the ancient ground level (the level of the H-shaped brick platform). These are most clear on the north side of the kiln (Plate 4.3) and are especially clear in the stereoscopic views taken of the excavation.[6] These protrusions are all that remained of the perforated floor or its supports.

Once the true nature of the excavated structure has been realised the structure and operation of the whole kiln becomes very much clearer. On top of the fire box would have stood a tower-like superstructure into which the saggars would have been placed. How tall such a structure would have been is not known but it can be estimated in a number of ways based on the depth of around 4.0m and on principles of kiln design (cf. Olsen 1983). Vernhet (1981) reconstructs the pottery kiln at La Graufesenque, France with a superstructure 1.6 times the height from the floor of the firebox to the top of the chequer though this cannot be used as a 'formula' since the firebox design will depend upon the type of fuel used, its volume and calorific value.

There remains some uncertainty as to the ground plan of the superstructure itself which may have been round or square. The latter is perhaps more likely (see below) but the size of the 'footprint' of the structure at ground level is debateable. A 1.60m square seems very small for such a deep fire box and one must consider whether the kiln itself was somewhat larger. Although supports for the floor can be seen projecting inwards it is also possible that, above this level, they may have angled outwards too, so allowing heat to be spread over a larger area than the size of the firebox top (Plate 4.4 and Colour Plate 1). Such an arrangement is clearly illustrated by Vernhet (1981: 38) in his reconstruction of the La Graufesenque kiln[7] and a similar feature is known from the kilns at Holt in Wales (Grimes 1930: 36). The size and depth of the firebox would have been determined through experience and designed for the specific fuel used (Bourry 1911: 193).

Comparison of the HAC3 structure with other kilns

Before comparing the HAC3 kiln with others it is worth considering the reasons why it is considered to be a kiln for faience production rather than for pottery making or some other purpose. One reason is that it is located in the general area where Petrie's faience kilns were found and there are numerous faience finds from around the kiln. However, this is not sufficient to prove that its function was faience production. More significant is that the kiln seems to have been designed for use with saggars and many of these have been found around it including making up the walls of the access pit on the west side of the structure.

The use of saggars is not generally associated with the production of unglazed pottery in the Roman world and there is no evidence at Kom Helul for the making of glazed (clay based) pottery. Although saggars are known from numerous locations world wide and through time for biscuit firing the author has found no evidence for their use in Roman Egypt. That pottery may have been made somewhere in the vicinity of Kom Helul is quite likely but it does not seem to have been the product fired in saggars in the HAC3 kiln.

Overall then, the location of the kiln, the use of saggars and the lack of non-faience products which would have required saggar firing all point to the likelihood that this is indeed a kiln for faience production.

To date, Petrie's excavation at Kom Helul is the only one to have produced well documented evidence of definite faience kilns. There are, of course, numerous pottery kilns known from the Roman world including those for the production of glazed or gloss wares.

As might be expected the majority of kilns excavated from the Roman period are simple updraught kilns and are mostly small in size. The work of Swan (1984) for Roman Britain provides a typical selection of these structures which were mostly used for the firing of pottery without saggars. There are, however, a few more complex kilns including the kiln for the production of sigillata ('Samian ware')[8] from Colchester (Hull 1963: 20-34). This kiln is circular in plan and has a perforated floor separating the ware from the firebox below. The sigillata was not fired in saggars but rather was separated from direct contact with the hot gases by an arrangement of clay pipes which channelled the gases through the stack of vessels, effectively enclosing the gases rather than the pots themselves.

A similar method of channelling the hot gases through the kiln using ceramic pipes is employed in the very large kiln at La Graufesenque, France (Vernhet 1981). The internal space was divided into a series of elongated cells using pre-fabricated tiles which fitted between the pipes (Vernhet 1981: 36, 38; Webster 1996: 11 see also Bourry 1911: 233).[9] The vessels to be fired were placed within these cells and no saggars were used. Since it is clear that the kiln at HAC3 employed saggars it is not surprising to find that this piped arrangement is not employed there. Sigillata is also known to have been fired in saggars as Mackensen (1993) has demonstrated at el Mahrine in Tunisia. Here the saggars are circular but can be open at bottom and top (Mackensen 1993: 90). They also appear to be wheel made and have thinner walls than the Type 12 saggars from Memphis (see Chapter 5).

Firing of glazed, rather than gloss, pottery was, however, a practice known in the Roman world, notably for the production of lead glazed pottery (Atik, 1995, Hochuli-Gysel 2002, Walton and Tite 2010). This ware was "never common" (Hayes 1997: 64) and though some of this pottery is imported into Egypt the distribution of Egyptian faience[10] outside Egypt is much more limited. Further east – in Mesopotamia - alkaline glazed pottery, often based on Hellenistic forms, was current from the 1st century B.C. and 3rd century A.D. but is used only on the eastern borders of the empire (Hayes 1997: 66). It does not have such a wide distribution as does the lead glazed material.

The lead glazed pottery was fired in saggars and mostly produced in Asia Minor (Atik 1995, Hochuli-Gysel 2002, Walton and Tite 2010). The sites at Perge (Atik 1995)

Plate 4.5. A pottery kiln at Fustat, Cairo. The lower of the two domed structures is covering the pit in which both firing and cleaning out take place, the uppermost is the tower structure into which the stacked vessels are placed for firing (see Plate 4.6). Photographed in 1998 at the workshop of Ahmed Abu Hassan. (Photo: P.T. Nicholson, courtesy of Ahmed Abu Hassan).

Plate 4.6. A pottery kiln at Fustat, Cairo (the same one as in Plate 4.5) showing the domed tower structure into which the pots are placed for firing, via the entrance door. No saggars are used in this industry. Photographed in 1998 at the workshop of Ahmed Abu Hassan. (Photo: P.T. Nicholson, courtesy of Ahmed Abu Hassan).

and Tarsus (Goldman 1950; Hochuli-Gysel 1977, 2002) are particularly well known in this area. Lead glazed ware was also produced at the site of Holt in Denbighshire[11] in the U.K. Here a bank of kilns for pottery and tiles was discovered (Grimes 1930).[12] All but one of the 8 kilns excavated is rectangular though even the smallest of the ground plans, that of kiln 1, measuring some 2.43m x 2.13m internally (Grimes 1930: 34)[13] is larger than HAC3. The area immediately above the stoke-hole is tapered, directing the hot gases up into the kiln itself.

That some of the pottery was fired in saggars is clear since they survive, though their shape is not that known from Kom Helul but rather takes the form of a lidded dish into which a vessel would be placed on a stand for glazing. This arrangement is less efficient than that used at Memphis since it requires a two part saggar whereas the cylindrical saggars used at HAC3 fit one above the other, each forming the lid of the one below. At Holt the lid of the saggar and the base of the bowl beneath are both flat and of similar diameter so that they could be stacked one on top of another as is suggested for Kom Helul, though unlike Kom Helul the stack would not have been straight sided since both the lid and saggar used at Holt are markedly flared.

Comparison of the kiln form might also be profitably made with some of the contemporary kilns of modern Cairo. In December 1998 the writer had the opportunity to visit the pottery owned by Ahmed Abu Hassan in the Fustat area of Old Cairo. Here were located a number of substantial updraught kilns which have features in common with the kiln at Kom Helul, HAC3 (Plates 4.5, 4.6).

Although time did not permit the measurement of the kilns in question the superstructures stood approximately 3m high at the centre of the dome and loading was facilitated by a doorway[14] which was bricked up during the actual firing. In the kilns observed the wares were all earthenware and no saggars were necessary but the superstructure gives a good impression of what the HAC3 kiln superstructure may have looked like. The substructure is separated from the superstructure by a chequer at about ground level – the doorway allows access straight onto this perforated floor for loading.

At the rear of the kilns, in a depression in the ground gives access to the substructure. This comprises a small domed building (Plate 4.5) which utilises the rear wall of the kiln as one of its walls and in which is a tall doorway like that seen on the west side of kiln HAC3. Looking through this doorway it was apparent that the walls of the firebox had undergone some vitrification, but this was not nearly as extensive as the massive slagging at HAC3. The fuel used in this modern workshop was mainly sugarcane or millet stalks and some wood chippings though some kilns were being fired with old car tyres.

A visit to a further Fustat workshop in 2005 revealed another type of kiln. This too was fuelled from below but was rectangular rather than round and instead of a dome it had a vault. Since the HAC3 substructure is approximately square and probably supported a square tower-like kiln it is likely that the top of this would have approximated to a dome rather than a vault.

A kiln visited at a workshop at Ezbet Makhmal near Mit Rahina (ancient Memphis) in 1986 is much smaller than the Fustat examples, and less well constructed. This kiln had a 'firing pit' in front of the stoke-hole. Whilst it is less deep and less well constructed than the access pit on the west side of HAC3 such pits are clearly common features.

In summary, it may be said that the HAC3 kiln would have resembled in its overall form the kilns seen at Fustat, except that there is little evidence for a domed structure covering the access pit at the rear which is seen on the Fustat examples. Whilst the superstructure of the Fustat kilns is circular that at Kom Helul was probably square.

Reconstructing the Kiln

Some indication of possible height of the kiln might be derived from figures for other kilns. Kiln designs are common in the literature for studio potters (e.g. Leach 1945/1971:181) but by their nature these are often much smaller than the industrial scale structure under consideration here. Exceptions are provided by the designs given by Olsen (1983) and this has been used alongside data from industrial kilns given by Sandeman (1921).

Sandeman (1921: 189-90) gives dimensions for a bottle kiln[15] of the early 20th century. Although his structure is coal fired and so has a differently proportioned fire box he does give the height of the firing chamber for a kiln of 14' 6" (4.42m) internal diameter (for summary see Table 4.2). It would have had a dome height (internal) of 17' (5.18m) and a shoulder height, from which the dome was sprung, of 12'6" (3.81m). The ground plan of the HAC3 kiln is approximately 1.6m (5.24 feet) square, considerably smaller than Sandeman's example. However, his figures are for a circular structure and in order to make a valid comparison it seems sensible to take the diagonal measurement of HAC3, 2.26m, and use it as a comparison measure for Sandeman's diameter.

Using the 2.26m diagonal length as a comparator for Sandeman's diameter figure of 4.42m makes the HAC3 kiln smaller than it by a factor of 1.96, thus giving an estimated dome height of 2.64m and shoulder height of 1.95m for HAC3. However, in estimating the size of the superstructure of HAC3 other factors must be taken into consideration and the proposed reconstruction be modified.

Table 4.2. Summary of Kiln Size (calculated figures in italics)

	Sandeman 1921	HAC3 Ground Plan*	HAC3 Projected Square Floor Plan**	HAC3 Projected Circular Floor Plan***
Diameter (m)	4.42	na	na	2.26
Length of side (m)	na	1.6	1.8	na
Diagonal (m)	na	2.26	2.32	na
Area (m2)	15.35	2.56	3.24	4.01
Height to shoulder (m)	3.81	*1.95*	*2.14*	*1.95*
Height at crown (m)	5.18	*2.65*	*2.71*	*2.65*

* *As excavated.*
** *Taking into account average saggar diameter.*
*** *Assuming a round firing chamber above a square fire pit.*

Modified Reconstruction

Most significant amongst the other factors to be considered is the question of the saggars contained in the kiln. The finds from HAC3 strongly suggest that Type 12 saggars were employed. These have an average height of 26.13cm (10.28 inches). The estimated kiln shoulder height of 1.95m would permit 7 saggars to be stacked on top of one another with a space of 0.12m remaining below the shoulder.

However, the mean average base diameter of a Type 12 saggar is 49.42cm (19.45 inches) with a modal average of 0.50m and the surviving brickwork of HAC3 is approximately 1.60m square.[16] If one assumes that the saggars had to fit within the 1.60m square of the preserved ground plan then three average saggars could comfortably be fitted side-by-side in each direction. Some 0.10m would remain as free space. However, given that the saggars, once placed, were plastered around this may not be sufficient and it may be assumed that a 3 x 3 saggar arrangement required a floor area of 1.8-2.0m square. This would be a larger ground plan than that which survives and requires further explanation.

The kiln at La Graufesenque (Vernhet 1981: 38) is reconstructed as channelling the heat to the firing chamber via a flaring arrangement of the perforated floor. Whilst HAC3 shows no trace of this it would be possible to construct a similar arrangement immediately above the preserved level of the kiln as shown in Plate 4.4. Even if this were not done it is likely that the footprint of the firing structure would be somewhat larger than the 1.6m square but this brickwork has now gone.

If one assumes a 1.8m square firing chamber and again uses the figures given by Sandeman (1921: 189-190) the diagonal of the square would be 2.32m making the HAC3 kiln smaller than Sandeman's by a factor of 1.91. This would give a new height for the kiln shoulder of 2.14m and 2.71m for the dome.

These calculations based on Sandeman (1921) are given added validity when Olsen's work is considered. He states (1983: 55) that "a cube is the best all purpose chamber shape"[17] and his figure 3-1 makes it clear that for updraught kilns a low dome should be added to this cube. He further states (1983: 24) that "an unsupported wall 9" (22.86cm) thick cannot be higher than 8 feet (2.44m)."[18] The superstructure of the kiln is unsupported and if built in alternate header and stretcher courses like the subterranean structure then a chamber approximating to 2.0m square appears entirely plausible.

These recalculated figures would allow 9 stacks[19] of 8 saggars tall up to the kiln shoulder, giving 72 saggars overall. To this should be added the saggars stacked into the dome. The number of these would, of course, depend on the proportions of the dome but if it were minimal, with a diameter of 1.8m and supported at the corners, it would be possible to stack a further 2 saggars of the average size on the centre stack to give a total of 74 overall. In practice, of course, smaller saggars would be used to fill up vacant space in the dome but these figures give some impression of the likely minimum capacity of the HAC3 kiln.

Examination of kilns at Fustat in Cairo suggests that the reconstruction proposed here is not improbable. It is worth noting also that some of these Fustat kilns have heights of around 3.0m (Plates 4.5 and 4.6) and similarly that a dome or vault is added to square/rectangular firing chambers as well as to round ones.

It is also worth considering whether or not the superstructure at HAC3 may have been circular rather than square. It is not impossible that the 1.6m square opening at the top of the kiln seen today served a circular structure of c.2.26m diameter (the smallest circle into which a square of 1.6m fits). If that were so then it would be possible to place 14 saggars on the floor area giving a total number for the circular structure of 98 when stacked 7 high to the 1.95m high shoulder. There are difficulties with the circular arrangement in that, unlike the square, the gaps between the average saggars are uneven and could create 'chimneys' leading to over-firing.[20] However, this arrangement of 14 saggars is based on the mean average base diameter: if this is ignored and a variety of sizes used, as would surely have been the case, then the chimney effect can be much reduced and the number of saggars increased. This is emphasised when taking the dome into account in that the best arrangement of saggars (Goldberg 1971)[21] would allow only 4 additional ones of average diameter to be placed directly on top of the stacks within the dome. Once again, in practice, saggars of smaller size would be used to fill up the space. A range of sizes was used in stacking saggars in the pottery industry of the 19th and early 20th centuries (see Chapter 5) and there is no reason to assume that the Roman practice would have been significantly different. Bonifay (2004: 63) suggests an arrangement whereby the holes in the chequer are always located between, rather than beneath, saggars but such an arrangement does not seem to be necessary, or always desirable, in practice.

However, square fire boxes with round superstructures are not common. Swan (1984) gives no evidence for such structures in Roman Britain although she does (1984: 83ff) list some rectangular kilns. These rectangular kilns are not, however, constructed in the same way or on the same scale as the Memphis kilns. It is notable that the great majority of pottery kilns dealt with by Swan (1984) and by Peacock (1982) are round and this seems to be the case not only for the Roman world but for traditional pottery kilns across the world as well as through time. One exception, however, is the brick kiln from Speicher, Germany, described by Loeschcke (1931, see also Peacock 1982: 71) which has a square substructure but was reconstructed by him as having a round superstructure. This is, however, misleading since the floor of the structure is itself square and supports a square tower which is then surrounded by a circular insulating coating but, as Peacock (1982: 73) points out, there is little archaeological evidence for such a coating. There are also square pottery kilns from the Legionary supply depot at Holt (Grimes 1930).

How the saggars were placed into the kiln must be a matter of conjecture. Their weight is a significant consideration here: an example of a Type 12 saggar of average size would weigh c.31.9 kgs. before any faience wares are placed inside it. Such a weight, and indeed diameter in this instance, would make loading them through an opening in the top of the superstructure extremely difficult and dangerous to both the loaders and to the saggar contents. It is therefore much more likely that they were loaded via an opening in the side of the superstructure (see Plate 4.6) and that this opening would then be walled up when the operation was complete and broken down after each firing. Given that there is an access pit on the west side of kiln HAC3 and a vent on the east side it is likely that any such opening would have been on the north or south sides. The mudbrick platform of the 'H' on the north side is very worn and is also the downslope side. Since it is likely that the workshop area would have been on the flat ground to the north of the kiln it might be supposed that the opening was also on the north in this instance.

Structural summary

The kiln can therefore be visualised as having a tower-like superstructure which was probably square in plan, closed at the top, probably with a dome, but with an opening

Plate 4.7. Looking into the HAC3 kiln showing part of the extensive slag unit [208] which adhered to the walls of the kiln. The timbers at left and right are part of the suspended shoring placed in the kiln to allow it to be excavated in safety. (Photo: P.T. Nicholson).

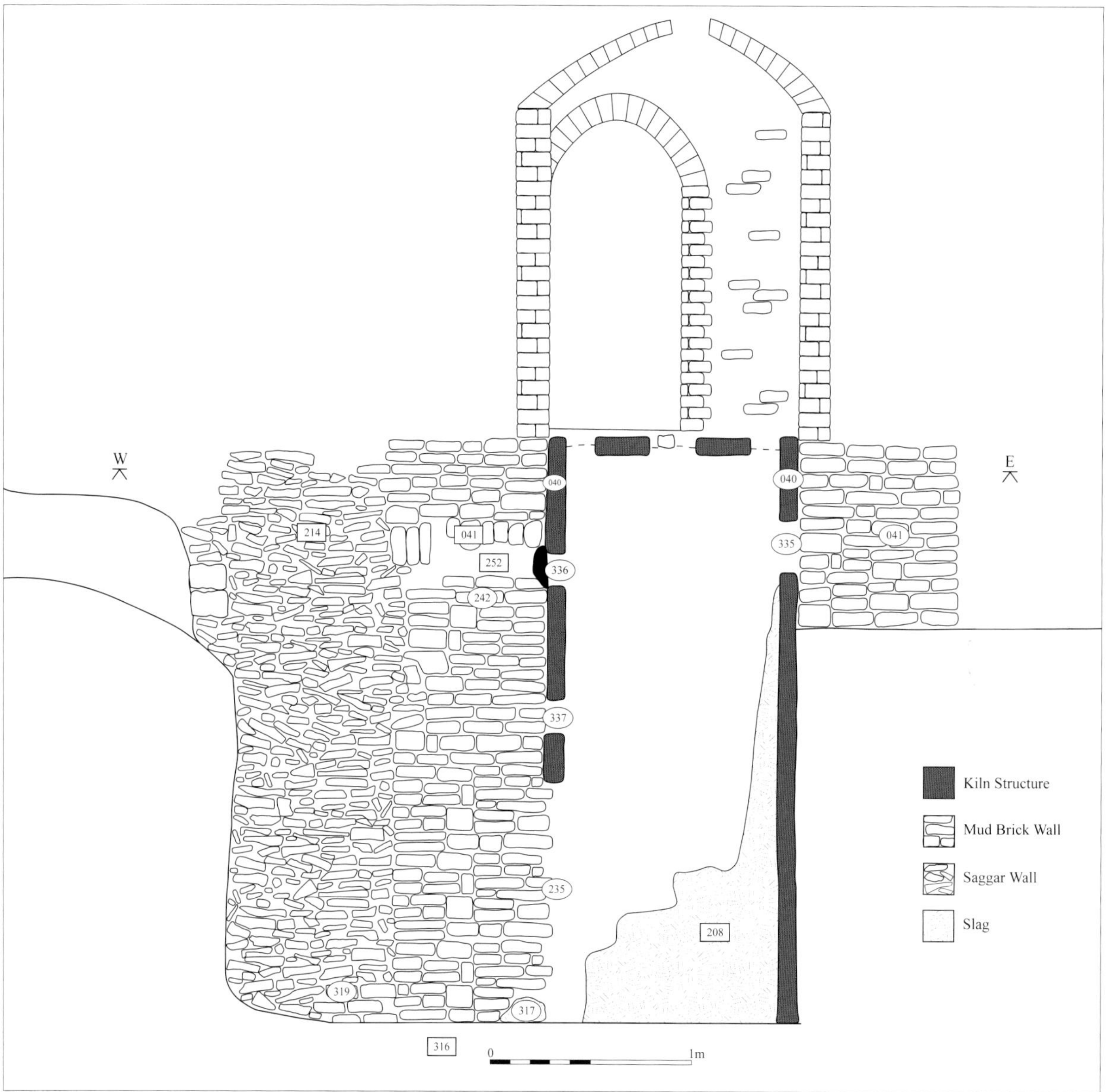

Figure 4.3. Reconstruction of the HAC3 kiln. The stoke-hole is on the east side [335] with two vents on the west [336] and [337]. Vent [336] was blocked in antiquity. The access doorway which also serves as a vent and possibly even a secondary stoke-hole is located at bottom west [235]. The domed top of the structure is hypothetical but based on ethnographic examples and kiln design. (Drawing: Tessa Baber).

on the north side which could be blocked during firing (Fig. 4.3). The superstructure was divided from the substructure by a perforated floor which was located just above a stoke-hole on the east side and above two vent holes and a vent/access hole on the west side. Extension of the chequer above the level of the preserved brickwork would allow for a somewhat larger floor area than that preserved. The vent/access hole and lowermost vent hole were located deep in the access pit which was itself bordered by revetted walls of saggar fragments. The access/vent hole was blocked at the end of each firing in order to retain heat within the structure and allow it to cool slowly. The same would doubtless be the case for the stoke-hole on the east side, though it was found open at the time of excavation.

Whilst the reconstruction is based on providing additional space around a 3 x 3 arrangement of Type 12 saggars it is possible that no such additional space was provided and that the tower measured only 1.60m square.

Fuel and 'slag'

The excavation at HAC3 was notable for the large amount of 'slag' discovered. This so-called slag is not in any sense related to metallurgical slag. However, Bachmann (1982: 1) defines a slag as "a once molten silicate or silicate mixture, sometimes including oxides, phosphates, borates, sulphides, carbides pure metals etc." This definition seems appropriate to the solid, vitrified material found within the excavated kiln and so is used here.[22]

Plate 4.8. A piece of the slag (V-21) from the HAC3 kiln preserving the impressions of halfa grass. Between the impressions small drips of vitreous slag are visible, emphasising how fluid it was during firing. (Photo: P.T. Nicholson).

Loose fragments of slag were found all around the site, and a very large quantity was found *in situ*, still adhering to the inner walls of the furnace, particularly on the east wall, opposite the main stoke-hole, and in the north east corner (Plate 4.7).

All of the slag from the excavation was examined, and samples kept for detailed study. This has allowed a reconstruction of the processes by which slag seems to have formed in the furnace. Sampling for scientific analysis has not been permitted, and as a result the following account is based on macroscopic examination of the many kilos of material recovered from the furnace and that which remains adhered to its walls.

How slag forms

Petrie (1911a: 35) states that "The fuel used was straw; we found much carbonised straw in the masses of slag, which had run down and covered it. No trace of sticks or of charcoal was found." Plant impressions were also discovered in the slag from the recent work, along with the carbonised remains of the fuel itself.

However, whilst the plant remains do look straw-like the writer believes that this was an unlikely fuel given that in Petrie's reconstruction it had to be thrown between the saggar stacks. There are two reasons for this doubt, first the difficulty of throwing straw between – and especially behind – the saggar stacks and second (perhaps more importantly) the likely cost of purchasing agricultural straw which would be required in very large quantities. Straw is an expensive commodity in Egypt today and is likely to have been so in the past, indeed Johnson (1936: 470) lists barley straw at the equivalent of between 8.5 and 10.45 *drachmae* per bundle.[23] The material is apparently not attested as a fuel in Roman Egypt either in lengths or chopped as chaff, although husk-chaff from winnowing[24] (Gk. *achuron*) is attested for the fuelling of brick kilns and baths[25] as described in *P.Lond.* 1166 which is a contract for heating baths at Hermopolis (Johnson 1936: 683-4) in AD 42.[26] In a clause of this contract some of the chaff is used to fuel a private brick kiln as well as to heat the baths. The cost of husk chaff fuel for a year was 2000 *drachmae*, this would be the equivalent of one rural labourer's wages for between c.5.5 and c11.0 years.[27] A bath building is, of course, considerably larger than a kiln but would (one hopes) have been heated to a considerably lower temperature and although size and heat comparisons are not very practical it is clear that the cost of providing the necessary heat to the baths, using husk chaff, is still high. Chaff is also the fuel suggested by Cockle (1981: 94) from one of the Oxyrynchus papyri of the 3rd Century A.D.[28] Kingery (1997:12) and Bourry (1911: 192) both list straw as common fuel for kiln firings, though not specifically in Egypt. Petrie may well have known of examples of straw/straw chaff being used as a fuel outside Egypt and assumed that his plant impressions were of that plant.

However, examination of the carbonised remains from HAC3 was undertaken by Dr. Mary Anne Murray

A

B

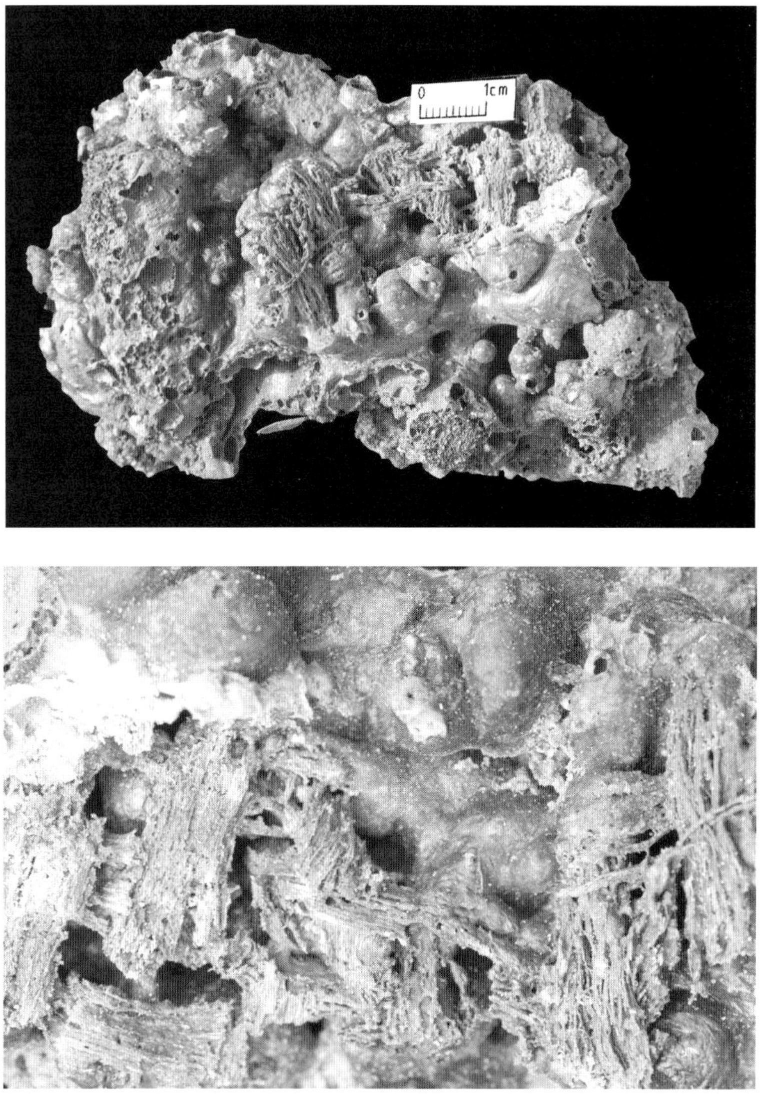

Plate 4.9. (A) Slag (V-22) preserving the impression of woven matting. (B) Detail of the weave. (Photo: P.T. Nicholson).

Plate 4.10. Detail of the fibrous texture left by the silica skeletons of halfa grass in the slag (V-31). (Photo: P.T. Nicholson).

who found that the fuel used was in fact halfa grass (*Demostachya bipinnata*) which still grows locally and so may have provided a cheap and convenient source of fuel. To fuel a furnace of this size over a prolonged period would have required considerable quantities of this plant so it is possible that some import of the material might also have been necessary. It is not unlikely that the locally available resource might have been managed in some way.

It is the reaction between this fuel and the structure of the furnace which is responsible for the production of the slag. The fuel seems to be particularly rich in silica and in alkalis and these react together to form a vitreous material which further reacts with the surfaces of bricks and sometimes with the saggars to yield the thick, grey-black slag so typical of the furnace.

Some work on the properties of grasses in relation to the use of biomass fuels has been carried out by Professor Nick Syred at the Institute of Energy, Cardiff University[29] who kindly provided data on tests on a number of materials including wheat straw and varieties of the perennial grass *Miscanthus,* a popular biofuel. *Miscanthus* is believed to be similar in its properties to the halfa grass used at HAC3. Among its characteristics is its high silicon content. "Silicon is a problematic constituent in ash as it combines with other metal oxides to form metal silicates which have lower melting points that reduce the ash melt flow temperature, for example Potassium silicates have melting points under 800ºC" (Steer *et al.* n.d.:29).[30] This effect is much less marked in wheat straw which needs higher temperatures (934ºC) before it begins to slag than does *Miscanthus* (894ºC; Syred pers. comm.). Given that temperatures in the firebox of the kiln may well have been around 900-1000ºC[31] the early formation of slag may have been a continual problem and – potentially – one which may have been avoided if wheat straw had been used rather than halfa grass.

Much of the slag contains the impressions of the grass as well as carbonised remains (e.g. V-24, V-26) and examination of these impressions clearly shows that the greatest vitrification took place in the areas immediately around the burning plants. Small pockets of vitreous material ran between the stems, and the ends of these 'stalactites' form small blobs which would have continually dripped had the temperature remained high (e.g. V-21) (Plate 4.8). As well as the usual straight plant stem impressions of c.2-3mm diameter there are much larger voids, up to 2.5cm across, and often almost square, which seem to have formed where the grass stems met[32] at the crown or where they were thrown in while tied into small bundles. Occasionally matting, probably from refuse, seems to have been burned as well as plant material and there is evidence of woven matting being preserved in the slag (e.g. V-22) (Plate 4.9).

Even the most dense slag has numerous oval vesicles in it ranging in size from 1mm across up to 2cm or so. However, although this is the most obvious form of the slag, it is not the way in which it begins to form. Examination of the slag shows that it forms in layers. What seems to happen is that quantities of fuel are thrown into the furnace and burn rapidly in an oxygen rich atmosphere leaving only a silica skeleton. This would usually be lost and melted into the slag, but where temperatures rise quickly and more fuel is thrown on top, a layer of silica skeletons can build up, resembling glass fibres (e.g. V-31) (Plate 4.10). As more fuel is thrown in and the temperature increases, probably in the presence of low oxygen levels, so the thick dark slag forms and runs over the ashy silica skeletons sealing them as layers within the slag. Gases are generated during this process and escape through the molten slag (e.g. V-7) frequently leaving its surface pitted.

From the kiln it was clear that there was a series of dense slag layers with silica skeleton layers between them, and these may represent different episodes of firing. However, because slag which had become adhered to the structure could not always be broken away after a firing it would soften again and might melt again in subsequent firings. As a result it was impossible to determine the number of firings to which the furnace had been subjected. The slag layers frequently become fused together and impossible to separate.

The slag, which overall is a very dark grey/black in colour frequently also has a reddish hue, probably from iron. In places the presence of iron is particularly obvious and rust patches can be seen in the slag where iron has formed and then rusted in the damp conditions prevalent after the kiln was filled in and the local water table rose. The iron is mainly derived from the Nile clay used to make the kiln bricks and mortar, and from that same clay, mixed with sand, which was used to form the 'red adhering clay' used to plaster over the stack of saggars, and sometimes to re-line areas of the kiln.

As well as the frequent red or reddish purple hue, yellow and a pale turquoise colour are also often observed in the slag. Some of these colours may derive from the iron or from contamination by copper used in the glazes for the faience vessels, fragments of which are sometimes found in the slag (e.g. V-28). Some contamination may also come from the non-plant fuels used in the furnace.

Amongst the non-plant fuel is bone, several pieces of which are embedded in the slag (e.g. 2002-V-0117).[33] This suggests that rubbish from the workshop environment was thrown into the fire. In one case a small piece of iron, probably an object of some sort, was found in the slag, suggesting that not all of the rubbish was carefully sifted. Initially more puzzling are many small fragments of lime, or pockets of lime powder (CaCO3), usually no more than 5cm long. Since the workshop is built on a mud sub-strate, and there is no rock outcrop in the immediate vicinity, this lime, which may have entered as limestone, must have been deliberately brought to the furnace.

The presence of lime amongst the slag can be attributed to its use as a flux. Because the plant fuel used, like most biomass fuels, is apparently rich in potassium and sodium, the formation of slag at relatively low temperatures is problematic (above). The throwing of handfuls of lime into the fire box during firing would help to flux the slag (Syred pers. comm.), helping it to run down the firebox and densify, rather than forming pockets which might otherwise block the flow of hot gases into the kiln proper. A negative effect of this, however, would be that the slag when solidified would be denser and harder to break up and remove – though the quantities of slag dumped around the site show that this was not an insuperable problem until late in the life of the structure. The number of firings which resulted in the mass of slag in HAC3 is not known but it may be derived from the last few episodes.

It seems likely that when the furnace was in operation the person fuelling it would have been able to hear not only the roar of the fire, but also a bubbling from the viscous slag which was forming, and spreading within the fire box.

After the furnace had cooled the large opening on the west which served as an access and vent hole would have been fully opened and raked out. At the same time the opportunity would have been taken to try to break away some of the now solidified slag from the walls. However, the slag set very hard and since the furnace does not have a sacrificial render, which would have allowed the slag to be pulled away and the furnace simply re-lined, it was never possible to clean it out fully. That attempts to remove the slag were made is apparent from the area of slag lumps piled on the north wall of the fire-pit entry ramp [239] and [241] (Fig. 3.10). It is likely that it was the quantity and immovable nature of the slag which eventually led to the abandonment of the furnace, the east wall and part of the north wall having become so slagged that it was no longer possible to obtain sufficient heat in these areas of the furnace to fire the faience vessels.

Firing Regime

The length of time for which the HAC3 kiln was fired and the temperatures it reached cannot be determined with certainty and one must look for comparison to similar kilns.

Olsen (1983: 140) describes an "Early Muslim Low-Fire Glaze Kiln" from New Delhi, India. This is used for firing blue glazed pottery and tiles, the pottery being fired in saggars. The kiln is of updraught type and is circular. It may also differ from the HAC3 example in being only 5 feet (1.52 m) tall above the perforated floor and having a similar internal diameter. The firebox is only 2 feet 6 inches high (0.76m) and is fed with hardwood. The nature of the fuel at HAC3 probably required a much larger space.

Despite the actual, and supposed, differences between the two structures the fact that this kiln uses saggars for firing a glazed ware may be instructive. Olsen (1983: 40) states that it took some 5 hours to "warm up" and a further 6-7 hours to fire, giving a total of 11-12 hours.

Olsen (1983: 145-147) also discusses the "Mirovet Medieval Kiln", actually a kiln in contemporary use but of Medieval pattern. This has a chamber of 8 feet (2.43m) square and 6 feet (1.82m) high to the shoulder with the dome reaching 9 feet (2.74m) at the crown. The firebox is not directly beneath this chamber, rather the area immediately beneath the chequer is actually a further firing chamber separated from the firebox by a low wall, known as a bagwall. The firebox forms a separate chamber built onto the front of the kiln beyond the bagwall and measures 6 feet (1.82m) by 8 feet (2.43m). Heat from the fire box is drawn over the wall, into the lower chamber and then upward through the chequer and into the firing chamber. The lower chamber also measures 8 feet (2.43m) square by 6 feet (1.82m) high. No saggars are used here and the firing lasts from 28 to 32 hours though Olsen gives no details of the temperatures reached.

The much larger bottle kilns used at the Gladstone Pottery in Stoke-on-Trent could take up to 48 hours to reach a maximum temperature of 1000-1250°C which would then be held for 2-3 hours (Gladstone Pottery Museum n.d.: 20) giving a total firing of up to 51 hours. Sandeman (1917: 232-233) says 45-55 hours are needed for biscuit firing in a kiln of 20 feet (6.0m) but notes that time is not a good guide to temperature as it is affected by the weather and the fuel quality.

The HAC3 kiln is closer in scale to Olsen's "Medieval" kiln though the HAC3 kiln uses saggars and has the fire directly below the vessels. Given that firing at HAC3 is in saggars and that biscuit firing normally requires higher temperatures than glost firing it does not seem unreasonable to suppose that a temperature of at least 1000°C was required. On the basis of the kilns examined by Olsen (1983) and Sandeman (1917) one might expect firings to have lasted between 18 and 24 hours.

Conclusion

It has been suggested that Petrie's (1909a, 1911a) descriptions of the kilns he excavated and the manner in which they may have operated is likely to be flawed. The shortcomings in these reports may stem from the incomplete excavation of the structures and particularly the lack of evidence for a perforated floor ('chequer') which would have separated the fire box from the firing chamber.

By following the rules suggested by Olsen (1983) for kiln design and making comparison with other kilns from the archaeological and ethnographic literature (among which may be considered industrial literature from the 19th and 20th centuries) a reconstruction of the HAC3 kiln can be proposed. This has a firebox separated from the firing chamber by a perforated floor on which stood more than 70 saggars of the average Type 12 size. The firing chamber had an entry door on one side through which the vessels were brought for stacking and which would be bricked up during firing. The chamber itself was probably square with a low dome.

By comparing this reconstruction with other kilns some indication of a firing regime and temperature may be made. It is suggested that temperatures of around 1000°C were probably employed at HAC3 in order to fire the faience body. As discussed later, the glazing may have formed a separate operation in a different kiln.

It has also been shown that at HAC3 halfa grass, rather than straw, was used as fuel and that this had significant drawbacks because of its propensity to form slag. To resolve this problem a lime flux was used, but this in itself led to difficulties with very dense, hard slag which had to be broken up and removed via the access on the west side of the HAC3 kiln.

Endnotes

1 See Chapter 1.
2 The vents in HAC3 are on the west and are below the level of the stoke-hole on the east. They are, however, above the vent/access hole on the west.
3 Or perhaps 'sites' since it is suspected that industrial material from Kom Qalama was treated as if from Kom Helul.
4 Also referred to as "English Bond".
5 In some cases Petrie probably had only a part of the subterranean structure.
6 These form part of the excavation archive.
7 The outermost stack of vessels in Vernhet's reconstruction is beyond the last floor vent making the footprint of the stack significantly larger than that of the perforated floor.
8 For a useful summary of Samian production see Webster (1996).
9 Bourry (1911:233) refers to these cells as "cupboards".
10 Hayes (1995:66) dislikes the term 'faience' but as a non-clay ceramic whose name is well established in the literature it seems appropriate to retain it here (see Chapter 2). He also implies that the Roman production is "self glazing" which generally it is not.
11 Now part of Wrexham, North Wales.
12 The excavator, Mr. T. Arthur Acton, died in 1925 before the material could be published. The work by Grimes (1930) is, of its time, a model example of industrial reconstruction.
13 The external dimensions are given as 18' x 11'9", internal 8'x 7' (Grimes 1930: 34).
14 Known as a 'clammin' amongst the potters of Stoke-on-Trent, U.K.
15 This name refers to the shape of the kiln, or more correctly its surrounding building or 'hovel'.
16 Somewhat smaller than recorded by Petrie for his kilns.
17 The cube is generally accepted as the best kiln shape – see Rhodes (1968).
18 Metric conversion added by the author.
19 That is a 3 x 3 arrangement on the perforated floor.
20 For an example of the damage caused by a chimney effect see Bailey (1976) plate 180.
21 A ring of 10 around the circumference with 4 in the central space as demonstrated by Goldberg (1971) see also www1.
22 It is stressed that the slag is neither the result of metallurgical processes nor derived from the ingredients of the faience glaze.
23 P.Lond.1177 from Arsinoe and dated to A.D. 133. The size of the bundle is not stated but it is unlikely to be more than could be carried as a single donkey load .
24 Rather than chopped straw which is sometimes called chaff in English (Rathbone: pers. comm.).
25 I am indebted to Professor Dominic Rathbone for this information and references.
26 Johnson (1936: 683) gives the date as A.D. 15 and I am indebted to Professor Rathbone for the corrected date.
27 A rural labourer at this time received 0.5-1.0 drachma per day (Rathbone: pers. comm.).
28 Inventory number 36 4B.99/J(6) dated to September 5th A.D.243.
29 Part of the School of Engineering. I am indebted to Professor Syred for his assistance in determining likely causes of slagging.
30 Unpublished report kindly provided by Prof. Syred.
31 Given that it is difficult to reach over 1000°C with an updraught kiln.
32 A feature typical of Halfa grass (Murray pers. comm.).
33 Not assigned a specialist number.

Chapter 5

Saggars and Kiln Furniture

P.T. Nicholson

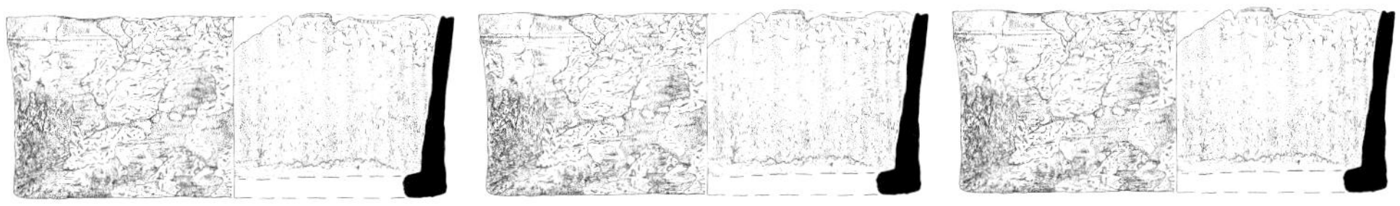

Introduction[1]

Coarse industrial ceramics constitute the biggest individual find group from Kom Helul, with the exception of domestic pottery, much of the latter being used to infill the kiln access ramp in trench HAC3 at the end of its life. The great majority of the industrial ceramic is in the form of saggar vessels.

The word 'saggar' (also spelled 'sagger') is believed to enter into English in the 17th Century and to be a contraction of 'safeguard' which well describes their function (OED 1989: XIV, 367).[2] They are a type of industrial pottery often, but not exclusively, circular in shape and used to contain other pots or faience items during firing. They serve to allow pieces of ware, some with complicated shapes, to be fired in large numbers without touching against one another and so becoming damaged. They similarly allow glazed items to be fired without the glaze becoming speckled with ash or affected by smoke. Their thick walls also have the effect of evening out the distribution of heat from the kiln and permitting gradual cooling (Godden 1992: 20). In effect, saggars act as small closed cells within the kiln, almost as kilns within a kiln.

Petrie (1909a: 14; 1911a: 34-37) found fragments of these saggar vessels in his excavations at Kom Helul where they had been used for firing faience vessels. It was his thinking on these vessels, fragments of which he had first seen lying around on the surface at Memphis in the 1880s, which led him to misinterpret similar cylindrical vessels at Amarna during his excavations there in 1891-2 (Petrie 1894: 26; 1909a: 14-15). At Amarna he believed the cylindrical vessels he found were used as stands rather than actual saggars whereas more recent research suggests that they were usually in fact crucibles or moulds for casting glass ingots (Nicholson *et al.* 1997; Nicholson 2007). The Amarna vessels are wheel thrown and show clear finger grooves on the inside of the base[3] whilst the Memphis vessels are handmade. Had Petrie better understood the manufacture of these vessels rather than relying only on their shape he would doubtless have realised that their function might be different.

After firing, particularly after a glaze firing, it would sometimes be necessary to break the saggar in order to remove its contents, although through the use of various supports etc. the workers would try to avoid this. Industrial sites may, nonetheless, be littered with worn out, broken, saggars and this is the case at Kom Helul.

Petrie describes the Memphis saggars as "cylinder jars 10 inches wide and 7½ inches high. The body was of coarse brown and yellow pottery fusing to a dirty yellow green" (1909a: 14). He further states that "The pottery to be glazed was stacked in saggars of cylindrical form. Two were found unused, 8 and 8½ inches wide, 5½ and 6 inches high. The largest sizes among the fragments of used saggars are 30 inches across and 8 high, another 19 inches across. The height was almost the same, whatever the diameter might be, because its limit was the height of the internal stack of glazed dishes…" (1911a: 35). Note that the size of saggar recorded by Petrie varies between these two accounts and that as well as the small saggars in the 8-10 inch bracket there are others in the range 19-30 inches. One of the unused saggars (Petrie 1911a: Pl.xix:239, UC33565) is now in the Petrie Museum, London, and has helped to contribute to the view that the saggars were generally of smaller rather than larger size.

Petrie states (1911a: 35) that the "the saggar fragments are flushed over with glaze and slag", but he is not specific about whether this applies to all three sizes or only to the smaller ones. As a result it is necessary to examine the saggars in some depth.

Field Processing of the Saggar Vessels

The remains of the saggar vessels are amongst the most difficult examples of ceramic manufacture ever examined by the writer. One would expect that it would be a fairly simple matter to differentiate between rims and bases, but on initial investigation it is not. This is largely a function of the handmade nature of these vessels (below).

When the saggars break they frequently do so along join lines, and their bases become detached from the walls. Because the bases are often chamfered they appear to be finished clay bats, whilst the similarly chamfered lower edges of the vessel walls appear to be rims. The picture is further confused because the clay strips used between the saggars (saggar joiners or 'wads')[4] can be of clay similar to that of the saggars. The joiners may also become fused to the saggars and so form artificial profiles to the rims, particularly where they are then covered by glaze. Flattening of the top of the saggar joiner, where it meets the base of the saggar above, only adds to the confusion by producing well profiled, flat-topped rims, which are in fact nothing of the kind. The biggest saggars are of such large diameter that it can be impossible to tell whether some small fragments come from rims or bases, particularly since the bases are made in such a way that they have a finished edge which receives the wall. Base fragments can also resemble bats.[5]

During excavation all the pottery was washed, dried and sorted on site. The industrial ceramics were sorted from the domestic, and the fragments weighed. It was decided that, with the exception of a very few contexts, the undiagnostic material should be discarded after weighing. This decision was justified on grounds of quantity and weight (both of which caused storage problems) and the difficulty of attempting to find joins in such coarse and similar material. Where joins were attempted by our conservators the process proved to be extremely slow and difficult since the vessels are handmade and vary sufficiently in their profile and circumference on a single vessel to make reconstruction awkward. The expenditure of time and resources was therefore felt to be unjustified. With hindsight this seems to have been the correct decision.

The more detailed processing of the industrial ceramics was developed over several seasons, and was finally completed in 2006. In earlier seasons time did not permit a great deal of material to be examined at any one time and as a result it was much more difficult to observe trends in the saggars. Several things became clear however. The amount of pottery and its coarseness precluded any attempt to number each and every individual sherd. The fabric meant that marker pens were rendered useless after as few as 20 sherds and bagging each individual piece would be extremely time consuming and prohibitively expensive. Instead a system was developed whereby every piece was examined, and any fragment which was felt to be of particular interest for any reason (fabric, form, adhering kiln furniture, etc.) was separated and given a specialist identification number. The rest were re-bagged with the material from their context.

The processing involved the identification of the piece and measurement of its diameter and the percentage of diameter preserved. The identification of the pieces was initially over-elaborate, with a number of different rim types being identified along with a series of different bat types. Several types of stands and possible drying trays were also identified. The combination of the complexity of this typology along with the relatively short periods available each season to examine the industrial material meant that no obvious trends were discerned, and that the system was extremely slow to apply. In the 2006 study season a major task for the writer, with substantial assistance from Hendrikje Nouwens, was to process those materials not previously examined, which was the bulk of the sherds, and if necessary to re-examine some of those done earlier.

Coming to the material afresh and spending long periods on it soon revealed areas of difficulty in the original system. Discussion with Janine Bourriau and Peter French, who were working on the domestic pottery, confirmed that the series of possible drying trays were in fact domestic pottery and known from non-industrial contexts, whilst the three-pointed stands, collected by Petrie, may be fire-trays and not usually connected with industrial use.[6] With these two categories removed, attention could be focussed on the saggars themselves.

It was quickly apparent that there were two broad types of saggar vessel. A small type, recorded by Petrie, which was normally coated with a brightly coloured glaze, and a much larger type, almost always in excess of 40cm diameter, in a very coarse red fabric, and which lacked glaze. Instead, this latter type frequently had a whitish interior and, more rarely, exterior and very often had up to 25cm of white powder in it. Quite commonly some of the white coating had reacted with the vessel wall and begun to form a very thin, colourless, incipient glaze.

The close examination of these large saggars in 2002 had already shown that the bases were made as a large disc of clay onto which the walls were pressed. As a result a finished edge could be seen on some of the wall, but often left no trace on the base. Further study in 2006 showed that there were variations on this method of adding a base, and that sometimes the disc of clay for the base could be chamfered around the edge and the walls chamfered to fit to it. Similarly, a groove of clay could be made around the base and the wall rounded at the bottom to fit into it. Clay was then smoothed down to the bottom to complete the join.

Once these variations were noted, it was realised that the variety of rims seen in the smaller saggars were in fact not rims at all, but smaller versions of the type of wall seen on the larger ones, and that the bats were actually bases whose finished edges were the result of their being separately made and then joined to the vessel walls. As a result the bat category was largely removed. This greatly simplified the typology. The vessels were reduced to two broad types, Type 3, generally small and glazed and Type 12, large, coarse and unglazed. As study continued it seemed that there was a distinction to be made at around 40cm, Type 3 being almost invariably smaller than this diameter, Type 12 greater than it.

It had been noted from early on that some of the Type 3 vessels at the smaller end of the diameter range were clearly of marl clay, and it seemed that there was at least some correlation between these and turquoise blue glazes. It was hypothesised that these were used for certain colours because the reduced iron in the clay meant that the glazes would not discolour.

As processing continued, the division between large coarse unglazed vessels and small, more dense, glazed vessels became less clear. Some large glazed vessels in coarse fabric were noted, but the most significant pattern to emerge was that large unglazed[7] vessels of Type 12 came almost exclusively from trench HAC3, whilst the full range came from trench HAC2.

Further examination revealed that these larger glazed vessels were themselves either marls or mixed marl-silt clays. In other words, there was a correlation between glazed saggars and calcareous clays and the white coated silts and lack of glaze. Janine Bourriau was able to confirm that the fine, pale firing, small saggars which had initially been noted as marl were essentially a type of Marl C in the Vienna System,[8] whilst those coarser glazed examples were coarser variations on this same fabric, with additional plant material, and sometimes a greater amount of ferruginous material.

Once this was realised, a coherent division became apparent. Trench HAC3 produced the large, mostly unglazed, Type 12 saggars, and therefore was engaged in a different part of the process to whichever kiln(s) had been responsible for the dump at trench HAC2 where glazed material was found. This glazed material was invariably of a marl or mixed clay, and any size divisions were to be made *within* the marl clay rather than between it and the coarse silt of Type 12.

General Typological Summary

Analysis has shown that whilst there are in fact several saggar types, they can best be divided into two broad categories. A smaller type which is here referred to as Type 3 and a larger one described as Type 12 (Table 5.1).

Table 5.1. Summary of saggar dimensions

Type 3

Total No. of Type 3	**629 including examples too small for diameter recording**		
Rim diam. range	15 - 70 cm	See Fig. 5.1	n=294
Base diam. range	15 - 64 cm	See Fig. 5.1	n=225
Wall height range	12 - 15 cm		n=3
Modal base diam.[9]	30 cm		n=57
Mean rim diameter	33.18 cm		
Mean base diameter	32.68 cm		
Mean wall height	13.33 cm		
Minimum number of vessels[10]	37 based on n=294		

Type 12

Total No. of Type 12	**1308 including examples too small for diameter recording**		
Rim diam. range	19 -70 cm	See Fig. 5.2	n=602
Base diam. range	18 -78 cm	See Fig. 5.2	n=507
Wall height range	21.5 - 28.5 cm		n=32
Modal base diam.[11]	50 cm		n=62
Mean rim diameter	48.33 cm		
Mean base diameter	49.42 cm		
Mean wall height	26.13 cm		
Minimum number of vessels[12]	52 based on n=566		

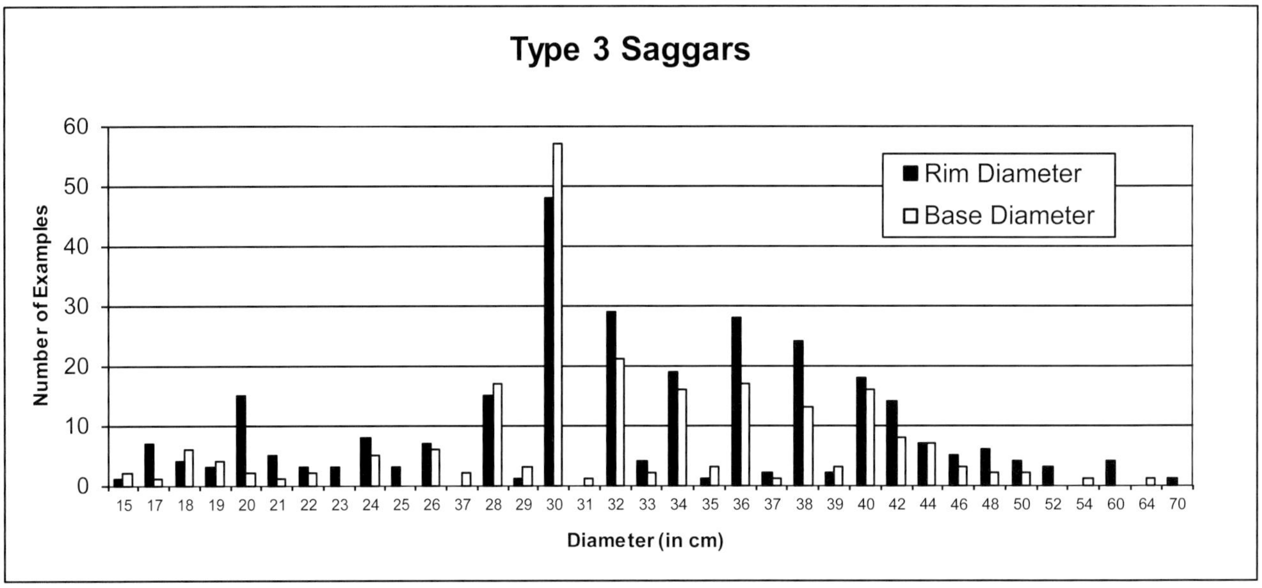

Figure 5.1. Bar chart showing the range of rim and base diameters for Type 3 saggars at Memphis.

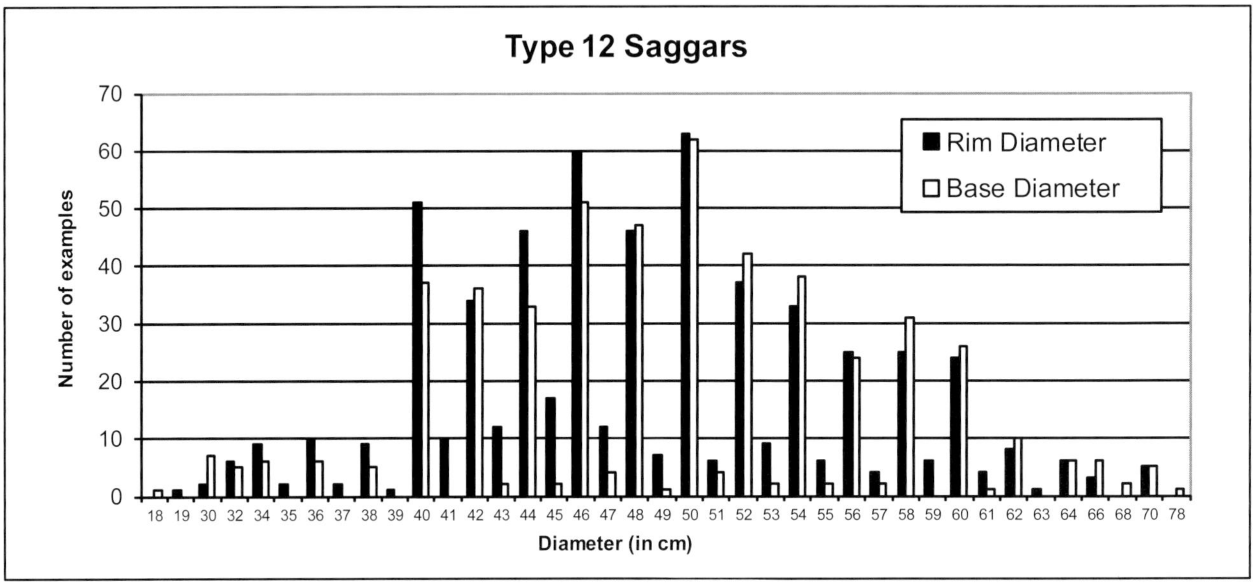

Figure 5.2. Bar chart showing the range of rim and base diameters for Type 12 saggars at Memphis.

In summary it may be said that the vessels can be characterized as follows:

Type 3 has a mean base diameter of 33cm (12.99 inches) and average height of 13cm (5.25 inches).

Type 12 has an mean base diameter of 0.49m (19.29 inches) and an average height of 26cm (10.28 inches).[13]

These measurements initially seem to confirm Petrie's observations. However, they also mask some important information. The smaller saggars tend to be made in a marl clay or a marl-silt mixture, they generally fire to a yellowish colour and are usually glazed on the inside and on their underside. The larger saggars are made from silt clay, often coarsely tempered and frequently have a thin whitish lining and up to 2.5cm of powdered lime (CaCO3) inside them. Both groups are handmade.

Whilst the concept of two broad classes of saggar vessel may hold, there is some overlap between the groups. Type 12 vessels from trench HAC3 are almost invariably unglazed, but the occasional finds of the same type from trench HAC2 may have glaze. Very few of the Type 3 saggars lack glaze, except on examples where it has obviously been pulled away in removing items or the piece has not been used.

The smaller class of vessel typically has a Type 3 rim, with at least a trace of a finger groove around it. The bases of these vessels were attached separately by a variety of means, sometimes chamfered, sometimes luted into a groove, sometimes by spreading clay over the join inside and pressing the wall against the curve of the base plate. One can assume that individual workers had their own preferred techniques and that this has led to a variety of joins on the same type of vessel, such that they are of no apparent typological significance.

The larger vessels generally have a Type 12 rim, and are of a more coarse fabric. Their walls are thicker, and they are altogether heavier than their glazed counterparts. Their bases too are added separately in a variety of ways. These large vessels sometimes bear a potter's or owner's mark inside them.

Types 3 and 12 account for virtually all the securely typed vessels and such others as exist are generally only variants of these, sometimes defined on the basis of fabric alone. Consequently the general saggar typology is much simpler than it initially appeared, and from 2006 bases were generally assigned either to Type 3 or Type 12 with reference to the rims. The bat typology was abandoned at this point.

Saggar Making: An Ethnoarchaeological Approach

Examination of the Memphis saggars raises a range of questions; for example why should they be handmade at a time when wheel manufacture of pottery is almost universal and how does this handmaking take place? Is Petrie's view that their height is governed by the maximum height of the vessel stack inside them correct?

Ideally one would ask present-day makers of saggars how they went about their work and why they made the technological decisions that they did. However, saggars today are made by machine using a powder press process and there are no surviving makers of handmade saggars who can be interviewed. Nonetheless it is well known that saggars were still being used in the pottery industry in Britain well into the 20th Century and it is possible to attempt some (near) contemporary ethnoarchaeology. Such approaches should be used wherever feasible, albeit with caution, in investigating technological processes. An attempt was therefore made to locate those with a knowledge of saggar making in Stoke-on-Trent, the centre of the British ceramic industry.[14]

In Britain the move to cleaner fuels following the *Clean Air Act* of 1956 (H.M.S.O. 1956) largely removed the need for saggars, which helped to protect the ware from smoke and dirt. The 'Bottle Kilns' of Stoke, which once existed in their hundreds, have now mostly been demolished. With the passing of the coal-fired kilns the traditional saggar making industry died out and with it, in the last decades of the 20th Century, the last of the makers of traditional saggars.

Fortunately there still remain individuals who worked alongside saggar makers or whose family were involved in the trade. There is also a 16mm film *Mau'ing the Saggar* made in 1981[15] which records most of the process. The author was fortunate enough to have access to this film and to the much longer sound recordings (which were later edited for the film's soundtrack). Along with reminisces from those who recalled saggar makers this information forms the basis for the reconstruction given below. A copy of the film has been included on the DVD accompanying this volume.[16]

Hand-Making Saggars In Stoke-on-Trent

One of the most interesting, if saddening, aspects of the current study is the realisation of how much knowledge has been lost of an industry which was still fully operational only 60 years ago. The account given below has been compiled from reminisces and from archive film as well as published accounts but these sources are sometimes at variance with one another. Whilst this sometimes reflects differing practices between workshops it also indicates details of practices which are now lost to the historical and archaeological record.

Clay

The clay used to produce saggars was known in Stoke as "Saggar Marl" and was mixed with grog. By grog archaeologists usually mean ground, fired pottery but in the pottery industry it can mean any aplastic material (see Hodges 1976: 20). In the case of saggar marl the grog often comprised pieces of brick, old saggar fragments and sand (Sandeman 1921: 202). The proportion of grog to clay varied according to clay type but could be as high as three parts grog to two parts clay (Sandeman 1921: 205). In recent times the clay was usually imported and according to Mr. Baggott (pers. comm.) who worked for *Wedgewood* it was imported to Stoke from many areas of Britain. However, he noted that in the 1770s one William Adams of Tunstall was fined for digging saggar clay from the road outside his factory. Local sources were confirmed by Mr. Glover (pers. comm.) who noted that marl was originally dug from a pit near *Hewitt's* works at Fenton but when this was exhausted it was bought in from elsewhere.

According to the unused parts of the soundtrack recorded by Mr. Mee in August 1981 and spoken by the late Mr. Ralph Wheeldon,[17] the saggar marl was delivered to the factory six or seven tons at a time, usually as lumps of 56lb each[18] (25.40 kg). It was of two distinct compositions, "side marl" which was used for the walls of the saggar and "bottom marl" used for the bases. Bottom marl had more grog mixed into it and the grog was of larger size than for the side marl. The six ton delivery would be divided into three tons of side and three of bottom marl.

The two types of marl were dumped on the workshop floor and each would then be "knocked with the mau"[19] until it stood about waist high. At this stage most of the air would have been knocked out of the clay and the individual blocks would have been amalgamated into a single pile of side marl and another of bottom marl.

However, in times before pre-mixed clay was brought to the factory the mixing of grog with clay was done on site. A layer of grog was spread on the floor, and on top of it a layer of ground clay, another of grog and so on "till the pile is 1 ft. 6 in. to 2 ft high" (Sandeman 1921: 205). It would then be "dug over" and sprinkled with water before being run twice through the pug mill (Sandeman 1921: 205).[20] Sandeman (1921: 205) recommends that as little water as possible be used "it means harder work in making, but it also means better saggers".

Making the saggar

Once the clay was prepared the first task was to work it on a bench. The bench was flat and had a metal frame which could be dropped over it (Plate 5.1). The bench was first wetted using a sponge and then sprinkled with sawdust until completely covered. Earlier in the 20th Century, and in the decades before, sand had been sprinkled on the bench but health and safety considerations had led to the use of sawdust as it gave rise to less dust and so reduced silicosis (Simcock, pers. comm.).

Individual slices of clay were now cut from the side marl pile, or "dump", using a tool known as a "grafter". This is a spade-like tool with a flat D-shaped blade, the curve of the D being uppermost and attached to the handle (or "stale"). These slices were cut to be only slightly thicker than the depth of the frame on the bench top. The slices were placed into the frame each running from the back toward the worker and each slightly overlapping the other by 1-1½ inches (2.5 – 3.8cm). The grafter was used to trim off excess thickness in a process known as "fettling off" and then the slices (or "bats")[21] were hammered down using the flat blade of the grafter such that the overlapped edges became compressed together and the whole sheet of clay was reduced to the thickness of the frame (Plate 5.2). The frame usually had only 3 sides, that nearest to the worker being open. It was not always necessary to fill the whole frame and the saggar maker used the grafter to trim the edges square where the frame was not completely filled as well as to trim the edge nearest to him. The normal depth of a frame was ¾ of an inch (19cm). Sandeman (1921: 206) recommends the same thickness though noting that it should be thicker for very large examples.

With this done, the edge nearest the saggar maker was thickened slightly with the fingers and the whole clay sheet again sprinkled with sawdust. A mau' was then used to strike along the clay, working across it horizontally, gradually moving in rows from back to front. The mau' itself was shaped like a bed-warming pan and comprised a cylindrical head made from heavy oak through which passed the shaft or stale (Plate 5.3). The flat ends of the cylinder were used to hammer the marl. The mau' was kept in a bucket of water to keep the oak head damp and to keep the wood expanded so that the stale did not come off. This practice of soaking the mau' led to handles becoming rotted and causing accidents when they broke. By the time saggar making ended as a practice the wooden handles had been replaced by metal ones. The wetting of the mau' also meant that the clay and sawdust did not stick to it when used to hammer them down into the frame.

Mr. Wheeldon describes the action of "mau'ing in" as striking the clay and pulling sideways and forwards, in other words drawing the clay to the side of the frame and toward him. Each blow overlapped the previous one to its left or right (depending on the direction of mau'ing) and one or more of those above it. The marks from each strike were very clear[22] and it was obvious to the worker where the next strike was to be.

Once the frame was filled the saggar maker took his measuring stick and marked the clay ready to cut into strips of the desired height for the wall. A rule, actually a wooden straight edge, was then aligned with the measured marks and struck so that it adhered to the clay whilst a blade was drawn through it to cut it into strips. The cutting was done with a tool known as a "splice". In recent times this tended to be an old hacksaw blade which had been bound with tape or otherwise given a handle (Plate 5.4). Mr. Wheeldon estimated that it took 8 minutes to fill the frame, mau' it in and then cut out the sides.

The individual strips, still lying in the frame, were once again dusted with sawdust. A blade, known as a "running under stick" was drawn underneath the first strip of clay, that nearest the saggar maker, to loosen it from the bench and it was then rolled around a wooden drum (Plate 5.5). These wooden drums had a circular, oval or other shaped cross-section with solid top and base (save for a hand-hole). Their walls were built up from laths to give the overall shape. The drum is placed onto the clay and rolled along the strip rolling the clay strip around it.

Whilst this process was going on another worker, the "bottom knocker",[23] working at a separate bench would be using the bottom marl to prepare the base of the saggar. He too used a metal frame but this time it comprised the complete shape of the base (Plate 5.3). He used a single piece of clay somewhat thicker than the frame ring and hammered it to the correct thickness using the mau'.

The frame was then used to help slide the finished bottom from the workbench onto a perforated metal plate known as a "shord".[24] Once on the metal plate the frame is removed and the plate carried over to the "wheelie",[25] a turntable on which the saggar will be completed (Plates 5.1 and 5.6). It took approximately three minutes to knock a bottom.

Plate 5.1. The saggar maker's workshop at the Gladstone Pottery Museum, Stoke-on-Trent (formerly the Gladstone Pottery). In the background is the saggar maker's bench, a metal frame runs around the back and two sides of it. In this exhibit a saggar drum and two finished saggars stand within the frame. A circular frame used for making saggar bases leans against the leg of the bench. The wheelie is in the foreground and has the perforated metal plate (shord) used to lift saggars, on top of it. A completed saggar stands on the plate. (Photo: P.T. Nicholson. Reproduced courtesy of the Gladstone Pottery Museum).

Plate 5.2. Mr. Fred Boulton using the 'grafter' to flatten down individual strips of side-marl into the frame. It would then be beaten using the mau'. Photographed at the Burgess and Leigh Factory, Middleport 1964. (Photo by and reproduced courtesy of Mr. Donald Morris).

Plate 5.3. Mr. Fred Boulton using the wooden mau' to flatten bottom-marl into a circular metal frame used for making the saggar base. The mau' is also used to flatten side-marl. Photographed at the Burgess and Leigh Factory, Middleport 1964. (Photo by and reproduced courtesy of Mr. Donald Morris).

Plate 5.4. Mr. Fred Boulton using a wooden straight edge – 'rule' – and blade to cut strips of side-marl to the appropriate width ready to be rolled onto a wooden drum. Photographed at the Burgess and Leigh Factory, Middleport 1964. (Photo by and reproduced courtesy of Mr. Donald Morris).

Plate 5.5. Mr. Fred Boulton rolling a strip of side-marl onto a wooden drum. Photographed at the Burgess and Leigh Factory, Middleport 1964. (Photo by and reproduced courtesy of Mr. Donald Morris).

Plate 5.6. Mr. Fred Boulton has placed the drum covered in side-marl onto a ready knocked bottom on the wheelie. The hand-hole in the top of the drum is clearly visible. Photographed at the Burgess and Leigh Factory, Middleport 1964. (Photo by and reproduced courtesy of Mr. Donald Morris).

Plate 5.7. Mr. Fred Boulton using a topping stick to finish the rim of the saggar. The vessel is still on the wheelie. Photographed at the Burgess and Leigh Factory, Middleport 1964. (Photo by and reproduced courtesy of Mr. Donald Morris).

The drum with clay wall wrapped around it was now carried over to the wheelie and placed on top of the prepared bottom, which was of slightly larger circumference than the drum and the wall wrapped onto it. The wall ("side") was now cut where the two ends met and moistened before being beaten back together. This was to ensure a strong join in the wall.

A small plank of wood about 30cm long and soaked in water was used as a paddle to beat the walls of the saggar, helping the join, and further evening out the wall thickness. The wheelie was revolved during this process serving as a revolving anvil in what was clearly a modern version of paddle and anvil work. The rim and walls were then moistened and the walls pressed against the bottom. The excess circumference of the bottom was then trimmed off using a piece of wood called a "peg" and the walls scraped upward using a "plucker" from the bottom so that they were fully joined. No distortion of the walls occured because the wooden drum was still in place. A piece of wetted oak, a "rib" is then used to wet-smooth the exterior of the walls before the drum was finally pulled upwards and out of the saggar. A "cant tool" was used to bevel the edges of the base.

A "topping stick" comprising of a piece of board tapered to a handle at one end was used to tap across and around the rim to compact it and to make sure that it was of the same height all around (Plate 5.7). A piece of strong tin[26] - a "topping tool" - is also used in this smoothing process. The join between the walls and base inside the vessel had not hitherto been touched but was now scraped with a tool as the vessel revolved and was wet smoothed.

Mr. Wheeldon explicitly pointed out that each saggar maker made many of his own tools from scraps of wood or metal. This helps to explain why it is so difficult to identify many craft tools in archaeological contexts – many of the tools were not standardised even if the processes for which they were used were.

The saggar was now almost complete. However, a final test was necessary. A flat board or "banner" was placed across the saggar and lifted off. The damp rim of the vessel left a ring on the board. If the ring was unbroken then the height of the walls was even and the job had been correctly done. A gap would mean a low spot on the wall. To ensure that the walls were even the board was given a slight tap as it was put in place.

It took 6 minutes to fit a saggar together so the whole process would take 16-17 minutes to complete. However, since the bottom knocker worked alongside the saggar maker the total time would be reduced to 14-15 minutes and if frame fillers were employed (below) a further six minutes could be removed from this time giving 8-9 minutes to produce a completed saggar.[27]

The now completed saggar, still on its shord, was then carried into the "hot house"[28] to dry. After drying they would be taken to the "placers" who would put the new saggars at the top of a stack of filled saggars so that they could be fired. For this first firing they would be empty but would be used filled in subsequent firings.

At the height of the industry the saggar maker would have been accompanied by a frame filler who would prepare a frame for the maker whilst the bottom knocker produced bottoms, keeping 6 or so ahead of the saggar maker. Often there would be two frames ("double end frame filling") so that one would be being filled whilst the other was being mau'ed, cut and rolled onto drums. The reason for the bottom knocker having to keep so far ahead was that each frame could produce several sets of sides and a delay in producing the correct number of bottoms would interrupt the work.[29]

The above account is based largely on the filmed recollections by Mr. Wheeldon and the unused soundtrack recordings made for it. However, what emerges from conversations with others is that there are areas about which even those who worked in the industry are unclear and which would have been clearly recalled only by those who were actually saggar makers. Amongst these was the question of why the saggars should be hand built. Explanations ranged from convenience, through size to shape. One likely explanation is that the saggars were not always circular, indeed many used in the Stoke industry were ovoid and could not have been wheel formed. Similarly, their great thickness and the quantity of grog would have made them difficult to wheel throw, particularly as the base is made with a coarser clay than the walls. Whilst such joins between clay pastes are not unknown the combination of shape, size and coarseness all tend to favour hand building as does the weight of the vessels. Interestingly Sandeman (1921: 207-8) notes that "There have been many appliances tried for making saggers completely by machinery, but up till the present they have not given sufficiently satisfactory results…and by far the greater number of saggers are still made solely by hand."

The reason for the height of the saggar is also difficult to determine. It seems that the base circumference is the most important factor as this determines the amount of ware which can be placed in the saggar. Deep narrow, saggars would have been difficult to fill and to empty, and unsteady to carry. Their weight would also have been very great. It therefore made more sense to produce vessels with a large footprint but with walls no more than about twelve inches (30cm) high.

The question of what happened to completed saggars was also problematic. Several informants thought that they were dried in the hothouse and then used straight away, whilst others thought that they might have been fired empty before use – as was in fact the case. The reason why an empty firing was not thought possible by some informants was that they believed that the saggar could be used only once because after a firing the clay had become so densified that it might vitrify and collapse if further used. In fact, it seems that saggars were usually used several times before becoming damaged (Sandemann 1921: 204). Saggars could supposedly be used up to 40 times at the Nantgarw pottery in south Wales.[30] Once damaged, saggars would be discarded on a "shordruck" – a pile of thrown away sherds from saggars and of ware which had been broken in manufacture. Such shordrucks were a feature of the potteries until recent times. Sandeman (1921: 211) estimates that in his time a 7% loss of saggars in biscuit firing and 6% loss in glost firing was normal.

Making Saggars at Memphis

Both main types of saggar found at Memphis are handmade. The larger ones, mostly Type 12, clearly had their bases and walls made separately (Plate 5.8). There does seem to be some evidence to suggest that the bases are often more coarsely tempered than the walls but this feature was not noted in initial recording and the difference between the two, where it exists, seems relatively slight. The clay is usually coarsely tempered[31] with plant material, sand and fragments of pottery grog up to 25cm long.

The process seems to have been to make a disc of clay – the Memphis examples are almost invariably round – though this may not have been done in a frame. Many fragments of base are thicker toward the centre than around the edges, suggesting that they were scraped downward from the centre. They were worked on a flat surface which was dusted with chaff or other plant material rather than with sawdust, but the effect was the same, in that it prevented the clay from sticking. The impressions of the chaff material are often clearly visible on the undersides of the vessels.

Just inside the circumference of the disc a shallow groove was usually made into which to seat the wall of the vessel. The impression of the groove is accentuated on many actual fragments because the clay from the interior of the base and the part of the disc protruding outside the wall have been drawn up, as in the modern examples, to help adhere the base to the walls. This may in fact entirely account for the groove but on some vessels it seems to be so marked as to have been deliberately made and may show thumb prints where the clay had been pressed down to form a groove. The joining of bases to walls seems to have been less well done on the ancient examples than on the modern ones since there are many examples where the wall has broken cleanly away from the base.

A variation on this technique is to bevel the edge of the disc and chamfer the bottom of the wall in the same way so that the two parts can be adhered (Plate 5.9). The simplest method is to simply make a butt joint between the flat upper surface of the disc and the flat lower edge of the wall and press the clay together, much as at Stoke.

Plate 5.8. Saggar (IM-144). The white powder layer can clearly be seen on the lower walls. The finger groove is also visible around the rim. Reconstruction by Nicole Stahl. (Photo: P.T. Nicholson).

Plate 5.9. Detail showing the bevelled joint between the disc forming the bottom of a saggar and the lower edge of its wall. The joint here is not perfect as parts from two different saggars have been used in the reconstruction (IM-17 & IM-27). (Photo: P.T. Nicholson).

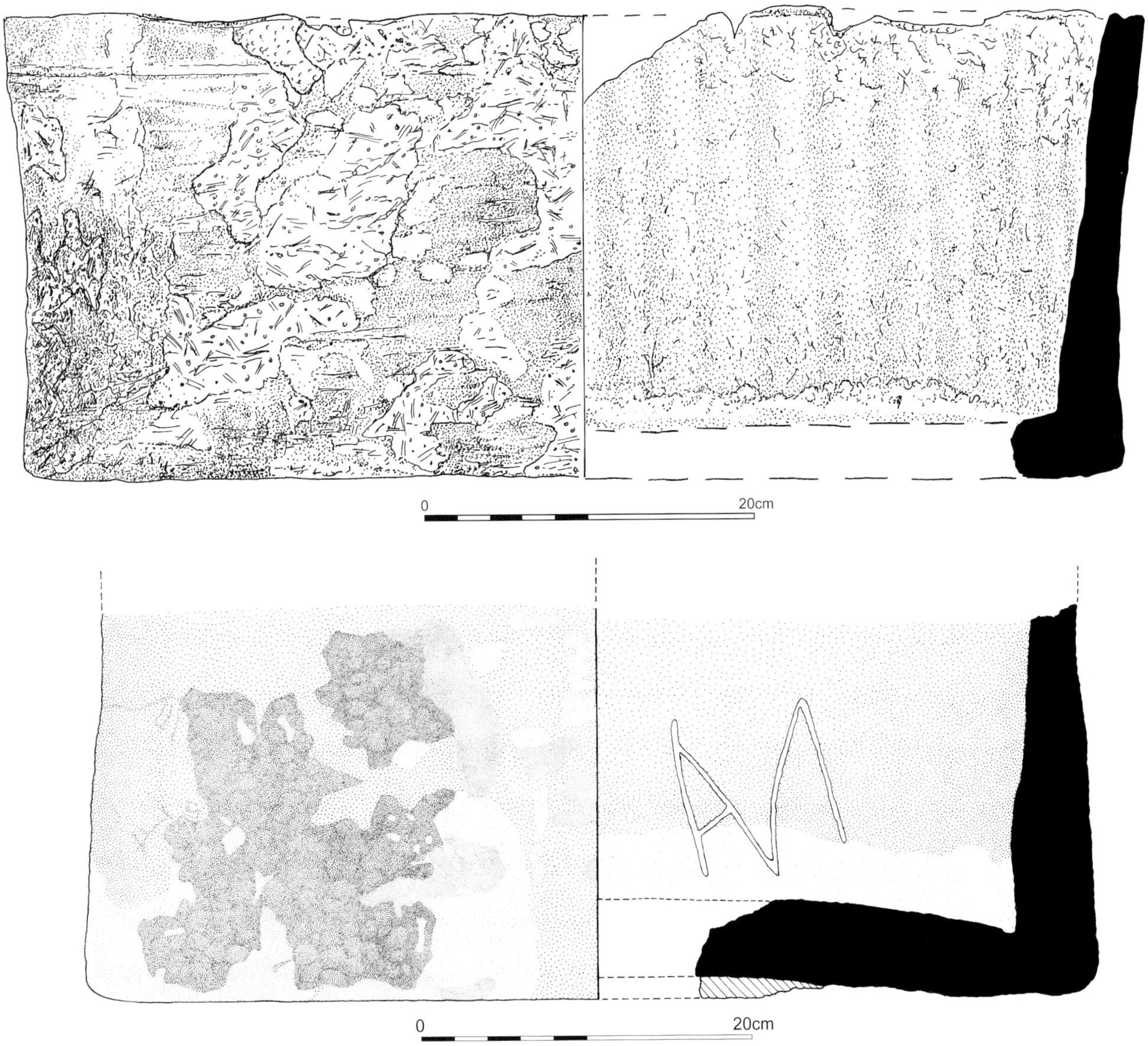

Figure 5.3. (Top) Saggar (IM-220) . The facets on the interior are clearly visible. (Drawing: Emily Stewart). (Bottom) Saggar (IM-145). Vitrification of the remains of red plaster is visible on the exterior while the interior bears an owner's mark. The lowest part of the interior has adhering white lime. (Drawing: Tessa Baber).

The making of the walls themselves may follow the same kind of procedure as that employed in Stoke. The exterior of the vessels excavated is often clay covered and vitrified, but where it is not there are traces of chaff impressions where the clay has been rolled out on a bench dusted with chaff to prevent sticking. The interior of the vessels is usually much better preserved and can be very smooth save for chaff impressions. It was initially believed that this smoothness came from pressing the clay between boards but it is much more likely that it derives from wrapping the clay walls around a wooden drum, as in the Stoke industry. Whilst no examples of such drums have yet been found at Memphis their existence seems highly probable.[32]

One difference between ancient and modern practice seems to be the joining of the walls to the base. The practice in Stoke was to cut away the excess circumference of the base to leave a join which was virtually right-angular on both outside and in. However, at Memphis it seems that the clay was scraped up the walls outside and perhaps only a small excess removed so that the bottom of the wall, where it meets the base, can be quite thick. The join on the inside is sometimes a right-angle but on other occasions slopes somewhat toward the outside.

Whilst the interior walls of most of the Memphis Type 12 saggars are very smooth, some have traces of faceting. These facets suggest that either the drum used on these examples did not have a very smooth profile or – perhaps more likely – the smoothing of the base into the walls was continued up the walls to leave corrugated facets (Figure 5.3).

The finishing of the walls of the Memphis saggars also differs from their modern cousins in that although attempts have clearly been made to ensure that the wall height is equal all round the circumference it does not seem to have been tested using a banner. There are two reasons for this observation, first that the wall heights are sometimes slightly uneven and second that the rim of the vessel has a groove around it which would be deformed if it were struck with a banner board. It may be objected that the rims may have become uneven as a result of deformation during use, and this is certainly true – some have become hugely deformed – but it is unlikely that noticeable yet minor deformity would occur on so many. It is suggested here that the height was determined simply by cutting the strip of clay for the walls carefully and then by roughly checking it with a stick.

The groove running around the top of the walls is also significant and may help to confirm that the wall heights were not so carefully monitored as they were at Stoke. The groove, made by running a finger around the top, can be very marked or barely visible and must depend upon how soft the clay was when this was carried out. It was probably the last stage in the forming process. Its purpose was to receive a strip of wet clay put onto the top of the saggar before it was used and which served to seal it to the saggar placed above it. This strip of wet clay – which has been recorded by the project as 'saggar joiner', but is more correctly a "wad", would ensure that there was a good seal between the saggars and so prevent ash entering them and would also serve to remove the effect of any slight irregularities in wall height around the circumference of the vessel. This may be further evidence to support the view that a banner was not used. According to Sandeman (1921: 219-20) wads were widely used in Europe both in firing biscuit ware and glost ware. The edges of the saggars were brushed with "calcined bone slip" (1921: 221) to prevent them sticking together when the wads were in place. In Britain wads were not widely used and especially not for biscuit firing, but instead handfuls of sand were rubbed around the join between saggars. Sandeman notes that "If the two systems are dispassionately discussed, the advantage will be found to be all on the side of the foreign system" (1921: 220). Clay strips were also used at Nantgarw and are attested in the Museum collection there, albeit of smaller size than most of those from Kom Helul.

A pot-mark is sometimes incised into the wet clay of the walls on the inside[33] of Type 12 saggars and their derivatives, though not on the smaller, glazed, vessels. The potmark 'AΛ' is particularly common, as well as a mark resembling an angular form of 'Ψ'. These marks are probably intended as owner's marks, rather than faience maker's marks, and may indicate that the kilns were shared, the marks denoting that they held the faience products of one particular workshop. The marks are probably on the interior because the exterior would be completely covered by the layer of clay applied over the finished stack (below). Mackensen (2009: 36) following Peacock *et al.* (1990: 79) notes that in the case of the central Tunisian pottery industry it may only have been the uppermost saggar in a stack which was marked. This same may be true of Kom Helul so that in unloading it would be apparent that all the saggars beneath belonged to the same workshop. This might account for the relative rarity of the potmarks.

It should also be considered whether the marks might represent the individual saggar makers. In this way their work could be identified for individual payment. However, if this were so there seems no reason to mark them on the interior rather than the exterior and their attribution to particular workshops, which might anyway be linked to particular saggar makers, seems the more likely.

It is noteworthy that the saggars are frequently broken along the line of part of the pot-mark, thus there are several examples of breaks running along the sloping sides of the 'A' or 'Λ' mark. It is interesting that such thick-walled vessels could be weakened sufficiently by inscribing a mark not more than 5mm deep that influenced the propagation of cracks on breaking. This is perhaps because the fabric of these saggars is normally so porous and open that the slight compacting and aligning of inclusions along these lines helped to direct cracking. Many of the saggars show clear vertical ridges inside where the clay has been smoothed upward with the fingers (above). The grooves between these ridges have a similar effect on breaking, and such vessels are usually found to have broken in long vertical strips.

The completed saggar was presumably moved from its place of manufacture, which may sometimes have been the ground rather than a bench or shelf, to dry. Many of the vessels found have a slightly domed underside, the outer circumference sitting well on a flat surface but the middle being raised somewhat. This is the opposite to what one might expect were it an effect of use – the heating and weight in the saggar would, if anything, tend to cause the base to slump slightly making the underside convex rather than concave. It might therefore be suggested either that for manufacture the bases were set on wooden discs or boards which were slightly convex or that they were placed to dry on ground which had been formed into slight mounds.

The suggestion of a mounded drying ground does not at first seem likely. However, given that saggar making would have been a large scale and a daily task it is certain that drying areas for the workshops must have existed. Sandeman (1921: 203) states that "it is very necessary to have a large stock of saggers in order to always have suitable sizes…" All those potters observed in Egypt today dry their wares on the ground, sometimes setting round-based vessels in pre-prepared depressions to stop them rolling away. The vessels observed are mostly fairly small and easily picked up by the rim or handles to be carried but Type 12 saggars are very large and have no handles. They are also heavy. Based on calculations from a saggar of 7cm diameter (the base disc of which alone weights 21.8kg) and with wall height of 28.5cm the empty weight of such a vessel would be 53.3kg[34] whilst a Type 12 of average size would weight 31.9kg A perfectly flattened drying area would soon become uneven as workers tried to pick up saggars by pushing their fingers underneath them or sliding a board beneath. Perhaps better then to have an area of very slight mounds on which the vessels could sit and from which they might more easily be removed?

A small, Type 3, saggar collected by Petrie (1911a: Plate XIX: 239) and now in the Petrie Collection[35] has a rim diameter of 22.3cm and height of 15.4cm, its weight is 4.58kg. Thus even small examples of saggars are of considerable weight. However, this vessel may suggest that these smaller saggars were treated differently since its base preserves clear impressions from having been placed on two timber planks, possibly a shelf. Since most of the vessels excavated by the writer are from Type 12 saggars and this is a Type 3 it may be that these smaller versions were placed on shelves to dry rather than on the ground.[36] It should also be noted that we have no information on the exact context of the Petrie Museum vessel and it may not only belong to another kiln but to an earlier or later period than most of those excavated by the writer.

It is worth noting that the saggar from Terenouthis (Kom Abu Billo) illustrated by Nenna and Seif el-Din (1999:79) has a similar diameter (50cm) and height (20cm) as well as wall thickness (2.5-3.4cm) to those known from Memphis. The overall appearance of the piece is also very similar and the same sort of manufacturing process may be inferred.

To judge by practice at Stoke and elsewhere the dried saggar would then be given an empty firing at the top of a stack of saggars filled with ware.

The Saggars in Use

Once the saggars had been given an initial firing they would be ready for use. The faience vessels and other pieces were fired in saggars of two broad types (Types 3 and 12) discussed above. They were used in somewhat different ways even though the purpose of their use remained the same, namely the firing of faience wares *en masse* free from the effects of smoke and ash.

Type 12

The first type to be used was the large, crudely made Type 12 which, when found in trench HAC3, lacks any coloured glaze. They are usually between 40 and 60cm in diameter (though a few up to 70cm are known) and have wall heights between 22 and 29cm high. Rim thickness is usually between 2 and 4cm, most being in the 2-3cm category.

The fired Type 12 saggars are given a calcareous slip on the interior, essentially a thick lime wash, before firing. On many vessels this slip is continued onto the top of the rim and is often seen splashed on the outside too. Since it is sometimes seen splashed over slagged areas of the saggar it may be suggested that it was reapplied when saggars were re-used.

The fired and slipped saggar was also given a layer of lime, up to 2.5cm deep on the inside, and the items to be fired were apparently placed onto this. It seems likely that these large, unglazed, saggars were used to give a first firing to the wares. It is known that the firing of Roman lead glazed ceramics was a two part operation (Hochuli-Gysel 2002: 306) and it is not unlikely that the same applies to the faience. Hochuli-Gysel (2002: 306) suggests a biscuit firing temperature of c.1000ºC and a glazing temperature of c.700ºC and similar temperatures for faience are plausible.

The question of when the wares were placed in the saggar is difficult to determine. With empty weights of 31.9kg or more for Type 12 saggars the vessels would be difficult to move around. In 19th and 20th Century Stoke the saggars were usually carried on the head and then lifted onto the stack, from a ladder if necessary. It is not impossible that the same technique was employed at Kom Helul and that the workmen were simply accustomed to carrying these very heavy weights. Carrying the saggars full would certainly be more practical, and so more likely, than loading them within the kiln where space was limited and light restricted.

Whether the faience vessels to be fired were placed directly onto the lime in the bottom tier or on cones is hard to say, but it seems likely that since the faience had no glaze at this stage the bottom layer of wares was seated directly into the lime. Subsequent vessels were then added, separated perhaps by clay cones, although as the faience objects were not glazed they were less likely to adhere to one another and so be archaeologically visible at this stage. It is also possible that unglazed vessels might be separated from another using sausages of clay, a practice attested from Holt in North Wales (Grimes 1930: 183 and Pl.79). Saggar firing would still be desirable in order to prevent smoke and ash contaminating the vessel surface, however, as that would make the subsequent glazing difficult.

Once the loaded saggar was placed in the kiln a strip of wet clay was added around the rim using the finger groove the help keep it in place. The next saggar was then placed on top of the first. This squashed the strip of clay, so that some was pressed to the inside of the vessel, some to the outside (Figure 5.4 and Plate 5.10). This clay outside is frequently augmented by a further strip, perhaps closing any gaps, or perhaps infilling the angle between the rim of one saggar and the base of the next where the upper one is of slightly larger diameter than the lower one. Once a stack (or "bung") is completed the whole thing is plastered with a very sandy, friable clay plaster containing large amounts of plant material. This red clay sometimes overlies areas of vitrification, suggesting that the saggars were re-used several times when possible, and that small areas where the

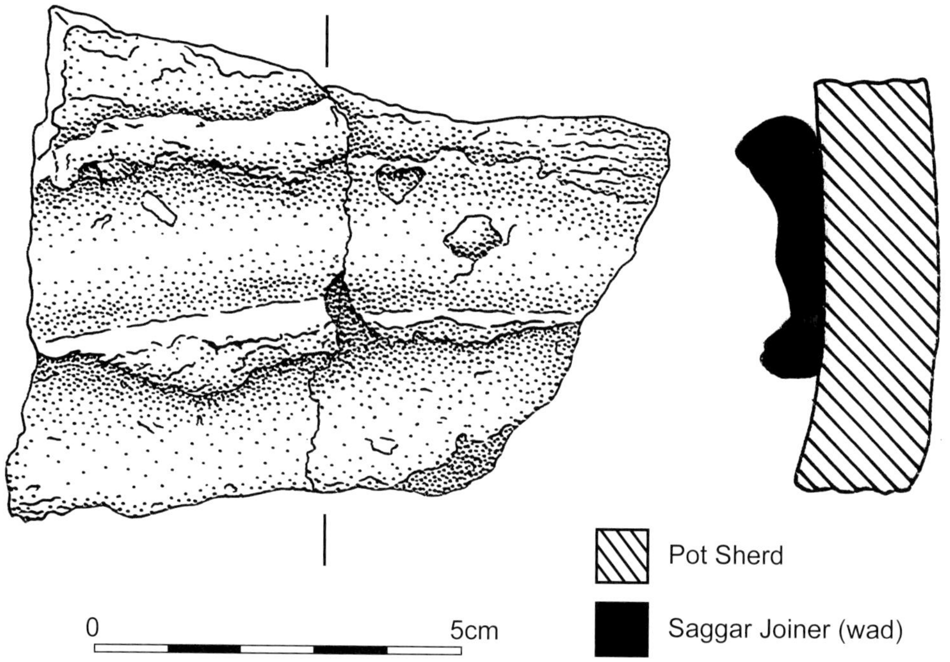

Figure 5.4. A saggar joiner or wad (P-353) adhering to the base of a saggar. The characteristic M-shaped profile is clearly shown in the section. (Drawing: F. Taylor).

Plate 5.10. Saggar joiner (P-226) viewed from the underside where it was pressed into the finger groove around the rim of a saggar. The upper surface is flat where it met the flat base of the saggar above it. (Photo: P.T. Nicholson).

Plate 5.11. Exterior of a Type 12 saggar (IM-175) showing lines where cord has been removed, bringing away some of the friable plaster which had been smoothed over the vessel as part of a stack. (Photo: P.T. Nicholson).

Plate 5.12. Detail of the plastered exterior of a saggar (IM-185) showing rope marks. Scale bar is 10cm. (Photo: P.T. Nicholson).

plaster, or even the vessel wall, had become vitrified were not regarded as major difficulties. The exterior coating of clay probably served to further protect the saggar contents from ash and smoke as well as prolong the life of the saggar by helping to prevent them becoming vitrified during firing. A similar process, using paper clay,[37] is sometimes used by contemporary studio potters (Duncan Ayscough pers. comm.). Whilst at Nantgarw (above) saggars might be reused up to 40 times, the writer suspects that the Kom Helul examples may have had a shorter use-life. In considering the sealing of saggars however, it should be noted that some small gap may have been left in the sealing and plastering during glaze firings in order to admit sufficient oxygen to render the copper colourant blue.

No regard seems to have been paid to the individual saggars during the plastering process, rather the plaster is run down the whole stack, covering the saggar joiners, and any additions to them, as it is smoothed down. However, a number of the saggars show distinct lines around the red plaster where a cord of some kind has been passed around them, probably to help the clay adhere (IM-175, Plate 5.11). Usually there is no indication as to whether this was a genuinely twisted rope or simply a large piece of plant material, however, a number of examples show clear cord impressions and that may be the norm. The gaps between the impressions suggest that the cord was put around as an individual loop, however, a few examples show areas where the cord slopes as though a single cord might be spiralled around the vessel. Since the vessels are not complete we see only a part of the cord impression, and so it may be that all were in fact spiralled but only a few vessels preserve clear evidence of this. It is apparent from IM-185 (Plate 5.12) that the cord was left on vessels during firing and burned out during the firing process. This can be seen from the fact that on this vessel small holes are left where the plaster ran over the cord which has now gone, rather than the clear impressions with no surface covering, normally associated with string marks.[38] The over-plastering of areas of cord was probably accidental. The voids left by the cords may have made it easier to break open the plaster and so remove it. One of the cord-voids is often located about 30cm below the saggar rim, although it seems unlikely that this was intended to indicate the whereabouts of saggar joiners, since once arranged in a tall stack individual vessels would be very hard to identify.

The question of exactly how the saggar stacks were covered in plaster is a problematic one.[39] There would be relatively little space within the kiln to attend to the plastering operation, and it must be supposed that one stack was built and plastered, before the next was constructed and so on. The final stack(s) may have required plastering by a small individual, perhaps a child, or might have had areas of their wall left uncovered. There are certainly examples of saggars with vitrified walls and little or no trace of plaster on the fragment.

Occasionally, and for reasons which are not understood, saggar joiners are attached to broken sherds of pottery which are placed around the rim of a saggar. It may be that these are intended to allow hot gases to circulate underneath certain saggars, perhaps to heat the stack more thoroughly. It may be that the saggar to which these sherds were attached was empty and served simply as a reservoir of hot gases helping to heat those saggars immediately above it. The friable plaster would not, of course, have been allowed to block the void in such cases. Examination of kilns at Stoke and Nantgarw shows the chequer to have been slightly convex so that sherds might have been used under stacks to help them to stand level. The Nangtarw works also used supports, taking the form of curved, L-profile pieces of clay (essentially sections of saggar wall with some base) beneath the lowermost saggar as a way of allowing heat to circulate beneath the stack (Plate 5.13). In preliminary publications the writer suggested that three-pointed stands were used at the bottom of saggar stacks and this remains a possibility. However, the form is usually found as part of the domestic pottery repertoire and so without further evidence this must remain uncertain. However, Olsen (1983: 111) illustrates the use of similar pots at the bottom of saggars used in downdraft kilns and also updraft (Olsen 1983:142). That a similar arrangement may have been employed in the kilns of Memphis therefore seems possible and may explain the presence of glaze on the 'ear' of at least one such stand.

It is also clear that saggars were sometimes stood on small pads or bats of clay which raised them from the chequer in the same way as the supports at Nantgarw, or were used to separate vessels in a stack (Plate 5.14).

The question of what was done with the top of the saggar stack is uncertain. It might have had an empty saggar on top, which would have provided a suitable opportunity for the initial firing of new saggars, or a broken base might have been luted into position as a lid.

During the overall process of firing, the saggar joiners and the red clay both became fired. The clay coating would attract any vitreous slag resulting from ash contact with the stack, suggesting that the workers were acutely aware of the propensity of their fuel to cause slagging. The lime coating on the inside and outside of the saggars might also become somewhat vitreous, giving an incipient glaze, perhaps as a result of particles of lime being carried around by the hot gas and fusing to the vessel walls.

It is possible that occasionally vessels for glazing were put into the large saggars as there are a very few examples with patches of pale blue, suggesting glaze. If we are correct in assuming that the lime formed an incipient glaze on the inside of the saggar then it must also have done so over the unglazed faience objects.[40] This may be of considerable significance, since it would help to harden them and would give a smoother, shinier surface to underlie the final glazing

Plate 5.13. Saggars at Nantgarw Pottery, South Wales, resting on L-shaped supports to allow hot air to circulate beneath them. (Photo: P.T. Nicholson. Reproduced Courtesy of the Nantgarw Museum).

Plate 5.14. The underside of a Type 12 saggar (IM-145) with a bat or pad of clay adhering (right) and another, found detached (left). Such pads would help to elevate the saggar above the floor of the chequer or to separate saggars within a stack. Note that here the saggar wall seems to have been added to the circumference of the vessel. (Photo: P.T. Nicholson).

of the objects. The lime may therefore play a particularly important role.

As firing proceeded the friable red clay, in the hottest places, would fuse and vitrify to become slag-like. At the end of the firing the stack would be allowed to cool. The thick, coarse walls of the saggars, themselves coated with a thick layer of porous plaster, would retain the heat for a considerable time, helping to make maximum use of the heat to fire the unglazed faience within. Cooling may have taken 24 hours or so based on comparison with Stoke (Gladstone Museum n.d.:11). Sandeman (1917: 236) allows 20 hours before the top of the doorway ("clammins") is opened and 30 hours before the fuel ash and clinker is cleaned out of the firebox.

Once the kiln had cooled, the workers would begin at the top of the stack, break away the plaster from around the saggars before removing them from the kiln and removing their contents. Where there had been a hot-spot in the kiln,

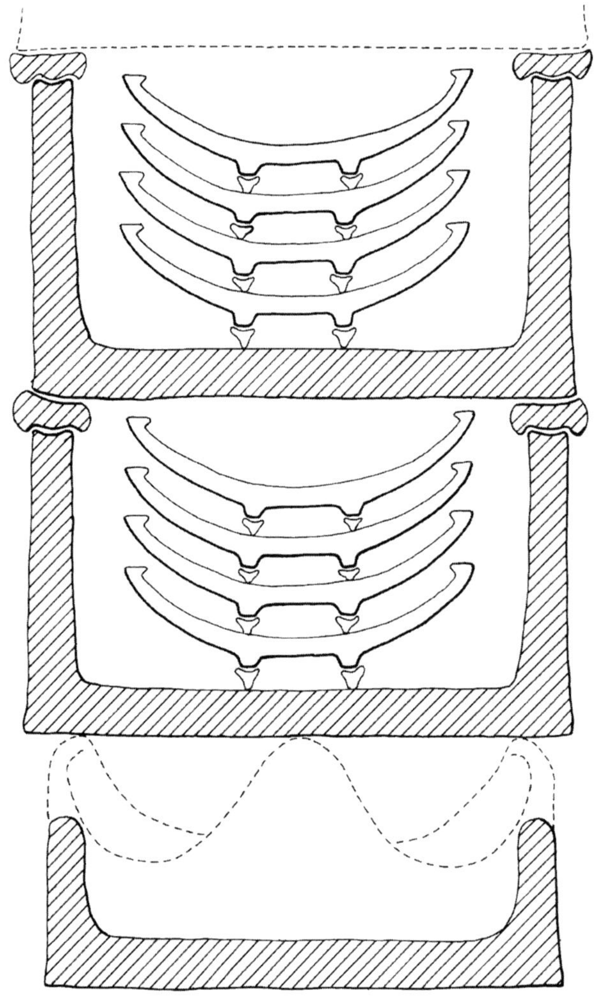

Figure 5.5. Schematic drawing showing the way in which vessels were stacked within saggars, separated one from another with small clay cones. The vessels and scales are illustrative only. (Drawing: Joanne Hodges).

the friable plaster might have become vitrified, but because of the friable nature of the coating it could usually be broken away from the saggar without damaging it. This was probably one of its major functions, prolonging the life of the saggar by preventing vitrification. Removal of the plaster would, perhaps, be facilitated by the calcareous coating which was sometimes added to the outside of the vessel as well as the inside. The broken up clay coating could be ground up and reused as grog in saggar making.

It is likely that most of the saggars were lifted out of the kiln and carried a little distance from it before the ware was removed from them. In cases where they were of exceptional weight they may have been emptied within the kiln.

As the saggars were emptied the workers would discard the small clay cones and clay strips which had served to keep stacks of vessels apart. The saggar joiners too would be broken away from the vessel rims and from where they had stuck to the bottom of saggars and would be discarded. These discarded joiners are very common at Kom Helul and can be seen in exposed sections of the site, especially on the west side of the mounds where a modern trackway has worn them away. It is likely that older saggars broke during removal or when the saggar joiners were broken away from them, accounting for the large number of fragments found in excavation.

The now fired - but as yet unglazed - faience would now require its (coloured) glaze coating. This could have been applied as a slip or as a powder, though in many cases a slip seems to be the most likely option (see Chapter 7). The glaze would be allowed to dry before further handling. The glost (i.e. glazing) firing would take place in smaller saggars, probably in a kiln other than that in trench HAC03, which – it may be suggested – served only to biscuit fire the raw pieces.

Type 3

The Type 3 glazing saggars were handmade (above). These are mostly smaller examples, and are usually made in a more dense fabric than their larger counterparts, though in much the same way, with the bases commonly being made separately. The bases are attached to the walls in a number

Plate 5.15. One of the carefully formed cones which seem to have been used in glazing. This example (F-140) has fallen sideways and become adhered to a faience fragment. (Photo: P.T. Nicholson).

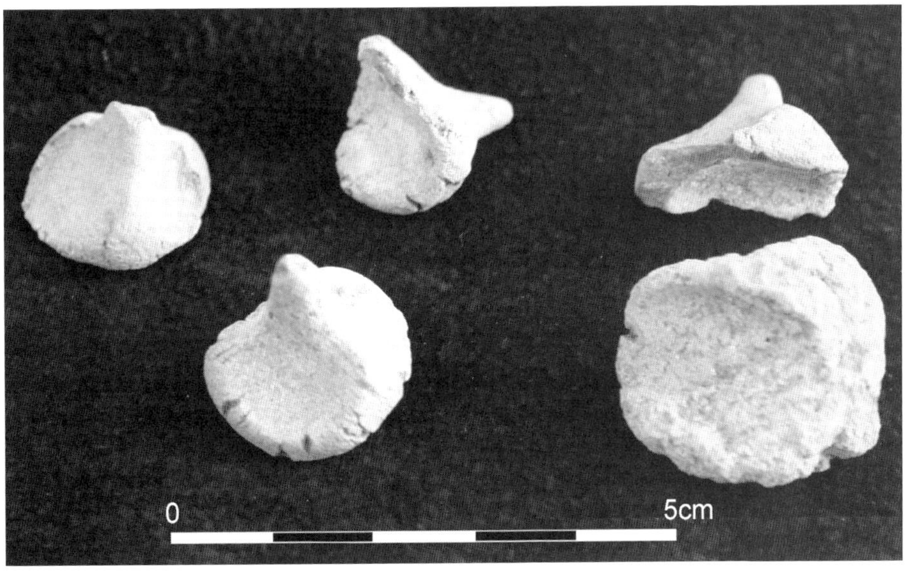

Plate 5.16. A selection of clay cones used to separate vessels in the stack. Such cones were certainly used during glazing and probably also during biscuit firing. (Photo: P.T. Nicholson).

of ways. Sometimes the edge of the base is rounded and the wall smoothed to it and over it, leaving a distinct lip in the vessel wall, sometimes the base has a marked chamfer where the wall meets it, and sometimes a groove is incised around the circumference of the base and the wall pressed into it. All of these techniques are attested more crudely on the large saggars, though the commonest method seems to be a version of the last technique, pressing the wall into a groove, or more precisely a series of thumb impressions around the circumference of the base. More rarely, the coarse Type 12 fabric, and size, is used for a glaze firing, presumably for larger objects than are the norm – for example the rectangular trays.

A finger groove was frequently added to the circumference of the rim so that sausages of clay could be used to cement the saggars together. The diameter range of these vessels fall mainly between 30 and 40cm, the mean average base diameter being 33cm. The wall height averages 13cm. It is noteworthy that there are both silt and marl/mixed clay fabrics used for these vessels, and there seems to be some correlation between the type of fabric and the colour of the glaze. It appears that marl clay is used for those vessels which contain pale turquoise glazed pieces whilst silt is used for darker greens and blues. It may be that the iron present in the Nile silt clays discolours the paler glazes to too great an extent to allow it to be used, at least without a special lining.

No pot marks have been found on the small saggars. This may mean that only one faience worker at a time fired his products in any given kiln. The fact that glaze usually covers the inside of the saggar would not of itself preclude potmarks, since the slightly raised edges of the marks scratched into the wet clay would remain visible, though the glaze would make them more difficult to see.

In these smaller saggars the bottom-most faience vessel in the stack was probably stood either on a small stand, or on cones, probably of the perfectly conical type with flat bases which would have adhered well to the flat bottom of the saggar (Fig. 5.5 and Plate 5.15). Other faience vessels would have stood within the first one, separated from it by small cones of clay attached to the footring and with their points down to the interior of the vessel below (Plate 5.16). Clearly these cones cannot have been attached and immediately inverted as the clay would simply have been deformed. Rather we must imagine trays of inverted bowls and other vessels each with three or four cones attached around the base with their points upward, drying in the sun. Once dry they could be stood one inside another in the saggar.

The vessels would have been put in the small saggars prior to stacking them in the kiln. It may be objected that the stacks of faience vessels would tend to topple as they were taken to the kiln, but this does not seem to have been a problem in the more recent European industries and could anyway have been overcome by putting two or three reeds or twigs into the space between the vessels and the saggar wall during transport, and removing them on arrival at the kiln (though this was probably unnecessary).

The saggars were then carefully luted together with saggar joiners, though a small gap may have been left to admit oxygen during firing. There is no evidence that any sherds were used to raise saggars here in order to let hot gases circulate although glaze on the ear of a three pointed stand may indicate their use for this process. The smaller size of these vessels may have rendered this unnecessary. It seems that, like their larger counterparts, the small saggars may also have been covered with a coating of red friable plaster. However, these smaller saggars are more carefully finished than the others and have smoother external surfaces, from which the plaster seems to have been easily removed. Hence there are very few examples with more than the smallest trace of red plaster on them.

Once a stack was complete it may have been adhered at certain points to its neighbour by pre-dried rods of clay and attached to the kiln walls in a similar way, thus giving tall stacks of small diameter greater stability than they might otherwise have enjoyed. This is much the same practice as used in loading saggars at Jingdezhen, China (Hu and Li 1997: 80-82 especially figure 7) where saggar fragments were used as supports. Such a practice might be less necessary with the heavier, broader saggars used for the unglazed pieces and might account for the numerous, apparently straight, rods of kiln furniture[41] which are common finds from the site.

During firing the hot gases would have gradually fused the glaze to the faience body. They were also sufficient to carry particles of glaze around inside the saggar and so glaze its interior walls as well as the underside of the saggar above which served as its lid. Each was thus a small glazing cell. The glaze could also form on the saggar joiner where it protruded into the saggar, but not until it had become fired. As a result, most saggar joiners have only a thin glaze, if any at all, though a few are as well glazed as are the saggar walls.

At the end of the firing the vessels would be left to cool in their saggars. Once cold the top saggars in the stack would be removed and opened by separating them along the line of the joiner. Usually the saggar joiner would part quite easily from the vessel, sometimes leaving a little ridge of glaze toward the rim of the vessel where it had run off the saggar joiner and collected in the angle between it and the saggar wall. The faience vessels, now much harder than before, could be gently levered to one side or the other so that they snapped off from their cones and so were removable. The cones themselves might show glaze near their tips (the actual tip remaining stuck to the inside of the faience vessel) and around the base circumference, but little else. The cones would then be discarded.

Because the vessels were fired right-way-up in most cases, a few might show the effects of glaze pooling on their interior, but most would be fairly evenly glazed. The saggars in which they had been glazed could probably be used once or twice until the layer of glaze built up to a considerable thickness. This may explain why the walls of the saggars are heavily glazed but the little cones, used only once, are not.

Eventually the saggars would become too heavily glazed to be useful and would tend to stick together very firmly as the glaze cooled, so that even the saggar joiner was not enough to separate them easily. At this time they would have to be broken in order to remove the vessels. The saggars often have straight, vertical breaks in their walls, perhaps suggesting that they were deliberately broken with a bladed tool or cracked along a predefined line of weakness.

The small glazing saggars, like the large saggars for unglazed ware, litter Kom Helul. The writer suggests that because of the problem of slagging and glaze sticking neither type had a life as long as the 40 firings suggested for Nantgarw (above). The large, heavy, fragments from the big saggars do not seem to have been moved far from the kiln in which they stood and are found re-used as walling on the entrance to the access doorway. The smaller ones may have been dumped at a little distance from the glazing kiln.

Summary

The finding of two major types of saggar (Types 3 and 12) suggests that the industry at Kom Helul may have been very specialised. The finding of Type 12 saggars almost exclusively around kiln HAC3 suggests that the kilns which utilised Type 3 for the actual glazing process remain to be found, at least by modern excavation. It may be reasonable to assume that the general form of the glazing kiln was the same as the biscuit kiln and that at least some of the examples excavated by Petrie were for this purpose. His general discussion on the kilns certainly suggests that those he found were the same in form as that excavated by us. However, his reports also imply that large saggar vessels were the exception rather than the rule and he does not seem to have collected them for U.K. museums. Whilst this may simply be because of their size and crudeness of manufacture, it might equally be because they were an exception on his excavation and that he was unsure of their function. If this latter is true, then we might safely imply that he worked in an area of Kom Helul separate from that which has been investigated here and which was concerned with glazing rather than with biscuit firing. The discovery of waste faience vessels thrown back into the kiln he excavated in 1908 (see Plate 4.1) might also suggest that it was used for glazing.

Other Roman Saggar Forms

Whilst the saggars found at Kom Helul are recognisably similar to those used in much later times in the ceramic industry in Britain, it is worth noting that cylinders with a closed base are not the only forms known from the Roman world.

From Tunisia come saggars with a cylindrical form but which are open at both ends. The rim (or arguably base) of these pieces is flattened into what is essentially a pierced flange. Peacock *et al.* (1990) make a good argument for the flange being at the top as these are sometimes marked, perhaps identifying a stack of saggars belonging to one individual. Mackensen (2009) takes the same view, using the weight of a full saggar as a reason why they could not have safely been carried full. It is, however, known from Stoke that saggars were carried when full, the wares carefully propped inside them to prevent collapse. The placing of these Tunisian saggars remains uncertain as does the placing of the wares inside them and some variation is certainly possible. More relevant for the purposes of this discussion is the fact that they are cylindrical and were placed one above the other as at Memphis.

From Holt in North Wales (Grimes 1930) come saggars which are essentially a pair of large bowls, one serving as the saggar and the other its lid. Inside these, glazed vessels could be fired on a three pointed support. It appears that only one glazed vessel at a time would be fired in such vessels and though they reinforce the use of saggars and supports in producing glazed ware they are of an entirely different type to those known from Roman Memphis.

Kiln Furniture

Processing

This category of object, designated as part of the P category in the Memphis system, comprises a large quantity of ceramic material believed to have been used within the kiln/furnace. The term kiln furniture is something of misnomer in that it is used by present day potters to refer to items such as stilts and setters used to position vessels in the kiln during firing, whilst here it is used to mean not only these items but also clay which was used for purposes such as closing saggars.

The examination of the kiln furntiture has been, of necessity, a fairly crude one. The recording of the cones was a simple matter, as they are clearly distinguishable from the other material and can readily be measured. Where a cone was folded over a stand ring the diameter of the base was measured along the fold line. The strips of clay used between saggars to join them into a continuous stack (or "bung") and termed here 'saggar joiners' were more difficult to examine. Flat sections of clay, and those with an 'M' profile were obvious as true saggar joiners, but rods or sausages of clay were less clearly so. When a whole range of material was seen together it was quite obvious that a flat piece of clay which was a definite saggar joiner at one end could become a round section piece at the other and might, had it lost its end, simply appear to be a rod of clay which had not actually been used to join saggars together. It therefore seemed to be an artificial and misleading exercise to try to 'type' what are in fact ephemeral artefacts used only once as part of an industrial process. Instead, the long sections of clay were divided into two classes, those of generally flat cross-section and those of generally round cross-section. The length of these was then measured. The purpose of such a measurement is simply to give the reader some idea of the quantity of clay used, given that the average cross-section of a round piece is about 15cm and about 25cm for a flat piece. It has no other significance and most of what is said about the kiln furniture below could have been arrived at by examining only a fraction of the total material. Nonetheless, the whole assemblage was examined in order that any significant fragments would not be missed.

Plate 5.17. "Bungs" of saggars in a bottle kiln at the Gladstone Pottery Museum, Stoke-on-Trent. It can be seen that bricks projecting from the wall (arrowed) have been used to anchor the bungs to the structure. Rods of clay would probably have been used in this way at Kom Helul. (Photo: P.T. Nicholson. Reproduced Courtesy of the Gladstone Pottery Musem).

Three-pointed Stands

Petrie (1911a: 35) states that the lowermost faience vessel in the stack to be fired in the saggars would be rested on a three pointed stand, examples of which he illustrates (1911a: Pl. xix nos.236-238).[42] Most such three pointed stands are believed to be domestic (French pers. comm. and this volume), however, as suggested above it is undoubtedly the case that some were used in connection with the faience making process.[43] This is especially clear in the case of UC33566 (see also Ashton 2003: 43)[44] where dark blue glaze can clearly be seen running down the inside of the points, each of which lacks its top. No saggar has yet been found with one of these stands adhering to the glaze inside nor are any known stands extensively glazed. Ashton (2003: 43) is correct in stating that glaze would be expected on the base of the stands were they inside the saggars.[45] It would appear that all those stands so far known were not used inside saggars but rather were sometimes placed underneath the lowermost saggar or, supported on a bat, part way up the saggar stack to allow gases to circulate. The glaze would adhere to the points not from the objects inside, nor –usually - from cracks to the base of the saggar but from the re-use of saggars whose bases were already glazed. In firing the glaze would again become molten and so run onto the three pointed stand. That the glaze drips are inside the points, rather than outside, may be because the outer circumference of glazed saggars is often lacking glaze because it had previously been protected by a saggar joiner. As a result the glaze is concentrated toward the centre of the saggar base and more likely to come into contact with the interior face of the points and so run to the interior of the stand. From the excavation itself is IM-80, one of the pointed 'ears' of such a stand with glaze, showing that use of this type in association with saggars is not confined to material from Petrie's work.

Shortland and Tite (2005: 43), however, show the three pointed stands being used *inside* the saggars with the vessels placed upside down over them. This arrangement is very unlikely as it would lead to major scars on the interior of the vessels which would damage the decoration/glaze. They do, however, note that this interpretation is open to question and that they may have been used beneath saggars (2005: 43, cf. Nicholson 2002b: 25).

In summary, the three-pointed stands would serve the same purposes as the L-profile curved pieces known from Nantgarw or the occasional insertion of sherds under the lowermost saggar in a stack to allow hot gases to circulate.

Cones

Whilst the purpose of some of the fired clay fragments from Memphis can only be guessed at, the most secure category are the clay cones, which were described by Petrie in some detail (1911a: 35). He believed that he could differentiate between Ptolemaic and Roman examples according to their size – the Roman ones being larger. However, examination of examples in the Petrie Museum suggested that this view may not be entirely correct and that cones of various sizes and configurations were used simultaneously. This view has been borne out by finds from the current excavations where a mixture of cone types has been found. The size may be related to the size of the object being fired rather than its date.

The fabric used for the cones is usually finer than that used for other so-called kiln furniture and often has a white firing surface suggesting that it is a marl clay, probably the same as used for the Type 3 saggars. The term cone is, strictly speaking, appropriate only for one type which is truly conical and flat based (for example P-198). Some of these may have been produced and dried in advance and used, point upward, to support items in the saggar. However, they most probably owe their flat base to having been adhered to a vessel with a broad footring so that the base did not deform around it. They would then be left to dry on the inverted vessel before the stack of vessels was assembled in the saggar. In this way the dry, hardened, points would not deform when placed in contact with the next vessel (Plate 5.15).

The more common type of cone, typified by P-199 and P-200, shows marked facets where it has been pinched up with the fingers and then the otherwise flat base has been folded over the stand ring of a faience vessel (Plate 5.16). It thus resembles a tack or drawing pin whose head has been bent around the stand ring. As a result of this folding the diameter of these pieces is sometimes uncertain. It is clear that this type of cone, which is also a white firing marl, was applied to the vessels whilst the clay was soft so that it could be bent onto the ring.

Petrie (1911a: 35) states that the vessels were first "inverted" on three pointed stands in the saggars and then had the cones stuck to their bases and this has led to some confusion. It seems that most of the stands are not industrial (below) and it is therefore worth reiterating that the cones must have been applied to a row or tray of unfired faience vessels standing upside down. They were then allowed to dry sufficiently to bear the weight of other vessels before being placed in the saggar right way up. Once the first bowl or plate was placed in the saggar others were added on top of it with the point of the cones touching the interior of the vessel beneath them. These vessels were fired right way up, as can be witnessed by the pooling of glaze in some of the mis-fired examples, including vessel UC47391 in the Petrie Collection.[46] This is particularly clear on a bowl from the Myers Museum Collection (Eton ECM 586; Plate 1.2) and on the bowl F-96 from the current excavations. Shortland and Tite (2005: 33-34) however, believe that they have evidence that some vessels were fired upside down. The author has not examined these pieces, but one of the criterion used to determine this stance is the adherence of pieces of "saggar base" to the rims of vessels. It is possible that this might, in some cases, come from contact with the underside of the saggar *above* that in which the vessels were fired, in which case they would be fired right way up. Slumping is also cited as showing inverted firing so the practice cannot be completely ruled out.

At least two individual makers of the cones seem to be represented by the collection from HAC3. The first pinches the cone up, usually leaving three distinct finger prints and a tall point, whilst the other worker fashions a 'cone' which is actually more like a three sided pyramid. Both types seem to have served the same purpose, but are the product of different hands.

After firing was complete and the kiln had cooled the saggars were removed and the vessels separated from one another by pulling, snapping off the point of the cone in the process. Only minor finishing of the vessel would be needed to remove any excess left from the cone. The ring stands were frequently left with quite obvious scars from the wide surface of the support but since this was not visible when the vessel was in use it was not considered necessary to disguise it and even the most accomplished pieces glazed with supports show such scars (e.g. MMA 1988.18).

Rods and Strips

The remaining 'kiln furniture' is much more difficult to classify. It comprises two broad groups, rods of clay, sometimes slightly tapering, sometimes with flattened ends, and flattish pieces of clay. The fabric of these pieces is generally red, though it sometimes has one white surface where it has been in contact with the white interior surface of a saggar vessel.

Often the rods appear to be quite straight but because the saggar vessels found around the excavated kiln are of such large diameter, short sections of handmade rod have such little curvature as to appear straight. Many of these pieces represent the excess clay left from making a long roll of clay to press around the rim of the saggar in order to close it as Petrie (1911a: 35) suggested. The end of the sausage might then be discarded on the chequer of the kiln. The saggars are of such large size and such great weight that they must have been luted closed *in situ* so that some of the excess clay would end up inside the kiln and not, as one might otherwise expect, outside it. As stated, the rim of the saggars very often has a finger-groove around its top. This groove served to hold the wet rod of clay which would then be pressed flat as the next saggar in the stack was put on top of it. The result of this stacking arrangement is to produce pieces of fired clay which have a roughly M-shaped cross-section, the middle of the M being where the clay pressed into the finger groove, and its legs being where it protruded down the interior and exterior wall of the vessel. The top of the M is usually quite flat where it was in contact with the flat base of the saggar above.

In pressing the clay sausage onto the rim of the saggar the kiln stacker was usually careful to overlap the two ends of the ring, and there are several examples where the flattened sausage preserves such overlaps (e.g. P-227, P-231). Sometimes a saggar joiner, applied into the groove on top of the vessel rim, has a sherd attached to it, and this might be indicative of several things. One possibility is that a gap was required between the top of one saggar and the bottom of another, perhaps to allow hot gases to circulate amongst the saggars more easily. If this is the case, one might suggest that the saggar to whose rim the sherds were attached was empty, since to leave it open would leave its contents open to soot and ash from the firing or that the gap was required to admit oxygen during glaze firing.

Some of the thick sections of rod may have been used to link saggar stacks together or to adhere a stack to the kiln wall (Hu and Li 1997: 80-82), this linking practice being evidenced in the Stoke potteries[47] (Plate 5.17).

It is probable, however, that not all of the clay rods owe their origin to an intended use for sealing the saggars. Some of them have the ends flattened and bent at an angle as though they either supported something or had been pressed with the thumb onto a flat surface with the rod coming off it at an angle. Examination of the material from Holt (Grimes 1930: 183 and Fig. 79) suggests that such clay sausages were there used to separate *mortaria* during firing. A similar process could have been used in the firing of unglazed faience vessels at HAC3. Since it is believed that HAC3 was the site of biscuit, rather than glaze, firings such sausages of clay would not stick to the vessels or pick up drips of glaze. It is also possible that some wares would have been fired in inverted position – as suggested for the Holt *mortaria* – during biscuit firing.

Those rods which have a flattened end might well have served as supports in a saggar, though it can also be suggested that this flattening comes from shearing off the end of a sausage of clay once the circumference of the saggar rim has been covered and that it is therefore nothing more than a bi-product of manufacturing the seal on the vessels. Examples where a rod is clearly held in friable clay are rare, but P-215 is such an example. It may be that it was used in the bottom of a saggar to lift a stack of vessels off the bottom of the saggar, or that it was used to fill up space within a saggar to help prevent a stack of faience vessels falling over within it where they were of a much smaller diameter than the container itself. Such rods might also have been used in carrying small saggars with vessels inside them and then discarded once the saggar was in position.

In summary it may be said that the rods of clay result from several different purposes and that because they are all of similar fabric it is not possible to be certain of the function of every individual piece. They have usually been described as 'saggar joiners' in the recording process because it is likely that many of them are the scrap pieces left over after completing a vessel circumference, the rest of the piece being flattened into an M-profile or similar. Some however, are clearly intended for other purposes.

Summary

Faience at Kom Helul was fired in handmade saggars. The larger (Type 12) used mostly for biscuit (bisque) firing and the smaller type (Type 3) primarily used for glaze (glost) firings. The kilns used in these processes may well have been separate so that the one known from HAC3 would be for biscuit firing only.

The fact that some saggars preserve potmarks on their interiors suggests that they may identify the contents as being the work of a particular workshop or individual, several such individuals sharing a single kiln. The marks are on the interior because the exterior of the saggars, once they had been luted together with clay strips (saggar joiners or "wads") would be plastered over so rendering marks invisible. Only when the stack ("bung") was dismantled would the marks be visible.

Within the saggars the faience ware was usually stacked right way up for glazing and separated by small cones of clay. In the case of biscuit firing the orientation of the ware is less certain and large open vessels might have been inverted and separated by sausages of clay as is known from Holt (Grimes 1930).

Saggars were probably used several times before they became too badly damaged and had to be discarded. The very large quantity of saggar material from Kom Helul attests the scale of the industry. Saggar making may well have been a full time occupation for some members of the workshop just as it was in the potteries of Stoke.

Endnotes

1 This chapter includes a revised and expanded version of material published by the writer as Nicholson (2011). The work presented here supersedes the preliminary reports Nicholson (2001, 2002a).

2 OED (XIV:367) note that it first enters English in 1696 as *schrager* perhaps an "etymological association with German *schragen* to prop up; it may have been invented by the German workmen employed in the Staffordshire potteries."

3 These grooves are reproduced on the glass ingots as ridges. For photographs see Bass (1987: 716).

4 Although known by us as "saggar joiners" these strips of clay were known as "wads" amongst pottery workers in the U.K.

5 The form of the saggars was mis-understood when first investigated and the figure in Nicholson (2001: 17) should be disregarded.

6 Though in a few instances the three pointed stands from Kom Helul may be industrial.

7 Type 12 vessels with incipient colourless glaze are included here as unglazed.

8 The Vienna System (Nordström and Bourriau 1993: 168ff.) is not intended to cover fabrics of the Roman period but here it provides an adequate and recognisable description.

9 Base diameter, rather than rim, has been chosen because this reflects the 'footprint' of the vessel in the kiln.

10 Estimating the numbers of vessels is not a straightforward process (Orton, Tyers and Vince 1993: 171-2). The method used here is based on taking the every secure example of either a Type 3 or Type 12 rim and using the measured diameter and its percentage. Thus where there are 3 rims of, say, 38cm diameter and their percentages added up to 150% they are treated as equivalent to 2 vessels. Similarly, if there is only 1 rim of 38cm diameter and it has 3% preserved the piece is recorded as the equivalent of 1 vessel. Because these saggar vessels are handmade, and are very coarse, variations of plus or minus 2cm in measuring their diameters are possible. Grouping vessels in a range may have the effect of lowering numbers but does not seem justified.

11 See note 9.

12 See note 10.

13 These figures are revised from those quoted in Nicholson 2011.

14 The author is grateful to the *Stoke Sentinel* for its help in attempting to locate these individuals.

15 This was made by Mr. Gerald Mee of *Stoke Amateur Cine Society* and I am indebted to him for his help.

16 I am indebted to Mr. Mee for permitting the film to be made available in this way.

17 Mr. Wheeldon described himself in the film as one of the last four remaining saggar makers.

18 Mr. Glover, a former maker of saggars by mechanical means, noted that pugs of clay were sent from the factory he worked in to others for saggar making in weights between 52 and 64 lbs. (23.58 – 29.03 kg.). This refers to the period after which Mr. Wheeldon would have retired.

19 Mau' is the local word for maul.

20 A pug mill is a mechanical device for mixing clay. It produces an homogeneous mixture free of air.

21 Note that this is a different use of the term "bat" than is common in ceramics where the bat is a disc of fired clay or plaster on which vessels are formed or moved.

22 Clearly visible in Mr. Mee's film.

23 Although less well paid than the saggar maker, the "saggar maker's bottom knocker" became immortalised for the British public by a now famous episode of the quiz show "What's My Line?" (1951-1962) hosted by Gilbert Harding.

24 It is tempting to see the etymology of this word as "sherd" and perhaps referring to a time when large fragments of saggar, perhaps discarded bases, were used as bats on which to form new vessels. Given that the local term for a pile of sherds, including saggars, is a "shordruck" such an origin is not impossible.

25 Or "whirlie" - Sandeman (1921: 207) refers to these as 'whirlers'.

26 Mr. Wheeldon used an old piece of metal from a *Coleman's Mustard* advertising sign.

27 Mr. Wheeldon states on one of Mr. Mee's tapes that a full team (saggar maker, frame filler and bottom knocker) could make 100 saggars in a day. Allowing 8 minutes per saggar this would be 800 minutes or 13.3 hours, longer than the normal working day in the post-war period. However, since each frame could produce enough sides for several saggars (6 in the film) the actual mau'ing process might have to be carried out only once per half dozen saggars which would substantially reduce production time. At five minutes per saggar 100 could be produced in 8.33 hours. Working alone and making all parts of the saggar, as sometimes happened toward the end of the industry, a man could produce 30 saggars which at 16 minutes per saggar would add up to an 8 hour day.

28 Also known as a "Green House" because the vessels placed there were green-hard.

29 Workers in the potteries tended to be paid a piece rate and delays were very unpopular with the saggar makers. In the case of saggar makers the piece was a score (i.e. 20) of vessels.

30 Information board at the Nantgarw Museum, source not attributed.

31 'Grogged' in the parlance of the Stoke and other potters.

32 The damp ground conditions at Memphis do not favour the preservation of organic material over most of the Kom Helul site and since wood is a valuable commodity in Egypt it is likely that it would be recycled and lost from the archaeological record.

33 That the clay is wet is evident from the raised edge of the letters where soft clay has been pushed aside.

34 By comparision a saggar from the Gladstone Pottery Museum, Stoke-on-Trent with an average diameter of 33.8cm and wall height of 27.2cm weighs only 12.9kg. These saggars are close to the mean average of the Memphis Type 3 vessels in base diameter though are twice as tall.

35 UC33565.

36 I am grateful to Dr. Geoffrey Killen for confirming that these marks are indeed from planks and for supplying the additional observation that they are from cleaved, rather than sawn, planks.

37 Paper clay is paper which has been soaked in clay.

38 The practice of leaving the cord on the vessel during firing is contrary to the process now employed by the makers of Ballas jars in Upper Egypt (see Nicholson and Patterson 1985) and by the makers of siltware milk containers at Ezbet Makhmal near Memphis. The removal of the cords from the vessels leaves a very clear mark, and no clay is put over the string, whereas it was sometimes smeared over it by those who were applying plaster to the saggar vessels.

39 I am grateful to Hendrikje Nouwens for drawing my attention to this point.

40 It should be noted that any such glaze on the objects would be very slight and not sufficient to prevent the adherence of the actual glaze coat.

41 These were classed as saggar joiners since it is not usually possible to differentiate them from some of the rods or strips of clay which were run around the rim of the saggars.

42 Examples in the Petrie Museum are UC33566, UC47323, UC47324, UC473426.

43 The difficulty in separating domestic from industrial wares is dealt with by Papadopoulos (1992).

44 Ashton (2003: 43) refers to these as "tripod stands" but Petrie's (1911a:35) term "three-pointed stands" is preferable since the points are not feet but are at the top of the object.

45 Although not if they were used in saggars whose purpose was purely biscuit firing.

46 Ashton (2003: 42) mistakenly states that it is the author's view that the vessels were fired inverted. My publication of this (1998: 255) was based on Petrie's work and was revised following the opportunity to examine the material from the Petrie Museum more fully. This reinvestigation was carried out in 2000 and was published in 2002 (Nicholson 2002a: 98).

47 Clearly visible in one of the displays at the Gladstone Pottery Museum.

CHAPTER 6
FAIENCE VESSELS AND OBJECTS

M-D. Nenna

INTRODUCTION

The excavations at Kom Helul, Memphis, between 2000 and 2005 gave the opportunity to examine the structures and processes of production of faience objects (i.e. the kiln and the kiln furniture – Chapters 4 and 5), as well as the objects that were produced there or in the vicinity. They offer a complementary picture of what can be extracted from the brief reports published by W.M. Flinders Petrie at the beginning of the 20th Century (Petrie 1909a, 1911, Ashton 2003). Knowledge of faience vessels and objects produced in the Ptolemaic and Roman periods has increased through the publications of numerous articles and books, mainly dedicated to pieces bearing decoration (see Nenna and Seif el-Din 2000, to which should be added Ashton 2003; Constandelou 2004; Di Gioia 2006; Hembold 2001; Mao 2000, 2001; Nenna 2001, 2002, 2003, 2005a-b, 2006; Nenna and Seif el-Din, forthcoming; Parlasca 2005 and 2010, Rodziewicz 2005; Shortland and Tite 2005; Silvano 2000, 2005; Welc 2011). However, the plain glazed ware still needs to be further explored in terms of typology and chronology. Whilst the corpus of forms of decorated vessels seems quite sound following the publication of the Graeco-Roman Museum of Alexandria[1] collection in 2000,[2] the corpus of forms of the plain glazed vessels is only now increasing following the exploration of sites occupied in the Graeco-Roman period. We have here relied on objects recently unearthed, or published, from Tell el-Herr (Nenna 2007a), Buto (Nenna 2007b and in press), Naukratis (Leonard 1997: 297-298, figs 7.11-12), Wadi Natrun (Nenna forthcoming a), Saqqara (Dayton 1981), Tebtunis (Nenna forthcoming b), Mons Claudianus and Mons Porphyrites (Tomber 2006; 2007; Whitcomb and Johnson 1979: 68-91 & 312-313), Coptos (Grataloup 1988), Elephantine (Rodziewicz 2005), Ahmeida (Cervi forthcoming) and Fezzan Oasis (Tagart 1983; Hoffmann and Tagart 2010) to try to be more precise on the chronology and on the spectrum of plain glazed vessels distributed in the Early Roman period. We propose here in Figures 6.1-6.13 an updated typology, following the same numbering as in Nenna and Seif el-Din 2000, but incorporating the plain glazed vessels more effectively.

DISTRIBUTION OF THE FINDS

During the excavation, trenches were opened in two main sections: HAD and HAC. The soundings in sector HAD were non-industrial in nature and the number of faience pieces found there was very small: eleven fragments have been unearthed of which two fragmentary beads and one plate of Nenna and Seif el-Din's type T13.3[3] are notable. The trenches in sector HAC have been much more prolific as shown by the tables 6.1 to 6.3,[4] especially in HAC3 where the kiln is located. The writer has tried here to give a general view of the functional distribution of the finds by units, as well as a broad chronology of the groups. For the detail, the reader should refer to the short entries catalogues by sector of excavation ordered by contexts), which contain all the finds, and to the long entries catalogue by sector of excavation, corresponding to the pieces which were the most demonstrative, ordered following the function and typology of the vessels.

The registration of even the very tiny fragments of faience has the potential to give a misleading view of quantities. In fact only 37 sherds were big enough to be attributed to a specific form (vessels, objects and wasters) in Trench HAC1, as opposed to 68 sherds in HAC2 and 407 in HAC3.

The finds from this region of Kom Helul have mostly consisted of three types: fragments of vessels, defective ('waster') vessels, and fragments of defective vessels found within the saggars, but in addition other kinds of objects are also attested, such as amulets, beads, furniture, lamps and

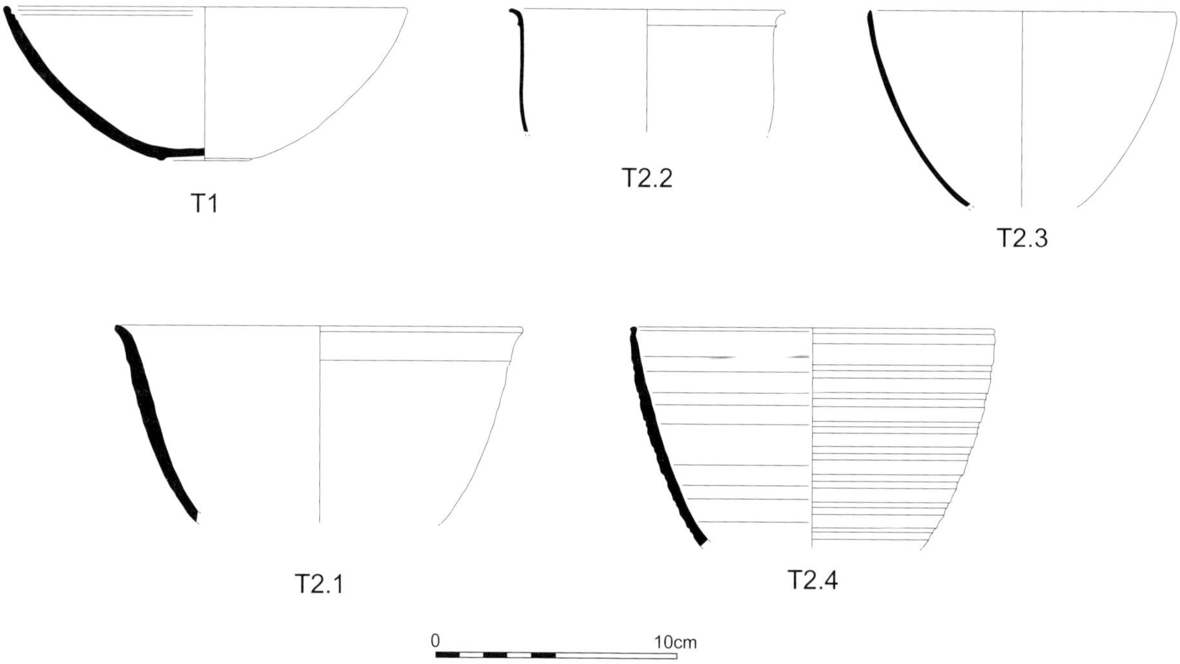

Figure 6.1

T1: Shallow hemispherical bowls (GRM, 16655, Nenna, Seif el-Din 2000, no. 3)

T1.1: light green or light blue or marbled glaze
Undecorated
3rd Century B.C.

T1.2: light and dark blue, or light and dark green glaze
Interior decoration in concentric bands and exterior limitedto a garland on the body and vegetal motif near the bottom
3rd Century B.C.

T1.3: light and dark blue glaze
Interior and exterior decoration in concentric bands
3rd Century B.C.

T1.4: white and light blue glaze, trichromatic glaze
Decoration in concentric bands, interior and exterior only a garland on bottom
2nd Century B.C.

T2: Deep bowls

T2.1: Deep bowl with flared lip (GRM, 32514, Nenna, Seif el-Din forthcoming, n° 657)
Light green / light blue / light and dark blue / trichromatic glaze
Exterior decoration: palm calyx / nelumbo calyx
3rd Century / 2nd-beginning 1st Century B.C.[1]

T2.2: Deep bowl with flared lip (GRM, P.14437, Nenna, Seif el-Din 2000, n° 138)
Light and dark blue / trichromatic glaze
Exterior decoration in bands
3rd-2nd Century B.C.

T2.3: Deep bowl with tapering walls (Tebtunis, 27127.19, Nenna 2002, fig. 7)
Light and dark blue / light green and dark blue / trichromatic glaze
a. Undecorated, b. vegetal calyxes cover major part of body (exterior), c. calyx of long thin leaves (exterior), d. geometric decoration covers entire body (exterior), e. freely organised decoration, f. exterior decoration in bands
3rd Century / 2nd-1st Century B.C.[2]

T2.4: Deep bowl made using bivalve mould (GRM, 32522, Nenna, Seif el-Din forthcoming, n° 670)
Light green / light green and blue glaze
Exterior decoration: horizontal fluting and strings of pearls; interior in bands
3rd Century B.C.

Notes

1 See Tebtunis, 7665 1st Century B.C. level for white and purple example, nelumbo calyxes seem to appear later than the palm calyxes.

2 Unpublished examples from Tebtunis in 2nd-1st Century levels.

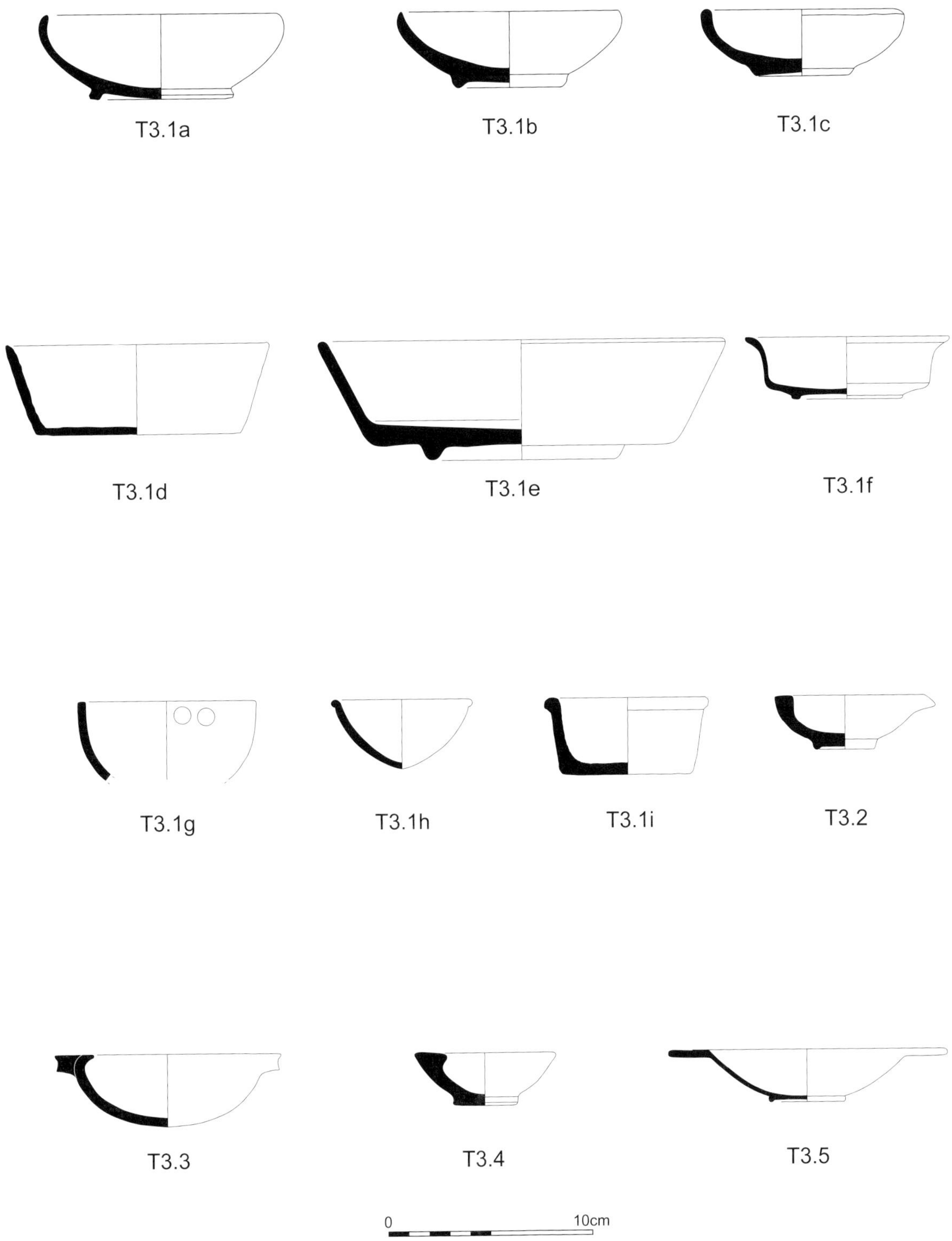
T3.1a
T3.1b
T3.1c
T3.1d
T3.1e
T3.1f
T3.1g
T3.1h
T3.1i
T3.2
T3.3
T3.4
T3.5
0
10cm

Figure 6.2

Figure 6.2

T3: Small bowls

T3.1a: Convex small bowl with fine, inward-turning lip and ring base (Tebtunis, 7536-12, Nenna, forthcoming b)
Light blue, light green, ultramarine blue glaze
Undecorated
3rd-2nd Century B.C.

T3.1b: Convex small bowl with tapering lip and ring base or reinforced bottom (Tebtunis, A20149-3, Nenna, forthcoming b)
Light blue, light green, ultramarine blue glaze
Undecorated
3rd- 2nd Century B.C.

T3.1c: Convex small bowl with flat lip and ring base or reinforced bottom (Tebtunis, A7310-48, Nenna, forthcoming b)
Light blue, ultramarine blue, white, marbled glaze
Undecorated
3rd-1st Century B.C.

T3.1d: Small bowl with oblique walls and flat bottom (Saqqara, Dayton 1981, pl. 8,1100)
Light blue, marbled (light and dark blue, purple and white) glaze
Undecorated
3rd-1st Century B.C.

T3.1e: Small bowl with oblique walls and ring base (Tebtunis, A7307-60, Nenna, forthcoming b)
Light blue, marbled (light and dark blue, purple and white) glaze
Undecorated
3rd-1st Century B.C.

T3.1f: Carinate small bowl with flaring lip (Louvre, DAE, E 10829b, Nenna and Seif el-Din 2000, fig. 9 and Nenna and Kaczmarczk forthcoming)
Light green glaze
Undecorated
3rd Century B.C.

T3.1g: Hemispherical small bowl with two suspension holes (Saqqara, Dayton 1981, pl. 8, n° G)
Light blue, marbled glaze
Undecorated
End of 4th-3rd Century B.C.

T3.1h: Conical small bowl (Cairo, CG 3832, Nenna, Seif el-Din 2000, fig. 9)
Light green glaze
Undecorated
3rd Century B.C.

T3.1i: Cylindrical small bowl with flattened lip (Saqqara, Dayton 1981, pl. 8,745)
Light blue glaze
Undecorated
End of 4th-3rd Century B.C.

T3.2: Low convex small bowl with flat rim and generally a spout (GRM, 32523, Nenna, forthcoming, no.: Seif el-Din in this volume, 673)
Light blue glaze
Laurel branch on rim, rosette on inner bottom, appliqués of recumbent lion
3rd Century B.C.

T3.3: Convex small bowl with moulded rim (GRM, P.14436, Nenna and Seif el-Din 2000, n° 214)
Light blue glaze
Varied decoration
3rd-1st Century B.C.

T3.4: Convex small bowl with wide flat inward-turning rim and recessed bottom (Tebtunis, 7501-735, Nenna, forthcoming b)
White, light blue or purple glaze
Saw teeth on rim, rosette on bottom
2nd-1st Century B.C.

T3.5: Convex small bowl with extending wide flat rim and ring base (Louvre, DAE, E 26095, Nenna and Seif el-Din 2000, fig. 10, formerly classed as T3.3)
Dark and light blue / white and purple glaze
Crude frieze of rosettes and lotus bundles on the rim, rosettes of varied form on the bottom
2nd-1st Century B.C.

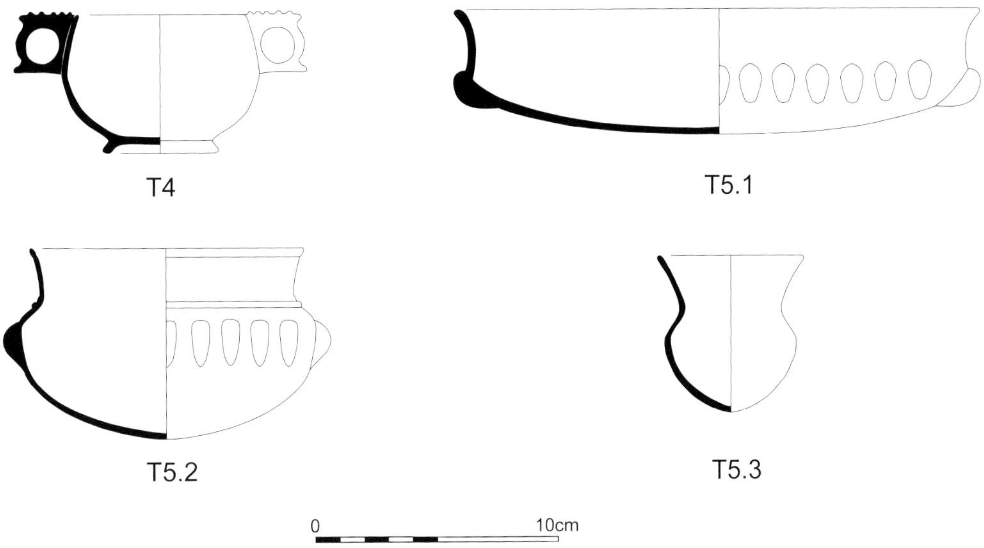

Figure 6.3

T4: ***Skyphos***

(GRM, 10479, Nenna and Seif el-Din 2000, n° 225)
Light and dark blue / light green and dark blue glaze
Rinceau of ivy leaves and berries / framed griffons / laurel branch
3rd Century B.C.

T5: ***Achaemenid inspired shapes***

T5.1: *Bowl with nodules (Cairo, JE 62956, Nenna, Seif el-Din 2000, fig. 10)*
Light green / light blue / light and dark blue / light green and dark blue glaze
Calyx of long leaves with nodules in between
End of 4th-3rd Century B.C.

T5.2: *Spherical bowl with cylindrical neck (Louvre, DAE, E 11159, Nenna and Seif el-Din 2000, fig. 10)*
Light and dark blue / light green and dark blue / marbled glaze
Calyx with long leaves with nodules in-between
End of 4th-3rd Century B.C.

T5.3: *Beaker with high neck and ovoid body (GRM, 25254, Nenna and Seif el-Din 2000, n° 236)*
Light green / light blue / light and dark blue / light green and dark blue glaze
Egg and dart motif on shoulder, vegetal calyx, decoration in bands one above the other, nodules
End of 4th-3rd Century B.C.

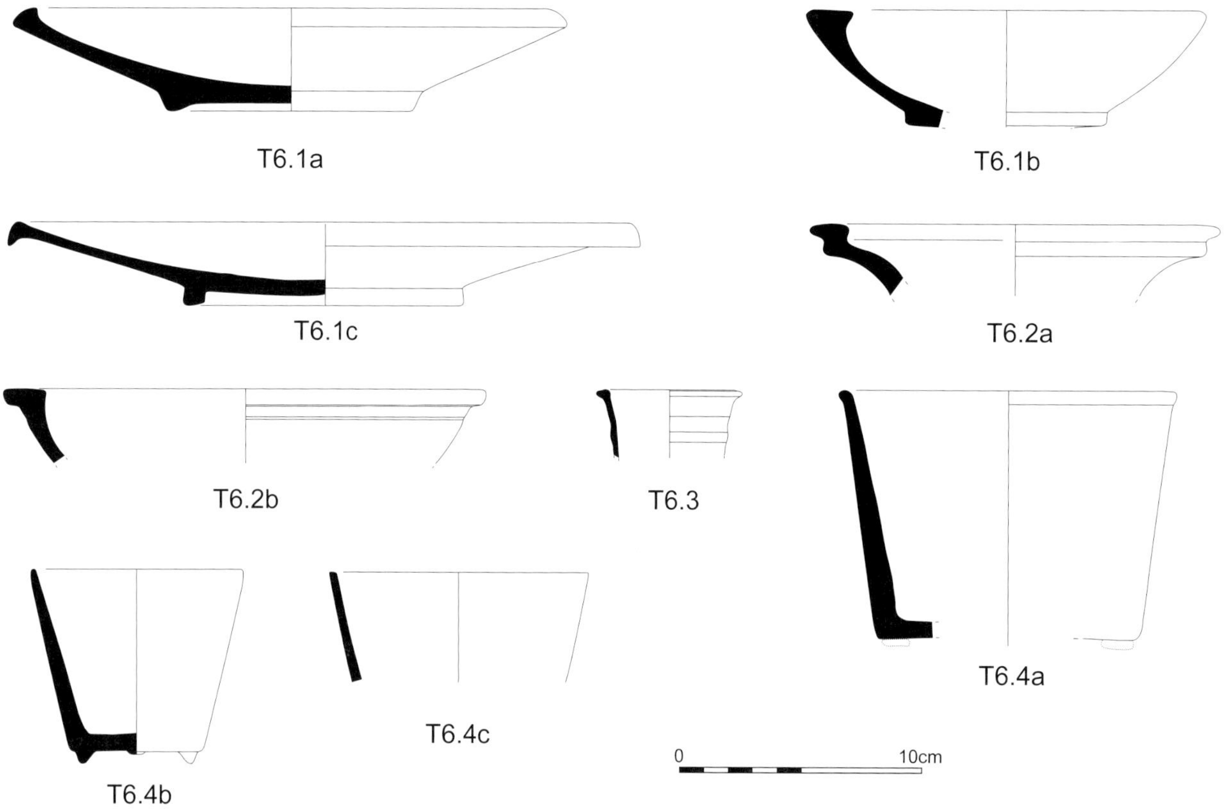

Figure 6.4

T6.1: Plates

T6.1a: Plate with internal lip, oblique walls and ring base (Tebtunis, A3236-2, Nenna 2002, fig. 1,6)
Light green / light blue / ultramarine blue / white and purple glaze[1]
Undecorated / large rosette
3rd-1st Century B.C.

T6.1b: Plate with flat inward-turning rim, convex walls and reinforced bottom (Tebtunis, A3255-1, Nenna 2002, fig. 1,5)
Light blue / ultramarine blue / marbled glaze
Undecorated
3rd-1st Century B.C.

T6.1c: Plate with downturned lip, oblique walls and ring base (Tebtunis, A3242-1, Nenna, forthcoming b)
Light green / light blue / white, purple, light green and dark blue glaze[2]
Undecorated or decoration of vine tendrils and rosette in the centre
3rd-1st Century B.C.

T6.2: Basins

T6.2a: Basin with moulded rim and concave walls (Tebtunis, 7601-820, Nenna, forthcoming b)
Ultramarine blue / light blue glaze
Undecorated
3rd-2nd Century B.C.

T6.2b: Basin with flat extending rim and convex (Tebtunis, 27120-1, unpublished)
Light blue / marbled / light and dark blue glaze
Undecorated / sometimes, laurel branch on rim and bands of decoration one above the other
3rd-2nd Century B.C.

T6.3: Rhytons (GRM, FA.51, Nenna, Seif el-Din forthcoming no., 692)
Light green and blue / light and dark blue glaze
Decoration in bands one above the other, lower opening modelled
3rd Century B.C.

T6.4: Beakers

T6.4a: Truncated cone beaker with flat bottom and reinforced lip (Tebtunis, 7701-136, Nenna, forthcoming b, with clay cones)
Light blue / ultramarine blue / marbled glaze
Undecorated
4th-1st Century B.C.[3]

T6.4b: Truncated cone beaker with flat bottom and tapering lip (Tebtunis, A7311-30, unpublished, with clay cones)
Light blue / ultramarine blue / marbled glaze
Undecorated
3rd-1st Century B.C.

T6.4c: Truncated cone beaker with flat bottom and flattened lip (Bouto, P5.2010.5271.58, unpublished)
Light blue / ultramarine blue / marbled glaze
Undecorated
3rd-1st Century B.C.

T6.5: Kantharos (not illustrated)

Notes

1. Only in 1st Century B.C. to 1st Century A.D. contexts.
2. This is a rare form in comparison with the two preceding types. The plate A3242-1 is the only one decorated with four colours of glaze.
3. This form is already attested in the Late Period, see Riefstahl 1968, n° 64 with inscriptions stating the contents.

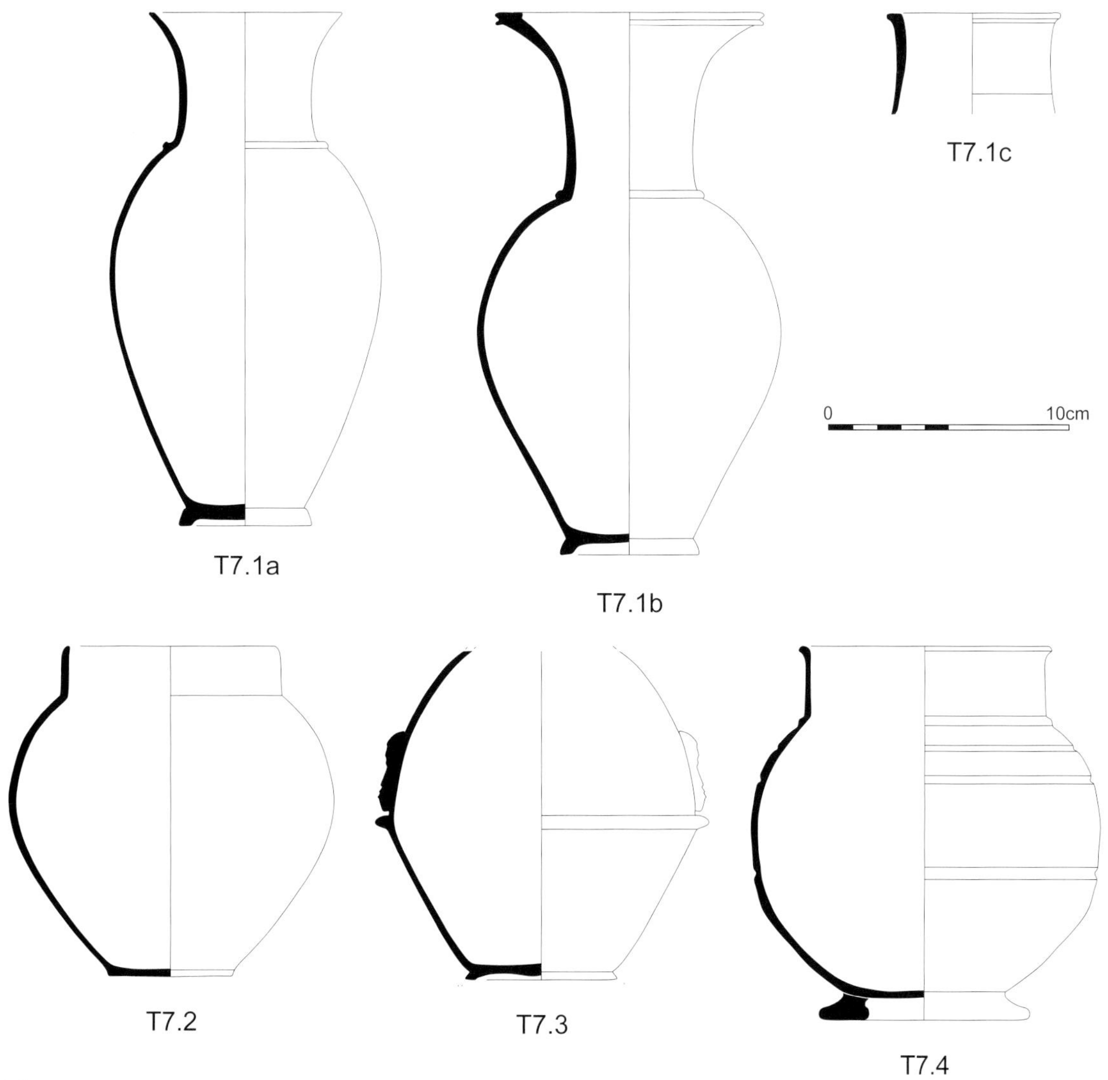

Figure 6.5

T7: Restricted vases with ovoid or spherical bodies

T7.1a: Restricted vase with fine lip, trumpet neck, ovoid body and ring base (Athens, National Museum, 1922, Nenna, Seif el-Din 2000, fig. 11)
Light and dark blue glaze
Decoration in bands one above the other
3rd Century B.C.

T7.1b: Restricted vase with flattened moulded lip, trumpet neck, ovoid body and ring base (Cairo, JE 45490 & 45491, Nenna and Seif el-Din 2000, fig. 11)
Light and dark blue glaze
Decoration in bands one above the other, appliqués
3rd Century B.C.

T7.1c: Restricted vase with flattened lip, cylindrical neck, ovoid body and ring base (GRM, FA.52, Nenna and Seif el-Din, forthcoming, no. 696)
Light and dark blue glaze
Decoration in bands one above the other, appliqués
3rd Century B.C.

T7.2: Restricted vase with short cylindrical neck, ovoid body and ring base (Cairo, JE 18/11/15/1, Nenna and Seif el-Din 2000, fig. 11)
Light and dark blue glaze
Decoration in bands one above the other, appliqués
3rd Century B.C.

T7.3: Restricted vase with ovoid body, medial protrusion and ring base (Cairo, JE 41300, Nenna and Seif el-Din 2000, fig. 11)
Light and dark blue / light green and blue / white and dark blue glaze
Decoration of appliqués
3rd Century B.C.-2nd Century B.C.

T7.4: Restricted vase with flared lip, short cylindrical neck, spherical body and added foot (Louvre, DAE, E 22582, Grimm 1972, 84, photo fig. 27)
Light and dark blue / white, light green and purple glaze
Decoration in bands one above the other in faint relief or no relief
1st Century B.C.-1st Century A.D.

Note: We did not create a specific form for the T7.4 vases in the 2000 catalogue. Since then, excavations at Memphis have provided evidence that would allow us to date their production to the turn of the 1st Century B.C. to the 1st Century A.D.. Distinguishing between the vases T7.2 and T7.4 is not always easy to do when one has only small fragments. One must bear in mind criteria of shape (transition from the neck to the shoulder and the ring base for T7.2 vases / protrusion at the base of the neck and added foot for T7.4 vases), of decoration (frieze of lotus bundles and of rosettes and faint relief on the T7.4 vases and not on the T7.2 vases), and of glaze (tendency towards combined use of green, purple and white glaze on T7.4 vases).

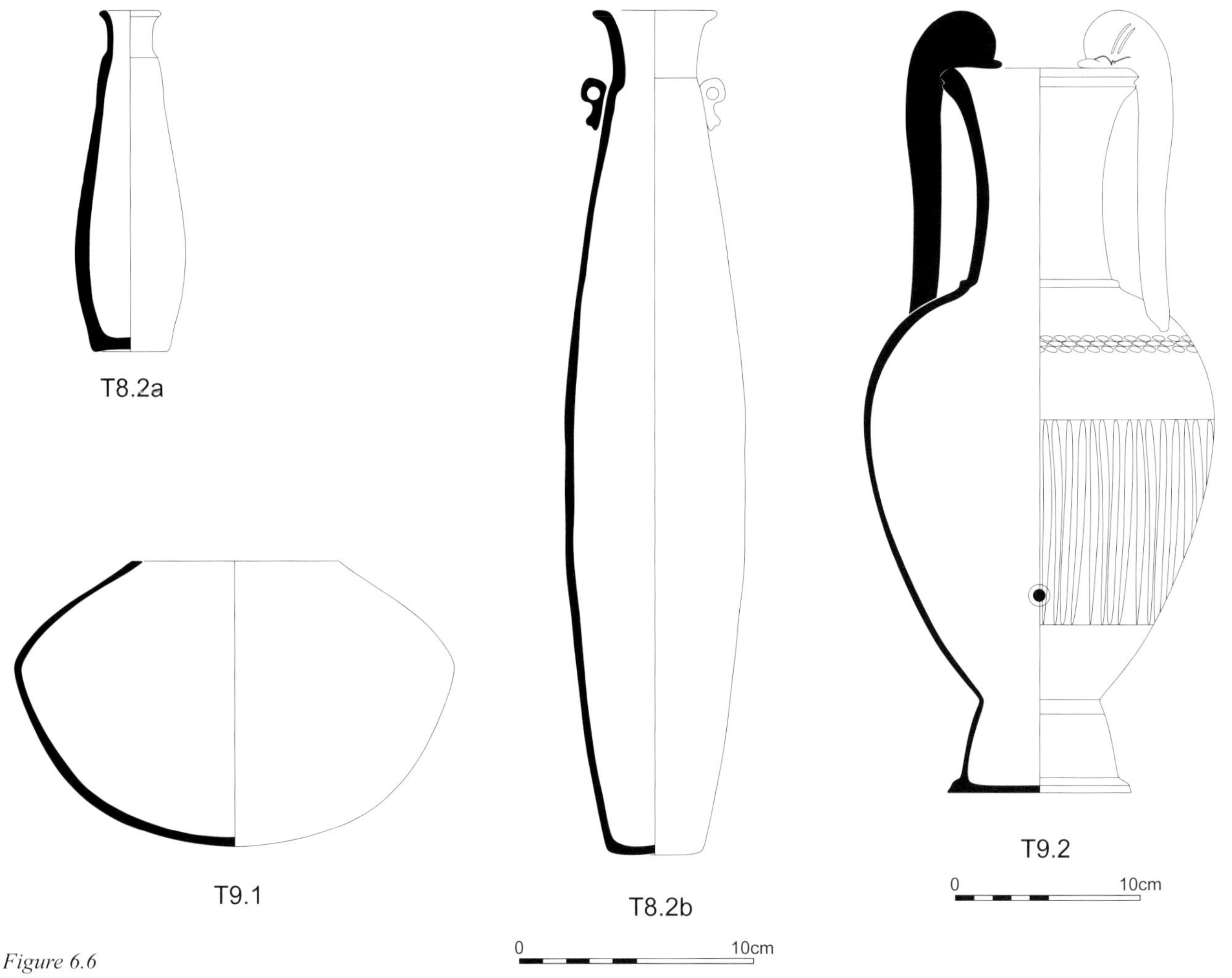

Figure 6.6

T8: Alabastrons

T8.1: Alabastron with a disc mouth, cylindrical body and knob or ring handles on the upper third of the body (not illustrated)
Light blue / light and dark blue / light green and blue glaze
a. Undecorated; b. decoration in bands one above the other
3rd Century B.C.

T8.2: Alabastron with splayed mouth, biconical body and flat bottom with small ring handles on upper part of body (GRM, 29505, Nenna and Seif el-Din 2000, n° 405 and Nenna and Seif el-Din, forthcoming, no. 715)
Light blue / light and dark blue / light green and blue / white and dark blue glaze
a. Undecorated; b. decoration in bands one above the other; c. decoration of appliqués with or without decoration in bands one above the other
3rd Century B.C. / 2nd-1st Century B.C.

T9: Restricted vases with floral appliqué decoration and fluted handles

T.9.1: Spherical vase (GRM, 18241, Nenna and Seif el-Din 2000, n° 407)
Light green glaze for the vase, yellow and/or blue from the appliqué decoration
Appliqué decoration of ribbon garland, fluting on the body.
3rd Century B.C.

T9.2: Amphora with trumpet neck, ovoid body, pedestal foot and dolphin-headed handles (The art market, Christie's London, Fine Antiquities, 27 October 2004: 70, n° 510, drawing by C. Edwar, from a photo)
Light green glaze for the vase, yellow and/or blue from the appliqué decoration
Appliqué decoration of ribbon garland, fluting on the body.
3rd Century B.C.

T10: Plastic vases (not illustrated)

T10.1: Plastic vase with animal representation
Light and dark blue / light green and dark blue / white and purple / white, purple, green, yellow and blue glaze
Realistic rendering of plumage for birds; of saddlecloth and harness for elephants
3rd Century B.C.

T10.2: Plastic vase with representation of divinity
Light and dark blue glaze
Rendering of body details and of hair (Eros) and beard (Bes)
3rd Century B.C.

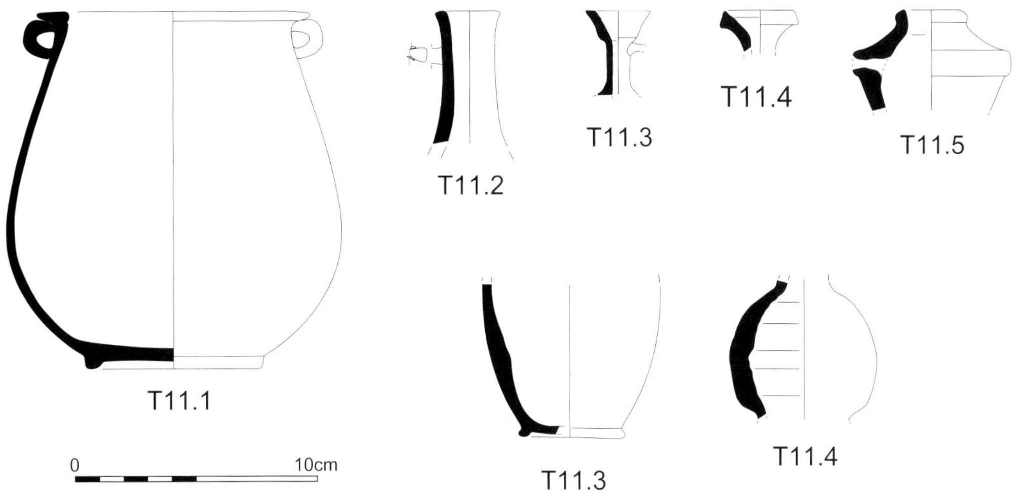

Figure 6.7

T11: Ovoid pots and flasks

T11.1: Ovoid pot with wide flat rim, ring base, and rounded or squared handles (GRM, 24341, Nenna and Seif el-Din 2000, n° 592)
Ultramarine blue, light blue, light green glaze
Undecorated
3rd-1st Century B.C.

T11.2: Lagynos with high cylindrical neck (Tebtunis, 27133-2, Nenna, forthcoming b)
Light blue / light green / light and dark blue glaze
Limited decoration or in bands one above the other
3rd-2nd Century B.C.

T11.3: Lekythos with funnel mouth, cylindrical neck and ovoid body with ring base[1] (Saqqara, Dayton 1981, n° 752, Tebtunis, 3255-15, Nenna, forthcoming b)
Light blue / light green / sometimes no glaze inside
Undecorated
End of 4th-2nd Century B.C.

T11.4: Squat lekythos or aryballos with flared mouth, rounded body and ring base[2] (Tebtunis, A2099-6, 2782-21, Nenna, forthcoming b)
Light blue / light green glaze
Undecorated
3rd-1st Century B.C.

T11.5: Vase with side spout – nemset vase[3] (Tebtunis, A3138-1, Nenna, forthcoming b)
Light blue / light green glaze
Undecorated
4th-2nd Century B.C.

Note: We had reserved the type T11 for a rare shapes of Hellenistic vases in the 2000 catalogue. The discoveries at Tebtunis led us to revise the classification. In fact, the ovoid pots that we had placed in an appendix for lack of parallels well connected to the Hellenistic era have turned out to be rather frequent containers on consumption sites (37 examples at Tebtunis).

Notes

1 A fine complete example can be seen at http://www.metmuseum.org: MET 44.4.44. An ensemble of fragments with no internal glazing is most probably from the same form; they are not moulded but fashioned around a core of perishable material. Ceramic vases of this form are dated to the 3rd-2nd Century B.C. at Tebtunis see Ballet and Poludnikiewicz 2012, nos. 473 and 482-484, however, similar pieces in faience have been found among the material from the Sacred Animal Necropolis at Saqqara dated to end of the 4th Century B.C. (Dayton 1981, nos. 752-753).

2 We have no complete piece. For corresponding ceramic forms, see Ballet and Poludnikiewicz 2012, nos. 474-480.

3 Two fragmentary examples from Tebtunis. For a complete example, see www.globalegyptianmuseum, Brussels MRAH, E. 2246.

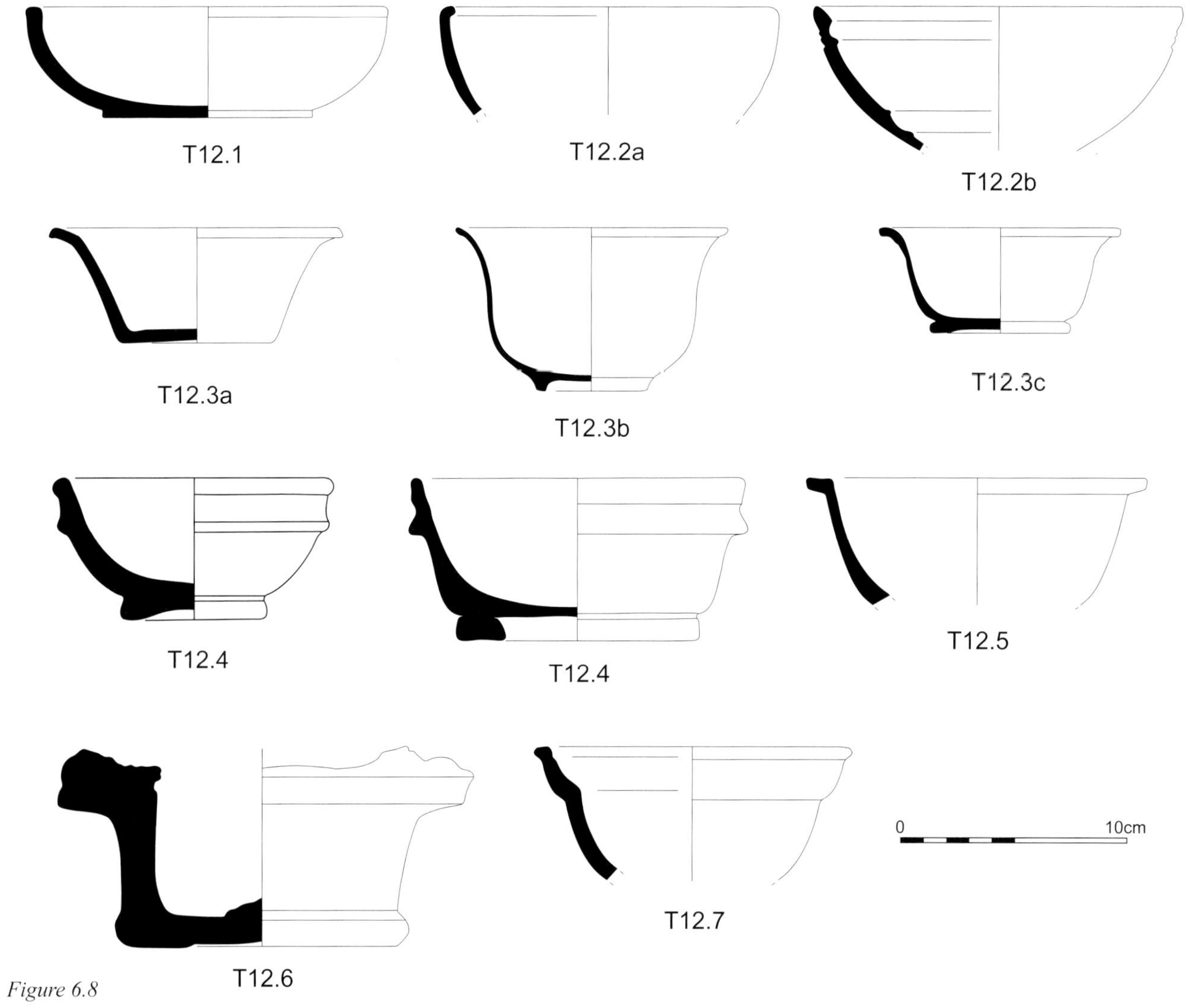

Figure 6.8

T12: Bowls

T12.1: Low bowl with convex walls and ring base (Louvre, DAE, without n°, Nenna and Seif el-Din 2000, fig. 12)
Turquoise glaze
Undecorated
1st-2nd Century A.D.

T12.2a: Deep hemispherical bowl with rolled internal lip (Tebtunis, 3701-219, Nenna, forthcoming b)
Turquoise glaze
Undecorated
1st-2nd Century A.D.

T12.2b: Deep hemispherical bowl with reliefs and hollows on interior walls (British Museum, GR 1910.11-16.5, Nenna, Seif el-Din 2000, fig. 12)
Turquoise glaze
Reliefs and hollows on interior walls
1st-2nd Century A.D.

T12.3a: Small bowl with flared rim, flared walls and flat bottom (Tebtunis, 2104-122, Nenna, forthcoming b)
Turquoise glaze
Undecorated
1st-2nd Century A.D.

T12.3b: Deep bowl with flared rim, flared walls and ring base (Cairo, JE 71980, Nenna and Seif el-Din 2000, fig. 12)
Turquoise glaze
Undecorated
1st-2nd Century A.D. (?)

T12.3c: Small bowl with flared rim, flared walls and recessed bottom (Beni Salama, Wadi Natrun, BSL05.20004.27.113, Nenna, forthcoming b)
Turquoise glaze
Undecorated
1st-2nd Century A.D.

T12.4: Hemispherical bowl with flanged rim and recessed bottom (small model: Tebtunis, 0000-52, unpublished) or added ring base (large model: Tebtunis, 2309-1, Nenna, forthcoming b)
Turquoise glaze
Undecorated
1st-2nd Century A.D.

T12.5: Deep bowl with wide flat rim (Tebtunis, A2082-185, unpublished)
Turquoise glaze
Undecorated
1st-2nd Century A.D.

T12.6: Cylindrical bowl with wide flat rim (Leiden, F1949 /5-3, Nenna and Seif el-Din 2000, fig. 12)
Dark green glaze
Appliqués of Erotes, lying on small appliqué leaves
1st-2nd Century A.D.

T12.7: Biconvex bowl (Tebtunis, A2104-121, Nenna, forthcoming b)
Turquoise glaze
Undecorated
1st-2nd Century A.D.

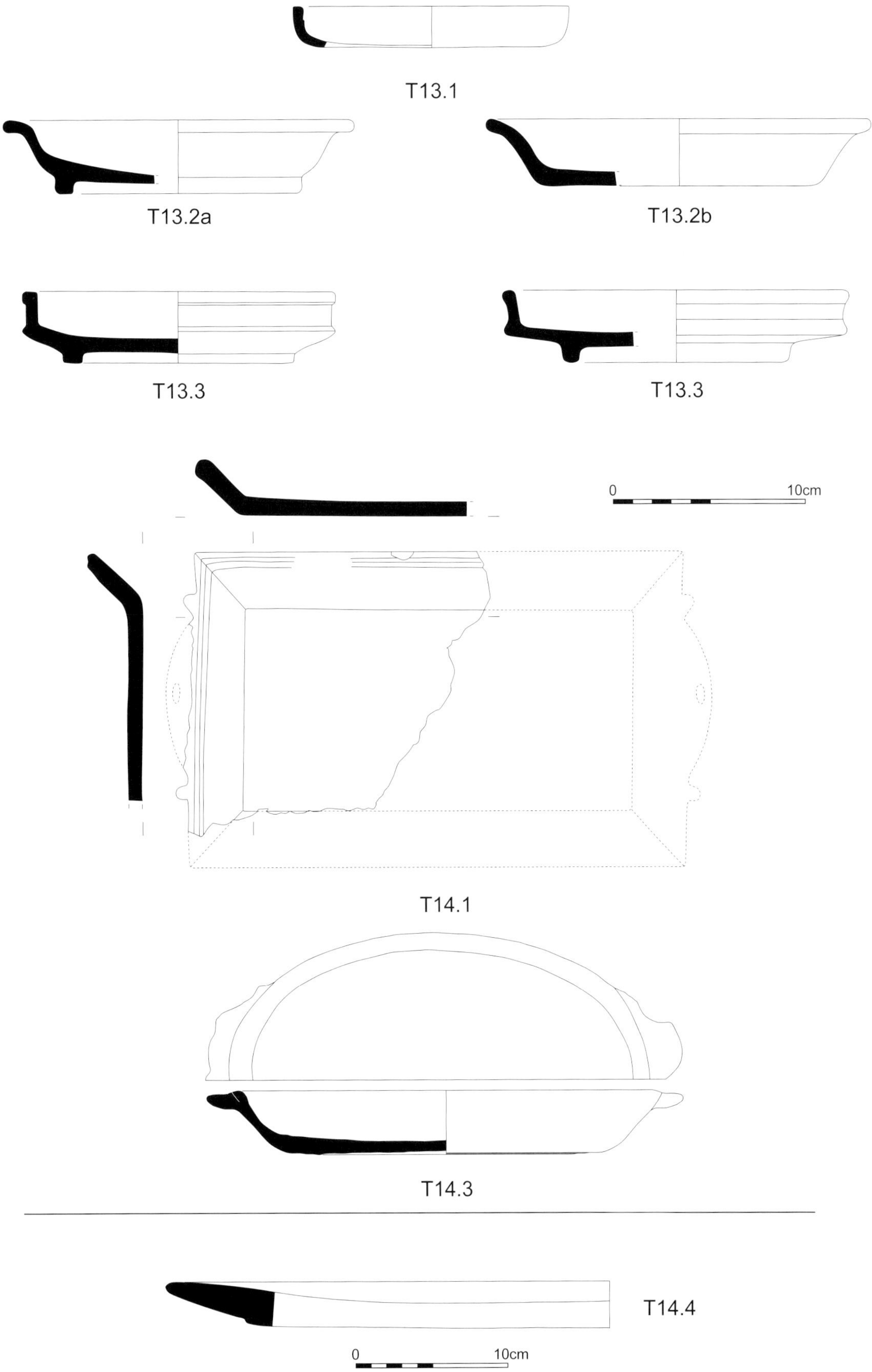

Figure 6.9

Figure 6.9

T13: Plates

T13.1: Plate with convex walls and a flat bottom (Petrie Museum, UC 33326, Nenna and Seif el-Din 2000, fig. 13)
Turquoise / dark green / light and dark blue / white and purple glaze
Decoration medallions on bottom (busts of divinities)
1st-2nd Century A.D.

T13.2a: Plate with flared rim, oblique walls and ring base (Tebtunis, A2082-190, Nenna, forthcoming b)
Turquoise glaze
Undecorated
1st-2nd Century A.D.

T13.2b: Plate with flared rim, oblique walls and flat bottom (Mons Claudianus, Tomber 2006, Type 5, fig. 1.16)
Turquoise and dark blue / purple and white glaze
Decoration of rosettes / figurative scenes
1st-2nd Century A.D.

T13.3: Carinate plate with rounded exterior lip and ring base (Tebtunis, A2082-189 7501-200, Nenna, forthcoming b)
Turquoise / purple and white glaze
a. Undecorated; b. central medallion with rosette or figurative scene
1st-2nd Century A.D.

T14: Platters

T14.1: Rectangular platter with flared walls, flat bottom and curved handles (Tebtunis, A2104-120, Nenna, forthcoming b)
Turquoise glaze
Undecorated
1st-2nd Century A.D.

T14.2: Platter with lion's head spout (not illustrated)
Turquoise glaze
Undecorated
1st-2nd Century A.D.

T14.3: Oval platter with flat bottom and worked handles (GRM, FA.08, Nenna and Seif el-Din, forthcoming, no. 727)
Turquoise / dark green glaze
Undecorated
1st-2nd Century A.D.

T14.4: Large flat circular platter with ring base (Ashmolean Museum, 1913.802, Nenna and Seif el-Din 2000, fig. 13)
Turquoise / white, light blue and purple undecorated / vegetal decoration
1st-2nd Century A.D.

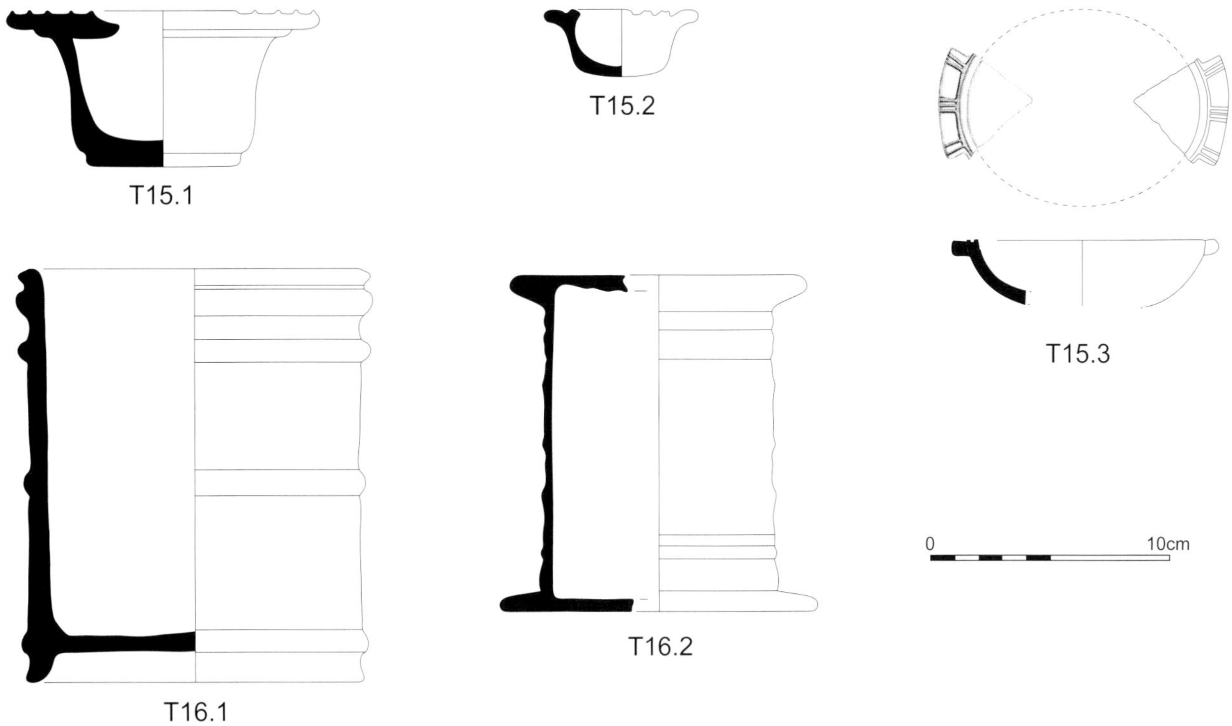

Figure 6.10

T15: Small bowls

T15.1: Deep small bowl with wide flat rim (Cairo, CG 18015, Nenna and Seif el-Din 2000, fig. 13)
Blue green and yellow / white, purple and blue glaze
Rim: recumbent lion appliqués; interior bottom: bunches of leaves and berries, exterior modelled nelumbo calyx
1st-2nd Century A.D.

T15.2: Deep miniature calyx-shaped small bowl (British Museum, EA 13166, Nenna and Seif el-Din 2000, fig. 13)
Dark blue glaze
Full vegetal calyx or appearing only as rows of pearls at the end of leaves on the rim
1st-2nd Century A.D.

T15.3: Oval small bowl with flat handles (Tebtunis, 7501-272, Neena, forthcoming b)
White and purple glaze
Indented lines on the handles
1st-2nd Century A.D.

T16: Cylindrical vases

T16.1 Cylindrical vase with ring base (GRM, P.13928, Nenna, Seif el-Din 2000, n° 487)
Yellow to dark green / white, green and purple / turquoise glaze
Decoration in bands one above the other / animal repertoire / calyxes of nelumbo leaves one above the other
1st-2nd Century A.D.

T16.2: Cylindrical vase with flat extending rim and base (Naples, 113022, Nenna and Seif el-Din 2000, fig. 14)
Yellow to dark green / white, green and purple / turquoise glaze
Decoration in bands one above the other
1st-2nd Century A.D.

T17: Rare open vessel forms, skyphos, krater, faceted beaker, ribbed bowl (not illustrated)

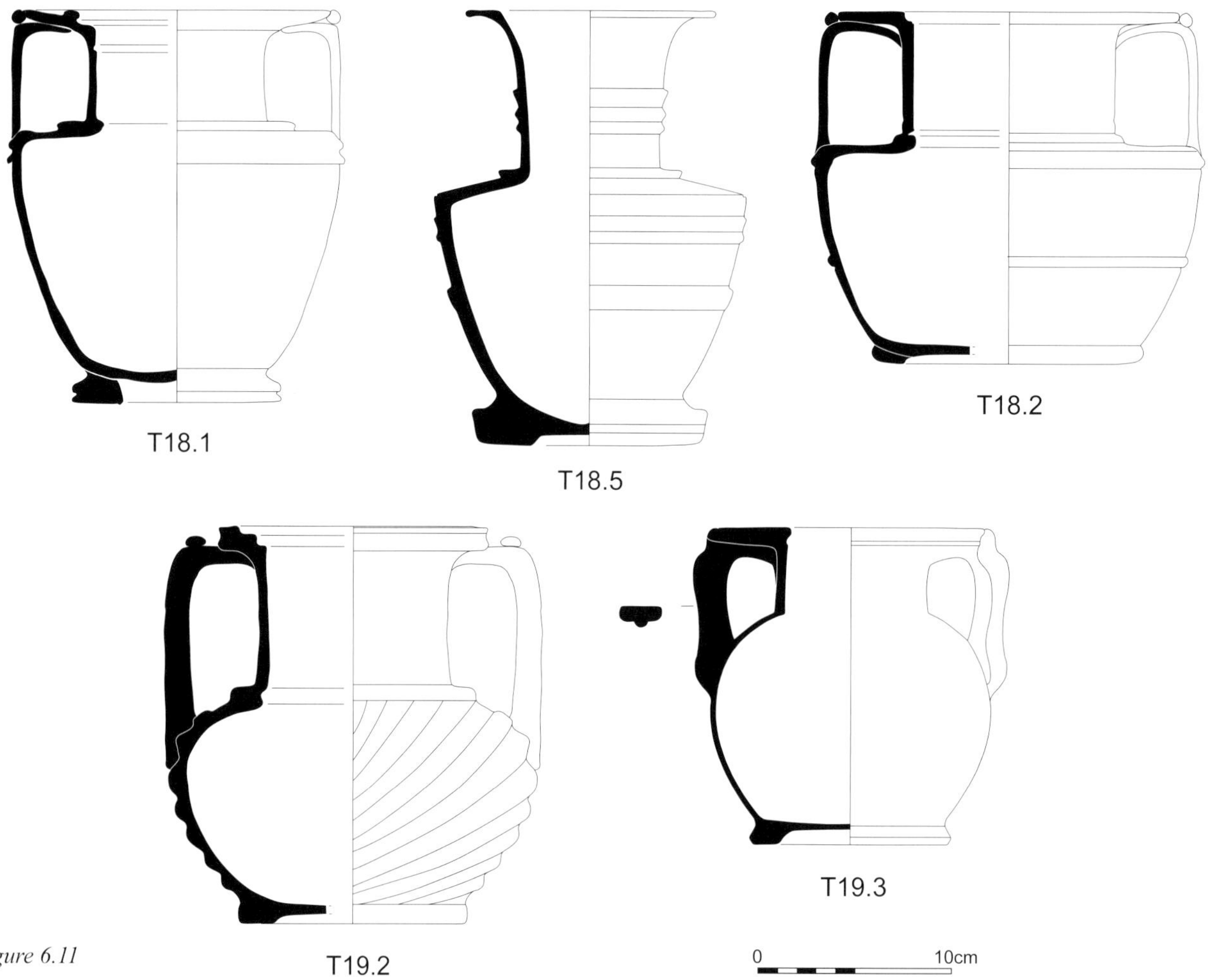

Figure 6.11

T18: Restricted vases with flat shoulders, truncated cone body and appliqué decoration

T18.1: Amphora with wide flat rim, cylindrical neck, flat shoulder and truncated cone body, strap handles (Louvre, DAE, E 22585, Nenna and Seif el-Din 2000, fig. 14 and Kaczmarczyk, and Nenna, forthcoming).
Purple exterior glaze, turquoise interior glaze, yellow or blue glaze for the decoration
Decoration of small appliqué leaves
1st-2nd Century A.D.

T18.2: Vase with flared lip, trumpet neck, flat shoulder and truncated cone body (Brooklyn 70.93.1, Nenna and Seif el-Din 2000, fig. 14).
Purple exterior glaze, turquoise interior glaze, yellow or blue glaze for the decoration
Decoration on the neck of appliqués of Aphrodite Anadyomene or of snakes / decoration on the shoulder and body of small appliqué leaves
1st-2nd Century A.D.

T18.3: Vase with cylindrical neck, flat shoulder and truncated cone body (not illustrated)
Turquoise exterior and interior glaze, yellow-green glaze for decoration
Decoration of appliqué leaves covering the body
1st-2nd Century A.D.

T18.4: Amphora with strap handles or vase with trumpet neck, flat shoulders and truncated cone body (not illustrated)
Light blue glaze
Decoration of appliqué leaves
1st-2nd Century A.D.

T18.5: Amphora with flat rim, flat shoulders, Truncated cone body, strap handles (Louvre, DAE, E 22581, Kaczmarczyk and Nenna, forthcoming)
Light blue glaze
Decoration of appliqué leaves where neck joins the body, nelumbo calyxes on the body
1st-2nd Century A.D.

T19: Amphorae with wide flat rim, cylindrical neck, spherical body and coiled handles

T19.1: (not illustrated)
Light blue glaze
Undecorated
1st-2nd Century A.D.

T19.2: (Louvre, DAE, E 11260 Kaczmarczyk, Nenna, in this volume)
Light blue interior and exterior glaze / purple exterior, blue interior glaze
Decoration of vertical or oblique spirals
1st-2nd Century A.D.

T19.3: (Hildesheim, 5155, Nenna and Seif el-Din 2000, fig. 14)
Light and dark blue glaze
Saw teeth or cabled moulding on the rim, on the body, rinceau of ivy and berries, cabling or waves, calyx of nelumbo leaves on a diamond background, an appliqué of a child's or woman's head at the base of the handles
1st-2nd Century A.D.

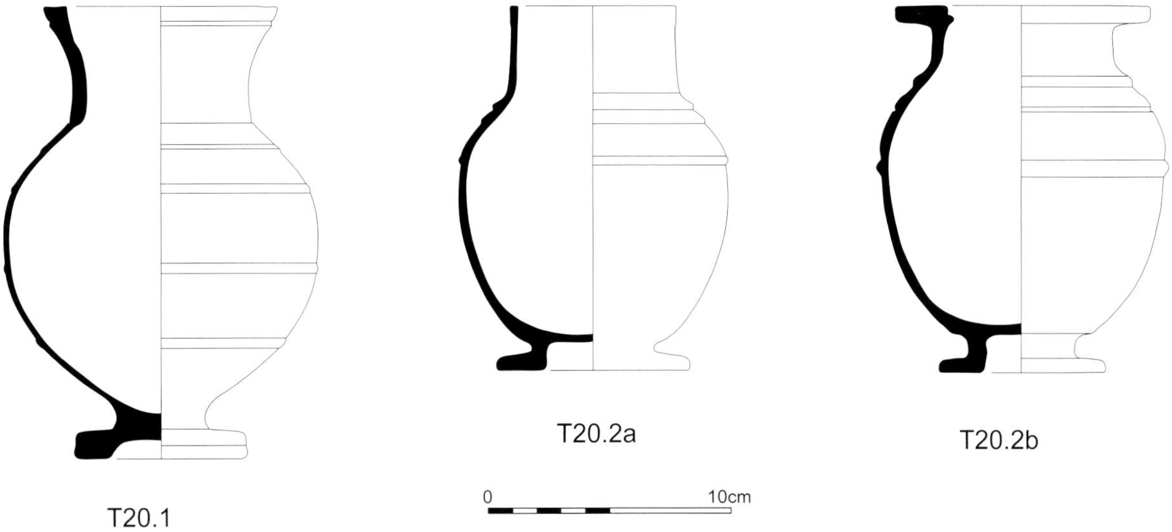

Figure 6.12

T20: **Restricted vases with ovoid body and high relief decoration**

T20.1: *Restricted vase with trumpet neck, ovoid body and added base (GRM, seized from Tzakos, Nenna and Seif el-Din 2000, n° 542)*
Blue / yellow to green glaze
Decoration in bands one above the other
1st-2nd Century A.D.

T20.2a: *Restricted vase with high cylindrical neck, ovoid body and added base (British Museum, EA62640, Nenna, Seif el-Din 2000, fig. 15)*
Light and dark blue glaze
Undecorated / decoration of nelumbo calyx
1st-2nd Century A.D.

T20.2b: *Restricted vase with wide flat rim, high cylindrical neck, ovoid body and added base (British Museum, EA 29352, Nenna and Seif el-Din 2000, fig. 15)*
Light and dark blue glaze
Decoration of nelumbo calyx
1st-2nd Century A.D.

T21: ***Rare forms of pitchers or restricted vases with conial or biconical body; plastic vases (not illustrated)***

Note: Painted decorations of the same inspiration set in bands appear on a series of painted vases of similar form discovered in the tombs of Antinoopolis, which have recently been the object of a detailed study. In the tomb of the "Prophetess", four vases close in form to T20 vases display a decoration set in bands above each other composed of garlands of ribbons and/or lattice patterns on the upper part of the body, friezes of birds and garlands or rows of diamonds on the mid section, and an egg and dart frieze below.[1] *In the tomb of the "Dionysian", two table amphorae present similar decoration.*[2] *The fact that in the two cases, these ceramic vases were associated with glass unguentaria of the 2nd-3rd centuries would suggest that they should be dated at the latest to the 3rd Century.* [3]

Notes

1. Ballet and Poludnikiewicz 2012; Dixneuf in press, nos. 25-28.
2. Dixneuf in press, nos. 22-23.
3. Since these notes were prepared a newly discovered burial from Antinopolis has shown that these vases should be dated to the 2nd Centrury.

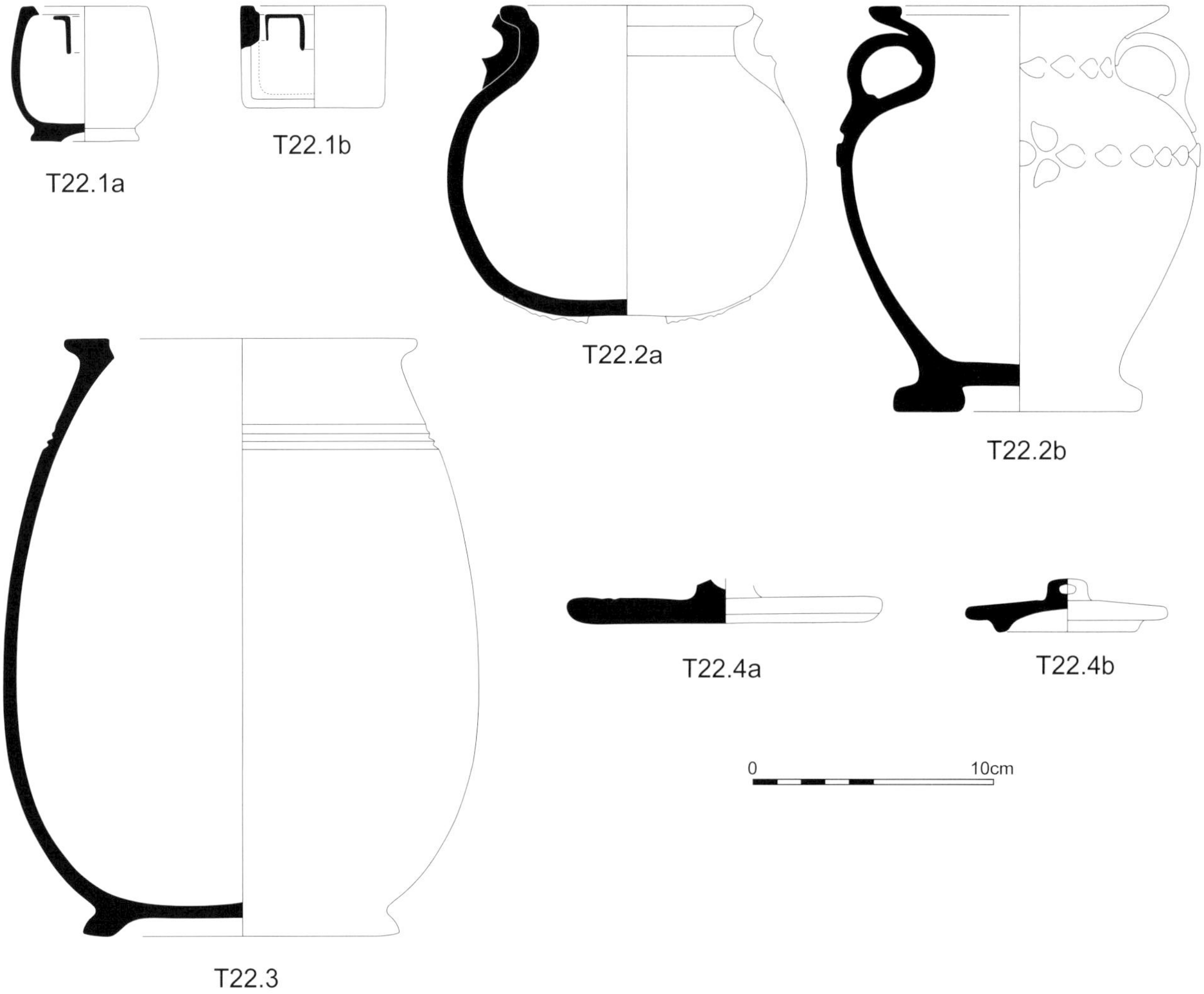

Figure 6.13

T22: Vases-containers

T22.1a: Inkwell with ovoid body (British Museum, EA 22015, Nenna and Seif el-Din 2000, fig. 15)
Light blue glaze
Undecorated
1st-2nd Century A.D.

T22.1b: Inkwell with cylindrical body (Louvre, DAE, E 22599, Nenna and Seif el-Din 2000, fig. 15)
Light blue glaze
Undecorated
1st-2nd Century A.D.

T22.2a: Spherical pot with two circular handles (British Museum, EA 37412, Hoffmann and Taggart 2010:. 427, fig. 8.2)
Light blue glaze
Undecorated
1st-2nd Century A.D.

T22.2b: Ovoid pot with flared lip, short neck, added base and two handles (Medinet Maadi, Silvano 2005, fig. 4b)
Purple exterior glaze, blue interior glaze, yellow-green for decoration
Decoration of appliqué leaves.
1st-2nd Century A.D.

T22.3: Large ovoid pot with flat rim and added base (British Museum, EA 22638, Nenna and Seif el-Din 2000, fig. 15)
Light blue glaze
Undecorated
1st-2nd Century A.D.

T22.4: Lids

T22.4a: with flat underside (Tebtunis, 3201.24, Nenna forthcoming b)
Light blue glaze
Undecorated
Hellenistic and Imperial period

T22.4b: with protrusion on underside (Tebtunis, 7905.43, Nenna, forthcoming b)
Light blue / green-yellow glaze
Undecorated
Hellenistic and Imperial period

Table 6.1. Faience from trench HAC1.

Area, Trench, Unit	Total number	Forms/glaze identified	Number of wasters	Amulets, beads and figurines	Furniture
HAC2000 Trench 1 Unit 1	69 sherds	1 Late Period 1 Ptolemaic 21 Early Roman	18	3	0
HAC2000 Trench 1 Unit 2	2 sherds	0	0	2	0
HAC2000 Trench 1 Unit 5	16 sherds	3 Early Roman	3	0	0
HAC2000 Trench 1 Unit 6	8 sherds	2 Early Roman	4	1	0
HAC2000 Trench 1 Unit 7	1 sherd	0	0	1	0
HAC2000 Trench 1 Unit 9	5 sherds	1 Late Period 1 Ptolemaic or Early Roman	0	3	0
HAC2000 Trench 1 CB	3 sherds	3 Early Roman	0	0	0
TOTAL	104 sherds				

Table 6.2. Faience from trench HAC2.

Area, Trench, Unit	Total number	Forms/glazes identified	Wasters	Amulets, beads and figurines	Furniture
HAC2000 Trench 2 Unit 10	214 sherds	11 Ptolemaic 45 Early Roman	53	1	2
HAC2000 Trench 2 Unit 11	35 sherds	11 Early Roman	6	0	0
HAC2000 Trench 2 CT	37 sherds	5 Ptolemaic 4 Early Roman	6	1	0
HAC2000 Trench 2 CB	1 sherd	0	1	0	0
TOTAL	287 sherds				

figurines. In order to establish the range of vessel forms and objects produced in this area, unfinished (i.e. unglazed) pieces, waste material in which identifiable vessels are stuck together, or are stuck to ceramic from saggars, have been taken into account in calculating the number of sherds. The low quality of the glaze has not been considered as a criterion since glaze quality seems to be a poor indicator, as indicated by the vessels found in consumption sites such as Tebtunis, with bubbly, decolorized red or even black glaze.

Amulets and beads

- Of the 17 amulets, 10 come from HAC1, one from HAC2 and six from HAC3. Most of them present conventional representations of Egyptian gods or symbols:

- Top of a papyrus sceptre (F-17, HAC1, unit 1)
  Papyrus column (F-16, HAC1, unit 6 ; F-26, HAC1, unit 7; F-32, HAC1, unit 2)

- Wedjet-eye (F-02201, HAC2, unit CT) (Anthes, 1965, no.338, pl. 47e)

- Anubis standing with jackal head and back pillar (F-18, HAC1, unit 2, F-19, HAC1, unit 9).

- Isis lactans with back pillar (F-21, HAC1, unit 9 ; F-1518, HAC3, unit 65, F-1791, HAC3, unit 189) (Anthes, 1959, no.263, pl. 35a)
  Ptah seated with back pillar (F-2186, HAC3, unit 189).

- Thoth standing with back pillar (F-1852, HAC3, unit 189) (Anthes, 1959, no.256, pl. 35b)

Except for the two Anubis amulets, which when complete would have had a height of 6 to 7cm, the other deities are of a smaller size and would have not have stood more than 3-4cm high.

Three of the amulets are of 'bead size' (height 1cm). The Bes bead with back pierced for suspension is very common (F-1486, HAC3, unit 65) in Ptolemaic and Roman contexts.[5] The recumbent lion, known since the Late Period, (F-17, HAC1, unit 9) is also known from several parallels (Petrie 1914, pl. 38, no.219h; Reisner 1907, no.12346-12359; Gabolde 1988, no.172; Schlick-Nolte and Droste von Hülstoff 1990, no.285-286 ; Constandelou 2004: 96, fig. 4) dated from the Late Period to the Ptolemaic Period. The griffin bead (F-01900, HAC3, unit 231) is more rare.

None of these amulets, except the Thoth-ibis, bears any trace of misfiring. The Thoth example is intriguing on account of the reddish colour of its glaze and it could well

Table 6.3. Faience from trench HAC3.

Area, Trench, Unit	Total number	Forms/glaze identified	Wasters	Amulets, beads and figurines	Furniture
HAC2001 Trench 3 Unit 33	161 sherds	15 Ptolemaic 18 Early Roman	8	1	1
HAC2001 Trench 3 Unit 34	1 sherd	1 Early Roman	0	0	0
HAC2001 Trench 3 Unit 36	549 sherds	26 Ptolemaic 45 Early Roman	19	2	0
HAC2001 Trench 3 Unit 37	73 sherds	22 Ptolemaic 2 Early Roman	3	0	0
HAC2001 Trench 3 Unit 38	18 sherds	2 Early Roman	0	0	0
HAC2001 Trench 3 Unit 39	88 sherds	9 Ptolemaic 16 Early Roman	3	0	0
HAC2001 Trench 3 Unit 44	6 sherds	0	3	0	0
HAC2001 Trench 3 Unit 48	4 sherds	1 Ptolemaic	0	0	0
HAC2001 Trench 3 Unit 50	42 sherds	1 Early Roman	18	1	0
HAC2001 Trench 3 Unit 51	19 sherds	0	1	1	0
HAC2001 Trench 3 Unit 52	16 sherds	4 Early Roman	2	1	0
HAC2001 Trench 3 Unit 53	3 sherds	0	2	0	0
HAC2001 Trench 3 Unit 56	9 sherds	2 Early Roman	4	1	0
HAC2001 Trench 3 Unit 60	1 sherd	0	0	0	0
HAC2002 Trench 3 Unit 65	11 sherds	1 Early Roman ?	0	2	0
HAC2002 Trench 3 Unit 66	16 sherds	3 Early Roman	2	0	0
HAC2002 Trench 3 Unit 68	2 sherds	0	0	0	0
HAC2002 Trench 3 Unit 70	1 sherd	0	0	0	0
HAC2002 Trench 3 Unit 74	127 sherds	4 Ptolemaic 17 Early Roman	16	1	0
HAC2002 Trench 3 Unit 75	2 sherds	0	0	0	0
HAC2002 Trench 3 Unit 76	10 sherds	0	0	0	0
HAC2002 Trench 3 Unit 77	2 sherds	1 Early Roman	1	0	0
HAC2002 Trench 3 Unit 80	1 sherd	0	1	0	0
HAC2002 Trench 3 Unit 184	1 sherd	0	1	0	0
HAC2002 Trench 3 Unit 188	10 sherds	3 Ptolemaic 1 Early Roman	0	0	0
HAC2002 Trench 3 Unit 189	277 sherds	5 Ptolemaic 38 Early Roman	7	4	0
HAC2002 Trench 3 Unit 193	2 sherds	0	0	0	0
HAC2002 Trench 3 Unit 204	2 sherds	1 Ptolemaic	0	0	0
HAC2002 Trench 3 Unit 207	9 sherds	3 Early Roman	0	0	0
HAC2002 Trench 3 Unit 208	2 sherds	0	2	0	0
HAC2002 Trench 3 Unit 209	1 sherd	0	1	0	0
HAC2002 Trench 3 Unit 215	13 sherds	0	0	0	0
HAC2002 Trench 3 Unit 218	2 sherds	0	0	0	0
HAC2002 Trench 3 Unit 231	93 sherds	1 Early Roman	0	1	0
HAC2002 Trench 3 Unit 232	1 sherd	1 Early Roman	0	0	0
HAC2002 Trench 3 Unit 233	35 sherds	0	0	0	0
HAC2002 Trench 3 Unit 234	6 sherds	0	0	0	0
HAC2002 Trench 3 Unit 238	28 sherds	2 Early Roman	3	0	0
HAC2002 Trench 3 Unit 244	9 sherds	1 Early Roman	0	0	0

Area, Trench, Unit	Total number	Forms/glaze identified	Wasters	Amulets, beads and figurines	Furniture
HAC2005 Trench 3 Unit 300	314 sherds	4 Ptolemaic 19 Early Roman	4	0	0
HAC2005 Trench 3 Unit 301	114 sherds	2 Ptolemaic 23 Early Roman	2	0	1
HAC2005 Trench 3 Unit 303	120 sherds	1 Ptolemaic 4 Early Roman	1	0	0
HAC2005 Trench 3 Unit 305	4 sherds	0	0	0	0
HAC2005 Trench 3 Unit 306	325 sherds	2 Ptolemaic 20 Early Roman	4	1	1
HAC2005 Trench 3 Unit 307	56 sherds	4 Early Roman	0	1	0
HAC2005 Trench 3 Unit 308	271 sherds	4 Ptolemaic 64 Early Roman	3	0	0
HAC2005 Trench 3 Unit 309	100 sherds	1 Ptolemaic 7 Early Roman	0	0	0
HAC2005 Trench 3 Unit 311	3 sherds	1 Early Roman	0	0	0
TOTAL	2960 sherds				

be a defective piece. But without any mould or substantial traces of other amulets from the vicinity, it is unlikely that this zone of Kom Helul produced the amulets.

Amongst the beads, one belongs to the very common miniature cylindrical type (F-1022, HAC3, unit 36) and one to the plain spherical type (F-1386, HAC3, unit 52). The two others are less frequent: the oval flat bead with indented edge (F-435, HAC3, unit 33) and the cylindrical bead with six rows of crenellations (F-1941, HAC3, unit 189) which finds parallels in Memphis,[6] as well as in Buto.[7]

For the amulets and the beads, it is difficult to be categorical on their chronology, as the types they include are produced throughout the Late Period and into the Graeco-Roman period. Most of them come from HAC1 (no F-11, F16-19, 21-22, 26, 32, 135), one is from HAC2 (F-2201). From HAC3, most of the pieces are not easily datable (F-1486, F-1518, F-1791, F-1826, F-1900), but the Thoth-ibis amulet (F-1852) has a reddish glaze which could indicate that it is a misfired piece.

Figurines

Only seven fragments of large figurines are attested and none is deformed or adhering to a saggar. Not all of them are easy to ascribe to known representations. They are usually made with two techniques (hollow and solid moulding), although a third technique, involving a perishable core is also attested. A fourth technique (involving only one mould) is also common for relatively small figurines with a flat back and is attested at HAC 3 by mould number Y-6.

The solid figurines are widely distributed in Early Roman Egypt. The most common representation is that of Harpocrates, as a crouching child without attributes (Nenna 2005a: 60; Kazmarczyk and Nenna forthcoming, no. E 22384, as well as four unpublished examples in the GRM collection) or holding a cornucopia (Petrie 1911b GRM 5502 and Petrie Museum UC 8796, see below), a duck (Nenna and Seif el-Din 1994: 295, fig. 2a and GRM 16256 unpublished; Kazmarczyk and Nenna forthcoming a, no. AF 10099), a basket (Nenna and Seif el-Din 1994: 295 fig. 2b and GRM FA.96 unpublished; Müller 1964, no. A165; Kazmarczyk and Nenna forthcoming, no. E 10952), a closed vase (3 unpublished examples in the GRM) or a lotus (Quibell 1907: pl. XXXV, 2-3).[8] Less frequent is, Harpocrates on a duck (Nenna and Seif el-Din 1994: 295, fig. 2c). To the same technical group belong Aphrodite Anadyomene kneeling (Adriani 1945: p. 41, pl. Xc; Schmidt 1997: no.187), Baubô (Nenna and Seif el-Din: 1994: 301, 297, fig. 3a), Bes (Nenna and Seif el-Din 1994: 299, pl. I,3-4), as well as representations of Horus-falcon (Musée de Marseilles, 1997, no.108), dogs (Petrie 1885: 43, pl. in frontispice nos. 3-4; Wallis 1898: fig. 139; Messiha and Elhitta 1979, no. 209, pl. XVII; Musée de Marseilles, 1997, no.109; Scheunert 1999, no. 242; Lunsingh Scheurleer 2002, fig. 20), horses,[9] dromedaries (Nenna and Seif el-Din 1994: 312, pl. IV,2; Nauerth 1996: 75, no. HD 1385, fig. 95 ; Ashton 2003, UC 40912 ; Louvre, Département des Antiquités égytiennes,[10] AF 10099). Remains connected to the production of this kind of solid figurine seem to have been found at Memphis, as shown by at least one misfired example kept in Petrie Museum (Harpocrates holding a cornucopia: UC 8796 see Ashton 2003: 46),[11] but their abundance in the Fayoum, as well as the analysis of one piece of the Louvre showing a different composition of the glaze (Kaczmarczyk and Nenna forthcoming, no. E 22384) points to the existence of other workshops.[12] To this technique, should be ascribed three fragments of figurines found during the excavations. F-2191 (HAC 3, unit 307) must be understood as part of the middle of the body of a standing Bes (thighs and left hand). F-1348 (HAC3, unit 51) could tentatively be identified as the left arm (the upper part was attached to the body, the lower part free) of a Bes statuette. F-2046 (HAC3, unit 306) is more tantalizing : at first sight it could be considered as the folds of the lower part of a woman's dress, but this type of iconography is not present in the faience figurines of the Early Roman period, and it should perhaps be seen as the paw of an animal.

In Memphis, the discards of hollow figurines are more numerous and this technique could well have been a speciality of the site and an invention of the Early Roman period. The most common type is the recumbent sphinx with the *nemes*. Numerous defective examples were found during Petrie's 1908 campaign and are today, at least in part, kept in United Kingdom museums.[13] Figurines of sphinxes are known in funerary contexts from Alexandria and Saqqara as well as in domestic contexts at Hermonthis.[14] Other types of hollow figurines are known such as rams,[15] lions (Dressel 1882, no.s 15 = Di Gioia 2006: 128-129, no. 10 from Pompei), griffins (Riefstahl 1968: 113, no.91; Gallois 1928: 11, fig. 7 = Lunsingh Scheurleer 2002, fig. 21), elephants,[16] crocodiles (Wallis 1898: 53, fig. 114; Nenna 2005c: 189, fig. 506, fig. 507 = Kaczmarczyk and Nenna forthcoming; Di Gioia 2006: 124-125, nos. 8.1-8.2 from Pompei), crocodiles with falcon head (Di Gioia 2006: 127-128, no. 10), frogs (Di Gioia 2006: 125-127, nos. 9.1-9.4) and canines (Wallis 1898: 63, fig. 140 = Grimm 1975, no a. 74, pl. 114). All these are supported by a rectangular or quadrangular base, manufactured separately from the figure. The object F-01305 (HAC3, unit 50) is tantalizing: it cannot be the back of the head of a sphinx with part of the *nemes*, because it is too spherical and lacks the ridges which can be observed on the faience sphinx from Saqqara (JE44228, Grimm 1972: 91-93, fig. 47-49); it could belong to the back of a head of a canine.

There are also deities that can reach 50cm in height as, for example, a large standing Anubis (now in the Cairo Museum and to the knowledge of the author unpublished), four representations of Ptah found in Pompeii (Dressel 1882: 24-26, no.17-19; Di Gioia 2006: 110-114, nos 4.1-4.4), as well as five Bes statuettes and one of a Thoth in the form of a baboon (Dressel 1882, p. 27-28, no. 20; Di Gioia 2006: 115-118, nos 6.1-6.6). The fragment of Serapis head (F-1616 HAC trench 3, unit 74) belongs to such a large figurine. It has a good parallel in a piece also unearthed in Memphis and now in the Petrie Museum (Ashton 2003: 46).[17] Nevertheless since they are only of *approximately* the same dimensions they cannot come from the same mould. Of the same excellent quality is a head of Herakles now in the Victoria and Albert Museum (Charleston 1955: 29, pl. 43B, C. 486.1891), as well as a head of Dionysos in the GRM of Alexandria (Nenna and Seif el-Din 1994: 303, pl. II,3). Parts of figurines of Isis and Isis-Aphrodite are also known (Grimm 1990 : 36, pl. XV ; Scheunert 1999, nos. 236-238).

The technique of building and moulding the figurines around a perishable core is attested by a fragmentary standing statuette of Aphrodite Anadyomene now in the Louvre (Kaczmarczyk and Nenna forthcoming, AF 10095) it is not yet well known. A new analysis of the series of Aphrodite Anadyomene standing on a flat circular base (Nenna and Seif el-Din 1994: 301-303, footnote 43, pl. II,1-2 and fig. 6b ; see also Davoli 2001: 102, fig. 93, Ashton 2003: 46 UC 33540) of which a good number come from Terenouthis should be undertaken, as well as of the standing Harpocrates, also on a flat circular base, nude or wearing a long tunic and leaning on a column (Nenna and Seif el-Din 1994: 295, pl. I,1-2 ; Musée de Marseilles, 1997, no.236; Nenna 2005c: 188, fig. 505). Several moulds discovered during a survey indicate that at least Aphrodite Anadyomene figurines were produced at this spot (Nenna and Seif el-Din 1999).

Furniture

There is one example of a cylindrical faience drum belonging to a column of a naos (F-1459), though it is a surface find. This type of object is well known in faience, as well as in glass and in gilded wood. It was fitted on a square bronze rod to constitute a column, often of two colours or materials. The top of the column was a palm or a Corinthian capital.[18] In Egypt, numerous examples were found in Tanis,[19] in Tebtunis,[20] as well as in Edfu in a foundation deposit.[21] Numerous examples exist in the Egyptian Museum Cairo as well as a complete column with glass and gilded wood drums.[22] Other examples are known from the Hadra Necropolis in Alexandria and from Kom el-Wist.[23] Outside Egypt, their presence is attested on the island of Delos, connected to one of the sanctuaries for Egyptian gods.[24]

Two fragments with perpendicular walls, one decorated with egg and dart motif (F-2036, trench 3, unit 306), the other with lotus buds (F-600, trench 3, unit 33) are reminiscent of rectangular or square boxes which are known in the Ptolemaic period. The rectangular boxes in the Louvre (Nenna 2005b: 172, fig. 147)[25] and in the Egyptian Museum Cairo[26] show a decor divided in two zones with egg and dart and a file of griffins, other fragments indicate a combination of waves and griffins or rosettes and griffins, or vegetal motifs (Nenna and Seif el-Din 2000, no. 323).[27] The square box from Musawarat es-Sufra (Hembold 2001) has various lively motifs (ducks between lotus, griffin between palmettes, human figures) occurring between the same decorative motifs: waves, row of dot, rosettes, and rope.

The production of lamps with triangular handle decorated with a palmette and the nozzle flanked by volutes is well attested in Memphis by finds from Petrie's 1911 campaign (Petrie 1911a: 36, pl. XIV; Ashton 2003: 54). Two fragments were found during the 2000-2005 excavations (F-139 HAC 2, unit 10 and F-2186, HAC 3, unit 301). The second one, part of one of the volutes near to the nozzle, is probably a defective piece, as it bears some hard brown concretions. Imitating Italian lamps dating to 1st Century B.C.– 1st

Century A.D., they must have been a quite rare production, as virtually all surviving examples come from Memphis.[28]

Vessels

The objects at our disposal are not part of a misfired load from the kiln, but belong to the filling of the kiln which took place during the 2nd Century, and to layers from the surroundings of the workshop. The difficulty of the study is thus to detect what objects are residual and what objects could have been produced in the kiln or in its vicinity if we suppose that the fillings of the kiln are not coming from very far away.

Late Period sherds

Only two fragments of vessels belong to the Late Period : the rim and neck of New Year flask (for new discoveries, see Yamani 2002, and Nenna 2007b, fig. 36.1) (F-20, HAC1, unit 9) and a body fragment with characteristic blue ware with no difference between the core and the cover (F-33, HAC1, unit 1).

Early and Middle Ptolemaic period sherds

One decorated fragment certainly dates to the Ptolemaic period : a rim fragment of a deep bowl (T2.3F) with external decoration in zones (F-534, HAC3, unit 37), typical of the 3rd Century B.C.

Also possibly of Ptolemaic date are a small number of body fragments with deep "ultramarine blue" glaze, which all come from HAC2, unit 10 (F-84 , F-251, F-312, F-335). One piece coming from the same unit is a waster composed of four rims of plates T6.1a stuck together (F-141) of this colour.

Gray blue, "lavender blue", glaze is attested by rims belonging to shallow convex cups (T3.1: HAC2, unit 10, F-75, HAC3, unit 36, F-1035 and F-1071, and unit 74, F-1875), as well as by body fragments coming from HAC2, unit 10 and CT, HAC3, unit 33, 39 and 189. This hue of blue seems mainly Ptolemaic, if we look at the finds contexts in Tebtunis.

There is only one body fragment of marbled faience (F-402, HAC3, unit 33), which was widely distributed in the Ptolemaic period.

Bichrome ware is attested by one fragment with the external wall ultramarine blue, and the internal wall apple green (F-1854, HAC3, unit 204). It belongs to a deep hemispherical bowl (T2.3a), which is dated in Tebtunis to the third-2nd Century B.C.

There are a discrete number of sherds which present an apple–green glaze (112 fragments, MNI 23),[29] which is typical of the early Ptolemaic period. More than half come from three units (HAC3, units 33, 36 and 37) and only three of them could be qualified as wasters, in particular F-1023, waster of a T6.1a plate. They are divided between:

— deep ovoid bowls with thin rim (T2.3a: F-439),
— shallow cups with in-turned rim (T3.1a: F-442, F-614, F-630, F-1027-28, F-1162, F-2111),
— plates with a flat rim protruding into the interior of the vase, oblique walls and annular base (T6.1a: F-158, F-697, F-827, F-1023, F-1036, F-1038, F-1047 and F-104, F-2014-2015),
— truncated conical goblets (T6.4: F-601),
— small *lagynos* (T11.2: F-772)
— as well as huge trays (T14.4: F-57, F-88, F-338, F-398;
— and HAC3, 2005, sherds in ID site finds 0002-F and 0035-F).

If the first forms are well attested in the Early Ptolemaic period, the huge trays are not easy to date. Some appear in Ptolemaic contexts, in Maresha (unpublished study by N. Sidi) and Samaria (Reisner 1924: 327, no.18, fig. 202, 18e) in Israel, while in Egypt, some were noted during the survey in Terenouthis (Nenna and Seif el-Din 1999, fig. 18), in an environment which seems to date to the Early Roman period. In Memphis, two sherds were found, one with apple green glaze, the other one with white, blue and violet glaze (Nenna and Seif el-Din, 2000 : 332, and 61, fig. 13).[30] It could be that, as for the plates T6.1a, these trays were produced during a long span of time, maybe till the 1st Century A.D. (see below).

Only one fragment could be assigned to a plate T6.1b with wide flat rim and convex body (HAC2, unit 10, F-62). Open vases with flat moulded rim and concave walls (T6.2a) are not a widely distributed form and it is difficult to be precise on their chronology. In Tebtunis, only three sherds were found, all in poorly dated contexts, but the deep blue colour of the glaze of one of them could suggest a Ptolemaic production. One sherd with decayed turquoise blue glaze was found in the 2000-2005 excavations (HAC3, unit 52, F-1385).

The flat bottomed truncated conical goblet (T6.4) was produced from the Late period and throughout the Ptolemaic period, as attested by the Tebtunis finds. Eight sherds have been found (HAC1, unit 5, F-114, HAC2, unit 10, F-76, HAC3, unit 36, F-685 and F-712, unit 37, F-601, unit 301, F-2185, unit 306, F-2038 and F-2053) as well as two wasters in HAC3, unit 300 (F-2145-2146).

Ovoid pots with two or three square or circular handles (T11.1) are attested by two handle sherds (HAC3, unit 33, F-1437; unit 36, F-710). This form originated in the Late Period and is attested in Tebtunis during all the Ptolemaic Period (Nenna and Seif el-Din 2000 : 395-396).

Small closed vases (*lagynos* type) are attested by sherds belonging to the neck or to the rim; the variety of their forms is not yet well known. In the 2000-2005 excavations, a turquoise blue glazed *lagynos* with cylindrical neck and rim was discovered (HAC3, unit 189, F-1714), attested in Tebtunis in Ptolemaic contexts (*cf.* above another one in apple green glaze), and another type with a funnel rim (HAC3, unit 300, F-2133) known in Tebtunis in second-1st Century B.C. contexts.

As well as apple green glaze and lavender glazes, the use of white, light blue and turquoise blue glaze is attested on the shallow convex cups (T3.1). Their abundance (34 sherds) is intriguing since they are a typical Ptolemaic ceramic form. There is no waster which can be connected with them, so we cannot be sure that they were still produced in this area in the Early Roman Period, but that could be possible as they are quite numerous in respect to the other types and as some of them have the same quality of turquoise blue glaze as have the plates, bowls and trays known from the workshop.

Late Ptolemaic sherds

The distinction between Early Ptolemaic and Late Ptolemaic sherds is not easy to make, as some of the plain glazed forms appearing in the Early Ptolemaic period are still produced in the 1st Century B.C. The colour of the glazes can help in some instances. The use of white glaze and its combination with violet or blue, or even green, go with the less pronounced relief of the decor, or even the absence of relief. The shallow (T1.4) and deep hemispherical (T2.3F) bowls, as well as small cups with wide rims (T3.4) showing these characteristics seems to appear in the 2nd Century B.C. and are widespread in the 1st Century B.C

On T6.1a plates, the white and violet glazes are used to provide a very low relief decor of which the composition remains unknown to us due to the small size of the fragments. It was probably combining violet line(s) near the rim with other motifs as a row of triangles and perhaps a central rosette, in some cases a garland of ivy could be used. Of the 20 fragments, 5 come from HAC2, unit 10 (F-146-147) and unit 11 (F-146-147; CT: F-110) and 14 from HAC3, unit 36 (F-731, F-747, F-1046), unit 231 (F-1905), unit 301 (F-2042, F-2188, F-2190), unit 306 (F-2097), unit 308 (F-2033, F-2064, F-2070, F-2096, F-2105, F-2109). One waster is also attested: F-142 (HAC2, unit 10), white and violet glaze plate stuck on a saggar. Petrie reports such a use of glaze on plates found in the excavation of 1910 (Petrie 1911a, pl. XVII,124-134, 139-144). To the same decorated group should be assigned a bottom fragment showing a large white rosette emerging from a deep blue background (F-117, HAC2, unit 10).

The 2005 excavations (units 300, 301, 306, 308) have brought to light a series of fragments which could attest the production in the vicinity of HAC3 of a transitional form of closed vase T7.4, which must be put between the Ptolemaic vases with a short cylindrical neck, ovoid body and a small annular base (T7.2) and the imperial vase (T20.1). They share with the first, the short cylindrical neck, the thin walls and the low relief decor and with the second the form of the vase with spherical body and high foot and the choice of the decorative repertoire (animals running in vegetation). The connection between the neck and the body is marked by a small projection. Morphologically, they are very near to painted vases recently studied by Bailey (2011), interpreted as drinking-goblets and dated, following the contexts in Alexandria and Athribis, between the 2nd Century B.C. and the 1st Century A.D. They all have a low cylindrical neck, decorated with two waves. Mainly, they are characterized by the use of a motif of rosettes and lotus bundles, which is peculiar to this form. The lotus bundle is already known in the Early Ptolemaic period, but is used alone on Achaemenid forms or as a filling motif when, in a freize of rosettes, there is not enough room to fit in only entire rosettes (Nenna and Seif el-Din 2000 : 71, fig. 17.6). In the Late Ptolemaic period, this motif is combined with rosettes of a special kind with eight petals. To the kind with light blue glaze, belong F-2124, F-2158, F-2184, F-2199, and sherd in ID site find 0155-F. A number of fragments show the use of white glaze combined with violet glaze: F-2039, F-2171, F-2087, F-2100, F-2174+F-2176, F-2177, F-2197, and sherds in ID site finds 002-F, 0104-F, 0140-F. Others bear a kind of glaze very similar to the one seen on T20.1 vases: F-2090, F-2194, F-2195, and sherd in ID site find 0140-F. Such fragments already appear in Petrie's report (Petrie 1911a, pl. XIV, 33-35) though in small numbers. Few complete vases are known; two with a high foot kept in the Louvre (Grimm 1972, fig. 25-27, Musée de Marseilles 1997, no128 ; Nenna 2005c: 172, fig. 446),[31] show on the neck a double wave, on the spherical body egg and dart, lotus bundles and rosettes, animals, *calyx* of plain *nelumbo* leaves on a diamond pattern. A third one in the Metropolitan Museum of Art (MET 26.7.1013, Grimm 1972: 83, fig. 22-24), seemingly without a foot, keep the frieze of rosettes, but has already acquired the typical decor of the vases of the Imperial period T20.1. Fragments are also known from Tebtunis, one in a 1st Century B.C. level, the other is from disturbed contexts (Nenna, forthcoming b) and one sample is now in the Hildesheim Museum (see www2. no. 4753).

The Early Roman decorated vessels

Three main techniques were used for the decoration of vases in the Early Roman period, moulding, incising and applying. There are no sherds from the 2000-2005 excavations, or those of 1908 and 1911 which testifies the production of ware with applied decoration.[32] Such wares mainly comprise vases (amphorae [T18.1], trumpet-neck vases [T18.2 and T18.3], ovoid jars [T22.2]) and flat rim bowls [T12.6] with violet or deep green glaze and applied green or small blue leaves in simple rows, lotus buds or vertical plants, or covering all the body, and more seldom turquoise blue glazed vases with decor of leaves of the same colour (T18.4 and 5). Most of these vases come from Alexandria, Fayum and Middle Egypt, and the rare fragments discovered in Memphis (UC40913) and in Saqqara should be considered as imports.[33] The analysis done by Kaczmarczyk shows that the composition of the violet, turquoise blue and yellow-green glazes of these vases does not fall within the glazes of similar colours produced in Memphis (Kaczmarczyk and Nenna forthcoming).

On the contrary, however, there is ample attestation of the production in Memphis of spherical bodied amphorae, with an incised decor consisting of triangles on the flat rim, and an ivy garland and a *calyx* of plain *nelumbo* leaves merging from a diamond pattern, separated by a row of squares on the body (T19.3) (Petrie 1911a, pl. 15, 73-81).[34] These are not very numerous amongst the finds of the 2000-2005 excavations (only 12 fragments) and are scattered between the different trenches (HAC1: F-92-93, HAC2: F-79, HAC3: F-406, F-411, F-696, F-1373, F-1793, F-1944, F-2125, and sherd SF: F-537). One could suppose that they were not produced in this part of Kom Helul.

This seems true also for the most widespread types of open and closed vases with moulded decoration in deep relief (T16.1 and T20.1). These vases, amply attested in Petrie's excavations, are here only represented by small fragments (15 examples), and - with a few exceptions - it is difficult to assign them to one or other form. To goblets T16.1, should be assigned F-115 and F-80 both coming from HAC2, unit 10; to vases T20.1, F-89 (HAC1, unit 1) and F-451 (HAC3, unit 33); all the other fragments could belong to both kinds of vases (HAC2, unit 10: F-72 and F-173, HAC3, unit 36: F-549, F-691, F-758, F-768, unit 244: F-1997, unit 308, F-2192-2193, unit 309: F-2196, HAD2, unit 131: F-1369).

The Early Roman plain glazed vessels produced in the area of the excavations 2000-2005

The plain glazed vessels are the category for which the greatest number of wasters have been found and there is no doubt that they were the main production of the HAC3 zone, though the excavated kiln seems to be for biscuit ware. Their homogeneity comes from the use of a thick turquoise glaze which is characteristic of the Early Roman period.

Three different kinds of plates were made in this area. The first one (T6.1a) is a wide plate with a flat rim protruding into the interior of the vase, oblique walls and annular base. The form is already attested in the Early and Late Ptolemaic periods as we have seen earlier, but the HAC excavation shows clearly that it is still produced in the Early Roman period[35] in thick turquoise blue glaze : 80 rims (total of fragments 84) can be counted, and to the wasters found by Petrie (Ashton 2003:55, UC33570 and UC47481), should be joined 3 wasters composed of pieces of this form found in the 2000-2005 excavations:

— F-129 (HAC2, unit 11) and F-2025 (HAC3, unit 308), turquoise blue glaze plates stuck on a saggar
— F-602 (HAC3, unit 36) fragment of the rim with concretions.

The second form belongs to a plate with an out-turned flat or slightly curved rim, convex body and annular base placed at the junction of the body and the bottom (T13.2) (Nenna and Seif el-Din 2000 : 322-323). It is covered with the thick turquoise glaze typical of the Early Roman period.[36] Though not very abundant in the finds (about 18 fragments), its production is attested in the area by wasters coming from the three trenches, HAC1, unit 6, F-056, HAC2, CT, F-106, unit 11, F-127, HAC3, unit 184, F-1706; unit 238, F-1945. Most of the fragments, however, were found in HAC3. Wasters were already found during Petrie's excavations.[37]

The third one is a form related to the sigillata pieces with a moulded rim (T13.3) and carinated body forming an sharp angle with the bottom and an applied foot-ring base (Nenna and Seif el-Din 2000 : 323-327). It is attested by 44 fragments, 18 of them rims. Two variants are known based on variation in thickness of the walls and the position and diameter of the base. The thick walls and widest base placed near to the carination of the body is one of the commonest forms produced in the early Roman period and is found on almost every Egyptian site occupied in this period.[38] Fragments from a mould preserved in the Petrie Museum show that the body of these plates was produced by moulding and that the annular base was applied in a second phase (Ashton 2003: 68).[39] Most of the time, they present a thick turquoise glaze, but decorated examples combining turquoise blue glaze, with white and violet glaze do exist (see HAC3, unit 300, F-2198 and a piece 'refunded'[40] from 0008-T). Their production is attested by numerous wasters composed of plates stuck together found in Petrie's 1908 excavations (Petrie 1909a, pl. XLIX ; Friedman 1998: 255, fig. 180; UC 43787; Shortland and Tite 2005, fig. 8). Four wasters attest the production of the turquoise blue glaze plates in the area of the 2000-2005 excavations:

— HAC1, unit 1, F-51, three plates stuck together, F-292, plates stuck together; and unit 5, F-70, two plates stuck together
— HAC2, unit 10, F-85, deformed rim
— HAC3, unit 80, F-1654, annular base covered with deformed glaze and ashes

It must be noted that most of the fragments coming from HAC present a bubbly glaze.

Three kinds of bowls were produced in this area. The first one is a hemispherical bowl with an annular base and a rim forming an inward fold (T12.2a) (Nenna and Seif el-Din 2000: 313) or with relief decoration on the interior. Bowls T12.2a are not represented by many pieces (22 fragments). Most of them come from HAC3, one from HAC1 and 3 from

HAC2. In addition, there are amongst them, pieces glazed on one side only (HAC3, unit 36, F-1034, unit 308, F-2056) showing small pinpoints under the fold and on the other, a waster (HAC2, unit 10, F-137) whose blue glaze has turned red and which has foreign bodies stuck to the wall. It is not a very widely distributed form, but it appears in Tebtunis in contexts dated from the 1st Century B.C. and in the early Roman period. It is, it seems, a transitional form between the Late Ptolemaic period and the Early Roman period. Bowls T12.2b are scarce in literature (Nenna and Seif el-Din 2000 : 60, fig. 12; Tomber 2006: 47, type 5) as well as in this excavation where the four pieces are coming from HAC2 (F-105, CT an F-123, unit 10) and HAC3 (F-755, unit 36 and F-2181, unit 301). They share the rare characteristic of having the internal walls with one or more depressions and reliefs reminiscent of the grooved glass bowls. To create this depressions and reliefs, a special tool seems to have been employed as for T12.2a, as shown by an unfinished piece (F-1436, HAC3, unit 33) with pinpoint holes under the relief.

Truly Roman, is the second type of bowl (T12.4) with a moulded rim and an hemispherical body (Nenna and Seif el-Din 2000 : 314-317), which along with the plate T13.3, is the most frequent form of the Early Roman period.[41] It is produced in two sizes: a small size with an indented base and a large size with a flat footring base, added after moulding the body. Forty-five rims were counted and both kinds of base are attested. The indented base is shared with another form of small bowl showing an everted rim (T12.3c),[42] hence the writer has indicated the two possibilities in the catalogues, but it seems, due to the lack of everted rim fragments of the T12.3c type (only two rims: HAC2, unit 10, F-64; HAC3, Unit 50, F-1317), that these fragments of bases belong mainly to small T12.4 bowls. Wasters attested that the two sizes were made there in the vicinity of HAC:

- — F-69, HAC1, unit 5: lower parts of the bodies of indented base bowls stuck together
- — F-71, HAC1, unit: two rims stuck together
- — F-1413, HAC3, unit 6: rims stuck together
- — F-1376, HAC3, unit 52: two rims stuck together
- — F-1581, HAC3, unit 74, indented bases stuck together
- — F-1596, HAC3, unit 74, applied base with ceramic cone still present.
- — F-1858, HAC3, unit 189, turquoise blue glaze over fired in reddish inside and outside of the rim fragment.
- — F-1790, HAC3, unit 209, glaze turned red on the internal wall, vanished on the external wall
- — F-1913, HAC3, unit 232: indented base of a T12.3c or T12.4 bowl with black slag stuck on.
- — F-1831, HAC3, unit 208: indented base of a T12.3c or T12.4 bowl with heavy overfiring of turquoise on the interior and mots of the glae lost in the exterior.

The third one is a biconvex rim bowl represented by 14 rims (Nenna and Seif el-Din 2000, no. 456), imitating a form known in sigillata and in glass. This form has been misidentified in Nenna and Seif el-Din 2000 and placed under T12.4 bowls. In fact, it is a type of its own (T12.7), not very widely distributed, but known, for example, in Tebtunis. All the rims are covered with turquoise blue glaze. Two wasters show rim fragments stuck together (F-290, HAC1, unit 1; F-1191, HAC3, unit 39); another one blue glaze turned red (F-131, HAC1, unit 1). Even if not very numerous, this type may have been produced in the area of HAC3.

Often occurring with T12.4 bowls and T13.3 plates, is the rectangular tray with volute handles (T14.1). This was also produced in Memphis as numerous wasters found by Petrie attest (Petrie 1909, pl. XLIX; Lunsingh Scheurleer 1990; Ashton 2003: 56, UC47397; Shortland and Tite 2005, nos. MEM10 and MEM14).[43] Two wasters (F-55, HAC1 in unit CB, F-2044, HAC3, unit 306) were also found in the 2000-2005 excavations. Attested by 12 fragments (9 rims), this type may have been produced in the area of HAC3.

The simply glazed vessels alien to the production of the HAC area

A series of forms are attested only by very few sherds and should be considered as alien to the types produced in the area of HAC3. The fragments F-153 (HAC1, unit 1) and F-357 (HAC2, unit 10) belong to cylindrical ink-wells (T22.1) of a type known in the early Roman period (Nenna and Seif el-Din 2000 : 387-388).

Three pieces attest also the presence of flat lids (T22.4). Two of them in turquoise blue glaze (HAC3, unit 74, F-1592; unit 77, F-1816) belong to a type that had been produced since the Late Period and was still made in the early Roman period. The third one (HAC3, unit 36, F-720) with a decor probably should be assigned to the early Roman period.

Additionally there are two sherds which do not fit into the known repertoire of forms, but which probably belong to the early Roman period. Both come from the same unit 301 (HAC3); F-2183 is a large flat plate in violet and white glaze with a vegetal decor, as well as F-2179 in turquoise blue glaze.

Conclusion

As stated above, the determination of the types of vessels produced in the area excavated is based on the presence of unfinished pieces, wasters, and on the relative number of sherds, the difficulty being that we are faced with pieces coming from the filling of the furnace and from layers surrounding the furnace. It is certain therefore that mainly plain glazed vessels with turquoise blue glaze dated to the early Roman period–plates T6.1a, T13.2 and T13.3, bowls

T12.2a-b, T12.4 and T12.7, trays T14.1–were produced in the area of HAC3. It also seems reasonable to assume that white and violet glazes were in use for the production of T6.1a plates, as well as shallow convex cups T3.1 and vases T7.4. The wasters of plates T6.1a with apple-green and deep blue glaze seem to stand alone, and could well be residual. The surprise is that no decorated vases, be they moulded or incised, neither hollow figurines or lamps seem to have produced in this spot. This could indicate that the workshops, even if they were localized in a quite restricted area of Memphis, were dedicated to particular forms.

Endnotes

1 Hereafter cited as GRM.

2 Nenna and Seif el-Din (2000) have attempted to build a chrono-typology of the faience vessels of the Ptolemaic and Roman period, and their numbering of the types is followed here, supplemented by the study of material from Tebtunis (Nenna 2002, Nenna and Seif el-Din, forthcoming).

3 See long entry catalogue in Section II and on DVD.

4 The contexts where faience pieces were absent are not included.

5 More than 20 examples are known from the Tebtunis excavations (see also Nifosi 2009, no.1-4, 10-12).

6 Petrie Museum, UC 55276.

7 Buto, French Mission, P1.2002.18.7.

8 See also for example Dasen 2008 in the tomb of a young girl of Hawara dated to the beginning of the 2nd Century A.D.; Nenna 2005a: 72.

9 For ex. GRM, 5519.

10 Hereafter DAE.

11 Note that there is no subsidiary application of a red glaze, as stated by the author, the red colour of the glaze is coming from a misfiring, this type of statuette is typical of the Early Roman period, and the colour of the glaze is surely not an argument for dating this piece to the 1st Century B.C.

12 I am not convinced that the Harpocrates with the *nemes* and the sceptre found in Elephantine (Rodziewicz 2005, no. 207) is a waster.

13 Petrie 1909a: pl. XLIX (= Oxford, Ashmolean Museum, E 4610); other defective pieces unpublished coming from the same excavation are also kept in the Ashmolean Museum (inv. E 4611, 4612, 4613, 4614, 4615), in the British Museum (GR.1910.11-16.11 (waster), GR.1910.11-16.13), in the Petrie Museum, UC 33475.

14 Nenna and Seif el-Din 1994: 304, fig. 6f and footnote 56 from Alexandria, Hermonthis, Saqqara (Grimm 1972: 91-93, fig. 47-49; Nenna 2003:.283-284, fig. 5, coming from the Necropolis of Gabbari, Alexandria; see also MMA 30.8.159, curiously dated on the website of the Museum to the 4th Century A.D. and also Louvre Museum, DAE, E 21468 (Guimet Collection, only the head is preserved).

15 For defective pieces coming from Memphis, see Oxford, Ashmolean Museum, 4616a and b; Petrie Museum, UC47420-47431, UC47387 (misidentified by Ashton 2003) and from Elephantine, Rodziewicz, 2005, no. 205 (defective piece?). For the rare complete pieces, see Arnold 1995, no.74 said to come from Medinet el Fayum, Fitzwilliam Museum, E.6.1964, Di Gioia 2006: 129-130 no. 12 from Pompeii.

16 Lunsing Scheurleer 1979: 105, no. 6, fig. 10-13 (private coll.), no.7 fig. 14-15 (Petrie Museum, UC 2322).

17 UC 2331.

18 For examples see Schmidt 1997: no.220 (Corinthian); Berman 1999, no. 365 ; Alexandria, GRM, 32572 ; Paris, Louvre, E 11142 ; Tebtunis, -A2086.1. Capitals could also belong to incense-burners, in the form of a column, such as a complete example in the Walters Art Gallery and a fragmentary one from the Necropolis of Gabbari in Alexandria, both of Hellenistic date (see Nenna 2001). Another example comes from the West Necropolis of Meroe dated to the Roman period (see Pierrat-Bonnefois 2010: 120, fig. 161).

19 29 examples unpublished.

20 7 examples found mainly in the rubbish zone of the temple Nenna forthcoming b).

21 Alliot 1933: 22, pl. XVII (2 ex.).

22 Inv. JE34109.

23 GRM, 16764 ; P. 649.

24 Deonna 1938: 245, pl. 64..

25 Also fragments AF 6850 and AM 1461 unpublished.

26 Inv. JE 37664, unpublished.

27 See no. Also GRM, 16684 and GRM, prov. FA.60.

28 Alexandria, GRM, P.10551; Tebtunis, 5203.8, A1793.4,

29 MNI = Minimum Number of Individuals (i.e. examples).

30 Oxford, Ashmolean Museum, 1910.562 (apple green glaze) ; 1913.802 (white, blue and violet glaze).

31 DAE, E11337 ; DAE, E 22582.

32 Ashton 2003: 56 misinterprets UC 47388-89 which are fragments of a saggar with deep blue glaze attached as well as fragments of vases (may be T13.3 or T12.4) stuck on it.

33 For the different types and bibliography, see Nenna and Seif el-Din 2000: 351-361, and Silvano 2005, fig. 1 and 4.

34 Also other fragments kept in the united Kingdom museums, see appendix of Nenna and Seif el-Din 2000.

35 This is also true for the ceramic type, at least in the Fayum, see Ballet and Poludnikiewicz 2012: 58-63.

36 Also produced in Elephantine, see Rodziewicz 2005, no.245-250.

37 Ashton 2003: 56 erroneously considers UC50000 as a waster of a T12.4 bowl, it is a waster composed of three T13.2 plates fused together, see also probably Shortland and Tite 2005, MEM13, Oxford, Ashmolean Museum, 1910.563.1.

38 Also produced in Elephantine, see Rodziewicz 2005, no. 251-260.

39 See in particular Ashton 2003 : 68, UC 50345 (illustrated), UC 50228 and UC 50268.

40 By 'refunded' is meant an item which was initially mis-identified in registration and subsequently returned to the correct category.

41 Also produced in Elephantine, Rodziewicz 2005, no. 261-284 and 304-310.

42 Produced in Elephantine, see Rodziewicz 2005, no. 239-244.

43 UC33324 cannot be considered as a waster, as prposed by Ashton 2003: 56, the misshapen handle occuring also on pieces from consumption sites.

Chapter 7
Faience Technology

M-D. Nenna and P.T. Nicholson

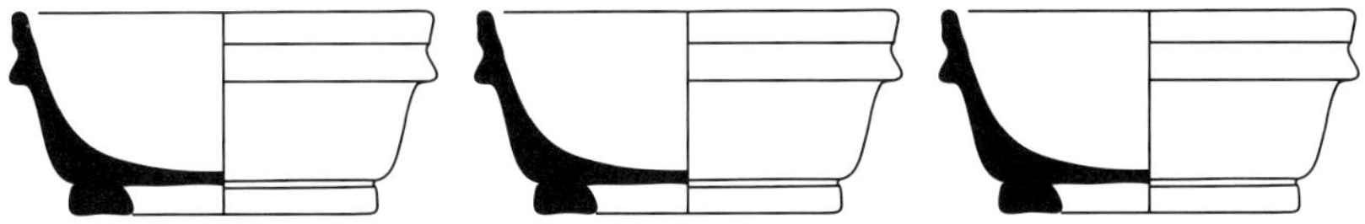

Introduction

Despite the amount of faience material known from Ptolemaic and Roman Egypt, relatively little is known about the workshops themselves. For the Ptolemaic period, apart from the Kom Qalama/Kom Helul area of Memphis investigated by Petrie (1909a, 1911a), a workshop is known from Athribis (modern Benha) in the central Delta (Myśliwiec 1996: 35-36) and dated to the time of Ptolemy IV (221-205 B.C.). Vessel remains (see Welc 2011), some with clay cones attached, are known but the kilns themselves have not been located and were probably destroyed during the reign of Ptolemy IV (Welc pers. comm. 2012). The workshop appears to have been close to an area producing pottery and coroplastic figures.

Despite excavations at Alexandria, where faience workshops are to be expected, none have yet been found (Nenna and Seif el-Din 1999: 77). Work by the S.C.A. and the joint project of the universities of Göttingen and Cologne in nearby Schedia has unearthed a craft quarter but as yet no faience workshops (Abd el-Fatah and Tezgör 1998; Ballet 1998; www3). The material is currently being studied by M. Seif el-Din and A. Martin.

Nenna and Seif el-Din (1999: 78) list three workshops of the Roman period in Egypt – Memphis Kom Helul, Terenouthis (Kom Abu Billo) where a workshop was found during a survey in 1996 (Nenna and Seif el-Din 1999: 79) and Elephantine (Rodziewicz 2005).

At Terenouthis (Kom Abu Billo), fragments of saggars, quartz pebbles and grinding stones/mortars were discovered. A dozen such mortar stones were found in an area of 50m^2 as well as a lump of glass which was perhaps intended to have been ground for glaze. Saggar joiners were also found. The photographs of the saggar given by Nenna and Seif el-Din (1999: 79) show that it had glaze on the interior though this is quite thin and has flaked in places. The glaze does not appear to be strongly coloured although this may be an effect of weathering. The survey also yielded a number of moulds for figurines which seem to have been the main product for the site. Vessels are not well known, although plain vessels seem to have been manufactured there. The finds themselves are unglazed suggesting that they underwent a first, biscuit, firing and would subsequently have gone on to be glazed. No excavation has yet been conducted on the site which is dated to the 1st-2nd Century A.D., but a topographical survey, hopefully followed by excavations, is forthcoming (Dhennin 2011).

The material from Elephantine has been published by Rodziewicz (2005) and comprises finds from simple glazed bowls, plates and lids as well as figurines of the Early Imperial period. The bowl types are Nenna and Seif el-Din's (2000)[1] T12.3a, T12.3c, T12.4, T12.5 and were certainly produced at the site, as were plates of types T12.2a, T13.3a. Rodziewicz (2005, 29) states that his 215 and 216 are semi-finished faience vessels, however, these forms do not belong to any currently known faience object.

Nenna and Seif el-Din (1999: 80) note that given the quantity of faience finds from Roman Egypt, from Alexandria, the Fayum, the regions around Oxyrhynchus and around Koptos as well as sites in the Western Desert oases, there must surely have been further workshops. This is an interesting observation because it may be assumed that for much of the pharaonic period there were small workshops producing amulets and simple pieces in most settlements of any size. The greater size of pieces and the standardisation introduced in Roman times may have had the effect of making faience production a more specialised venture than in earlier times and making its technology more closely allied to pottery production than to stone or glass making/working (Nicholson 2012).

Analyses prepared by Kaczmarczyk in the 1990s (Kaczmarczyk and Nenna forthcoming) show that recipes for violet, turquoise blue and yellow-green glazes made in Memphis differ from others of the same colour made elsewhere, probably the Fayum or Middle Egypt. Examples of this latter are categories of vase with external violet glaze and applied yellow-green decoration. It is clear that faience recipes were not standardised between regions of Egypt.

It is notable that whilst researchers speak of workshops in most cases they are actually referring to areas where only the presence of kilns denotes the proximity of the areas where the raw material was prepared. It is worth noting that the lack of physical workshop buildings may not be as surprising as it first seems. Scholars from the temperate west are accustomed to activities taking place indoors whereas, as Shaw (2004: 16) points out it is likely that many craft activities took place in courtyards and other open areas. Although Shaw is focussing on the pharaonic era it is not unlikely that, despite the large scale of Ptolemaic and Roman production, work may have gone on in the open or under ephemeral shelters rather than in workshop buildings *per se*.

The Making of Faience

Faience manufacture has a long history in Egypt (see Friedman 1998, Kaczmarczyk and Hedges 1983, Lucas 1962, Nicholson and Peltenburg 2000) but it is worth attempting to reconstruct the *chaîne opératoire* (Lemmonier 1993) (i.e. stages in the manufacturing process) in so far as it relates to faience of the Ptolemaic and Roman period as evidenced at Memphis.

It is worth noting that although numerous attempts have been made to replicate faience (e.g. Brandt 1999; Busz and Sengel 1999; Vergès 1992), especially of the pharaonic period, little work has been done on vessel manufacture and none has been done on vessels of the Roman period.

Raw material

The raw materials of faience are essentially the same as those known since prehistoric times, namely silica for the body material and an alkaline glaze using a soda of some kind mixed with lime and silica (see Kaczmarczyk and Hedges 1983). However, the way in which these materials are procured and treated changes over time (see Chapter 2), most notably in the Ptolemaic and Roman periods.

The Core

Silica

Silica could be procured in several ways. The most obvious is to use quartz sand, abundant in Egypt's deserts. However, this material is often high in impurities such as iron and so could lead to discolouration where these were high enough to affect the applied glaze. A higher quality source was available in the form of rock-crystal, though this was highly prized in its own right and so unlikely to be used, or as the more readily available white quartz pebbles (Nenna and Seif el-Din 2000: 17).

Analyses of faience glaze suggest that both quartz sand and ground quartz pebbles were used (Shortland and Tite 2005: 35) in its production. Given that both materials are used for the glaze it is not inconceivable that in areas with a ready sand source this might also be commonly used for the body material. Nenna believes that the pebbles found at Kom Abu Billo were intended as a source of core material but this is yet to be demonstrated by excavation. At Kom Helul no significant numbers of quartz pebbles were found, but this is not especially surprising given that excavation was focussed around the kiln. It may be that the preparation area was located at some little distance away from it. Nonetheless stray finds of quartz pebbles at Kom Helul are not common perhaps indicating the use of sand. A number of possible stone mortars or grinding/pounding stones were located during excavation (e.g. T-67, T-59) but were not directly associated with quartz powder.

Natron

The principal alkali used in pharaonic times for faience varied between plant ashes and natron. Its purpose is to act as a 'flux', allowing the partial melting of the silica at lower temperatures than would otherwise be possible. By this means the silica grains become cemented together at their edges helping to give the faience material its strength.

By the Roman period natron had become the standard alkali source used in glass (Freestone 1991: 40) and the same seems to be true of faience from most of the Delta (Kaczmarczyk and Hedges 1983: 280). It would have been obtained from the Wadi Natrun as well as other minor sources within Egypt. We know little of the preparation of natron for use in faience manufacture but it is safe to assume that it would have been crushed to a fine powder and any impurities such as plant debris removed from it. Because the material is soluble it is unlikely to have survived in the damp conditions prevalent at Memphis and none was found. However, there may be other reasons for its absence.

The Memphis faience examined by Kaczmarczyk and Hedges (1983: 280) is high in potassium suggesting that plant ashes were still in use as an alkali source there. Kaczmarcyk and Hedges (1983: 280-281) were unable to give a convincing explanation as to why this was still in use, however, it may be that the site itself had an abundance of suitable plants (perhaps halfa grass) and so chose to use that rather than import natron from a distance and at a cost.[2]

Lime

The use of lime is well known in faience and Vandiver (1982: 162) estimates its presence (CaO) at between 1 and 5% of the body. However, she does not comment specifically on the levels in Roman faience. Lime would have been obtained from the burning of limestone or dolomite or might occur naturally in certain sand sources.

Clay/Organic binders

It has been suggested for some time that at least some faience vessels, especially of the Roman period, were formed by throwing (Vandiver 1982: 177; 1983: A-124-5) and because faience paste is low in plasticity, the addition of clay or an organic binder has been suggested (Vandiver 1983: A-125).[3] The suggestion of throwing is repeated by Tite *et al.* (2008: 60).

Whilst the presence of clay cannot be discounted there are several reasons to believe that its use was not common, if used at all. First, faience had been produced in Egypt since prehistoric times apparently without the need for clay. Second, much of the Roman material studied comes from Memphis or the Delta, whose mud adheres to the broken sections making them look more like pottery than faience. When a fresh break is visible the underlying material is usually white or greyish and there is no macroscopic trace of clay. Third, the underlying assumption has been that much of the Roman material was wheel thrown and that the clay was necessary for this process.

However, the authors are uncertain that Roman faience vessels were thrown, or at least that they were free-thrown, that is without the use of a mould. Closed form pottery vessels frequently preserve corrugations, or rills, from the throwing process – potters do not try to remove these as they are on the interior of the vessel and so unseen. The same logic might be expected to apply to closed form faience vessels. When Nenna has examined vessels she has found that where ridges exist they are from the joining of separately moulded parts such as shoulder garlands and necks. This can be clearly seen in some of the vessels presented in Kaczmarczyk and Nenna (forthcoming fig. 6, Louvre DAE E 22593).

If clay were required then it is readily available from the banks of the Nile. This is iron-rich clay, firing red in colour and so might be apparent macroscopically. A white firing marl clay is also available at several places in Egypt (Arnold 1981) and would be less obvious amongst the silica body.

It has also been suggested (Nenna and Seif el-Din 2000: 18; Vandiver 1983: A-125) that organic binders may have been used to assist with the cohesion of the paste during forming. They would add to the plasticity/workability of the material. However, as Vandiver (1983: A-125) points out, such organic binders would burn out during firing and so leave no trace macroscopically or for chemical analysis. Their usefulness has been attested in experimental work but has not yet been proven archaeologically (Manti 2004).

Glaze raw materials and preparation

The raw materials used to make the glaze would include silica, either from quartz pebbles or sand, natron as a flux and lime as a stabilising material. The lime may not have been deliberately added but could have been present with either the sand or the natron flux. These are the same materials as used for the core, though mixed in a different ratio – using a higher proportion of flux relative to the silica.

This mixture, on its own, would yield only a dirty greenish or brownish glaze and in order to give it colour it would be necessary to add a colourant in the form of copper oxide for the turquoise blue colours or cobalt for the very dark blues. Shortland and Tite (2005: 36) believed that the colouring material was probably derived from the use of bronze scrap as it had 10% tin content. If this was so then it may be suggested that the faience workers were obtaining bronze waste from metal smiths or were recycling domestic metal scrap.

Other glaze colours, notably violet and white and the (earlier) apple green glaze, would require a different range of colourants. According to Kaczmarczyk and Nenna (forthcoming, Table 3) copper formed the colourant for apple green which was also high in lead and tin, iron and copper were used in the indigo/violet and purple/brown was achieved using manganese, iron and copper. The work by Kaczmarczyk and Hedges (1983) does not cover the Roman material sufficiently for reliable comparisons to be made.

The reacting together of the ingredients for the glaze presents several questions. One of the most fundamental is whether or not this process took place at the Memphis workshops or whether the glaze was imported. There are several reasons for believing that it was a local operation. First, the Memphis industrial area at Kom Helul is quite extensive (see Appendix 1) and at nearby Kom Qalama Nicholson believes that Egyptian blue was being manufactured on a large scale.[4] Given that the technology to produce frit already existed at the site it seems unnecessary to propose that the glaze would need to have been imported. From Terenouthis comes a large block of fritted material (Nenna and Seif el-Din (1999: 81 top right) and it might be supposed that similar material was made at Memphis.

It is worth considering whether Egyptian blue itself could have been used as a colourant. Vandiver (1982: 178) believed that the balls of Egyptian blue were themselves intended as the glaze. This is possible but in the view of the authors it is more likely that they were simply the colourant to be added to the frit to give it colour. Their production in standard sized balls would allow much greater colour control than would the addition of powdered metal scrap whose composition – and therefore precise colouring properties – were unknown to the faience workers. Analyses by Tite and Hatton (2007: 77-78) show that tin is present in the frit balls from Memphis, though not at the 10% level recorded by Shorland and Tite (2005). Tin is, however, present at up to 4.38% in the glassy phase of the frit balls and without a greater number of analyses their use should not, perhaps, be ruled out.

The production of the coloured frit for glazing could be achieved at temperatures of around 900-1000°C (see Pradell *et al.* 2006; Tite *et al.* 2008), lower than might be necessary for the production of a fully formed glass. Once the ingredients had been fritted together they would need to be reduced to a form suitable for application as a glaze. This would be achieved by crushing the frit to a powder which would then need to be mixed with water or an organic binder in order to be applied to the surface of the faience objects.

Shaping the Body

The crushed silica, either from sand or quartz pebbles, would be mixed with the natron, lime and water to make a paste. Organic binders might also be added at this stage. The Roman paste is generally less finely powdered than that used in Ptolemaic times and individual sand grains can be distinguished (Nenna and Seif el-Din 2000: 17).

The consistency of faience paste is usually described as being like firm pastry, though there are no published measurements of its viscosity (this, of itself, might argue against the use of the material for throwing – potter's clay is frequently soft when used on the wheel).

The paste used at Memphis seems to have been formed primarily by (1) moulding, (2) hand forming and (3) assembling from pre-moulded elements. During the excavation a number of fragments of plaster likely to have formed parts of moulds were unearthed. However, most of these fragments cannot be assigned to particular vessel forms or figurines with any certainty.

The use of moulds in shaping vessels is known from the end of the 4th Century B.C. with the arrival of the Macedonians in Egypt and is one of the great technological novelties brought by the Greeks to the faience industry (Nenna 2006, 199-200). Prior to this time faience vessels were mainly formed around a core as Tait (1963: 131) suggests (see also Vandiver and Kingery 1987b; Felder 1988) and this technique was still in use at the beginning of the Hellenistic period as shown by some closed vases unearthed in Tebtunis (Nenna pers. comm.).

Shaping Vessels: Open Forms

From Kom Helul there is relatively little evidence for the moulds for vessels themselves, though Y-242 and Y-243 may be examples. There are several pieces in the Petrie Museum collection, notably UC50228, UC50268 and UC50345 (Figure 7.1). Unlike the pharaonic moulds which are usually made of Nile clay and used for the making of amulets and tiles the moulds from Memphis are all made of plaster (see Ashton 2003: 59-70).

The use of plaster moulds is well attested in the manufacture of ceramics (cf. Bailey 1976: 98-100; Noble 1988: 75-76) and is still in use for the slip casting of modern, industrially produced wares. The use of plaster here may suggest a closer link with the pottery industry, including coroplastic manufacture, than was the case in faience making in earlier periods. Plaster moulds are also known for metallurgy (Reinsberg 1980; Cheshire 1996; Seif el-Din 1998).

Examination of the moulds in the Petrie Museum suggests that they were made over a form,[5] either an extant vessel or a wooden model. The plaster was first applied as a fine, even coat between 6 and 9mm thick and allowed to dry almost completely. At this point it was reinforced by dripping blobs of thick plaster – perhaps the remains of the mixture originally used to make the even coating – onto the back of the mould. That this was done whilst the mould was still inverted over the form is evident in that some of the plaster blobs have run down toward the vessel rim.

The moulds were made in sections. For example UC50268 is half of a two-part mould. It preserves the remains of a tenon at the centre and another at one edge. It is suggested that these would have been created by first making a mould of half of the vessel using a piece of wood or metal to give a sharp defining line midway across the diameter. Once dry and with plaster blobbed onto the back to reinforce it, the half-mould would be removed from the form and mortises cut into it. The exposed edge, along with the mortises, would then be coated in oil or resin and the half mould returned to the form. The other half of the form would then be carefully covered with plaster, allowing it to penetrate into the shallow mortises. Once it had partly dried the original half mould would be removed allowing the new one to dry completely.

When fully dried the two half-moulds would fit together to give the complete circumference of the vessel to be produced and would be ready to receive the faience paste.

We have no precise archaeological context for the moulds in the Petrie Museum, other than that they are known to have come from Petrie's work at Memphis and are included with the industrial finds from Kom Helul/Qalama. It is not certain that the moulds discussed above are definitely for faience production, however, UC50268 may correspond to a plate of Nenna and Seif el-Din's (2000) type T13.3. UC50228 is less certain but may be from a cup known from the end of the Late Period T3.1 (Dayton 1981: Plate 8 nos. 1099 and 1100). UC50345 is enigmatic but may belong to a wide rimmed shallow bowl T3.5. The examples from HAC3, Y-242 and Y-243 appear to belong to moulds for shaping plates. Only the lower part of the profile is preserved.

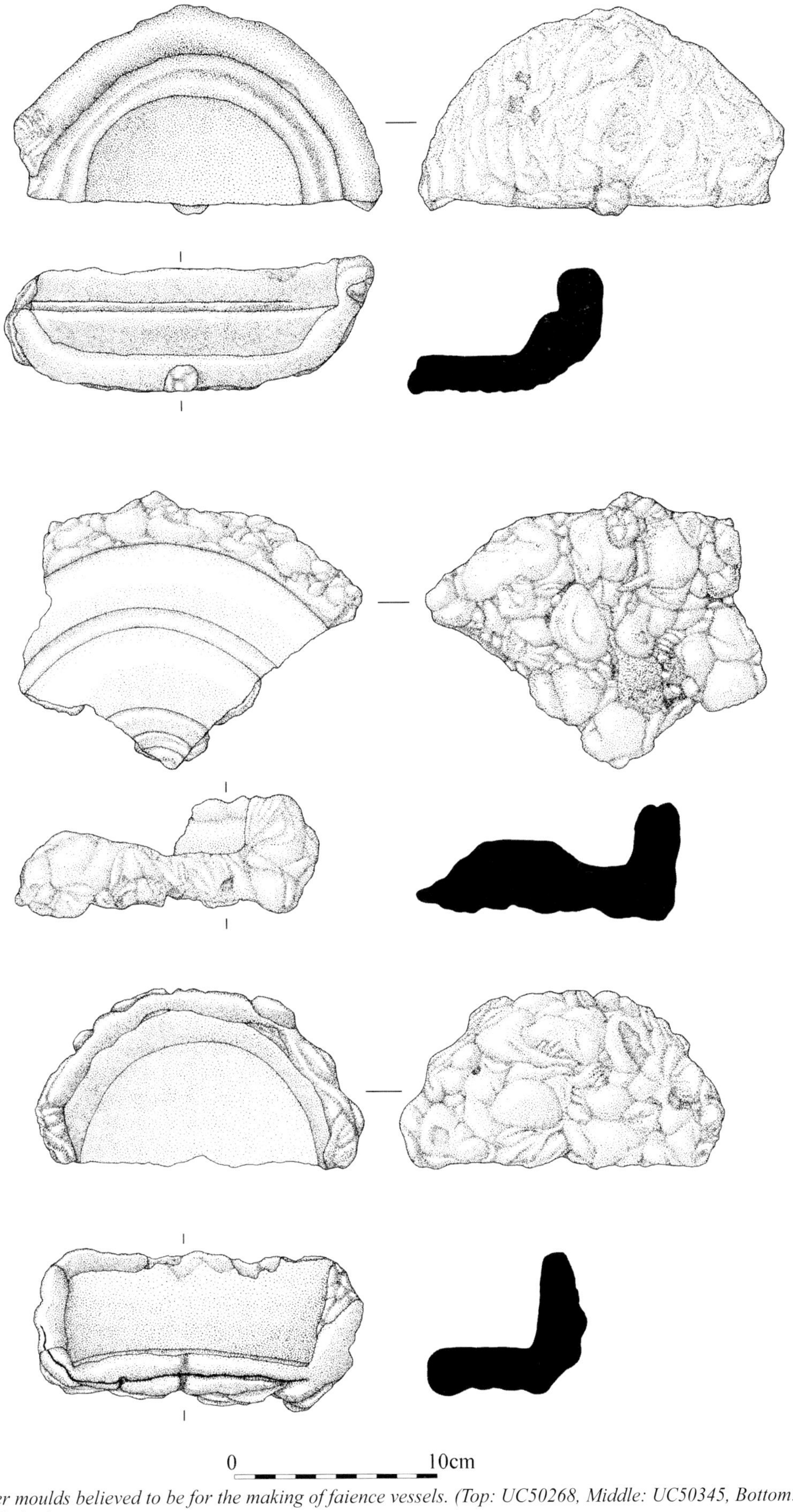

Figure 7.1. Plaster moulds believed to be for the making of faience vessels. (Top: UC50268, Middle: UC50345, Bottom: UC50228). (Drawing: Tessa Baber).

Into the completed mould would be put the faience paste. This would be smoothed into the mould and then, perhaps, the whole might be placed on the potters' wheel and revolved slowly to smooth the interior of the form.[6] This might have been achieved in part by using a template of some kind[7] (Hodges 1976: 27-28). So, although a potter's wheel or similar device might have been used, it is not being used for throwing but rather for regularising the interior profile of the vessel. For this reason it seems less likely that clay would have been needed to increase plasticity. This kind of process is attested for the manufacture of Samian ware (Brown 1976: 78-80) and African Red Slip (Hayes 1997:18; Bonifay 2004, 59; Bonifay also refers to Schuring 1988, 34-35). Once removed from the mould, stand rings would be made and added separately to the moulded vessels. This view is valid for the open forms with straight walls and those with out-turned rims as well as for trays. However, those bowls like T12.2a with internal thickening of the rim would require further finishing perhaps by turning on a turntable whilst still supported in the exterior mould.

Shaping Vessels: Closed Forms

Three main closed forms are attested from the excavation. These are T7.4, T19.3 and T.20, all of them made up from pre-moulded elements. T7.4 produced at, or near, HAC3 comprises four different elements: the cylindrical neck, upper part of the body, lower part of the body and the foot. All these parts were manufactured in moulds and then luted together using faience paste. The joint between the neck and the body is masked by a projecting band forming the lower part of the neck. The wave decoration of the neck, and the complex decoration in registers one above the other on the body, derive from the mould. The mould would thus have had relief *en creux* derived from an archetype which had the decoration already on it. The complicated decoration may itself have been carved or moulded onto a plaster archetype. It should be noted, in the absence of any actual moulds for these pieces, that some of the floral roundels on the shoulder of T7.4 appear to have been individually stamped into the mould. If this is the case then it is likely that the mould was made of clay rather than plaster since the process of stamping into wet plaster would be a difficult one. Nevertheless there are very few known ceramic moulds from Memphis whereas there are numerous plaster moulds and archetypes. T7.4 is a transitional form linking the Ptolemaic and Early Imperial vases (see Chapter 6).

T19.3 and T20 are Memphite productions but not, on present evidence, attested at HAC3. T20 is the succeeding form to T7.4 with deep relief decoration always zoned in successive registers and was probably manufactured in the same way as its predecessor – namely as four moulded parts assembled as one vessel.

T19 was also made in three or four different moulds: the rim plus neck (or rim and neck separately), the upper part of the body and the lower body comprising the base. The handles were made separately and applied under the rim down to the shoulder. A small cylinder was applied where the top of the handle met the rim and a medallion in the form of a child's face was applied at the base of the handle. The question of how the homogenous decoration of the body was made remains open. On the upper part of the body this decoration comprises ivy branches etc. and on the lower the *calyx* of the *nelumbo* plant. The decoration might have been incised in the mould or be derived from the archetype; alternatively it may have been directly incised into the faience paste once the element had been removed from the mould.

Figurines

There are four broad types of faience figurine. These comprise (1) flat-backed, (2) hollow (3) solid and in the round and (4) solid but formed around a perishable core.

1. From HAC3 the flat-backed type is represented by the plaster mould Y-6 showing Bes with his plumed headdress (Figure 7.2). The mould measures 16.7cm long by 9cm wide with a maximum thickness of 3.7cm. This flat-backed type is the traditional pharaonic method of moulding inlays and small amulets. The paste is pressed into the mould and after a few moments the object is tipped out, onto its back, on a flat surface in order to dry.

2. Solid in the round. This requires a two-part mould and is reserved for small figurines such as those of Harpocrates. It is normally found on pieces of less than 15cm high. The paste is pressed into the face of one mould and then more paste into the second. They are joined by either luting with a slurry or are sufficiently damp when put together to join without further effort.

3. Solid but formed around a perishable core. This is reserved for larger pieces such as statuettes of Aphrodite Anadyomene. These can reach 50cm in height. No examples of this type are recorded from the current excavations.

4. Hollow figurines are a speciality of Memphis. The paste is pressed into two halves of the mould and the two halves pressed together. Sometimes, especially in the case of animal figures, the creature is set on a platform; this can be made in separate pieces (e.g. Petrie Museum UC47387) and then luted together. The fragment of a head of Serapis F-1616 belongs to such a hollow figurine. F-1305 is also a hollow figure of part of an unidentified animal.

First Firing

Once the objects had been produced and allowed to dry they would have been fired. The initial (biscuit) firing of the objects seems to have taken place in the excavated kiln at HAC3, but this does not seem to have been used for glazing.

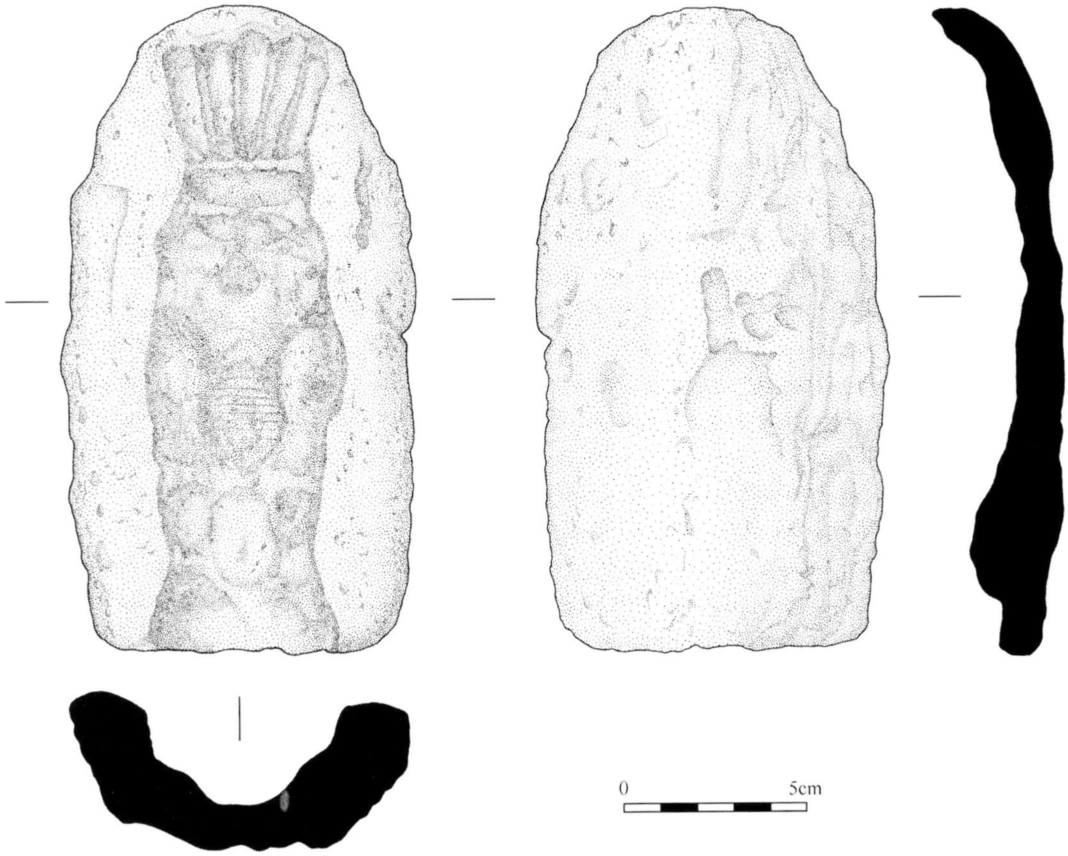

Figure 7.2. Plaster mould for a flat-backed figure of Bes (Y-6). (Drawing: Tessa Baber).

The products would have been placed into the large saggars of Type 12 which have an average diameter of 49cm and height of 26cm (see Chapter 5), the lowest objects in the saggar resting on lime as a separator. The individual pieces of ware would perhaps have been separated from one another in stacks using the same sort of clay cones that are well attested from glazed examples (below).[8] Closed form vases would fit comfortably within the saggars and several would fit within the diameter of the Type 12s. The saggars would then be carried into the kiln (see Chapter 4) and stacked one on top of the other, each being closed by a ring of wet clay, forming the so-called 'saggar joiner'. The whole stack would then have been plastered over with coarse clay before the firing chamber itself was closed up by bricking up the doorway.

The duration of the firing itself is not known although it can be estimated that it might have lasted for most of a day (18-24 hours, see Chapter 4) based on evidence from similar kilns. The openings in the kiln, notably the stoke-hole and (secondary) stoke-hole at the lowermost west side, would be given temporary blockings at the end of the firing so that the kiln would be allowed to cool slowly, perhaps for up to two days.

The saggars would then be removed from the kiln by opening the doorway and chipping off the coarse, friable clay with which the saggar stacks were covered. The individual saggars would then be carried away and their contents removed for the next stage in the process. The saggars themselves would be put to one side ready for re-use in subsequent firings.

Application of the Glaze

The products removed from the saggar would now be ready to be prepared for glazing. There are several examples of unfinished faience from HAC3; these are pieces which have undergone first firing but have not been glazed. These include F-1436, F-1034, F-2056, from the excavation, along with the surface find Y-5 (Fig. 7.3).

These unglazed finds were probably broken as they were removed from the saggar or were found to be deformed in some way after first firing and so discarded. It is not surprising that there are less unfinished waster pieces than glazed ones since the opportunities for misfiring unglazed faience are much less than for glazed, there being no glaze to cause the adherence of vessels. Those pieces which were undamaged, representing the majority of the fired product, would now be given a coating of glaze.

Shortland and Tite (2005: 38, 42) suggest that the glazes were applied in liquid form, i.e. as a slurry or slip (see also

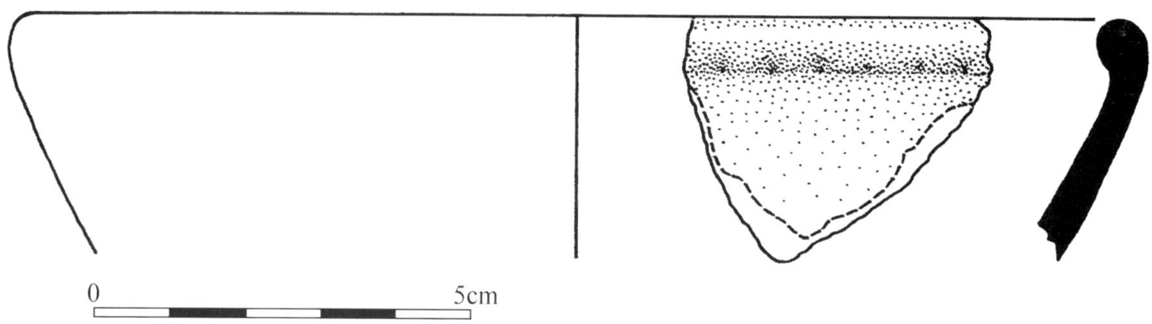

Figure 7.3. Unglazed faience vessel (F-2056). A series of small holes, quite regularly spaced, are visible under the thickening on the inside of the rim, but the purpose of these is not clear. Similar holes are found on the bowls with internal mouldings such as F-1436. (Drawing: Frances Taylor).

Plate 7.1. Misfired fragment (F-451) from a plate of type T6.1a, showing different colours of glaze. (Photo: P.T. Nicholson).

Mao 2000: 191). Drips and runs observed by Shortland and Tite (2005: 38) confirm that most of the glazing was applied, that is brushed onto the surface or the object dipped into a slurry. Incidentally, the fact of applying a wet slurry or dipping an object into it, may argue for a biscuit firing since otherwise a piece which was only air dried might tend to distort or dissolve if re-wetted for more than a few moments (see Appendix 4).

In discussing application glazing Vandiver (1983: A27) notes that this refers to the applying of a glaze to a vessel surface. This is generally assumed to mean the applying of a pre-fritted glaze which is then added as a suspension or powder to the surface of the vessel before firing. However, she also notes that it is possible to apply a separate layer of efflorescent material to an object. In other words, the glaze might be developed by efflorescence but is actually an applied glaze.

If this latter technique is used at Memphis it raises interesting questions, not least about the position of the craft of faience making. Why should faience makers produce the object and then add a separate layer of efflorescent material to it rather than make the whole body efflorescent as was usual in pharaonic times (although some tiles seem to have been given a separate efflorescent layer in this period)? It may be that the makers found it more economical to add only a thin layer rather than make the whole body paste efflorescent – although for crockery this seems unlikely since it would make a less strong body. If the layer was added

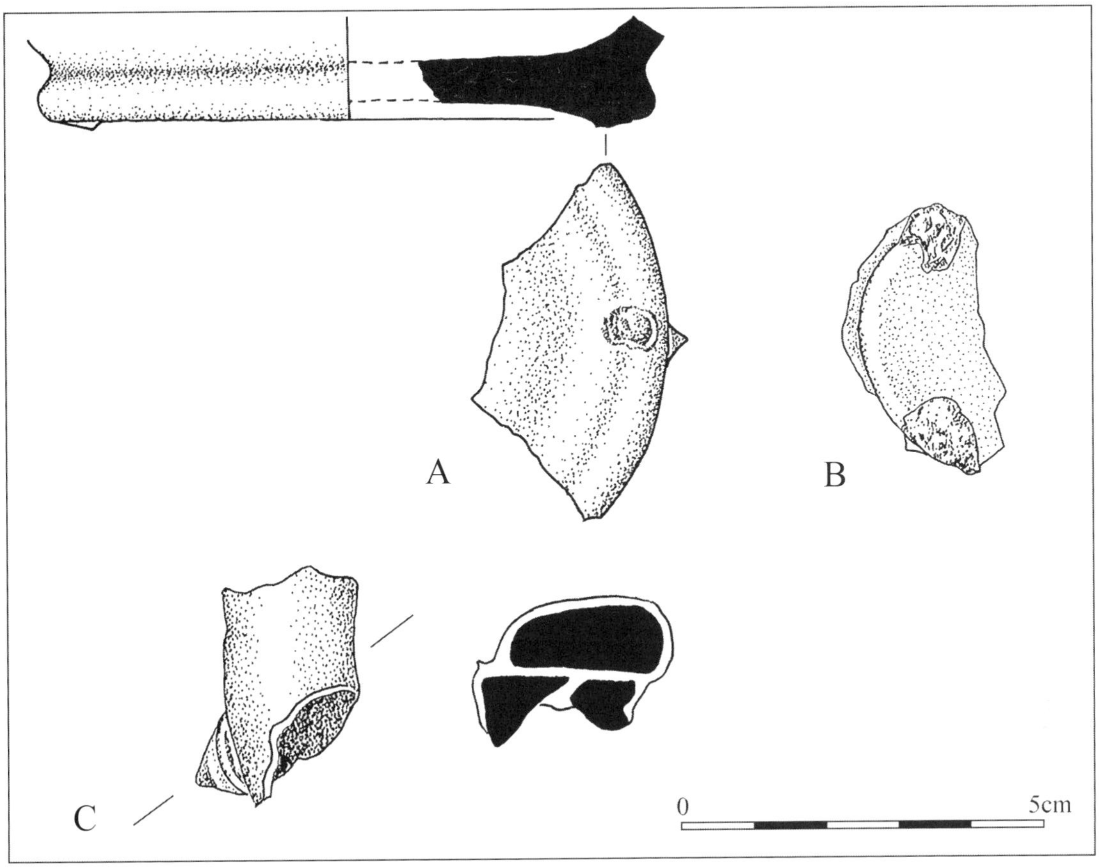

Figure 7.4. (A) Fragment of vessel of type T3.1 with adhering cone (F-68). (B) Underside of the base of a type T12.3c or T12.4 (small) bowl (F-207) with adhering cones. (C) Part of the standring of a type T12.4 bowl with cone still attached (F-1350). (Drawings: Joanne Hodges).

Plate 7.2. Fragment of the base of a type T13.2 vessel (F-127) with the remains of a pad of clay adhering just inside the footring (left lower edge). Scale bar is 5cm. (Photo: P.T. Nicholson).

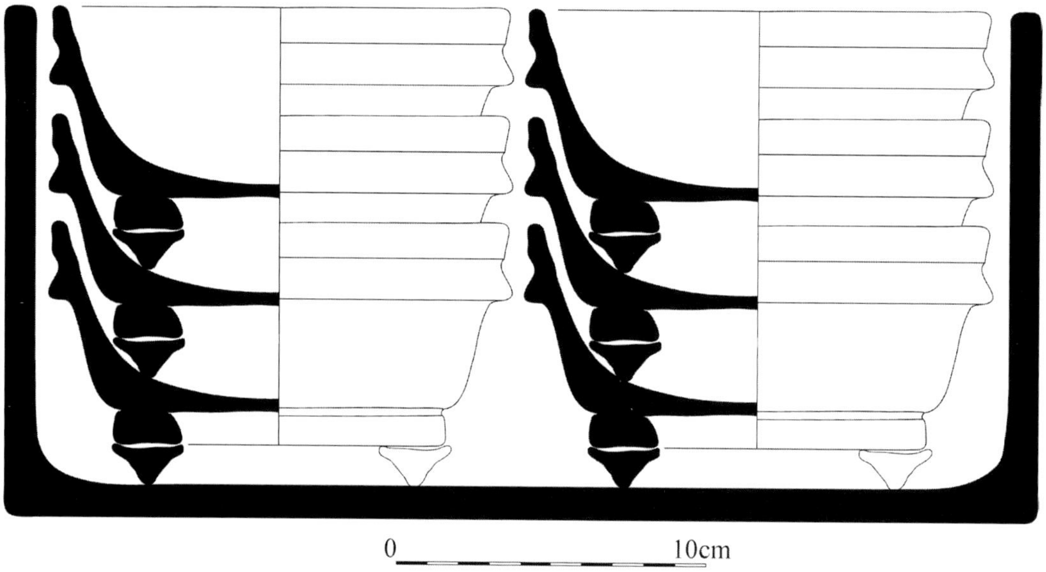

Figure 7.5. Vessels of Type T12.4 shown inside a type 3 saggar. (Drawing: M-D Nenna & K. Harding).

to biscuit fired wares it would also mean an unnecessary biscuit firing. However, if the makers of this Roman faience were themselves from a pottery tradition where glazes were added separately to biscuit fired wares then their addition as an efflorescent layer might be seen as simply another form of glaze and be thought of as essentially the same as adding a pre-fritted glaze layer.

Once the glaze had been applied to the object it would be allowed to dry. This would be the only stage necessary for the plain turquoise blue glazed pieces which are well attested. However, for those pieces with several colours of glaze, which are also known to have been made at Memphis, a more complicated process was necessary. This process has been highlighted by the works of Mao (2000) and Shortland and Tite (2005). Ptolemaic vessels with bichrome glaze of deep blue and apple green, or deep blue and light blue, show two strata of glaze implying two applications of the glazing slurry. Previous work on the two-tone blues (e.g. Kaczmarczyk and Hedges 1983 followed by Nenna and Seif el-Din 2000) suggested that only one application of glaze was necessary and the two tones of blue were derived from the differing thickness of the single glaze colour, in other words that it showed as a darker colour where the relief was deeper.

Forms such as T7.4, a transitional form bearing decoration inherited from the Ptolemaic period, or plates such as T6.1a which seem to have been produced until the Early Imperial period, have three different glaze colours. The colours are turquoise blue for the interior with white and violet for the exterior (T7.4) or *vice versa* for plates of type T6.1a (F-451; Plate 7.1). Alternatively turquoise blue is used for the interior, turquoise – deep blue and yellow for the exterior. For example on F-2174 the first colour applied seems to have been violet.

Forms such as T19.3 are also decorated using a monochrome blue which varies in thickness giving a deep blue in the deeper relief and a somewhat more turquoise shade elsewhere (see Metropolitan Museum of Art 44.4.45 for colour variation). Form T20 is produced in monochrome turquoise and monochrome dark blue, and also follows the Ptolemaic practice of applying an underglaze of turquoise first into the areas of deep relief and wiping it from the higher ones before applying a second glaze of yellowish green over the whole surface. The final product has variations of shade on individual pieces as well as between pieces (Shortland and Tite 2005).

Most figurines of the early Roman period, whether solid or hollow, are covered with thick turquoise blue glaze which shows a deeper colour in areas of deeply sunk relief. A yellow glaze may be used to enhance details such as jewellery elements (see for example Louvre AF 10095, Kaczmarczyk and Nenna forthcoming), vegetal elements and ram horns (see MMA 26.7.1019). Some figurines such as Louvre AF 10097 are covered in a whitish and violet glaze (e.g. Kaczmarczyk and Nenna forthcoming).

Once the glaze slurry had been allowed to dry on the objects they were ready to be placed in saggars. However, the most efficient way to do this with many vessel types was to stack them one inside the other. In order to do this without the vessels becoming stuck to one another, it was necessary to add clay cones as separators. The cones were usually added to the footring of the bowls (e.g. F-68 Fig.7.4a of Type T3.1) with the broad end of the cone on the ring or to the underside of bowls with an indented foot (e.g. F-0207 Fig. 7.4b T12.3c or the T12.4 [small]). The larger form of T12.4 is made with a separate footring to which three cones were attached (F-1350 Fig. 7.4c). In the case of shallow bowls/plates the cones may be attached directly to the base of the object inside the footring. For example F-0127 (form T13.2) from HAC2 shows such an arrangement, the clay 'cone' in this case being more like a small clay pad (Plate 7.2). For the carinated plates such as T13.3, whose shape does not allow them to sit easily within one another, slightly longer cones were needed for the footring. All these cones would be allowed to dry in position on the vessel for some time until hard. The vessels would then be placed one inside the other in the saggar with the point of the cone touching the inside of the vessel below it (see figure 7.5).

The saggars used for the glazing operation seem to have been mainly of Type 3 (see Chapter 5). These have an average size of 33cm diameter and 13cm height. They are generally made of marl clay or a marl-rich mixed clay. The lack of iron in their fabric would help to prevent discolouration of the glazes of the vessels they contained.

Since the Type 3 saggars are smaller than Type 12 they must have held correspondingly less ware. However, this is not necessarily a disadvantage since firing faults at the glazing stage, causing vessels to adhere together, are much more common than during the biscuit firing. By grouping the vessels into smaller batches the loss resulting from such a mis-firing in one of the smaller saggars would have been much less than had many vessels been together in a large one. Bowls are seemingly stacked in threes or fours as UC47394 demonstrates and the same is true of BM GR1980.10-17.1 (Petrie 1909a pl. xlix; Nicholson 1988: 255 entry 180) whilst the shallower plates may be stacked in greater numbers; T6.1a plates for example would stack five deep in an average Type 3 saggar and their average diameter is approximately 23cm making them easily suited to this type. It should be noted that these figures are based on the average, and that saggars of Type 3, like Type 12, exhibit some variation. Where the diameter of vessels is much smaller than the usual diameter of the saggars it is possible that two or three stacks may have been placed within a single saggar so that space was not wasted.

The placing of closed form vases must also be considered. Vase T7.4 averages c.16cm high, T19 is 16-22cm, and T20.1 is 16-20cm, while T20.2 is 14-16cm high, in other words most of these vessels are less than 20cm in height and the greatest width of any of them is 17cm. From HAC3 we have too few complete profiles of Type 3 saggars to know if they extended to 20cm in height, but such does not seem unlikely. If this were so then they would fit, individually, into some of the Type 3 saggars. In order that they did not become adhered to the bottom of the saggar they were generally stood on three small pads, rather than on true cones, of clay. These can be clearly seen on some of the examples in the Myers Museum collection at Eton College, for example ECM 570 (see Plate 1.4) or ECM 576.

Glost Firing

Once the vessels had been correctly stacked in their saggars they would be carried to the kiln. It is believed that the kiln excavated at HAC3 was used primarily, and perhaps

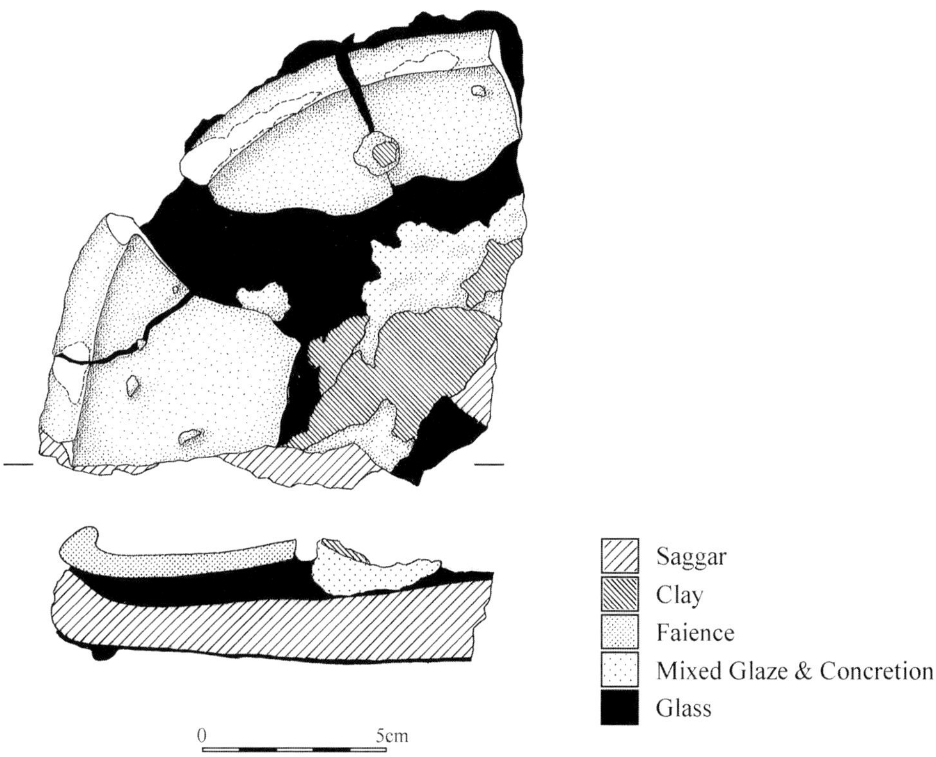

Figure 7.6. Fragments of faience vessel (F-2025) of type T6.1a adhering to the base of a saggar. (Drawing: Frances Taylor).

exclusively, for the first stage of the process, the biscuit firing of the ware. Other kilns in vicinity would then be used for the glost (or glaze) firing.

It seems reasonable to suppose, on the basis of Petrie's excavations, that the glost kilns were of identical design to the biscuit kiln. He found numerous glazed saggars in the area of some of his kilns (though frustratingly we do not have details of which or in what relationship to the kiln) suggesting that some or all of those which he excavated were for this purpose. The geophysical survey (Appendix 1) shows numerous kilns at Kom Helul and there is no need to suppose that the biscuit-fired wares needed to be carried very far.

The saggars used for glost firing were of Type 3, and like their larger counterparts they too were coated in friable clay during the firing. However, this coating seems to have been less thick and survives less often on the saggar fragments. One reason for the coating being less well evidenced is probably that the Type 3 saggars were not re-used as often as their larger counterparts and as a result there was less opportunity for the coating to become fused to the vessel or to build up in layers. The Type 3 saggars probably enjoyed a shorter life because their interiors often became quite thickly glazed during firing. This is the result of glaze particles being carried around in the hot atmosphere of the saggar and so glazing the walls, as well as from glaze running down the faience vessels, especially the lowermost in the stack, and pooling on the saggar floor. It is likely that after only one or two firings they would be deemed useless and were therefore discarded. At first sight the build up of glaze in the saggar may not seem problematic until one considers that it would become molten during each successive firing. As a result vessels would be much more prone to sticking to the walls and base of the saggar. Since the undersides of the saggar bases also become glazed as a result of serving as the 'lid' of the saggar beneath them in the stack, there is also the possibility of glaze of one colour dripping from the saggar above and landing on faience vessels of a different colour in the saggar below. That dripping was a problem is very clear from the remains of drips visible on the undersides of many Type 3 saggars.

The temperature of the glost firing is likely to have been lower than that for biscuit firing, possibly in the order of 800°C. The duration of these firings may well have been considerably shorter than those used for biscuit firing. The duration and temperature would, of course, be sufficient to fuse the frit which had been applied as a slurry, making it into a true glaze. Where temperatures became only slightly too high the glaze would run and pool, causing the faults so often encountered. At the end of the firing the kiln would be left to cool for the requisite period of time, perhaps 24 hours or so.

The intended colour for the glazes was usually turquoise or dark blue and was achieved in an oxidising atmosphere. Occasionally there seem to have been localised areas of reduction in the saggar stack and these sometimes result in streaks of red on what were otherwise turquoise vessels.

Once cool the firing chamber of the kiln would be emptied and the saggars carried to a nearby area so that the ware could be unloaded. At this stage it would become evident whether there had been any misfirings leading to vessels distorting or becoming stuck together. There is considerable evidence for vessels becoming fused in their stacks such as the vessels mentioned above in the Petrie and British Museum collections.[9] From the HAC excavations come examples of vessels fused to their saggars notably F-2025 (T6.1a) and F-0129 (T6.1a) (Fig. 7.6 and Plate 7.3). Such waster vessels would generally be discarded on a waste dump located near or around the kilns.

The faience workers seem to have dismantled the vessel stacks quite rapidly and items were sent for sale with cones still adhering. It would have been for the customer to remove any cone still adhering to the finished vessel; this is clearly witnessed by finds from consumption sites such as Tebtunis (Nenna personal observation). It should therefore be noted that vessels with cones or partial cones, still adhering are not of themselves sufficient to indicate a workshop site.

Those pieces of ware that were undamaged would have been prepared for sale. They were probably packed in the same way used for ceramics – namely in baskets filled with straw. The distribution of the material was largely within Egypt but a certain amount was sent to Libya, Sudan, Greece, Turkey, Cyprus, Italy and France (see Nenna and Seif el-Din 2000, 41-45, di Gioia 2006 (Pompeii); De Caro 2002, 74 (Pouzzoli); Hermary and Nenna 2006, 142, no Fa2 (Amathus); Scarfi 1974-1975 (Altino)).

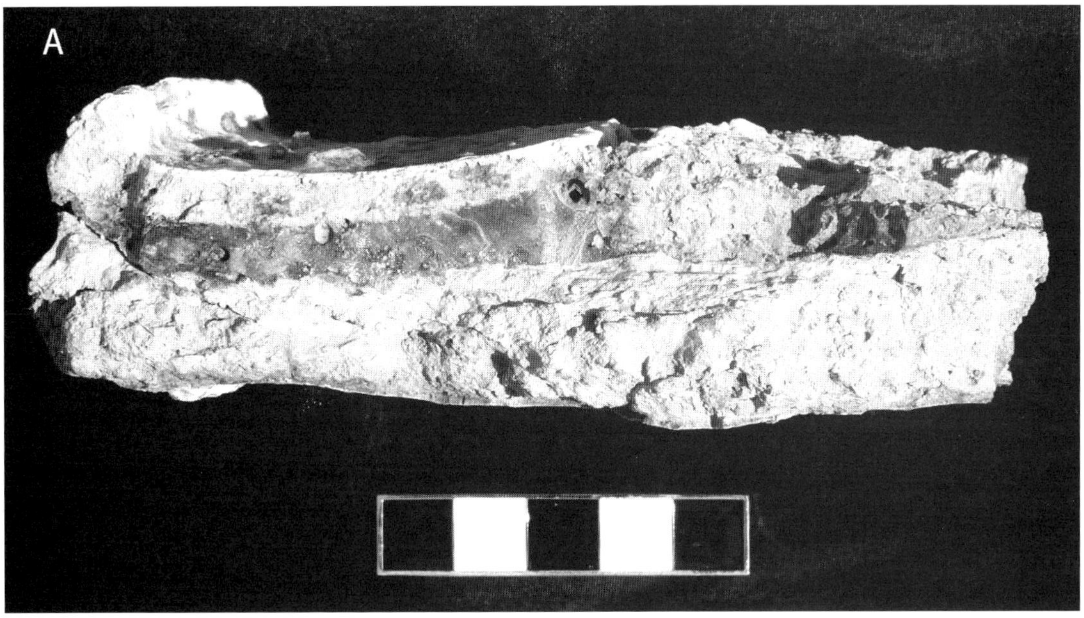

Plate 7.3. (A) Cross section showing a faience vessel (F-2025) of type T6.1a adhering to the base of a saggar. The thick layer of dark glaze can clearly be seen over the saggar base cementing the faience to it. (B) Fragments of faience vessel (F-129) of type T6.1a adhering to the base of a saggar. (Photos: P.T. Nicholson).

Endnotes

1 All references to types prefixed T are from Nenna and Seif el-Din (2000), see here typological plates in Chapter 6.

2 Plant-ash based glasses are known to have been produced in the nearby Wadi Natrun in the Imperial Period, see Picon *et al.* 2008.

3 Interestingly, Vandiver (1983: A-125) does not say that clay was added to the faience paste but that it could have been, and that this might be detected in analyses. So far as the authors are aware clay has not certainly been shown in Roman faience.

4 Petrie's finds from Memphis, now in the Petrie Museum, London, include substantial evidence for the production of Egyptian blue. For the type of crucibles, see Cavassa forthcoming. The work published here has recovered some related finds from Kom Helul but these seem to be stray finds, probably from Kom Qalama.

5 Also known as *patrix.*

6 Whether this was truly a potter's wheel and used at speed as if to throw or was simply a turn-table device is uncertain.

7 If the template is applied to clay/faience which is over a form or mould it is known as a jigger whilst a template which is used to shape clay/faience within a mould is a jolley. The moulds from Memphis suggest that a jolley would most commonly be employed.

8 There is no trace of such cones being used on the unglazed vessels, but their trace would be hidden by subsequent glazing. However, cones are known from HAC3 and may well have been used in saggars employed at the site.

9 For example UC47394 and BM GR1980.10-17.

Chapter 8

Discussion and Conclusions

P.T. Nicholson

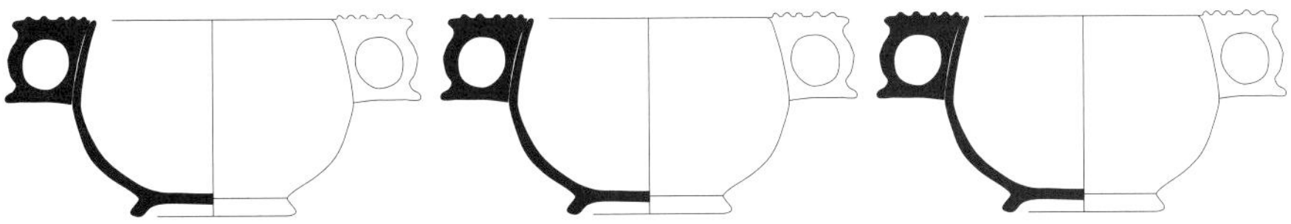

Introduction

The work at Kom Helul has demonstrated that although Petrie (1909a, 1911a) was correct to describe the area as for the manufacture of faience (or in his words "glazed pottery" Petrie 1911a) his reconstruction of how the kilns functioned is not correct.

Rather than stacks of saggars standing on the floor of the kiln with fuel thrown in around them as his accounts (1909a, 1911a) imply, the kilns were much larger than he supposed with a superstructure, probably at least 3.0m tall, standing on top of what he took to be the whole kiln, but which is actually only the firebox. Similarly, it has been suggested that the fuel was probably not agricultural straw but was halfa grass, rich in silica and potassium and which consequently caused extensive slagging (Chapter 4). This may have been the reason for the great depth of the firebox which, as Bourry (1911: 193) notes, would have been specifically designed to cope with the properties of the fuel.

Similarly it seems that two broad types of saggar were used, a large one for biscuit firing and a smaller one for glazing and that these operations may have gone on in separate, but probably structurally similar (if not identical) kilns (see Chapter 7). The operation at Kom Helul was clearly a large one and seems to have taken place alongside the production of Egyptian blue at Kom Qalama. Pottery production, perhaps including the manufacture of terracotta figurines, may well have taken place in the near vicinity as the dumping of some – virtually unused – pottery indicates (see Appendix 2).

Kom Helul and Kom Qalama were clearly part of a large industrial quarter of Roman Memphis and would no doubt have supplied goods well beyond the city itself.

The question of the market for the faience made at Memphis and its relation to other industries is one which is worth considering.

Faience Ancestry at Kom Helul

Insufficient is known about the diachronic development of ancient Memphis, let alone the evolution of particular areas of the city, for us to speak with any confidence about the formation of industrial areas of the city. However, there are hints from the excavation that the Roman faience factories on the site were not the first to be located there.

Petrie's excavations (Petrie 1909a, 1911a) found evidence of faience production of the Ptolemaic era and the present project unearthed some sherds of that date, including pieces with characteristic early Hellenistic apple green glaze and waster pieces such as F-1023. The excavated kiln at HAC3 had probably been built over an existing installation as suggested by the mid-4th Century B.C. coins from the site and although it cannot be said with certainty that a Ptolemaic kiln stood on this site, it does seem highly probable that such kilns were present in the vicinity and the geophysical results (Appendix 1) clearly show such kilns – though their date must remain unknown until excavated.

A number of moulds from the site are, apparently, earlier than the kilns and include a mould for a multiple wedjat eye amulet (P-5), a product known from the New Kingdom but most common in the Late Period.[1]

It is tempting to see Kom Helul, perhaps along with the southern part of Kom Qalama, as a long established industrial quarter of ancient Memphis. Kom Helul certainly has a mass of debris which covers earlier remains that are now affected by the water table and were not excavated. That Late Period and Ptolemaic finds relating to faience production come from the site lends some credibility to this view of the Roman production having a more ancient ancestry. What this might have meant in terms of the adoption of new techniques by a local workforce is discussed below.

Craft Relationships: A Discussion

Petrie (1909a) describes the faience as "glazed pottery" and his subsequent paper (Petrie 1911a) is specifically entitled *The Pottery Kilns at Memphis*. In *Tell el-Amarna* (1894) Petrie also speaks of "glaze" and "glazing works" and his chapter dealing with faience in *The Arts and Crafts of Ancient Egypt* (Petrie 1909c) is entitled "Glazed Ware". In this latter he states that "The use of pottery ware for covering with glaze begins with beads…The pottery base for glazing is never a clay in Egypt but always a porous body of finely ground silica either sand or quartz rock. This was slightly bound together, but the whole strength of the object was in the soaking of glaze on the outer surface" (Petrie 1909c: 108).

One must question why Petrie chose these terms given that 'faience' was already a widely accepted term and was the one later used by Lucas (1962: 156ff) to describe the material. The reason is probably that Petrie saw the material as what would now be called a "non-clay ceramic" (Vandiver and Kingery 1987: 19) and wished to avoid confusion with the various clay based ceramic products being sold as "faiences" in his own time (see Bourry 1911: 366ff) or the tin glazed earthen wares which are now usually referred to as majolica (Nicholson and Peltenburg 2000: 177).

The present author has suggested a close link between the working of stone and the making of faience and glass (Nicholson 2012) during the New Kingdom (1550-1069 B.C.) and the link with stone goes back still further. The situation may begin to change during the Late Period (747-332 B.C.) as Egypt was increasingly drawn into the Mediterranean world (see Lloyd 1983 and 2000), though our knowledge of faience production at this time is far from complete. What is clear is that already during Ptolemaic times the models for faience forms had begun to shift away from those usually produced in stone toward the shapes made in silver, pottery and glass and this trend is continued into Roman times. According to Greene (2007: 659) the arrival of the Ptolemies led "faience (to become) adapted to Hellenistic forms, notably tall jugs decorated with appliqués representing Ptolemaic queens" (see also Thompson 1973). The very common convex bowl undergoes similar Hellenisation. Other faience forms, including elaborate bowls based on metalwork as well as traditional amulets were also produced. It is noteworthy, however, that this production although Hellenised in style retains the Egyptian tradition of faience vessels that are 'special' and much of the production remains of luxury items. Plain wares are found too but the scale of their production seems to change significantly with the coming of the Romans. However, some caution is needed here since as Nenna (pers. comm.) points out more work has been done on Roman than on Ptolemaic sites over the last two decades and good quantification of forms is lacking.

The types of faience product made in the Roman period, at least at Memphis, are often larger, plainer and more utilitarian than those made in pharaonic times. Elaborate and luxurious vessels continue but they have undeniably been joined by common wares (e.g. Nenna and Seif el-Din 2000 forms T12, T13). The making of figurines, although well known from the pharaonic era, is expanded under the Romans to include the types of hollow formed figures which are more usually associated with coroplastic production. These, then, are the kinds of items which are commonly produced in pottery elsewhere in the Roman world. They can also be of larger size than most of the pharaonic productions. The diversity of products seems reduced and production placed in the hands of large specialised workshops which imitate the products made in clay ceramic in Egypt and elsewhere in the Roman world.

One must ask why the link with pottery becomes stronger as the Roman era is reached. The clustering together of high temperature industries is already apparent at least as early as the 18th Dynasty (1550-1295 B.C.) (see Nicholson 2007) and these industries include pottery and faience. The coming of the Ptolemies opened Egypt to a wider world and the products of the 3rd Century B.C. are regarded by Nenna (pers. comm.) as the height of production in terms of range of forms and decoration. Less is known of the 2nd and 1st Century B.C. products though the repertoire of decorated forms is decreased while plain ones continue. With the Roman occupation of Egypt the country is opened to a still wider world than that of the Ptolemies.

Nenna and Seif el-Din (2000: 36) conveniently show the distribution of Hellenistic faience from Egypt. This is mainly through the Levant and eastern Mediterranean as far as Italy and Corsica. This distribution of wares produced in Egypt is greater than the distribution found in Roman times. However, under Roman rule, rather than being open simply to the wider Mediterranean and Near East, Egypt became part of a great empire ultimately stretching as far north as the British Isles. Trade extended even beyond the boundaries of Empire reaching to the shores of the Indian Ocean (Sidebotham 2011, Tomber 2008) and although Egyptian-made faience did not reach all such areas, being focussed mainly on Italy and the Mediterranean, Egypt herself was open to new ideas and new people. These ideas seem to have become incorporated into traditional craft practices.

This is not an insignificant change. Greene (2007: 653) has coined the term "cognitive synchronization" to refer to synchronous developments "among workers in different materials" and it is tempting to see here the importation of industrial, mass-production, techniques associated with Roman pottery workshops to the Ptolemaic Egyptian faience industry. What is not yet clear is how far the Ptolemaic industry had already gone beyond that of Pharaonic times. Saggars seem to have already been in use and some of the changes may have been ones of scale and simplification.

From the late Hellenistic Period into the 1st Century A.D. lead glazed pottery was produced in northern Syria and Asia Minor in imitation of metal prototypes (Hochuli-Gysel 2002) and production spread across the empire extending beyond the 4th Century A.D. (see Walton and Tite 2010). However, "Glazed pottery was not particularly common in the Roman period though the techniques were known throughout the Empire and at one time or another nearly every province had workshops producing it" (Brown 1976: 86). Some of this glazed pottery found its way to Egypt and is represented at sites such as Alexandria (Nenna, Seif el-Din 2000: nos. 624-632 and also a curious sphinx statuette in Gabbari, Nenna 2003: 521-522 no.11 fig.57), Berenike on the Red Sea coast[2] (Tomber, pers. comm.) though in no great quantity. Similarly, alkaline glazed pottery is produced on the eastern borders of the Roman Empire by the Parthians (c.238 B.C.- A.D. 224) and Sassanians (A.D. 224 -651) and (Brown 1976: 87 see also Simpson 1997) but was not widely used beyond their borders though an example is known from the Hadra necropolis of Alexandria (Nenna and Seif el-Din 2000: no. 633).

The glazed pottery of the Roman, Parthian and Sassanian empires is limited in its distribution and is largely confined to its country of production with only small amounts being exported. It may be that lead glazed pottery never became popular in Egypt because the country already had a glazed ware in the form of faience and that under the Romans that material was coming to serve the same purposes as lead glazed pottery elsewhere. Greene (2007) criticises Courby (1922: 257) and Jeammet (2005: 191) for their view that lead glazed pottery in Asia Minor was "a local expedient aimed at reproducing the colour, brilliance and impermeability of imported Egyptian faience…" (Greene 2007: 659) since this does not explain the invention of lead glazing. However, it does perhaps explain why lead glazed wares were not required in Egypt and reinforces the fact that relatively little faience was imported from Egypt, though some reaches as far as Italy where it is known at Pompeii and elsewhere (Mangone *et al.* 2011 and Chapter 7 here).

The reasons why faience is not widely exported are not immediately clear. However, it seems likely that (1) its potential market niche elsewhere in the Roman empire was effectively taken by local lead glazed wares and that (2) it was strongly identified with Egypt (though limited local production of faience had long been established in the Mediterranean and on a larger scale in the Near East and Sudan cf. Andreu- Lanoe *et al.* 2010).

As noted, however, the incorporation of Egypt into first the Ptolemaic and then the Roman empires had a major effect on production. The Roman production of faience frequently uses the material to produce utilitarian shapes which are well known from Terra Sigillata or other ceramics. Thus we find bowls, drinking vessels and plates being produced along with trays and inkwells. These are far removed from the specialised faience vessels made for votive and decorative purposes during the pharaonic period. However, there remains a production of Roman decorated ware which enjoys a wide distribution within and beyond Egypt. Many of these decorated products are found in funerary contexts. The Roman plain wares are also produced in a way and on a scale not previously known. It may be supposed that these vessels were aimed, initially, at the non-native Egyptian population, those who were familiar with Mediterranean taste and style but who wanted a little local colour. At the same time the material itself and its predominantly blue and green colours were familiar to the Egyptians and held a symbolic significance for them as having the brilliance and dazzling qualities of the sky through being related to Hathor (Pinch 1993; Nicholson 2012). In this way the vessels might still have found a market amongst the native Egyptian population. However, it is too early to say for certain which sections of the population used what kinds of faience vessels and at what time. It is certain, however, that faience amulets remained in production and likely that they had a wide appeal, not least as aspects of Egyptian religion were adopted by Ptolemaic and Roman settlers and visitors.

In summary it may be said that faience vessels sat well in their local, Egyptian market but were either duplicated in, or not to the taste of, other regions of the empire. As a result they became a part of a regional 'pottery' tradition often serving similar functions to those met by fine clay ceramics.

A New Kind of Ceramic?

If the faience of Egypt had become largely like 'pottery ceramics' in its shapes and was fulfilling some of the roles which were otherwise taken by glazed or unglazed (but perhaps gloss)[3] pottery, how far had its production become influenced by that of pottery? It seems to the writer that there is a very significant connection with pottery manufacture in the faience workshops of Memphis and elsewhere in Roman Egypt.

Whilst it is certain that pottery production went on alongside the making of faience and glass at pharaonic sites such as Tell el-Amarna (Nicholson 2007), where the kilns for faience and for pottery seem indistinguishable,[4] there is a noticeable change at Roman Kom Helul. The kilns at Kom Helul are square in plan, while those at Amarna and other pharaonic sites are usually round or ovoid. Round pottery kilns are common in the Roman world too, though square ones are also known. However, so far as the writer is aware pharaonic faience production does not seem to have made use of saggars within the kiln in which to fire the ware, true saggars may be a Ptolemaic development.[5] The saggar-like cylindrical vessels from Amarna are wheel made and quite small. Frequently they have also been found to contain traces of glass and are believed to be crucibles for the manufacture of raw glass. However, the fact that glass and faience making were happening in close proximity does not mean that they might not sometimes have been used as convenient containers for firing small faience objects, indeed it would be surprising if they were never used in this way. Critical, however, is the fact that they were not luted together by saggar joiners and there is no evidence for the kind of saggar stacks discussed in Chapter 5. The same is clearly not true of Memphis where two types of saggar have been identified, along with masses of fragments of saggar joiners, and where they were apparently used in association with the square kilns.

As discussed in Chapter 5, saggars have been identified on pottery making sites elsewhere in the Roman world (see Grimes 1930; Mackensen 1993; 2009) and so are clearly part of the production of pottery. Their function, however, goes beyond merely protecting the ware from the effects of smoke and ash in the kiln. Saggars can be regarded as a sign of industrialised mass production since they allow large quantities of ware to be moved more easily and conveniently than would otherwise be the case. In this way they share some of the features of palletised or containerised distribution in the modern world (Headrick 2009: 146) something implied by their French title: "Cassettes."

Not only is the ware conveniently moved in saggars but it can be arranged by shape type and by colour for glazing. As a result different shapes and, more especially, colours can be fired together in the same firing. Thus, in dismantling a saggar stack, saggars could be taken to the appropriate area of the workshop yard for unpacking into lots ready for distribution. This would have been a much more efficient process than dismantling a stack of mixed vessels from a traditional kiln.

The ability to fire wares of different shapes and colours together should also mean a greater efficiency in fuel use since the number of firings for different wares could be reduced and the amount of ware fired could be geared to the anticipated demand. It is not necessary to fire all the dark blue wares separately from the green ones or plates separately from bowls. As a result the amount of ware loaded into a kiln can be larger and, presumably, the number of kilns smaller. This leads to the question of the number of kilns.

It has been argued that there were kilns for biscuit firing (like that excavated) and others for glost firing, however, the total number at Kom Helul is not known. The geophysical survey shows many potential kilns but how many are actual kilns and how many were contemporary is, of course, unknown. Nonetheless, it is likely that two or more biscuit kilns and a similar number of glost kilns might have operated contemporaneously over the site. So far no evidence for the production of decorated wares has been found, but if such wares were made at Memphis then it is likely that they would have had their own kiln complexes.

A New Way Of Forming?

The forming of the actual vessels has also changed toward that of pottery production. The use of moulds for making faience in pharaonic times is well attested and, in the view of the author, extends back at least as far as the making of the tiles of the Step Pyramid complex at Saqqara under Djoser (2667-2648 B.C.) and is especially well known for the making of amulets and inlays from Akhenaten's Amarna (1352-1336 B.C.) as well as other New Kingdom sites. However, there is a significant difference between these moulds and those used in Hellenistic and Roman times. The pharaonic moulds are usually made in fired clay and are for the production of small flat-backed objects such as amulets or tiles. The writer is unaware of any multi-part moulds for making vessels during pharaonic times. They are, however, known from Roman Memphis.

Whether the use of multi-part moulds can be attributed to the Romans is more problematic. It is possible that the multi-part moulding technique is introduced into Egypt by the Greeks during the Late Period or Ptolemaic era.

Greek and Roman moulds are commonly made from plaster (Ashton 2003: 59) rather than clay and it is these which have been found at Memphis. As discussed in Chapter 7, the Petrie Museum has several plaster moulds for vessels and these are clearly multi-part. It has been suggested above that once the faience paste had been pressed roughly into them the moulds may have been seated on the potter's wheel where the excess paste could be removed and the interior shaped whilst further pressing the material into the mould. After a short period of drying the mould could be taken apart and itself be dried before being reused. The making of pottery in plaster moulds, albeit by slip casting,[6] is still in use amongst pottery manufacturers today.[7] Interestingly, most of the moulds used for making Hellenistic relief bowls are made of fired clay (Rotroff 1982; Bailey 1984: 351) as are those for Roman Terra Sigillata, and are single piece moulds, while those for pottery lamps are most commonly plaster (Bailey 1997: 168). The difference may be because the elaborate decoration stamped into the clay moulds could not be achieved in the same way using plaster and because plaster would wear more rapidly than fired clay. This would not be a problem in moulding plain faience wares.

Once again, it seems that the workshops were designed to produce large amounts of ware by reducing the production processes into operations which could be achieved without great craft skill. "Mass production is the focussing on a manufacturing project of the principles of power, accuracy, economy, system, continuity and speed" (Ford 1926)[8] and these principles generally require the simplification of complex tasks into a series of shorter, simpler ones.[9] The filling of moulds, if not their final trimming on the wheel, their unloading, drying and stacking into saggars could all have been achieved with a minimum of training. These are classic features of mass production and are known from the pottery industry of the Roman Period. This is also a very different approach to mass production than that taken by the Egyptians.

The ancient Egyptian way of making something in large quantities was to examine how a single item of such a thing might be produced and then multiply that production unit sufficient to produce the number of items wanted. Thus if the amount of flour required for a labour gang in a day is 10 times that which can be produced in a normal household quern emplacement then ten quern emplacements and labourers are needed. This is very clearly seen in a Middle Kingdom (2055-1650 B.C.) model of bakers and brewers now in the British Museum.[10] There is never any attempt to increase the size of the quern stone or to power it differently. Labour was evidently sufficiently cheap and in sufficient supply to continue to do more of the same. With the coming of the Romans the infrastructure of Egypt is somewhat revised from the changes already instituted under the Ptolemies and technologies in use elsewhere in the empire are imported.

This raises the interesting question of whether those who made faience at Memphis were regarded as faience makers or just another kind of potter and whether they were native Egyptians or came from outside. One might guess that, given that there were moves toward greater production in the Ptolemaic period, those who worked in the industry then continued, albeit under new management, in the Roman era. We do not need to assume that new workshops were set up at Memphis with new people. Instead it simply seems likely that it was necessary to adopt new technologies in order to meet new demands. It is possible that the first to set up a workshop with such new methods was a non-Egyptian but that his production methods were rapidly adopted by his neighbours. That there may have been foreign influence in the industry might be indicated by the name used for faience workers during Ptolemaic times – namely kalleinopoioi (καλλάϊγοποιων)[11] (Bogaert 1998-1999: 66).

Conclusions

This publication has tried to bring together the evidence excavated by both Petrie and the writer and to combine it with museum and other evidence to give an account of the making of faience at Roman period Kom Helul, Memphis.

It has been shown that Petrie's reconstruction of the kilns and their fuelling was wrong, but was wrong for good reasons, namely the technique of excavation available and the state of technological knowledge in his time. His attempt at reconstruction must be regarded as a model of its time. It must also be said that the present attempt at a reconstruction is not a complete picture. The kiln excavated appears to have been used only for biscuit firing and though, on the basis of Petrie's work, it seems that glost kilns were of the same form this is not absolutely certain.

Evidence from actual workshops has come not from buildings but from debris found around the furnace. It is unclear what form any workshop buildings may have taken but given the favourable climate in Egypt and the need to dry faience paste, plaster moulds and unfired glazed vessels, it may be that they took the form of open areas with only a shelter for those involved in working on the moulding process, be that filling the moulds or trimming their contents on a wheel, if such were done. Shaw (2004) has suggested that much work went on in the open and that may well be as true of Roman Memphis as it was in pharaonic times. Only large-scale open area excavation at Kom Helul would reveal whether any workshop structures survive. Such an operation would undoubtedly yield a very great deal of pottery, including industrial pottery, and would be a worthwhile but expensive operation.

It is hoped that a much clearer impression has been gained of the physical appearance and operation of kilns at Memphis and of the stages of production of the vessels which were the main products of the workshops. The relationship between faience production, an old established Egyptian craft, and mass production of pottery, a Roman development, seems to be a significant one. Petrie is not explicit about whether he viewed production in the same way as suggested here, but it is evident from the titles of his publications that he saw some such connection in the making of "glazed pottery" at Memphis.

The coming years will surely see the excavation of further faience production sites of both Ptolemaic (see for example Desbordes and Brissaud 2013: 73) and Roman date and these will add significantly to our understanding of the development of the faience industry in these periods.

Endnotes

1 See for example Boston Museum of Fine Arts 25.2365 and 72.1105, the latter in stone.

2 The Berenike examples are of 1st Century A.D. date and belong to the 'Tarsus' type. I am indebted to Roberta Tomber for this information and her permission to include it here.

3 Greene (2007:655) rightly notes that the Greek pottery specialists' practice of referring to "black glaze" or "red glaze" pottery is misleading, and teh term 'gloss' is better used instead of glaze. The term "glaze" is often erroneously applied to Terra Sigillata and other gloss-surface ceramics and should be restricted to those products which actually have a glaze (i.e. glassy) layer on their surface.

4 In addition to pottery/faience kilns at site O45.1, two very large furnaces are thought likely to have been for glass production.

5 The writer is assuming that at least some of the saggars found by Petrie are Ptolemaic, but as these were not collected and because we do not have certain saggars of this date from Kom Helul the matter must remain speculative. It is possible, but perhaps unlikely, that saggars are a wholly Roman development in Egypt.

6 A process in which liquid clay is poured into a mould, usually of multi-part type, and removed once sufficiently dry. Moulds used in slip casting would take longer to dry before re-use than would those for faience as the slip clay is liquid.

7 For example at the Burleigh factory, Stoke-on-Trent.

8 Although conventionally cited, as here, as by Ford, since the article is initialled (H.F.) it is believed by Batchelor (1994: 6 n.4) that the text is actually that of one of Ford's ghost-writers, one William J. Cameron.

9 In defending mass production against charges of monotony and lack of skill this paper goes on to state that "the need for skilled artisans and creative genius is greater under mass-production than without it" (Ford 1926: 823) though there seems little evidence for the statement and many of the early principles of the method have been abandoned.

10 BM EA 40915.

11 Literally workers in blue and green materials.

APPENDIX I

GEOPHYSICAL INVESTIGATION OF AN INDUSTRIAL SITE AT KOM HELUL, MEMPHIS (EGYPT)

R. Hart

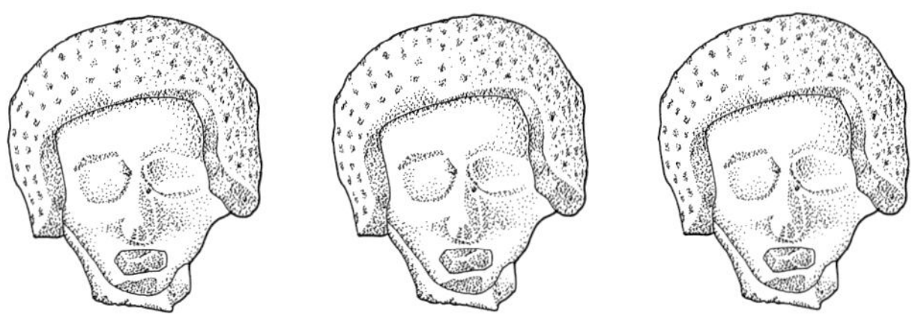

INTRODUCTION

Kom Helul is a site of approximately 14,000m^2 divided into two distinct areas (designated HAC and HAD) by a modern irrigation canal. It is located to the south-east of the Memphis Open-Air Museum and within the Memphis Antiquities Area. Geophysical survey was conducted using a *Geoscan* FM36 magnetic gradiometer. The topography of the area HAC, and of the canal, was surveyed by EDM.

The results of the geophysical survey in the HAC area suggest the presence of kiln structures within the survey area, with some displaying little sign of disturbance. It is uncertain whether any of the kilns, the original targets of this survey, are those that Petrie described (Petrie 1909a; 1911a) though that subsequently excavated at HAC3 is certainly not. The anomalies interpreted as relatively undisturbed faience kilns are situated in the south-east region of HAC, to the south-east and on top of the southern mound (25.28m above sea-level). The four kilns in this area form a diamond shape approximately 20 x 20m. Vitrification products, alongside domestic and industrial pottery and faience can be found in abundance over the whole site; although the slag was more concentrated in the area where the kilns were highlighted by the survey. There were other anomalies in the HAC area that are likely to be kilns, although less prominent as a result of being less well preserved.

The results in the HAD area, located south of the canal, suggested a large structure approximately 25.0 x 23.0m which had a trench dug through part of its north side during the E.E.S. excavations in 2000, revealing a robber trench. The extraordinarily thick edges of this feature are of particular note. There were no kilns obvious on this side of the site.

METHODS

Survey area

The area of the geophysical survey covered approximately 200.0m north-south and 140.0m east-west. This was divided into 70 grids each of 20.0m square. Within this area 36 grids were surveyed using magnetic gradiometry. A topographic survey was also undertaken covering those 70 grid squares.

Survey techniques

The geophysical technique employed was magnetic gradiometry, using a *Geoscan* FM36. The survey was carried out in 20m grid squares with 0.5m sample intervals and 1m parallel, traverse intervals. Each data point (d.p.), therefore, covers an area of 1 x 0.5m and an average of the magnetic gradiometry measured in nT (for more information on the scientific terms and data handling programmes used refer to the Geoplot Instruction Manual (2001), an explanantion of technical terms used here appears at the end of this Appendix). Due to the size of these d.p.s a small feature within a d.p. would not show itself in detail, it would, however affect the overal average of the value of that d.p.. The direction of the traverses was northerly, beginning in the south-west corner of the grid square.

Coordinate system

The site grid was laid out with respect to magnetic north, with the south-west corner having the coordinates (0,0). To re-establish the grid at any time the south-west corner of grid M11, (or coordinate 100,120) has a permanent grid peg that can be lined up with the corner of the military boundary fence and this will provide the north-south grid line.

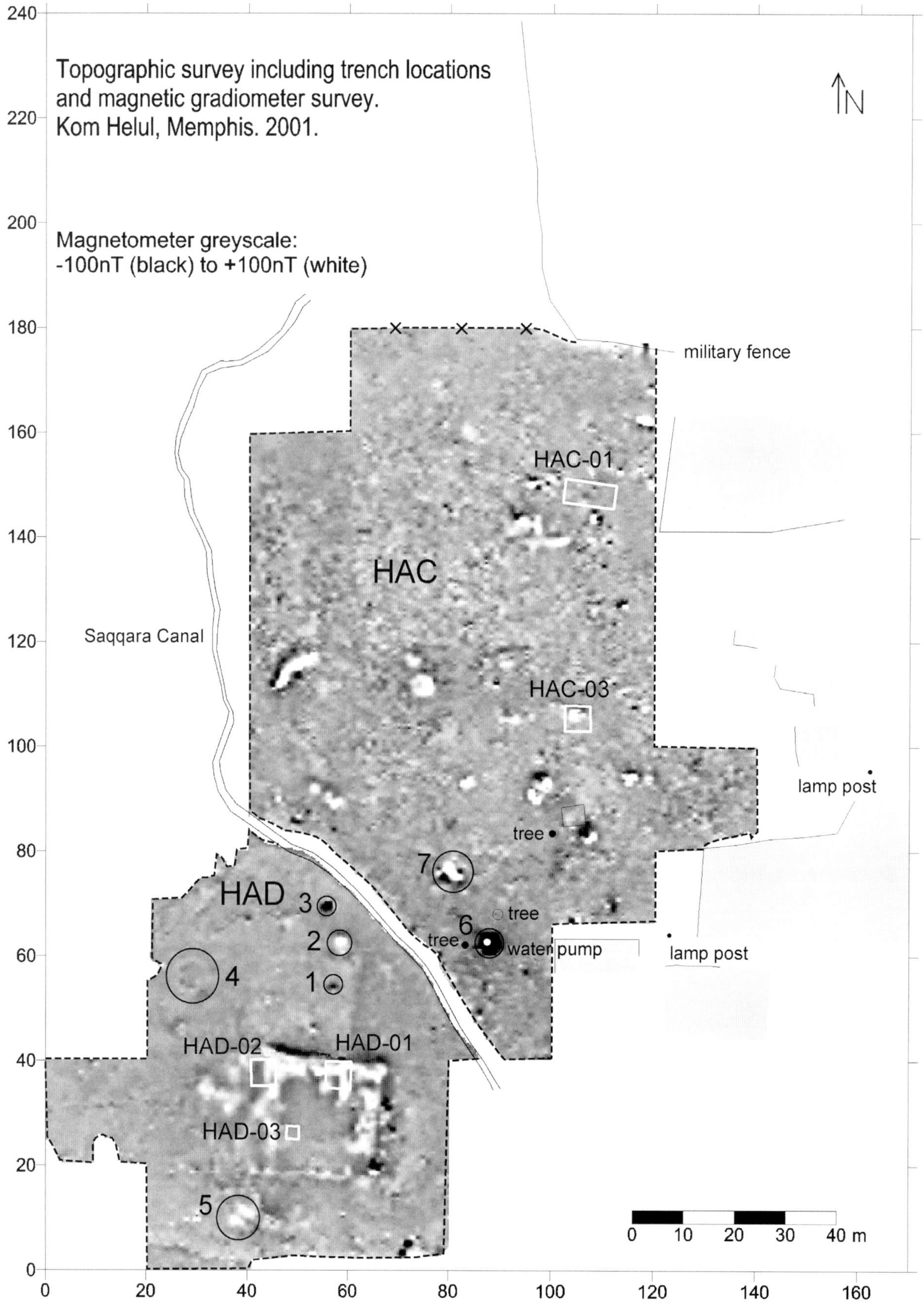

Fig. A1.1. Kriged dataset output from Surfer. Data clipped at +100nT and –100nT.

Results

The survey data were of a high quality throughout the surveyed area, with only a few minor interferences due to the abundance of modern ferrous metal littering the site, especially so in the HAC part of the site. A small number of high magnetic readings were the result of small depressions filled with scrap metal. Mud brick houses delimited the eastern edge of the site on HAC, a large, steel military fence delimited most of the northern edge and these added some interference to the edges of the survey. The archaeological features associated with this industrial area were well imaged by the survey, some detail was noted especially on HAD where a trench was dug in the 2000 season that was clearly imaged by the magnetometer.

Discussion of Figure A1.1

This figure shows the position of the Saqqara Canal and how it divides the site into the areas HAC and HAD outlined by the dashed lines. It also shows the features of the results that could be interpreted as archaeological, but are in fact modern:

1-3. Three piles of bricks and large pieces of ferrous metal.

4. A recent ring of bricks used to contain small fires.

5. A large concentration of ferrous metal including barbed wire.

6. A water pump, supplying the village with clean drinking water.

7. A concentration of mud bricks and large amounts of metal.

The dashed and crossed line represents the military boundary fence.

Discussion of Figure A1.2

The grid square markings can be seen on the axis of this figure. This figure primarily introduces some linear features: **AA^1.** This internal wall in this complex structure adds another dimension to it. It is possible that this internal wall was initially an external wall before the structure was rebuilt or extended. It shows as a particularly strong feature at the east and west sides (+88nT), gradually reducing and almost disappearing as a feature in the centre (5nT (42.25,49.5)). Could this be an entranceway into the structure or, internally into another part of the structure? Equally, the wall could have in some way been damaged, or the fired bricks robbed and used for building elsewhere.

BB^1 & CC^1. These two parallel lines that run from south-east to north-west can be seen as a general pattern for the distribution of kilns in this industrial area (the detail of kiln locations is discussed in Fig.A1.4). There is a high proportion of anomalies on these lines although there are many kiln features that deviate from this rule.

DD^1. This linear feature begins running in a south-easterly to north-westerly direction and so parallel to BB^1 and CC^1, however at approximately (157.25, 94.5) it curves to the west-north-west. It is unclear what this feature might be, however where it does begin to turn from its original direction it disappears into a the southern edge of a large feature and so it is difficult to say whether it is associated with it.

EE^1. This feature marks the edge of HAD, where the ground level drops considerably. This line marks the difference in these heights.

Discussion of Figure A1.3

Here we can see most clearly, the largest number of features, all but the large structure are found on HAC.

1. This imposing structure is situated on HAD and measures approximately 25.0 x 23.0m. Its walls vary in thickness from 2m to 8m. The readings range from +216nT to -100nT. Its north-west corner is particularly thick, with what appears to be an additional feature running away from its west wall in a westerly direction. The internal wall also adds detail to this structure. Its south wall is by far the thinnest and the reason for this must be held by that internal wall. The westerly wall does infact appear to be a double wall also with a niche or semi-circular recess in the internal wall.

2. A large negative anomaly (-138nT) with positive areas to the east (+55nT) and west (+134nT). The pattern of this feature suggests, especially due to the values that this is unlikely to be a kiln.

3. This feature could include three kilns, with the western most being 1.0m away from the other two that are touching, possibly sharing a wall. This is a 'figure 8' shape feature, where either two contemporary kilns are built 'back-to-back' and therefore share a wall, or one kiln was built using a surviving wall of a disused kiln. The westerly kiln has readings of between +88nT and –64nT. The 'figure 8' shape has a range of +149nT and –60nT.

4. This is the most southerly of the four kilns (4, 5, 6 and 11) forming a 20.0 x 20.0m diamond shape. Its range of values are +291nT to -178nT, and measures approximately 7.0 x 7.0m.

5. This is the most easterly kiln in the diamond shape, measuring 5.0 x 5.0m with extreme values of +315nT and –112nT.

6. The most westerly of the kilns in the diamond shape. This follows the typical 'figure 8' shape (see 3). It measures

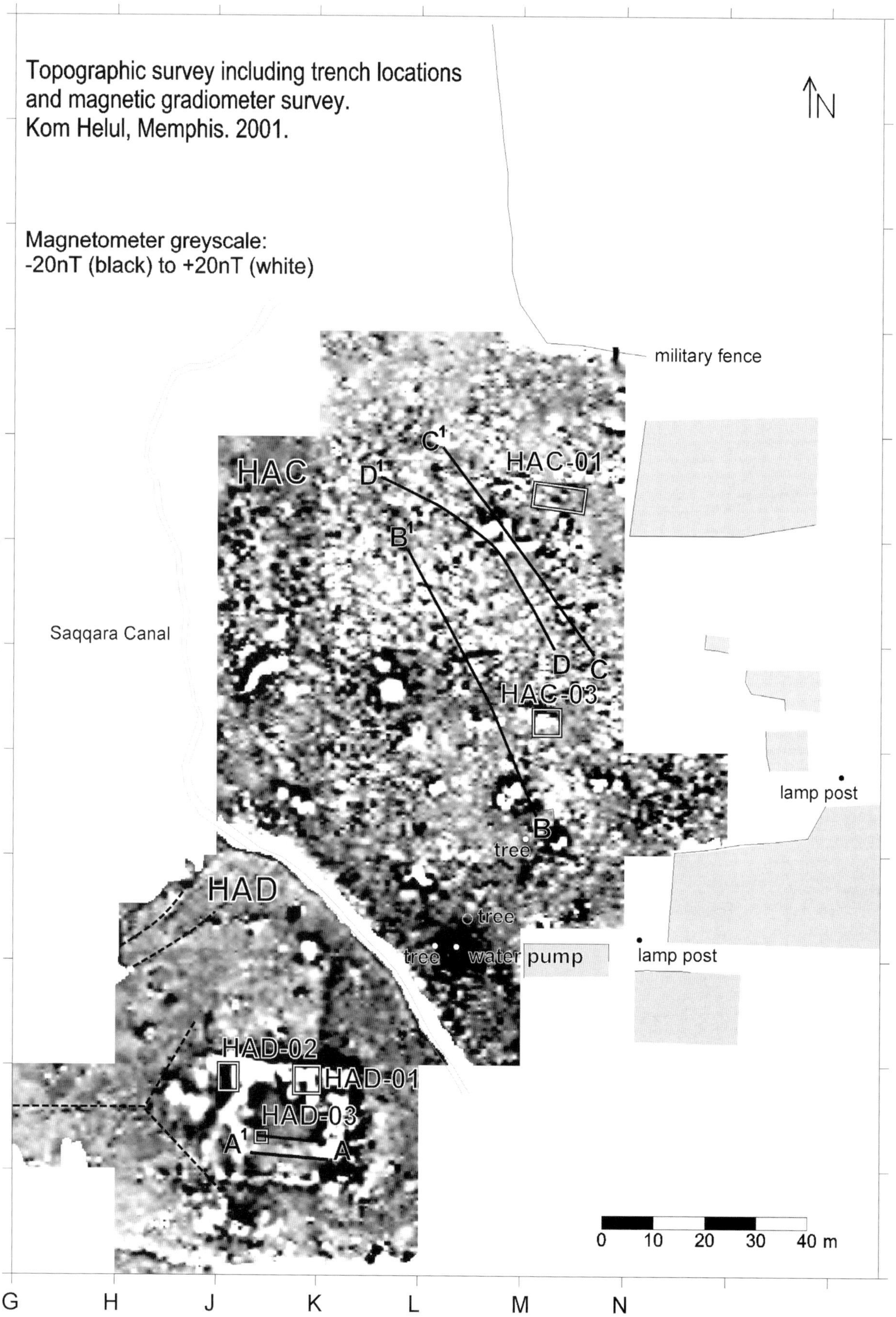

Fig. A1.2. Kriged dataset output from Surfer. Data clipped at +20nT and –20nT.

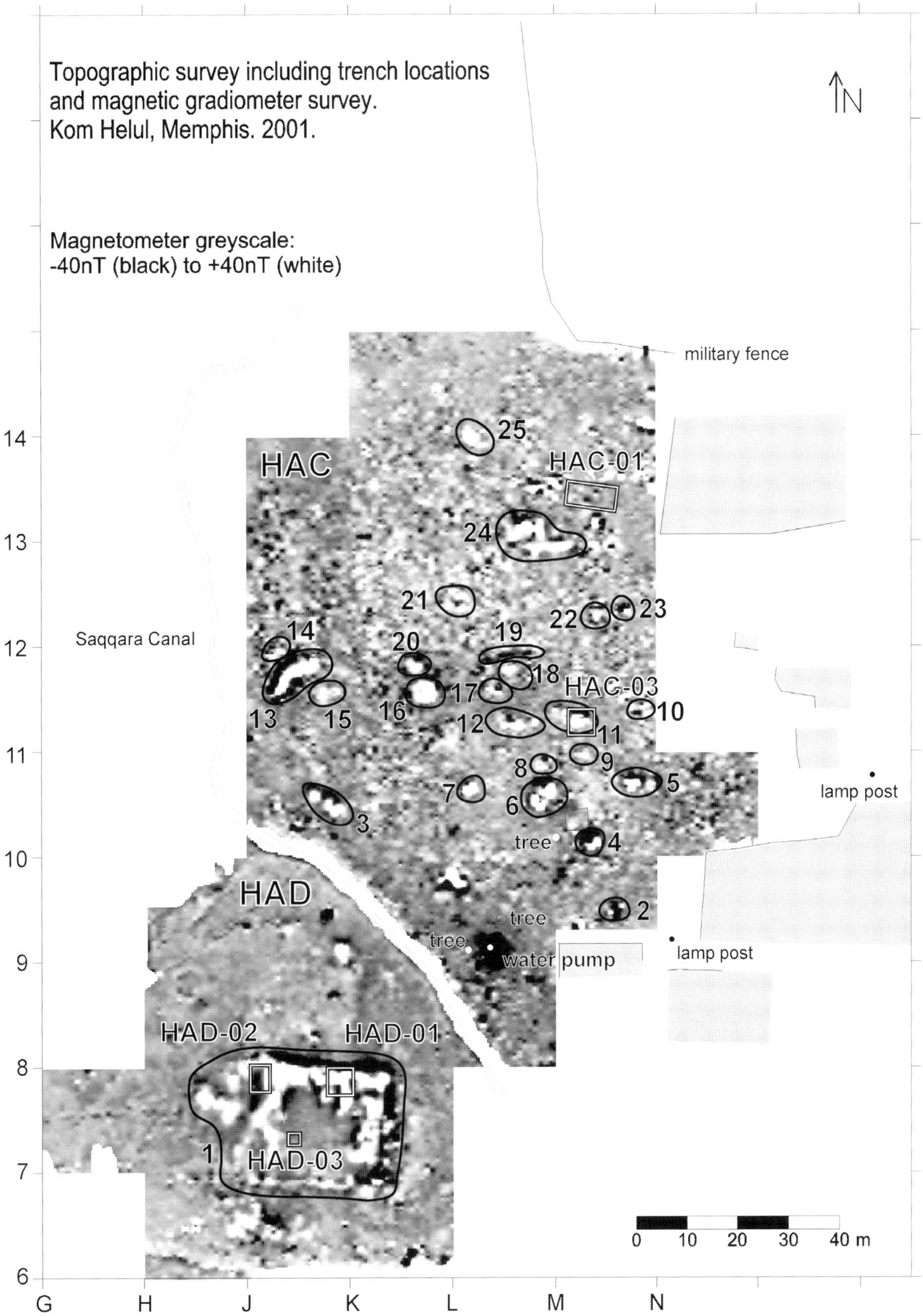

Fig. A1.3. Kriged dataset output from Surfer v7. Data clipped at +40nT and –40nT.

approximately 9.0 x 6.0m, with values ranging from +460nT and –168nT. This is a very high positive reading.

7. This feature is a large positive value (+309nT) with little negative signature around it. It measures approximately 3.0 x 3.0m.

8. A small positive/ negative feature probably associated with 6.

9. A small positive feature probably associated with 11.

10. A small positive/negative feature.

11. The northerly kiln in the diamond shape, measuring 4.0 x 4.0m, with a range of readings from +245nT to -197nT. This was the kiln excavated during the 2001 season (HAC-03).

12. A 'figure of 8' shaped feature (kiln?), with a small negative signature. High readings of +108nT and lows of -65nT.

13. A remarkably long feature measuring 11.0m in length and approximately 3m wide. It has high values of +680nT (the highest value on the site) and negative values of -182nT. This feature is situated on the west side of a long mound and may be the material of a kiln running down the slope and therefore creating this pattern.

14. A small positive feature associated with 13.

15. A small positive feature associated with 13.

16. A large positive feature approximately 6.0m square, with moderate readings between +179nT and -88nT, with the negative signature outlining the west and north sides of the positive square. It is possible that this is a large kiln, if so it would be the largest on the site.

17. A small, negative/positive anomaly, possibly associated with 18 and 19.

18. A positive, oval feature, 1.0m wide and 2.0m long, with a high value of 91nT

19. A narrow, negative feature approximately 8.0m long with readings above -59nT. Probably associated with 18.

20. A feature associated with 16. This possible kiln feature is unlike those in the diamond pattern (4, 5, 6 and 11) as it lacks the right angled corners that the others have. This could be a plundered kiln, or possibly it material from feature 16, excavated (by Petrie?) and the spoil tipped beside it?

21. This is a circular feature with a positive signature with a small negative interior. The diameter is approximately 3.0m.

22. A small positive feature with a negative ring around it.

23. A small positive feature similar to 22.

24. A complex of features including a long (10.0m), thin positive line running east-west, with a shorter positive line (5.0m) leaving it at right angles to the north with highs of +177nT. To the west of this shorter line is a possible kiln feature with high values of 90nT and a strong negative signature to the north of it.

25. This is a positive feature, roughly circular with a diameter of 4m and highs of +61nT.

Discussion of Figure A1.4

This figure shows the geophysical data set as shown in figure A1.1 with a contour and feature survey overlaid. This allows interpretation of the major geophysical anomalies and their associated location within the topography of the site and their proximity to modern features including housing and the canal.

Geophysical terms used in the text

Kriged dataset: In plotting data different methods of gridding will provide different interpretations of the data because each method calculates the grid node using a different algorithm. Kriging is the default gridding method used by the *Surfer 7* computer program (see below) "because it generates a good map for most data sets" (Golden Software Inc. 1999: 103). It can be used for gridding most kinds of geophysical data set.

nT: NanoTesla. The Tesla is the SI unit of magnetic flux density, defined as the density of one weber of magnetic flux per square metre. A nanoTesla is therefore one thousand millionth of one weber of magnetic flux per square metre. This is the unit used to record the readings from the magnetometer.

Surfer: Computer program used for contouring and 3D surface mapping. Commonly employed for the processing of geophysical results.

weber: SI unit of magnetic flux, defined as the flux that, linking a circuit of one turn, produces in it an E.M.F. (electromotive force) of one volt as it reduces to zero at a uniform rate in one second.

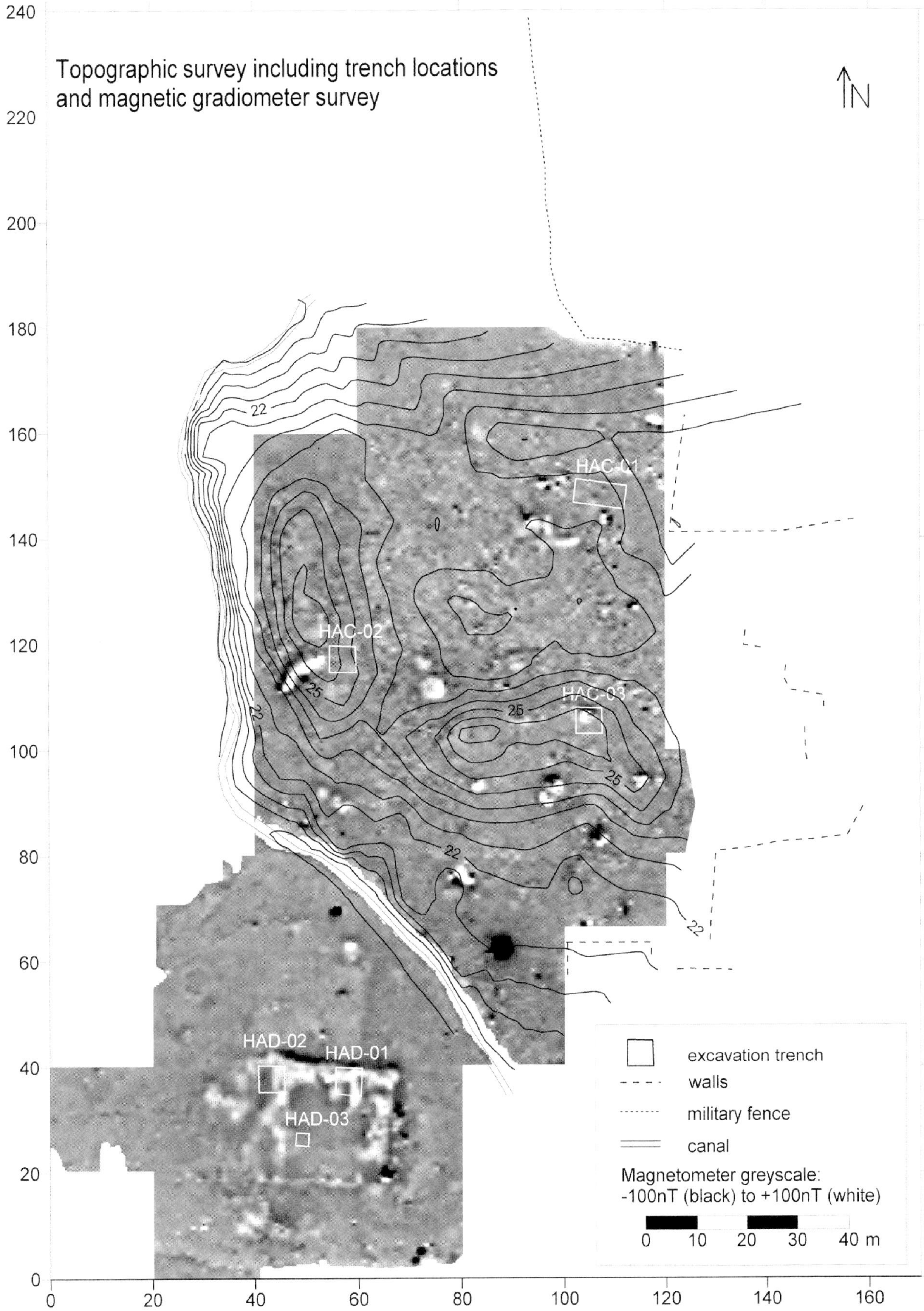

Fig. A1.4. Kriged dataset output from Surfer. Data clipped at +100nT and –100nT. Overlain with topographic and feature survey including all trench locations.

APPENDIX 2

Domestic Pottery

P.G. French

Introduction

This Appendix offers a small selection of the domestic pottery recorded from the excavations, to demonstrate the range of material present and to provide a chronological framework for the work. The present writer and Janine Bourriau catalogued the material in the field and intend to publish it in full when it has been studied further, to include both a more detailed description of the ceramics themselves and full bibliographical references to comparative examples from other excavations. The choice of pottery for the present chapter has been guided by a wish to show a representative selection from every period in each of the various areas without undue duplication, whilst concentrating on the ceramic types which are stratigraphically and statistically the most informative. Pottery specifically related to the operation of the kiln(s) is dealt with elsewhere (Chapter 4).

The major dimension is most commonly the rim diameter, specified as 'top' or 'maximum' according to which was measured, as appropriate to the vessel form. It should be borne in mind that very few of the vessels were complete, so a vessel which originally had handles may not reveal this on the preserved sherd(s). Polish on the surface is mentioned where visible, but may have been lost elsewhere through weathering. Where a fabric designation is included (e.g. Marl D (H1)), the reference is to the Vienna system followed by the Saqqara system classification (French 2013, 19-22).

The six excavated trenches are dealt with in alphabetical and then numerical order, and within each, the material is described and illustrated chronologically.

Chronological summary

Old Kingdom (2686-2181 B.C)

Parallels for the few sherds included in the present chapter were readily available among the published material from the Polish excavations at Saqqara (Rzeuska, 2006, *passim*), and from the Anubieion in another part of the Saqqara necropolis (French, 2013, *passim*). They belong to the later part of the Old Kingdom, probably the Sixth Dynasty, or to the first years of the First Intermediate Period. The vessels were hand made but the rims were probably finished on a slow wheel. The slipped and polished surfaces are typical of their period.

Middle Kingdom (2055-1650 B.C)

No sherds of the Middle Kingdom have so far been recognised.

New Kingdom (1550-1069 B.C)

The New Kingdom sherds derive from the Ramesside Period (1186-1069 B.C)., and some perhaps from the Third Intermediate Period (1069-747 B.C)., rather than earlier, and tend to confirm in a small way the view that this part of the city was not settled until that time. Much the most interesting and unusual are the two open forms 31 and 51 from HAC1, which appear to be Egyptian copies of Mycenaean vessels.

Late Dynastic Period (747-332 B.C)

Almost all the pottery of this period could fit comfortably within the sixth and 5th Centuries B.C, though the absence of evidence for the preceding and succeeding centuries need not imply that adjacent areas of the city were unoccupied. The second half of the 6th Century, which witnesses a great increase in the popularity of polished red slips on the Nile clay forms, is more fully represented than the first half. 'Pigeon Pots' 1023/95, of a type already evolving during the 7th Century B.C. (author, personal observation), display the developed rim-form of the 6th Century and the base has the low collar around the hole characteristic of the same period (French, 2007, 111 and Abb. 16.5/6.). Marl bowl 1103 matches a 6th Century series (Aston, 1999, 210-12 and Pl. 65, Nos 1906-10) very well. The bulge in the neck of 1062 probably places it in the first half of the same century

(French, 2007, 113-14 and Abb. 19.1), whereas the cordons on the neck of 1072 do not develop until the second half (French and Ghaly, 1991, 118, No. 83). Saucer-lamp 1235 is attested from the first half of the 6th Century at Buto (French, 2007, 108-09 and Abb. 15.3) but apparently continues to be produced throughout the century according to examples from the Saqqara Anubieion (French, in preparation). The Chian amphora 100 is in accord, as Greek transport vessels of this and related forms were probably not manufactured until after c.650 B.C (Cook and Dupont 1998, 146) and are unlikely to have become common in Egypt immediately. At Elephantine shallow bowls like 889, which are known in both Nile and marl clay versions, are variously dated from as early as 550-400 B.C. onwards (Aston 1999, 224 and Pl. 70, No. 2000; 241 and Pl. 76, No. 2106; 250 and Pl. 78, No. 2168; 258 and Pl. 82, Nos 2245/46), parallels from the Saqqara Anubieion probably confirming at least the 6th Century date (French, in preparation). Torch bases 938 and 1218 are also consistent with this time (French and Ghaly, 1991, 124, Nos 114/15), although their whole period of currency is not yet firmly established. The Levantine amphora 124 is exceptional in being more likely to fit into the 4th or early 3rd Century B.C. than earlier.

Ptolemaic and Roman Periods (332 B.C. – A.D. 395)

Some sherds appear to belong to the later Ptolemaic Period or the beginning of the Roman Period. Pending further work, these are catalogued as Ptolemaic or Roman, as are some which may be later in the Roman Period. Where there is good reason to regard others as specifically Ptolemaic or specifically Roman, they are so described. Parallels from other sites indicate that those described as Roman are of the 2nd or 3rd Century A.D., when ribbing the bodies of non-amphora vessels became much more general.

Summary of the excavation of Area HAC in relation to the ceramics

Three trenches were opened in this area, designated HAC1, 2 and 3. HAC1 and 2 were worked on only in the first excavation season (2000), when the author and Janine Bourriau were not present, and were discontinued in favour of HAC3 following geophysical evidence which located a kiln there. The sherds from HAC1 and HAC2 were found to have been pre-sorted, with only those 'of interest' saved, so there is uncertainty as to how representative they are of the total assemblage; in particular, the light-coloured marls would have stood out and are probably over-represented. However, since they derive from surface or immediately sub-surface contexts and display the mixture of periods usual in such material, this is of no great significance.

Unfortunately, some misunderstanding had also taken place in 2000. When seen by the ceramicists in 2001, all sherds marked as HAC2 had also been marked as from a joint context [010/011], whereas the excavation report states that the only context in HAC2 was [010] and that [011] was the 'cut' for HAD1. These sherds are assumed to be from HAC2, but as it happens the matter is of little significance.

At HAC3 far more sherds were excavated, and from a stratigraphic sequence which related to the large excavated kiln; furthermore, for most of the work in this trench, pre-sorting was discontinued.

Discussion and catalogue by individual trenches

Trench HAC1

Contexts with pottery were [001], [002], [006], [007] and [009], plus a few sherds from trench cleaning and effectively without context; as is normal, there was no pottery from the wall [008]. The material from contexts [006] and [007] consisted almost entirely of large pieces, indicating that pre-selection, even of the diagnostic[1] sherds, had taken place, and this may have affected [009] also. However, there proved to be no discernible difference between the assemblages, confirmed by joins between sherds from different contexts. There were a few sherds of the Old Kingdom, probably derived from bricks manufactured later since this part of Memphis is thought to have been settled only in the later New Kingdom, after the Nile had changed its course. There were also some of the New Kingdom to Third Intermediate Period, which are more likely to relate to activity in the area. Otherwise, there is a large component of the 6th-5th Century B.C. and a smaller but still substantial one of the Ptolemaic and Roman Periods, some of it from the lower level [009]. It is not possible to tell, from the pottery alone, how the mixing came about. There appear to be two possibilities:

1. The entire mixed assemblage was deposited in one or more episodes, the last being in the Roman Period or later.

2. A deposit of the Late Dynastic Period was already present when later material was dumped upon it, and mixing has subsequently taken place.

Catalogue of representative pottery in HAC1

No. 973 (Fig. A2.1:a). Late Old Kingdom. Context [009]. Bowl with groove below rim. Maximum rim diameter 17cm. Nile clay, with polished thick red slip on all surfaces.

No. 45 (Fig. A2.1:b). Late Old Kingdom. Context [001]. Bowl with maximum diameter on the body. Rim diameter (top) c.22cm. Nile clay with polished pink slip on all surfaces.

No. 1102 (Fig. A2.1:c). Ramesside (-Third Intermediate Period?). Context [006].
Storage Jar. Rim diameter (top) 18cm. Marl D (H1) fabric. Self-slip firing white on exterior and top of rim, orange-pink on interior. Polished where slipped, except interior below minimum diameter.

No. 31 (Fig. A2.1:d). New Kingdom(?). Context [001]. Thin-walled bowl with flat rim. Maximum rim diameter 21cm. No handles as preserved. Nile clay with red-brown slip on exterior and on top of rim, extending 2 cms down on interior; below this, too weathered to show. Polish on outer edge of rim only. Two white painted bands on body, one sinuous, one straight. Perhaps an Egyptian copy of a Mycenaean vessel.[1](See 51).

No. 51 (Fig. A2.1:e). New Kingdom(?). Context [002]. Thin-walled bowl with two opposed vertical handles. Rim diameter (top) 21cm. Nile clay with light red-brown slip on all surfaces. Exterior polished, and traces on interior. Sinuous white painted band on body, and narrow white painted band around rim showing on both surfaces. Perhaps an Egyptian copy of a Mycenaean vessel.[2] (See 31).

No. 1103 (Fig. A2.1:f). Late Dynastic Period (6th Century B.C.). Context [006].
Bowl. Rim diameter (top) 18cm. Marl clay. Interior pale brown, exterior pale grey shading to pale brown in some areas. Smoothed but not coated. Not polished or burnished.

No. 1054 (Fig. A2.1:g). Late Dynastic Period (6th Century B.C. or slightly later). Context [006].
Globular bowl or jar with slightly undercut rim. Maximum rim diameter 18cm. Nile clay with highly polished red slip on exterior and on top of rim, slip extending just over rim and running down inside.

No. 1023 (Fig. A2.1:h). Late Dynastic Period (6th Century B.C. or slightly later). Context [002].
'Pigeon Pot'. Rim diameter (top) 27cm. Nile clay. Uncoated. Not polished or burnished.

No. 1095 (Fig. A2.1:i). Late Dynastic Period (6th Century B.C. or slightly later). Context [001].
Base of 'pigeon pot' (not same vessel as 1023), with 'collar' and pre-firing central hole. Collar diameter 6cm, hole c.2.5cm. Nile clay. Uncoated. Not polished or burnished.

No. 1051 (Fig. A2.1:j). Late Dynastic Period. Context [002]. Neckless jar. Rim diameter (top) 15cm. Exterior lightly grooved. No handles as preserved, but probably had two opposed. Marl clay. Exterior white, interior pale pink. Uncoated. Not polished or burnished. (See 1052).

No. 1052 (Fig. A2.1:k). Late Dynastic Period. Context [002]. Neckless jar with widely spaced shallow grooves on exterior. Rim diameter (top) 11cm. No handles as preserved, but probably had two opposed. Nile clay with white slip on exterior and top of rim, presumably in imitation of a marl fabric, interior uncoated. Possible traces of polish on exterior only. (See 1051).

No. 1062 (Fig. A2.2:a). Late Dynastic Period (6th Century B.C. or slightly later). Context [001].
Jar with bulge on neck. Rim diameter (top) 8cm. Nile clay with unusually large number of limestone inclusions. Probably uncoated. Possible trace of polish on top of rim.

No. 1080 (Fig. A2.2:b). Late Dynastic Period (6th Century B.C. or slightly later). Context [002].
Jar with groove around rim. Rim diameter (top) 8cm. Nile clay with polished thick red slip on exterior and on top of rim, and down 0.3cm on interior to a straight edge.

No. 1082 (Fig. A2.2:c). Late Dynastic Period (6th Century B.C. or slightly later). Context 'trench cleaning'.
Jar/bottle with shoulder shaped to take a lid. Rim diameter (top) c.8cm. One small vertical lug handle, assumed to be one of two opposed, set across a shallow groove for string-tying before firing. Nile clay with red slip on exterior and on top of rim. Traces of polish on top of rim, only.

No. 1050 (Fig. A2.2:d). Late Dynastic Period (6th Century B.C. or slightly later). Context [002].
Cylinder-necked jar. Rim diameter (top) 8cm. Nile clay, with polished red slip on exterior and on top of rim where unweathered surface survives.

No. 1072 (Fig. A2.2:e). Late Dynastic Period (second half of 6th Century B.C. or slightly later). Context [002].
Cylinder-necked jar with two cordons around neck. Rim diameter (top) 8cm. Nile clay with thick red slip on exterior and rim top, continuing down interior to an irregular depth, max 1.5cm. Highly polished where slipped, except interior.

No. 938 (Fig. A2.2:f). Late Dynastic Period(?). Context [009].
Base of a torch. Maximum base diameter 5.5cm. String-cut from the clay lump. Interior burnt black. Nile clay. Probably uncoated. Not polished or burnished. (See 1218 of HAC2).

No. 956 (Fig. A2.2:g). Ptolemaic Period. Context [006]. Neck and rim of spindle-shaped unguentarium. Maximum rim diameter 3.5cm. Marl clay. Polished grey slip, probably intended to be red but misfired, on exterior and top of rim. (See base 8).

No. 30 (Fig. A2.2:h). Ptolemaic Period. Context [001]. Shallow carinated bowl with rolled rim. Maximum rim diameter 14cm. Nile clay with polished black slip on all surfaces. No rouletted or stamped decoration.

No. 944 (Fig. A2.2:i). (Late?) Ptolemaic Period. Context [006].
Shallow dish with grooved rim. Maximum rim diameter 23cm. Nile clay with red slip on interior and top of rim. Polished on rim, and two thin lines of burnish on the interior ridges.

No. 965 (Fig. A2.2:j). Ptolemaic Period. Context [006]. Base and lower body of deeper carinated bowl. Maximum base-ring diameter 8.3cm. Nile clay with highly polished black slip on all surfaces, decorated with good quality fine rouletting partly overlain by four stamped palmettes.

No. 48B (Fig. A2.2:k). Ptolemaic or Roman Period. Context [001].
Bowl with almost hammer-headed rim. Maximum rim diameter c.15cm. Nile clay with areas of red slip, perhaps polished, on exterior just below rim; surfaces otherwise weathered. (See 959).

No. 959 (Fig. A2.2:l). Ptolemaic or Roman Period. Context 'trench cleaning'.
Bowl with almost hammer-headed rim. Rim diameter (top) 15cm. Nile clay with red slip on all surfaces. Polished on top of rim and traces on interior. (See 48B).

No. 901 (Fig. A2.2:m). Ptolemaic or Roman Period. Context [001].
Large bowl with short, thick rim. Maximum rim diameter c.28-32cm. No handles as preserved. Nile clay with white slip on exterior, and probably also interior and top of rim but weathered. Probable traces of polish on exterior where slip survives. (See 1195 of HAC2).

No. 953 (Fig. A2.2:n). Ptolemaic or Roman Period. Context [006].
Globular bowl with inward-sloping rim. Maximum diameter c.19cm. No handles as preserved. Nile clay with thin red slip on exterior and top of rim, interior unslipped. Faint traces of polish on exterior only. (See 360 of HAC3).

No. 900 (Fig. A2.2:o). Ptolemaic or Roman Period. Context [001].
Bowl or jar with distinctive wide rim. Maximum rim diameter 22cm. No handles as preserved. Nile clay with red slip on all surfaces. Not polished or burnished.

No. 931 (Fig. A2.2:p). Roman Period. Context [009].
Thin-walled ribbed jar or cooking-pot. Maximum rim diameter 18cm. No handles as preserved, but may have been present. Nile clay with red slip on exterior and rim, polished on concave surface of rim and traces on exterior of vessel.

No. 917 (Fig. A2.2:q). Ptolemaic or Roman Period. Context [001].
Jar with one surviving handle, assumed to be one of two opposed. Maximum rim diameter c.9cm. Nile clay, exterior probably red slipped. Not polished or burnished, but weathered.

No. 8 (Fig. A2.2:r). Ptolemaic Period. Context [001].
Well-made base of spindle-shaped unguentarium. Maximum base diameter 2.6cm. Not string-cut from the clay lump but with secondary shaping. Nile clay with thick red slip on exterior, polished where slipped, except under base. (Contrast 196 of HAC3).

Trench HAC2

There was much less pottery from this trench than from HAC1, and only two contexts were represented (but see note above), i.e. [010] and [011]; furthermore, almost all sherds were marked as derived from a combination of the two, so there is no possibility of distinguishing between them. Otherwise, there were also a few sherds from 'trench cleaning', as in HAC 1. As a whole, the assemblage was similar to that from HAC1, but the proportions differed, the Ptolemaic/Roman constituting the majority. A few sherds of the Old Kingdom were again present, and at least two of the New Kingdom. The same explanations for the deposition pattern as in HAC1 are possible, though it seems more likely that the Ptolemaic/Roman pottery was superimposed upon that of the Late Dynastic Period. The differing proportions may reflect the fact that the excavation was halted before much depth of deposit had been removed.

Catalogue of representative pottery in HAC2
No. 1248 (Fig. A2.3:a). Late Old Kingdom. Context [010/011].
Jar, distorted and abraded. Rim diameter (top) c.13cm. Nile clay with red slip on exterior, over rim and down 2.5cm inside to an edge near base of neck. Traces of polish where slipped.

No. 1178 (Fig. A2.3:b). Ramesside to Third Intermediate Period (?). Context [010/011].
Bowl. Rim diameter (top) 15cm. Nile clay, smoothed but probably uncoated. Trace of possible polish in exterior grooves only.

No. 1236 (Fig. A2.3:c). Ramesside to Third Intermediate Period. Context [010/011].
Jar. Rim diameter (top) 18cm. Marl clay. Thick polished slip on all surfaces, exterior fired pink, interior cream.

No. 100 (Fig. A2.3:d). Late Dynastic Period. Context [010/011].
Rim and upper neck of a Chian amphora. Rim diameter (top) 14cm.

No. 1254 (Fig. A2.3:e). Late Dynastic Period. Context [010/011].
Bowl with groove in exterior of rim. Rim diameter (top) 20cm. Nile clay with red slip on exterior and on rim, running irregularly down interior. Traces of polish where slipped, except interior.

No. 1260 (Fig. A2.3:f). Late Dynastic Period. Context [010/011].
Dish (or lid) with groove around rim. Rim diameter (top) 16cm. Nile clay, with lightly polished pale pinkish red slip on exterior only.

No. 1235 (Fig. A2.3:g). Late Dynastic Period (6th Century

B.C. or slightly later). Context [010/011].
Saucer-lamp. Maximum rim diameter c.10cm. Rim abraded. Nile clay with small surviving area of polished red slip on interior; exterior weathered.

No. 1218 (Fig. A2.3:h). Late Dynastic Period(?). Context [010/011].
Base of a torch. Maximum base diameter 4.2cm. Distorted by handling before firing. Cannot tell whether string-cut because underside has deep impress of straw, acquired before firing. Nile clay. Uncoated. Not polished or burnished. (See 938 of HAC1).

No. 1230 (Fig. A2.3:i). Ptolemaic or Roman Period. Context 'trench cleaning'.
Saucer-lamp, successor to the Late Dynastic form 1235 (above). Maximum rim diameter 11cm. Grooves on underside from reshaping on the wheel. Burning along the rim, acquired in use. Nile clay with red slip on interior, and probably also exterior. Traces of polish on interior only.

No. 1175 (Fig. A2.3:j). Ptolemaic Period. Context [010/011].
Plate with rolled rim, its inner edge slightly hooked. Maximum rim diameter 15cm. Nile clay with polished red slip on interior and rim, extending patchily just on to exterior. (See 321 of HAC3 and 1323 of HAD2).

No. 1184 (Fig. A2.3:k). Ptolemaic or Roman Period. Context [010/011].
Bowl. Rim diameter (top) 15cm. Nile clay with highly polished thick red slip on interior, and small area on exterior, which is otherwise weathered.

No. 1207 (Fig. A2.3:l). Ptolemaic or Roman Period, or perhaps Ramesside. Context [010/011].
Large thick-walled shallow bowl. Rim diameter (top) c.35cm-40cm. Nile clay with polished slip on exterior and top of rim, fired pale brown and red respectively. The interior has a thin coating of white plaster.

No. 1152 (Fig. A2.3:m). Ptolemaic Period. Context [010/011].
Deep bowl with low-set ledge to support a lid. Rim diameter (top) 25cm. The lower break is horizontal, perhaps along a ridge or change of angle. No handles as preserved. Nile clay with polished red slip on all surfaces.

No. 1195 (Fig. A2.3:n). Ptolemaic or Roman Period. Context [010/011].
Large bowl with thick rim. Maximum rim diameter 35cm. No handles as preserved. Nile clay with brown slip on exterior of body and rim, otherwise weathered. Not polished or burnished. (See 901 of HAC1).

No. 1161 (Fig. A2.4:a). Ptolemaic or Roman Period. Context [010/011].
Jar or cooking pot. Rim diameter (top) c.18cm. Stump of one unengaged loop handle, assumed to be one of two opposed. Nile clay with polished red slip on exterior, rim and interior of neck.

No. 1197 (Fig. A2.4:b). Ptolemaic or Roman Period. Context [010/011].
Wide-mouthed jar with bifurcated rim. Maximum rim diameter 18cm. No handles as preserved. Nile clay, all surfaces weathered. (See 739 of HAC3).

No. 1165 (Fig. A2.4:c). Ptolemaic or Roman Period. Context [010/011].
Large carinated bowl with bifurcated rim. Maximum rim diameter 36cm. No handles as preserved. Nile clay with polished red slip on all surfaces, exterior somewhat weathered.

Trench HAC3

Much the most significant trench from the excavations on Kom Helul, being the most extensive and the best stratified, and (as regards the pottery) the most fully documented. It also produced an important structure, the deep kiln. The stratigraphy is more complex than that of the other trenches, and the details of the ceramic typology and its relation to the pre-kiln, kiln and post-kiln phases must wait for full analysis in the projected volume on the domestic pottery. What can certainly be said is that the fills of the access pit, consisting of material dumped after the kiln went out of use, contain large quantities of pottery of the Roman Period, probably of the 2nd (or less probably the 3rd) Century A.D. There is so much of this, and it is so uniform and so unweathered, that a short period of deposition is certain and re-deposition from another dump site can almost certainly be ruled out. The circumstances that led to its deposition can only be guessed at, but it does not consist of kiln rejects ('wasters'), nor were the sherds damaged by fire, as they would have been if the victims of an accidental conflagration; yet we recorded a minimum of 84 of the small jugs of Types 625 and 623 (Fig. A2.8:d and A2.8:e) and at least 40 of the cooking pots of Type 627 (Fig. A2.6:a), almost all from the access pit fills. These are not the normal breakages of a single house or even a group of houses, but might be evidence of the physical collapse of a pottery warehouse or some similar catastrophe.

Catalogue of representative pottery in HAC3
No. 124 (Fig. A2.4:d). Late Dynastic or Ptolemaic Period. Context [033].
Transport amphora. Import, probably from southern Lebanon or Palestine. Rim diameter (top) 10cm. Angular shoulder with trace of handle, assumed to be one of two opposed. Marl clay, probably uncoated. Not polished or burnished.

No. 889 (Fig. A2.4:e). Late Dynastic Period, late 6th Century B.C. or later. Context [308].
Shallow bowl with flat rim. Maximum rim diameter c.17cm. Marl clay, polished thick creamy white slip on all surfaces.

No. 580 (Fig. A2.4:f). Ptolemaic or Roman Period. Context [036].
Jar/table amphora? with elaborate folded rim. Maximum rim diameter 14.5cm. Marl clay, badly mixed, with red streaks in a yellow matrix. Surface treatment not recorded.

No. 560 (Fig. A2.4:g). Ptolemaic or Roman Period. Contexts [303]+[306] joining.
Neck of jug. Rim diameter (top) 3.0cm. Stump of (probably the only) handle. Marl clay or import. Surface treatment not recorded.

No. 643 (Fig. A2.4:h). Ptolemaic or Roman Period. Context [308].
Large shallow dish or tray. Maximum rim diameter c.34cm. One loop handle, assumed to be one of two opposed. Imported ware(?), probably Levantine, and probably for a specialised function. Many poorly sorted inclusions. Moderate quantity fine and medium sand, with rounded grains, similar to the coarsest fraction found in Nile fabrics. Moderate quantity of hard, opaque white grits, not limestone, to 0.1cm. Small quantity of red-brown and black mineral fragments to 0.1cm. No visible plant remains. No certain limestone, but sparse (shell?). Small quantity grog(?). Perhaps self-slipped, but no coloured slip. Wipe-marks indicate smoothing, but only possible traces of polish, on interior only. Handle, and both surfaces from mid-wall to rim, grey, probably smoke-stained.

No. 637 (Fig. A2.4:i). Roman Period. Context [189].
Plate. Maximum rim diameter 23cm. One of a type very common in HAC3, diameter range c.13-25cm. Nile clay with thin (probably self-) slip on all surfaces. Not polished or burnished.

No. 321 (Fig. A2.4:j). Ptolemaic Period. Context [303].
Plate with rolled rim, of a type common in HAC3. Maximum rim diameter 22cm. Diameter range of this smaller version c.16-25cm. Nile clay with red slip on interior and rim, running over on to exterior down to maximum depth of 3.0cm. Irregularly band burnished on interior only. (See 1175 of HAC2 and 1323 of HAD2).

No. 177 (Fig. A2.4:k). Ptolemaic or Roman Period. Context [039].
Shallow flat-based bowl. Maximum rim diameter 12cm. One of a series numerous in HAC3, the top of the rim concave to a variable extent. Diameter range c.11-20cm. Nile clay. Uncoated. Not polished or burnished. (See 178).

No. 178 (Fig. A2.4:l). Ptolemaic or Roman Period. Context [033].
Shallow bowl. Maximum rim diameter 18cm. Nile clay. Uncoated. Not polished or burnished. (See 177).

No. 317 (Fig. A2.5:a). Roman Period. Context [189].
Incurved dish or shallow bowl. Rim diameter (top) 22cm. Very numerous in HAC3, with the unusually wide diameter range 13-c.32cm. Flat or lightly rounded base where preserved. One to four grooves on exterior. Nile clay, unweathered examples preserving red slip on all surfaces. Not polished or burnished. (See 315).

No. 315 (Fig. A2.5:b). Roman Period. Context [189].
Incurved dish or shallow bowl. Rim diameter (top) 20cm. A few examples have impressed (as here) or slashed pre-firing decoration, which did not always extend around the entire circumference. Nile clay, unweathered examples preserving red slip on all surfaces. Not polished or burnished. (See 317).

No. 343 (Fig. A2.5:c). Roman Period. Context [207].
Small bowl. Rim diameter (top) 11cm. Numerous in HAC3. Diameter range well standardised, 10-13cm. Base shaped at second throwing, not string-cut. Nile clay with probable thin self-slip on all surfaces. Not polished or burnished.

Nos. 332/31/29 (Fig. A2.5:d/e/f). Ptolemaic or Roman Period. Contexts [074/308/308].
Small incurved bowls. Rim diameter (top) 6/11/11cm. Very numerous in HAC3. Diameter range 6-13cm. Surviving bases are flat and string-cut from the clay lump. Nile clay. Uncoated. Not polished or burnished.

No. 340 (Fig. A2.5:g). Ptolemaic or Roman Period. Context [308].
Larger incurved bowl. Rim diameter (top) 20cm. Nile clay with red slip on all surfaces. Not polished or burnished.

No. 393 (Fig. A2.5:h). Ptolemaic or Roman Period. Contexts [309] (7 sherds) + [311] (2 sherds) joining; two sherds from [306] probably from the same vessel.
Bowl. Rim diameter (top) 16cm. Nile clay. All surfaces probably slipped but largely obscured by a thin plaster coating (for waterproofing?). Not polished or burnished.

No. 826 (Fig. A2.5:i). Ptolemaic or Roman Period. Context [189].
Bowl or cooking pot, blackened in use. Maximum rim diameter 16cm. Nile clay. Lower interior unslipped, remainder not visible. Not polished or burnished.

No. 751 (Fig. A2.5:j). Ptolemaic or Roman Period. Context [033].
Wide-rimmed bowl. Maximum rim diameter c.26cm. No handles as preserved. Nile clay, with possible trace of red slip on interior but all surfaces weathered. Not polished or burnished.

No. 360 (Fig. A2.5:k). Ptolemaic or Roman Period. Context [300].
Globular bowl with inward-sloping rim. Maximum rim diameter 20cm. No handles as preserved. Nile clay with red slip on exterior and top of rim, interior uncoated. Not polished or burnished. The interior is covered with white

plaster (for waterproofing?). (See 953 of HAC1).

No. 379 (Fig. A2.5:l). Ptolemaic or Roman Period. Context [215].
Large carinated bowl with *cavetto* rim. Rim diameter (top) 32cm. No handles as preserved. Nile clay with thin red slip on all surfaces. Trace of polish on exterior only.

No. 364 (Fig. A2.5:m). Ptolemaic or Roman Period. Context [074].
Large cooking pot. Rim diameter (top) 32cm. No handles as preserved. Nile clay, with probable thin red slip on exterior and down interior as far as least diameter. Not polished or burnished.

No. 627 (Fig. A2.6:a). Ptolemaic or Roman Period. Context [238].
Carinated cooking pot with ledge for a lid. Maximum rim diameter 22cm. Very numerous in HAC3 with wide diameter range 14-30cm. Normally no handles, as here. Nile clay, examples not burnt in use often showing red slip on exterior and sometimes on interior. Probably not polished or burnished.

No. 310 (Fig. A2.6:b). Roman Period. Context [189].
Small cooking pot with lightly ribbed, rounded body. Rim diameter (top) 14.5cm. Scars from one vertical handle on rim and upper body (arrowed). Nile clay, perhaps self-slipped. Not polished or burnished.

No. 188 (Fig. A2.6:c). Ptolemaic or Roman Period. Context [036].
Jar with wide, flat hammer-headed rim. Maximum rim diameter 20cm. Nile clay with red slip on exterior and on rim, and trace of polish on top of rim.

No. 361 (Fig. A2.6:d). Ptolemaic or Roman Period. Context [189].
Jar. Rim diameter (top) 15cm. Nile clay, with possible brown slip and polish on exterior.

No. 248 (Fig. A2.6:e). Ptolemaic or Roman Period. Context [074].
Jar with flanged rim and cordon on shoulder. Rim diameter (top) 13.5cm. Nile clay with brown slip on exterior and rim, extending irregularly down interior. Not polished or burnished.

No. 634 (Fig. A2.6:f). Roman Period. Context [189].
Small jar or cooking pot. Maximum rim diameter 11cm. Out-turned rim, ribbed body and two opposed strap handles. Numerous in HAC3, diameter range 11-20cm. Nile clay with thin (probably self-) slip on exterior and rim, extending down inside neck. Not polished or burnished.

No. 629 (Fig. A2.6:g). Roman Period. Context [309].
Cooking pot. Maximum rim diameter 11cm. Ribbed body and two opposed strap handles. Very numerous in HAC3, diameter range 10-16cm and one example each of 19 and c.20cm. Nile clay, uncoated or perhaps self-slipped. Not polished or burnished.

No. 374 (Fig. A2.6:h). Ptolemaic or Roman Period. Context [306].
Cooking pot. Maximum rim diameter 14cm. Two opposed strap handles. Nile clay. Most examples have red slip on exterior and on interior of neck, and areas of light polish on exterior.

No. 226 (Fig. A2.7:a). Ptolemaic or Roman Period. Context [033].
Krater. Maximum rim diameter 24cm. No handles as preserved. Nile clay. Exterior probably red slipped. Not polished or burnished.

No. 844 (Fig. A2.7:b). Ptolemaic or Roman Period. Context [036].
Jar with concave interior to neck. Maximum rim diameter 15cm. No handles as preserved. Nile clay, burnt so cannot tell whether or not slipped. Not polished or burnished.

No. 385 (Fig. A2.7:c). Roman Period. Context [074].
Neckless jar, perhaps a *qadus* pot from a water-wheel. Maximum rim diameter 19cm. Exterior ribbed. No handles as preserved, and a *qadus* would not have had any. Nile clay, apparently with a red slip on all surfaces. Not polished or burnished.

No. 647 (Fig. A2.7:d). Ptolemaic or Roman Period. Context [308].
Large jar. Maximum rim diameter 14cm. Two opposed strap handles. Vestigial ledge for a lid in interior of rim. Nile clay with red slip on exterior and on top of rim. Not polished or burnished.

No. 373 (Fig. A2.7:e). Ptolemaic or Roman Period. Contexts [189] (35 sherds)+[207] (10 sherds)+[215] (4 sherds)+[218] (1 sherd), joining.
Jar. Rim diameter (top) 12cm. Two opposed vertical handles. Grooves, made with the fingers or with a tool, run from the centre of the base to the upper body, around the entire circumference. These were made pre-firing, after shaping of the base and while the vessel was inverted on the wheel. They may be intended to increase the surface area available when heated on a fire. Nile clay. Uncoated. Not polished or burnished.

No. 372 (Fig. A2.7:f). Ptolemaic or Roman Period. Context [306].
Barrel-jar with thickened rim. Rim diameter (top) 13.5cm. No handles as preserved. Nile clay with carelessly-applied polished red slip on upper 6cms of exterior, over the rim and down about 1cm on interior.

No. 739 (Fig. A2.8:a). Ptolemaic or Roman Period. Context [189].
Neck of a very large jar with out-turned rim. Maximum rim diameter 25cm. No handles on the neck. Nile clay with red slip on exterior, and black and white painted decoration on neck and top of rim. Not polished or burnished. (See 1197 of HAC2).

No. 377 (Fig. A2.8:b). Ptolemaic or Roman Period. Context [300].
Jar with cordon on neck and groove in rim. Rim diameter (top) 7cm. One strap handle, and part of a second on a separate sherd apparently from the same jar. Nile clay with red slip on exterior and on top of rim, probably also down interior to midway. Not polished or burnished.

No. 631 (Fig. A2.8:c). Roman Period. Contexts [189]+[207] joining.
Jar with complex rim, one of several all slightly different. Maximum diameter (flange) 9cm. No handles as preserved. Nile clay. Uncoated and not polished or burnished, but two others have red slip and traces of polish.

No. 625 (Fig. A2.8:d). Roman Period. Context [189].
Small jug. Rim diameter (top) 6cm. Very numerous in HAC3. Highly standardised form but two series, as here, recognisable by consistent minor differences in form and firing, perhaps the output of two potters in the same workshop. Nile clay, perhaps self-slipped. Not polished or burnished. (See 623 for an example from the other series).

No. 623 (Fig. A2.8:e). Roman Period. Contexts [074]+[188]+[189] joining.
Small jug. Rim diameter (top) 6cm. Nile clay, perhaps self-slipped. Not polished or burnished. (See 625 for further details).

No. 345 (Fig. A2.8:f). Roman Period. Contexts [189]+[238] joining.
Jar with strainer-neck and spout. Maximum rim diameter 10.5cm. Two opposed handles, imitating metalwork. Nile clay with thick white slip on exterior and handles and on interior of neck. Not polished or burnished._

No. 194 (Fig. A2.9:a). Roman Period. Context [056].
Neck and rim of two-handled jar or bottle. Maximum rim diameter 3.2cm. Two opposed handles. Nile clay with thick white slip on all surfaces as preserved. Not polished or burnished.

No. 344 (Fig. A2.9:b). Roman Period. Contexts [189]+[207] joining (most sherds were from [189]).
Lower body with base-ring from a jug of the same type as 311. Maximum body diameter 21-22cm. Nile clay with white slip on exterior including under base. Light polish on shoulder only. Incised decoration in horizontal rows, probably made with a wheel.

No. 311 (Fig. A2.9:c). Roman Period. Contexts [074]+[189] joining (most sherds were from [189]).
Upper body, neck and rim from a jug of the same type as 344. Maximum body diameter 22cm. One vertical handle and spout. Nile clay with white slip on exterior including handle, also interior of neck. Light polish on shoulder only. Incised decoration in horizontal rows, probably made with a wheel.

No. 537 (Fig. A2.9:d). Roman Period. Vessel [310] in context [309].
Amphora. Rim diameter (top) 10cm. Two opposed handles wholly on ribbed neck, body unribbed. Numerous in HAC3. Nile clay. Uncoated. Not polished or burnished. No pitch on interior.

No. 628 (Fig. A2.10:a). Roman Period. Context [238].
Jar or bottle. Maximum body diameter 15cm. Opposed handles from shoulder to high on neck. Nile clay. Thick white slip on exterior and handles, but unslipped below maximum diameter of body. Black painted horizontal bands with zigzag (snake?) motif above. (Another example has the same motif above only three narrow bands).

No. 312 (Fig. A2.10:b). Ptolemaic or Roman Period. Context [207].
Small deep jar. Rim diameter (top) 6cm. Very numerous in HAC3. Nile clay. Uncoated. Not polished or burnished.

No. 195 (Fig. A2.10:c). Ptolemaic Period. Context [033].
Neck and rim of spindle-shaped unguentarium. Maximum rim diameter 2.8cm. Nile clay with red or brown slip. Not polished or burnished.

No. 196 (Fig. A2.10:d). Ptolemaic Period. Context [036].
Base of spindle-shaped unguentarium, same Type as 195 but not from the same vessel. Base diameter 1.3cm. Poorly made. Nile clay with red or brown slip. Not polished or burnished. (See 8 of HAC1 for a less typical well-made example).

No. 635 (Fig. A2.10:e). Roman Period. Context [306].
Lid with ribbed interior. Maximum rim diameter 11cm. Very numerous in HAC3. Diameter range, apart from 635, 13-25cm. Probably had a knob on top, of which many were found but none was attached. Nile clay, perhaps self-slipped. Not polished or burnished. (See 636).

No. 636 (Fig. A2.10:f). Roman Period. Context [189].
Lid with ribbed interior. Maximum rim diameter 18cm. Probably had a knob on top, of which many were found but none attached. Nile clay, perhaps self-slipped. Not polished or burnished. (See 635).

No. 245 (Fig. A2.10:g). Ptolemaic or Roman Period. Context [037].

Large shallow basin. Rim diameter (top) c.42cm. Nile clay. Uncoated. Not polished or burnished.

Summary of the excavation of Area HAD in relation to the ceramics

The smaller area HAD, was the subject of only very limited excavation (in 2000/01), and produced few sherds. The three trenches HAD1, 2 and 3 were close together and for present purposes may be thought of as a single unit. The sherds from HAD1 and 2 had been pre-sorted before the ceramicists saw them, with only diagnostics[3] saved, but this is unlikely to have had any significant effect on the assemblage, since they derived from surface and immediately sub-surface deposits. No sherds were recovered from HAD3, where the excavated area was very small.

As usual, the sherds were of various dates. Those of the Old Kingdom were small and probably derived from bricks manufactured later; where they can be dated, they appear to be of the 5th or Sixth Dynasty rather than earlier. They certainly cannot, in the absence of further evidence, be taken as proving an occupation of that date in the area. The lack of recognisable sherds of the New Kingdom is not considered significant. That the Late Dynastic rims were mostly from marl clay vessels, which in Lower Egypt are much less common than those of Nile clay, probably means that the latter were relatively numerous but discarded; where those retained can be dated they are again of about the 6th Century B.C., and should attest to activity of that time in the area. It is not possible to say whether or not this was continuous into the Ptolemaic Period, but many sherds of the latter date were small, usually an indication (since they are unlikely to derive from bricks) of trampled surfaces, so of either intensive activity or an actual occupation in the vicinity. This appears to have continued into the early Roman Period.

In general, the history of area HAD is not, on present evidence, significantly different from that of area HAC.

Discussion and catalogue by individual trenches

Trench HAD1

Most of the few sherds seen were from surface context [084], where Old Kingdom rims predominated but a few Late Dynastic marl clay rims and one Nile clay 'Pigeon Pot' were recognisable, together with a black ring-base and part of a long amphora handle, both Ptolemaic. Another surface context [012] yielded three Old Kingdom rims, but also a body sherd from a Roman amphora. Contexts [015] and [016] each produced a Late Dynastic marl rim, while from [015] there came a Ptolemaic or Roman base-ring fragment and from [016] a Ptolemaic cooking pot fragment with burnished bands, proving the late date of these deposits.

Trench HAD2

More sherds were available than from HAD1, derived from three contexts. Those from surface context [131] were mostly tiny and worn, and probably of the Old Kingdom; in addition, a fragment of a Samian amphora, two tiny sherds of Attic black-glazed ware and three marl rims attested to the Late Dynastic Period and there were a few Ptolemaic or Roman rims, including one Mareotis amphora (probably early Roman), together with some base-ring fragments. Context [132] was represented by two small rims only, one certainly and one probably of the Old Kingdom. The basal deposit [133] had fewer sherds than [131], but again one certainly and six probably Old Kingdom, together with a number of small fragments of Ptolemaic to early Roman rims and handles, including one bifid amphora handle probably of that date. However, a thin green glazed cup rim was probably Islamic and a tiny china sherd probably modern, betraying more recent contamination.

Catalogue of representative pottery in HAD1 and HAD2

No. 1300 (Fig. A2.10:h). Late Old Kingdom. Context [012] (HAD1).
Bowl, perhaps drawn with sides too steep. Maximum rim diameter c.30-35cm. Nile clay, with polished slip fired black.

No. 1323. (Fig A10:i). Ptolemaic or Roman Period. Context [131] (HAD2).
Plate with rolled rim, of a type common in HAC3. Maximum rim diameter c.18cm. Nile clay with polished black slip on all surfaces, fired black. (See 1175 of HAC2 and 321 of HAC3).

No. 1330. (Fig. A2.10:j). Ptolemaic or Roman Period. Context [133] (HAD2).
Cooking pot with ledge for a lid. Maximum rim diameter c.20-30cm. No handles as preserved. Nile clay with polished red slip on exterior, on top of rim and on interior down to the lid-ledge.

No. 1326. (Fig. A2.10:k). Ptolemaic or Roman Period. Context [133] (HAD2).
Jug. Maximum rim diameter 9cm. Stump of a single handle which would have risen in a loop above the level of the rim. Nile clay. Grey-black slip, probably intended to be red but misfired, on all surfaces. Polish visible on top of rim only.

No. 1314. (Fig. A2.10:l). Ptolemaic or Roman Period. Context [016] (HAD1).
Part of the base of a carinated cooking pot. Diameter at carination 18cm. Underside blackened. Nile clay with polished red slip on all surfaces and additional band burnish on interior.

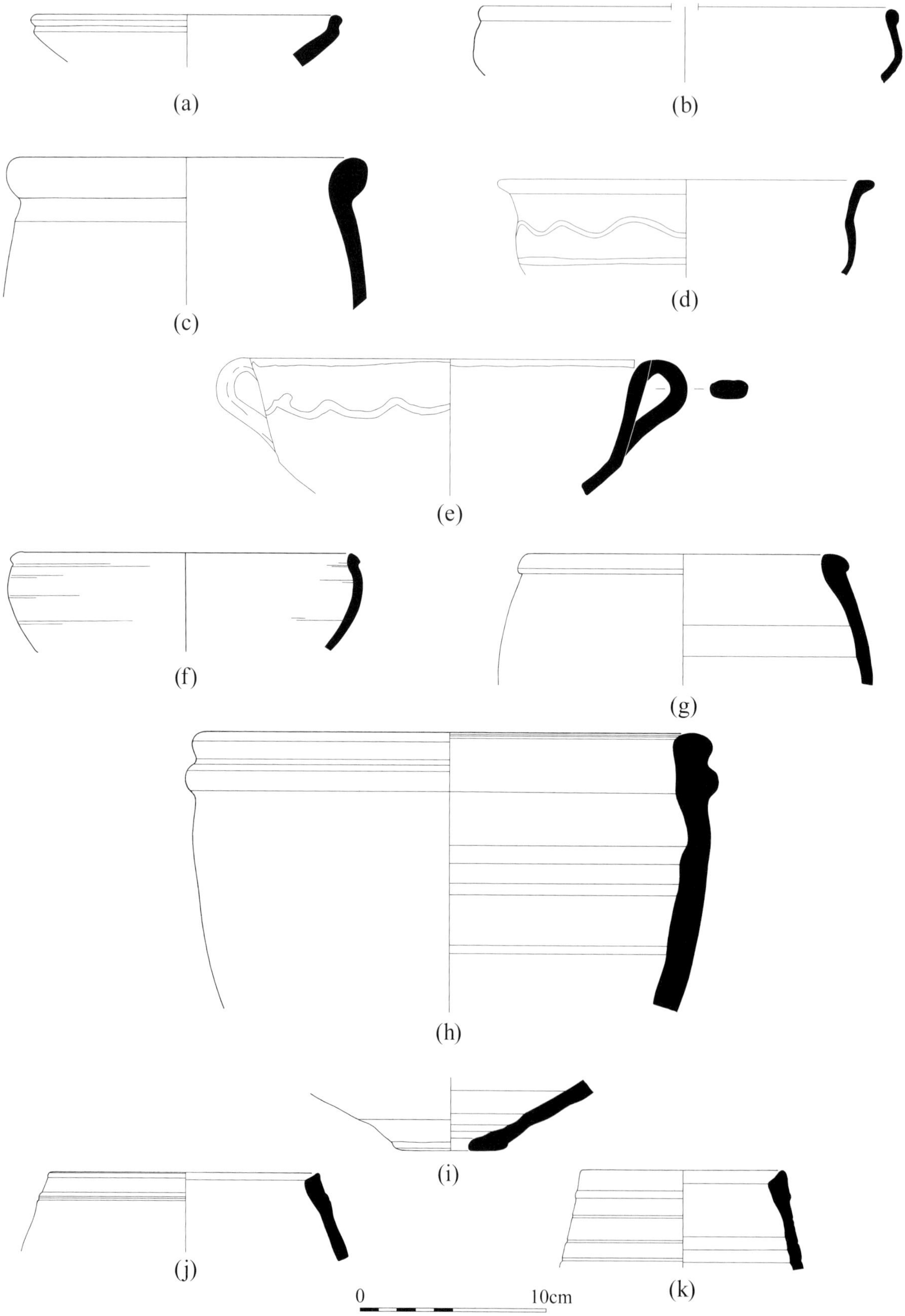

Fig. A2.1 Pottery from HAC1. (a)973;(b)45;(c)1102;(d)31; (e)51; (f)1103; (g)1054; (h)1023; (i)1095; (j)1051; (k)1052. Scale 1:3

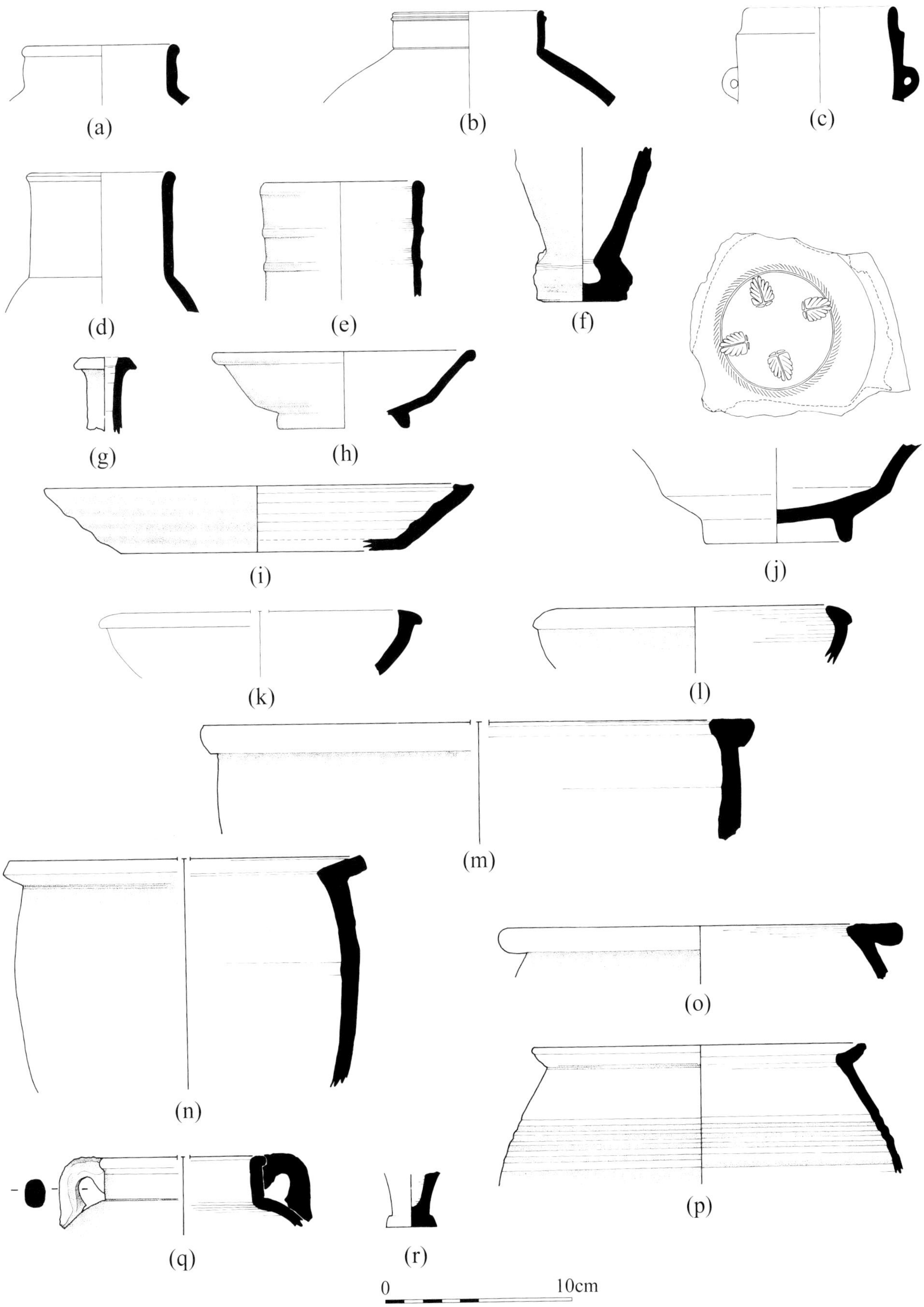

Fig. A2.2. Pottery from HAC1. (a)1062; (b)1080; (c)1082; (d)1050; (e)1072; (f)938; (g)956; (h)30; (i)944; (j)965; (k)48B; (l)959; (m)901; (n)953; (o)900; (p)931; (q)917; (r)8. Scale 1:3

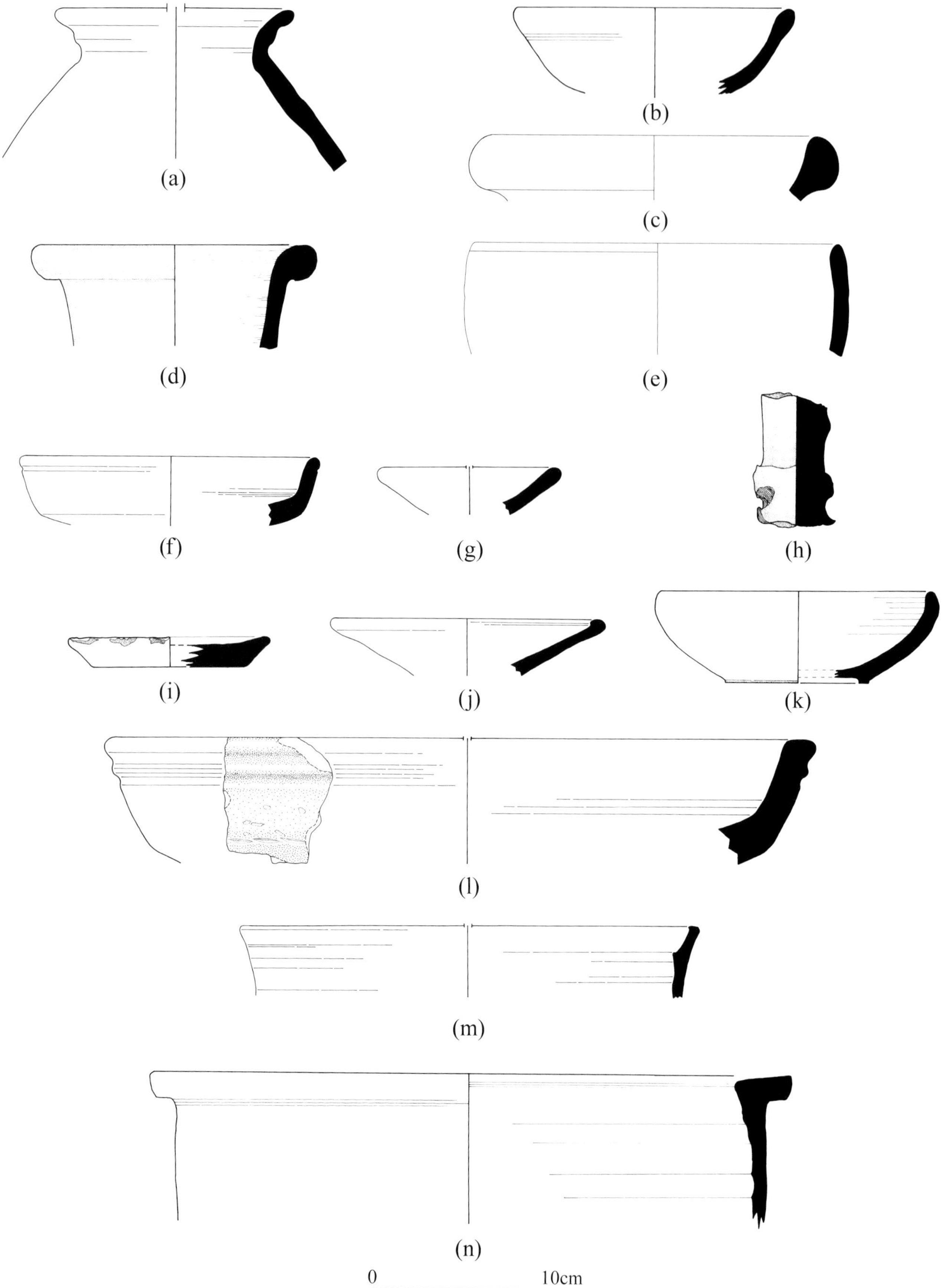

Fig. A2.3. Pottery from HAC 2. (a)1248; (b)1178; (c)1236; (d)100; (e)1254; (f)1260; (g)1235; (h)1218; (i)1230; (j)1175; (k)1184; (l)1207; (m)1152; (n)1195. Scale 1:3

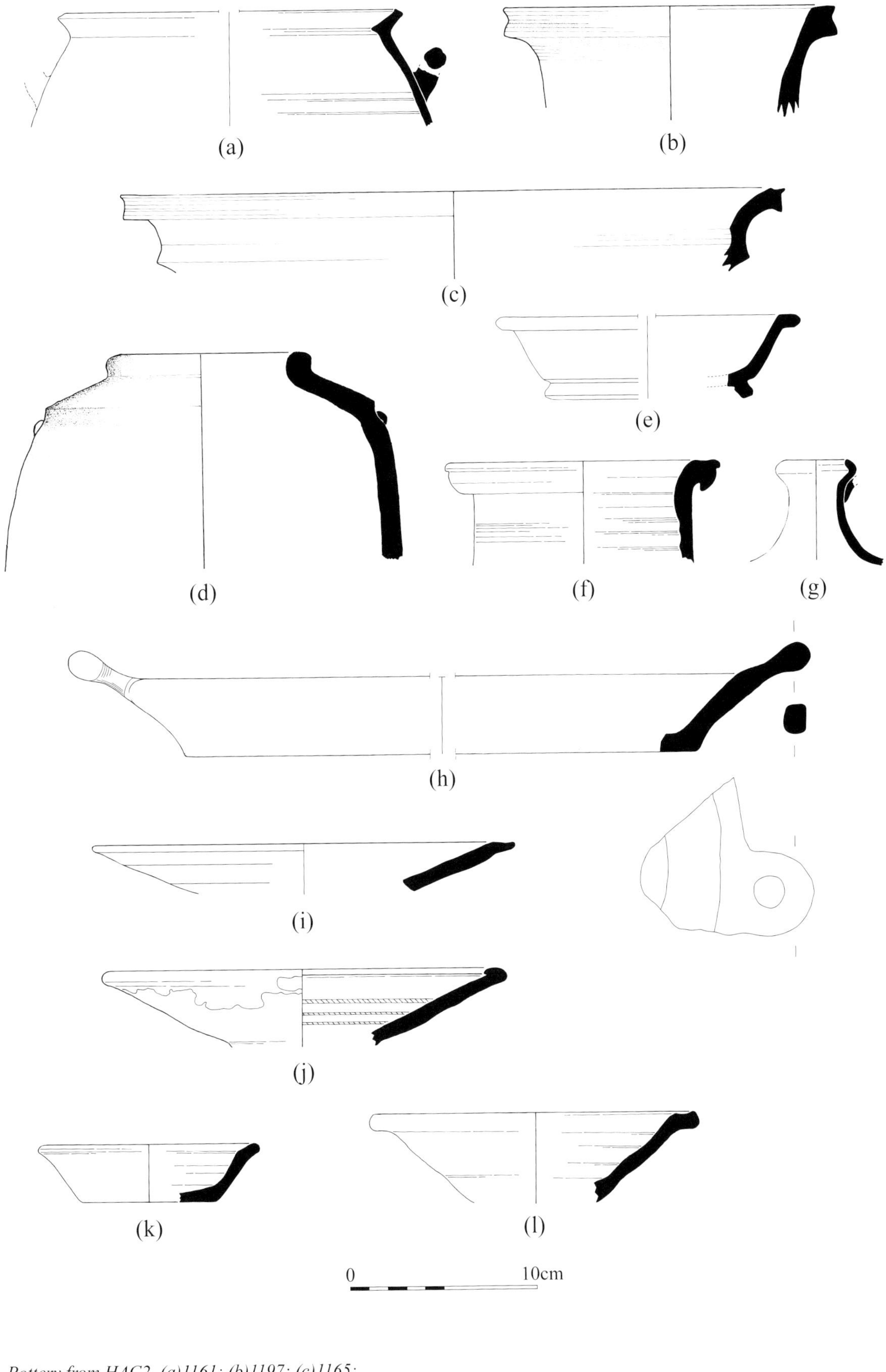

Fig. A2.4. Pottery from HAC2. (a)1161; (b)1197; (c)1165;
Pottery from HAC3. (d)124; (e)889; (f)580; (g)560; (h)643; (i)637; (j)321; (k)177; (l)178. All scale 1:3

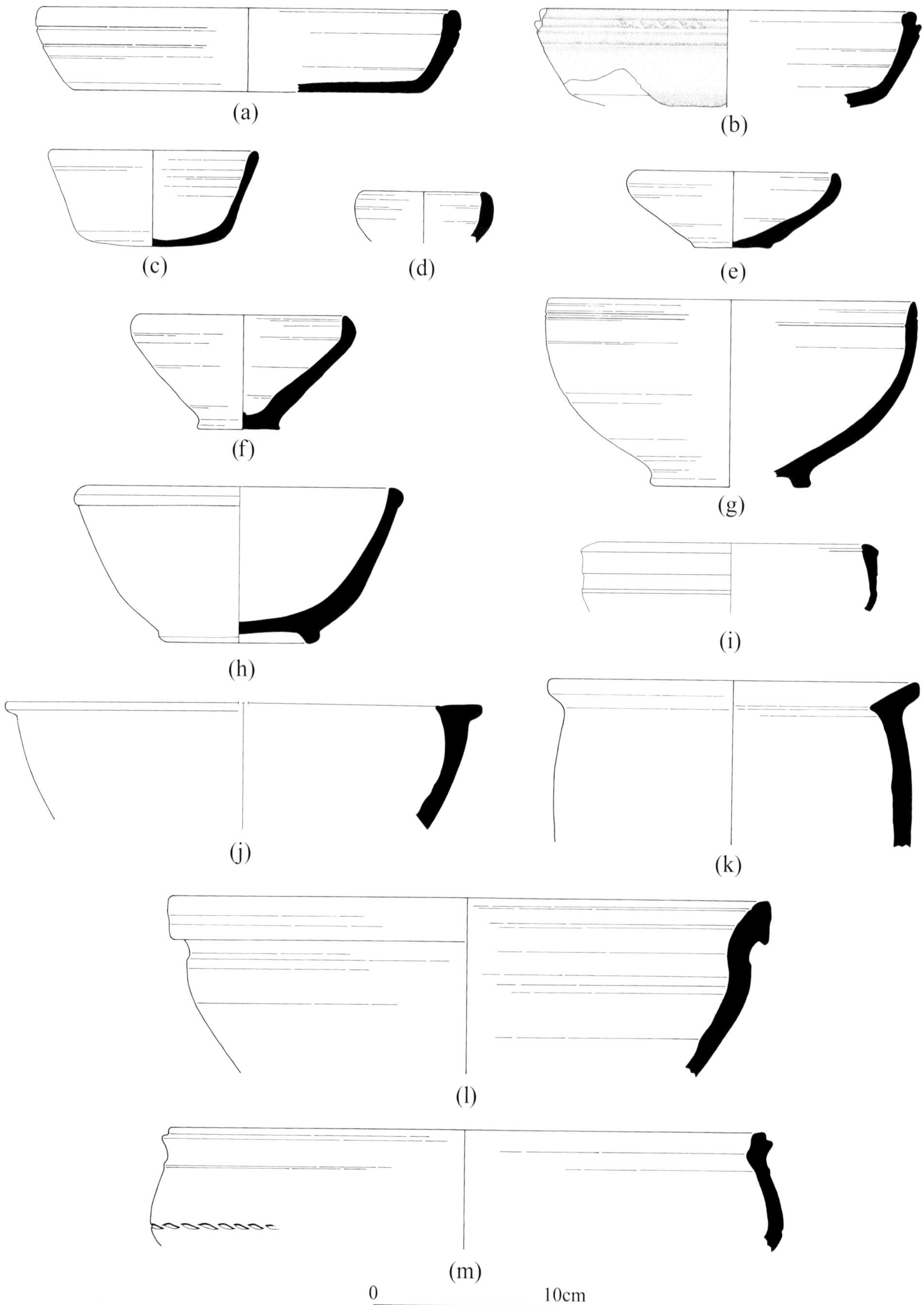

Fig. A2.5. Pottery from HAC3. (a)317; (b)315; (c)343; (d)332; (e)331; (f)329; (g)340; (h)393; (i)826; (j)751; (k)360; (l)379; (m)364. Scale 1:3

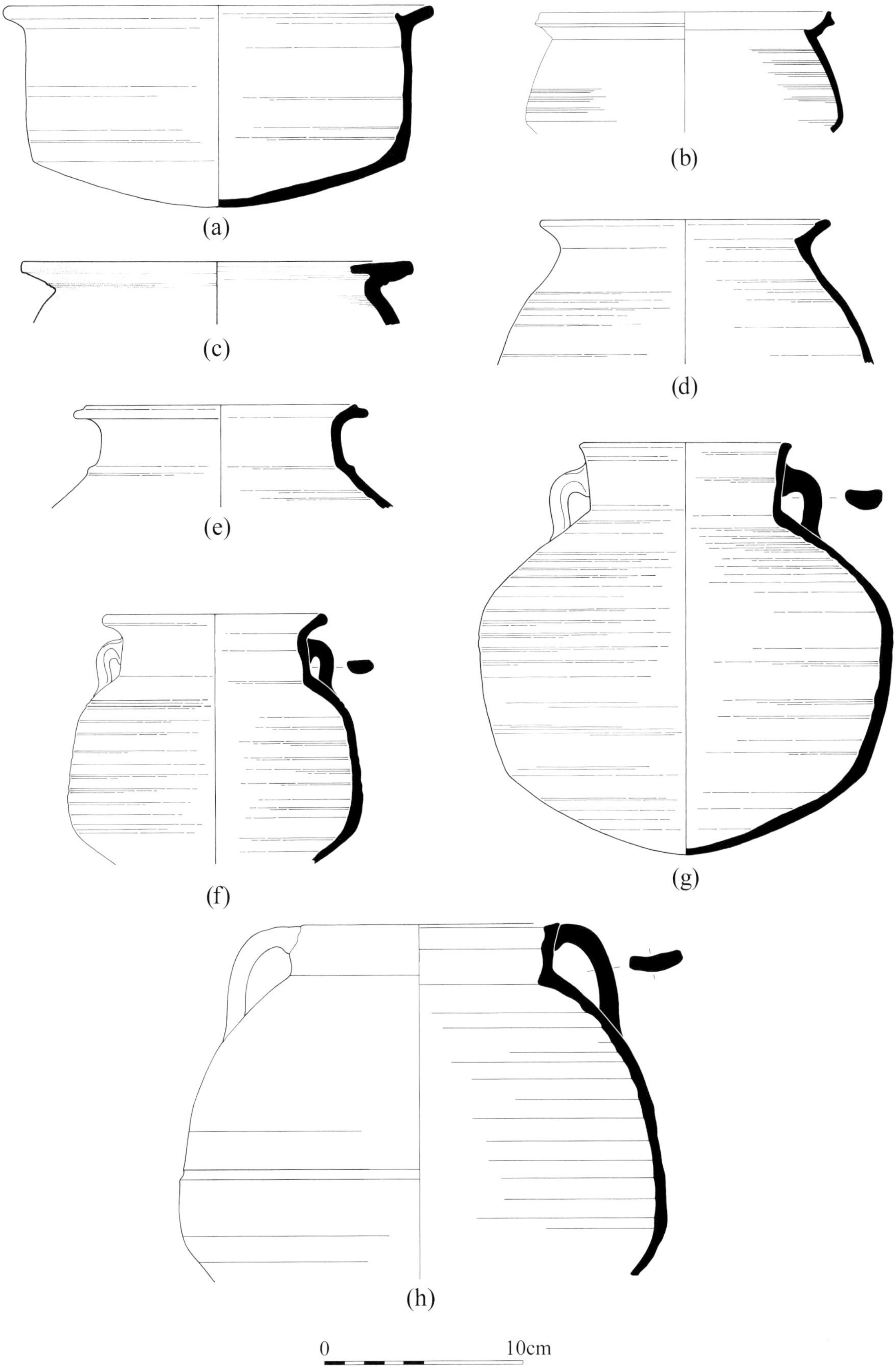

Fig. A2.6. Pottery from HAC3. (a)627; (b)310; (c)188; (d)361; (e)248; (f)634; (g)629; (h)374. Scale 1:3

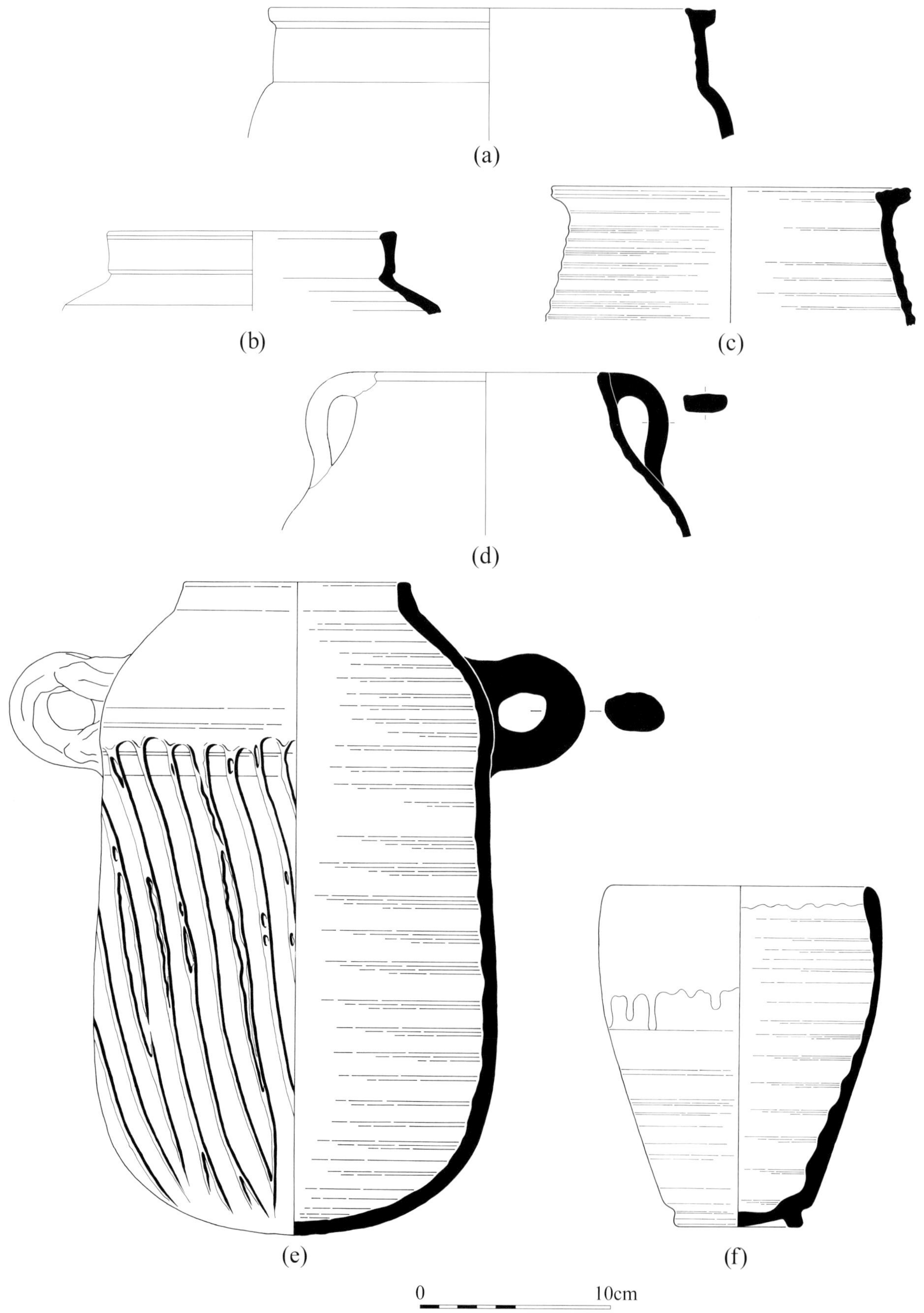

Fig. A2.7. Pottery from HAC3. (a)226; (b)844; (c)385; (d)647; (e)373; (f)372. Scale 1:3

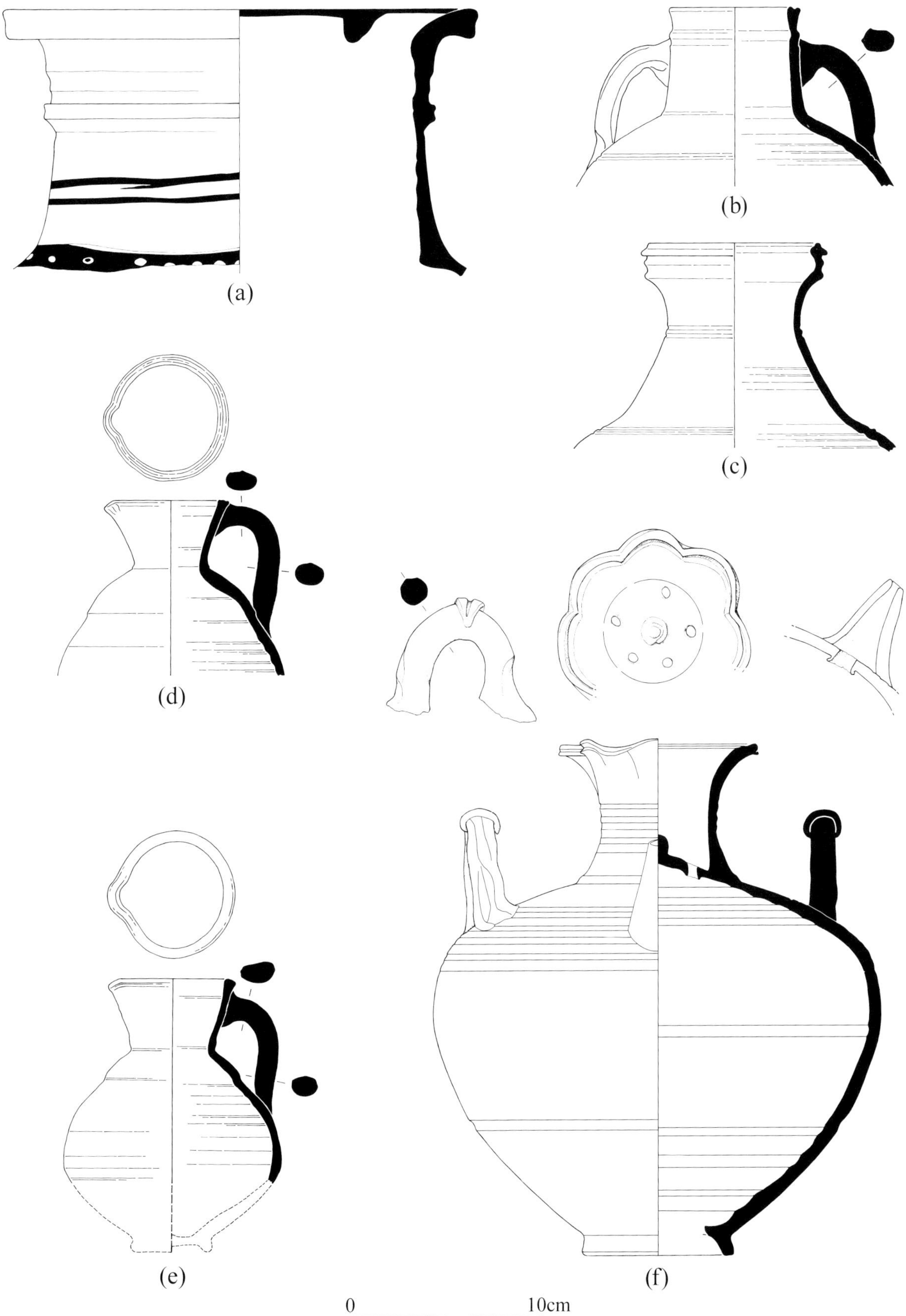

Fig. A2.8. Pottery from HAC3. (a)739; (b)377; (c)631; (d)625; (e)623; (f)345. Scale 1:3

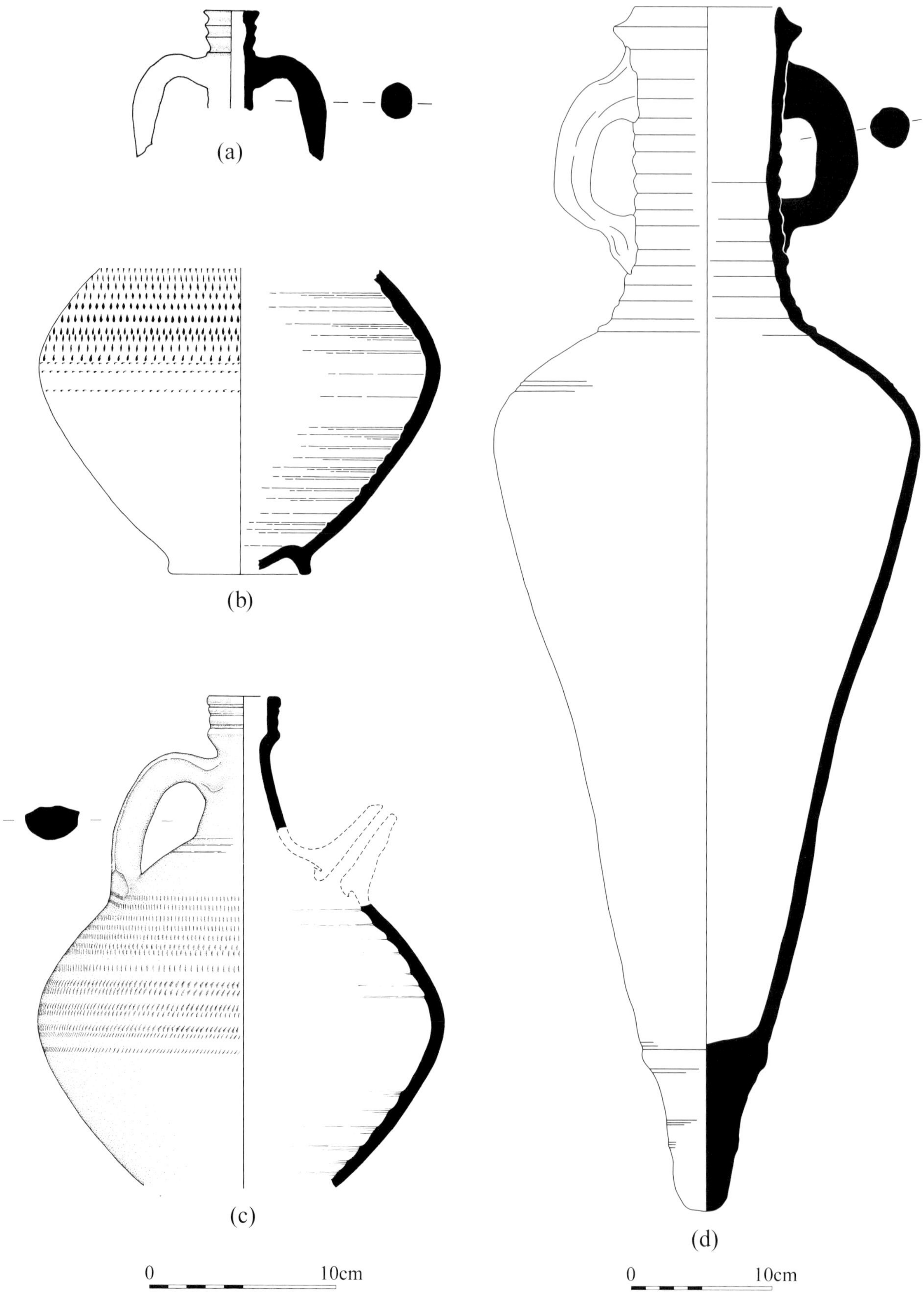

Fig. A2.9. Pottery from HAC3. (a)194; (b)344; (c)311. Scale 1:3
(d)537. Scale 1:4

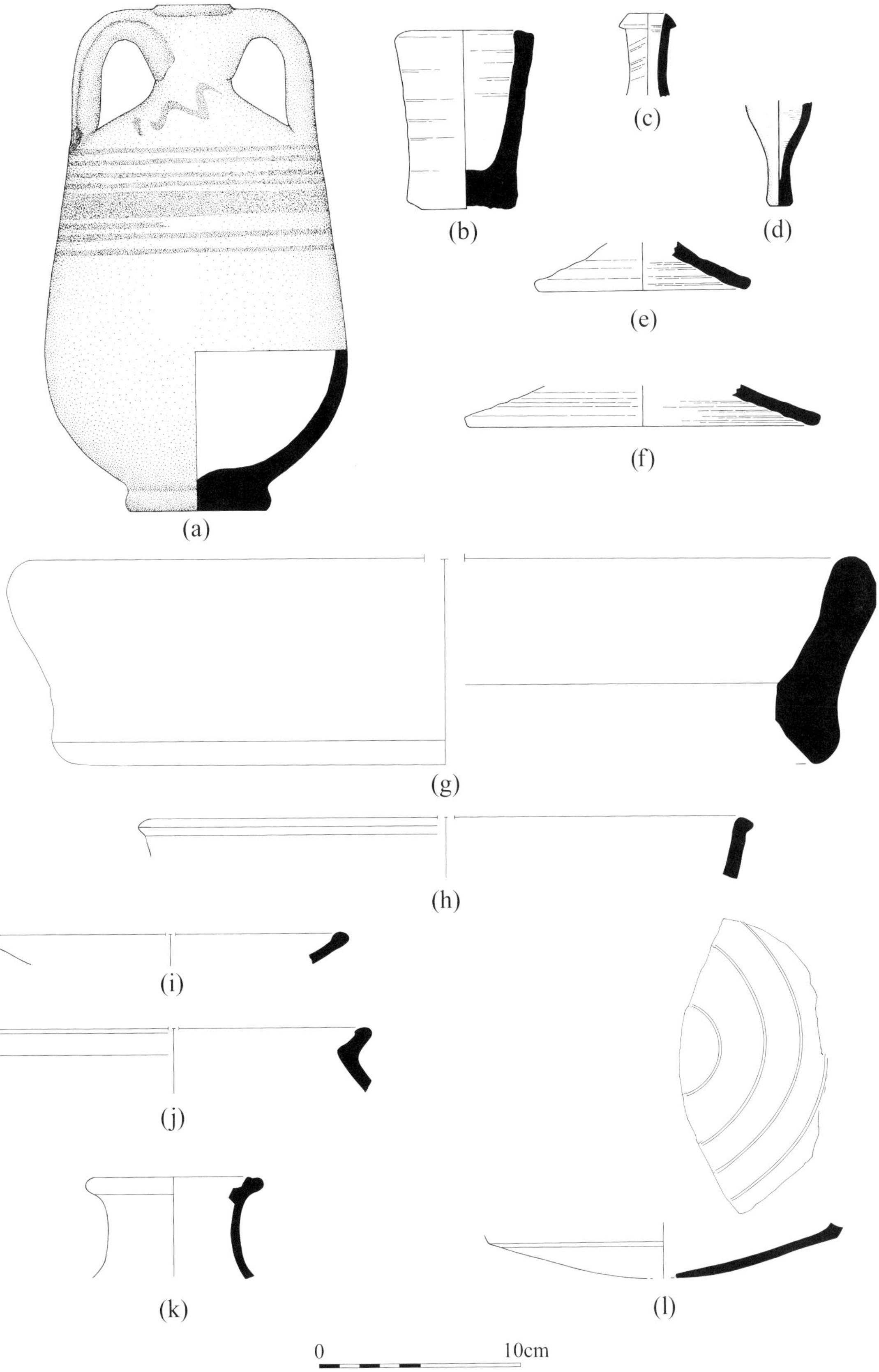

Fig. A2.10. Pottery from HAC3. (a)628; (b)312; (c)195; (d)196; (e)635; (f)636; (g)245.
Pottery from HAD1 and HAD2. (h)1300; (i)1323; (j)1330; (k)1326; (l)1314. All scale 1:3

Endnotes

1 Rims, bases, handles and decorated sherds.

2 As this Appendix went to press, the author was shown by Sabine Laemmel a drawing of a rim sherd almost identical to No.51, from the Russian excavations at Memphis (Kom Tuman). The number is 05-06/0015/50; the sherd is undecorated but the ware is not known The date is uncertain but it is more likely to be of the Persian Period than earlier. Further work is needed to establish any Greek prototype but none has so far been found.

3 See note 1.

APPENDIX 3

Basic Archaeozoological Report on Kom Helul Remains

S. Ikram

Introduction

A total of 220 bone fragments from Kom Helul were examined and identified. The bones had been collected by hand and sieve and came from the Ptolemaic and Roman levels of the site. The examination of the specimens was carried out on-site at the Mit Rahina workroom of the Egypt Exploration Society using a limited comparative collection and publications.

The information recorded for each bone included: taxon, element, portion, side, age, butchery, work, gnawing, burn marks, erosion, and breakage patterns. Fragments (measuring over 1.0cm at least) of limb bones, ribs, and vertebrae that were identifiable only by mammal size (medium, medium to large, and large) were counted. The ageing systems used for bones and teeth were Silver (1969), Grant (1982) and Payne (1973). Measurements follow Von Den Driesch (1976).

Virtually all of the bones from the different contexts showed signs of burning and erosion. Only a few fragments showed no evidence of being burnt. Some of the bones were very burnt, attaining colours that ranged from grey to blue, well beyond being burnt black. Either these bones were involved in a huge conflagration that devastated the site, or were used as fuel. As some of the specimens that were burned were quite large, it is less likely that they were used as fuel, although it is not beyond the realm of possibility. Most of the bones also were quite eroded, with the surfaces of some being rather powdery.

Below is summarised the information for each area, providing taxa lists for each, as well as a brief archaeozoological summary of the assemblages whenever possible.

HAC1 2000

A total of 19 bones were retrieved from this area. The majority came from a horse and consisted of a group of connected bones: the metatarsals and tarsals from the right hind-leg, as well as portions of a phalanx and a humerus. Medium mammals were represented by fragments of limb bones and possibly belonged to ovicaprids, although some fragments might have been from pigs. Three positively identified pig bones (fragments of a right tibia, the pelvis of a male pig, and part of the atlas vertebra) were also recorded. Aquatic creatures were represented by a fragment of the skull of a catfish and a portion of the shell of a freshwater mussel.

Table A3.1 Identified specimens from HAC1 2000

Taxa	Total
Horse (*Equus caballus*)	8
Large Mammal	1
Medium Mammal	4
Medium-Large Mammal	1
Pig (*Sus scrofa*)	3
Catfish (*Synodontis schall*)	1
Freshwater Mussel (*Unio* sp.)	1
Grand Total	19

Table A3.2 Measurable bones from HAC1 2000

Taxa	Bone	Side	Measurement
Horse	Astragalus	R	GB 75, BFd 51
Horse	Metatarsal	R	Bd 53
Pig	Tibia	R	Bd 28

HAC2 2000

Only two bones were recorded from this area. One was a fragment of the ilium of a mature pig, and the other was a long-bone fragment from a medium sized mammal, more likely an Ovicaprid than a pig.

HAC1 2000

Only one bone was recovered from this context: a vertebral fragment from a mature Large Mammal.

HAC3 2001

This trench yielded a total of 41 bones. All of them showed different degrees of burning, and all were eroded, save one bird bone and a fragment of a large mammal bone. A few of the bones looked as if red ochre might have been applied to them; it is possible that this is residue from pot dust. Unfortunately there was insufficient evidence from the mammals to determine the age at death of the various animals represented in this assemblage.

Table A3.3 Species recovered from HAC3 2001

Taxa	Total
Bird	2
Cattle (*Bos taurus*)	4
Goat (*Capra hircus*)	1
Donkey (*Equus asinus*)	1
Large Mammal	2
Medium Mammal	14
Medium-Large Mammal	6
Ovicaprid	7
Pig (*Sus scrofa*)	1
Catfish (*Synodontis schall*)	1
Catfish (*Clarias* sp.)	1
Turtle (*Trionyx triunguis*)	1
Grand Total	41

Table A3.4 Measurable bones from HAC2 2001 (in cm)

Taxa	Bone	Side	Measurement (cm)
Goat	1st phalange	L	GL40, Bp12.75, Bd 11
Bird	Tibiotarsus	L	Bd 3
Cattle	1st phalange	L	GL57, Bp26, Bd 22.5

The greatest number of bone fragments from the excavations at Kom Helul came from HAC3, numbering a total of 148. This locale also yielded the most diverse group of fauna from all those recorded at the site. All the specimens were very burnt and eroded, with several bones exfoliating due to the burning and depositional history.

Most of the bones came from Medium Mammals, either ovicaprids or pigs, with fish (different sorts of catfish, primarily) also contributing significantly to the deposit. The number of bones coming from 'high status' animals, such as cattle and horse was very low here, suggesting that this area was not used by the elite, but by lower income groups who, in addition to rearing animals for food consumption, also exploited the river and canals for food.

Table. A3.5 Species list for HAC3

Taxa	Bones
Bird	4
Cattle (*Bos taurus*)	1
Goat (*Capra hircus*)	1
Donkey (*Equus asinus*)	1
Medium Mammal	54
Medium-Large Mammal	3
Sheep (*Ovis aries*)	1
Ovicaprid	17
Shell (*Unio* sp.?)	1
Snail shells	2
Pig (*Sus scrofa*)	12
Catfish (*Synodontis schall*)	25
Catfish (*Clarias* sp.)	3
Catfish	6
Nile Perch (*Lates niloticus*)	3
Fish (unidentified)	14
Grand Total	148

Table A3.6 List of measurable bones from HAC3

Taxa	Bone	Side	Measurement
Ovicaprid	Phalange 2	L	GL21, Bp10, Bd7
Pig	Humerus	L	Bd 30
Goat	Phalange 3	R	GL 25
Pig	3rd Metatarsal	L	Bd 14
Donkey	Radius	L	Bfd 41, Bd 46
Pig	3rd Metatarsal	L	Bp 12
Ovicaprid	Scapula	R	GLP 29
Pig	4th Metacarpal	L	Bp 14
Bird (domestic fowl?)	Femur	L	Bd 14

Discussion

The taxa represented at the various areas within the site were: cattle (Bos taurus), donkey (Equus asinus), horse (Equus caballus), pig (Sus scrofa), Ovicaprid (Capra hircus/ Ovis aries), Catfish (Synodontis schall and Clarias sp.), Nile Perch (Lates niloticus), turtle (Trionyx triunguis) in the form of carapace fragment, mussel shells (Unio sp.), snail shells, and a few unidentified birds. The medium sized mammals (ovicaprids and pigs) accounted for the largest number of animal bones collected from the site. These point to a less elite population as well as less state sponsored activities here. Evidence for more elite or state oriented supplies and activities came in the (limited) form of cattle and horse bones. In addition to pigs, sheep, and goat, the inhabitants of this area exploited the wet environment of ancient Memphis, consuming fish, fresh mussels and possibly turtles.

Table A3.7 Distribution of species at Kom Helul

Taxa	Total
Large Mammal	12
Medium Mammal	73
Medium-Large Mammal	10
Horse (*Equus caballus*)	8
Donkey (*Equus asinus*)	2
Pig (*Sus scrofa*)	18
Cattle (*Bos taurus*)	5
Goat (*Capra hircus*)	2
Sheep (*Ovis aries*)	1
Ovicaprid	24
Catfish (*Clarias* sp.)	4
Catfish (*Synodontis schall*)	27
Catfish	6
Nile Perch (*Lates niloticus*)	3
Fish (unidentified)	14
Turtle (*Trionyx triunguis*)	1
Shell (*Unio* sp.?)	1
Snail shells	2
Freshwater Mussel (*Unio* sp.)	1
Bird	6
Grand Total	220

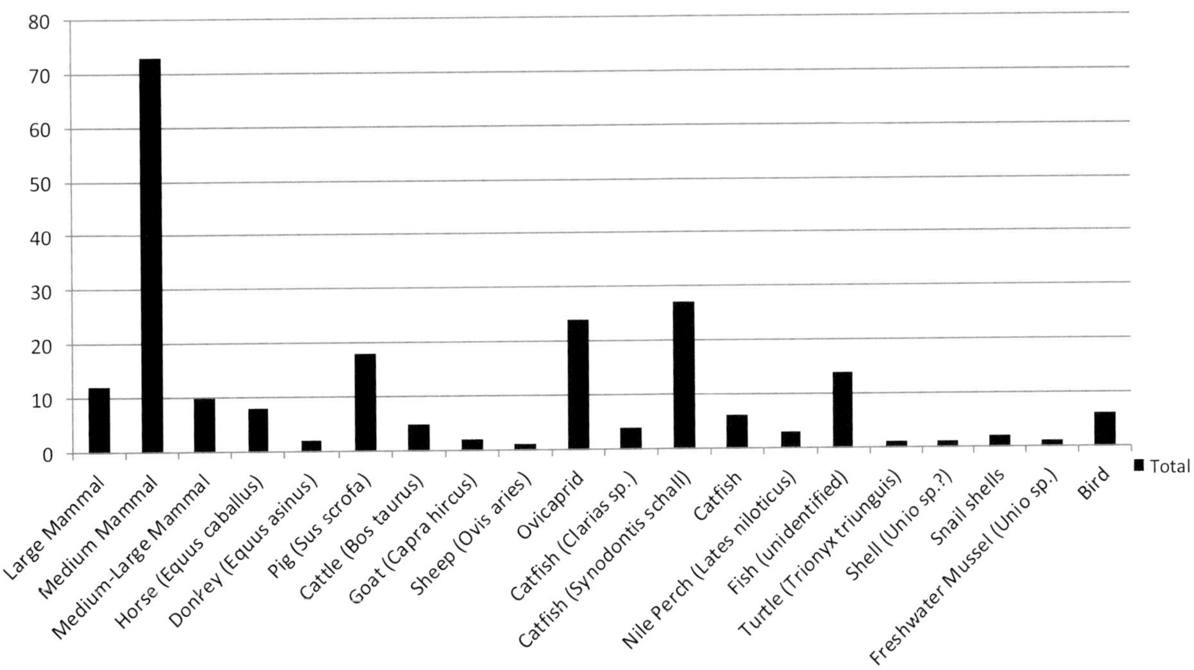

Figure A3.1. Distribution of fauna from the site of Kom Helul, showing total speices represnted.

APPENDIX 4
Analyses Of Selected Faience Objects

P. Manti

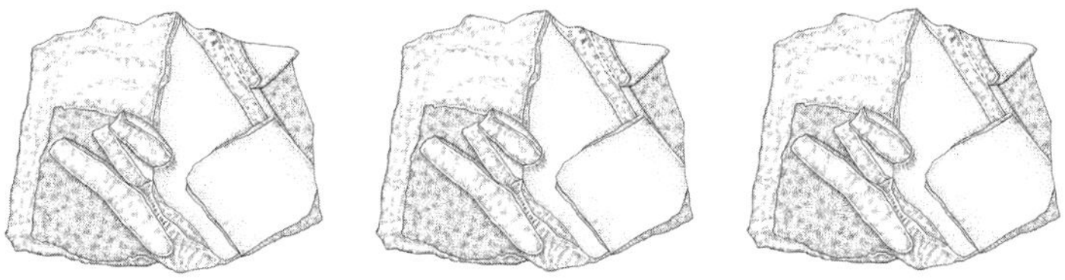

Introduction

Several scientific investigations and experimental replication studies have led to our current understanding of Egyptian faience materials and manufacture (for example Kaczmarczyk and Hedges,1983; Tite, Freestone and Bimson, 1983; Tite and Bimson, 1986; Vandiver, 1998). Despite this, there is only a small number of research focusing on the technology of faience production during the Ptolemaic (332-30 B.C.) and Roman (30 B.C. - 311 A.D.) periods in Egypt. Most of the archaeological evidence derives from excavations at Memphis and only a limited number of archaeometric investigations have been conducted. Vandiver (1983:A123-A131; C53-C58) includes investigation of about 47 objects predominantly from the Hellenistic period and offers the most extensive list of macroscopic evidence and XRF composition analyses of glazes from a range of object types. Work by Shortland and Tite (2005) centres on analyses of 14 small vessels and trays (their objects MEM1, MEM3, MEM4, MEM9, MEM15 were also analysed by Vandiver 1983). This work is coupled with analyses of Egyptian blue pigment or frit balls from Memphis and elsewhere (Tite and Hatton 2007), which had been associated with faience glazing by application (Vandiver 1983: A128), a glazing method that was used extensively during the Hellenistic period (*ibid* A124). Variation in the techniques of making different object types is previously noted for the making of large vessels and ushabtis; this could be combined with adjustments in the formulation of the body composition and particle size (Vandiver, 1983: A124). These technological adjustments are unclear merely due to the analyses of a handful of objects.

Relationships to other craft technologies are still being investigated (see Chapters 7 and 8). A systematic scientific investigation of archaeological evidence and selected object types is required to investigate shaping technologies and glazing techniques involved during this period and their development over time. A forthcoming PhD research programme at Cardiff University is designed to address these and other hypotheses for wheel thrown faience vessels during this period. This would enable placing the production of Hellenistic and Roman faience within the broader technological framework of ceramic production in Egypt and the Mediterranean world.

This report includes scientific analyses of two representative objects from Petrie's work at Memphis, contributing to the small list of analysed Hellenistic and Roman faience objects. The analysis aims to examine the materials used for shaping and glazing and the nature of the glaze colourant used.

Material examined

Since the removal of material from Egypt is not permitted, the analyses reported on here are based on two objects from museum collections in the U.K. The samples comprised a stack of faience waster vessels from Memphis held at Rochdale Museum (ROCH 103.22) and a fragment from an open faience vessel from Memphis now held at the Petrie Museum (UC 47410) (Fig. A4 .1). Both objects have a well preserved, patchy light blue colour glaze and exhibit evidence of damage during firing. The adherent material from the saggar at the base of the waster assemblage and the mode in which the faience trays are stacked (ROCH 103.22) indicate that the objects were fired in the kiln the right way up. UC 47410 shows glaze drips and imperfections to the external surface from contact to other pieces or the saggar. Macroscopically the body of the faience in both cases appears white.

Experimental Details

Cross-sectioned samples were removed from the objects and prepared by mounting in *Struers Epofix*™ epoxy resin,

Figure A4.1: Images of investigated fragments from Memphis. (Left) Stack of waster vessels from Memphis, Rochdale Museum 103.22 and (Right) fragment from a vessel, University College London UC 47410.

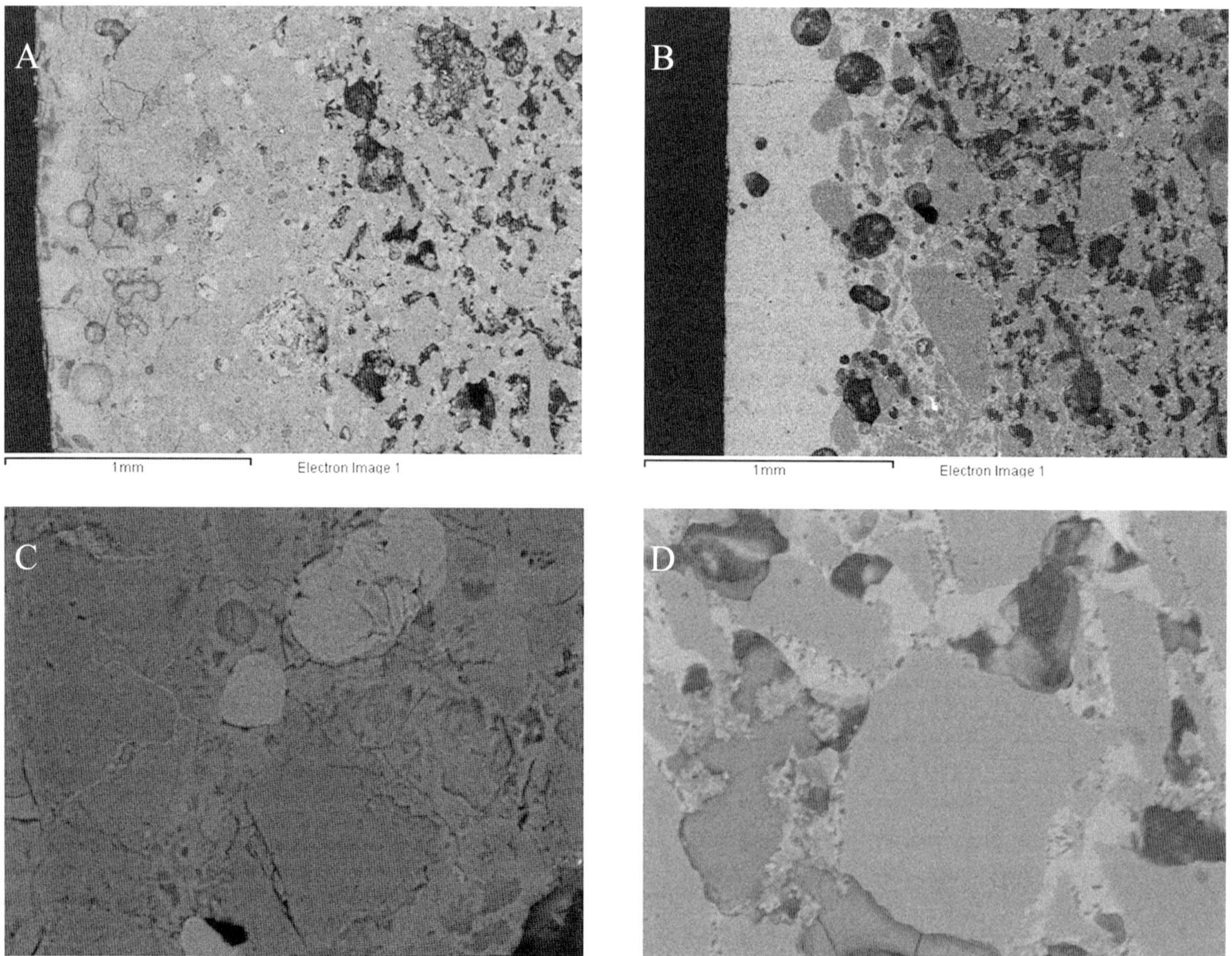

Figure A4.2: SEM-BSE images of (upper left, A) ROCH 103.22 and (upper right, B) UC 47410 at low magnification showing glazing profile. (lower left, C) BSE of sintered interaction zone with rounded Ca- based inclusions in ROCH 103.22. (lower right, D) Ca-based compound between the silica grains in the body of UC 47410.

followed by grinding and polishing using a *Struers Labopol-5*™ machine with progressively finer grit of silicon carbide papers (180, 320, 1600, 1200, 2500, 4000) and *Metadi*™ aqueous diamond polishing pastes (3-1/4 μm). The resin blocks were carbon coated prior to SEM observation using the *Emitech K450*™ Carbon Coater with carbon fibre strands. Samples were examined using the CamScan 2040 Scanning Electron Microscope, which is coupled with the Oxford Link Pentafet 5518 Energy Dispersive X-ray spectrometer for composition analyses, situated at the Department of Archaeology and Conservation, Cardiff University. The spectrometer's super thin atmosphere window (ATW2) permits X-ray detection of light elements (Z>4).

The SEM-EDX system calibration involved pure elements and mineral standards (No. 4629, *Micro-Analysis Consultants Ltd*). The system was optimised on cobalt and verified for accuracy by regular analyses of Corning B glass standard and on wollastonite mineral standard (No. 4629). EDX analyses of features of inclusions and the glass phase was conducted at 20KV, 100 seconds, using spot beam size typically at 500x magnification unless if otherwise stated. EDX analyses of the glass phase are presented combined by stoichiometry oxides normalised wt%. Backscattered electron (BSE) images show compositional contrast of phases present that are distinguished due to differences in their atomic number.

Results

Microstructure

BSE imaging shows that the ROCH 103.22 (Fig. A4.2a) exhibits a thin glaze layer (about 20-30 μm) free of silica grains which is situated over a thick interaction zone (c. 800 μm). The interaction zone is very compact, predominantly composed of silica grains (smaller than 100 μm), with only few and small voids, a small amount of glass and rounded Ca-based grains (Fig. A4.2c). Relatively small voids are present in the body where silica grains seem to be held in place by a Ca-based phase; there is a small amount (if any) of interparticle observed in the body. Larger roundish voids are along the interface between the core and the interaction zone.

UC 47410 (Fig. A4.2b) exhibits a thick glaze layer free of silica inclusions (300-500 μm) with a clear interaction zone between the glaze and the body (c. 400-600 μm thick). The silica grain size in the body varies but is smaller than 200 μm and some coarser grains are present (larger than 600 μm). The body is porous with little interparticle glass if any connecting the silica grains. Spot EDX analyses of areas between the silica grains in the body show the presence of a Ca-based compound most likely calcite (Fig. A4.2d). The glaze has small round voids caused likely by air bubbles trapped in the glaze during firing. Larger round voids are across the interaction zone.

Composition

Spot EDX analyses (Table A4.1) of the glaze of the cross sectioned samples shows that the glazes are of the soda-lime type containing typical amounts of Na_2O and CaO for blue faience in agreement with other blue faience from Memphis (Shortland and Tite, 2005). The CaO values are increased in the glass phase of the interaction zone in both samples. UC 47410 has unusually high K_2O and elevated MgO and SrO content. The high K_2O with the relatively high MgO may indicate the use of desert plant ash as the source of alkali for UC 47410. The high alumina (>2 wt%) and FeO content suggest the use of quartz sand in the case of UC 47410. Alumina (>1 wt%), and FeO are lower in ROCH 103.22 but high enough to suggest the use of quartz sand.

Both samples are coloured by copper (CuO 1.4-2.5 wt%); the CoO concentrations are below the detection limit of the technique. A small amount of SnO is present in the glaze with higher SnO content in UC 47410 glaze (c. 1wt%) which also has high PbO in the interaction zone glass. SnO and PbO have been previously associated with the use of a leaded bronze as a source of colourant in the glaze (Shortland aand Tite 2005).

Discussion

The presence of drips (UC 47410) and macroscopic evidence of the stacked vessels (ROCH 103.22) indicate that the application glazing method was employed on both objects. This is in agreement with previous findings from the appearance of glazes and the factory evidence from Memphis that applied glazes were extensively used (Vandiver, 1983:A124; Shortland and Tite, 2005). The thick interaction zones seen in BSE images indicate that the glazing material was applied as a wet mixture onto a dry core, which allowed the glazing material to penetrate well into the body. Penetration of the glazing material during the firing is possible but the round bubbles present in the glaze may suggest that a relatively viscous glaze was developed during firing. The presence of voids at the interface between interaction zone/body (ROCH 103.22) or the interaction zone (UC 47410) may be significant; more experimental work is necessary to aid understanding of the properties of the glazing materials used. This could offer evidence to elucidate if glazing was undertaken in a second firing step in the production of faience of this period adopting practices from other ceramic crafts.

EDX data suggest the use of quartz sand as the source of silica in the glaze mixture, and desert plants as the source of alkali for UC 47410, which were likely used also for the making of ROCH 103.22. This is in agreement with the less angular silica grains observed at the BSE images (UC 47410). It is unclear if the glazing materials were applied as a wet mixture in their raw form or if they were pre-fired. The use of a frit has been previously proposed to explain

Table A4.1: Normalised spot EDX analyses of the glaze (GLZ) and glass phase in the interaction zone (IAZ) in polished cross sections. Values below the detection limit of the technique are left blank.

	Analyses / Norm. Oxide wt%	Na_2O	MgO	$Al2O_3$	SiO_2	SO_2	K_2O	CaO	TiO_2	FeO	CoO	NiO	CuO	ZnO	SrO	SnO	Sb_2O_3	PbO
ROCH103.22	GLZ 1	15.5	1.2	1.3	72.1	0.7	0.5	4.4		0.7			2.5			0.3		
ROCH103.22	GLZ 2	15.6	1.3	1.5	70.8	1.0	0.4	4.7	0.5	0.9			2.5			0.3	0.5	
ROCH103.22	GLZ 3	16.4	1.2	1.5	71.7	0.6	0.3	4.1		1.1	0.3	0.4	2.3					
ROCH103.22	**GLZ Mean n=3**	**15.9**	**1.2**	**1.5**	**71.5**	**0.7**	**0.4**	**4.4**		**0.9**			**2.4**					
	Std. Dev.	0.5	0.0	0.1	0.6	0.2	0.1	0.3		0.2			0.1					
ROCH103.22	IAZ 1		0.4	0.8	92.5	0.3		4.7		0.4			1.2		0.3			
ROCH103.22	IAZ 2	0.2	1.0	1.4	85.4	0.4	0.3	8.1		0.8			1.8				0.2	0.4
ROCH103.22	IAZ 4	0.3	0.7	1.4	91.8		0.5	4.3		0.9			0.7			0.3		
ROCH103.22	IAZ 5		0.8	0.5	88.0	0.6		9.5		0.4			0.4			0.4		0.3
ROCH103.22	**IAZ Mean n=5**	**0.2**	**0.7**	**1.0**	**89.5**	**0.4**		**6.6**		**0.6**			**1.0**					
	Std. Dev.	0.1	0.2	0.4	3.3	0.2		2.6		0.3			0.6					
UC47410	GLZ 1	9.0	2.0	2.9	66.2	0.4	8.9	5.2		1.5		0.3	1.1			0.9		0.7
UC47410	GLZ 2	8.5	2.5	3.0	64.9	0.7	8.8	5.4	0.4	2.2			1.2	0.5	0.2	0.5	0.7	
UC47410	GLZ 3	8.9	1.8	2.3	66.9	0.5	8.9	5.8	0.3	1.3			1.1			1.6		0.4
UC47411	**GLZ Mean n=3**	**8.8**	**2.1**	**2.7**	**66.0**	**0.5**	**8.9**	**5.4**		**1.6**			**1.1**			**1.0**		
	Std. Dev.	0.3	0.4	0.4	1.0	0.2	0.1	0.3		0.5			0.1			0.5		
UC47410	IAZ 1	9.4	1.0	1.2	67.9	0.2	7.6	6.8		1.4			1.3		1.2			1.4
UC47410	IAZ 2	9.8	0.6	1.2	69.5		7.4	7.3	0.2	0.9			1.4		1.3			1.6
UC47410	IAZ 3	9.3	1.0	1.8	68.6		7.1	6.5		0.8			1.2		1.0		0.4	1.8
UC47410	IAZ 4	9.6	0.7	1.8	68.7	0.3	6.8	6.6	0.2	0.7	0.2		1.6		2.3			1.8
UC47411	**IAZ Mean n=4**	**9.5**	**0.8**	**1.5**	**68.7**		**7.2**	**6.8**		**0.9**			**1.4**		**1.4**			**1.6**
	Std. Dev.	0.2	0.2	0.4	0.6		0.3	0.3		0.3			0.2		0.6			0.2

the use of blue spheres (c.1cm diameter) found in Memphis in contexts associated with faience making and containing quartz, cristobalite and calcite (Si, Ca, Fe, Cu, Mg, Zn) (Vandiver 1983:A128). There is clear analytical evidence to support the view that these balls are of Egyptian blue, which was used as a pigment (Tite and Hatton, 2007). The use of balls of Egyptian blue as a pigment is however not restrictive; it may have been employed as a source of colourant in the glaze mixture with the addition of alkali to form a slurry. EDX bulk composition analyses of the balls from Memphis show a composition high in SiO_2 (c.60-70 wt%), PbO (c. 3-6 wt%), CuO (8.5-10.7 wt%), CaO (c. 9-14 wt%) and FeO (2.5-3 wt%) the rest of the components being in low concentrations (Tite and Hatton, 2007).The addition of alkali would be necessary to form a glaze and if only a small amount of Egyptian blue was sufficient to colour the glaze, the compositional signature of the final glaze would be significantly different. Experimental work could offer insights as to how cristobalite or Egyptian blue crystals would transform in an alkaline environment during melting in a second firing.

The absence of glass in the core suggests that little (if any) alkali was mixed in the preparation of the body but the presence of calcite or a Ca-based phase is interesting. Calcite in the core has been previously found in similar objects and it was attributed to post-burial weathering (Shortland and Tite, 2005; sample MEM6). In this case it is deposited between silica grains in the core of both samples and it may equally be due to the burial conditions. However, the rounded Ca-based inclusions in the interaction zone of ROCH103.22 are more difficult to interpret because they are absent from the porous core of the sample. More work is necessary to understand the deterioration patterns of faience and the deposition of calcite in its pores. Acicular SiO_2 crystals are absent from both samples, signifying absence of a high temperature phase such as cristobalite (Vandiver 1983: A45 and Fig. 27f), which has been previously found in a similar faience waster (Shortland and Tite 2005; sample MEM13) but not in other (*ibid.* sample MEM14). Absence of high temperature SiO_2 polymorphs may point toward lower temperatures of firing, X-Ray diffraction analyses is planned to verify absence of SiO_2 polymorphs and the nature of the Ca-based inclusions.

Conclusions

The analysed samples fit well within previously published work. The objects are glazed by the application method and most likely formed by moulding. The presence of Ca-based inclusions is enigmatic and experimental work is important to understand if this is an outcome of deterioration during the burial. A systematic investigation of more faience vessels is needed to understand the use of frit for glazing and technologies involved in their making including cross-fertilisation between faience and pottery manufacture as previously suggested by Vandiver (1983) and in Chapters 7 and 8 of this volume.

Section II

Finds Catalogue

Section II

Finds Catalogue

P.T. Nicholson

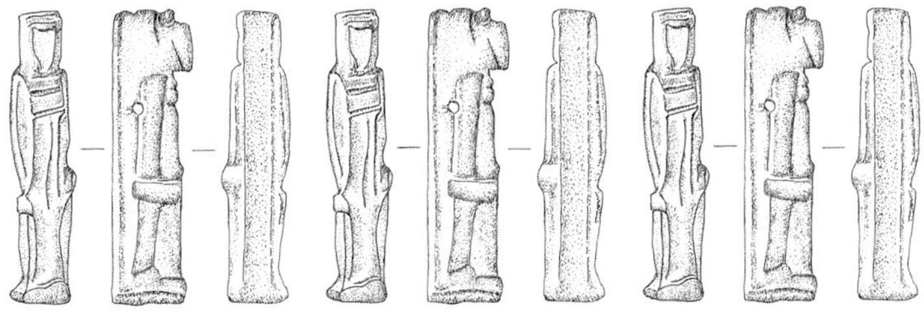

Introduction

All finds from the excavation are presented on the DVD along with relevant illustrations of them. However, a number of categories which are likely to be of most interest to researchers either because of their utility for dating or their relevance to the products made at Kom Helul are presented in this section.

All finds were recorded at the time of excavation and those deemed most important were either photographed or drawn then or shortly afterwards. Less significant finds were photographed or drawn as necessary during the study seasons. However, the destruction of the E.E.S. workroom at Memphis and the finds it contained put an end to this process and accounts for any gaps in illustration. Many of the drawings have been worked on by two or more illustrators and so are not individually credited in the text. All illustrators are credited in the acknowledgements section of the main text.

Dimensions are given in millimetres unless otherwise stated. Weights are in grams.

The database system used for processing and recording the finds is described by Nouwens below. Note that each unique specialist number (= object number), for example H-1, comes under a general Find ID number e.g. 2002-H-0352 and the trench and context information is given in this section since each Find ID may include multiple ojects.

Finds Registration System

H.M. Nouwens

General introduction

There are numerous ways in which archaeological finds may be registered following their excavation. The decision on which system to use is partially a matter of personal choice and partly determined by the nature and aims of the excavation itself, namely the type of material likely to be excavated, its quantity and the requirements of specialists and the site director.

However, all registration systems share the same purpose: they are designed to accurately record and describe finds according to criteria such as material type, quantity, form and possible function as well as recording the trench number, context and excavation date of each find. Effective systems both enable efficient recording and facilitate the ease of relocating archaeological material once processed and stored. This is especially important as finds may need to be (re-) examined, often at a later date, and not necessarily by those who conducted the actual excavation.

Although individual registration systems may differ in their design, all require good organisation. Data which are not recorded by the registrar, or specialist using the registration system, cannot be regained without recourse to the actual object, and since objects cannot be removed from Egypt the record must be as complete as possible.

The registry system developed for use at Kom Helul is typical in that it has undergone a series of changes and modifications during the duration of the project, resulting in a complex finds registration system with many cross references, which were necessary to give the registrar in the field the maximum amount of information at any time.

The Memphis Faience Project initially recorded its finds directly onto paper. The decision to record to paper was dictated by difficulties with the electricity supply in the field. At a later stage all data were transferred to an electronic medium, resulting in the Memphis database.

Finds registration

Introduction

The Memphis finds registration is divided into two broad levels. It has a general numbering system which was used to identify *groups* of excavated finds and a specialist numbering system for specialists to refer to some of those finds in further detail. On the first level the so-called Finds Identification Number (Finds ID) plays the key role; on the second level, which is cross-referenced to the first one, the Specialist Identification Number (Spec ID) is most important and is the one used to refer to those finds with an extended description or individual note.

Finds Identification Number (Finds ID)

All finds excavated in the field were initially treated in the same manner in that they were separated according to material type, contextual information and excavation date before being placed in a container. After the details of each find bag were confirmed and recorded, the Finds Identification Number was allocated by the registrar. All finds at Kom Helul were registered by material category, meaning that all finds of the same material and from the same unit and excavation date were recorded together under one and the same Finds Identification Number. Thus the excavated finds were not registered individually at this stage of registration. This batch processing of materials allowed more rapid processing of the large volume of finds. Furthermore, it allowed the find specialists to assign their own numbers at a later time: some finds acquired their own Specialist Identification Number (see below) as a supplement to their Finds Identification Number. This general number may be thought of as a kind of 'stock control' system allowing groups of finds to be located when in storage.

The Finds Identification Numbers, which were ascribed by the registrar to the excavated finds, comprise three parts, separated by hyphens:

1. The year of excavation (for example 2000)

Since the Memphis Faience Project continued over several years, the first part of the Finds Identification Number is either 2000, 2001, 2002 or 2005. This first part of the Finds Identification Number makes immediately clear in what year certain finds were excavated.

2. A letter code for the material type (for example F = Faience)

The second part of the Finds Identification Number refers to the material contained in the finds bag. The materials categories (see below) were created by the registrar and underwent minor modifications between seasons, yet remained largely the same. Each category is denoted by one or two letters of the alphabet, from A to Z, and it is this abbreviation indicating the material that constitutes the second part of the Finds Identification Numbers, joined to the preceding and following number by a hyphen. So in the example given here, this would result in: 2000-F, which refers to a bag with faience, that was found in 2000.

The materials categories used were as follows:

A Unworked Bone
B Worked Bone
C Clay
D Charcoal
E Organic Other
F Faience
G Glass
H Fibres
IM Industrial Material
L Pigment
M Ferrous Metal
N Non- Ferrous Metal
O Botanical Remains
P Pottery
Q Unworked Shell
R Worked Shell
S Unworked Stone
T Worked Stone
U Textile
V Vitreous Slag
W Unworked Wood
X Worked Wood
Y Plaster
Z Soil Samples
Zz Unknown

3. An identifier of four digits (for example 0041)

This third part of the Finds Identification Number is only unique when combined with the year, since it runs consecutively, starting from 0001 *each* excavation season. Thus, the first find of each year of excavation was assigned number 0001, the second 0002 and so on. Therefore, there are in total four identifiers numbered '0041' incorporated in the database, one in each excavation year. For example, in 2001, identifier 0041 is referring to some industrial finds (2001-IM-0041), while for 2005 the database contains 2005-N-0041 (a bag containing 4 fragments of non-ferrous metal). To avoid confusion with the Specialist Identification Number (below), finds from the Memphis Faience Project should not be referred to by only the second and third part of their Finds Identification Number, such as F-0041, rather 2000-F-0041 should be used.

It is important to stress that the Finds Identification Number does not necessarily represent just one single piece of a certain material (e.g. faience); the number may represent a whole bag of fragments or objects from the same material, all from the same area, trench and context. In the example of 2000-F-0041 there were actually 11 fragments in the bag.[1]

Any finds which were initially misidentified were re-registered to the correct category when the error became apparent. Sometimes they could be allocated to an existing Finds Identification Number because they came from the same context as other finds of the same material, at other times a new number had to be issued.

Specialist Identification Number (Spec ID)

In addition to, and cross-referenced with, the Finds Identification Number there is a second level of finds registration; the so-called Specialist Identification Numbers. After the details of each find bag were recorded and the Finds Identification Number designated, a decision was made regarding whether any of the pieces within the registered finds bags should be allocated a Specialist Identification Number (Spec ID). Normally, a specialist, responsible for a certain category of finds, would make such a decision, but the registrar was also able to make this distinction.

A Specialist Identification Number was allocated to all finds considered to have a particular importance or significance, and included those which needed to be conserved, drawn or photographed or a combination of the above. In contrast with the Finds Identification Number, which may refer to a whole bag containing several finds, the Specialist Identification Number refers to an individual piece from a certain area, trench and context.

The Specialist Identification Numbers comprise two parts, separated by hyphens:

1. A letter code for the material type (for example P = Pottery)

The first part of the Specialist Identification Number refers to the material of the find. Here the same materials categories (above) were used as in the second part of the Finds Identification Numbers. Each category is denoted by one or two letters of the alphabet, from A to Z, as described above, and joined to the following number by a hyphen.

2. An identifier of one to four digits (for example 3)

For example P-3 is a solid figure of a quadruped that originated from a bag which was allocated the Site Identification Number 2000-P-0111. The second part of the Specialist Identification Number, the identifier, is only unique in combination with the first part, the letter code, since it runs consecutively, starting from '1' within each material category. Depending upon the last entry made, a find would receive for its Special Identification Number the number which followed on consecutively, regardless of the year of excavation. By consequence Specialist Identification Numbers are unique within their category and can be used without reference to their Finds Identification Number.

It follows that from a given bag that was allocated a Site Identification Number, more than one piece could be assigned a Specialist Identification Number. For example the bag with Finds Identification Number 2000-F-0012 contained six pieces, which were all given Specialist Identification Numbers, in this case F-35 to F-40.[2]

The Processing of Finds

Labelling and storage

All finds from the field were separated according to material type and placed into a container according to their contextual information and excavation date. Each container, be it bag or bucket, was labelled by the site supervisors with the find material 'type', 'Area', 'Year', 'Trench', 'Unit' and 'Excavation Date'. These were entered onto the relevant sections of the pre-printed finds labels. At the end of each day the labelled containers with finds were brought into the workroom from the trench to be weighed and further processed. The bulky finds, however, such as all industrial material, vitreous slag and domestic pottery, were temporarily kept in the field. This was due to the fact that most of them required washing.

Washing

The washing of industrial material, vitreous slag and domestic pottery took place each day. In order to prevent labels becoming lost or finds from one unit and date becoming confused with those of another, the washing of the materials was carried out on separate mats: one for industrial material and slag, the other for domestic pottery. The contents of each bucket were laid out in the sun to dry. From the domestic pottery a division was made between diagnostic and non-diagnostic pieces and labels made for both categories. Once dry, the industrial material and vitreous slag were returned to buckets while the diagnostic and un-diagnostic domestic pottery was stored in cotton bags.

Weighing

Once the contents of the containers were checked and the labels were confirmed, all finds were weighed. Weighing of the bulky finds occurred whilst they were still in the field. These were weighed on a large set of scales in kilograms, whereas all other finds were weighed in the workroom on a smaller set of scales in grams. Since the scales could not accurately weigh any objects of less than five grams the weight of these pieces was recorded as '0' grams; = "too light to be accurately recorded." All weights were recorded onto the relevant finds labels, attached to the buckets and bags, and then incorporated in the registration system. If more than one bag was to be registered under the same Finds Identification Number, their total weight was incorporated in the registration system.

Area

For all finds that were excavated in context the registrar recorded what area they came from: HAC or HAD.

Trench and Unit Number

As with the area, the trench and unit numbers already appeared on the find labels coming in from the field to the registry and were recorded by the registrar. The trench numbers were fixed, numbered consecutively and followed on year from year; thus, as there were two trenches in area 'HAC' in 2000 – HAC1 and HAC2, the first trench in that same area in 2001 was known as HAC3. The stratigraphic units, of course, changed regularly and were given a unique number; they were numbered consecutively and followed on year from year. The registrar noted short descriptions of the units, including the soil type, the alignment, any inclusions, the effects of any modern activity, colour and the position in relation to other contexts as recorded by the supervisors.

Object type

The description of the object type was essential to clarify the type of find, as a variety could be included within the same category and material. For example, category 'A', 'Unworked Bone', could refer to either ivory, horn, antler or hoof. Likewise, category 'C', 'Clay Sample', included clay stoppers, fired brick or, for example, unfired brick and it is such information which was registered under object type.

Description and Extended Description

All finds entered into the registration system were given a description and in some cases an extended description. The description was made by the registrar and was meant, in the first place, to quickly identify certain fragments or objects in a bag which was allocated a certain Finds Identification Number. Normally, the entries that recur relate to the quantity of bags which were registered under the same 'Finds Identification Number,' as well as the approximate amount of objects in each bag, the total amount and the size and type of fragments. Thus, if there were two bags of kiln furniture within the P-category, the quantity of bags would be recorded first, followed by an estimate of the amounts in each. It may then be stated whether the bags contained mostly saggar joiners or cones, or if there were any unusual pieces. For the faience finds some object details were, whenever possible, noted, e.g. 'technological faience', 'some waster pieces stuck together'.

The extended descriptions of the finds were written by the specialists and go beyond the simple initial descriptions in that they include detail about the registered individual finds allocated a Specialist Identification Number, including accurate measurements and sometimes a suggested date.

Conclusions

The finds processing system used at Memphis is a somewhat modified version of one in use on a number of other sites in Egypt, though the Memphis system has material category at its core rather than find-type. Although the system has proved extremely efficient at locating objects in storage and its in-built cross-checks have made it possible to identify and correct errors quickly, it has proved complicated. Although variants of this system are in use elsewhere in Egypt finds specialists are not usually familiar with this type of system. It also proved to be over-complex for use on relatively small excavations. For these reasons, although the system served its purpose well in the current excavations, it will not be used again by the excavators. However, the focus on material is certainly one which the director might wish to retain.

Endnotes

1 Exceptions to the material code normally used are SF to indicate a surface find or DC for finds from a drill core. These exceptions are rare. In some instances especially notable finds were registered under category , for example 'P', pottery, and the Finds Identification Number was lengthened by adding a letter after the identifier (e.g. A, B or C). For example: 2005-P-0012A. This sub-division within the Finds Identification Number made it easier to handle and relocate the great variety of object types which shared the same Finds Identification Number.

2 Within the Specialist Registration process faience formed an exception, in that every individual piece was automatically given its own Specialist Identification Number.

Figurines

R. Thomas and P.T. Nicholson

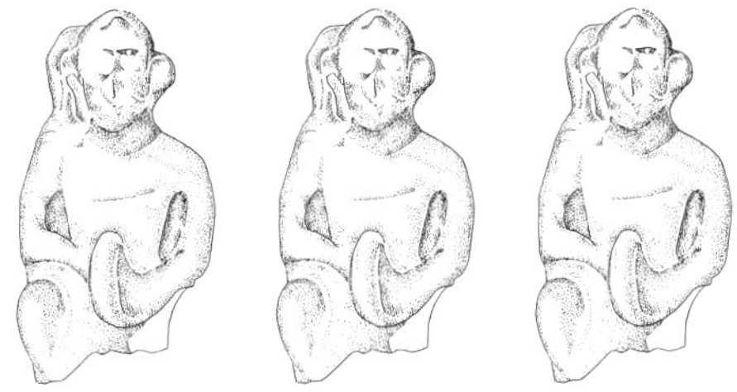

Introduction

The character of the assemblage is representative of two periods with different coroplast technologies. Firstly, Late Period figures, specifically of the 5th and 4th centuries B.C., are represented by hand-made and single piece mould-made figures or plaques. Secondly, Roman Period figures of around the 2nd Century A.D., which are hollow and made in at least two moulds. The Late period material is concentrated in area HAC Trench 1 (contexts 001. 002, 005 and 006) and Trench 2 (context 010). A small amount of Late Period and early Ptolemaic material is residual within HAC Trench 3 (contexts 058, 065, 218, 300 and 306). The majority of the figurine fragments from HAC Trench 3 are of types typical of the mid-1st through to early 3rd Century A.D., but with good 2nd Century A.D. parallels.

Both the Late Period and Roman material is very similar to that already found in Memphis by Petrie, including pieces from the same mould (see below for unpublished pieces in the Petrie Museum; Petrie 1909a; 1909b; 1910). The Late Period material has good parallels from nearby Saqqara and Lower Egypt, specifically Naukratis (Villing *et al.* 2013 and see forthcoming additions by Thomas to the catalogue), with Isis-Hathor figures and plaques, erotic scenes, phallophorous and ithyphallic Harpocrates figures and the so called 'Persian Riders' (see below). Whilst some of these Late Period types may creep into the very beginning of the Ptolemaic period, there is a notable absence of mid to late Ptolemaic material in this assemblage, which, in the case of both Memphis and Naukratis, had a more naturalistic representation of a greater variety of subjects represented before or after (Villing *et al.*2013 and forthcoming).

The Roman material is quite different, being heavily dominated with beneficent demon figures (Bailey 2008: 43-50; see P-55, P-57, P-62, P-70, P-74, P-372, P-110, P-50 and P-66), though figures of Isis enthroned with Harpocrates, Sothic dogs and riders were also found. These all have good parallels from catalogues (see below), but of most interest are the fragments from sites with secure independent dating of mid 1st to early 3rd centuries A.D., especially contexts dating to the Trajanic and Antonine periods (Bailey 2006; Thomas 2011).

These objects have been grouped together as a conventional finds class rather than being grouped by material since they are of interest beyond the main, industrial, scope of this work.

Find ID: 2000-P-0023 Area: HAC Trench: 01 Unit: 001
Material(s): Pottery
Object type: Figurine
Description: 2 fragments of terracotta figurines.

Specialist code P-2 (Figure II.1)
Length: 73 Breadth: 48 Thickness: 38 Diameter: 0 Weight: 55
Specialist description: Solid modelled figure of an animal, probably from a group. A bird, or horse. Not well modeled for either. The head has lost its beak or muzzle. The neck is long and there is a pronounced bulge to the crop or breast bone (if

a bird). The leading edge of a wing(?) is indicated and the leg is stumpy and ends in an inverted Y shape, perhaps meant to suggest the claw. From the left side of the animal comes a projection suggesting that it was attached to something, possibly a similar animal. There is also a suggestion of another leg on its left side, or it may have relied on the second animal to balance. Although the overall shape of the figure as preserved resembles a pigeon, the lack of a beak makes the type of bird uncertain and the closest parallels for such groups are from chariot models of the Late Period.

Comparanda: Parallel for Late Period chariot groups from Memphis show similar features, fabric and technology (Petrie Museum UC48057-9, dated Late Period), however, the chest is poorly executed if this is the intended subject. Alternatively a number of bird figures dated to the late Roman period are known from Memphis (Petrie Museum UC48344) and in the British Museum (Bailey 2008: no.3731), although the date, technique and the subject makes such parallels unsatisfactory.

Specialist code P-398 (Figure II.1)
Length: 43 Breadth: 0 Thickness: 0 Diameter: 24 Weight: 17
Specialist description: Tapering clay cone with slight modelling suggesting that it is meant as the leg or arm of a Figure It is solid and where broken at the narrow end has a slight angle suggesting a knee or elbow. Max.D.24mm Min.D.14mm.

Find ID: 2000-P-0100 Area: HAC Trench: 01 Unit: 005
Material(s): Pottery
Object type: Figurine
Description: 1 fragment of a terracotta figurine.

Specialist code P-8 (Figure II.1)
Length: 75 Breadth: 52 Thickness: 28 Weight: 88
Specialist description: Solid modelled clay figure of a horseman. The figure has lost his head, arms and legs, though the stumps of the latter survive sufficient to show that the figure had his legs apart so as to be seated on a horse. The stumps of his arms show that they were lowered and forward facing. The curvature of the opening of the legs would allow him to sit on P-3 which comes from the same trench, though there is no certainty that he did so, and he is forward leaning when placed upon it.

The navel of the figure is shown much enlarged and was probaby made by the tip of the index finger rather than with a tool of similar size. On his left side the rider has a stump, apparently the remains of a sword or scabbard worn at the waist. The figure is painted in a pinkish yellow slip. It is uncertain whether the rider was entirely hand-made, or whether he originally had a mould made face, consistent with 'Persian Riders', labelled 'Scythian Riders' by Petrie (1909a: 17).

Comparanda: Numerous 27th to 31st Dynasty parallels from Memphis Include 'Persian Riders' with mould made riders (Petrie Museum UC38503-6, UC49906, UC47802-7, UC48123-4, UC48039-46, UC47808-10, UC30155-6; Ashton 2003: 72; Petrie 1909: Pl.xl, no. 44-6; Petrie 1909a: Pl.xliv, Pl. xl, nos. 42, 45, 46; Petrie 1909b: Pl.xxix, no. 78-82, 84; Petrie 1910, Pl.xlii, 136-8; Cairo Egyptian Museum SR5/6260, CG43519) There are numerous 'Persian Rider' parallels from Naukratis (Edgar in Hogarth *et al.* 1905, 129; Higgins 1954, 407, no. 1549; Villing *et al.* 2013; British Museum GR1888,0601.90; Cairo Egyptian Museum: CG32804; CG43442; Cambridge Museum of Classical Archaeology: NA595, NA603, NA602), Tanis (Dunand 1990, 215-6, no. 583-592 and 594-595), Tell Basta (Vaelske 1912: 13; Cairo Egyptian Museum: CG32810 , TR26/11/22/2), Tukh el-Karamus (Cairo Egyptian Museum: CG32806), Deir el-Bahari (Cairo Egyptian Museum:CG32807, CG32808) and unprovenanced (Cairo Egyptian Museum TR26/11/22/3, CG32903, CG32907, CG32904, TR22/11/22/1, TR22/11/22/2, TR22/ 11/ 22/3, CG32902). A date associated with Achaemenid rule is confirmed by parallels from Persian period sites in Syria (Pruss 2000: 54), Dura Europos (Downey 2003: 142-53, no. 91), Uruk (Ziegler 1962: Pl.39-42, no. 482-536) and Nippur (McCown 1967: Pl. 47-49, no. 245-262), though some prefer a 4th to 3rd Century B.C. date (Dunand 1990: 215; Vaelske 2012: 13).

Alternatively, this may be from an entirely hand-made copy of a 'Persian Rider', with parallels from Memphis (Petrie Museum UC48297, UC48060-7; Petrie 1909a: Pl.xliv), Naukratis (British Museum GR1886,0401.1468; Bolton Museum 1966.93.A; Bristol, City Art Gallery & Museum H2223; Cambridge Museum of Classical Archaeology NA599), Toukh el Karenis (Cairo TR14/1/34/5) and unprovenanced (Cairo TR14/1/34; CG32901).

Find ID: 2000-P-0111 Area: HAC Trench: 01 Unit: 006
Material(s): Pottery
Object type: Figurine
Description: 3 fragments of terracotta figurines.

Specialist code P-1 (Figure II.1)
Length: 55 Breadth: 50 Thickness: 42 Weight: 105
Specialist description: Head of a male Figure Modelled in solid clay. The hair/wig hangs down over the ears and has the texture indicated by dots, perhaps intended to suggest a Nubian hair style. The forehead juts out and the eyes are large discs of clay which have been pressed into the sockets as balls. The nose is long, rather than Negroid, and the lips are shown as a single protruding 'V' of clay. The back of the head is damaged and the hair there is lost. The head is probably intended as that of an Egyptian and has similarities to the types illustrated by Petrie (1909a: Pl.xxxv).

Comparanda: From Memphis there are many parallels of this diverse group of hand-made figures dated between the 27th Dynasty and the 4th Century B.C., and are probably within 500 B.C.- 300 B.C. (Petrie Museum UC47754, UC47756-7, UC47873, UC47894-5, UC48136-9, UC48514-6, UC48567, UC49900; Petrie 1909a: Pl.xliv; Petrie 1909b: Pl.xxviii, no. 72; Pl.xxxiv, no.127; Petrie 1910: Pl.xliv, no.188; Vaelske 2012: 13).

Specialist code P-3 (Figure II.2)
Length: 67 Breadth: 47 Thickness: 88 Weight: 103
Specialist description: Solid modelled figure of a quadruped. The head survives as a crude rhomboid, the ears or perhaps horns, having been snapped off. The front left leg survives for most of its length and the right for part. The rest of the body is lost from the base of the neck. Behind the neck is a scar in the clay which may indicate that a seated figure was once luted into place here. If so the animal would probably have been a horse, perhaps the mount for a so-called 'Persian' or 'Scythian Rider' (Petrie 1909a: 17). The whole appears to have been.red slipped.

Comparanda: if this is from a rider figure, see parallels listed under P-8. Alternatively, this may be from another hand-made quadruped figure, which also has Late Period parallels from Memphis (Petrie Museum: UC48296, UC48322; Petrie 1909a: Pl.xliv; Petrie 1909d: Pl. xix; Anthes 1965: Pl.49 c.252).

Specialist code P-4 (Figure II.2)
Length: 94 Breadth: 64 Thickness: 44 Weight: 286
Specialist description: Fragment of a solid clay male figure, broken below the chest and also above the knees. The left leg is slightly forward of the right. The belly is quite bulbous with deeply impressed navel. The genitals are modelled though the phallus has been broken off. The back of the figure is modelled, though less carefully than the front. There is smoothing to the back which has traces of red, suggesting that it may have been red-slipped.

Comparanda: Later, finer, hollow parallels of this figure are dated to the Ptolemaic, or more generally to the Graeco-Roman Period (Fischer 1994: 261, nos. 363-6) including an example from Memphis (Petrie Museum UC30205). Ashton (2003: 72-73) notes that Egyptian figures are normally solid rather than hollow moulded and this is likely to be an example and as such probably dates from the Late Period or 4th Century B.C. A solid, but seated, parallel from Naukratis was found with 'Persian Period' pottery (Ashmolean AN1896-1908-E.4653; Hogarth *et al.* 1905: 125) and a kneeling solid muscular torso also from Naukratis (AN1896-1908-E.4714) is probably early Ptolemaic in date, but looks later than the present example.

Find ID: 2000-P-0195 Area: HAC Trench: 02 Unit: 010
Material(s): Pottery
Object type: Figurine
Description: 1 fragment of terracotta figurine.

Specialist code P-12 (Figure II.2)
Length: 68 Breadth: 67 Thickness: 33 Weight: 104
Specialist description: Part of a solid moulded plaque. The subject is a man exposing himself. The left leg of the figure is preserved as far as the ankle and is carefully moulded. The phallus survives as little more than a lump, whilst the folds of the raised toga are clearly visible. The back of the piece is flat.

Comparanda: A near exact parallel for this piece is given by Manniche (1987: 11, fig. 2), though probably not from the same mould series.

Find ID: 2000-P-0223 Area: IIAC Trench: 02 Unit: 010
Material(s): Pottery
Object type: Figurine
Description: A terracotta plaque with the head of a woman, incomplete.

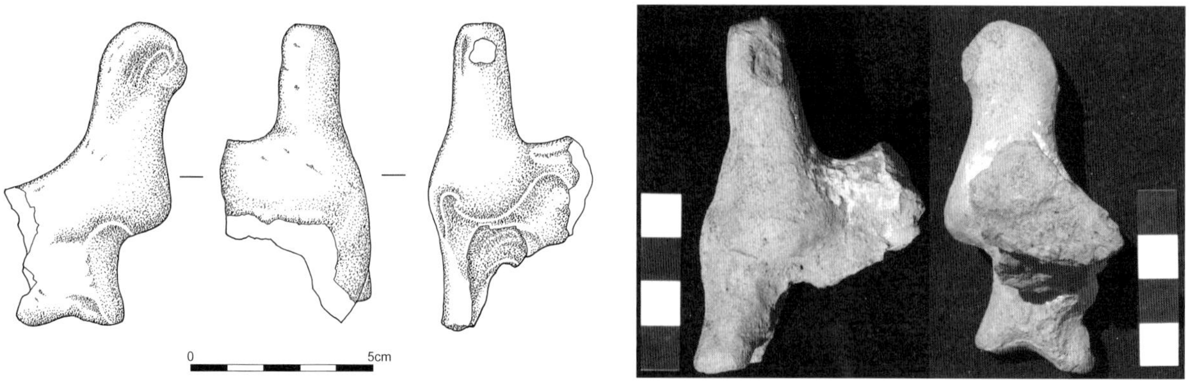

P-2

P-398

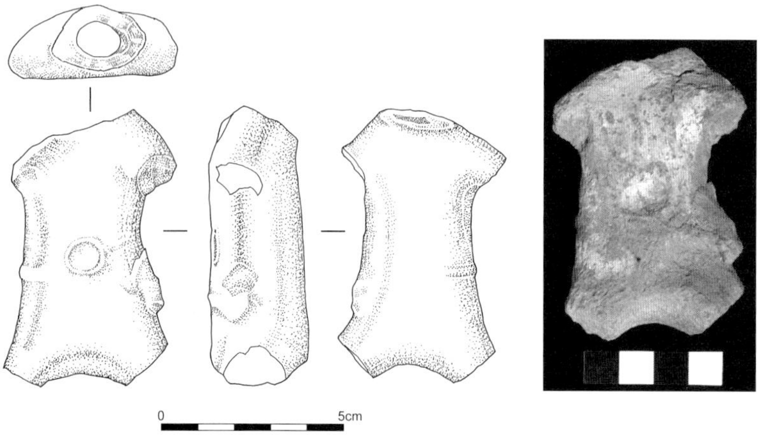

P-8

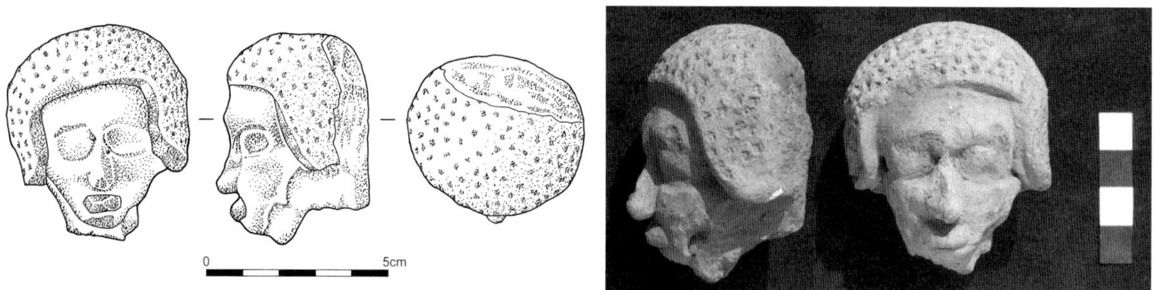

P-1

Figure II.1

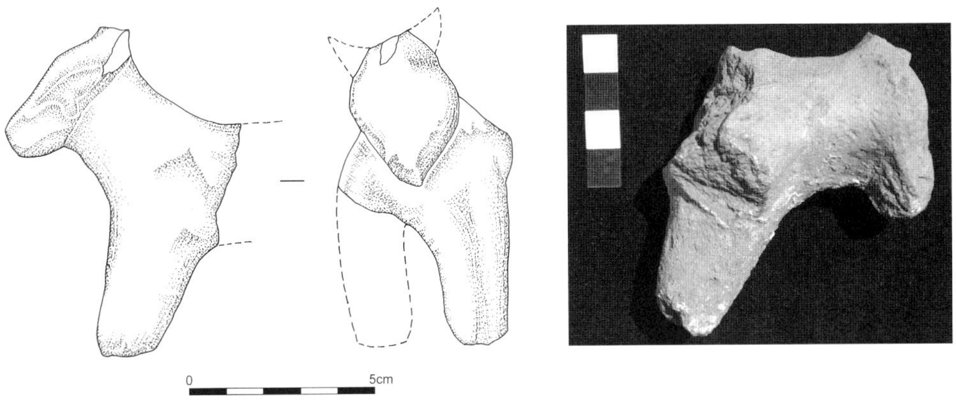

P-3

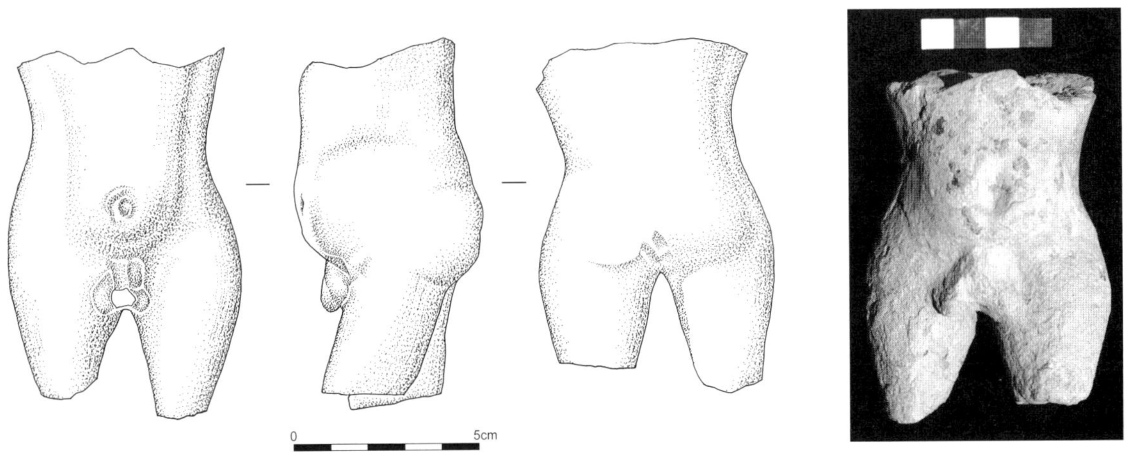

P-4

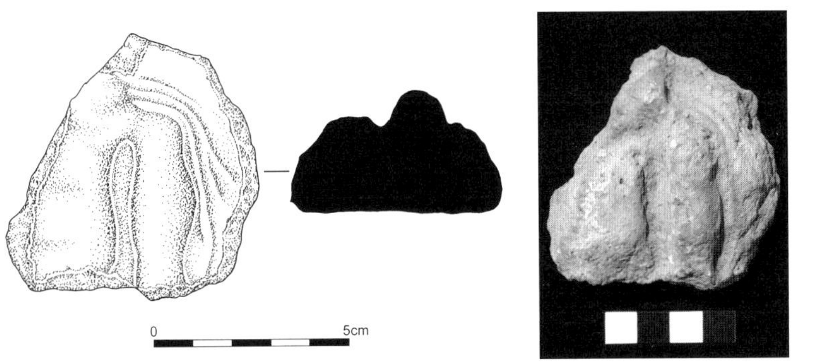

P-12

P-11

Figure II.2

Specialist code P-11 (Figure II.2)
Length: 82 Breadth: 61 Thickness: 25 Weight: 119
Specialist description: Upper part of a plaque with figure of a female (based on parallels) standing in a shrine.[1] The top of the plaque has a cavetto cornice supported by two pillars. These have a plain rounded section at the very top where they meet the cornice, but the actual capitals are in plant form, probably intended as lotuses. The figure is centred between the columns, but only the head remains. It wears a simple wig and though the face is damaged it is clear that it originally had some detail. The back of the plaque is flat, save for some undulations from the surface on which it rested during manufacture.

Common figure plaque form found in Late Period sites in Lower Egypt, that have close parallels found in Achaemenid period Phoenician sites in the Levant (Pruss 2000: 52-4; Rotté 2012: 13), showing foreign influences on the established 'Pharaonic tradition' of Egyptian so-called 'concubine' (Hogarth *et al.* 1905, 128) or 'fertility' figures (Pinch 1983; 1993; 2006; Teeter 2010) without pillars, often associated with domestic religion, healing and apotropaic rites concerning the cults of Isis, Mut, Hathor and Anuket, associated with, but not exclusively, women and childbirth (Bayer-Niemeier 1988, 148; Teeter 2010, nos. 1 to 9 and 25 to 26; Waraksa 2009, no. 3; 2008, 2; 2007; Hogarth *et al.* 1905, 128; Del Vesco 2009). Late Period examples can be shown with or without pillars, children and vessels. Parallels are generally dated to the Late Period and early Ptolemaic periods in Egypt and thought to be fertility figures or *ex-voto* in honour of, but not representing, Hathor.

Comparanda: Parallels from Memphis (Petrie Museum UC30186-8, UC33574; Petrie 1909a: Pl.xxxv, no. 6-12; Ashton 2003: 73, UC30186; Rotté 2012: 13; see also Dunand 1973: 20-1), unprovenanced but also likely Memphis (UC30190-9). Note UC30190 is from the same mould, whilst UC30191, UC30187 and UC30198 are from a very close mould series. Dated to the Late Period or early Ptolemaic. Parallels from Naukratis dated to the late 6th to 4th centuries B.C. (Bailey 2008: nos. 3108 to 3110; Higgins 1954: 404; Hogarth *et al.* 1899, 82, nos. 51-55; Villing *et al.* 2013; City Art Gallery and Museum, Bristol H2223.b; Bolton Museum 1966.92.A; Cambridge Museum of Classical Archaeology NA580 and NA578; NA582, see also NA576, NA577, NA579, NA581, NA583, NA584; British Museum GR1886,0401.1543, GR1886,0401.1458, GR 1888,0601.113, ME1885,1010.28; Ashmolean Museum, Oxford, no. 1896-1908.E4679; Boston 86.395; Brussels A.1849). Figure plaques were found in late 5th to 4th Century B.C. contexts at Tell el-Muqdam (Redmount and Friedman 1997, Fig. 6) and several figure plaques, including those within shrines were found in 4th to 3rd Century B.C. context at Mendes (Redford 1988, 67, Pl. 22d). A similar example comes from the Fayum (Kaufmann 1915: fig. 69,3, no. 269). Unprovenanced (Egypt) parallels are usually given Late Period or early Ptolemaic dates (Török 1995: 137-9, Pl. 109, nos. 202-9, particularly 205; Bayer-Niemeier 1988: 148-9, Pl.50, nos. 263 to 267; Weber 1914: no.199).
Probably the same type as 0230-P-10.

Find ID: 2000-P-0230 Area: HAC Trench: 02 Unit: 011
Material(s): Pottery
Object type: Figurine
Description: A fragment of a terracotta plaque showing a woman.

Specialist code P-10 (Figure II.3)
Length: 89 Breadth: 72 Thickness: 20 Weight: 113
Specialist description: Plaque showing a naked female wearing a shoulder length wig and holding her right breast with her left hand. Her face has been carefully modelled. The piece was probably of the same type as 0223-P-11, though here the top of the plaque has broken away so that any cornice has been lost. However, the poles or columns supporting the cornice are shown. That on the left of the figure has lost its capital, but the right one is a papyrus umbel. The top of the umbel has a round projection where it originally met the cornice. The front is slightly blackened from burning. The back of the plaque is flat, though it has the contours of the surface on which it was manufactured.

Comparanda: Parallels from Memphis (Petrie Museum UC30186-8, UC33574; Petrie 1909 Memphis I: Pl.xxxv, no. 6-12; Ashton 2003: 73, UC30186), unprovenanced but also likely Memphis (UC30190-9). Dated to the Late Period or early Ptolemaic.
For other parallels see P-11 above.

Find ID: 2000-P-0288 Area: HAC Trench: 01 Unit: 001
Material(s): Pottery
Object type: Figurine
Description: Terracotta figurine, possibly a Scythian rider.

Specialist code P-41 (Figure II.3)
Length: 92 Breadth: 48 Thickness: 40 Weight: 183
Specialist description: Fragment of a male figure made from poorly fired solid clay. Only the torso is preserved, the lower body is missing from the waist down, and so are both arms, though the shoulder of the left one is present. The navel is modelled and there is some indication of the spine on the back. The lower part of the torso, as preserved, curves forward slightly, suggesting that it might originally have been seated. The figure has been painted red.

Comparanda: This may be another rider like figures P-8 and P-3. See notes for comparanda for P-8 of the late 6th to 4th centuries B.C.

Find ID: 2000-P-0289 Area: HAC Trench: 01 Unit: 002
Material(s): Pottery
Object type: Figurine
Description: Terracotta figurine.

Specialist code P-42
Specialist description: Defunct.

Specialist code P-399 (Figure II.3)
Length: 61 Diameter: 21 Weight: 29
Specialist description: Solid modelled fragment of figurine. The piece is not especially well shaped, but is probably meant to represent an arm or leg. It has been coated in a pink slip.
Comparanda: Late Period parallel from Memphis (Petrie Museum UC48339).

Find ID: 2001-P-0012-B Area: HAC Trench: 03 Unit: 033
Material(s): Pottery
Object type: Figurine
Description: Fragment of a figurine.

Specialist code P-397 (Figure II.3)
Length: 35 Breadth: 29 Thickness: 10 Weight: 9
Specialist description: Fragment of a hollow moulded figurine. There is one straight, finished edge which may be part of the base, though could also be where two halves of the moulding were joined. The fragment is roughly triangular in shape and has an inverted L-shaped raised area with three small ridges to its left (as viewed). The subject is unidentified.

Find ID: 2001-P-0022-C Area: HAC Trench: 03 Unit: 036
Material(s): Pottery
Object type: Figurine
Description: Fragment of a figurine.

Specialist code P-409 (Figure II.3)
Length: 66 Breadth: 45 Thickness: 9 Weight: 31
Specialist description: Badly weathered fragment from the base of a hollow moulded figurine. The fragment is roughly triangular on the largest preserved face and has a finished edge around the bottom on which the piece probably stood. No original surface remains.

Find ID: 2001-P-0044-B Area: HAC Trench: 03 Unit: 037
Material(s): Pottery
Object type: Figurine
Description: Roughly square fragment, possible figurine.

Specialist code P-396 (Figure II.3)
Length: 45 Breadth: 35 Thickness: 30 Weight: 58
Specialist description: Orange/red block of solid clay, apparently part of a figurine. No clear detail remains, but there is a pre-firing hole through the piece, and it has broken along the line of this. It is possible that this is part of a loom weight but the fabric is consistent with that used for figurines.

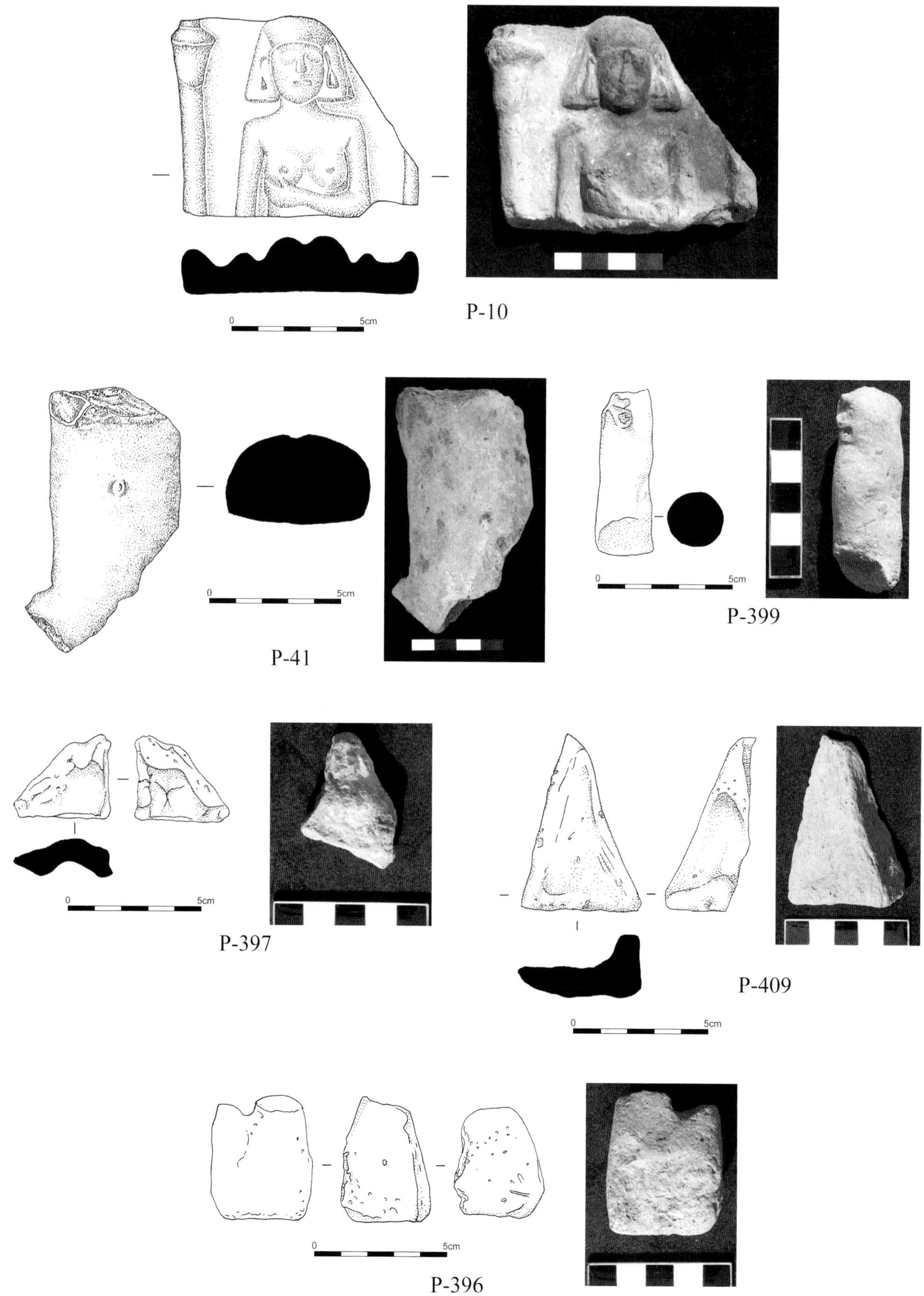

Figure II.3

Find ID: 2001-P-0060-C Area: HAC Trench: 03 Unit: 036
Material(s): Pottery
Object type: Figurine
Description: Possible fragment of a figurine.

Specialist code P-47 (Figure II.4)
Length: 40 Breadth: 27 Thickness: 6 Weight: 6
Specialist description: Fragment of hollow, moulded figure in fine hard fired silt clay. The fragment is covered by radiating fine ridges which disappear toward the top (?) of the piece. It may be intended as pleated drapery with the pleats pressed out near the wearer's shoulder. Less convincingly it could also be intended as part of a wig.

Find ID: 2001-P-0068-B Area: HAC Trench: 03 Unit: 036
Material(s): Pottery
Object type: Figurine
Description: Fragment of a figurine.

Specialist code P-79 (Figure II.4)
Length: 52 Breadth: 35 Thickness: 20 Weight: 51
Specialist description: The corner of a rectangular plaque. Slightly raised one edge and with a thickening beyond that, but no detail visible.
Probably Late Period, from an erotic, Harpocrates or nude female figure plaque.

Find ID: 2001-P-0105-B Area: HAC Trench: 03 Unit: 050
Material(s): Pottery
Object type: Figurine
Description: Possible Bes-figurine.

Specialist code P-45 (Figure II.4)
Length: 40 Breadth: 34 Thickness: 23 Weight: 18
Specialist description: Part of a hollow moulded figure, possibly of Bes. The piece is made in two halves and joined, and has broken along the seam at what is presumed to be the top of the head. The top has a series of dimples, perhaps intended as hair, there is then a band and a series of ridges, perhaps a fringe. A projection sticking up to the left (as viewed) is probably part of a headdress. The fragment seems to have been covered in a fine red slip or paint.

Find ID: 2001-P-0115-B Area: HAC Trench: 03 Unit: 051
Material(s): Pottery
Object type: Figurine
Description: Fragment of a figurine.

Specialist code P-51 (Figure II.4)
Length: 45 Breadth: 44 Thickness: 9 Diameter: 0 Weight: 22
Specialist description: Fragment of what appears to be a standing figure. The piece is hollow and moulded. The base is roughly finished and there is a possible finished edge running up the back where two moulded halves may have been joined. The piece apparently shows the left leg of a standing figure, and since the leg is painted yellow it may be assumed that it was female. From the side the leg is in front of a large column which would have allowed the otherwise slim figure to stand upright. The clay is quite coarse with much chaff, but has been given a fine coating of slip.

Find ID: 2001-P-0161-B Area: HAC Trench: 03 Unit: 052
Material(s): Pottery
Object type: Figurine
Description: Fragment of a figurine.

Specialist code P-48 (Figure II.4)
Length: 72 Breadth: 50 Thickness: 25 Diameter: 0 Weight: 39
Specialist description: Fragment of a figurine, showing the mould line along the inside. Probably the back and part of the front of a head and left shoulder, but the face and other details are missing.

Find ID: 2001-P-0187-C Area: HAC Trench: 03 Unit: 056
Material(s): Pottery
Object type: Figurine
Description: Defunct.

Specialist code P-395
Defunct.

Find ID: 2001-P-0211 Area: HAC Trench: 03 Unit: 053
Material(s): Pottery
Object type: Figurine
Description: Fragment of a figurine.

Specialist code P-46 (Figure II.4)
Length: 70 Breadth: 52 Thickness: 50 Weight: 101
Specialist description: Fragment of solid modelled ithyphallic figure/phallophorous Figure Lower torso has a separately modelled phallus added. The clay has broken away at the junction of the two pieces. Thickness at break = 16mm. The legs/support have been broken away. The piece is not well preserved, but it appears to represent a ithyphallic figure, with the phallus carried in procession by a pair of priests and Bes as illustrated by Martin (1981: Pl.23) in an example from Saqqara, a procession discussed by Herodotus in the 5th Century B.C. (*History*: ii.48).

Comparanda: P-53 may come from the same figure. Many parallels are known from Memphis (same mould series as P-53: Petrie Museum UC48384; lower half UC33595-601; different mould series UC33410, UC33602, UC47868, UC48382, UC48385, UC48391, UC33605; Anthes 1959, Pl.30, no.206; Anthes 1965, 129 nos. 255 and 256), Naukratis (Gutch 1899, Pl.12.143; Hogarth *et al.* 1905: 130, n.6; Cambridge, Museum of Classical Archaeology NA576, NA581, NA601; Bristol, City Art Gallery & Museum H2805; Boston, Museum of Fine Arts 86.389; Bolton Museum 1886.31.17, 1886.31.16 and 1886.31.15; Brussels, Musées Royaux d'Art et d'Histoire A.1837; British Museum GR 1886,0401.1458; Oxford, Ashmolean Museum AN1896-1908-E.4694) and Saqqara (Martin 1981: 29, Pl.23, no.306 probably early 4th Century B.C., see also nos. 307 and 1331). All date to the (probably late) 5th to 4th Century B.C.

Find ID: 2001-P-0228-B Area: HAC Trench: 03 Unit: 044
Material(s): Pottery
Object type: Figurine
Description: Fragment of a figurine.

Specialist code P-50 (Figure II.4)
Length: 35 Breadth: 20 Thickness: 25 Weight: 12
Specialist description: Foot/feet of a hollow moulded figurine. This may be a single foot of a figure or be intended to represent two feet bound together as in a mummiform Figure Two horizontal lines on the left of the leg (as viewed) give the impression of bandages, or more likely clothing concealing the back of the Figure The foot/feet rest against what seems to have been a square back pillar. The bottom part shows secondary burning.

Comparanda: See P-66. Standing beneficient demon wearing anklet, of Roman period (Bailey 2006: 270: 22, 2nd to early 3rd Century A.D.; Dunand 1979: no.122; see also Dunand 1990: 209, no. 570).

Find ID: 2002-P-0020-B Area: HAC Trench: 03 Unit: 066
Material(s): Pottery
Object type: Figurine
Description: Fragment of a figurine.

Specialist code P-52 (Figure II.5)
Length: 58 Breadth: 23 Thickness: 11 Weight: 14
Specialist description: Part of a hollow moulded figurine. The fragment comprises the back part of a naked figure. The left buttock, half of the right buttock and the lower back are preserved. A break down the left side suggests that this was the location of the seam. The figure is incomplete making certain attribution difficult. However, the angle of the leg and torso are closely matched by the figure of Aphrodite given by Bailey (2008: Pl.63, no. 3354) dated to the 1st Century B.C.. It is, however, possible that this could have been intended as a recumbent figure.

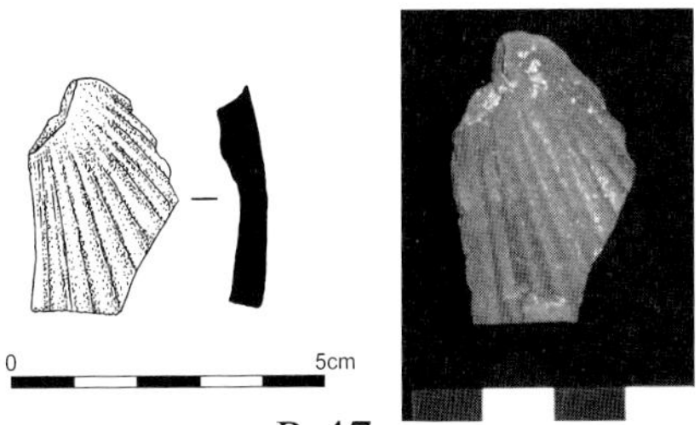

P-47

P-79

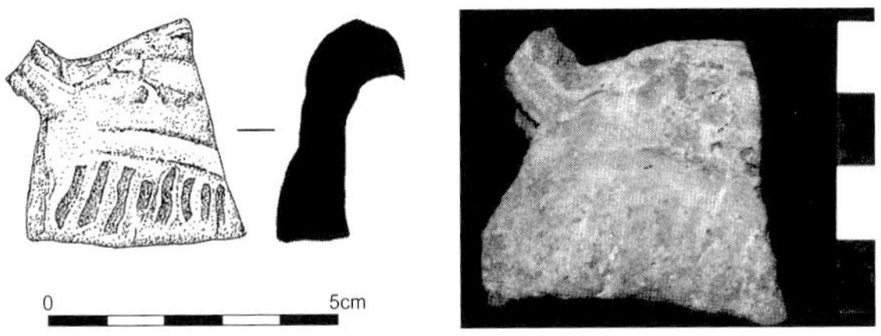

P-45

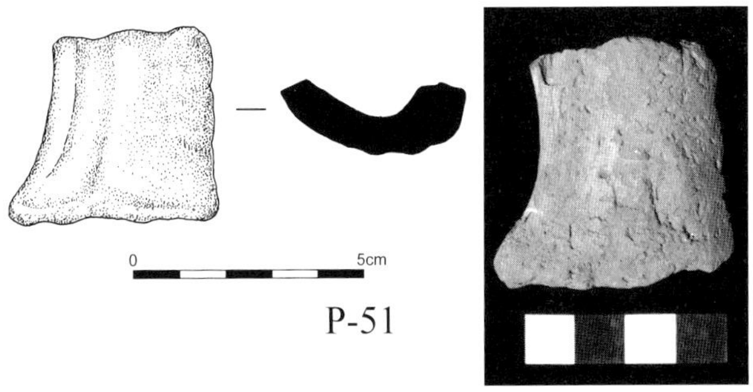

P-51

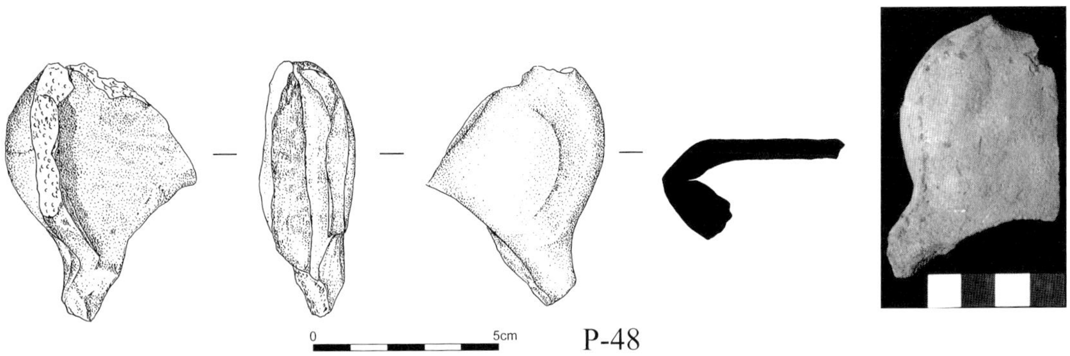

P-48

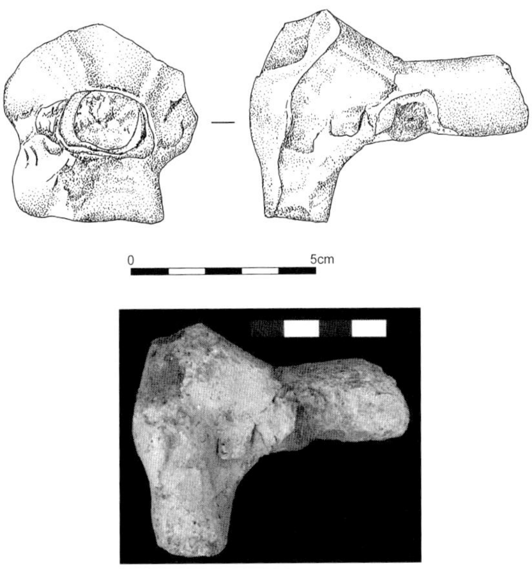

P-46

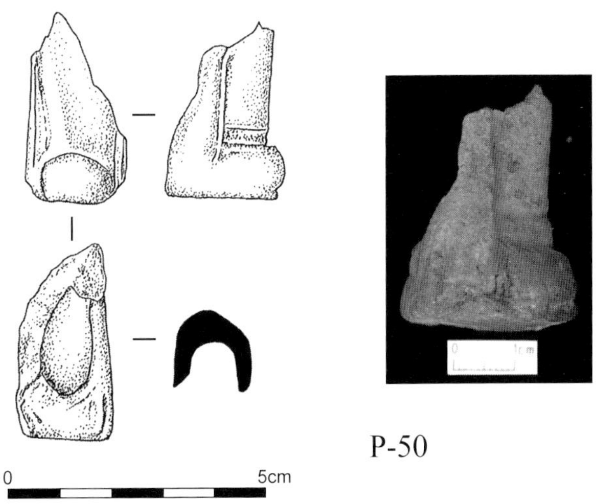

P-50

Figure II.4

Comparanda: Bailey (2008) Pl. 63, no. 3354. Dated to the 1st Century B.C.

Find ID: 2002-P-0025-B Area: HAC Trench: 03 Unit: 065
Material(s): Pottery
Object type: Figurine
Description: Fragment of a figurine.

Specialist code P-53 (Figure II.5)
Length: 117 Breadth: 62 Thickness: 40 Weight: 156
Specialist description: Figure of ithyphallic Harpocrates, with tambourine, as part of a phallophorous group. The figure is solid moulded. The solid moulded figure was standing, broken below the rather wide hips typical for this type (hip on the the right is not to be confused with a drawn up knee also known from squatting ithyphallic figures). There is a small lump at the top of the forehead. A sidelock of youth hangs down the right side of the head and is counter-balanced by a particularly large ear on the left. The face of the figure is not especially well modelled though the eye brows, eye sockets, nose and lips are clear. The nose is damaged. The chest and the muscles of the arms are well modelled though the hands are little more than blobs. The figure has been over-fired, probably secondarily and this has caused surface cracking as well as burning what seems to have been a red slip. The back is flat. In his hands he holds what is shown as a half-round object, possibly intended as a tambour. The tambour rests over the now lost phallus. Parellels may be drawn with ithyphallic Harpocrates figures playing tambour (Bailey 2008: nos. 3204, 3209). This is an ithyphallic Harpocrates, with the phallus carried in procession by a pair of priests and Bes (Martin 1981: Pl.23), a procession discussed by Herodotus in the 5th Century B.C. (*History*: ii.48). This is confirmed by parallels from the same and other mould series discussed below.

Comparanda: P-46 may come from the same figure. Many parallels are known from Memphis (same mould series as P-53: Petrie Museum UC48384; lower half UC33595-601; different mould series UC33410, UC33602, UC47868, UC48382, UC48385, UC48391, UC33605; Anthes 1959, Pl.30, no.206; Anthes 1965, 129 nos. 255 and 256), Naukratis (Gutch 1899, Pl.12.143; Hogarth *et al.* 1905: 130, n.6; Cambridge, Museum of Classical Archaeology NA576, NA581, NA601; Bristol, City Art Gallery & Museum H2805; Boston, Museum of Fine Arts 86.389; Bolton Museum 1886.31.17, 1886.31.16 and 1886.31.15; Brussels, Musées Royaux d'Art et d'Histoire A.1837; British Museum GR1886,0401.1458; Oxford, Ashmolean Museum AN1896-1908-E.4694) and Saqqara (Martin 1981: 29, Pl.23, no.306 probably early 4th Century B.C., see also nos. 307 and 1331). All date to the (probably late) 5th to 4th Century B.C.

Find ID: 2002-P-0076-B Area: HAC Trench: 03 Unit: 072
Material(s): Pottery
Object type: Figurine
Description: Fragment of a figurine.

Specialist code P-58 (Figure II.5)
Length: 37 Breadth: 43 Thickness: 37 Weight: 17
Specialist description: Part of a hollow moulded figurine. This is probably from a canine, the right ear and half of the right eye are preserved and show careful modelling, especially around the eye. The piece has broken away on, or close to, the seam line. The subject is a Sothic dog of Isis associated with the New Year and the beginning of the inundation.

Comparanda: See P-60. Contemporary parallels from Memphis (Petrie Museum UC48304, UC48333, see also UC48330-4), From Naukratis (Ashmolean Museum: 1872.1047, 1949.746) and in Museum collections (Bailey 2008: nos. 3707 and 3709; Bayer-Niemeier 1988: nos. 643 and 627; Besques 1992: no. D/E 4540; Fischer 1994: no. 1125). Mostly dated to the 2nd Century A.D. or Roman Period. This dating confirmed by excavations of fragments of this type (Thomas 2011: no. C214, context dated Mid 1st to early 2nd Century A.D.; Bailey 2006: 275, no.37, Antonine period).

Find ID: 2002-P-0134-B Area: HAC Trench: 03 Unit: 074
Material(s): Pottery
Object type: Figurine
Description: 9 fragments of figurines.

Specialist code P-59 (Figure II.5)
Length: 24 Breadth: 19 Thickness: 5 Weight: 7
Specialist description: Fragment of a hollow moulded figurine, made in two parts. It seems to be the muzzle of an animal, perhaps a horse or camel. The mould seam runs at a right angle to the mouth making it appear that the creature wears some

kind of muzzle or unusual bridle. The punctate texture on the top of the piece may suggest that the animal was a camel. Thickness of wall 5mm.

Comparanda: Similar muzzles from hollow horse figure are dated to the mid 1st to 3rd Century A.D. (Petrie 1910 Pl.xl.52; Bailey 2008: no. 3751).

Specialist code P-60 (Figure II.5)
Length: 67 Breadth: 41 Thickness: 13 Weight: 20
Specialist description: Part of a moulded figurine, probably hollow. The piece preserves a well modelled eyelid and ear of an animal, apparently a canine. The form looks more jackal-like than any of the dog figurines illustrated by Bailey (2008: Pl.126, 128-129) and may be intended to represent Anubis. However, Sothic dogs are more commonly represented in the Graeco-Roman period and this may be another example.

Comparanda: See P-58.

Specialist code P-61 (Figure II.6)
Length: 56 Breadth: 36 Thickness: 15 Weight: 17
Specialist description: Fragment of a solid clay figurine. Probably a human foot, though this is uncertain.

Specialist code P-383 (Figure II.6)
Length: 83 Breadth: 39 Thickness: 5 Weight: 28
Specialist description: Part of a hollow moulded figurine. The preserved fragment is from the back or side of the figure and has no moulded detail at all. The bottom edge is finished and shows string cutting, but there is no indication as to the type of figure to which this belonged.

Specialist code P-384 (Figure II.6)
Length: 39 Breadth: 22 Thickness: 14 Weight: 7
Specialist description: Solid moulded or modelled fragment but one which may have come from a hollow moulded figure. It is probably the foot or claw of an animal or perhaps a bird, since only three toes seem to be indicated. The back of the piece appears to have been pressed against the surface of the figurine.

Specialist code P-403 (Figure II.6)
Length: 43 Breadth: 40 Thickness: 18 Weight: 22
Specialist description: Part of a hollow moulded figurine. The finished edge of the fragment seems to be the bottom of the base rather than a seam line. The surface has very little relief but has an equilateral triangle (perhaps a Delta sign?) moulded in very low sunk relief in the middle of the base, which appears to be a plinth. No other decoration/letters are visible.

Specialist code P-404 (Figure II.6)
Length: 47 Breadth: 36 Thickness: 9 Weight: 13
Specialist description: Part of a hollow moulded figurine. There is a finished edge which may be the bottom of the base or a seam line. No moulded detail is visible.

Specialist code P-405 (Figure II.7)
Length: 38 Breadth: 30 Thickness: 7 Weight: 9
Specialist description: Part of a hollow moulded figurine. The piece has several curves on it, though what is represented is unclear.

Specialist code P-413 (Figure II.7)
Length: 53 Breadth: 35 Thickness: 14 Weight: 15
Specialist description: Fragment of a hollow moulded figurine. The fabric is a deep red, pottery-like silt clay and has a finished edge which looks like a rim. However, the rim is probably to be seen as the edge of the base, and is not from an actual vessel, as confirmed by the ceramicists. The piece has a moulded decoration in high relief, comprising what appears to be a twisted rope or cord ending in a flower head, or - more likely - a rosette. it is possible that this design was repeated around the whole of the base. Above the cord and flower are a series of shallow horizontal corrugations.

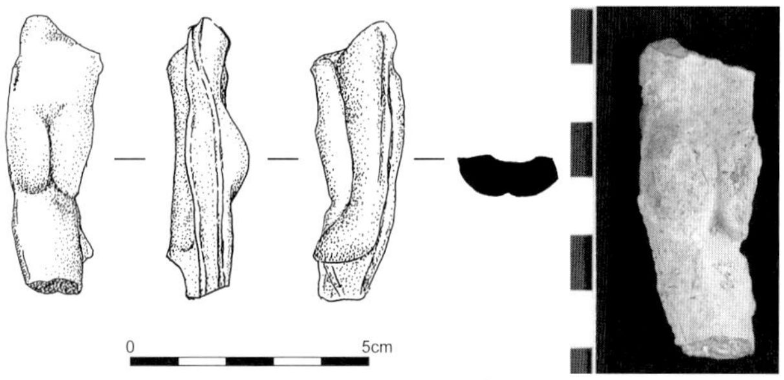

P-52

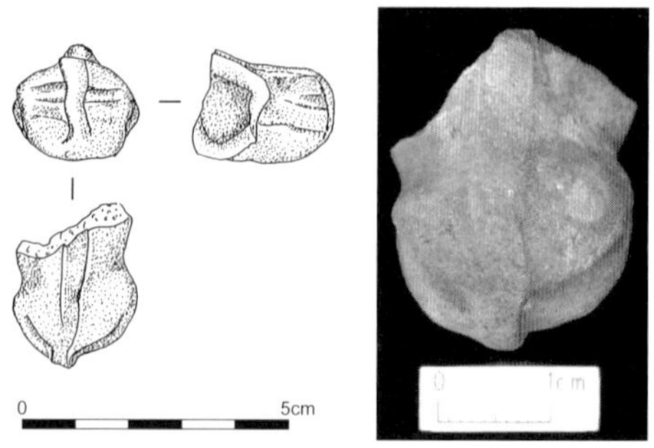

P-59

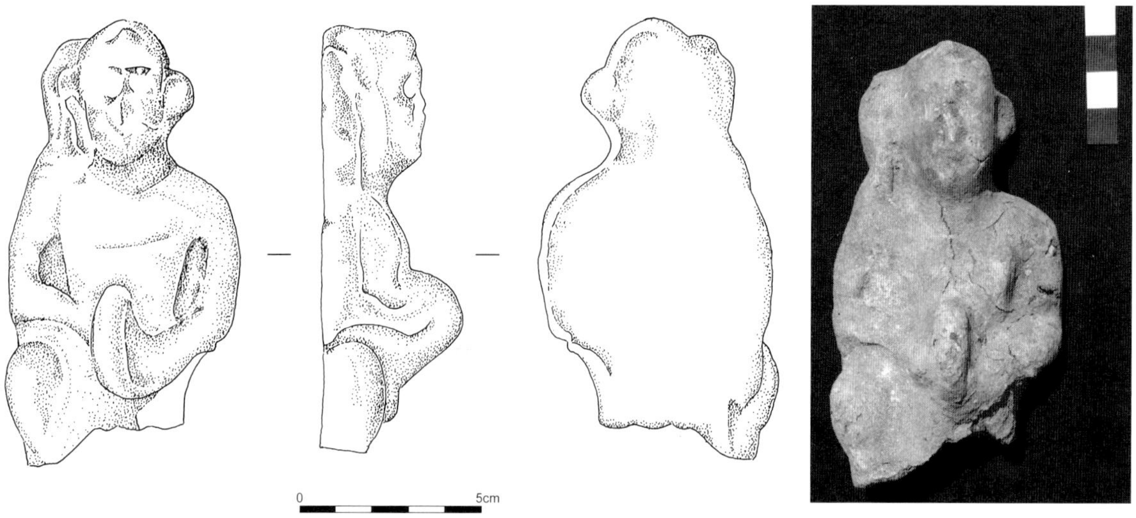

P-53

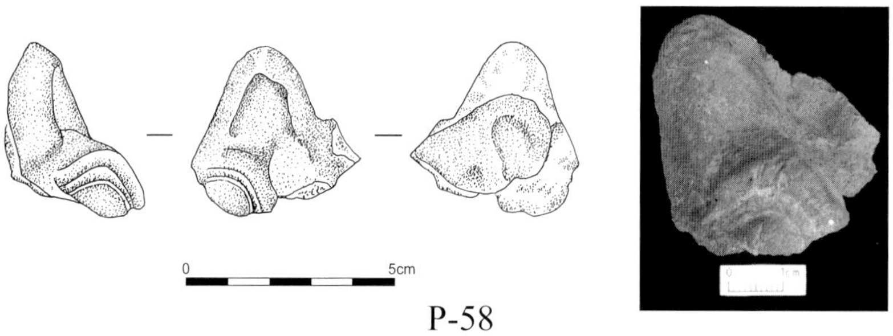

P-58

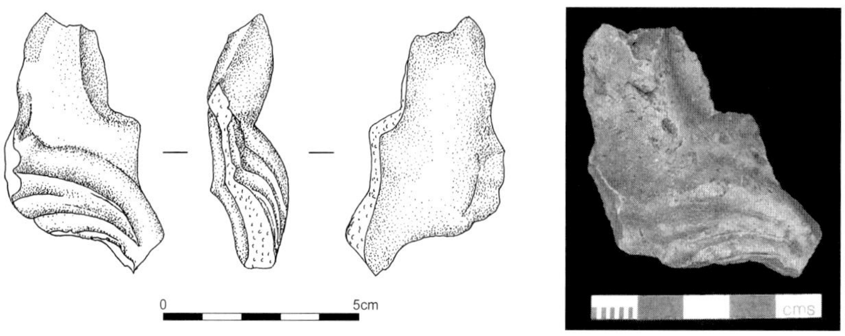

P-60

Figure II.5

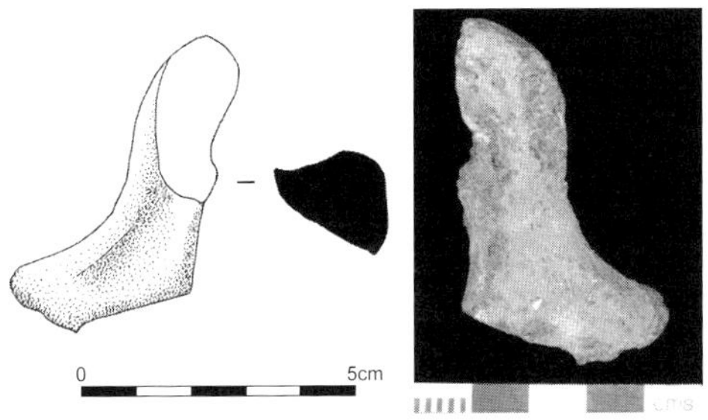

P-61

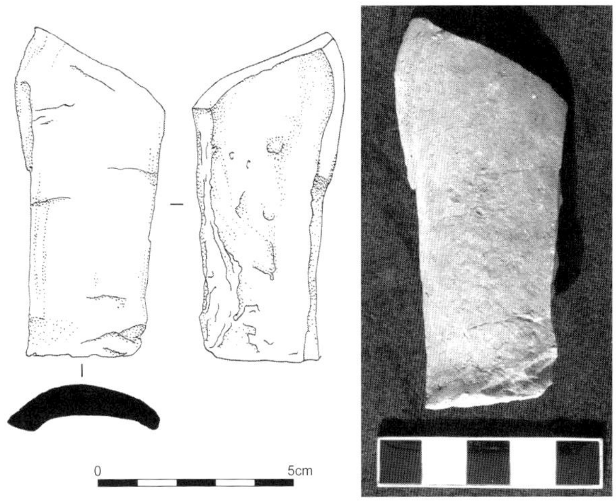

P-383

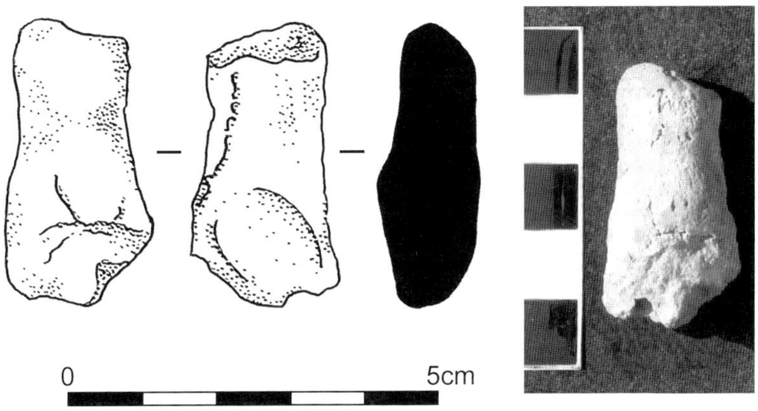

P-384

P-403

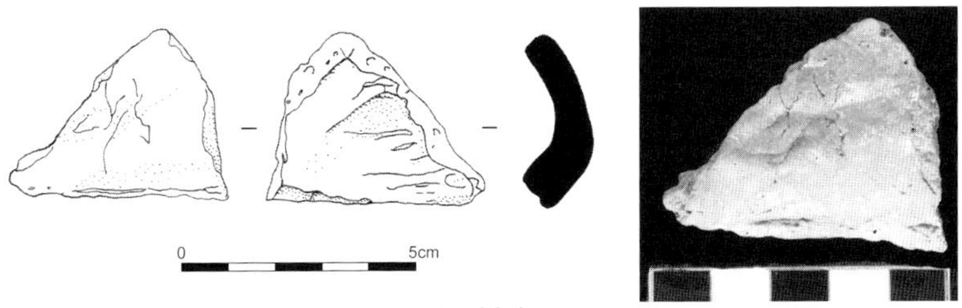

P-404

Figure II.6

Find ID: 2002-P-0162-B Area: HAC Trench: 03 Unit: 189
Material(s): Pottery
Object type: Figurine
Description: 3 fragments of figurine.

Specialist code P-62 (Figure II.7)
Length: 42 Breadth: 20 Thickness: 19 Weight: 12
Specialist description: Part of a hollow moulded figurine. The fragment is of a hand, wearing a bracelet and has a short forearm. The piece is very similar to 0273-P-74 which comes from the same context. The arm is broken along the seam and suggests that it may have been attached to the figure at this point. This is the hand of what Bailey (2008: 48-50) classifies as a beneficient demon, of which many fragments were found during this excavation (hands P-55, P-57, P-62, P-70, P-74, P-372 and head P-110).

Comparanda: This style of beneficient demon figure has good 1st, probably late 1st to 2nd Century A.D. parallels (Bailey 2008, 43-5, 48-50, nos. 3115-9, especially no. 3115 with the arm and hand being modelled in the same way, dated to the late 1st or early 2nd Century A.D). However, P-62 may be from a 3rd Century A.D. type (Bailey 2008, no. 3117). They are found across Egypt and examples from Museum catalogues are commonly dated to the 1st to early 3rd Century A.D. (Allard Pierson Museum 7468; Ashmolean Museum, 1966.1060; Bayer-Niemeier 1988: nos. 261, 307, 316, and 328; Besques 1992: no. E 392; British Museum EA49531; EA68547, EA37599; Castiglione 1969: Pl. xic; Török 1995: nos. 174–7). This dating is confirmed by excavated parallels from 1st to 2nd Century A.D. contexts (Bailey 2006: 268, nos. 9-21; Thomas 2011: nos. C247, C252, C257, C260, C261, C264).

Specialist code P-411 (Figure II.7)
Length: 56 Breadth: 36 Thickness: 8 Weight: 21
Specialist description: Fragment of a hollow moulded figurine. The piece is probably the back of the head of a figure who was wearing a pointed head covering of some kind, such as a Phrygian cap or hooded cloak. The curvature of the piece is fairly crude, confirming that this was the back and was not intended to be seen. The piece has broken along the seam.

Specialist code P-412 (Figure II.7)
Length: 41 Breadth: 31 Thickness: 9 Weight: 8
Specialist description: Fragment of a hollow moulded figurine. The fragment is pentagonal, and has decoration which may be intended to be the folds of a garment or, perhaps more likely, vegetation.

Find ID: 2002-P-0171-B Area: HAC Trench: 03 Unit: 189
Material(s): Pottery
Object type: Figurine
Description: 4 fragments of figurines.

Specialist code P-63 (Figure II.7)
Length: 50 Breadth: 25 Thickness: 9 Weight: 13
Specialist description: Part of a moulded figurine, probably hollow. The fragment shows the hair, one eye and one ear of a face, probably female. The ear is large and rather low down the face. The clay extends beyond the edge of the face suggesting that there may have been a headdress higher up. The hair is arranged in Isis-locks undeneath a wreath or headdress. The figure may be intended as a beneficient demon, although the hair resembles that found on Isis figurines.

Comparanda: Similar arrangement of the hair is seen on P-67 and Roman variants of Isis-Hathor and Isis lactans figures (Bailey 2008: nos. 3000, 3004, 3133, 3013). Naukratis (Ashmolean AN1896-1908-E.4712).

Specialist code P-64 (Figure II.7)
Length: 57 Breadth: 35 Thickness: 29 Weight: 32
Specialist description: Fragment of a hollow moulded figurine. The piece represents a leg, the outer side is almost straight whilst the inside is markedly curved suggesting a figure with legs apart, possibly intended as a rider for a horse or camel. The pieces are modelled but without any careful attention to musculature.

Comparanda: Riders dated to Roman period (Dunand 1990: 214, no.580) and an example was found in a 2nd Century A.D. context in Tell Atrib (Szmańska 2005, Pl.xxviii, No. 225).

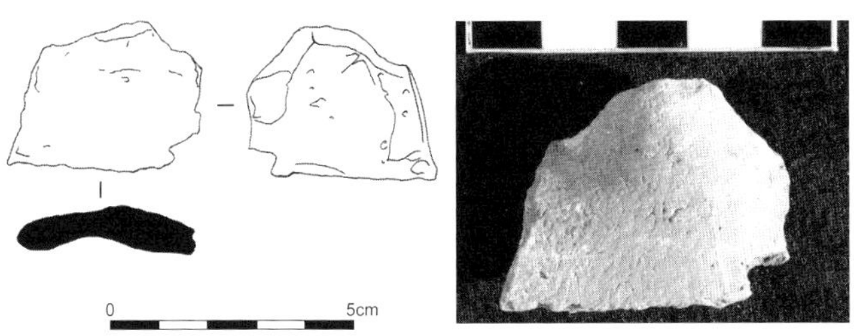

P-405

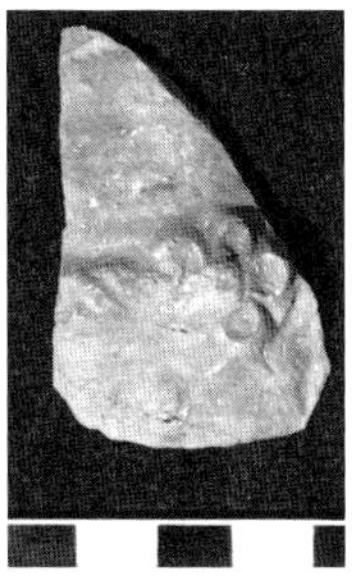

P-413

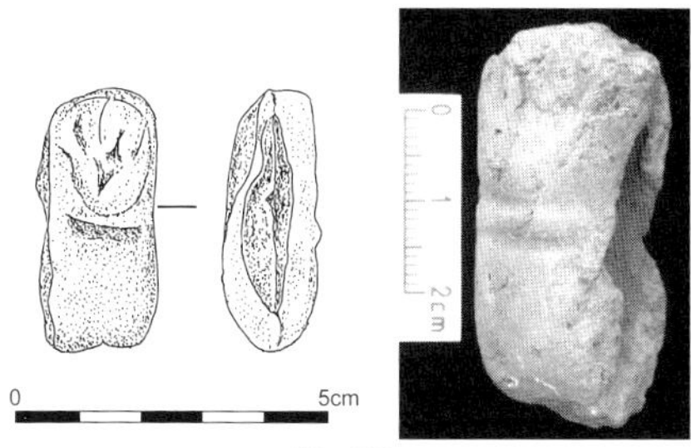

P-62

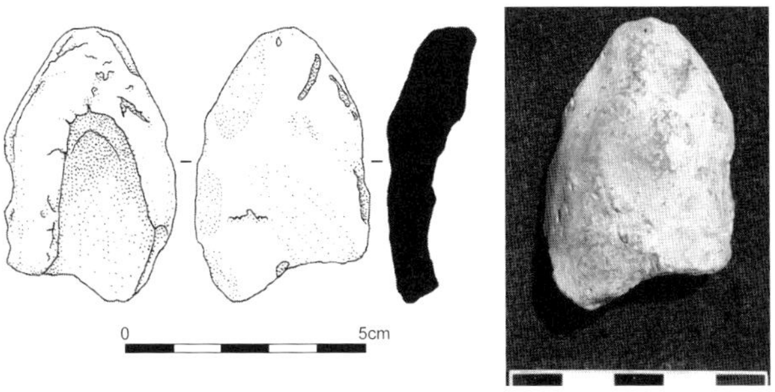

P-411

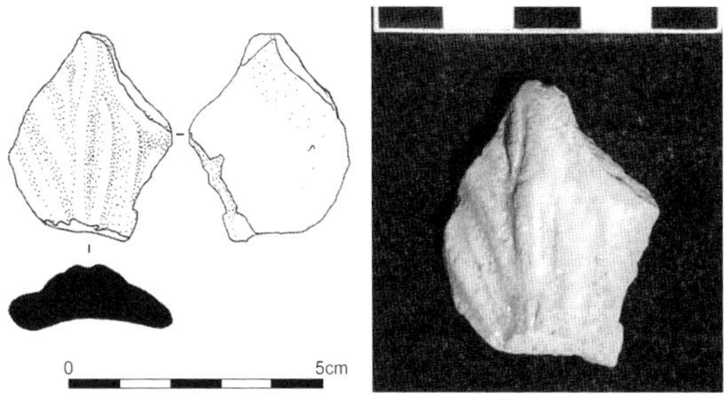

P-412

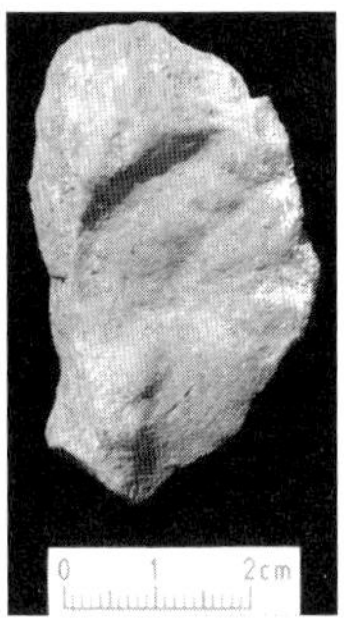

P-63

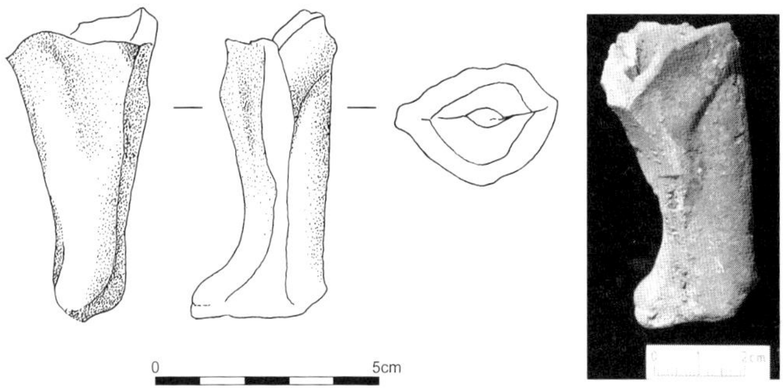

P-64

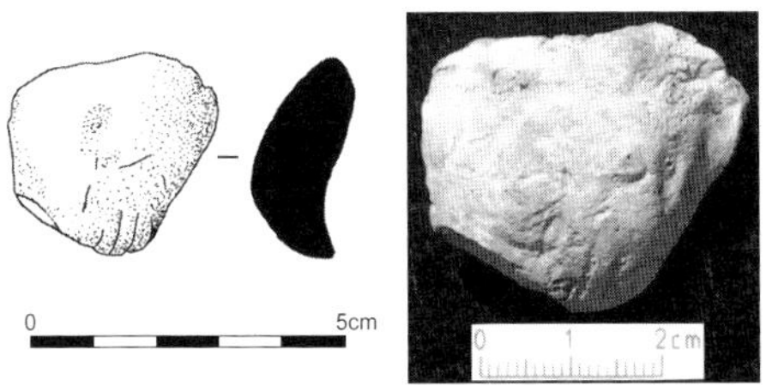

P-65

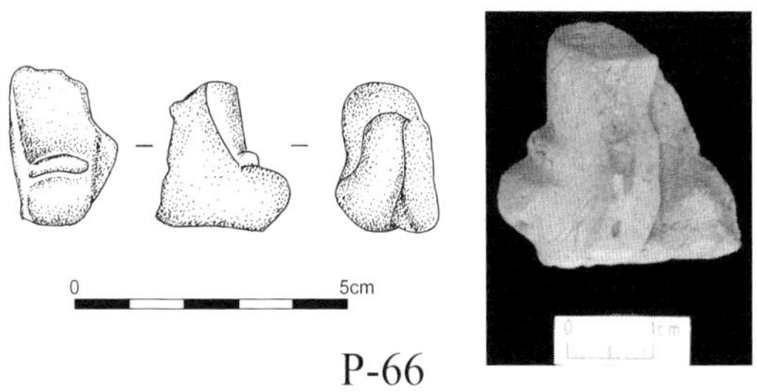

P-66

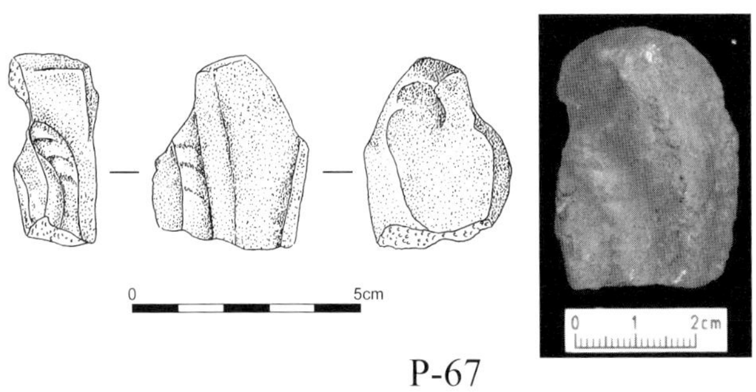

P-67

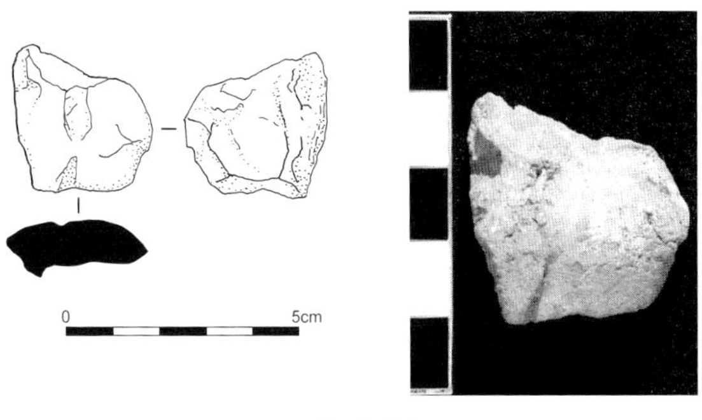

P-367

Figure II.7

Specialist code P-65 (Figure II.7)
Length: 35 Breadth: 26 Thickness: 9 Weight: 11
Specialist description: Fragment of a hollow, moulded figurine. The piece is a hand held against a knee or breast. The fingers are well modelled but no other detail is visible. A seam runs vertically behind the hand. This may be from an Isis enthroned with Harpocrates (lactans), but is too fragmentary to be certain of parallels.

Specialist code P-66 (Figure II.7)
Length: 26 Breadth: 26 Thickness: 17 Weight: 8
Specialist description: Fragment of a hollow moulded figurine. The fragment seems to represent a foot wearing an anklet. However, the foot is not unambiguously human and may be the foot of an animal or animal form chair leg. The piece itself is solid, but is almost certainly from a hollow figurine and is in the fine micaceous clay typical of such hollow figures. The underside of the base is flat. This form is typical of Roman standing beneficient demon figures.

Comparanda: See P-50, hand P-55, P-57, P-62, P-70, P-74, P-372 and head P-110 fragments that may come from similar, contemporary figures. Standing beneficient demon wearing anklet, of Roman period (Bailey 2006: 270: 22, 2nd to early 3rd Century A.D.; Dunand 1979: no.122; see also Dunand 1990: 209, no. 570).

Find ID: 2002-P-0204-B Area**:** HAC Trench: 03 Unit: 189
Material(s): Pottery
Object type: Figurine
Description: 2 fragments of figurines.

Specialist code P-67 (Figure II.7)
Length: 41 Breadth: 18 Thickness: 28 Weight: 14
Specialist description: Part of a hollow moulded figurine. The subject is not clear. There is one finished edge. The main part of the composition comprises what appears to be a coil around a cone. Alternatively, it resembles P-63 and may be from a human face with hair arranged in Isis–locks under a wreath. Such hair arrangement is common on Isis-Hathor figures and Isis lactans figures of the Roman period.

Comparanda: This may be from the same, or similar figure as P-63, with rather crude depiction of the eyes typical of these Roman variants (Bailey 2008, nos. 3000, 3004, 3133, 3013, 3143).

Specialist code P-367 (Figure II.7)
Length: 31 Breadth: 31 Thickness: 13 Weight: 8
Specialist description: Fragment of a hollow moulded figurine. The subject is unclear, though a seam line runs through it.

Find ID: 2002-P-0218-A Area**:** HAC Trench: 03 Unit: 189
Material(s): Pottery
Object type: Figurine
Description: 2 fragments of figurines.

Specialist code P-54 (Figure II.8)
Length: 56 Breadth: 38 Thickness: 46 Weight: 55
Specialist description: Head of a hollow moulded figurine. The face is shallowly moulded, though all the features are clear. Below the lower lip and slighlty to the figure's right something is attached to the face, probably a finger coming up to the mouth to indicate Harpocrates.

The hair seems to be in ringlets around the face and is topped by a headress whose ends are painted red, whilst the rest of the figure has a whitish wash. The back of the head is plain. The seam line runs through the head from side to side.

Comparanda: Though of the same style and date as the 'beneficent demons' produced at Memphis (see P-110), the headdress confirms this is the representation of Harpocrates. There are close 1st (probably late) to 2nd Century A.D. parallels from Memphis (Petrie Museum UC8769-70, UC8776, though too damaged to tell if from same mould series; see also P-71 below and Petrie Museum UC8767-8). Parallels in Museum collections (Dunand 1979: no. 191; Dunand 1990: 76, no. 148; Török 1995: 73, no.79) dated 1st or 2nd Century A.D.

Specialist code P-410 (Figure II.8)
Length: 53 Breadth: 23 Thickness: 13 Weight: 15
Specialist description: Fragment of a hollow moulded figurine. The fragment is not very clear and it is debateable which is the face side. It may show part of a foot or claw of an animal.

Find ID: 2002-P-0232-B Area: HAC Trench: 03 Unit: 074
Material(s): Pottery
Object type: Figurine
Description: 3 fragments of figurines, two of them joining.

Specialist code P-55 (Figure II.8)
Length: 27 Breadth: 22 Thickness: 18 Weight: 9
Specialist description: Part of a hollow moulded figurine. The fragment is a hand wearing a bracelet and has broken just below the bracelet. The detail of the fingers has been sharpened after removal from the mould. The piece has fractured along the seam line so that the two moulded halves are easily examined. The back is plain. It closely resembles P-62 and could have come from the same figurine. This is the hand of what Bailey (2008: 48-50) classifies as a beneficient demon, of which many fragments were found during this excavation (hands P-55, P-57, P-62, P-70, P-74, P-372 and head P-110).

Comparanda: This style of beneficient demon figure has good 1st, probably late 1st, to 2nd Century A.D. parallels (Bailey 2008, 43-5, 48-50, nos. 3115-9, especially no. 3115 with the arm and hand being modelled in the same way, dated to the late 1st or early 2nd Century A.D). However, P-62 may be from a 3rd Century A.D. type (Bailey 2008, no. 3117). They are found across Egypt and examples from museum catalogues are commonly dated to the 1st to early 3rd Century A.D. (Allard Pierson Museum 7468; Ashmolean Museum, 1966.1060; Bayer-Niemeier 1988: nos. 261, 307, 316, and 328; Besques 1992: no. E 392; British Museum EA49531; EA68547 EA37599; Castiglione 1969: Pl. xic; Török 1995: nos. 174–7). This dating is confirmed by excavated parallels from 1st to 2nd Century A.D. contexts (Bailey 2006: 268, nos. 9-21; Thomas 2011: nos. C247, C252, C257, C260, C261, C264).

Specialist code P-370 (Figure II.8)
Length: 33 Breadth: 23 Thickness: 11 Weight: 6
Specialist description: Part of a hollow moulded figurine. There are two ridges with diagonals across them suggesting that they might be meant to represent hair.

Find ID: 2002-P-0273-B Area: HAC Trench: 03 Unit: 189
Material(s): Pottery
Object type: Figurine
Description: 6 fragments of figurines.

Specialist code P-56 (Figure II.8)
Length: 54 Breadth: 26 Thickness: 8 Weight: 11
Specialist description: Fragment of a hollow moulded figurine, or possibly a lamp. The piece is in marl clay, which is unusual for a figurine, and shows a vine leaf and bunch of grapes, some of which may have been added separately and pressed on. Details of the leaf have been added by hand after moulding.

Comparanda: In the British Museum (Bailey 2008, no. 3654), though this is unclear.

Specialist code P-74 (Figure II.8)
Length: 37 Breadth: 21 Thickness: 16 Weight: 12
Specialist description: Part of a hollow moulded figurine. The fragment comprises a hand with open palm and wearing a bracelet, and part of the arm. The break at the edge of the piece confirms that the hand may originally have been held upright as if waving. The forearm is short, but the elbow is definitely present. The back of the fragment has no detail and is simply rounded off. This is the hand of what Bailey (2008: 48-50) classifies as a beneficient demon, of which many fragments were found during this excavation (hands P-55, P-57, P-62, P-70, P-74, P-372 and head P-110), though the modelling of this one is slightly different to P-55 and P-62.

Comparanda: This style of beneficient demon figure has good 1st, probably late 1st to 2nd Century A.D. parallels (Bailey 2008, 43-5, 48-50, nos. 3115-9, especially no. 3116 with the arm and hand being modelled in the same way, dated to the 2nd Century A.D). However, P-62 may be from a 3rd Century A.D. type (Bailey 2008, no. 3117). They are found across

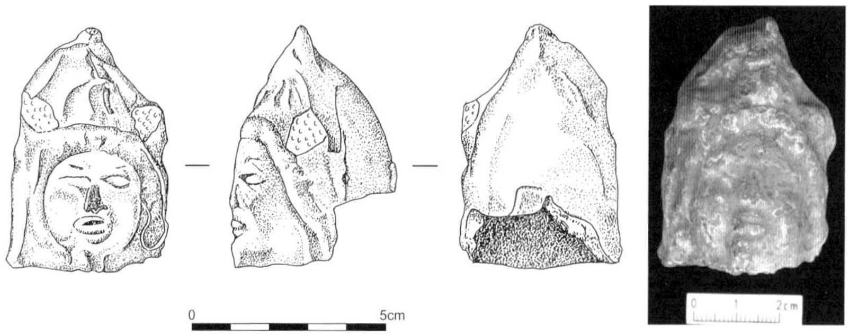

P-54

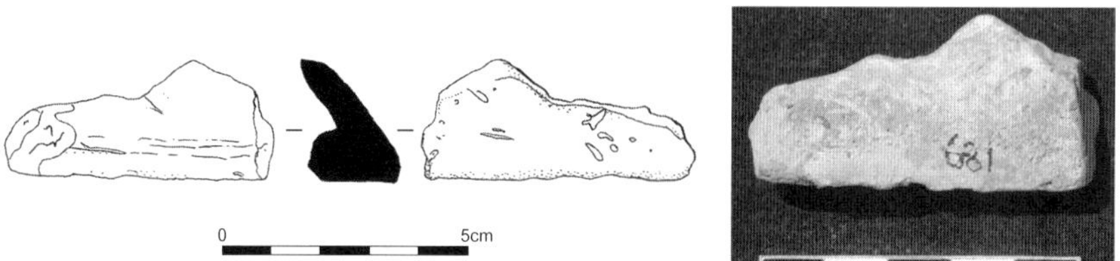

P-410

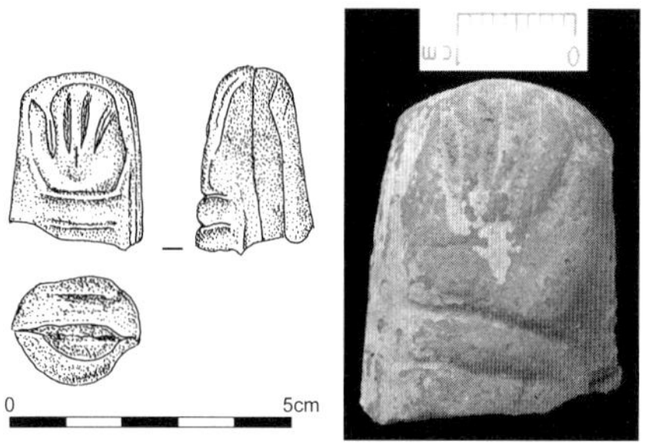

P-55

P-370

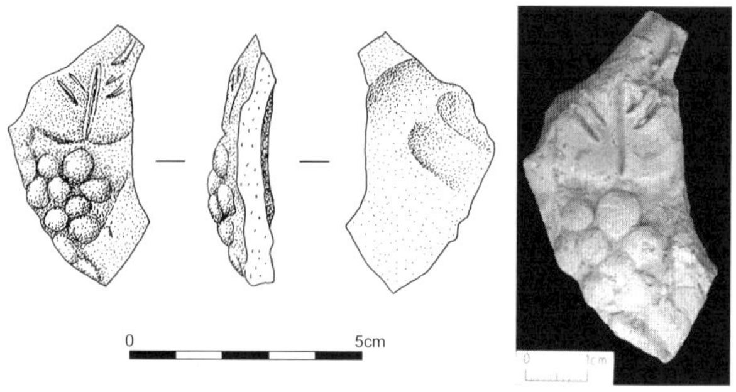

P-56

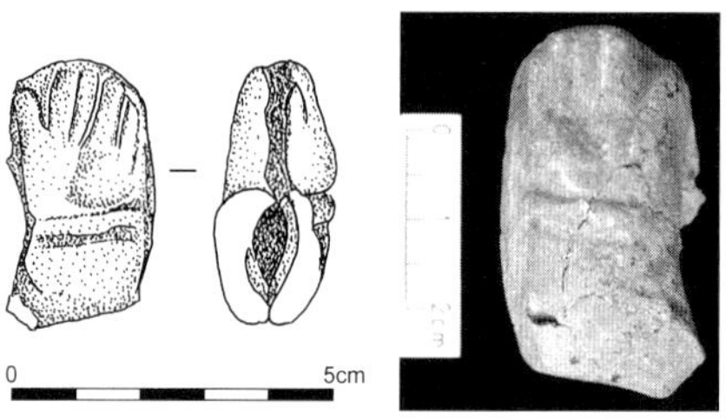

P-74

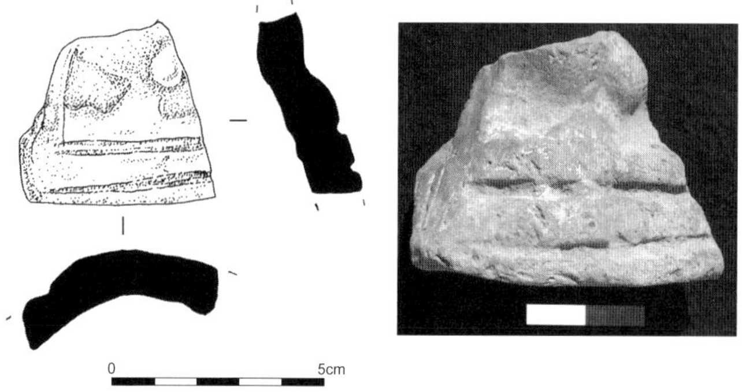

P-75

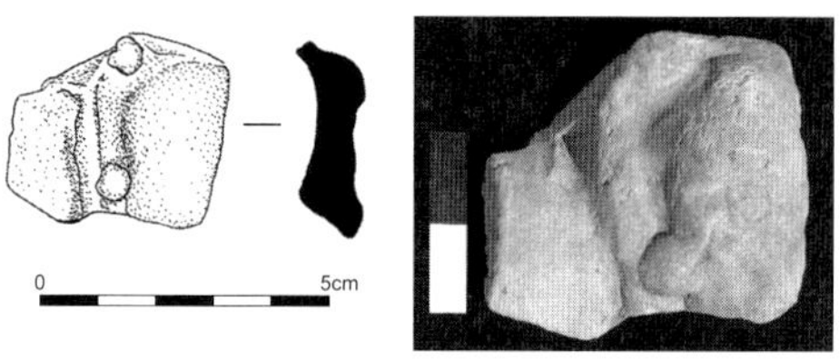

P-76

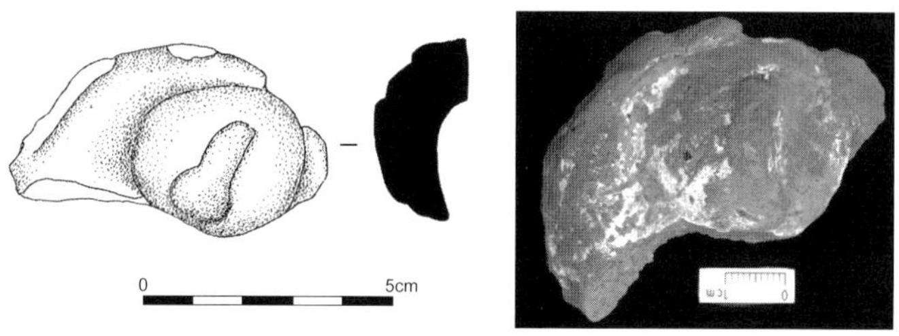

P-77

Figure II.8

Egypt and examples from museum catalogues are commonly dated to the 1st to early 3rd Century A.D. (Allard Pierson Museum 7468; Ashmolean Museum, 1966.1060; Bayer-Niemeier 1988: nos. 261, 307, 316, and 328; Besques 1992: no. E 392; British Museum EA49531; EA68547 EA37599; Castiglione 1969: Pl. xic; Török 1995: nos. 174–7). This dating is confirmed by excavated parallels from 1st to 2nd Century A.D. contexts (Bailey 2006: 268, nos. 9-21; Thomas 2011: nos. C247, C252, C257, C260, C261, C264).

Specialist code P-75 (Figure II.8)
Length: 50 Breadth: 37 Thickness: 10 Weight: 23
Specialist description: Part of the base of a hollow moulded figurine. The lowest part is simply a plinth decorated in three bands. Above it is what seems to be part of a creature with coils or perhaps short limbs. The fragment is too small to offer any certain comparanda. A second finished edge suggests that the piece was to be viewed only from the front.

Comparanda: Traces of coils of Isis-Thermuthis and the style of base are similar to figures in the British Museum and Cairo (Bailey 2008: no. 3019; Dunand 1979 174, Pl. xviii, no.26). 1st or 2nd Century A.D.

Specialist code P-76 (Figure II.8)
Length: 35 Breadth: 30 Thickness: 6 Weight: 8
Specialist description: Fragment of a hollow moulded figurine. One edge is flat and finished, though it may be a seam line along which the piece has broken cleanly. The relief design is not clear. it may be a head with a sidelock of youth, but this is uncertain.

Specialist code P-77 (Figure II.8)
Length: 55 Breadth: 45 Thickness: 12 Weight: 20
Specialist description: Part of a hollow moulded figurine. The fragment is probably part of an elaborate uraeus headdress, possibly from an Isis Figure The centre of the piece is evidently a sun disc, in whose centre is a uraeus with its own , smaller, disc. To the left is part of what is probably another, larger cobra. A matching one to the right is broken away.
Gypsum has been used to coat the piece, and is also present inside, though not over the break, suggesting that it comes from the use of the object rather than post-depositionally.

Specialist code P-78 (Figure II.9)
Length: 60 Breadth: 36 Thickness: 10 Weight: 23
Specialist description: Badly weathered fragment of a hollow moulded figurine. The piece has a finished edge, but this may be a seam line. The decoration is in the form of ridges, representing hair from the back of a female figure of the Roman period.

Comparanda: Though too fragmentary for any precise parallels, similar indications of hair can be found on a number of Roman 'beneficent demon' and other female figures in museum collections (Bailey 2008, no. 3113; Besques 1992: 117, Pl. 73 no. E393; Dunand 1990: 202-4; nos. 551-2, 558; Fischer 1994: 378, no.966p. 378; Török 1995: 127-30, no.169-180, esp 170,-174) dated to the 2nd or 3rd centuries A.D.

Find ID: 2002-P-0291-C Area: HAC Trench: 03 Unit: 189
Material(s): Pottery
Object type: Figurine
Description: 6 fragments of figurines.

Specialist code P-368 (Figure II.9)
Length: 83 Breadth: 33 Thickness: 11 Weight: 38
Specialist description: Part of a hollow moulded figurine. It is not clear what is represented, though it could be part of an animal since the surviving moulding may represent hair. Alternatively, if the piece is rotated through ninety degrees it is possible to see the decoration as a hand with elongated fingers. There are some tiny streaks of white which may be supposed to be nails. A seam runs around the piece.

Specialist code P-369 (Figure II.9)
Length: 44 Breadth: 26 Thickness: 18 Weight: 12
Specialist description: Probably part of a hollow moulded figurine. It is not clear if the finished edge is part of the base or a rim of some kind. Another edge has what may be a seam. No modelling is evident.

Specialist code P-372 (Figure II.9)
Length: 33 Breadth: 19 Thickness: 17 Weight: 8
Specialist description: Part of a hollow moulded figurine. The fragment is of a hand, but is damaged on the palm side and has become blackened. A seam runs around the hand. This is the hand of what Bailey (2008: 48-50) classifies as a beneficient demon, of which many fragments were found during this excavation (hands P-55, P-57, P-62, P-70, P-74, P-372 and head P-110).

Comparanda: This style of beneficient demon figure has good 1st, probably late 1st to 2nd Century A.D. parallels (Bailey 2008, 43-5, 48-50, nos. 3115-9, especially no. 3115 with the arm and hand being modelled in the same way, dated to the late 1st or early 2nd Century A.D.). However, P-62 may be from a 3rd Century A.D. type (Bailey 2008, no. 3117). They are found across Egypt and examples from Museum catalogues are commonly dated to the 1st to early 3rd Century A.D. (Allard Pierson Museum 7468; Ashmolean Museum, 1966.1060; Bayer-Niemeier 1988: nos. 261, 307, 316, and 328; Besques 1992: no. E 392; Bailey 2008: 43-50, nos. 3112-4, British Museum EA49531; EA68547 EA37599; Castiglione 1969: Pl. xic; Török 1995: nos. 174–7). This dating is confirmed by excavated parallels from 1st to 2nd Century A.D. contexts (Bailey 2006: 268, nos. 9-21; Thomas 2012: nos. C247, C252, C257, C260, C261, C264).

Specialist code P-373 (Figure II.9)
Length: 52 Breadth: 48 Thickness: 16 Weight: 25
Specialist description: Part of a hollow moulded figurine. The piece is probably the right side of a bird such as a cockerel. The head is gone, but the neck has a chevron design in black paint as if to suggest the uneven rim of feathers at the base of a cock-bird's neck. The body has shallow striations running down it as if to suggest feathers. The back slopes downward somewhat, though is rather thicker than might be expected for a bird. No exact comparison has been found but the form is similar to Bailey (2008) no.3360, although the preserved example has no obvious trace of a rider.

Specialist code P-381 (Figure II.9)
Length: 51 Breadth: 34 Thickness: 21 Weight: 15
Specialist description: Part of a hollow moulded figurine. The subject is unclear, it preserves a raised, curved band, perhaps intended as an arm or leg. There are no finished edges.

Specialist code P-382 (Figure II.9)
Length: 55 Breadth: 41 Thickness: 43 Weight: 35
Specialist description: Base of a hollow form figure, apparently square or rectangular in section. Fragment of cloven hoof and leg from a ram or sheep, with rectangular base. The edge of the base is flat.

Comparanda: Figure of Harpocrates riding a ram in the British Museum (Bailey 2008: no. 3084, dated to the Ptolemaic Period, though previously considered to the Roman; Fischer 1994: 279, nos. 620-2, dated 2nd to 3rd Century A.D.). Roman Period.

Find ID: 2002-P-0312-A Area**:** HAC Trench: 03 Unit: 218
Material(s): Pottery
Object type: Diverse
Description: 3 fragments of figurines.

Specialist code P-68 (Figure II.10)
Length: 30 Breadth: 30 Thickness: 15 Weight: 11
Specialist description: Part of a limestone (erroneously classified as pottery and hence P designation) figure of a naked female. The front of the figure is lost, but the poise with arms straight by the sides and carefully modelled legs and buttocks suggests that this may be a small erotic figurine.

Comparanda: Parallels of naked women in solid terracotta, gypsum and limestone, are often interpreted as representations of Isis-Hathor, and are dated to the Late Period or early Ptolemaic periods from Memphis (Petrie Museum UC33572-3 in terracotta), Naukratis (Bailey 2008, no. 2992; Villing *et al.* GR 1886,0401.1469; Cambridge, Fitzwilliam Museum: E.SU.147; Amsterdam, Allard Pierson Museum: 7936), Saqqara (Martin 1981: nos. 793 and 406) in Gypsum Late Period - Ptolemaic dump. A fine example in limestone was found at Naukratis, which shares the elongated hands (Petrie 1886: 33; British Museum EA1886,0401.1394) dated to the early Ptolemaic period based on stratigraphy by the excavator.

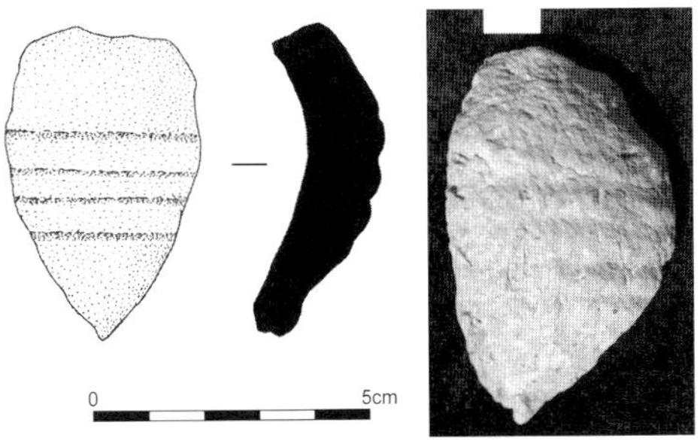

P-78

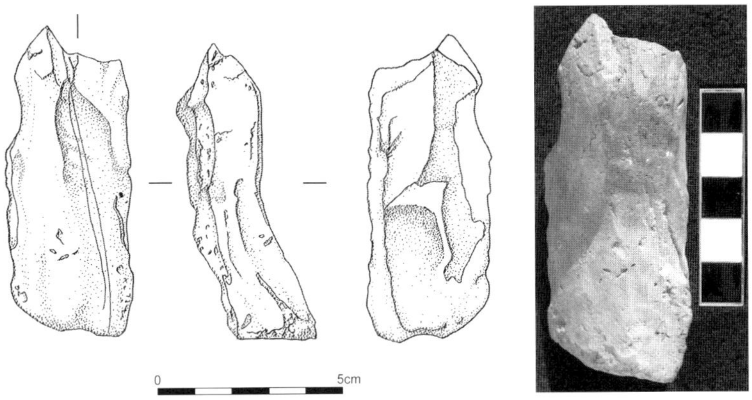

P-368

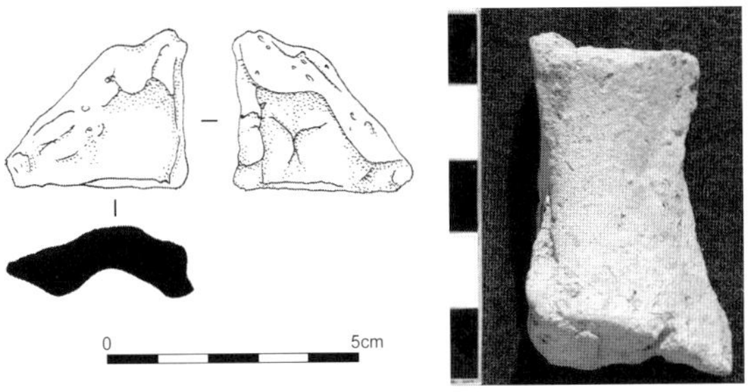

P-369

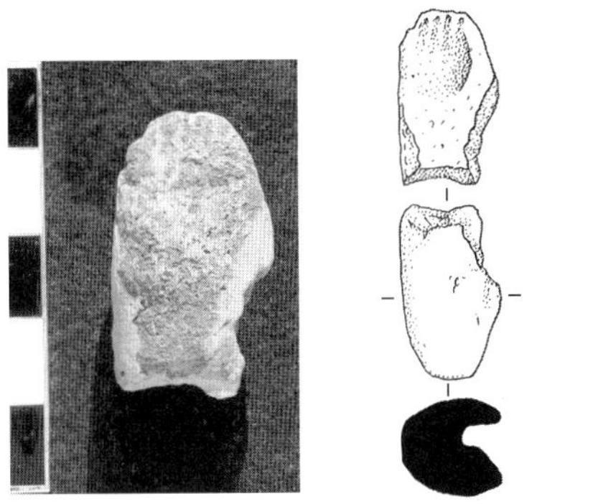

P-372

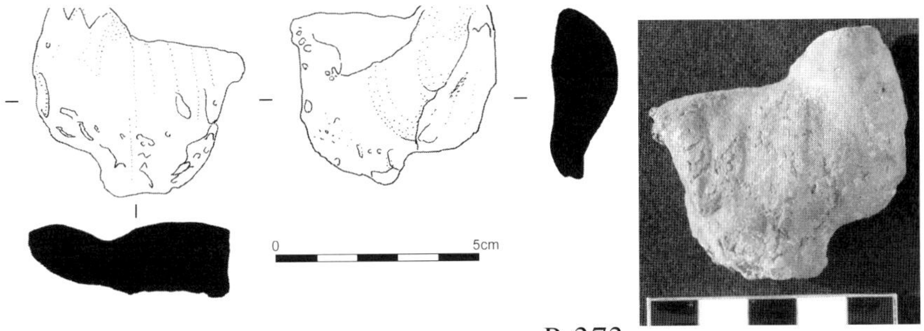

P-373

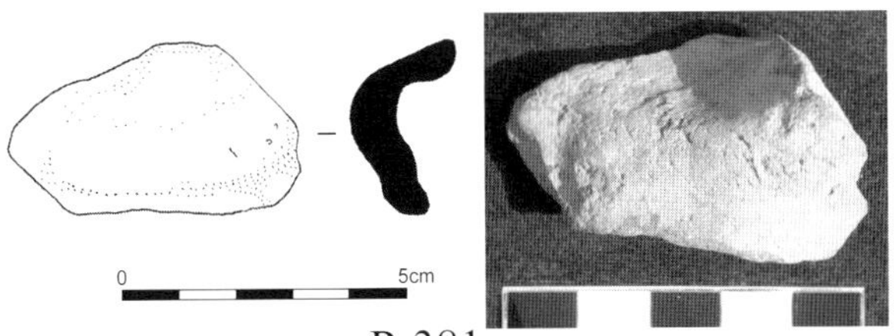

P-381

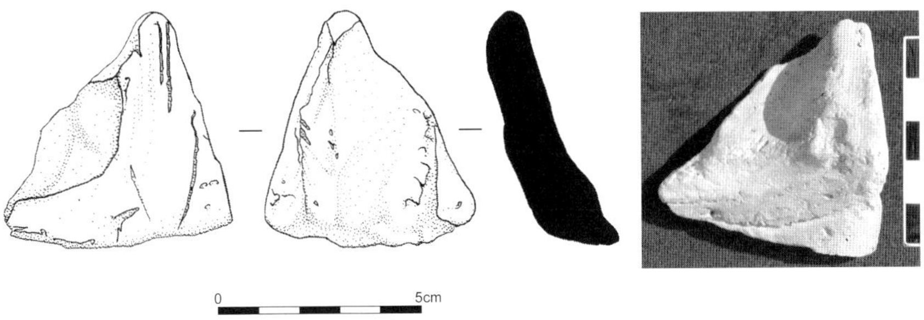

P-382

Figure II.9

Specialist code P-69 (Figure II.10)
Length: 25 Breadth: 22 Thickness: 20 Weight: 7
Specialist description: Part of a hollow moulded figurine. The fragment comprises a small dome with seam, to which has been added a separate suspension loop running at a right angle to the seam, above what appears to be the head of a figure amulet. At either side of the dome there are small protrusions, possibly small horns or ears. Diameter of dome 20mm.

Comparanda: Early Roman parallel from Memphis (Petrie Museum UC48102), may be from a fertility amulet (see Petrie Museum UC33447 where loop is attached to the back).

Specialist code P-378 (Figure II.10)
Length: 40 Breadth: 34 Thickness: 8 Weight: 17
Specialist description: Solid, moulded, fragment of a plaque or figurine. The piece seeems to be intended to represent hair and possibly the temple of a head, but the rest is broken away.
The rear is almost flat, and the left edge (as viewed) seems finished suggesting a plaque. The whole is covered in a dark red slip or paint.

Find ID: 2002-P-0320-A Area: HAC Trench: 03 Unit: 219
Material(s): Pottery
Object type: Figurine
Description: 1 fragment of a figurine.

Specialist code P-57 (Figure II.10)
Length: 25 Breadth: 20 Thickness: 7 Weight: 3
Specialist description: Part of a hollow moulded figurine. The fragment comprises an open hand whose general shape has been moulded and the details of which have then been incised into it, so that the digits are very clear. The back of the piece has broken away where it has split along the seam line. This is likely the hand from a beneficient demon figure, of which many fragments were found (hands P-55, P-57, P-62, P-70, P-74, P-372 and head P-110).

Comparanda: This style of beneficient demon figure has good 1st, probably late 1st, to 2nd Century A.D. parallels (Bailey 2008, 43-5, 48-50, nos. 3115-9, especially no. 3115). However, P-62 may be from a 3rd Century A.D. type (Bailey 2008, no. 3117). They are found across Egypt and examples from museum catalogues are commonly dated to the 1st to early 3rd Century A.D. (Allard Pierson Museum 7468; Ashmolean Museum, 1966.1060; Bayer-Niemeier 1988: nos. 261, 307, 316, and 328; Besques 1992: no. E 392; British Museum EA49531; EA68547 EA37599; Castiglione 1969: Pl. xic; Török 1995: nos.174–7). This dating is confirmed by excavated parallels from 1st to 2nd Century A.D. contexts (Bailey 2006: 268, nos. 9-21; Thomas 2011: nos. C247, C252, C257, C260, C261, C264).

Find ID: 2002-P-0342-B Area: HAC Trench: 03 Unit: 189
Material(s): Pottery
Object type: Figurine
Description: 3 fragments of figurines.

Specialist code P-70 (Figure II.10)
Length: 36 Breadth: 21 Thickness: 8 Weight: 5
Specialist description: Fragment of a hollow moulded figurine. This is probably part of an arm and the back of the hand, though there are no modelled details. The piece is smaller than 0320-P-57 which is the front of a similar hand. This is likely to be the hand from a beneficient demon figure, of which many fragments were found (hands P-55, P-57, P-62, P-70, P-74, P-372 and head P-110).

Comparanda: This style of beneficient demon figure has good 1st, probably late 1st to 2nd Century A.D. parallels (Bailey 2008, 43-5, 48-50, nos. 3115-9, especially no. 3115). However, P-62 may be from a 3rd Century A.D. type (Bailey 2008, no. 3117). They are found across Egypt and examples from museum catalogues are commonly dated to the 1st to early 3rd Century A.D. (Allard Pierson Museum 7468; Ashmolean Museum, 1966.1060; Bayer-Niemeier 1988: nos. 261, 307, 316, and 328; Besques 1992: no. E 392; British Museum EA49531; EA68547 EA37599; Castiglione 1969: Pl. xic; Török 1995: nos. 174–7). This dating is confirmed by excavated parallels from 1st to 2nd Century A.D. contexts (Bailey 2006: 268, nos. 9-21; Thomas 2011: nos. C247, C252, C257, C260, C261, C264).

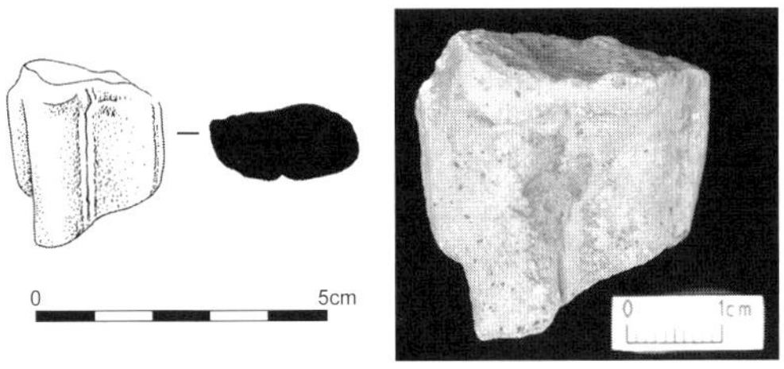

P-68

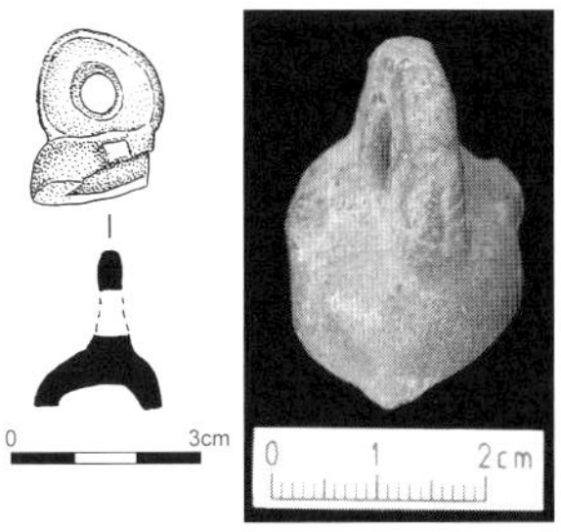

P-69

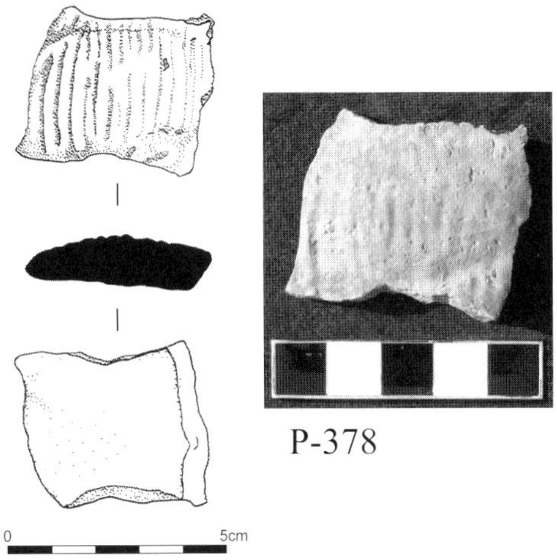

P-378

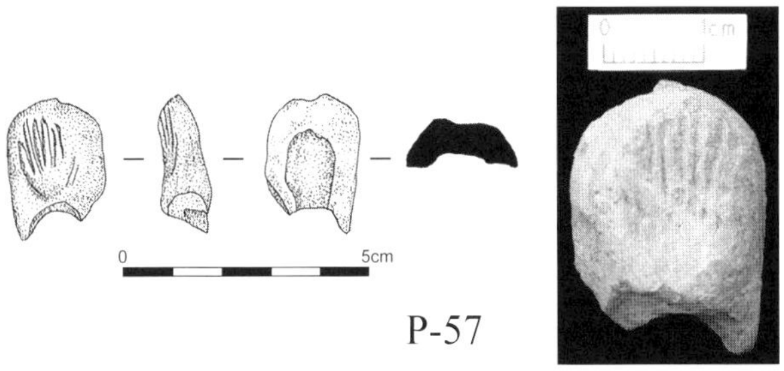

P-57

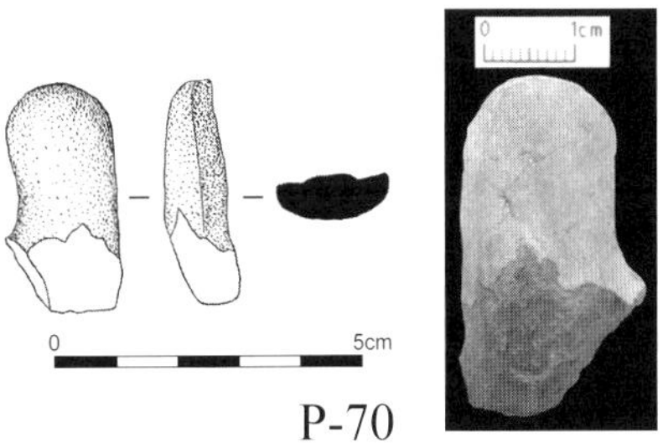

P-70

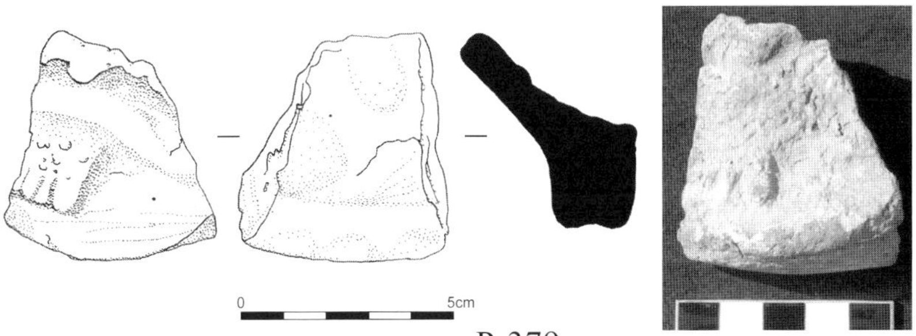

P-379

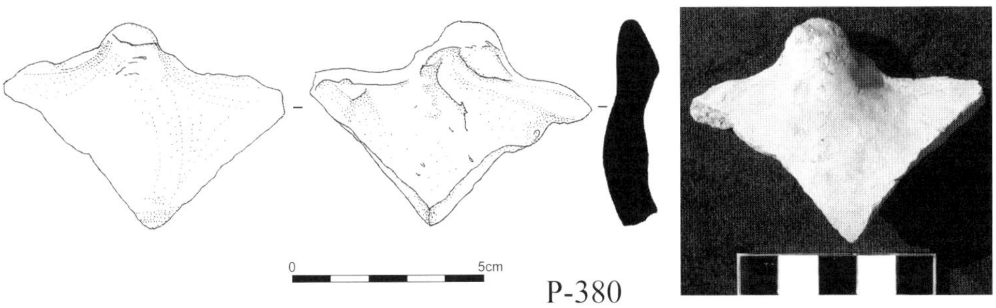

P-380

P-376

P-377

Figure II.10

Specialist code P-379 (Figure II.10)
Length: 50 Breadth: 30 Thickness: 15 Weight: 44
Specialist description: Base of a hollow moulded figurine. The detail is not clear, but seems to be the right foot of a person wearing a sandal. If so, then the figure would have been quite large. The edge of the base has been cut flat in order to stand firmly on a flat surface.

Specialist code P-380 (Figure II.10)
Length: 74 Breadth: 55 Thickness: 11 Weight: 23
Specialist description: Part of a hollow moulded figurine, broken along the seam line. The subject is not clear, but appears to be an animal. To judge from the shape of the piece it is probably the hump and part of the back of a camel figurine. There is a distinct dip next to the hump as if intended to take a rider Figure

Find ID: 2002-P-0422-B Area: HAC Trench: 03 Unit: 231
Material(s): Pottery
Object type: Figurine
Description: 2 fragments of figurines.

Specialist code P-376 (Figure II.10)
Length: 41 Breadth: 44 Thickness: 15 Weight: 21
Specialist description: Part of a hollow moulded figurine. The fragment is from the side of the base of a figurine. As a result there is little detail, though the front, where it joins the side, has a modelled human foot and part of a leg on it. The leg is joined to the side with a seam which is clear on the inside.

Specialist code P-377 (Figure II.10)
Length: 36 Breadth: 34 Thickness: 6 Weight: 8
Specialist description: Part of a hollow moulded figure. The fragment preserves the head, with the left side of the face and hair visible. The features are clearly modelled in low relief, but the gender of the figure is uncertain. The hair suggests that it is probably female.

Comparanda: Poorly moulded, but typical style for some beneficient demons (Bailey 2008: 3127; Dunand 1990: 209, no.570) dated Roman, 1st, 2nd and 3rd Century A.D.

Find ID: 2002-P-0447-B Area: HAC Trench: 03 Unit: 238
Material(s): Pottery
Object type: Figurine
Description: 5 fragments of figurines.

Specialist code P-371 (Figure II.11)
Length: 40 Breadth: 35 Thickness: 18 Weight: 17
Specialist description: Part of a hollow moulded figurine. The piece preserved is part of a head and was joined laterally at the back, which has now been lost. What remains is a face surrounded by an elaborate coiffure. The eyes and nose are only shallowly moulded, but the mouth is deep, possibly artificially so as a result of damage to whatever was raised to the mouth on the left side (as viewed). It may be that this was a finger, and the statue may therefore be intended as a Harpocrates.

Comparanda: Though of the same style, and date as the 'beneficent demons' produced at Memphis (see P-110), the headdress confirms this is the representation of Harpocrates. There are close 1st (probably late) to 2nd Century A.D. parallels from Memphis (Petrie Museum UC8767-8, though too damaged to tell if from same mould series; see also P-54 above and Petrie Museum UC8769-70, UC8776). Parallels in museum collections (Dunand 1990: 76, 103, nos. 148 and 236; Török 1995: 73, no.79) dated 1st or 2nd Century A.D.

Specialist code P-72 (Figure II.11)
Length: 37 Breadth: 45 Thickness: 38 Weight: 36
Specialist description: Part of the base of a hollow moulded figurine. The fragment shows the right front and hind legs of an animal, probably a dog.. Although the fragment is preserved at the other side there is no corresponding moulding, suggesting that the rest of the 'round' served only to allow the piece to stand up, and that it was to be viewed from the front only. The piece shows signs of burning.

Comparanda: From a lying Sothic dog with head turned to the right found on figure and lamp types dated to the Roman Period (Dunand 1990: 290, no.867; Fischer 1994: nos. 1120, 1128).

Specialist code P-73 (Figure II.11)
Length: 40 Breadth: 32 Thickness: 6 Weight: 14
Specialist description: Part of a moulded, perhaps, hollow, figurine. The fragment has the right shoulder of a person over which is draped a cloak. The right breast, apparently female, is exposed. Below it is the right arm, bent beneath the breast and across the waist. Fragment of a Roman variant of Isis enthroned with Harpocrates (lactans). A yellowish coating suggests that the piece may originally have been painted, consistent with this type.

Comparanda: Too small to be certain of parallels but various examples in museum collections can be suggested (Bailey 2008: nos. 3013 and 3014 from Saqqara, British Museum EA1849,0811.6; Dunand 1979: nos. 1-4; 1990: no.372; Török 1995: 89, Pl. lvii, no.107; Fischer 1994: 342, nos. 844, 849, 850) dated between the 1st and the early 3rd Century A.D.

Specialist code P-374 (Figure II.11)
Length: 52 Breadth: 22 Thickness: 10 Weight: 11
Specialist description: Fragment of a hollow moulded figurine. No trace of moulded detail remains, though the fabric and thickness of the piece make it clear that this is part of a figurine.

Specialist code P-375 (Figure II.11)
Length: 55 Breadth: 40 Thickness: 29 Weight: 18
Specialist description: Part of a hollow moulded figurine. The piece has a lateral seam and little of the original detail remains. It is the top of the head of a figure perhaps wearing a hooded cloak, the back being better preserved than the front. A similar cloak is illustrated by Bailey (2008: nos. 3778 and 3779) but these cannot be used as general comparanda.

Find ID: 2002-P-0458-B Area: HAC Trench: 03 Unit: 234
Material(s): Pottery
Object type: Figurine
Description: 1 fragment of a figurine.

Specialist code P-366 (Figure II.11)
Length: 47 Breadth: 33 Thickness: 18 Weight: 16
Specialist description: Part of a hollow moulded figurine. The piece probably represents an arm, though the hand is missing and seems to have been made separately. A seam line is visible beneath the forearm.

Find ID: 2002-P-0504 Area: HAC Trench: 03 Unit: 189
Material(s): Pottery
Object type: Figurine
Description: 1 fragment of figurine.

Specialist code P-371 (Figure II.12)
Length: 57 Breadth: 43 Thickness: 5 Weight: 13
Specialist description: Fragment of a hollow moulded figurine. A small part of a finished edge survives, though it may be a seam rather than the edge of the base. The piece is curved in several directions but with no indication of what is intended which makes identification uncertain.

Find ID: 2005-SF-0001-B Area: HAC Trench: Surface Unit: Surface
Material(s): Pottery
Object type: Figurine
Description: 1 fragment of a figurine.

Specialist code P-389 (Figure II.12)
Length: 23 Breadth: 20 Thickness: 10 Weight: 3
Specialist description: Probably the stylised feet of a small standing figure. The piece is solid and flat bottomed. In plan view it is C-shaped.

Comparanda: Similar to foot fragment of a Roman period Hathor figure, found in Trajanic or later levels in Mons Claudianus (Bailey 2009: 267, no.7).

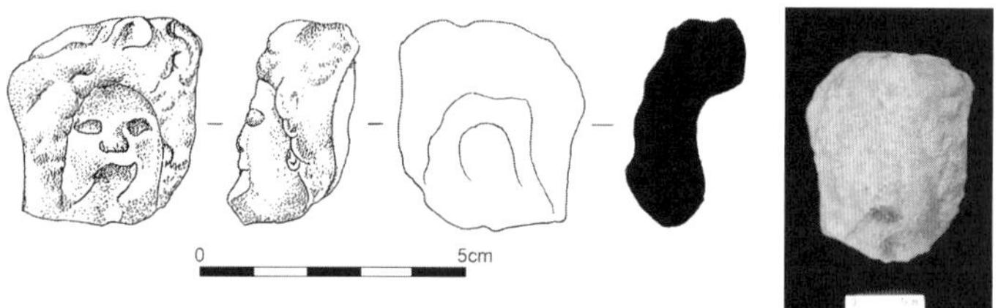

P-371

P-73

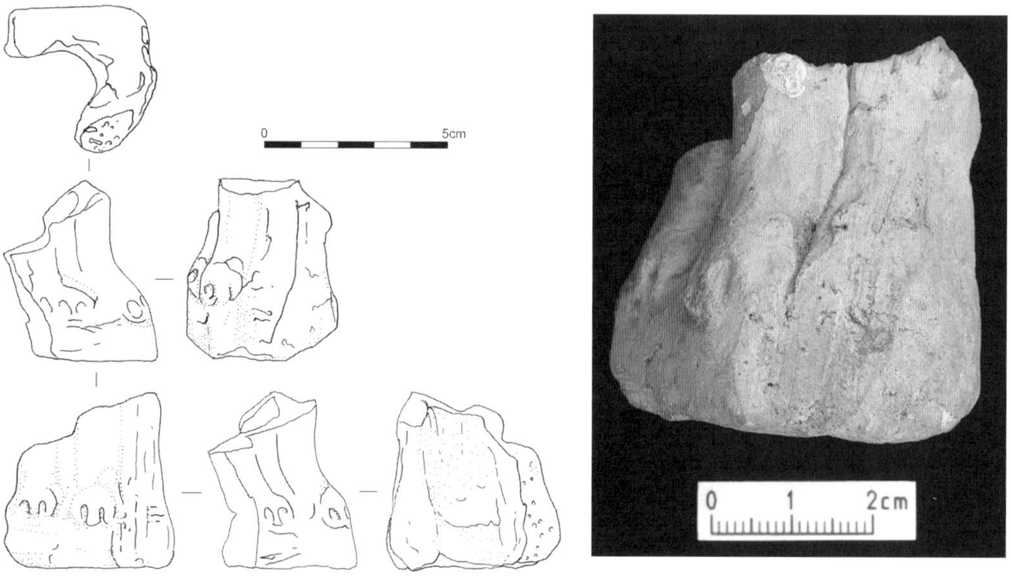

P-72

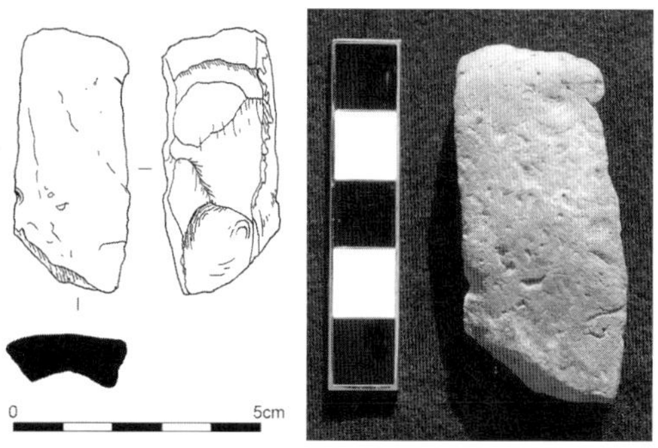

P-374

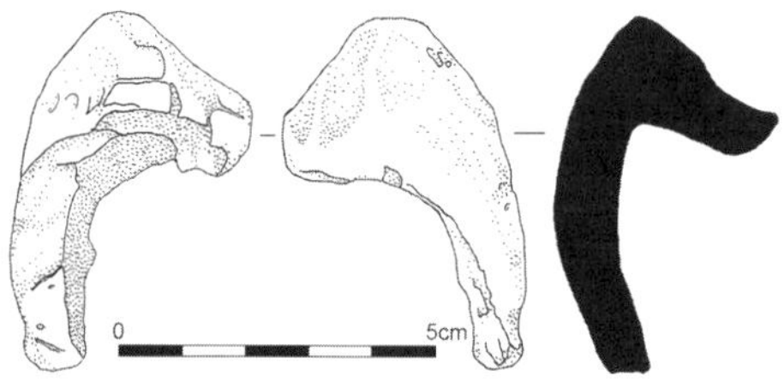

P-375

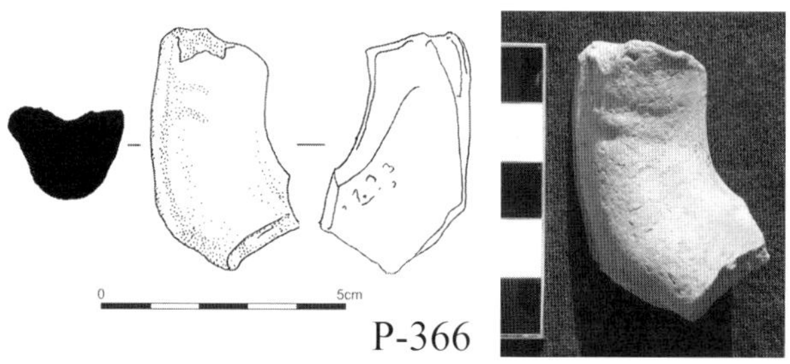

P-366

Figure II.11

Find ID: 2005-P-0001-C Area: HAC Trench: 03 Unit: 300
Material(s): Pottery
Object type: Diverse
Description: 5 fragments of figurines.

Specialist code P-109 (Figure II.12)
Length: 33 Breadth: 21 Thickness: 14 Weight: 7
Specialist description: Small, solid clay figure of a squatting male figure. One knee is drawn up higher than the other, and the phallus is exposed. The head of the figure is carefully modelled and there is a suggestion of a side lock of youth, so that this may be a figure of Harpocrates. The chest is modelled, as are the arms. The right arm rests on the lower knee, the left on the raised knee. The exposed phallus has been broken away. The bottom part of the figure seems to have been shaped onto a base of some kind, as it is flared somewhat. The back of the figure has almost no detail, and the clay has simply been scraped to give a rounded profile.

Comparanda: Parallels from Naukratis (Bailey 2008: no. 3206; Villing et.al. 2013: GR1973,0501.18), another was based on a Rhodian style temple boy (Oxford, Ashmolean Museum: AN1896-1908-E.4761) is dated to the 5th Century B.C. Contemporary hand-made variants (Boston 86.386; Cambridge, Fitzwilliam Museum E.98.1914; Cambridge, Museum of Classical Archaeology: NA599) also date to the Late Period. A parallel from Tell el-Muqdam was found in late 5th Century B.C. context (Redmount & Friedman 1997: 76-7, fig. 18).

Specialist code P-385 (Figure II.12)
Length: 25 Diameter: 12 Weight: 5
Specialist description: A small cone of solid modelled clay with a modelled band around it. The surface has been painted pinkish. It could be intended as an animal horn or, more probably, the tip of a phallus.

Comparanda: Bailey (2008: Pl.44 & 45) illustrates a number of clay phalluses ranging in date between the Late and Roman Periods.

Specialist code P-386 (Figure II.12)
Length: 60 Breadth: 17 Thickness: 15 Weight: 17
Specialist description: A long rod of solid clay shaped like an arm. It is possible that this is in fact no more than a piece of kiln furniture, but it is more dense than is normal for such pieces and has traces of pinkish colour on one side suggesting that it is actually from a figurine. Breadth and thickness given above are at thickest end, the smaller end is 17 x 14 mm.

Specialist code P-392 (Figure II.12)
Length: 45 Breadth: 31 Thickness: 7 Weight: 9
Specialist description: Fragment of a hollow moulded figurine. There are no finished edges. The design is uncertain and the texture suggests the skin of a reptile. However, this pattern of indentations seems to be more widely used to indicate plumage as illustrated by Bailey (2008) nos. 3073 and 3324. The same technique is used in both Ptolemaic and Roman work such that it is not possible to suggest a form or date for this piece with any certainty.

Specialist code P-408 (Figure II.12)
Length: 34 Breadth: 23 Thickness: 20 Weight: 15
Specialist description: Fragment of a hollow moulded figurine. The piece is broken at the back to reveal that it is hollow and has a slight curve. It may be a leg from a seated horse/camel-rider figure, but if so the foot is badly moulded. Alternatively it may be the bound feet from a mummiform figure, although the curvature of the piece and the fact that the underside of the feet is not flat argues against this.

Find ID: 2005-P-0012-B Area: HAC Trench: 03 Unit: 300
Material(s): Pottery
Object type: Figurine
Description: 3 fragments of figurines.

Specialist code P-387 (Figure II.12)
Length: 47 Breadth: 32 Thickness: 10 Weight: 13
Specialist description: Part of a hollow moulded figurine. Probably the side or back of the figure, since no details are visible.

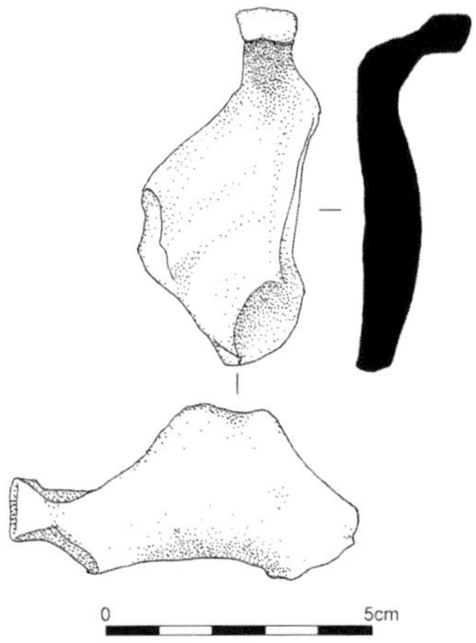

P-371

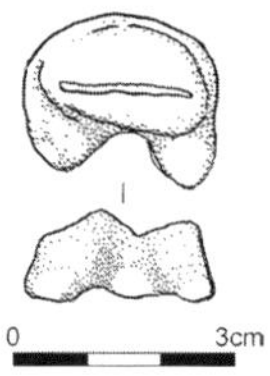

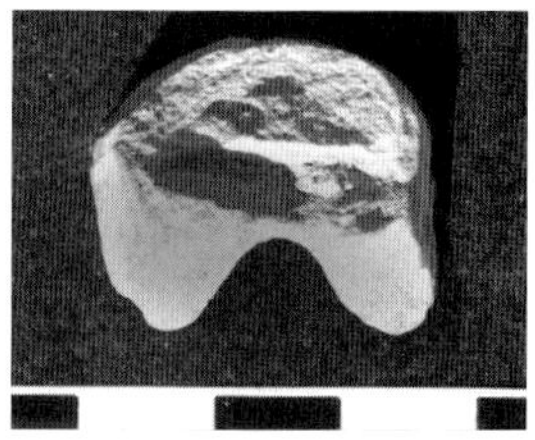

P-389

P-109

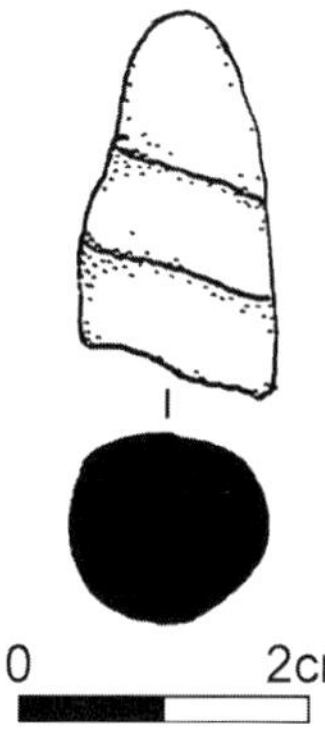

P-385

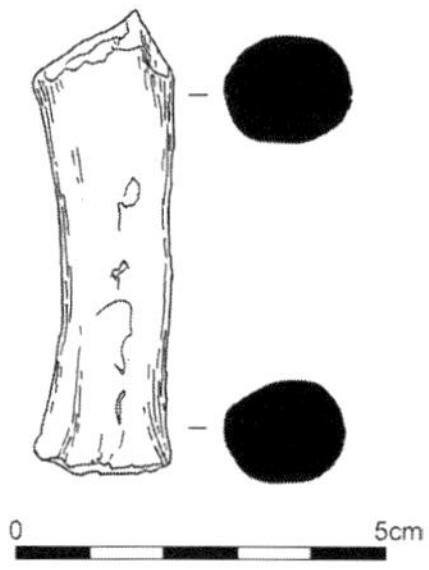

P-386

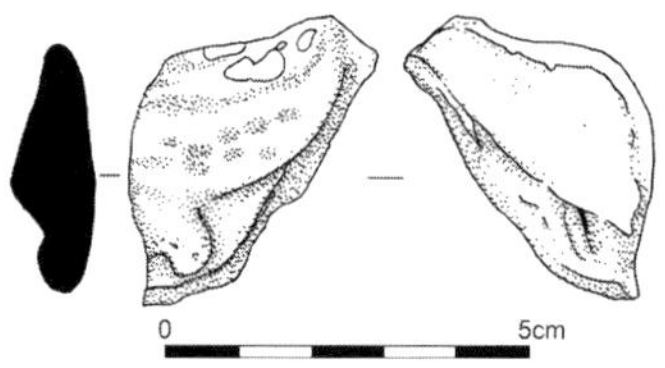

P-392

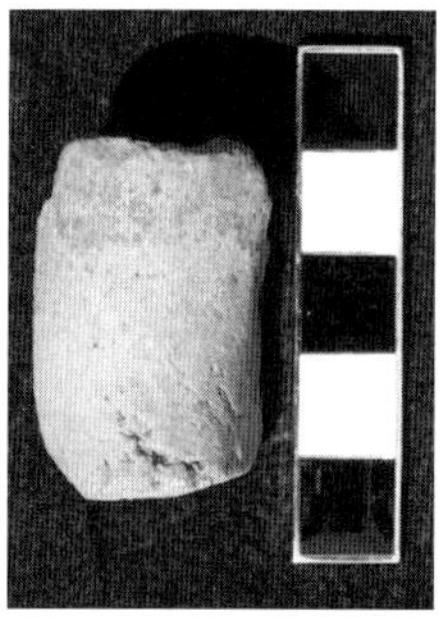

P-408

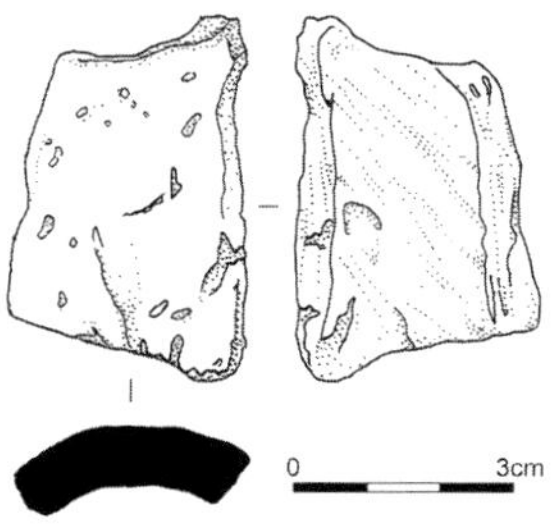

P-387

P-388

P-407

Figure II.12

Specialist code P-388 (Figure II.12)
Length: 31 Breadth: 25 Thickness: 10 Weight: 7
Specialist description: Part of a hollow moulded figurine. Probably from the side or back as no details are visible.

Specialist code P-407 (Figure II.12)
Length: 35 Breadth: 19 Thickness: 9 Weight: 6
Specialist description: Fragment of a hollow moulded figurine. There are two angled depressions as if intended to suggest the twist of a rope or cord, or perhaps the leaves of a garland. The subject is not clear.

Find ID: 2005-P-0034-B Area: HAC Trench: 03 Unit: 306
Material(s): Pottery
Object type: Figurine
Description: 1 fragment of a figurine.

Specialist code P-394 (Figure II.13)
Length: 40 Breadth: 55 Thickness: 12 Weight: 29
Specialist description: Part of a hollow, moulded figurine. Probably the leg of a horse standing on a plinth, facing left.The modelling of the leg is very similar to rider figures of the Roman periods, usually carying Isis or Harpocrates. The base is flat, the other details are moulded in high relief. The piece has been given a beige slip. It has a mould flaw by the hoof.

Comparanda: Bristish Museum pieces dating to the Ptolemaic, of types that extend into the 2nd Century A.D. (Bailey 2008: 35, nos. 3068 and 3069), an example from Cairo (Duannd 1979: no.242) and various examples in Paris (Dunand 1990: nos. 169-177), but none with the mould flaw present in this example.

Find ID: 2005-P-0089-B Area: HAC Trench: 03 Unit: 303
Material(s): Pottery
Object type: Figurine
Description: 1 fragment of a figurine.

Specialist code P-414 (Figure II.13)
Length: 47 Breadth: 34 Thickness: 9 Weight: 16
Specialist description: Part of a hollow moulded figurine. There is a finished edge, apparently of the base, with relief detail above it in the form of small C-shaped curls. These are probably meant to represent waves so that the piece is probably the base to a marine scene or deity.

Find ID: 2005-P-0096 Area: HAC Trench: 03 Unit: 189
Material(s): Pottery
Object type: Figurine
Description: 2 fragments of figurines.

Specialist code P-107 (Figure II.13)
Length: 37 Breadth: 25 Thickness: 27 Weight: 22
Specialist description: Head of small female figurine with elaborate hair style. Hollow moulded. The face has very deep pierced eyes and the head may be intended to represent a tragic theatre mask. The nose and lips are also modelled. The back of the head is shaped and has detailed wavy lines on it. There is no real neck, though a small flange may represent the join to the sholders or a necklace. The head is hollow and has a seam running laterally. The opening at the neck is 13mm.

Comparanda: Roman theatre masks from the British Museum (Bailey 2008: nos. 3564; 3286) although the coiffure of the present example may be intended to denote a female. 1st to 3rd Century A.D.

Specialist code P-464 (Figure II.13)
Length: 69 Breadth: 48 Thickness: 13 Weight: 31
Specialist description: Fragment of a figurine in silt fabric with red slip on exterior. There are two finished edges, one of them leads into a roll decoration which may be the back of a Classical chair, but appears more like the back of a couch, as the angle seems too curved for a chair. The cushion roll, if such it is, is bound by two strands of rope. If this is not a couch cushion, then it may be a column and should be viewed vertically.

P-394

P-414

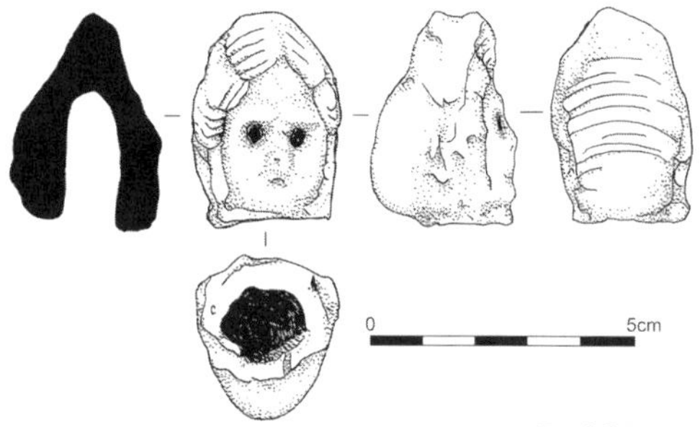

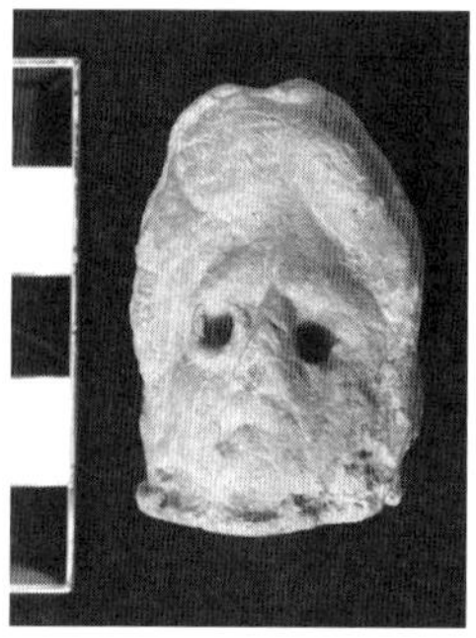

P-107

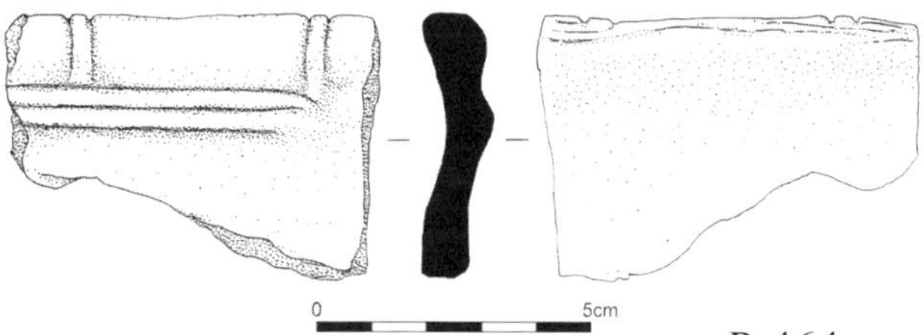

P-464

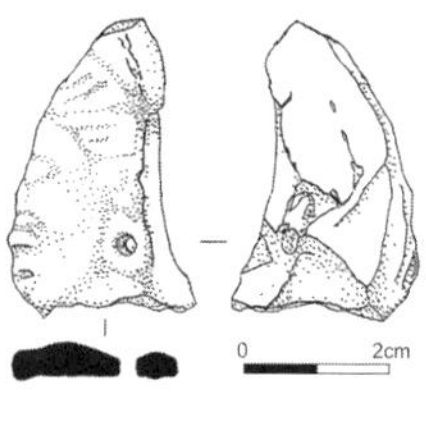

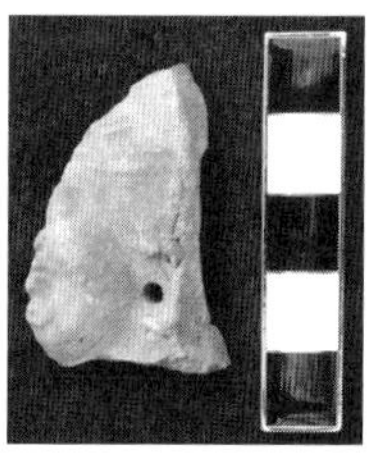

P-110

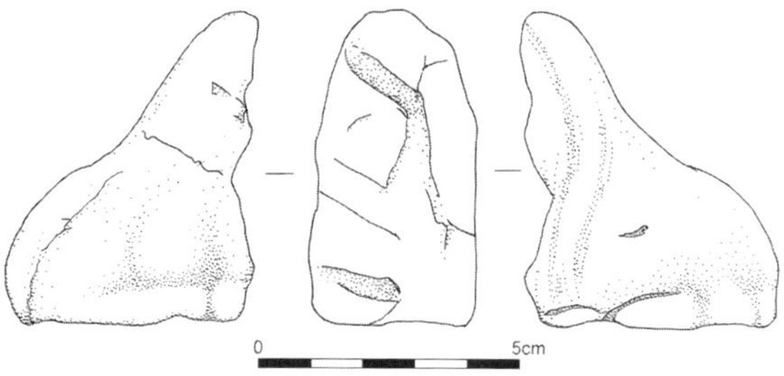

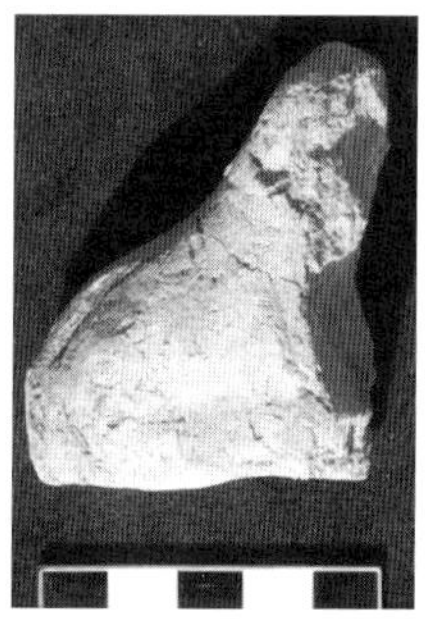

P-390

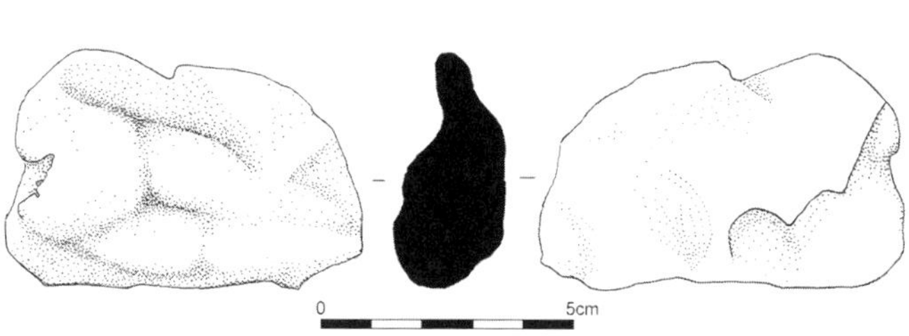

P-393

Figure II.13

Find ID: 2005-P-0102-B Area: HAC Trench: 03 Unit: 308
Material(s): Pottery
Object type: Figurine
Description: 2 fragments of figurines.

Specialist code P-110 (Figure II.13)
Length: 37 Breadth: 26 Thickness: 40 Weight: 5
Specialist description: Hollow moulded fragment of a female figure. Only the left half of the face survives. The face is quite full and the lips are thick and rather down curved. The ear has a hole of 2mm diameter pierced through it. This may have been intended to take an earring of metal when the piece was complete. The hair is shown in diagonal lines as if it were tied back. Above the hair the clay continues in a slight curve suggesting that the figure would have had a headdress of some kind, supported by the clay backing when complete. This is the head of what Bailey (2008: 48-50) classifies as a beneficient demon, of which many fragments were found during this excavation (hands P-55, P-57, P-62, P-70, P-74, P-372 and head P-110).

Comparanda: This style of beneficient demon figure has good 1st, probably late 1st to 2nd Century A.D. parallels (Bailey 2008, 43-5, 48-50, nos. 3115-9, especially no. 3115). However, P-110 may be from a 3rd Century A.D. type (Bailey 2008, no. 3117). They are found across Egypt and examples from museum catalogues are commonly dated to the 1st to early 3rd Century A.D. (Allard Pierson Museum 7468; Ashmolean Museum, 1966.1060; Bayer-Niemeier 1988: nos. 261, 307, 316, and 328; Besques 1992: no. E 392; British Museum EA49531; EA68547 EA37599; Castiglione 1969: Pl. xic; Török 1995: nos. 174–7; Dunand 1979: nos. 111-117). This dating is confirmed by excavated parallels from 1st to 2nd Century A.D. contexts (Bailey 2006: 268, nos. 9-21; Thomas 2011: nos. C247, C252, C257, C260, C261, C264).

Specialist code P-391
Specialist description: Defunct as a figurine. Fragment of what is probably kiln furniture, two sherds stuck in a piece of red adhering clay.

Find ID: 2005-P-0118-B Area: HAC Trench: 03 Unit: CT
Material(s): Pottery
Object type: Figurine
Description: Fragment of a figurine.

Specialist code P-390 (Figure II.13)
Length: 47 Breadth: 57 Thickness: 28 Weight: 66
Specialist description: Solid clay figure of what is perhaps intended as a recumbent lion on a small plinth. Although solid, the piece seems to have been moulded and a seam is visible. The legs and belly of the creature are only lightly moulded. The face is missing. Probably originally a crude sphinx or lion.

Comparanda: One example dated to the Late Roman period, or thought to be a fake (Török 1995: 98-9, Pl.lxv, no. 129), though neither of these possibilities seems likely for this piece.

Find ID: 2005-P-0125-B Area: HAC Trench: 03 Unit: 306
Material(s): Pottery
Object type: Figurine
Description: 1 fragment of a figurine.

Specialist code P-393 (Figure II.13)
Length: 72 Breadth: 45 Thickness: 21 Weight: 57
Specialist description: Solid moulded figurine or plaque. The fragment seems to represent a naked female resting on her right arm and inclining her body slightly upward. Her left arm is lost but the clay between it and her body survives and runs up to a thickened area toward the knees. The lower edge is slightly irregular but the figure will stand on this edge, suggesting that it may be the original base. Probably from an erotic scene.

Comparanda: Parallel, probably from Memphis, dated to the 29th Dynasty (Petrie Museum UC35953) and another, probably from Naukratis (Bailey 2008: no. 3266; Villing *et al.* 2013: GR1973,0501.54).

Find ID: 2005-P-0001-C Area: HAC Trench: 03 Unit: 300
Material(s): Pottery
Object type: Diverse
Description: 4 fragments of figurines 4 lamp fragments.

Endnotes

1 Ashton (2003: 73) considers these females to be on a bed rather than in a shrine (e.g. 30186) while Petrie (1909a:16) describes them as on a couch. However, the pillars and cavetto cornice suggest that a shrine rather than a bed is intended, though of a less elaborate type than those illustrated by Bailey (2008). The origin of such figures may, however, lie in the pharaonic tradition of models of females on beds.

Faience

M-D. Nenna

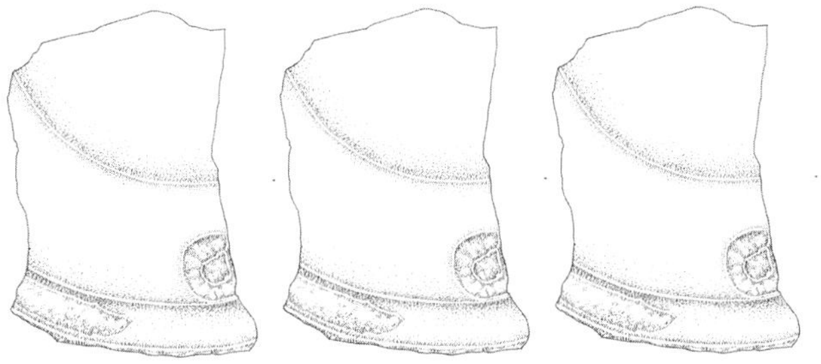

HAC I

Vessels

New year flask
Find ID: 2000-F-0177 Area: HAC Trench 1 Unit 9
Material: Faience
Object type: Vessel
F-20 ***(Figure II.14)***
Diameter of the rim: 2.5 Pres. Height 3.9
Rim and neck of a small New Year flask, made separately and then fitted into the body. The rim is in the form of a papyrus capital with Calyx of pointed leaves with central nervure and pointed leaves. Large curved rim and a small filling hole. The neck is cylindrical and bears two vertical appendages which should represent the baboons in this position. Glaze worn away.

T12.2
Find ID: 2000-F- 221 Area: HAC Trench 1 Unit 6
Material: Faience
Object type: Vessel
F-96 ***(Figure II.14 and Colour Plate 5)***
Diameter rim: 18 Diameter base: 10
Fragment presenting the complete profile of a large convex bowl with inward curving rim and annular base T12.2. Bubbly turquoise blue glaze. Traces of cones on the internal and external walls.

T12.3c/T12.4
Find ID: 2000-F-0012 Area: HAC Trench 1 Unit 1
Material: Faience
Object type: Vessel
F-68 ***(Figure II.14)***
Diameter: 8.5
Pushed-in-base of a small bowl type T12.3C or T12.4. Turquoise blue glaze. Trace of an oval-base cone on the external wall of the base and of the pointed end of a cone on the internal wall.

Find ID: 2000-F-0089 Area: HAC Trench 1 Unit 1
Material: Faience
Object type: Vessel
F-133 ***(Figure II.14)***
Diameter: 5
Pushed-in base fragment of a bowl T12.3c or T12.4. Turquoise blue glaze. Trace of the circular part of a ceramic cone on the external wall of the base.

Find ID: 2000-F-0105 Area: HAC Trench 1 Unit 5
Material: Faience
Waster
F-69 ***(Figure II.14)***
Base Diameter: 6.8 Pres. Height: 3.3.
Two lower parts of the pushed-in base bottom and body of bowls of T12.3c/T12.4 piled and stuck together. In addition fragments of rims stuck to the piece. Turquoise blue glaze. On the inferior base, remains of the circular part of the three cones.

T12.4
Find ID: 2000-F-0012 Area: HAC Trench 1 Unit 1
Material: Faience
Object type: Vessel
F-47
Diameter: 16
Rim fragment of a T12.4 bowl. Turquoise blue glaze.

Find ID: 2000-F-0041 Area: HAC Trench 1 Unit 1
Material: Faience
Object type: Vessel
F-130 ***(Figure II.14)***
Diameter: 15.5
Rim fragment of a T12.4 bowl. Turquoise blue glaze.

Find ID: 2000-F-0079 Area: HAC Trench 1 Unit CB
Material: Faience
Waster
F-71 ***(Figure II.14)***
Diameter: c.10.5
Rim and body fragment of a T12.4 bowl. Turquoise blue glaze. Under the moulding of the wall, remains of another bowl are stuck to the piece.

T12.7
Find ID: 2000-F-0041 Area: HAC Trench 1 Unit 1
Material: Faience
Object type: Vessel
F-131 ***(Figure II.14)***
Diameter: 15.5
Rim fragment of a T12.7 biconvex bowl. Turquoise blue glaze which has turned red on part of the external wall through defective firing.

Find ID: 2000-F-0041 Area: HAC Trench 1 Unit 1
Material: Faience
Waster
F-290 ***(Figure II.14)***
Max. dimension 4
Three adhering rim fragments of T12.7 biconvex bowls with a flat moulded edge and a groove under the edge. Turquoise blue glaze.

Find ID: 2000-F-0175 Area: HAC Trench 1 Unit CB
Material: Faience
Object type: Vessel
F-50 ***(Figure II.15)***
Diameter: 12
Out-turned rim fragment of an open form, may be T12.7 bowl. Turquoise blue glaze.

T13.2
Find ID: 2000-F-0104 Area: HAC Trench 1 Unit 5
Material: Faience
Object type: Vessel
F-112 ***(Figure II.15)***
Base Diameter: 13
Lower part of the body of a plate T13.2 with annular base. Turquoise blue glaze.

Find ID: 2000-F-0116 Area: HAC Trench 1 Unit 6
Material: Faience
Object type: Waster
F-56 ***(Figure II.15)***
Base Diameter: 13 Height: 4.2
Three plates T13.2 with annular base piled and stuck together. Turquoise blue glaze.

T13.3a
Find ID: 2000-F-0027 Area: HAC Trench 1 Unit 1
Material: Faience
Object type: Waster
F-51 ***(Figure II.15)***
Length: 7.8 Diameter of one of the plates: 17
Three plates T13.3a stuck together, rim in contact with angle of the body, fragment of the annular base inside. Turquoise blue glaze.

Find ID: 2000-F-0060 Area: HAC Trench 1 Unit 1
Material: Faience
Object type: Vessel
F-90 ***(Figure II.15)***
Diameter unknown.
Rim fragment of a plate T13.3a. Turquoise blue glaze.

Find ID: 2000-F-0105 Area: HAC Trench 1 Unit 5
Material: Faience
Object type: Waster
F-70 ***(Figure II.15)***
Max. Dimension: 4 Diameter of one plate: 17.
Two plates of T13.3a with thin wall bodies stuck together. Turquoise blue glaze.

T13
Find ID: 2000-F-0012 Area: HAC Trench 1 Unit 1
Material: Faience
Object type: Vessel
F-48 ***(Figure II.15)***
Diameter: 9.5
Bottom fragment of an annular base of a plate T13. Turquoise blue glaze.

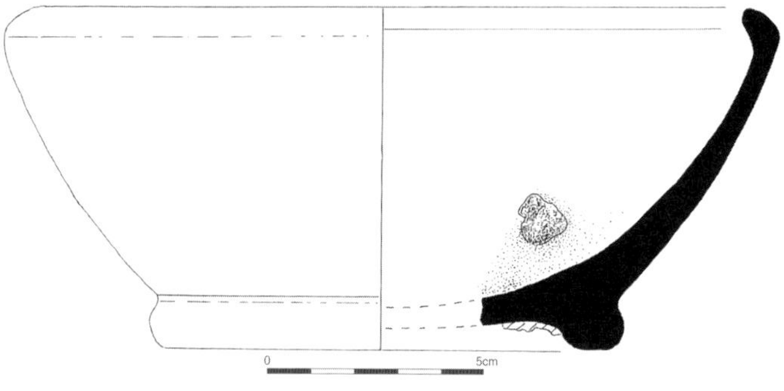

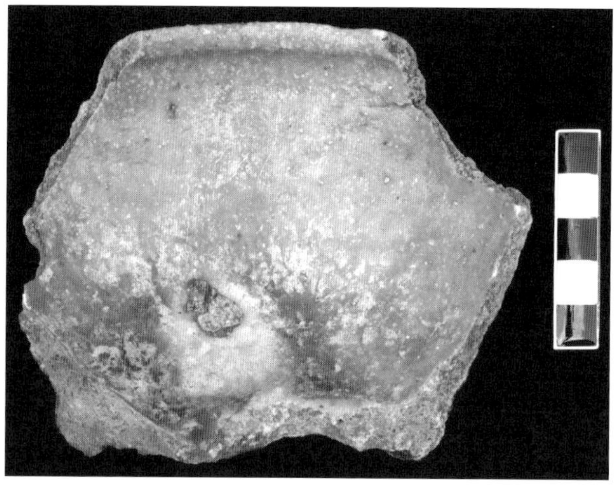

F-96

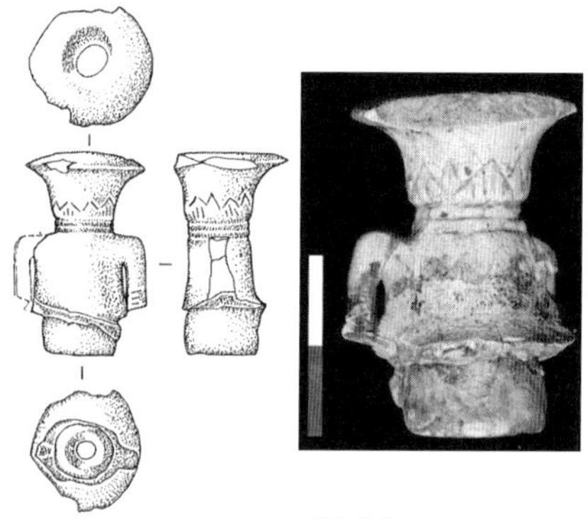

F-20

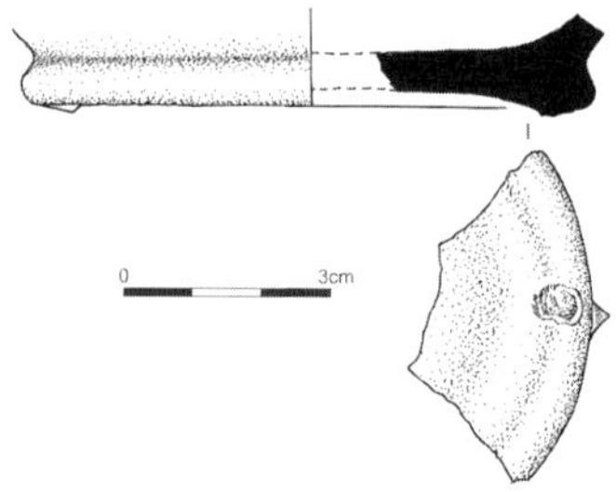

F-68

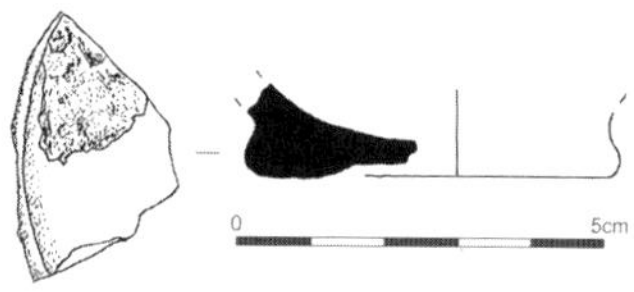

F-133

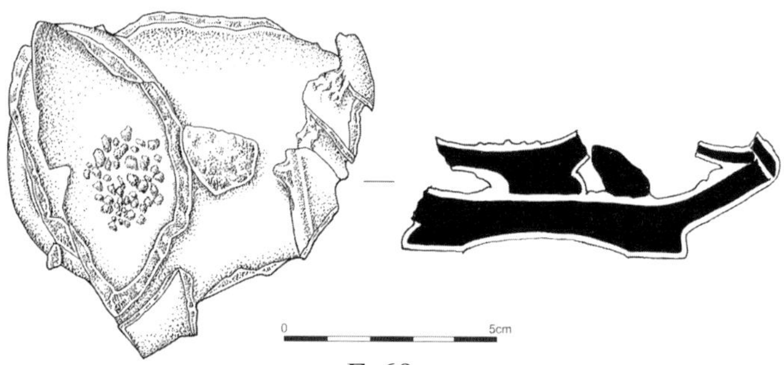

F-69

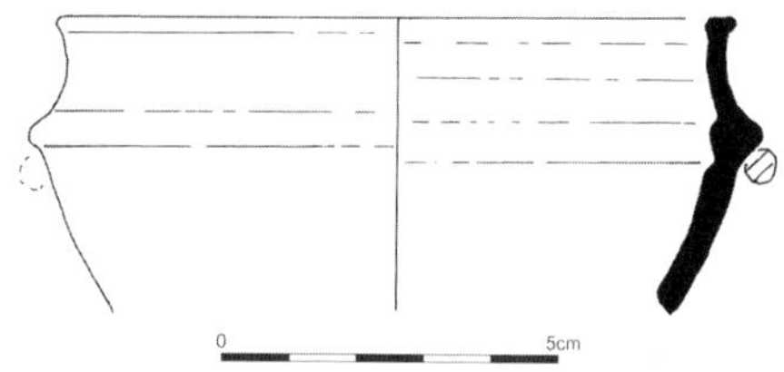

F-71

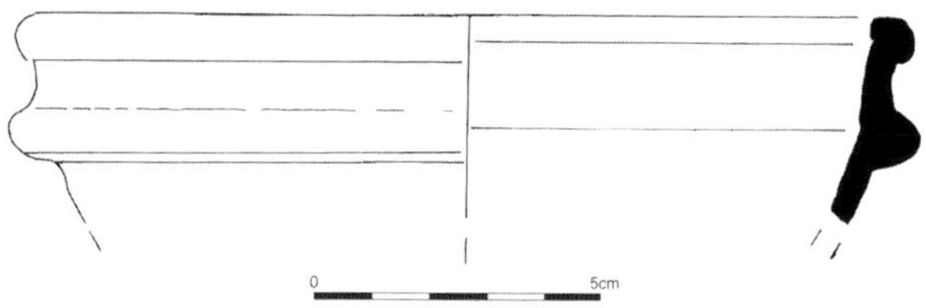

F-130

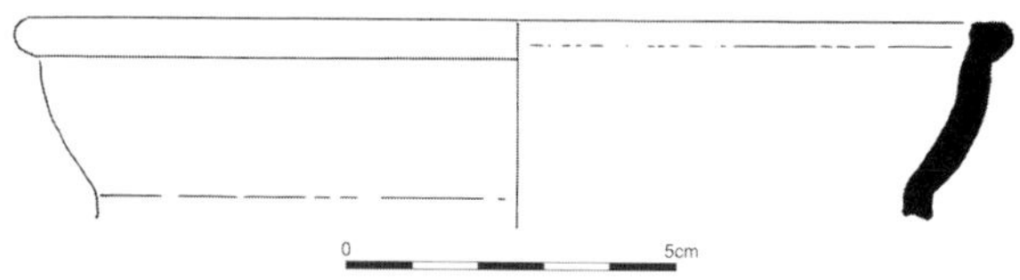

F-131

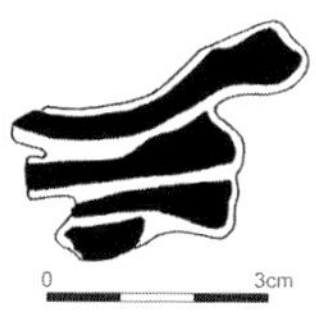

F-290

Figure II.14

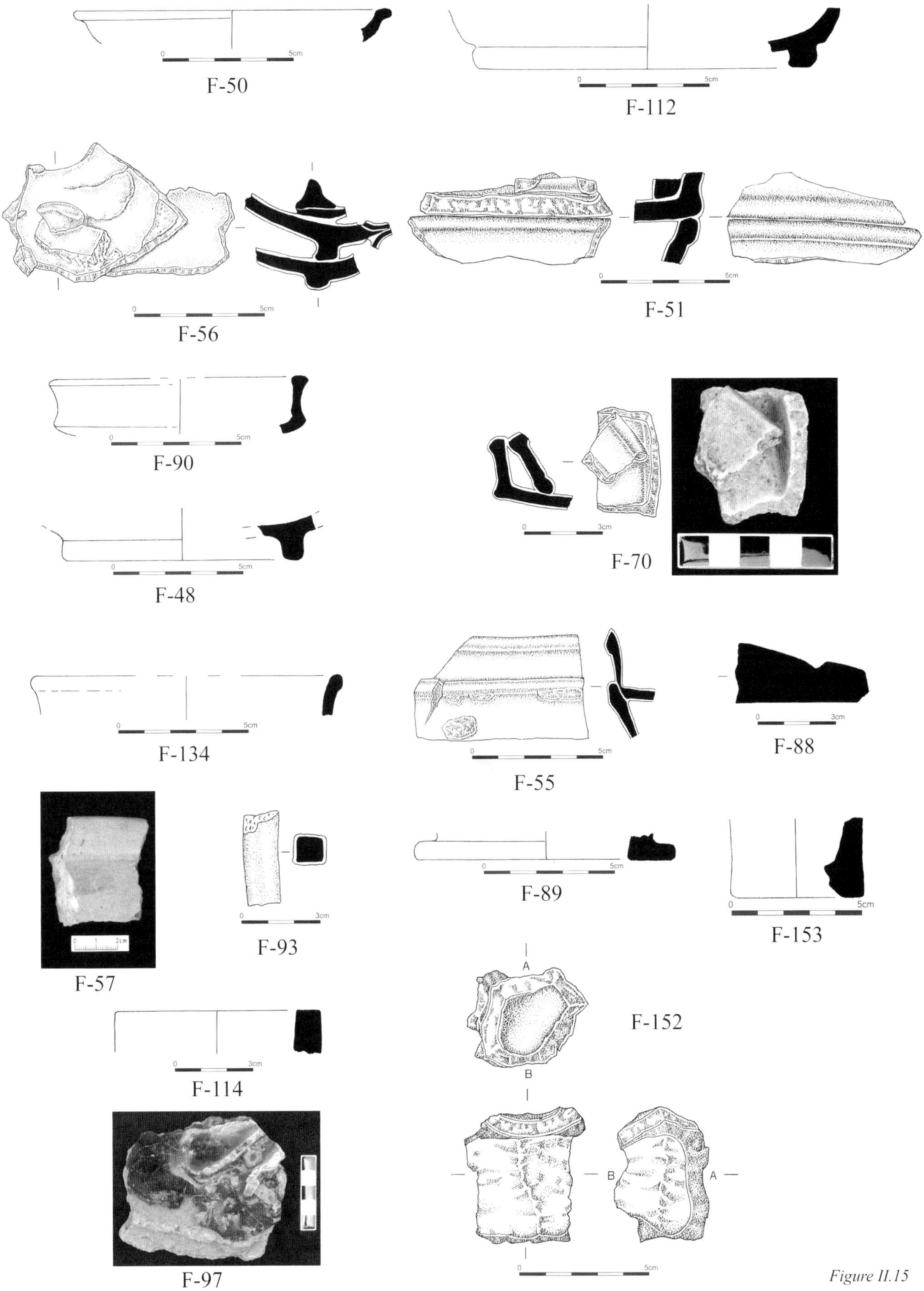
F-50
F-112
F-56
F-51
F-90
F-70
F-48
F-134
F-55
F-88
F-57
F-93
F-89
F-153
F-152
A
B
F-114
F-97

Figure II.15

T14.1
Find ID: 2000-F-0089 Area: HAC Trench 1 Unit 1
Material: Faience
Object type: Vessel
F-134 ***(Figure II.15)***
Max. Dimension: 3
Rim fragment of tray T14.1. Thickened rim. Blue green glaze.

Find ID: 2000-F-0129 Area: HAC Trench 1 Unit CB
Material: Faience
Object type: Waster
F-55 ***(Figure II.15)***
Max. Dimension: 6.5
Two rim fragments of rectangular trays type T14.1 stuck together. Turquoise blue glaze.

T14.4
Find ID: 2000-F-0060 Area: HAC Trench 1 Unit 1
Material: Faience
Object type: Vessel
F-88 ***(Figure II.15)***
Diameter: 42
Rim fragment of a large tray. Pale green glaze, quite thin. Rim with rounded edge and a slight fold. Flat internal wall; rounded external wall.

Find ID: 2000-F-0081 Area: HAC Trench 1 Unit 1
Material: Faience
Object type: Vessel
F-57 ***(Figure II.15)***
Diameter: 35
Rim fragment of a large tray. Light green glaze. Rim with rounded edge. Flat superior surface; curved inferior surface.

T19.3
Find ID: 2000-F-0080 Area: HAC Trench 1 Unit 1
Material: Faience
Object type: Vessel
F-92
Max. Dimension: 2.7
Appliqué at the base of the handle in the form of an oval visage of which none of the features has been kept. Turquoise blue glaze. Perhaps belonging to a T19.3 vase.

Find ID: 2000-F-0080 Area: HAC Trench 1 Unit 1
Material: Faience
Object type: Vessel
F-93 ***(Figure II.15)***
Max. Dimension: 4 Section: 1.5
Handle fragment with square section perhaps belonging to a T19.3 vase. Turquoise blue glaze.

T20.1
Find ID: 2000-F-0060 Area: HAC Trench 1 Unit 1
Material: Faience
Object type: Vessel
F-89 ***(Figure II.15)***
Diameter: 9.5 Pres. Height:1.3
Applied ring base of a closed vase type T20.1-2. Turquoise blue glaze. Remains of the circular part of the ceramic cone.

T22.1
Find ID: 2000-F-0081 Area: HAC Trench 1 Unit 1
Material: Faience
Object type: Vessel
F-153 ***(Figure II.15)***
Diameter: 5 Pres. Height 2.8
Bottom fragment of a cylindrical inkwell T22.1. Turquoise blue glaze.

Find ID: 2000-F-0104 Area: HAC Trench 1 Unit 5
Material: Faience
Object type: Vessel
F-114 ***(Figure II.15)***
Diameter: 8
Rim of a cylindrical inkwell with thick flattened edge rim. Turquoise blue glaze.

Wasters belonging to unspecified types of vessel

Find ID: 2000-F-0046 Area: HAC Trench 1 Unit 1
Material: Faience
Object type: Waster
F-152 ***(Figure II.15)***
Max. Dimension: 4.8
Fragment of an open vase stuck in a vitrified ceramic ware.

Find ID: 2000-F-0221 Area: HAC Trench 1 Unit 6
Material: Faience
Object type: Waster
F-97 ***(Figure II.15)***
Max. dimension: 10 max. Thickness: 3.5
Bottom of a saggar with black/green glaze on the interior and on the exterior. On the inside of the saggar, two fragments of body with turquoise blue glaze stuck to the saggar.

Amulets and beads-amulets

Find ID: 2000-F-0061 Area: HAC Trench 1 Unit 1
Material: Faience
Object type: Amulet
F-17 ***(Figure II.16)***
Diameter: 1.5 Pres. Height: 1.7
Upper part of an amulet (in the form of a mushroom or nail) with a suspension loop placed on one side. Light blue glaze.

Find ID: 2000-F-0089 Area: HAC Trench 1 Unit 1
Material: Faience
Object type: Amulet
F-11 ***(Figure II.16)***
Max. Dimension: 0.7
Part of an amulet of a deity with a head of a ram with two large horns curving. Apple green glaze.

Find ID: 2000-F-0089 Area: HAC Trench 1 Unit 1
Material: Faience
Object type: Amulet?
F-135 ***(Figure II.16)***
Max. Dimension: 1.4
Fragment of an amulet ? Light blue glaze.

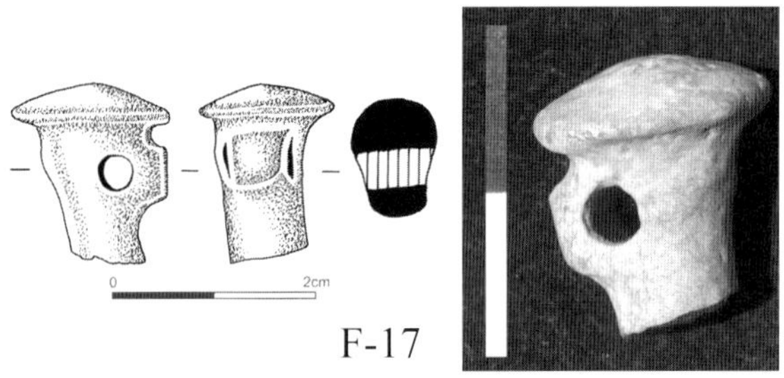

F-17

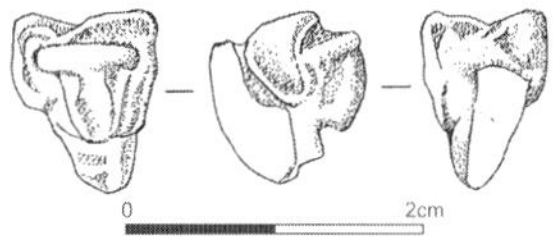

F-11

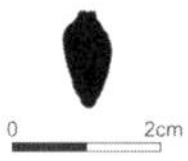

F-135

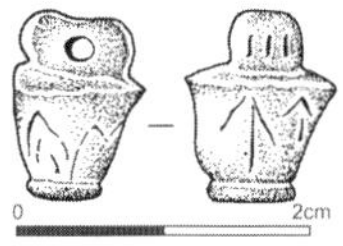

F-32

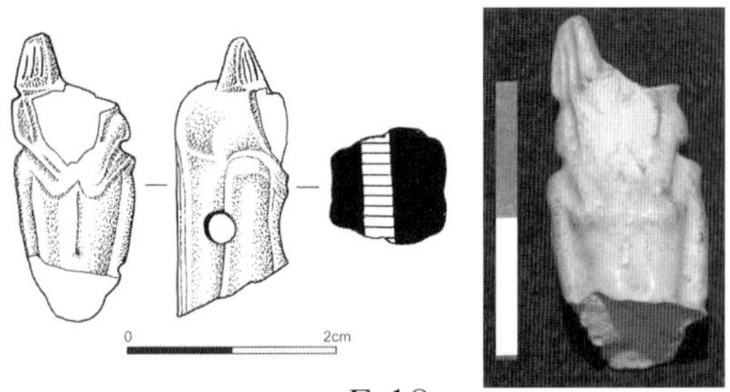

F-18

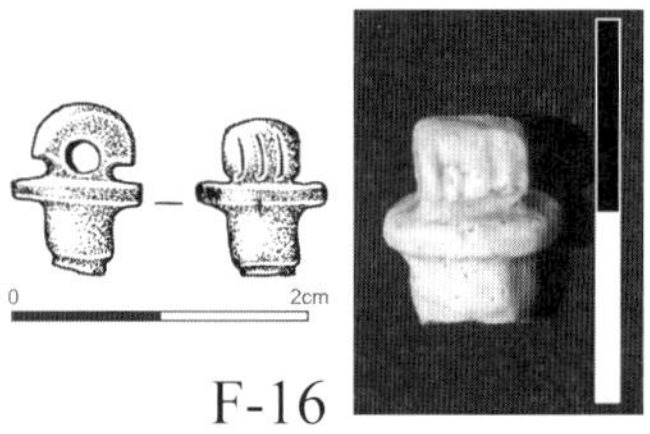

F-16

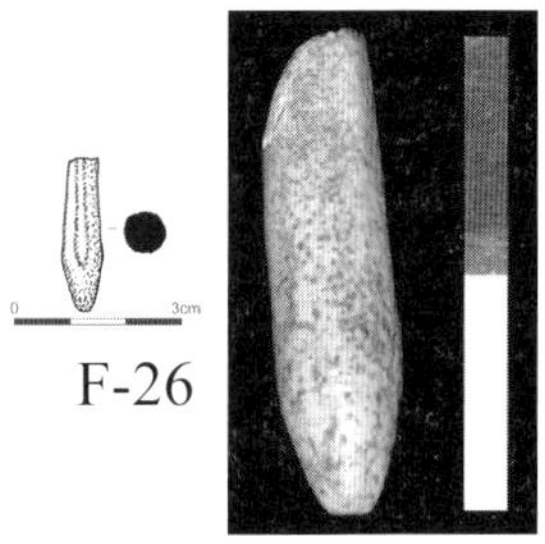

F-26

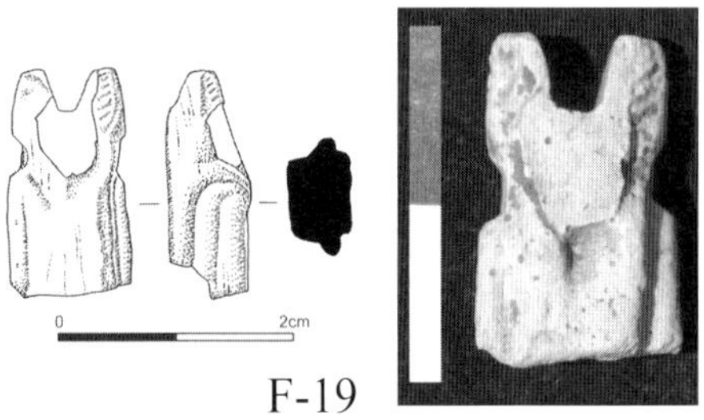

F-19

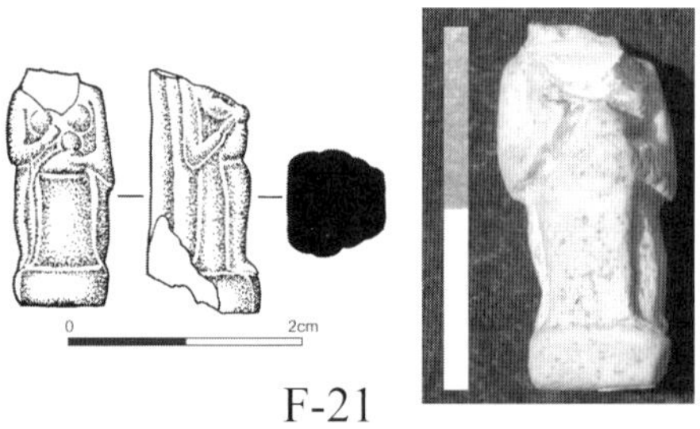

F-21

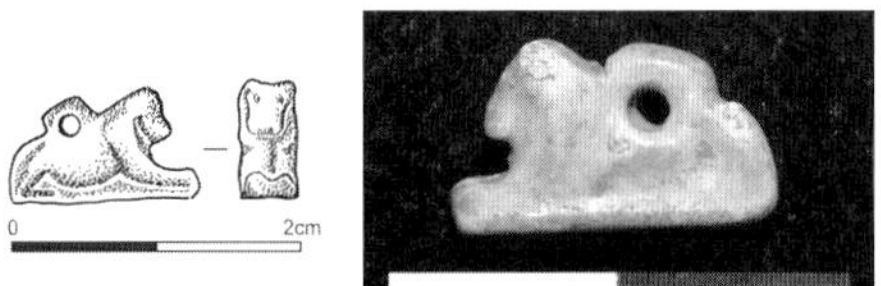

F-22

Figure II.16

Find ID: 2000-F-0070 Area: HAC Trench 1 Unit 2
Material: Faience
Object type: Amulet
F-32 ***(Figure II.16)***
Diameter of the shaft: 0.5 Diameter of the capital: 1 pres. Height: 1.5
Superior part of a papyrus column amulet. Suspension loop with three vertical lines incised. Only the capital is preserved with the incised representation of a calyx of six central ribs triangular leaves. Light blue glaze worn out.

Find ID: 2000-F-0138 Area: HAC Trench 1 Unit 2
Material: Faience
Object type: Amulet
F-18 ***(Figure II.16)***
Pres. Height 2.9
Upper part of an Anubis amulet. Anubis with a human body and a dog head of which is preserved one tall incised vertical ear, standing against a dorsal pillar. Pillar has the hole for suspension. Light blue glaze.

Find ID: 2000-F-0117 Area: HAC Trench 1 Unit 6
Material: Faience
Object type: Amulet
F-16 ***(Figure II.16)***
Max. Diameter: 0.8 Pres. Height: 1
Upper part of a papyrus column amulet. Rectangular suspension loop with incised lines. Only the capital is preserved (with no decor). Light blue glaze.

Find ID: 2000-F-0147 Area: HAC Trench 1 Unit 7
Material: Faience
Object type: Amulet
F-26
Max. Diameter: 0.5 Pres. Height: 2.
Lower part of a papyrus column amulet. Light blue glaze. ***(Figure II.16)***

Find ID: 2000-F-0160 Area: HAC Trench 1 Unit 9
Material: Faience
Object type: Amulet
F-19 ***(Figure II.16)***
Pres. Height: 2
Upper part of an Anubis amulet. Anubis with a human body and a dog head of which are preserved the two tall incised vertical ears, standing against a dorsal pillar. Light blue glaze.

Find ID: 2000-F-0171 Area: HAC Trench 1 Unit 9
Material: Faience
Object type: Amulet
F-21 ***(Figure II.16)***
Pres. Height: 2
Fragmentary amulet representing Isis lactans (the superior part of the torso and the head are missing). Seated on a stool, she holds on her knees the child Horus that she is nursing. Light blue glaze.

Find ID: 2000-F-0171 Area: HAC Trench 1 Unit 9
Material: Faience
Object type: Amulet
F-22 ***(Figure II.16)***
Length: 1.3 Height: 0.75
Small bead-amulet in form of a laying lion on a rectangular pedestal. Suspension loop on the back. Turquoise blue glaze.

HAC2

T3.1a
Find ID: 2000-F-0202 Area: HAC Trench 2 Unit 10
Material(s): Faience
Object type: Vessel
F-73 ***(Figure II.17)***
Diameter: 9
Rim and body fragment of a small bowl type T3.1a with inward curving rim. Bubbly turquoise blue glaze.

Find ID: 2000-F-0202 Area: HAC Trench 2 Unit 10
Material(s): Faience
Object type: Vessel
F-75 ***(Figure II.17)***
Diameter: 10
Rim fragment of a T3.1a small bowl with inwards curving lip. Bubbly gray blue glaze.

T6.1a
White and violet/deep blue glaze
Find ID: 2000-F-0220 Area: HAC Trench 2 Unit 10
Material(s): Faience
Object type: Vessel
F-65 ***(Figure II.17)***
Diameter: 19
Rim fragment of a plate T6.1a. White glaze on the internal and external walls. Violet glaze for the decor. Circular violet line, probably a calyx of white pointed leaves merging from a violet ground or a row of triangles.

Find ID: 2000-F-0226 Area: HAC Trench 2 Unit 11
Material(s): Faience
Object type: Vessel
F-146 ***(Figure II.17)***
Base diameter: 12.5
Lower part of the body of a T6.1A plate. White glaze on the exterior, bluish glaze on the interior with violet decayed in brown. Motive of light colour triangles merging from a deeper colour, framed by a line of light colour glaze.

Find ID: 2000-F-0226 Area: HAC Trench 2 Unit 11
Material(s): Faience
Object type: Vessel
F-147 ***(Figure II.17)***
Diameter: 23
Rim fragment of T6.1a plate. White glaze.

Find ID: 2000-F-0245 Area: HAC Trench 2 Unit CT
Material(s): Faience
Object type: Vessel
F-110 ***(Figure II.17)***
Diameter: 26 Pres. Height 2
Rim fragment of a T6.1a plate. White glaze on the internal and external walls. Violet glaze for the decor. Motifs of the decor are hardly discernible (may be the summit of a leaf or of a triangle).

White and deep blue glaze

Find ID: 2000-F-0207 Area: HAC Trench 2 Unit 10
Material(s): Faience
Object type: Vessel
F-117 ***(Figure II.18)***
Base diameter: 14

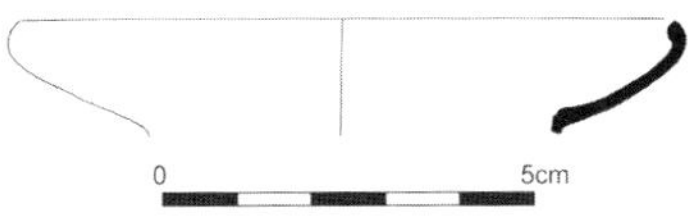

F-73

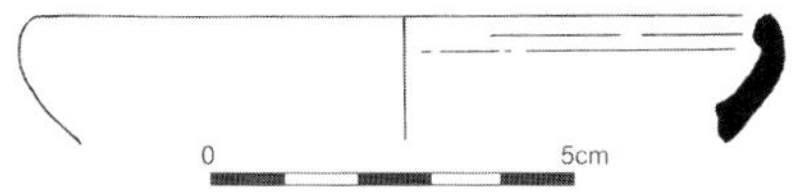

F-75

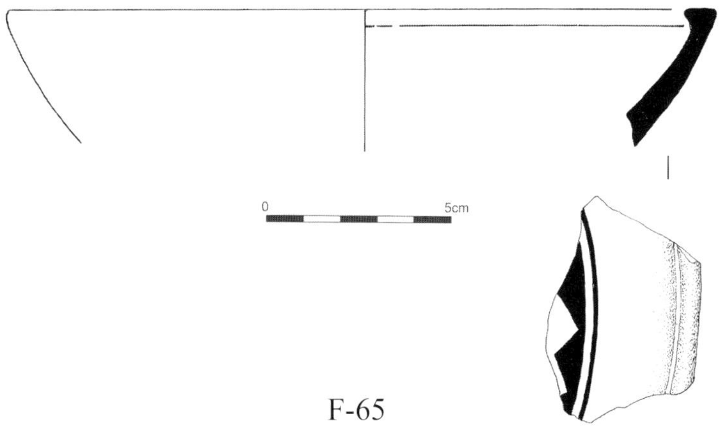

F-65

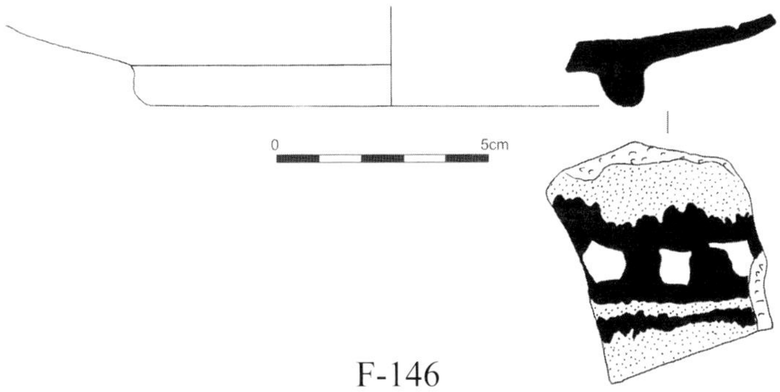

F-146

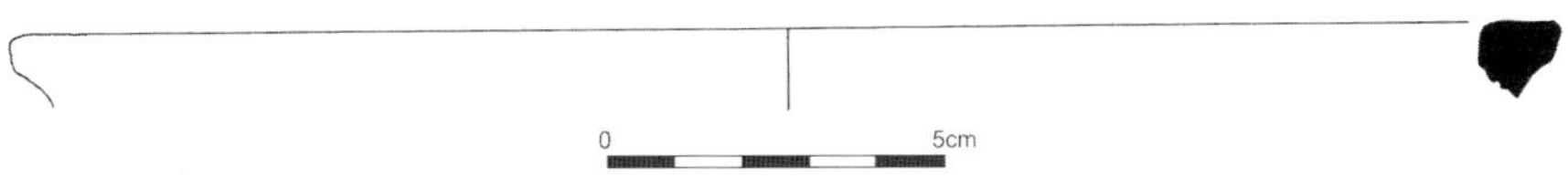

F-147

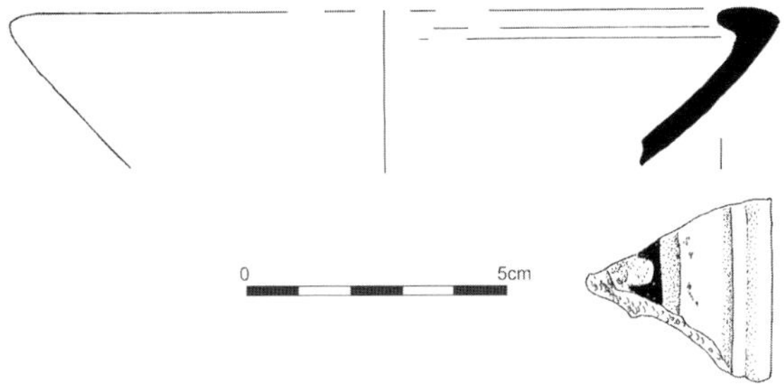

F-110

Figure II.17

Lower part of the body of a plate with an annular base (perhaps T6.1a). Light blue glaze on the exterior. Light and deep blue glaze on the interior. On the internal wall of the base of the plate, light blue/white rosette with hexagonal petals merging from a deep blue ground. Traces of the pointed end of a cone on the internal wall, of the circular part of the cone on the exterior wall.

Blue glaze

Find ID: 2000-F-0220 Area: HAC Trench 2 Unit 10
Material(s): Faience
Object type: Vessel
F-66 ***(Figure II.18)***
Diameter: 25
Rim fragment of a plate T6.1a. Bubbly turquoise blue glaze.

Find ID: 2000-F-0208 Area: HAC Trench 2 Unit 10
Material(s): Faience
Object type: Waster
F-141 ***(Figure II.18)***
Max. Dimension: 7.5
Four rims of plates T6.1a piled stuck together. Upper walls are of a deep blue ultramarine, lower ones of a lighter colour probably caused by over-firing.

Find ID: 2000-F-0208 Area: HAC Trench 2 Unit 10
Material(s): Faience
Object type: Waster
F-142
Max. Dimension: 4
Rim fragment of a T6.1a plate. White glaze, violet decor. Very small part of the decor is preserved. Fragment of saggar attached on the external side.

Find ID: 2000-F-0227 Area: HAC Trench 2 Unit 11
Material(s): Faience
Object type: Waster
F-129 ***(Figure II.18)***
Max. Dimension: 12 max. thickness of saggar 2.5
Fragment of the base of a saggar on which a series of turquoise blue glazed T6.1a plates which slipped, are glued to each other and stuck to the black glaze layer developed on the saggar.

Find ID: 2000-F-0245 Area: HAC Trench 2 Unit CT
Material(s): Faience
Object type: Vessel
F-109 ***(Figure II.19)***
Diameter: 22 Pres. Height: 1.8-2
Rim fragment of a T6.1a plate. Light blue glaze.

T6.1b
Find ID: 2000-F-0220 Area: HAC Trench 2 Unit 10
Material(s): Faience
Object type: Vessel
F-62 ***(Figure II.19)***
Diameter unknown
Rim fragment of a T6.1b plate. Wide flat rim, slightly concave walls. Turquoise blue glaze.

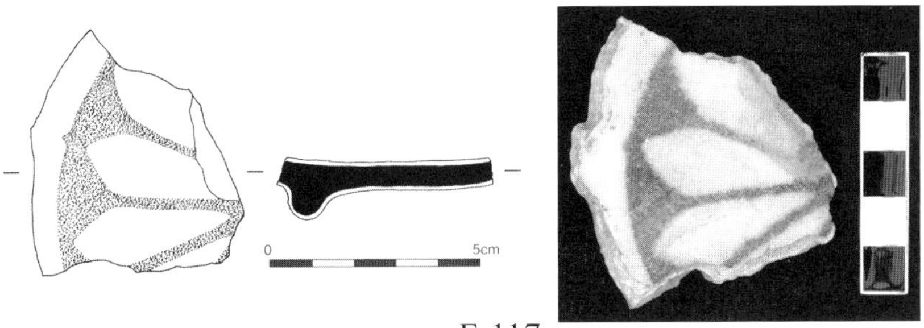

F-117

F-141

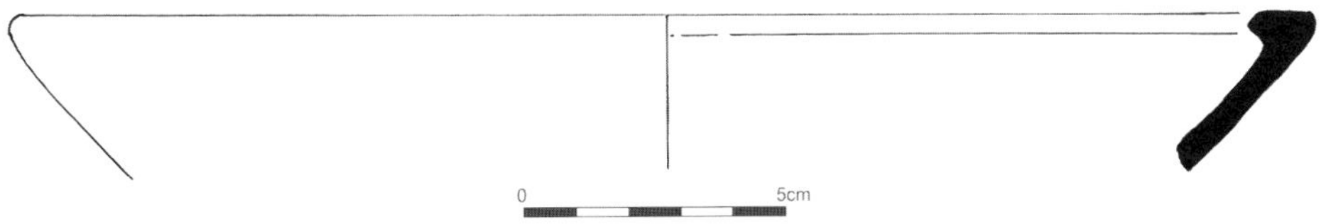

F-66

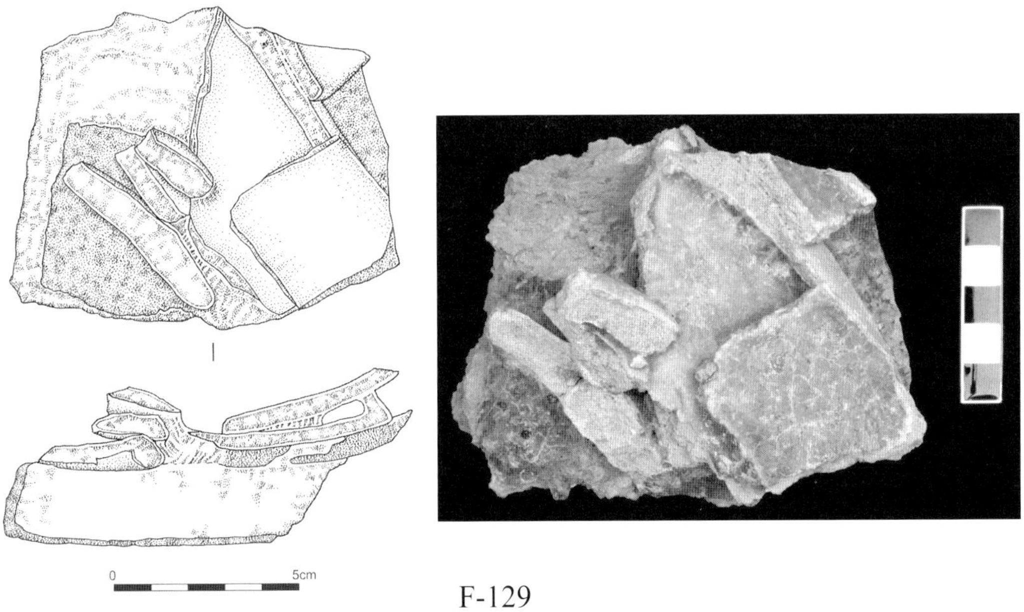

F-129

Figure II.18

T6.4
Find ID: 2000-F-0202 Area: HAC Trench 2 Unit 10
Material(s): Faience
Object type: Vessel
F-76 ***(Figure II.19)***
Diameter: 9
Rim fragment of a cylindrical goblet with flat lip (T6.4c). Turquoise blue glaze.

T12.2a
Find ID: 2000-F-0208 Area: HAC Trench 2 Unit 10
Material(s): Faience
Waster
F-137 ***(Figure II.19)***
Diameter unknown
Lower part of the body with annular base of a T12.2a bowl. Mis-firing has the glaze turned red on the external wall. The glaze on the internal wall has lost its shininess and some extraneous fragments are adhering to the piece.

T12.2b
Find ID: 2000-F-0204 Area: HAC Trench 2 Unit 10
Material(s): Faience
Object type: Vessel
F-123 ***(Figure II.19)***
Diameter: 18
Rim fragment of a bowl with a flat moulded edge and a groove under the edge (T12.2b). Decayed blue glaze.

Find ID: 2000-F-0245 Area: HAC Trench 2 Unit CT
Material(s): Faience
Object type: Vessel
F-105 ***(Figure II.19)***
Diameter: 26
Rim fragment of a big bowl with a flat moulded edge and a groove under the edge, oblique wall (T12.2b). Turquoise blue glaze.

T12.3a/c
Find ID: 2000-F-0220 Area: HAC Trench 2 Unit 10
Material(s): Faience
Object type: Vessel
F-64 ***(Figure II.19)***
Diameter unknown
Rim fragment of a bowl T12.3a or c. Flat Rim slightly moulded. Turquoise blue glaze.

Find ID: 2000-F-0207 Area: HAC Trench 2 Unit 10
Material(s): Faience
Object type: Vessel
F-118 ***(Figure II.19)***
Diameter: 12
Out-turned rim of a T12.3a or c bowl. Dark blue green glaze.

T12.3c/T12.4
Find ID: 2000-F-0202 Area: HAC Trench 2 Unit 10
Material(s): Faience
Object type: Vessel
F- 78 ***(Figure II.19)***
Diameter: 7
Pushed-in base of a T12.4 or T12.3c bowl. Decayed turquoise blue glaze.

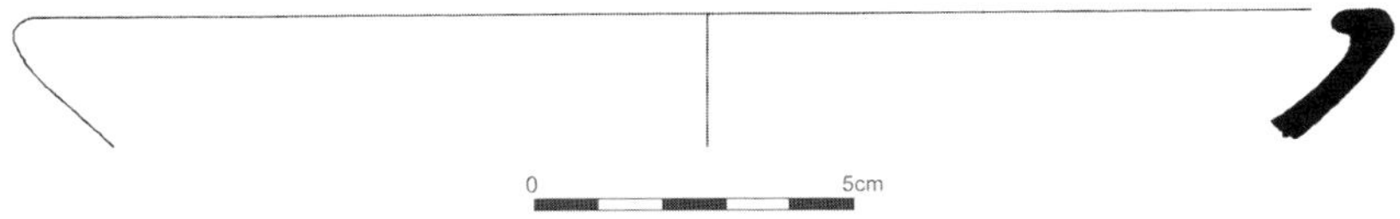

F-109

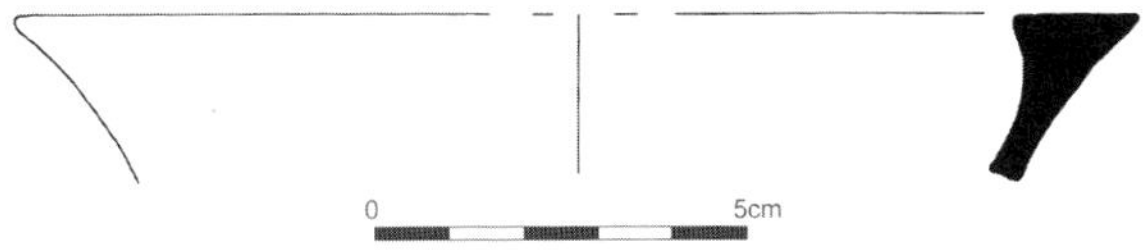

F-62

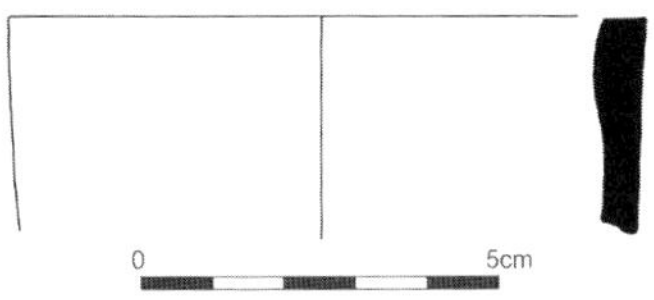

F-76

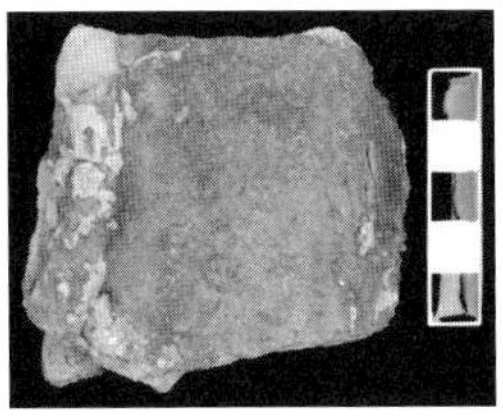

F-137

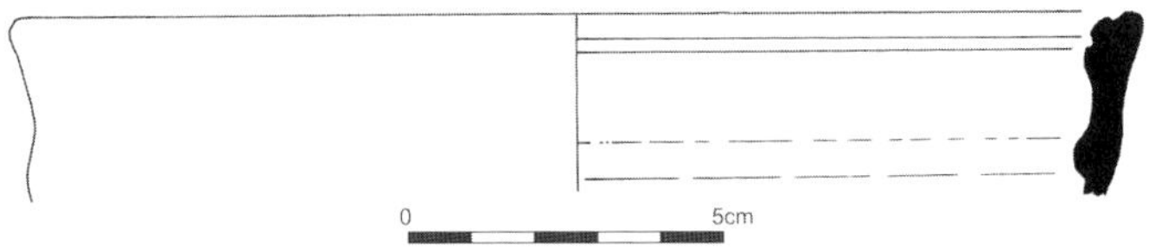

F-123

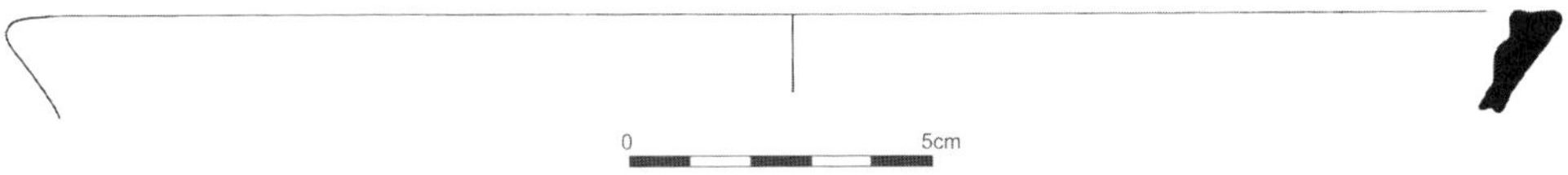

F-105

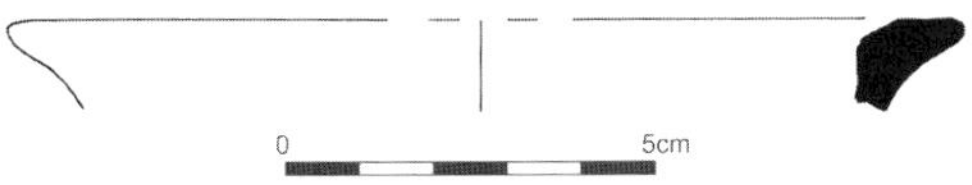

F-64

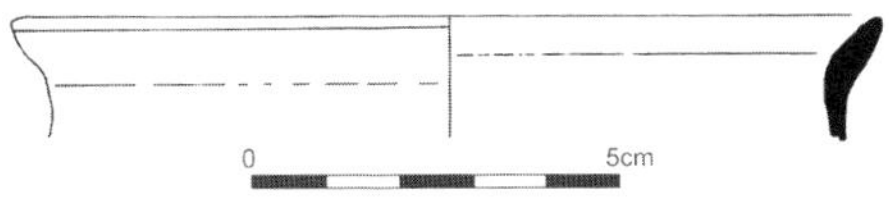

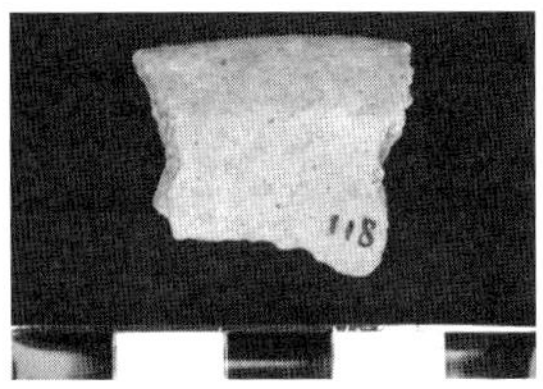

F-118

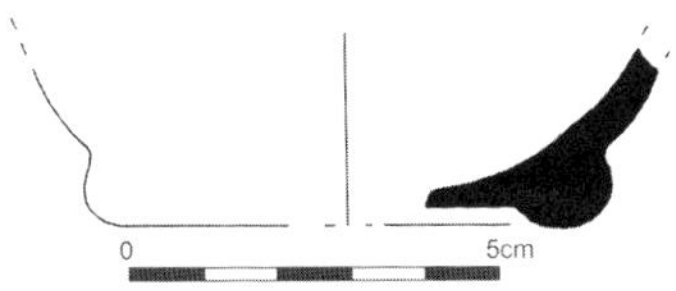

F-78

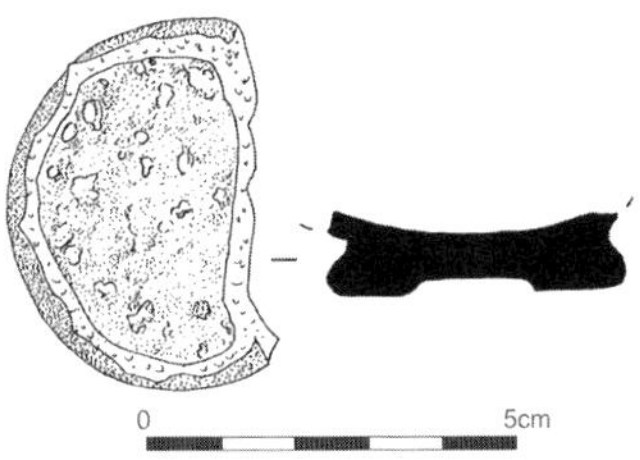

F-120

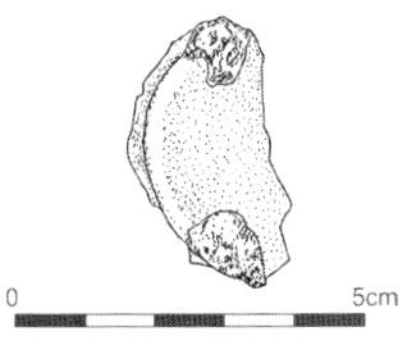

F-124

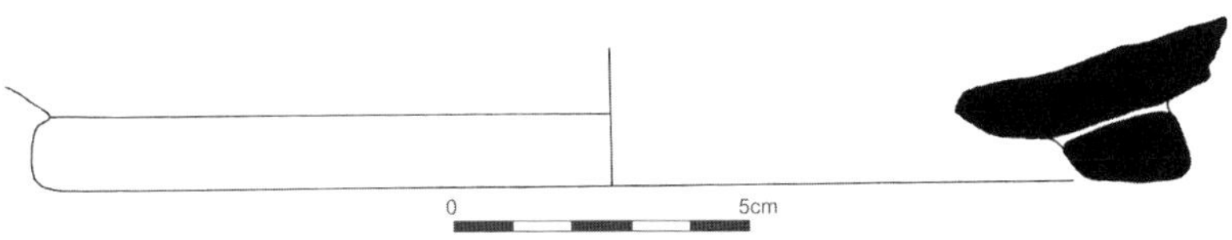

F-148

Figure II.19

Find ID: 2000-F-0207 Area: HAC Trench 2 Unit 10
Material(s): Faience
Waster
F-120 ***(Figure II.19)***
Diameter: 5
Defective pushed-in base body fragment belonging to a small bowl T12.4 or T12.3c. Bubbly turquoise blue glaze.

Find ID: 2000-F-0207 Area: HAC Trench 2 Unit 10
Material(s): Faience
Object type: Vessel
F-124 ***(Figure II.19)***
Diameter: 3.5
Flattened base fragment of a small bowl T12.4 or T12.3c. Scars of the circular part of two cones. Light blue glaze.

T12.4
Find ID: 2000-F-0226 Area: HAC Trench 2 Unit 11
Material(s): Faience
Object type: Vessel
F-148 ***(Figure II.19)***
Diameter: 19
Lower part of body and applied base ring of a T12.4 bowl. Decayed glaze or bluish red glaze.

T12.7
Find ID: 2000-F-0202 Area: HAC Trench 2 Unit 10
Material(s): Faience
Object type: Vessel
F-77 ***(Figure II.20)***
Diameter: 14
Rim fragment of a T12.7 with a biconvex profile. Turquoise blue glaze.

Find ID: 2000-F-0207 Area: HAC Trench 2 Unit 10
Material(s): Faience
Object type: Vessel
F-116
Diameter: 15
Rim fragment of a T12.7 bowl with a biconvex profile. Turquoise blue glaze.

Find ID: 2000-F-0226 Area: HAC Trench 2 Unit 11
Material(s): Faience
Object type: Vessel
F-143 ***(Figure II.20)***
Diameter: 11
Rim fragment with flat edge and biconvex profile. Turquoise blue glaze.

Find ID: 2000-F-0226 Area: HAC Trench 2 Unit 11
Material(s): Faience
Object type: Vessel
F-145 ***(Figure II.20)***
Diameter: ca 13-15
Rim fragment of a biconvex bowl. Turquoise blue glaze.

T13.2
Find ID: 2000-F-0245 Area: HAC Trench 2 Unit CT
Material(s): Faience
Object type: Waster
F-106 ***(Figure II.20)***
Max. Dimension: 5
Two out-turned rim plate type T13.2 stuck together. Light blue glaze.

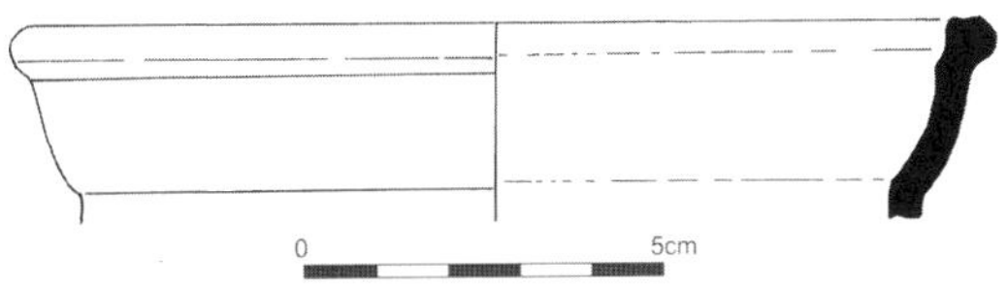

F-77

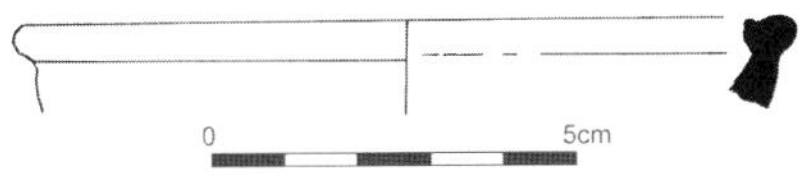

F-143

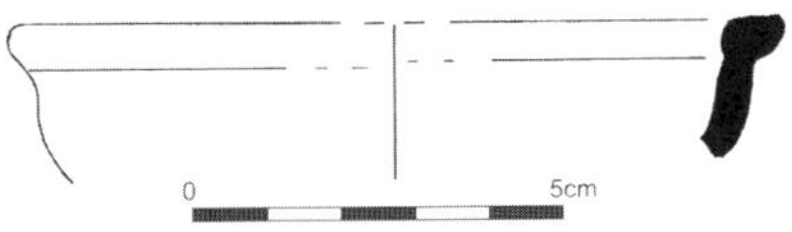

F-145

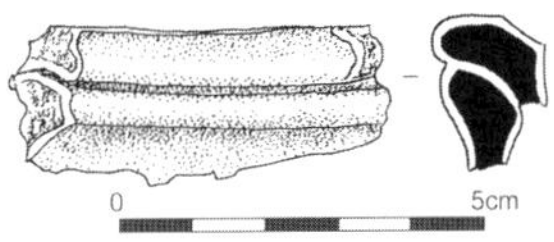

F-106

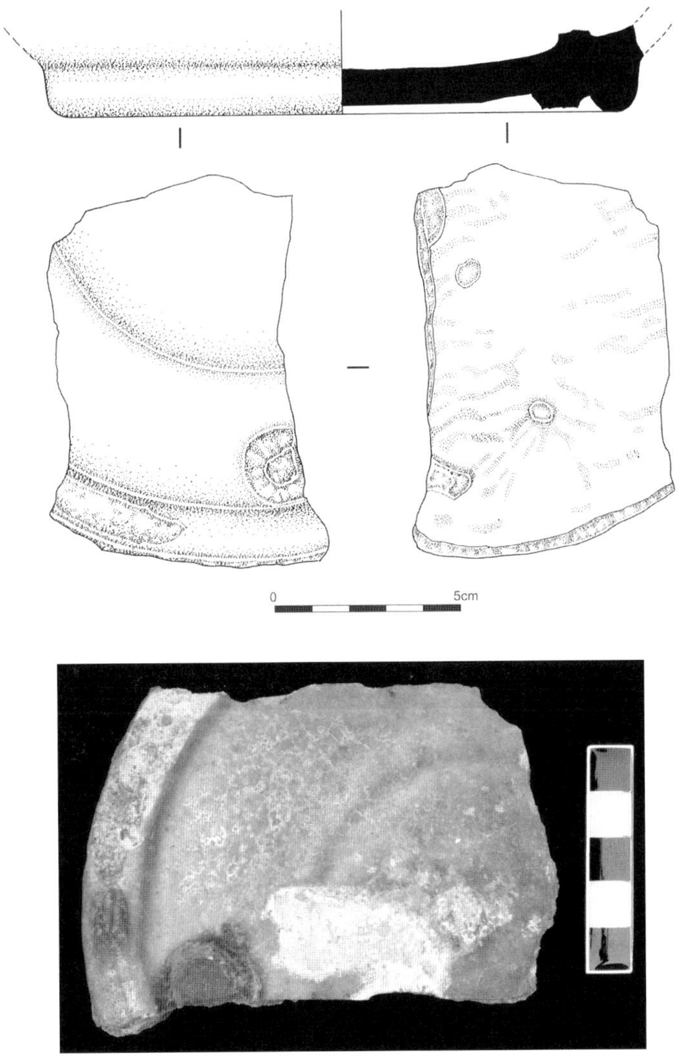

F-127

Figure II.20

Find ID: 2000-F-0227 Area: HAC Trench 2 Unit 11
Material(s): Faience
Object type: Vessel
F-127 ***(Figure II.20)***
Base diameter: 16
Lower part of the body with annular base of a plate T13.2. Traces of the cones obvious on internal (pointed part) and external walls (circular 1.5), one of the cones is still partly *in situ*. Circle on the lower part of the bottom (diam. 9). Turquoise blue glaze.

T13.3a
Find ID: 2000-F-0202 Area: HAC Trench 2 Unit 10
Material(s): Faience
Object type: Vessel
F-83 ***(Figure II.21)***
Diameter: 16
Rim fragment of a plate T13.3a with thin walls. Bubbly light blue glaze.

Find ID: 2000-F-0202 Area: HAC Trench 2 Unit 10
Material(s): Faience
Object type: Waster.
F-85
Max. Dimensions: 3.5
Deformed rim of a T13.3a plate. Turquoise blue glaze.

T13.3b
Find ID: 2000-F-0221 Area: HAC Trench 2 Unit 10
Material(s): Faience
Object type: Defective Vessel
F-99 ***(Figure II.21)***
Base Diameter: 11
Fragment of the lower part of a plate with annular base T13.3b. Four concentric grooves on the interior. Bubbly and defective glaze turquoise blue turned red.

T13
Find ID: 2000-F-0221 Area: HAC Trench 2 Unit 10
Material(s): Faience
Object type: Defective Vessel
F-100 ***(Figure II.21)***
Max. Dimension: 4
Fragment of the lower part of a defective plate with annular base T13 worn away. Bubbly and defective glaze. Turquoise blue glaze turned red on the internal wall. Chips of other material adhering to the surface.

Find ID: 2000-F-0221 Area: HAC Trench 2 Unit 10
Material(s): Faience
Object type: Defective Vessel
F-101 ***(Figure II.21)***
Max. Dimension: 6.5
Fragment of the lower part of a defective plate with annular base. Bubbly and defective turquoise blue glaze. Chips of other material adhering to the surface.

Find ID: 2000-F-0208 Area: HAC Trench 2 Unit 10
Material(s): Faience
Object type: Waster
F-138 ***(Figure II.21)***
Max. Dimension: 5.5
Fragment of the lower part of a defective plate with annular base. Bubbly and defective turquoise blue glaze. Chips of other vessels adhering to the surface.

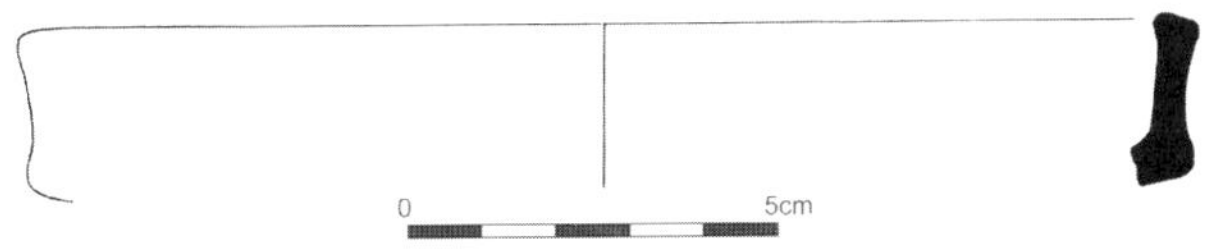

F-83

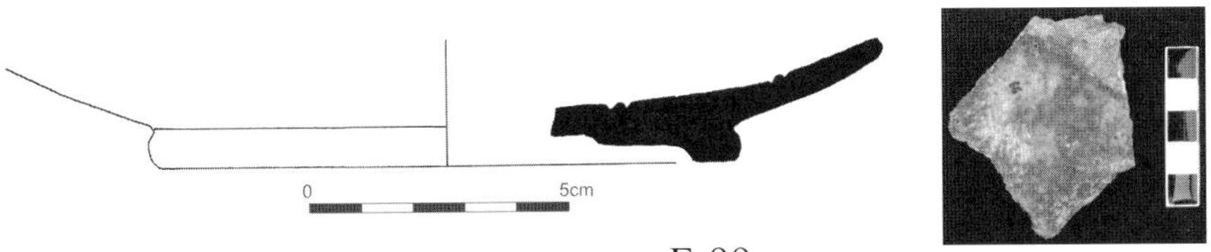

F-99

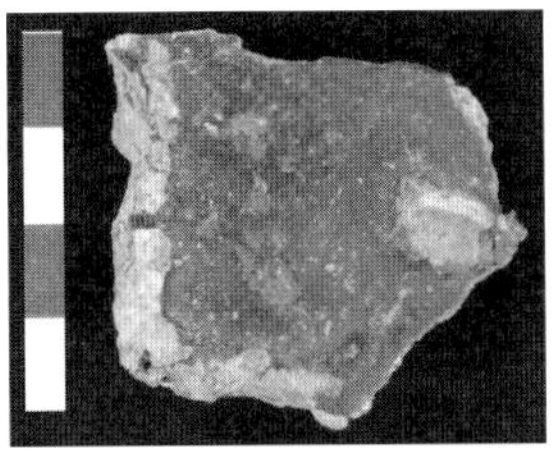

F-100

F-101

F-138

F-140

F-128

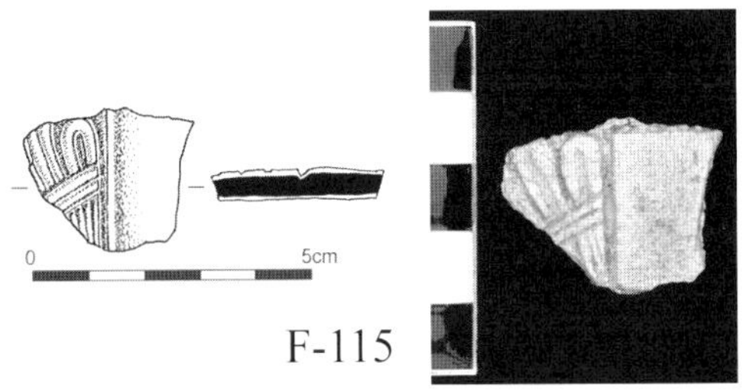

F-115

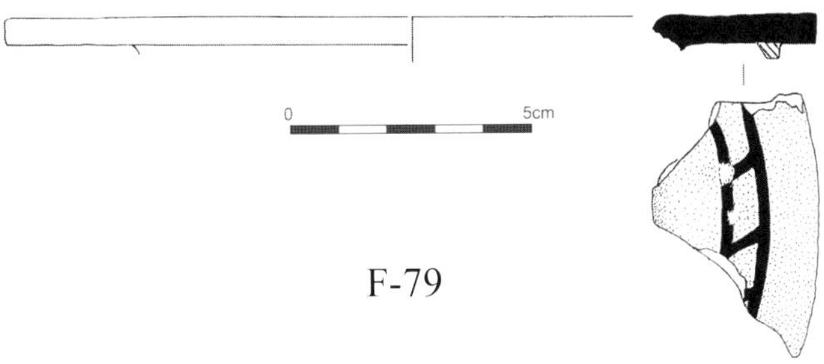

F-79

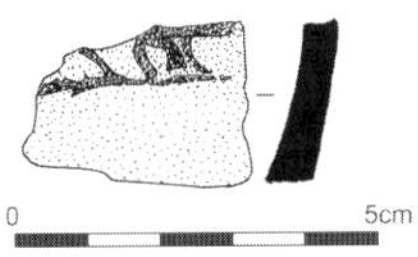

F-107

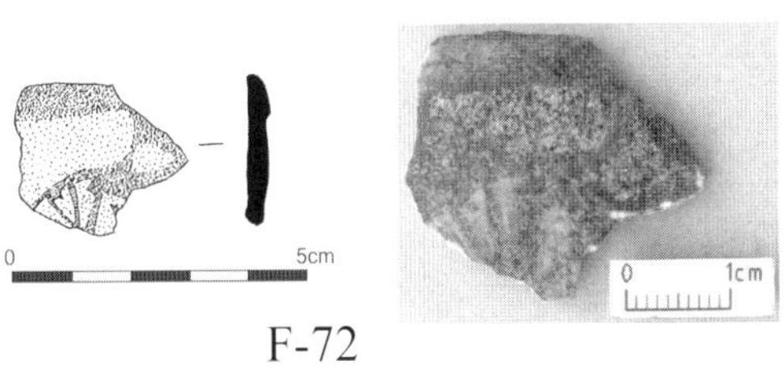

F-72

Figure II.21

Find ID: 2000-F-0208 Area: HAC Trench 2 Unit 10
Material(s): Faience
Object type: Waster
F-140 ***(Figure II.21)***
Diameter of the cone: 1.5 Height: 2.1
Body fragment of vessel. Turquoise blue glaze with a cone attached to it (not in the position for firing).

Find ID: 2000-F-0227 Area: HAC Trench 2 Unit 11
Material(s): Faience
Object type: Waster
F-128 ***(Figure II.21)***
Diameter base: 11
Bottom fragment with annular base of a T13 plate. Bubbly turquoise blue faience turned red.

T16.1
Find ID: 2000-F-0202 Area: HAC Trench 2 Unit 10
Material(s): Faience
Object type: Vessel
F-80
Diameter: 12
Rim fragment of a goblet with moulded decoration. Row of dots in relief under a reinforced rim. Internal grove under the lip. Turquoise blue glaze.

Find ID: 2000-F-0207 Area: HAC Trench 2 Unit 10
Material(s): Faience
Object type: Vessel
F-115 ***(Figure II.21)***
Max. Dimension: 3
Body fragment of moulded goblet T16.1. Turquoise blue glaze. Decoration one with a bundle of wheat and one zone without decoration.

T19.3
Find ID: 2000-F-0202 Area: HAC Trench 2 Unit 10
Material(s): Faience
Object type: Vessel
F-79 ***(Figure II.21)***
Diameter: 17
Rim fragment of an amphora type T19.3. On the superior part of the lid, rope in a deeper blue colour. Under the rim, traces of the departure of the handle. Turquoise blue glaze; except the decor in a deeper tone.

Find ID: 2000-F-0245 Area: HAC Trench 2 Unit CT
Material(s): Faience
Object type: Vessel
F-107 ***(Figure II.21)***
Neck diameter: 10
Neck fragment of a T19.3 vase. Turquoise blue glaze on the interior, violet and white glaze on the exterior. Motif of rope on the neck.

T20
Find ID: 2000-F-0202 Area: HAC Trench 2 Unit 10
Material(s): Faience
Object type: Vessel
F-72 ***(Figure II.21)***
Max. Dimension: 3
Lower part of body of T20.1 vase with moulded decoration. Light blue glaze on the interior, on the exterior the colours of the glaze are altered, and were violet and white at the origin. Animal running to the left.

Lamps

Find ID: 2000-F-0208 Area: HAC Trench 2 Unit 10
Material(s): Faience
Object type: Lamp
F-139 ***(Figure II.22)***
Height : 9 Width: 2
Fragment belonging to a defective lamp, part of the volute flanking the side of the burner.

Amulets

Find ID: 2000-F-0291 Area: HAC Trench 2 Unit CT
Material(s): Faience
Object type: Amulet
F-2201 ***(Figure II.22)***
Dimensions: 2.2 x 1.4 Thickness: 0.4
Wedjet-eye with perforation under the brow. No special decoration. Light blue glaze worn out and covered with a blackish crust.

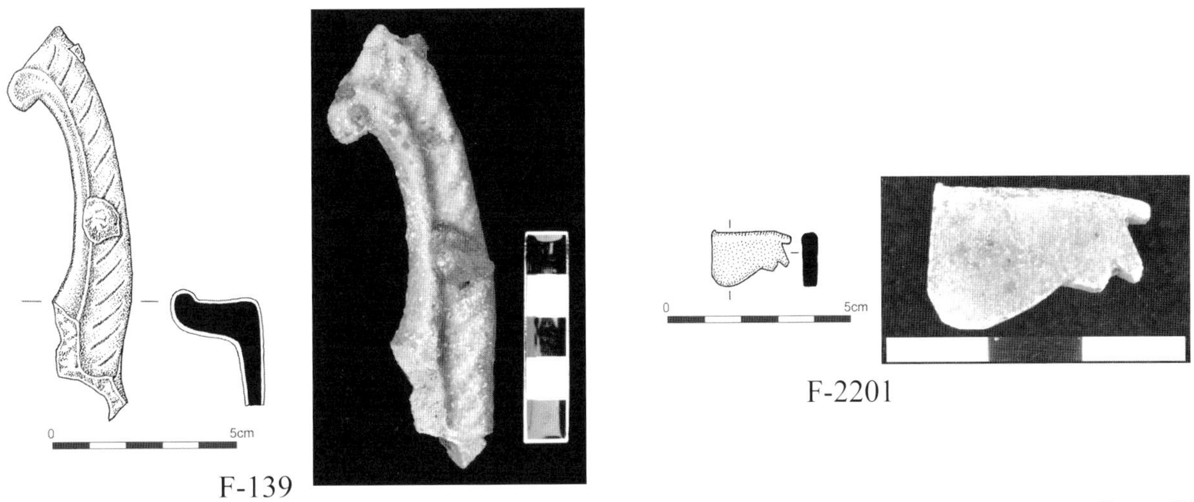

Figure II.22

HAC3

T2.3a
Find ID: 2001-F-0017 Area: HAC Trench 3 Unit 33
Material(s): Faience
Object type: Vessel
F-439 ***(Figure II.23)***
Diameter: 12
Rim fragment of a T2.3a bowl. Light green glaze.

T2.3f
Find ID: 2001-F-0027 Area: HAC Trench 3 Unit 37
Material(s): Faience
Object type: Vessel
F-534 ***(Figure II.23)***
Diameter: unknown
Fragment of the rim of a bowl T2.3f with thin lip slightly inturned. Light blue and medium blue glaze on the exterior, light blue glaze on the interior. Decor divided into zones separated by large bands with no decor: waves, band without decor, below may be a frieze of griffins.

T3.1a
Find ID: 2001-F-0017 Area: HAC Trench 3 Unit 33
Material(s): Faience
Object type: Vessel
F-440 ***(Figure II.23)***
Diameter: 11
Rim fragment of a T3.1a small bowl. Light blue glaze.

Find ID: 2001-F-0059 Area: HAC Trench 3 Unit 36
Material(s): Faience
Object type: Vessel
F-738 ***(Figure II.23)***
Diameter: 9.5
Rim fragment of a T3.1a small bowl. Turquoise blue glaze.

Find ID: 2005-F-0136 Area: HAC Trench 3 Unit 308
Material(s): Faience
Object type: Vessel
F-2111 ***(Figure II.23)***
Diameter unknown
Rim fragment of a T3.1a small bowl with inwards curving lip. Apple green glaze.

T3.1b
Find ID: 2001-F-0070 Area: HAC Trench 3 Unit 36
Material(s): Faience
Object type: Vessel
F-1035
Diameter: 11
Rim fragment of a T3.1b small bowl. Grey blue glaze.

Find ID: 2001-F-0047 Area: HAC Trench 3 Unit 37
Material(s): Faience
Object type: Vessel
F-614 ***(Figure II.23)***
Diameter: unknown
Rim fragment of a T3.1b small bowl. Light green glaze.

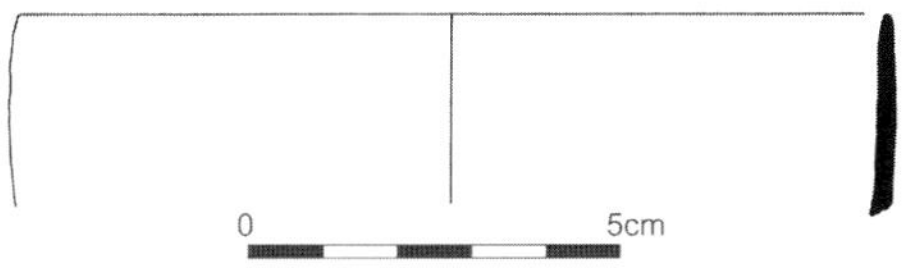

F-439

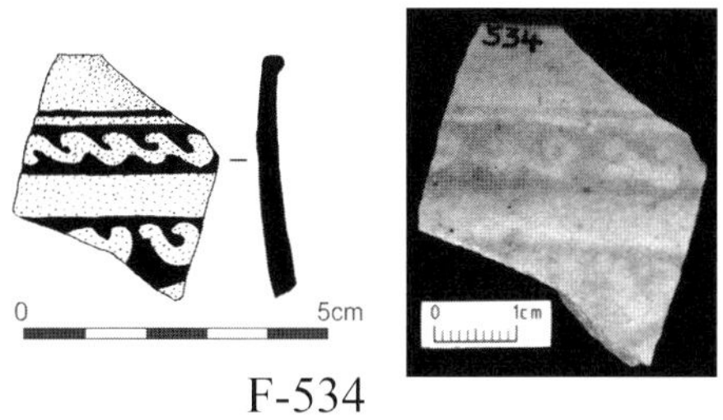

F-534

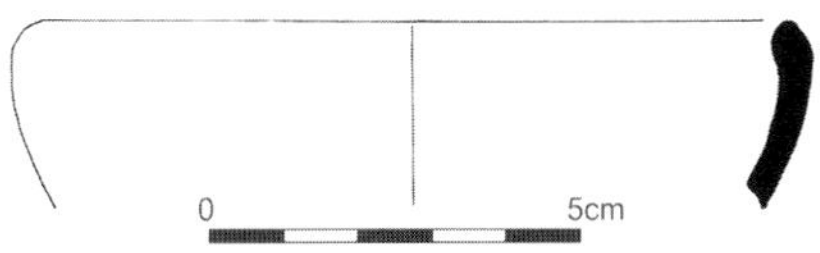

F-440

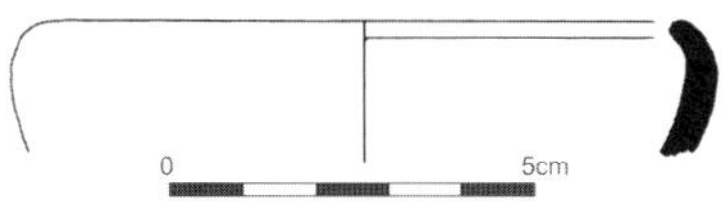

F-738

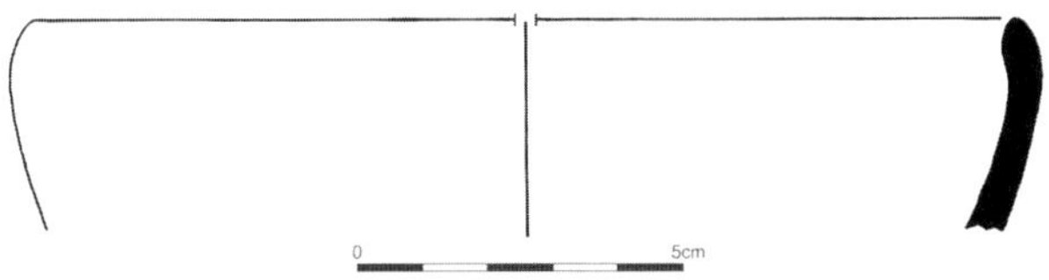

F-2111

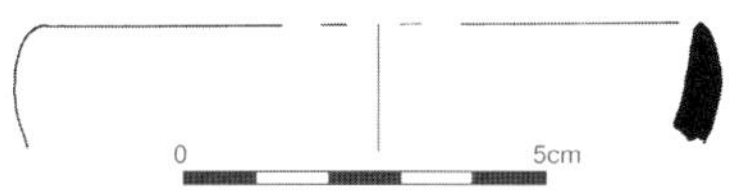

F-614

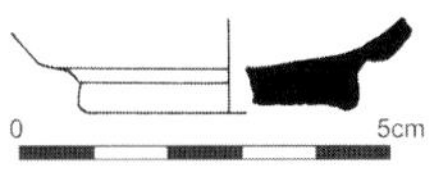

F-715

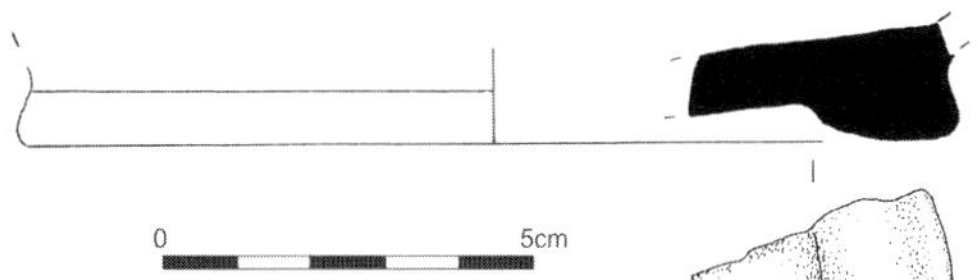

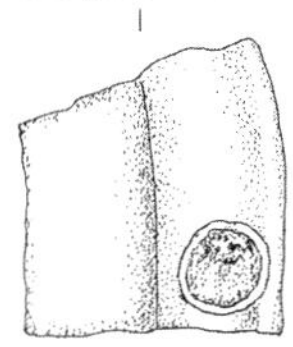

F-683

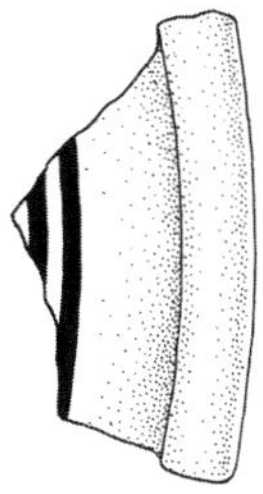

F-2042

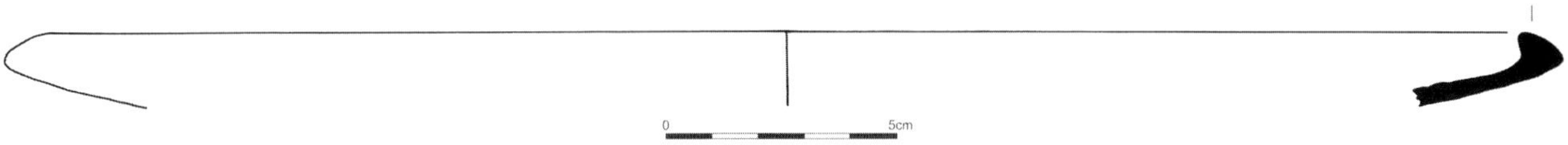

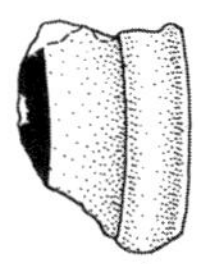

F-2097

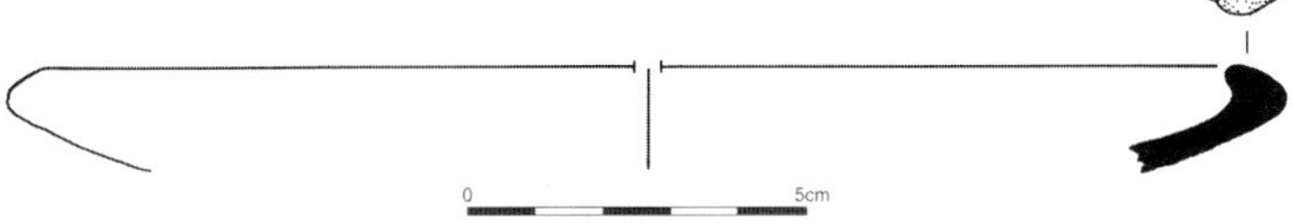

Figure II.23

T3.1c
Find ID: 2001-F-0059 Area: HAC Trench 3 Unit 36
Material(s): Faience
Object type: Vessel
F-715 ***(Figure II.23)***
Diameter: 4
Flattened base fragment of a small bowl T3.1c. Light blue glaze.

T6.1a
White and violet glaze
Find ID: 2001-F-0059 Area: HAC Trench 3 Unit 36
Material(s): Faience
Object type: Vessel
F-683 ***(Figure II.23)***
Base diameter: 13
Body fragment with a low annular base (Dim. 1.8) of a plate. White glaze. Traces of the circular part of the cone on the base.

Find ID: 2005-F-0016 Area: HAC Trench 3 Unit 300
Material(s): Faience
Object type: Vessel
F-2042 ***(Figure II.23)***
Diameter: 35
Two rim fragments of a T6.1a plate. White and violet glaze. Two concentric violet lines preserved.

Find ID: 2005-F-0074 Area: HAC Trench 3 Unit 306
Material(s): Faience
Object type: Vessel
F-2097 ***(Figure II.23)***
Diameter: unknown
Rim of a T6.1a plate. White glaze violet glaze for the decor.

Find ID: 2005-F-0030 Area: HAC Trench 3 Unit 303
Material(s): Faience
Object type: Vessel
F-2028 ***(Figure II.24)***
Diameter: c.15-16
Rim and body fragment. Blue glaze turned to green and concretions, should be considered as a waster.

Turquoise blue glaze

Find ID: 2001-F-0059 Area: HAC Trench 3 Unit 36
Material(s): Faience
Object type: Vessel
F-602 ***(Figure II.24)***
Diameter: 16
Rim fragment of a T6.1a plate. Turquoise blue glaze.

Find ID: 2001-F-0059 Area: HAC Trench 3 Unit 36
Material(s): Faience
Object type: Vessel
F-699
Diameter unknown
Rim fragment of a plate T6.1a. Turquoise blue glaze.

Find ID: 2005-F-0155 Area: HAC Trench 3 Unit 308
Material(s): Faience
Waster

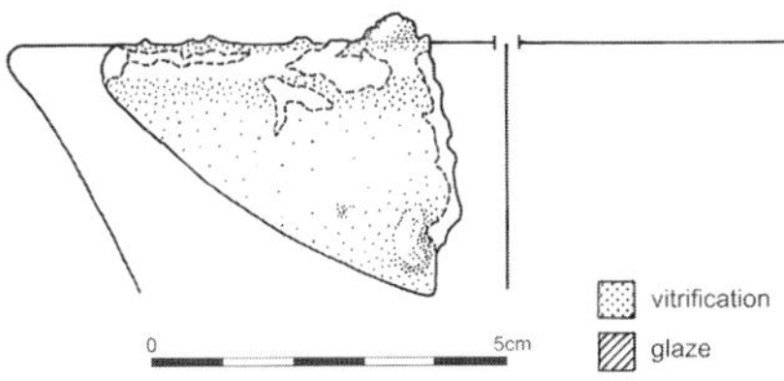

F-2028

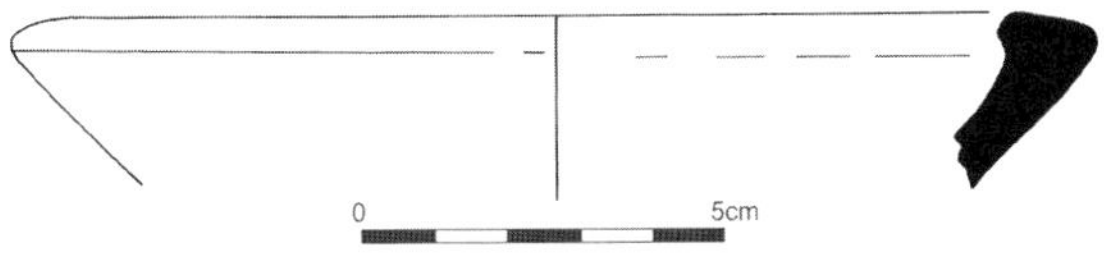

F-602

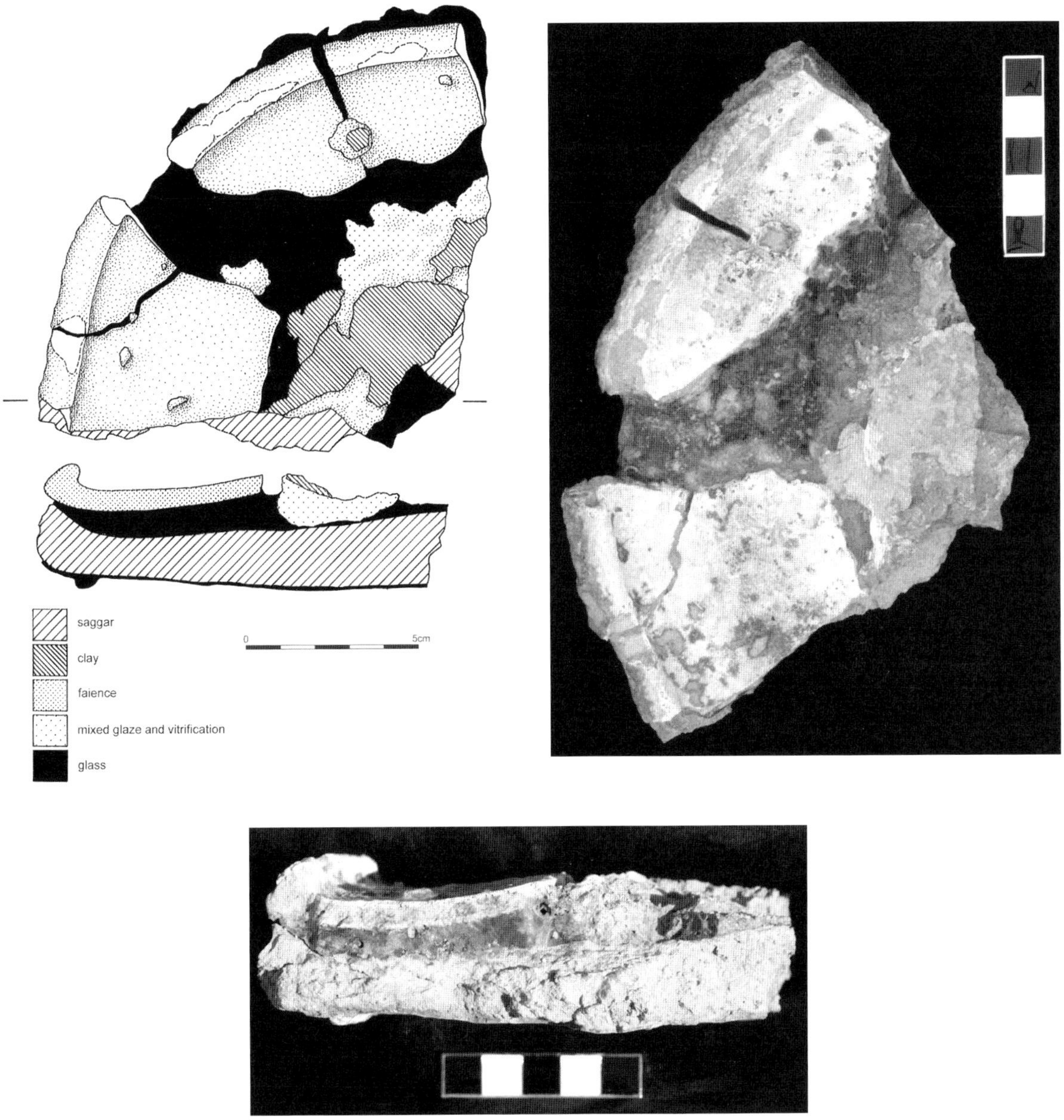

F-2025

Figure II.24

F-2025 ***(Figure II.24)***
Diameter of the saggar: around 20-25
Fragment of the bottom of a saggar containing a thick layer of glaze, then the remains of a T6.1 plate. On the side in the middle, is a gritty surface. The walls of the saggar are not preserved, only the bottom thickness from 1.5 to 2 in the middle, glaze going up on the side, thickness 1, on the lower surface of the saggar, glaze is preserved.

Find ID: 2005-F-0104 Area: HAC Trench 3 Unit 308
Material(s): Faience
Object type: Vessel
F-2069
Diameter unknown width of the rim: 1.2
Rim fragment of a T6.1a plate. Turquoise blue glaze.

T6.2a
Find ID: 2001-F-0162 Area: HAC Trench 3 Unit 52
Material(s): Faience
Object type: Vessel
F-1385 ***(Figure II.25)***
Diameter: 15
Rim of a T6.2a plate. Flat rim with two mouldings on the superior lip. Turquoise blue glaze decayed.

T6.4
Find ID: 2001-F-0059 Area: HAC Trench 3 Unit 36
Material(s): Faience
Object type: Vessel
F-712 ***(Figure II.25)***
Diameter: 10
Rim fragment with thick out-turned edge of a goblet (T6.4a). Turquoise blue glaze.

Find ID: 2001-F-0047 Area: HAC Trench 3 Unit 37
Material(s): Faience
Object type: Vessel
F-601 ***(Figure II.25)***
Diameter: 10
Rim fragment with thick out-turned edge of a goblet (T6.4a). Turquoise blue glaze.
Light green glaze.

T7.4
Blue glaze
Find ID: 2005-F-0002 Area: HAC Trench 3 Unit 300
Material(s): Faience
Object type: Vessel
F-2124 ***(Figure II.25)***
Max. Dimension:. 2
Shoulder fragment of a T7.4 vase. Turquoise blue glaze for the parts in depth and light blue for the relief. Decor in zones: Upper: frieze of rosettes-stars (8 pointed petals) and lotus bundle; lower zone: probably ivy branch.

Find ID: 2005-F-0050 Area: HAC Trench 3 Unit 301
Material(s): Faience
Object type: Vessel
F-2184 ***(Figure II.25)***
Max. Dimension: 2
Shoulder fragment of a T7.4 vase. Blue turquoise glaze decayed. Decor: frieze of lotus bundles and rosettes with very thin petals.

Find ID: 2005-F-0050 Area: HAC Trench 3 Unit 301
Material(s): Faience
Object type: Vessel
F-2199-F-2200 ***(Figure II.25)***
Max. Dimension: 1
Two shoulder fragments. Rosette-star and lotus. Turquoise blue glaze on the interior; blue greenish glaze on the exterior.

White and violet

Find ID: 2005-F-0016 Area: HAC Trench 3 Unit 300
Material(s): Faience
Object type: Vessel
F-2197 ***(Figure II.25)***
Max. Dimension: 1
Shoulder fragment of a T7.4 vase. Turquoise blue glaze on the interior, white and violet glaze on the exterior. Decor in zones: upper zone rosettes alternating with degenerate lotus motif; lower zone: ivy branch.

Find ID: 2005-F-0050 Area: HAC Trench 3 Unit 301
Material(s): Faience
Object type: Vessel
F-2174 (+F-2171, F-2176, F-2177, F-2202) ***(Figure II.25)***
Joining and non-joining fragments belonging to a closed vase T7.4. Internal glaze turquoise blue, external glaze white and violet.
Rim with a thin everted rim (light blue), short cylindrical neck decorated with two waves motifs. Shoulder marked by two lines in relief decorated by a frieze of eggs and darts, and by a frieze composed alternatively of a lotus bundle and of a pointed petals rosette.
Lower part of the body. Turquoise blue glaze on the interior, violet and white glaze on the exterior. Decoration divided in two zones: frieze of animals wandering in nature, then calyx of nelumbo plain leaves on a diamond pattern back (F-2177)
Fragment of the annular base of diameter 8.5. White glaze.

Find ID: 2005-F-0104 Area: HAC Trench 3 Unit 308
Material(s): Faience
Object type: Vessel
F-2087 ***(Figure II.25)***
Max. dimension: 3
Body fragment belonging may be to the inferior part a T7.4 vase. Diamond motif composed of lines inter-crossing. Turquoise blue glaze on the interior, violet and white glaze on the exterior.

Find ID: 2005-F-0136 Area: HAC Trench 3 Unit 308
Material(s): Faience
Object type: Vessel
F-2100 ***(Figure II.25)***
Neck: diameter: 10 Height: 3 Thickness: 0.5
Body: Max. dimension: 2
Neck fragment and body fragment of a T7.4 vase. Turquoise blue glaze on the interior, violet and white on the exterior, probably over-fired, turned black. On the neck, double wave pattern separated by a line hardly visible and framed by two lines. On the body fragment, lotus bundle motif degenerated.

Greenish glaze

Find ID: 2005-F-0002 Area: HAC Trench 3 Unit 300
Material(s): Faience
Object type: Vessel
F-2158 ***(Figure II.25)***
Max. Dimension: 3.5 Thickness: 0.6
Shoulder fragment. Turquoise blue glaze on the interior; decayed greenish blue glaze on the exterior. Decor in zones separated by bands without decor: frieze of degenerated lotus motif (and rosettes), then ivy branch.

Find ID: 2005-F-0074 Area: HAC Trench 3 Unit 306
Material(s): Faience
Object type: Vessel
F-2090 ***(Figure II.25)***
Max. Dimension: 4 Thickness: 0.8.
Body fragments of a T7.4 vase. Deep greenish-bluish glaze, with yellow dots in relief. Lotus bundle and rosette.

Find ID: 2005-F-0104 Area: HAC Trench 3 Unit 308
Material(s): Faience
Object type: Vessel
F-2194 - F-2195 ***(Figure II.25)***
Max. Dimension: F-2194: 4.5; F-2195: 2
Neck and body fragment of T7.4. Turquoise blue glaze on the interior; greenish glaze decayed on the exterior. On the neck, two lines of waves separated by a line framed by two bands. On the shoulder, decor in zones : upper zone frieze of rosettes: with centre in relief and lotus bundles, lower zone: calyx of plain nelumbo leaves on a diamond backing.

T11.1
Find ID: 2001-F-0017 Area: HAC Trench 3 Unit 33
Material(s): Faience
Object type: Vessel
F-1437 ***(Figure II.25)***
Height: 3.5
Fragment of a circular handle with three vertical lines belonging to a pot type T11.1. Decayed glaze worn out.

Find ID: 2001-F-0059 Area: HAC Trench 3 Unit 36
Material(s): Faience
Object type: Vessel
F-710 ***(Figure II.25)***
Dimensions: 2.5 x 2
Fragment of a square handle with moulding of the upper side, may be belonging to a T11.1 pot. Turquoise blue glaze.

T11.2
ind ID: 2002-F-0221 Area: HAC Trench 3 Unit 189
Material(s): Faience
Object type: Vessel
F-1714 ***(Figure II.25)***
Pres. Height: 2.3 Diameter: 2.3
Fragment of a cylindrical neck of a close vase perhaps Lagynos T11.2 . Turquoise blue glaze.

T11.4
Find ID: 2005-F-0002 Area: HAC Trench 3 Unit 300
Material(s): Faience
Object type: Vessel
F-2133 ***(Figure II.25)***
Diameter: 3 Pres. Height: 1.7
Funnel-shape rim and cylindrical neck fragment of an unguent bottle. Turquoise blue glaze.

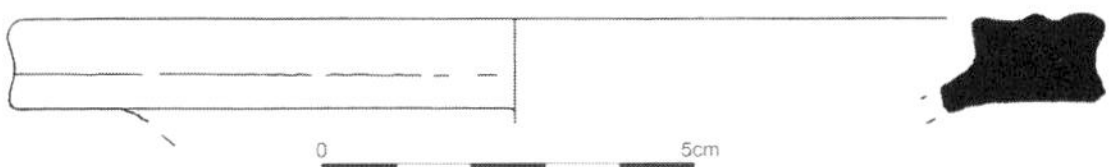

F-1385

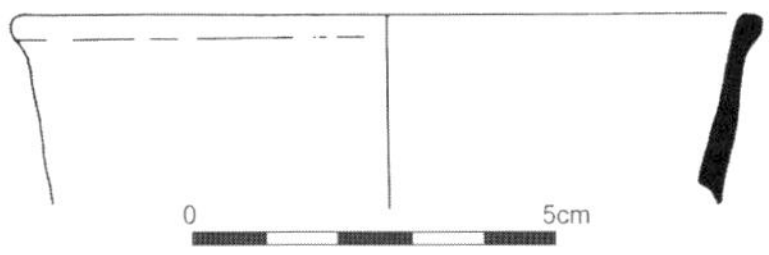

F-712

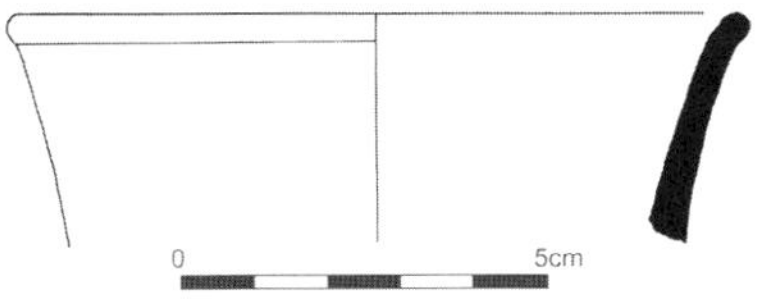

F-601

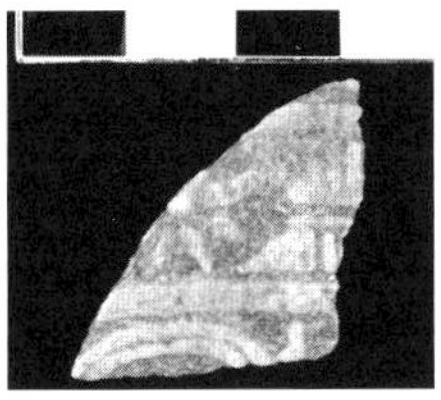

F-2124

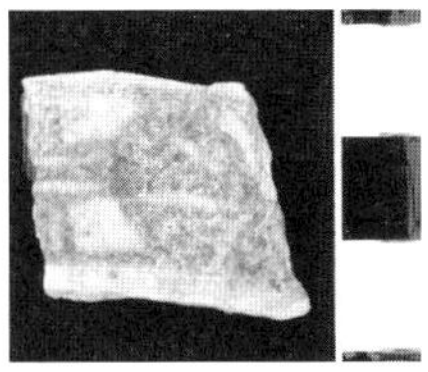

F-2184

F-2199

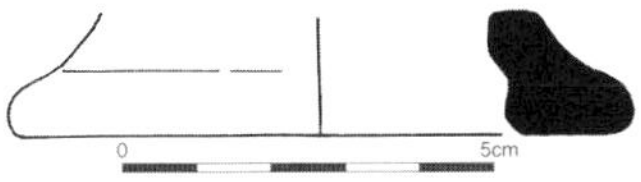

F-2171

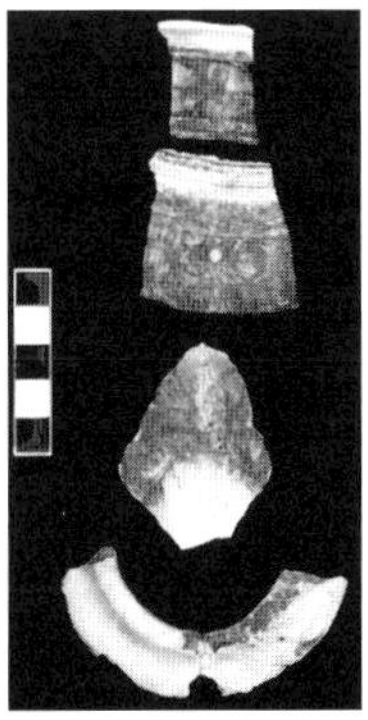

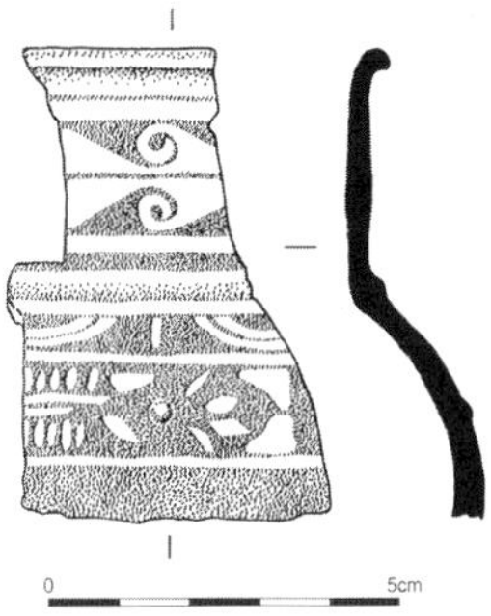

F-2174

F-2197

F-2087

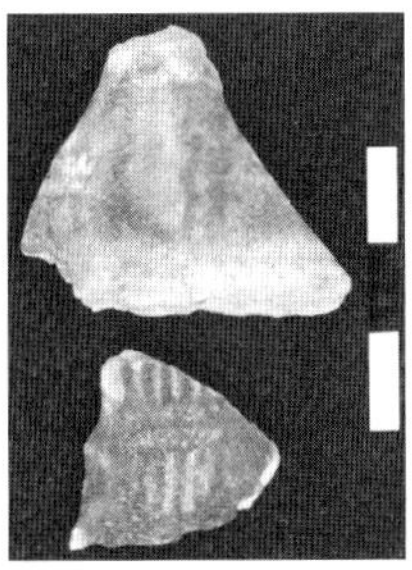

F-2100

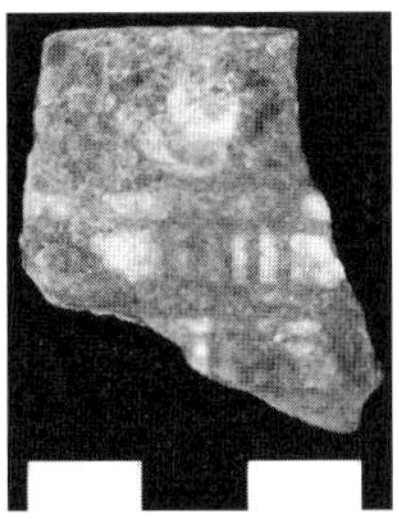

F-2158

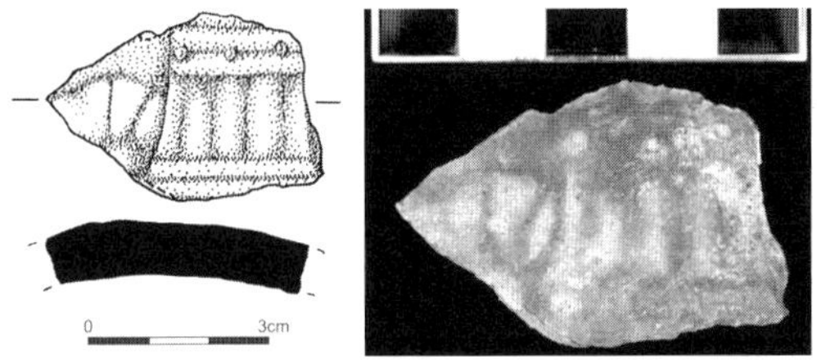

F-2090

F-2194

F-2195

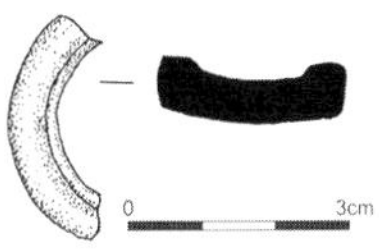

F-1437

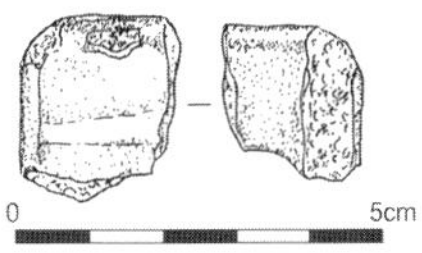

F-710

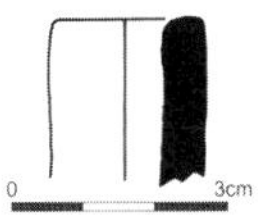

F-1714

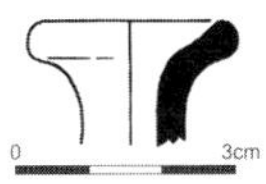

F-2133

Figure II.25

T12.2a
Find ID: 2005-F-0016 Area: HAC Trench 3 Unit 30
Material(s): Faience
Object type: Vessel
F-2098
Diameter: unknown
Rim fragment of a T12.2a bowl with inwards curving lip. Turquoise blue glaze.

Find ID: 2001-F-0070 Area: HAC Trench 3 Unit 36
Material(s): Faience
Unfinished Vessel
F-1034
Diameter: unknown
Rim fragment of an unfinished T12.2a bowl. No glaze.

Find ID: 2001-F-0080 Area: HAC Trench 3 Unit 39
Material(s): Faience
Object type: Vessel
F-1188 ***(Figure II.26)***
Diameter: 15
Rim fragment of a T12.2a bowl. Glaze worn away, small bubbles surface.

Find ID: 2005-F-0104 Area: HAC Trench 3 Unit 308
Material(s): Faience
Unfinished Vessel
F-2056 ***(Figure II.26)***
Diameter: 15
Rim fragment with inwards curving rim forming a fold. Unfinished piece: whitish paste with some open bubbles. On the internal wall, on the lower line of the fold, small holes disposed regularly 0.5cm, may be traces of a tool to create the fold.

T12.2b
Find ID: 2001-F-0059 Area: HAC Trench 3 Unit 36
Material(s): Faience
Object type: Vessel
F-755 ***(Figure II.26)***
Diameter: 10
Fragment of a thin rim with two mouldings on the internal wall belonging to a conical bowl. Turquoise blue glaze.

Find ID: 2005-F-0050 Area: HAC Trench 3 Unit 301
Material(s): Faience
Object type: Vessel
F-2181
Diameter unknown
Rim fragment of a bowl with two internal moulding under the lip. Turquoise blue glaze.

Find ID: 2001-F-0006A Area: HAC Trench 3 Unit 33
Material(s): Faience
Object type: Unfinished piece
F-1436 ***(Figure II.26)***
Diameter: 15
Rim of a bowl T12.2b. Moulded edge with groove under it.

T12.3a
Find ID: 2001-F-0070 Area: HAC Trench 3 Unit 36
Material(s): Faience
Object type: Vessel
F-1029
Diameter: 8
Out-turned rim fragment of T12.3a bowl. Bubbly turquoise glaze.

Find ID: 2001-F-0047 Area: HAC Trench 3 Unit 37
Material(s): Faience
Object type: Vessel
F-612 ***(Figure II.26)***
Diameter: unknown
Out-turned rim fragment of T12.3a bowl. Light blue glaze.

T12.3c
Find ID: 2005-F-0050 Area: HAC Trench 3 Unit 300
Material(s): Faience
Object type: Vessel
F-2172 ***(Figure II.26)***
Diameter: unknown
Everted rim fragment of a T12.3c. White glaze.

Find ID: 2005-F-0050 Area: HAC Trench 3 Unit 301
Material(s): Faience
Object type: Vessel
F-2187 ***(Figure II.26)***
Diameter: 10
Rim fragment of a T12.3c bowl. Turquoise blue glaze.

Find ID: 2002-F-0108 Area: HAC Trench 3 Unit 74
Material(s): Faience
Object type: Waster
F-1593 ***(Figure II.26)***
Diameter: 11.5 Pres. Height: 3.2
Wide rim and vertical walls of T12.3a or T12.3c. Bubbly turquoise blue glaze.

T12.3c/T12.4
Find ID: 2002-F-0108 Area: HAC Trench 3 Unit 74
Material(s): Faience
Object type: Waster
F-1581 ***(Figure II.26)***
Max. Dimension: 5
Pushed in-base with another one stuck on it of a T12.3c or T12.4 bowl. Turquoise blue glaze.

Find ID: 2002-F-0319 Area: HAC Trench 3 Unit 208
Material(s): Faience
Object type: Waster
F-1831 ***(Figure II.26)***
Base Diameter: 7
Pushed-in base and body fragment of a T12.3c or 12.4 bowl. No glaze at all on the exterior, reddish glaze and incrustations on the interior. Probable unfinished piece, left and burnt before the application of the glaze. Slag adhering to the exterior.

T12.4

Find ID: 2001-F-0017 Area: HAC Trench 3 Unit 33
Material(s): Faience
Object type: Vessel
F-437 ***(Figure II.26)***
Diameter: unknown
Rim fragment of a T12.4 bowl. Turquoise blue glaze. Two faint grooves on the interior.

Find ID: 2001-F-0116 Area: HAC Trench 3 Unit 51
Material(s): Faience and ceramic
Object type: Waster
F-1350 ***(Figure II.26)***
Max. Dimension: 4
Fragment of a annular base of a T12.4 bowl, with a ceramic cone still attached on one of the surfaces. Turquoise blue glaze.

Find ID: 2001-F-0149 Area: HAC Trench 3 Unit 52
Material(s): Faience
Object type: Waster
F-1376 ***(Figure II.26)***
Diameter: c.11-12
Two rims fragments of T12.4 bowls stuck together; piling with the moulding of the body on the rim of the inferior fragment. Turquoise blue glaze.

Find ID: 2001-F-0202 Area: HAC Trench 3 Unit 56
Material(s): Faience
Object type: Waster
F-1408-1409 ***(Figure II.27)***
Diameter: 12
Applied base of a large T12.4 bowl. Upper surface with no glaze on the contact point, lower surface with irregular glaze and traces of a cone. Turquoise blue glaze. Probably detached at the moment of the firing.

Find ID: 2001-F-0202 Area: HAC Trench 3 Unit 56
Material(s): Faience
Object type: Waster
F-1413 (+ F-1415, 17, 19-23) ***(Figure II.27)***
Diameter: 20
Rim fragment of a T12.4 bowl with part of another bowl stuck on under the moulding. Bubbly turquoise blue glaze.

Find ID: 2001-F-0338 Area: HAC Trench 3 Unit 189
Material(s): Faience
Object type: Vessel
F-1858 ***(Figure II.27)***
Diameter: 16
Rim fragment of a T12.4 bowl. Turquoise blue glaze over-fired, reddish inside and out.

Find ID: 2005-F-0002 Area: HAC Trench 3 Unit 300
Material(s): Faience
Object type: Vessel
F-2150 ***(Figure II.27)***
Diameter: 22
Rim fragment of a T12.4 bowl. Turquoise blue glaze.

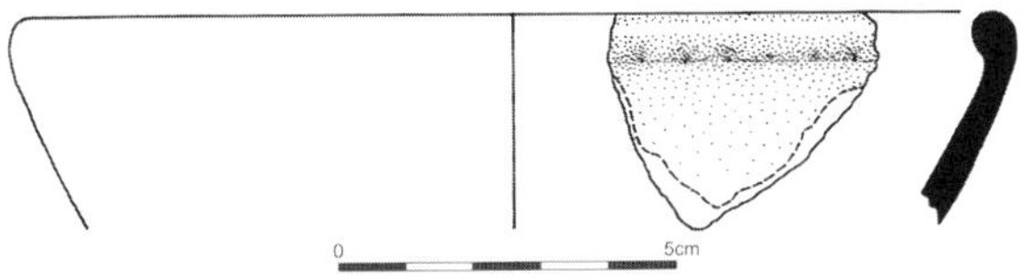

F-2056

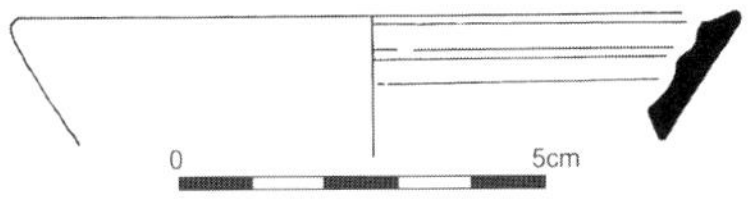
F-755

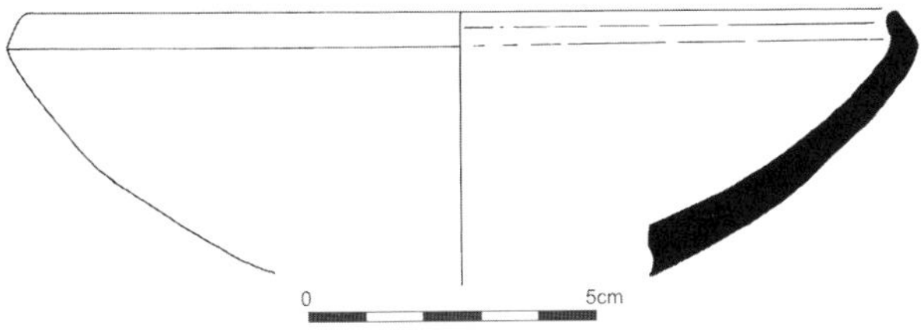
F-1188

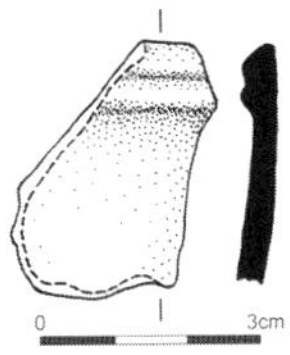
F-2181

F-1436

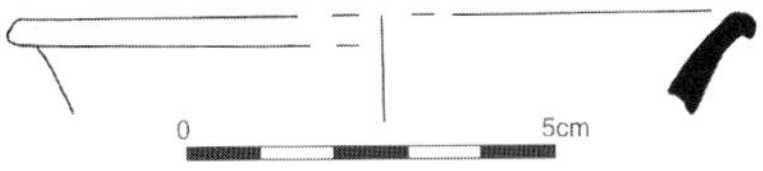
F-612

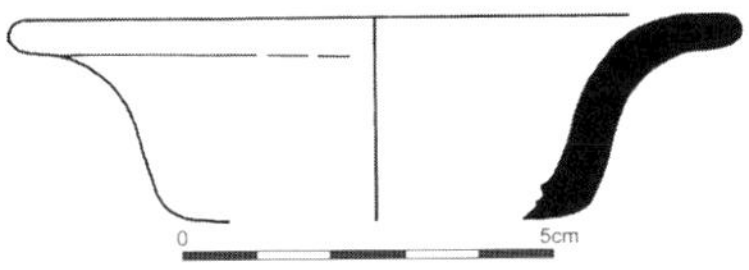
F-2187

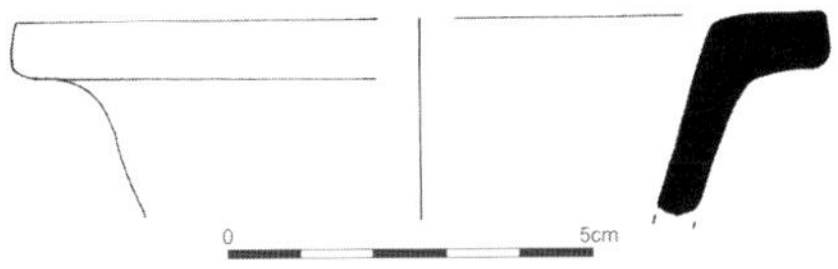
F-1593

F-2172

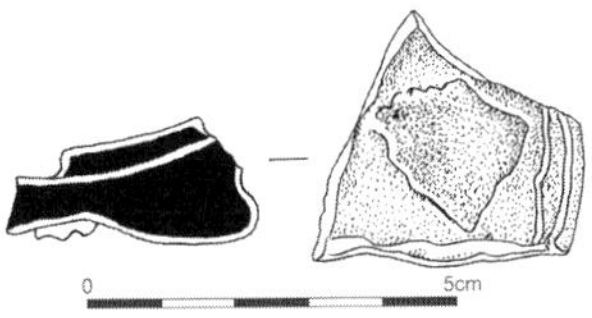
F-1581

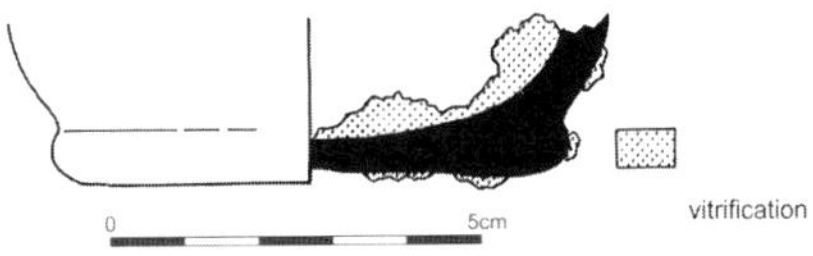

F-1831

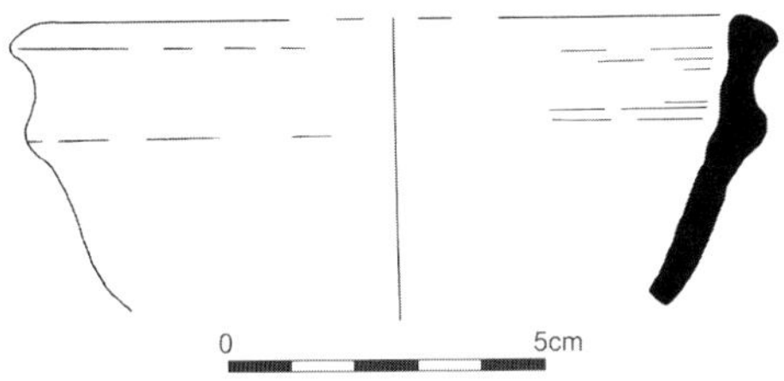
F-437

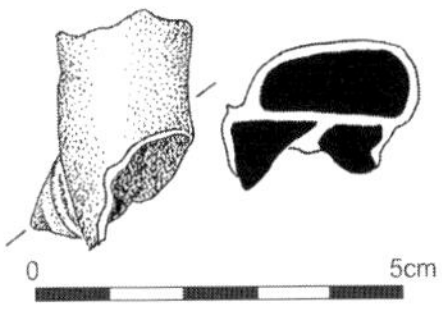
F-1350

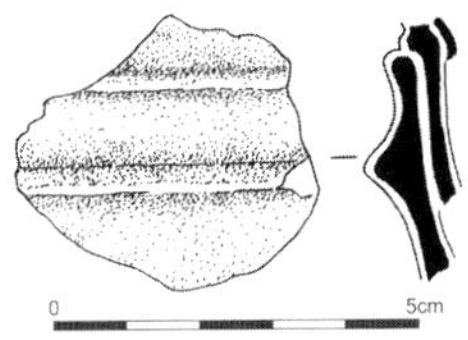
F-1376

Figure II.26

Find ID: 2005-F-0016 Area: HAC Trench 3 Unit 300
Material(s): Faience
Object type: Vessel
F-2094 ***(Figure II.27)***
Diameter: 10.8 Width: 2
Applied large annular base and bottom fragment of a T12.4 bowl. Turquoise blue glaze.

T12.7.
Find ID: 2001-F-0006 Area: HAC Trench 3 Unit 33
Material(s): Faience
Object type: Waster
F-1191 (+ 1196, 1220 1234, 1257, 1267, 1270, 1279) ***(Figure II.27)***
Diameter: 16
Two rim fragments of biconvex bowls stuck together. Moulded edge. Light blue green glaze.

Find ID: 2001-F-0006 Area: HAC Trench 3 Unit 33
Material(s): Faience
Object type: Vessel
F-405
Diameter: 10
Rim fragment of a biconvex bowl T12.7. Glaze mostly lost.

Find ID: 2001-F-0059 Area: HAC Trench 3 Unit 36
Material(s): Faience
Object type: Vessel
F-700 ***(Figure II.27)***
Diameter: 9
Rim Fragment of a T12.7 bowl with reinforced lip and carinated body. Bubbly turquoise blue glaze.

Find ID: 2001-F-0107 Area: HAC Trench 3 Unit 50
Material(s): Faience
Object type: Vessel
F-1317 ***(Figure II.27)***
Diameter: 10
Flat rim fragment of a T12.7 bowl. Turquoise blue glaze.

Find ID: 2002-F-0087 Area: HAC Trench 3 Unit 74
Material(s): Faience
Object type: Vessel
F-1557 ***(Figure II.27)***
Diameter: 8
Rim fragment of a small biconvex bowl. Moulded lip. Turquoise blue glaze.

T13.2
Find ID: 2001-F-0006 Area: HAC Trench 3 Unit 33
Material(s): Faience
Object type: Vessel
F-409 ***(Figure II.27)***
Diameter: 16
Flat rim fragment of a plate T13.2. Turquoise blue glaze gone reddish.

Find ID: 2002-F-0338 Area: HAC Trench 3 Unit 189
Material(s): Faience
Object type: Vessel
F-1835 ***(Figure II.27)***
Diameter: 19
Rim fragment of a T13.2 plate. Bubbly turquoise blue glaze turned whitish.

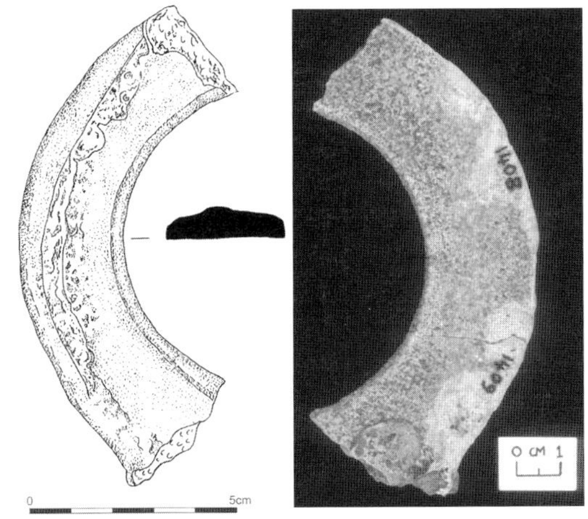

F-1408/1409

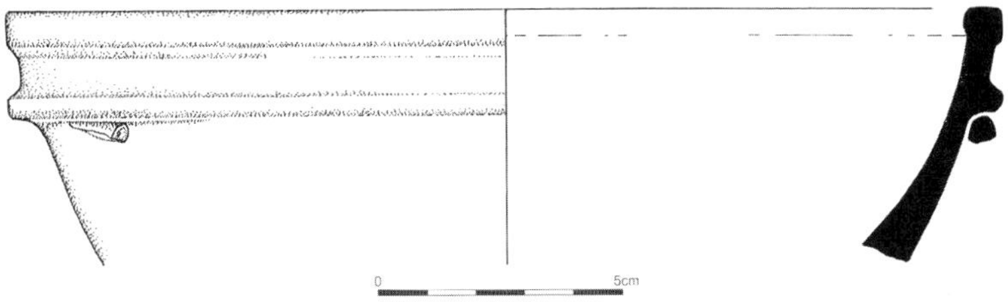

F-1413

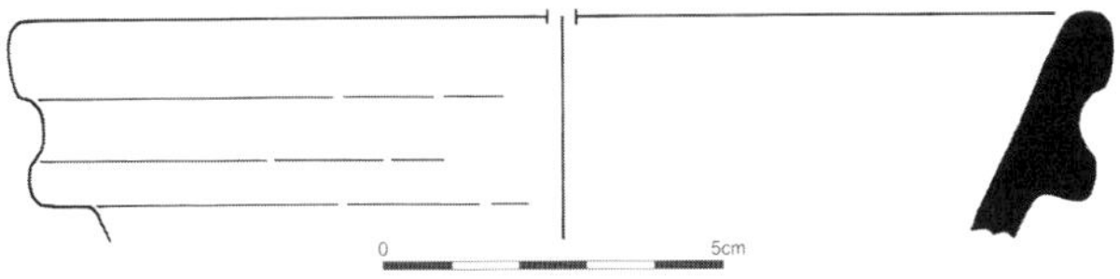

F-1858

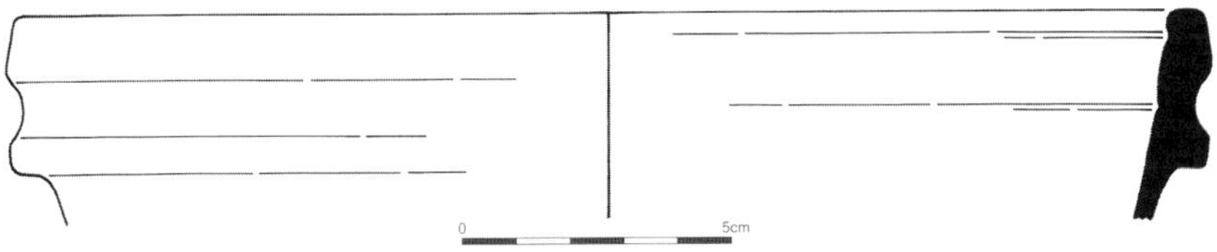

F-2150

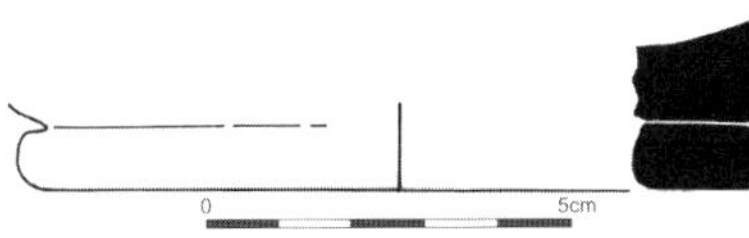

F-2094

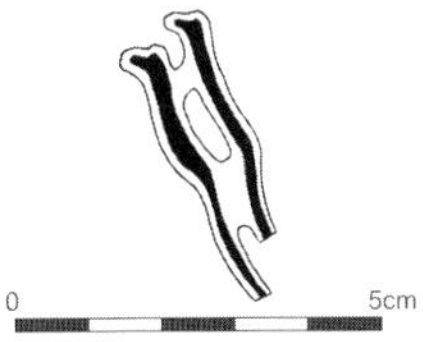

F-1191

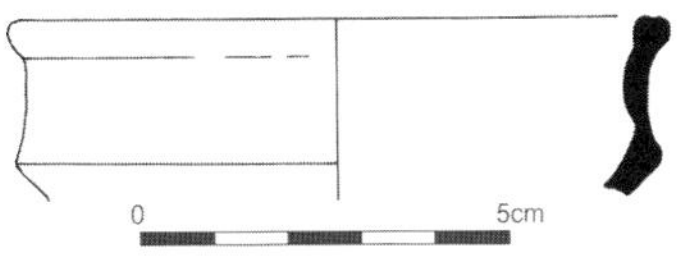

F-700

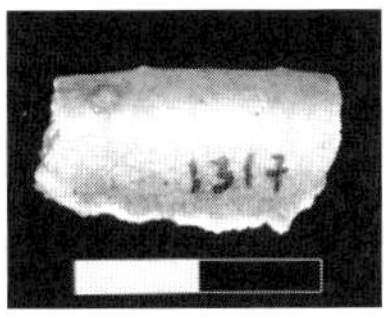

F-1317

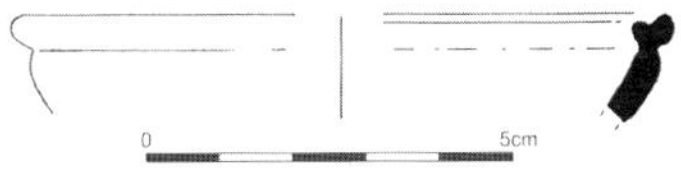

F-1557

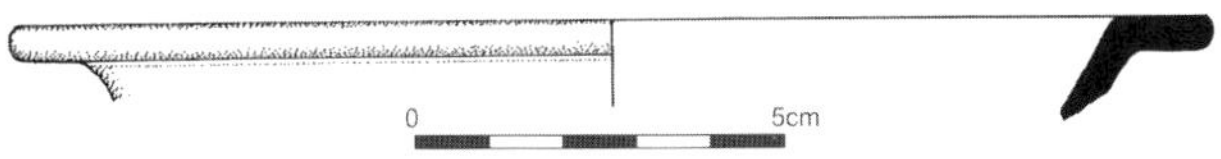

F-409

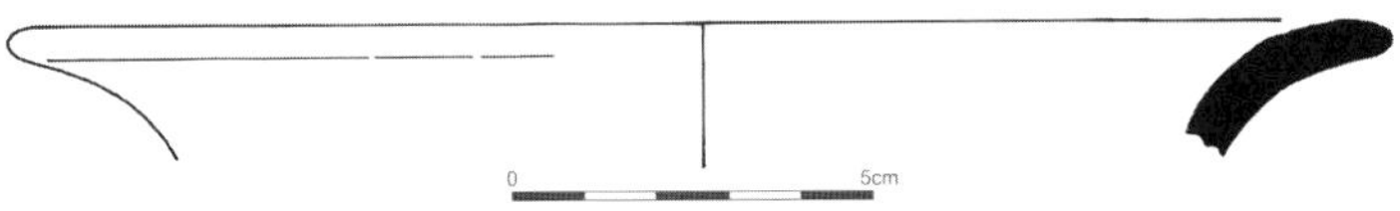

F-1835

F-1945

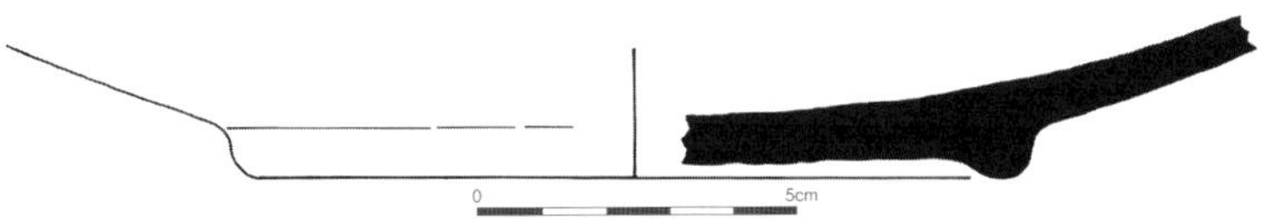

F-2030

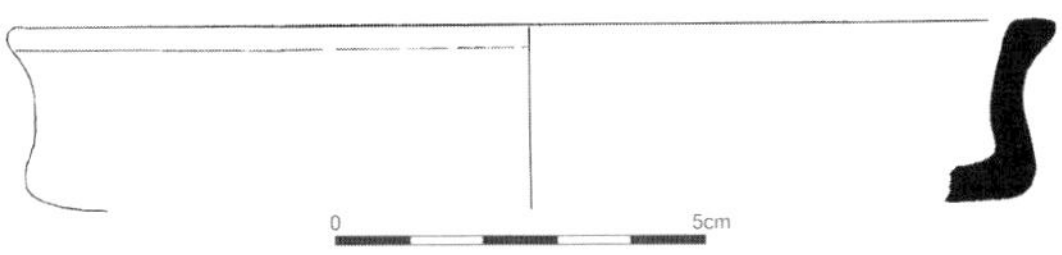

F-1375

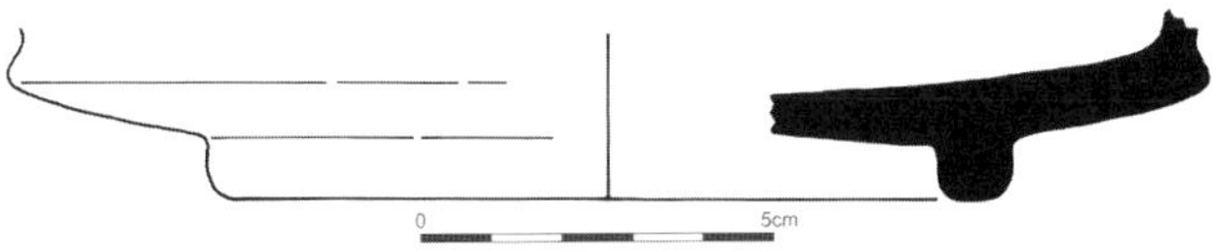

F-1862

Figure II.27

Find ID: 2002-F-0445 Area: HAC Trench 3 Unit 238
Material(s): Faience
Object type: Waster
F-1945 ***(Figure II.27)***
Base diameter: 12
Bottom and body fragment of a T13.2 plate of which the glaze has been reduced to a wavy surface with bubbles. Pointed extremity of the cone still in place on the internal wall; ceramic powder coming from it and splitting around.

Find ID: 2005-F-0155 Area: HAC Trench 3 Unit 308
Material(s): Faience
Object type: Waster
F-2030 ***(Figure II.27)***
Base diameter: 12
Body and bottom fragment with annular base of a T13.2 plate. Turquoise blue glaze. Remains of the cylindrical part of a cone on the bottom.

T13.3a
Find ID: 2001-F-0149 Area: HAC Trench 3 Unit 52
Material(s): Faience
Object type: Vessel
F-1375 ***(Figure II.27)***
Diameter: 14.5
Rim fragment of a T13.3 plate (thin walls). Decayed turquoise blue glaze.

Find ID: 2002-F-0383 Area: HAC Trench 3 Unit 74
Material(s): Faience
Object type: Vessel
F-1862 ***(Figure II.27)***
Base Diameter: 11
Lower body fragment with ring-base of a T13.3a plate. Turquoise blue glaze.

Find ID: 2002-F-0161 Area: HAC Trench 3 Unit 80
Material(s): Faience
Object type: Waster
F-1654 ***(Figure II.28)***
Base diameter: 13
Bottom and body fragment with annular base of a T13.3a plate, covered with deformed glaze and ashes.

T13.3b
Find ID: 2005-F-0002 Area: HAC Trench 3 Unit 300
Material(s): Faience
Object type: Vessel
F-2198 ***(Figure II.28)***
Max. dimension: 5
Body fragment of a T13.3b plate. Exterior glaze white; interior glaze violet and turquoise blue. Decoration: large rosette with rounded petals turquoise blue on a violet backing. Conical point of the ceramic cone still adhering.

T13
Find ID: 2002-F-0265 Area: HAC Trench 3 Unit 208
Material(s): Faience
Object type: Waster
F-1789 ***(Figure II.28)***
Max. Dimension: 7.5 Base diameter: 13
Waster composed of the bottom of a plate T13.2 or T13.3 with annular base and a fragment of a unspecified vessel stuck on it. Faience completely turned blackish with ash-like appearance, glaze turned red.

T14.1
Find ID: 2005-F-0035 Area: HAC Trench 3 Unit 306
Material(s): Faience
Object type: Waster
Max. Dimensions: 6 x 3 Pres. Height 2.5
F-2044 ***(Figure II.28)***
Waster of a rectangular tray T14.1 (one angle preserved) with extraneous element stuck on it. Turquoise blue glaze.

T14.4
Find ID: 2001-F-0059 Area: HAC Trench 3 Unit 36
Material(s): Faience
Object type: Vessel
F-682 ***(Figure II.28)***
Base diameter: 32.5 Max. Thickness: 3.
Part of the body with annular squarish base of a big tray T14.4. Turquoise blue glaze.

T14
Find ID: 2005-F-0155 Area: HAC Trench 3 Unit 308
Material(s): Faience
Object type: Vessel
F-2035 ***(Figure II.28)***
Max. Dimension: 2.5
Fragment of the wall of a tray with a circular hole. Decayed turquoise blue faience.

T19
Find ID: 2002-F-0443 Area: HAC Trench 3 Unit 189
Material(s): Faience
Object type: Vessel
F-1944 ***(Figure II.28)***
External Diameter: 14.5 Internal diameter 8.3 Height: 6
Wide flat rim and cylindrical neck of a T19 vase. Rim bearing the traces of two ribbon handles (3-3.5). The surrounding of the neck is in relief. Cylindrical neck quite low. Turquoise blue glaze everywhere but over-burnt on the exterior and turned to black. The glaze is everywhere even in the contact zone with the shoulder which could mean that neck and body were fired separately or that body and neck separated during the firing.

T19.3
Find ID: 2001-F-0006 Area: HAC Trench 3 Unit 33
Material(s): Faience
Object type: Vessel
F- 406 ***(Figure II.28)***
Pres. Height: 3.5
Lower part of the body fragment of a T19.3 vase with moulded decoration mostly worn out. Calyx of plain nelumbo leaves merging from a diamond backing. Glaze worn away.

Find ID: 2001-F-0139 Area: HAC Trench 3 Unit 34
Material(s): Faience
Object type: Vessel
F-1373 ***(Figure II.28)***
Diameter: c.10
Rim fragment of the large amphora type T19.3. Turquoise blue glaze, the two grooves on the superior part of the fragment are deep blue.

Find ID: 2001-F-0059 Area: HAC Trench 3 Unit 36
Material(s): Faience
Object type: Vessel
F-696 ***(Figure II.28)***
Pres. Height: 2.3
Fragment of the upper part of handle of a vase T19.3. Turquoise blue glaze.

Find ID: 2005-F-0002 Area: HAC Trench 3 Unit 300
Material(s): Faience
Object type: Vessel
F-2125 ***(Figure II.28)***
Max. Dimension: 2.5
Body fragment of a T19.3 vase. Turquoise blue glaze. Row of squares between two lines, diamond pattern.

T16.1/T20.1
Find ID: 2001-F-0017 Area: HAC Trench 3 Unit 33
Material(s): Faience
Object type: Waster
F-451 ***(Figure II.28)***
Max. Dimension: 3
Two fragments of vessels fused together : part of the neck of T20.1 vase with decor of ivy.

Find ID: 2001-F-0059 Area: HAC Trench 3 Unit 36
Material(s): Faience
Object type: Vessel
F-691 ***(Figure II.28)***
Maximum Dimension: 4.2.
Deformed body fragment of a moulded decoration belonging to T16.1 or T20.1 type. Vegetal decoration. In the centre, sort of a pomegranate surrounded by a plant with circular leaves on the left, and on the right by thin leaves with nervures.

Find ID: 2001-F-0059 Area: HAC Trench 3 Unit 36
Material(s): Faience
Object type: Vessel
F-758 ***(Figure II.28)***
Max. Dimension: 2
Body fragment of a moulded vase, with the decor of two small grapes T16.1 or T20.1 type. Light bluish-green glaze on the exterior, light blue glaze on the interior.

Find ID: 2002-F-0492 Area: HAC Trench 3 Unit 244
Material(s): Faience
Object type: Vessel
F-1997 + F-2001 ***(Figure II.28)***
Max. Dimension: 2 Thickness: 0.5
Two body fragments joining of a T16.1 goblet or a T20.1 vase. Greenish and yellow glaze. From two vegetal motifs, wheat on the left and pomegranate on the right, comes a flower with two long petals.

Find ID: 2005-F-0104 Area: HAC Trench 3 Unit 308
Material(s): Faience
Object type: Vessel
F-2192-F-2193 ***(Figure II.28)***
Maximum Dimensions: F-2192: 2.3; F-2193 : 2
Two body fragments of a T16.1 goblet or T20.1 vase. Greenish and bluish glaze on exterior. Turquoise blue glaze on interior. Ivy cordiform leaf on both fragments.

Find ID: 2005-F-0198 Area: HAC Trench 3 Unit 309
Material(s): Faience
Object type: Vessel
F-2196 ***(Figure II.28)***
Max. Dimension: 1.5
Body fragment of a T16.1 goblet or T20.1 vase. Greenish yellow faience. Vegetal decoration.

T22.4
Find ID: 2001-F-0059 Area: HAC Trench 3 Unit 36
Material(s): Faience
Object type: Vessel
F-720 ***(Figure II.28)***
Diameter: 8
Rim fragment of a lid (?) : decor of a volute ending in a relief dot. Turquoise blue glaze.

Find ID: 2002-F-0108 Area: HAC Trench 3 Unit 74
Material(s): Faience
Object type: Waster
F-1592 ***(Figure II.29)***
Max. Dimension: 2 Diameter: unknown.
Conical lid with lower projection. Turquoise blue glaze.
.
Find ID: 2002-F-0280 Area: HAC Trench 3 Unit 77
Material(s): Faience
Object type: Vessel
F-1816 ***(Figure II.29)***
Diameter: 7.7
Flat lid. Light blue glaze. Inferior surface flat, small hole under the handle, probably to help to fix the handle. The upper surface has a groove 5mm from the lip. Semi-circular applied handle with tongs on both sides.

Wasters belonging to unspecified types of vessel

Find ID: 2002-F-0108 Area: HAC Trench 3 Unit 74
Material(s): Faience
Object type: Waster
F-1596 ***(Figure II.29)***
Width: 2.
Fragment of applied base with cone still attached on and vitrified

Find ID: 2005-F-0035 Area: HAC Trench 3 Unit 306
Material(s): Faience
Object type: Waster
F-2045 ***(Figure II.29)***
Max. Dimensions: 5.5 x 4.5
Waster of an unspecified open form, probably a bowl. Two pieces stuck together. Turquoise blue glaze.

Find ID: 2005-F-0104 Area: HAC Trench 3 Unit 308
Material(s): Faience
Object type: Waster
F-2057 ***(Figure II.29)***
Block (Height: 3.5) of glaze applied to a body fragment of a plate (Height: 4.5; Thickness: 1).

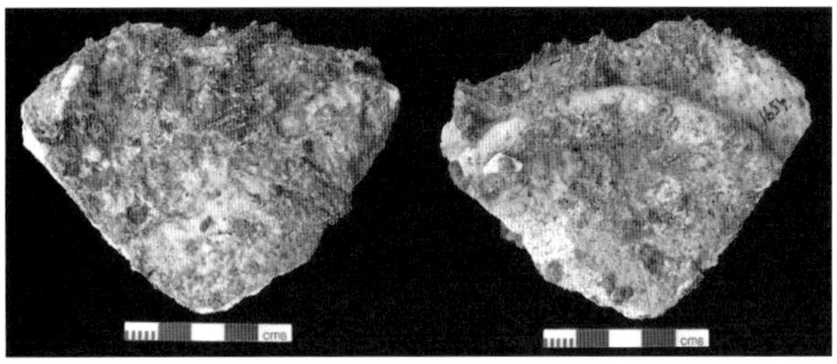
F-1654

F-2198

F-1789

F-2044

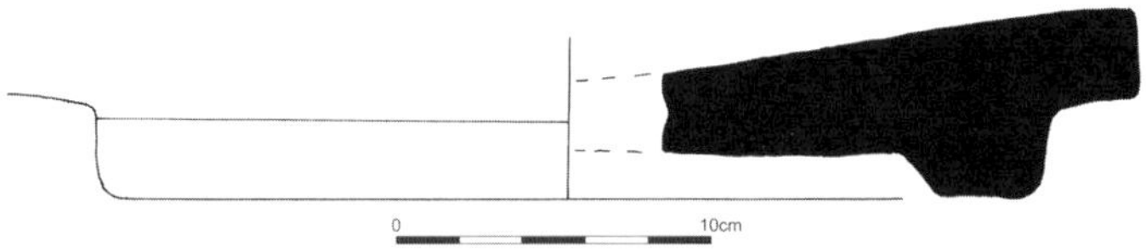
F-682

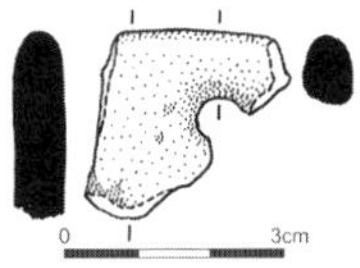
F-2035

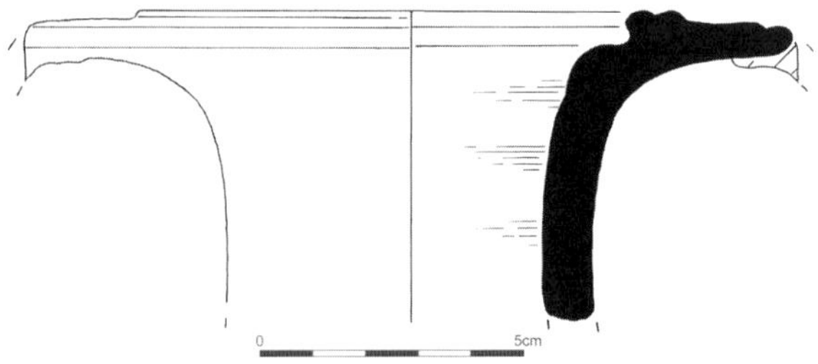
F-1944

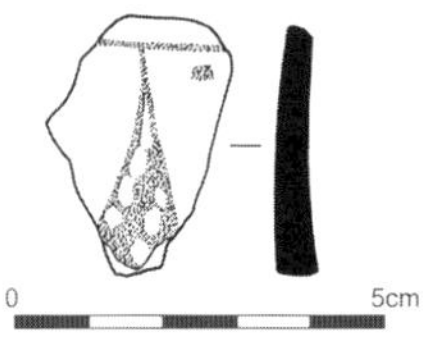
F-406

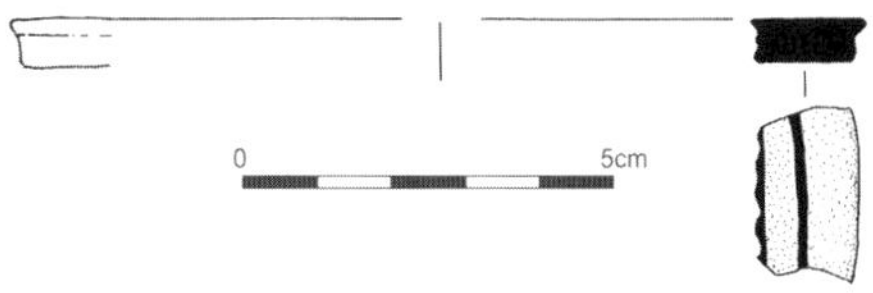
F-1373

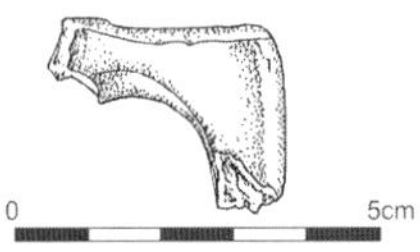
F-696

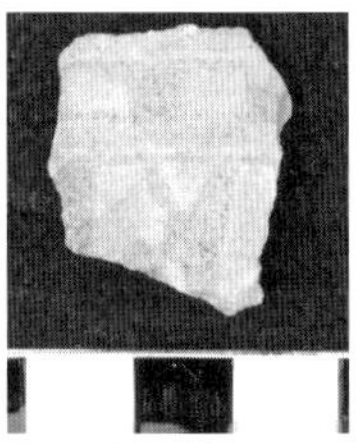
F-2125

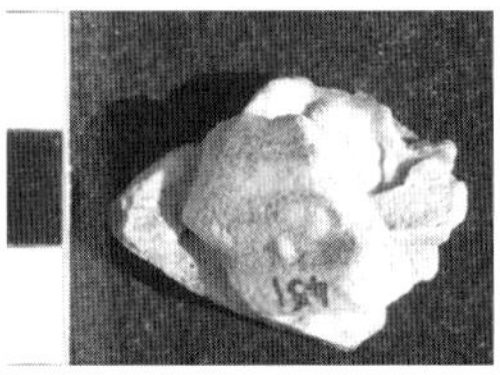
F-451

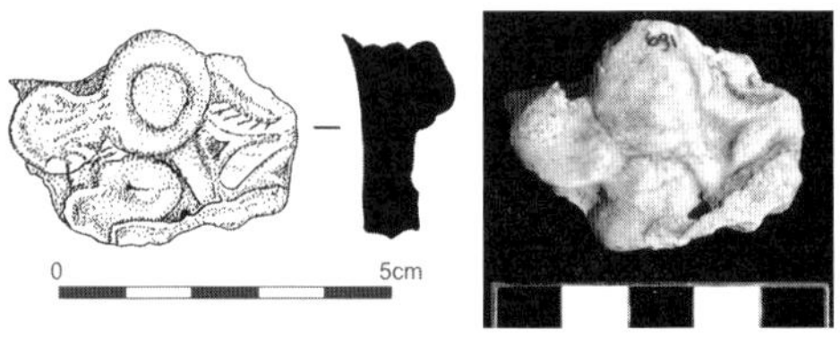
F-691

F-758

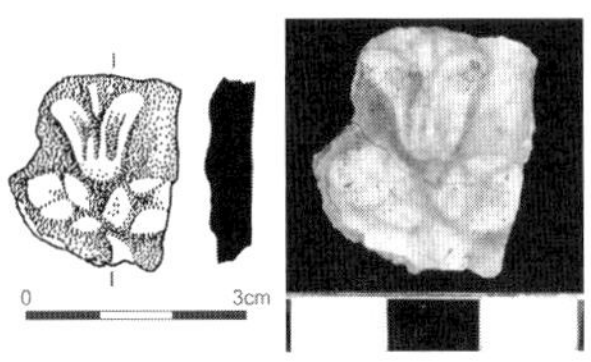
F-1997

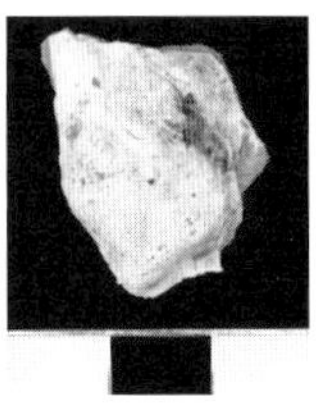
F-2192

F-2196

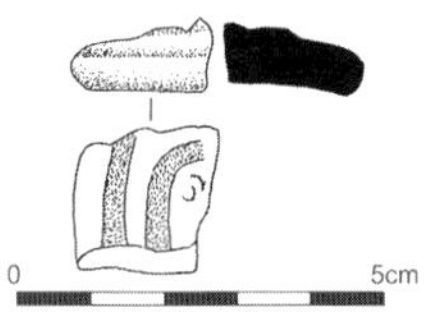
F-720

Figure II.28

Vessels of unknown types

Find ID: 2001-F-0059 Area: HAC Trench 3 Unit 36
Material(s): Faience
Object type: Vessel
F-755 ***(Figure II.29)***
Diameter: 10
Fragment of a thin rim with two mouldings on the internal wall belonging to a conical bowl. Turquoise blue glaze.

Find ID: 2005-F-0050 Area: HAC Trench 3 Unit 301
Material(s): Faience
Object type: Vessel
F-2179 ***(Figure II.29)***
Diameter unknown
Rim fragment of a big flat plate slightly going up. Turquoise blue glaze.

Find ID: 2005-F-0050 Area: HAC Trench 3 Unit 301
Material(s): Faience
Object type: Vessel
F-2183 ***(Figure II.29)***
Diameter unknown
Rounded rim fragment of a big tray. White glaze on the exterior, white and violet glaze on the interior. Ivy and berries incised.

Furniture

Lamp

Find ID: 2005-F-0050 Area: HAC Trench 3 Unit 301
Material(s): Faience
Object type: Lamp
F-2186 ***(Figure II.29)***
Max. Dimension: 4
Side body fragment of a lamp. Side is without decor, top with moulded decoration: part of the volute? Turquoise blue glaze.

Boxes (?)

Find ID: 2001-F-0047 Area: HAC Trench 3 Unit 33
Material(s): Faience
Furniture
F-600 ***(Figure II.29)***
Dimensions: 4 x 2
Part of a box (?) showing on the front side a row of lotus buds. The back is not glazed.

Find ID: 2005-F-0035 Area: HAC Trench 3 Unit 306
Material(s): Faience
Object type: Vessel or furniture
F-2036 ***(Figure II.29)***
Pres. Height: 1.4
Bottom and body fragment of a box. Flat base. Vertical walls with decor of eggs and darts. Turquoise blue glaze for the interior and the parts in relief in the decor, deep blue glaze for the parts in recess.

Figurines

Find ID: 2001-F-0107 Area: HAC Trench 3 Unit 50
Material(s): Faience
Object type: Figurine
F-1305 ***(Figure II.29)***
Max. Dimensions: 6.6 x6.
Fragment of a hollow figurine, may be a sphinx, a dog or a Bes. On the front, mane (?) on the back rounded part. Blue turquoise glaze.

Find ID: 2001-F-0116 Area: HAC Trench 3 Unit 51
Material(s): Faience
Figurine
F-1348 ***(Figure II.29)***
Height: 7.8
Forearm and arm belonging to a big masculine figurine (solid). Whitish glaze.

Find ID: 2002-F-0139 Area: HAC Trench 3 Unit 74
Material(s): Faience
Object type: Figurine
F-1616 ***(Figure II.29 and Colour Plate 6)***
Pres. Height: 5.5 Thickness: 1 to 1.3
Fragment of a hollow figurine of Serapis preserving only part of the head. Very neatly moulded piece, particularly in the details of the hair and the beard. Beige fabric, light blue glaze, partly decayed. Four waves of hair on the right temple which end in twists, on the top of the head, a circle in relief which may belong to the calathos. Big eye widely opened and cheek in relief. Triangular moustache and small mouth. Oval beard with locks. The internal surface is smooth and regular.

Find ID: 2005-F-0140 Area: HAC Trench 3 Unit 306
Material(s): Faience
Object type: Figurine
F-2046 ***(Figure II.30)***
Pres. Height: 3 Max. Dimension base: 3.5
Lower part of a feminine figurine with a long dress making folds or fragment of the paw of an animal. Light blue glaze. Oval base.

Find ID: 2005-F-0084 Area: HAC Trench 3 Unit 307
Material(s): Faience
Object type: Figurine
F-2191 ***(Figure II.30)***
Height: 7 Width of the pillar: 5 Thickness: 3
Lower part of a figurine of a standing Bes, standing on a back pillar. The two legs and the left hand coming on the left are visible. Turquoise blue glaze on the front, light blue glaze for the dorsal pillar.

Amulets

Find ID: 2002-F-0015 Area: HAC Trench 3 Unit 65
Material(s): Faience
Object type: Amulet
F-1486 ***(Figure II.30)***
Pres. Height 0.5
Upper part of a miniature bead of a standing Bes. Light green glaze. Upper half is preserved with head, beginning of the crown and perforation.

Find ID: 2002-F-0029 Area: HAC Trench 3 Unit 65
Material(s): Faience
Object type: Amulet
F-1518 ***(Figure II.30)***

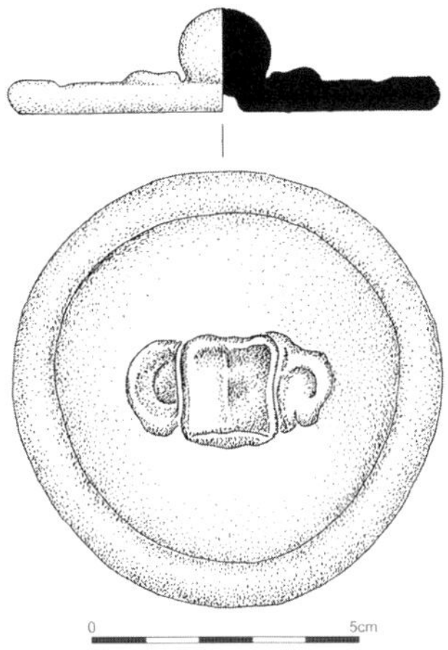

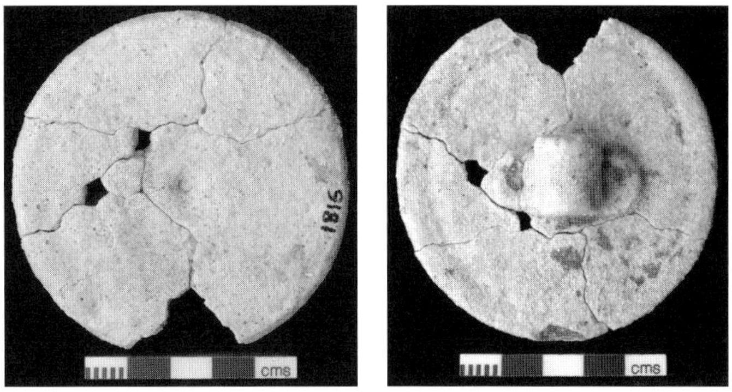

F-1816

F-1592

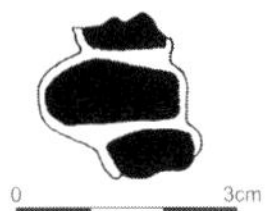

F-1596

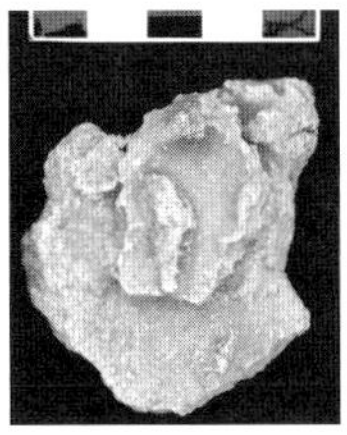

F-2045

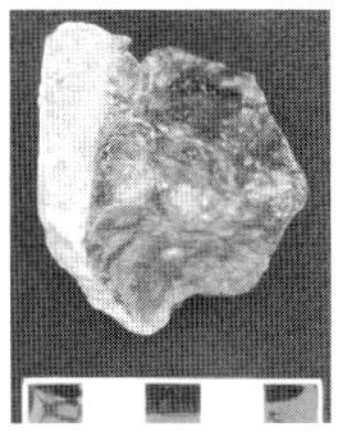

F-2057

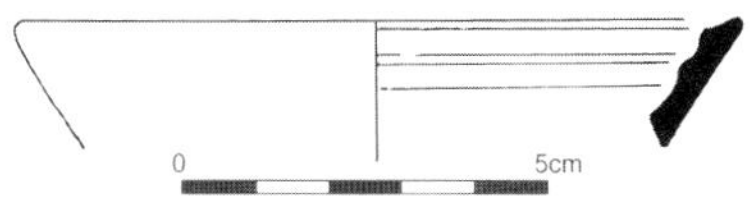

F-755

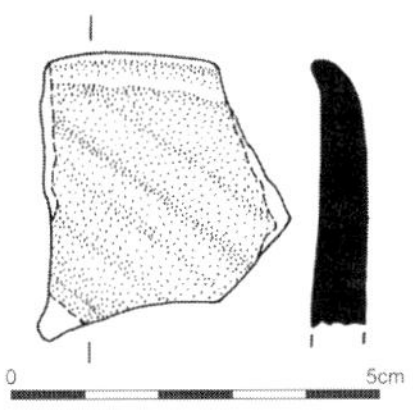

F-2179

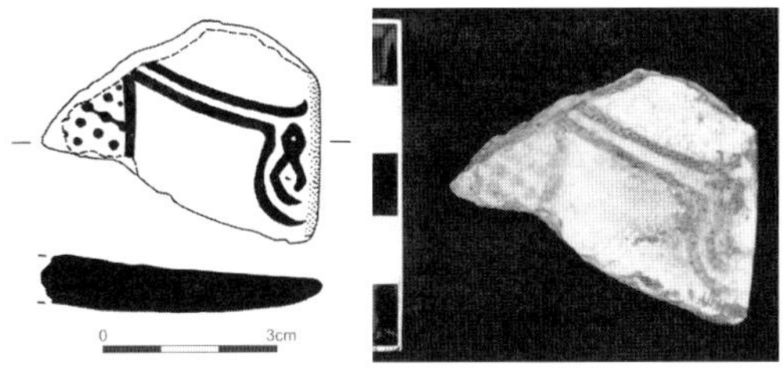

F-2183

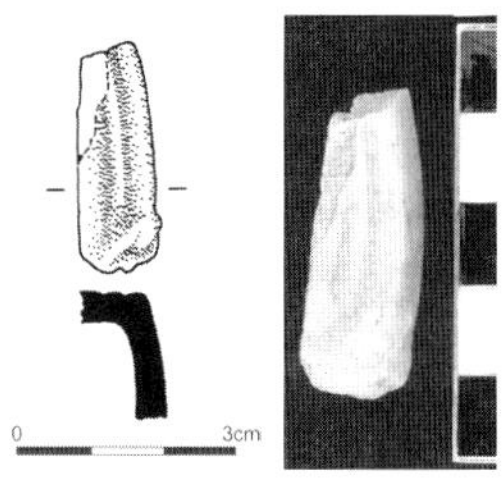

F-2186

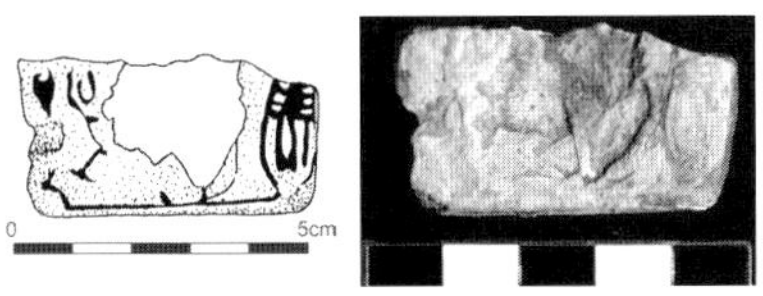

F-600

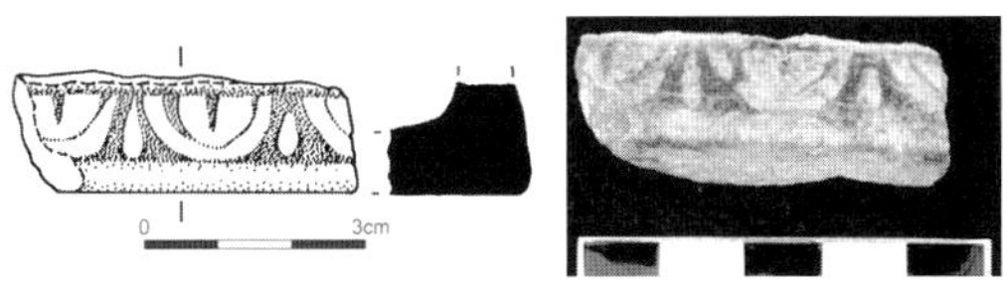

F-2036

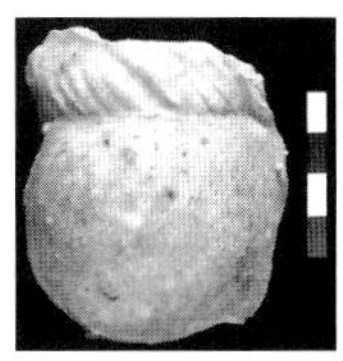

F-1305

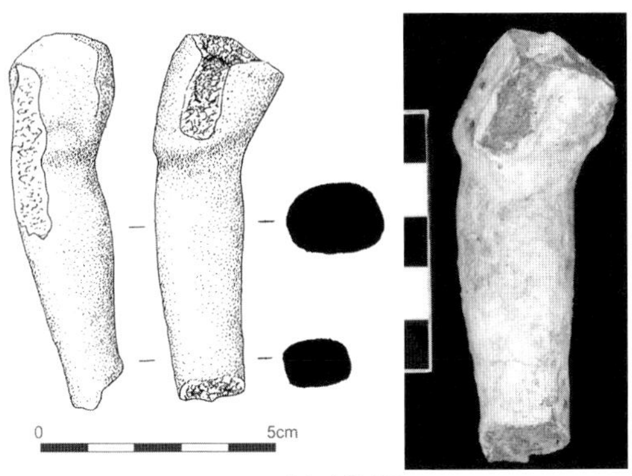

F-1348

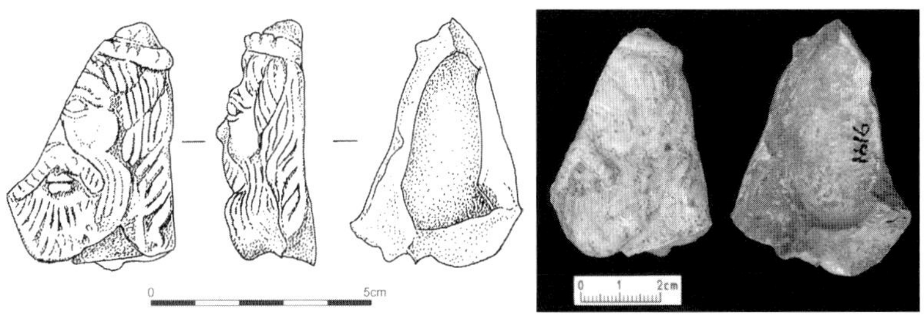

F-1616

Figure II.29

Pres. Height: 1.6 Dim. of base 1,3 x 0.6
Lower part of a amulet of a seating deity with legs and feet clasped together on the base. Light blue glaze mostly worn out.

Find ID: 2002-F-0272 Area: HAC Trench 3 Unit 189
Material(s): Faience
Object type: Amulet
F-1791 ***(Figure II.30)***
Pres. Height: 1.2
Inferior part of an Isis Lactans amulet. Sitting on a stool decorated with incised hexagons, legs are separated from the stool. The legs of the child Horus are visible. Rectangular base. Light blue glaze.

Find ID: 2002-F-0285 Area: HAC Trench 3 Unit 189
Material(s): Faience
Object type: Amulet
F-1826 ***(Figure II.30)***
Pres. Height: 1.5
Inferior part of a seated deity. The figure is seated on a stool, no special decor on the piece. Small rectangular pedestal and back pillar.

Find ID: 2002-F-0338 Area: HAC Trench 3 Unit 189
Material(s): Faience
Object type: Amulet
F-1852 ***(Figure II.30)***
Height: 4 Pedestal dimension: 1.3 x 0.8.
Amulet of Thot standing very schematic against the back pillar. Back pillar pierced from suspension. Over-fired object, glaze has turned Bordeaux-red.

Find ID: 2002-F-0404 Area: HAC Trench 3 Unit 231
Material(s): Faience
Object type: Amulet
F-1900 ***(Figure II.30)***
Height: 1 Pedestal dimension 0.8 x 0.5
Bead-amulet representing a griffin, seated on his back legs, loop suspension on the back. H. 1; pedestal 0.8 on 0.5.

Beads

Find ID: 2001-F-**0006** Area: HAC Trench 3 Unit 33
Material(s): Faience
Object type: Bead
F-435 ***(Figure II.30)***
Length: 1.5 Width: 1.25 Max. Thickness: 0.3
Flat oval bead with cut edge. Light blue glaze. Horizontal suspension canal.

Find ID: 2001-F-0070 Area: HAC Trench 3 Unit 36
Material(s): Faience
Object type: Bead
F-1022
Diameter: 0.4 Thickness: 0.15
Cylindrical miniature bead. Glaze worn out.

Find ID: 2002-F-0443 Area: HAC Trench 3 Unit 189
Material(s): Faience
Object type: Bead
F-1941 ***(Figure II.30)***
Length: 1.5
Part of a cylindrical bead with six rows of crenulations. Glaze almost vanished.

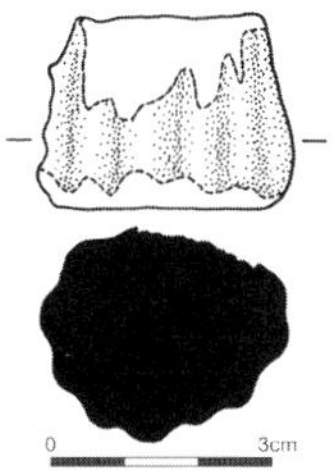

F-2046

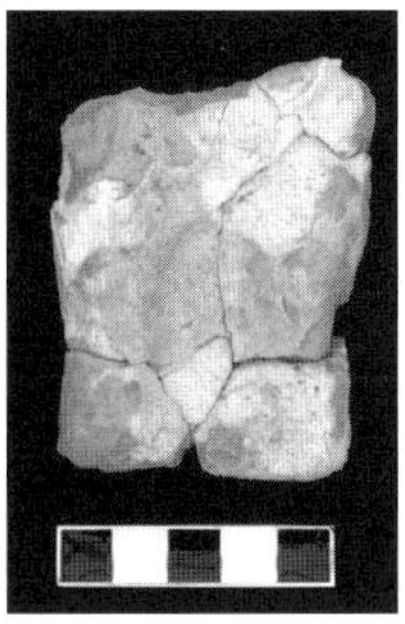

F-2191

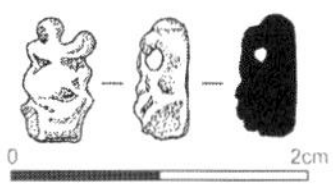

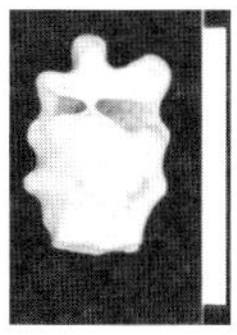

F-1486

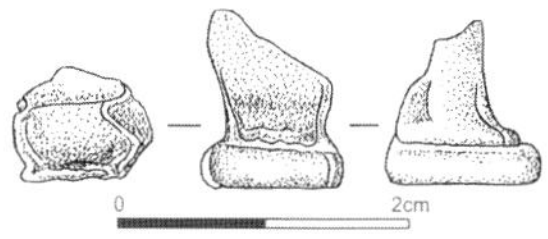

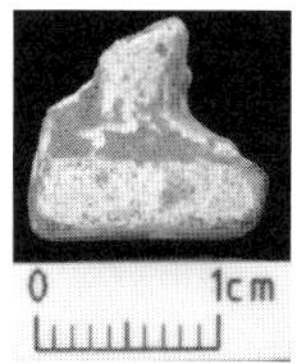

F-1518

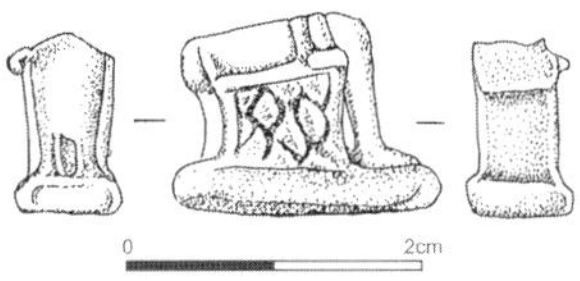

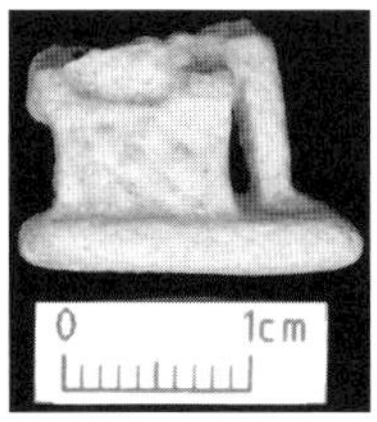

F-1791

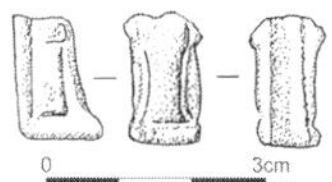

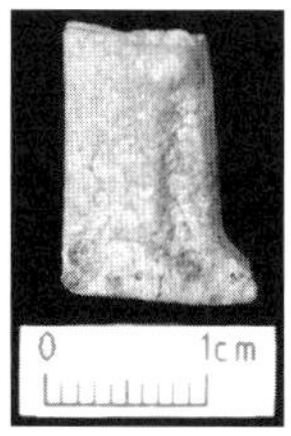

F-1826

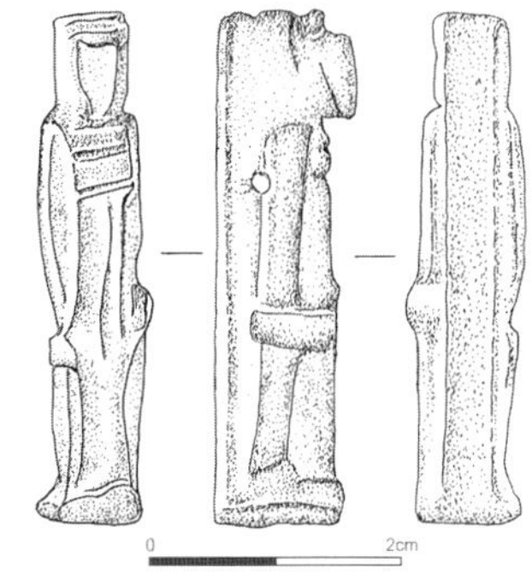

F-1852

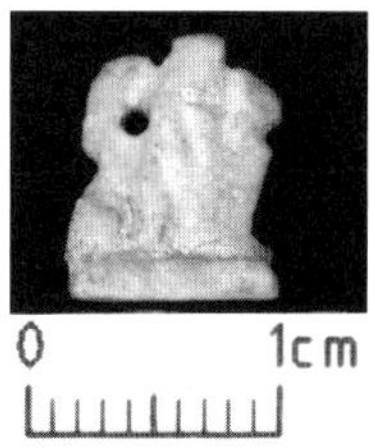

F-1900

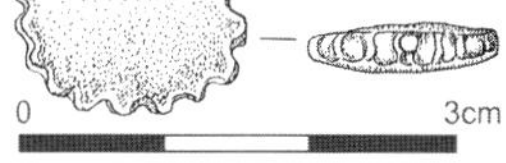

F-435

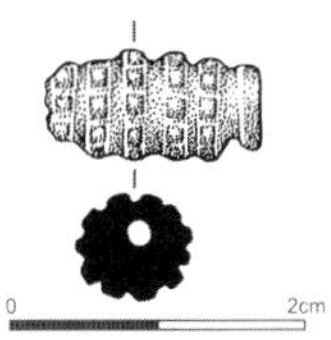

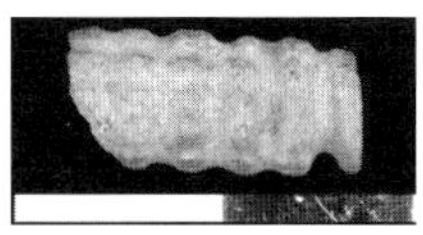

F-1941

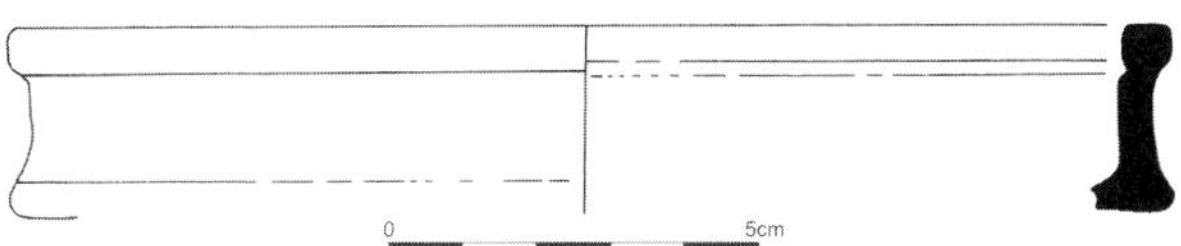

F-164

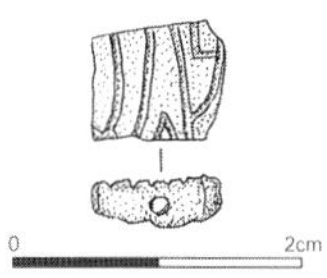

F-1370

Figure II.30

HAD

Find ID: 2000-F-0261 Area: HAD Trench 1 Unit 17
Material(s): Faience
Object type: Vessel
F-164 ***(Figure II.30)***
Diameter: 16.
Rim fragment of a T13.3A plate. Turquoise blue glaze.

Find ID: 2001-F-0129 Area: HAD Trench 2 Unit 131
Material(s): Faience
Object type: Bead
F-1370 ***(Figure II.30)***
Max. Diameter: 1. Dim. max. 1.4; diameter: 0.6
Bead fragment. Incised (?) decoration of triangular leaves.

Find ID: 2001-F-0207 Area: HAD Trench 2 Unit 133
Material(s): Faience
Object type: Bead
F-1411
Diameter: 0.4, th. 0.15
Miniature cylindrical bead. Turquoise blue glaze.

Surface finds

T3.2
Find ID:SF-0004
Faience
Unfinished vessel.
Y-5 ***(Figure II.31)***
Max. Dimension: 2
Base fragment with annular base-ring of a shallow bowl, may be adorned with recumbent lions (T3.2). Decor of a rosette on the internal wall. The fragment shows no trace of glaze at all and seems to be an unfinished vessel, broken before glazing.

T13
Find ID: 2001-F-0002 SF
Faience
Vessel
F-538 ***(Figure II.31)***
Base Diameter: 10,5.
Fragment of the lower part of the body of a plate with annular base. Glaze worn out. Two concentric grooves still containing light blue glaze.

T14.1
Find ID: 2000-F- 0002 SF
Faience
Vessel
F-58 ***(Figure II.31)***
Height: 2,1
Rim fragment of a rectangular tray T14.1 with one angle. Turquoise blue glaze.

T19
Find ID: 2001-F-0003 SF
Faience
Vessel

F-537 ***(Figure II.31)***
Max. Height: 4
Surface find. Deformed fragment of a big and thick closed vase with incised vegetal decoration (?)Bubbly greenish glaze.

Furniture

Find ID:2002-F-0003 HAC SF
Faience
Furniture
F-1459
Diameter: 6 Pres. H. 3,8.
Fragment of a drumshaft , central orifice not preserved. White core, grey blue glaze.

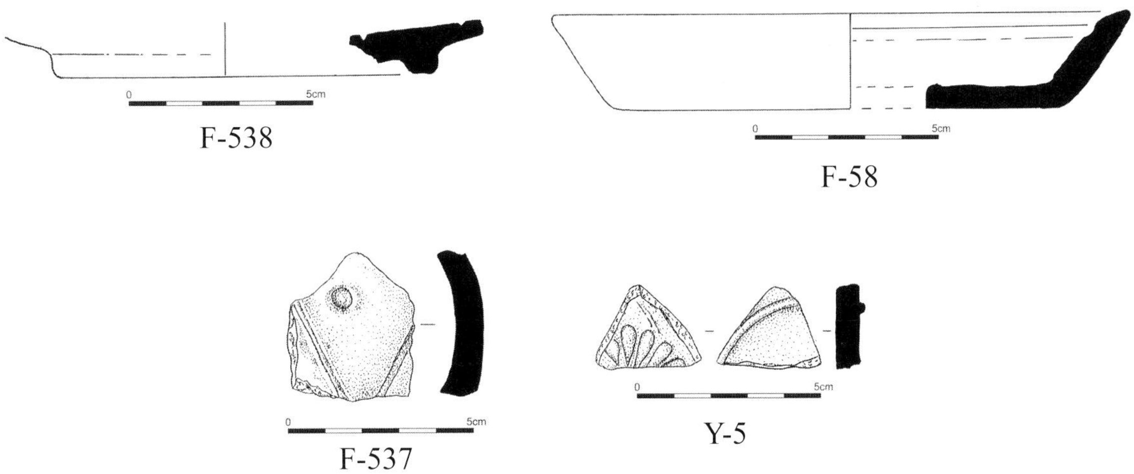

Figure II.31

Coins

Find ID: 2001-N-0101 Area: HAC Trench: 03 Unit: 034
Material(s): Non-Ferrous Metal (Copper Alloy/Lead)
Object type: Coin?
Description: 1 round object. Possible coin or button.

Specialist code N-4 (Fig. II.32)
Length: 0, Breadth: 0, Thickness: 2, Diameter: 19 , Weight: 3
Specialist description: Round object possibly a coin or button.

Find ID: 2002-N-0129 Area: HAC Trench: 03 Unit: 186
Material(s): Non-Ferrous Metal (Copper Alloy/Lead)
Object type: Coin
Description: Coin of silver, lead or Cu Alloy. Obverse: portrait of man. Reverse: Owl or eagle.

Specialist code N-5 (Fig. II.32)
Length: 0 Breadth: 0 Thickness: 5.95 Diameter: 25.5 Weight: 17.05g
Specialist description: Coin of silver, lead or Cu Alloy. Obverse: portrait of Athena. Reverse: Owl. Thickness at centre including raised decoration 5.95mm, thickness at edge 3.46mm. Max. D.25.5mm, Min. D.24.47mm.
A cast and description of this coin were sent to Dr. Andew Meadows, Curator of Greek Coins at the British Museum who believes it to be either a genuine Athenian tetradrachm or a local imitation. The weight should be approximately 17g suggesting that this coin may be genuine. Irrespective of whether the coin is genuine or imitation the date is mid-late 4th Century B.C.

Find ID: 2002-N-0387 Area: HAC Trench: 03 Unit: 068
Material(s): Non-Ferrous Metal (Copper Alloy/Lead)
Object type: Coin
Description: Coin, made of silver, lead or Cu Alloy. Obverse: portrait. Reverse: Owl and inscription.

Specialist code N-8 (Fig. II.32)
Length: 0 Breadth: 0 Thickness: 5.83 Diameter: 25.45 Weight: 16.81g
Specialist description: Coin, made of silver, lead or Cu Alloy. Obverse: portrait of Athena. Reverse: owl and inscription. Thickness including decoration 5.83mm, thickness at edge 3.04mm. Max. D. 25.45mm, Min. D.23.93mm.
A cast and description of this coin were sent to Dr. Andew Meadows, Curator of Greek Coins at the British Museum who believes it to be either a genuine Athenian tetradrachm or a local imitation. The weight should be approximately 17g suggesting that this coin may be genuine. Irrespective of whether the coin is genuine or imitation the date is mid-late 4th Century B.C.

Find ID: 2005-SF-0002 Area: HAC Trench: Surface Unit: Surface
Material(s): Non-Ferrous Metal (Copper Alloy/Lead)
Object type: Coin
Description: Coin of Arabic origin, made of Cu alloy.

Specialist code N-9 (Fig. II.32)
Length: 0 Breadth: 0 Thickness: 0 Diameter: 17 Weight: 0
Specialist description: Coin, made of Cu Alloy, Arabic origin (text in Arabic reads 'made in Egypt', 4/10 of piasters, with a 'stamp' of Mohammed Ali.

Find ID: 2005-N-0108-B Area: HAC Trench: 03 Unit: 308
Material(s): Non-Ferrous Metal (Copper Alloy/Lead)
Object type: Coin
Description: Coin of Arabic origin with a small hole. made of Cu alloy.

Specialist code N-10 (Fig. II.32)
Length: 0 Breadth: 0 Thickness: 0 Diameter: 20 Weight: 0
Specialist description: Coin of Arabic origin with a small hole, made of Cu alloy. The Arabic text reads 'made in Egypt', the year that is mentioned on the coin is 1223 (1808 A.D.) . It has a 'stamp' of Mohammed Ali. Possibly not an original coin as this type is sometimes copied for decoration on veils.

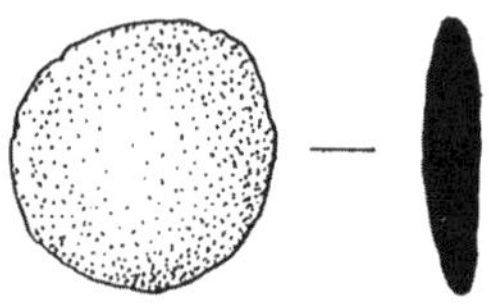

N4

N5

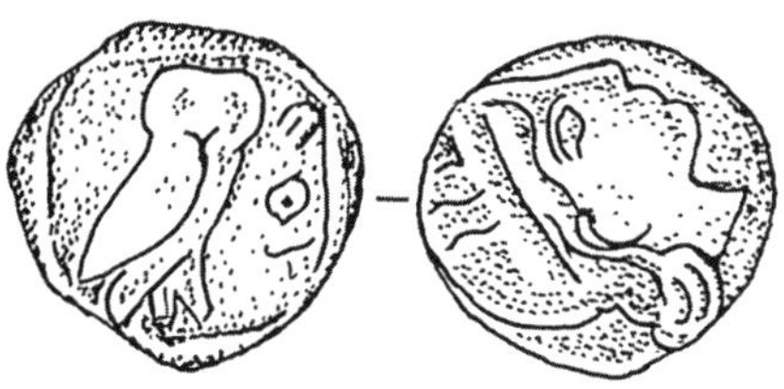

N8

N9

N10

Figure. II.32

Seals and Stoppers

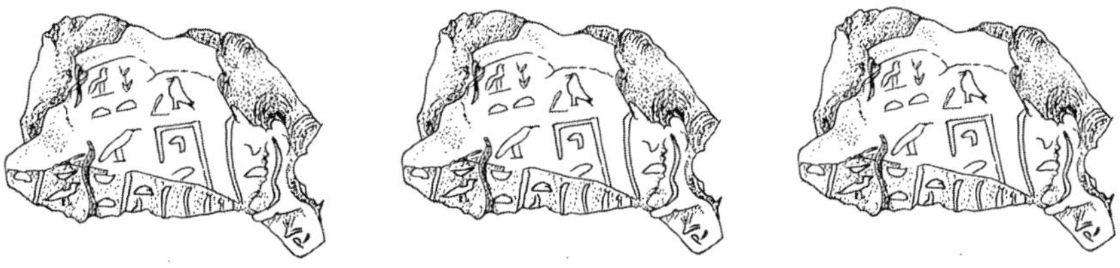

Seals and Stoppers

Find ID: 2000-P-0292 Area: HAC Trench: 02 Unit: 010
Material(s): Pottery
Object type: Seal
Description: Defunct.

Find ID: 2000-P-0293 Area: HAC Trench: 02 Unit: CT
Material(s): Pottery
Object type: Seal
Description: Defunct.

Find ID: 2001-P-0030-C Area: HAC Trench: 03 Unit: 036
Material(s): Pottery
Object type: Seal
Description: Fragment of mud sealing with string impressions.

Specialist code P-462 (Fig. II.33)
Length: 44 Breadth: 25 Thickness: 23 Diameter: 0 Weight: 0
Specialist description: A clay seal (?) which has become fired after use. One edge preserves impressions believed to be from basketry, and the other a semi-circular depression which may be from a basketry fastener.

Find ID: 2001-P-0182 Area: HAD Trench: 01 Unit: 084
Material(s): Pottery
Object type: Seal.
Description: 1 fragment of seal.

Specialist code P-463
Length: 25 Breadth: 12 Thickness: 16 Diameter: 0 Weight: 0
Specialist description: Fragment of clay seal which has become fired after use. Fine dense red clay. Apparent impressions on the surface are actually the result of later damage.

Find ID: 2002-SF-0007 Area: HAC Trench: Surface Unit: Surface
Material(s): Clay
Object type: Seal
Description: 1 incomplete crude clay seal.

Find ID: 2005-C-0013 Area: HAC Trench: 03 Unit: 300
Material(s): Clay
Object type: Seal
Description: Clay seal with hieroglyphic inscription, incomplete.
L.3.0cm, W.2.0cm.

Specialist code C-1 (Fig. II.33)
Length: 30 Breadth: 20 Thickness: 0 Diameter: 0 Weight: 0
Specialist description: Fired clay seal with hieroglyphic inscription, incomplete. On the back of the seal, straw impressions are visible.

The inscription is difficult to read and I am indebted to Drs. Robert Morkot and Campbell Price for the suggestion that the piece may be Old Kingdom in date and particularly to Dr. Richard Bussman who suggests that the name may be that of Neferirkare (2475-2455 B.C.) of the 5th Dynasty and therefore a residual piece. Dr. Bussman suggests that one might read the Horus name as *Wsr-xaw* where the *wsr*-sign is much compressed (which happens quickly when rolling a cylinder seal over a piece of mud) and the *xaw* is rather abbreviated. The preserved signs in the cartouche might be *nfr, jrj* and *kA* adding up to *Nfr-ir-kA-Ra*. The cartouche (if correctly identified as such) could be part of a private name or title rather than belonging to the royal titulary. Below the niswt-bit group on the left hand side, he suggests reconstructing the the nb.ti-group, i.e. vulture and cobra.

Comparanda: Kaplony (1981) Tafel 65- 70 especially nos. 7, 18, 19 and 20. It is difficult to match the reading of the front side with the signs on the lateral side and so is difficult to say to what extent these two inscriptions represent the same part of the sealing pattern.

Find ID: 2002-C-0038 Area: HAC Trench: 03 Unit: 065
Material(s): Clay Charcoal
Object type: Stopper
Description: 1 fragment of a possible mud stopper, some charcoal inclusions.

Find ID: 2005-C-0042 Area: HAC Trench: 03 Unit: 306
Material(s): Unfired Clay
Object type: Stopper
Description: Unfired clay-object, possibly a stopper. With thumb impression.

Specialist code C-2 (Fig. II.33)
Length: 0 Breadth: 0 Thickness: 19 Diameter: 42 Weight: 33
Specialist description: Jar stopper with detached fragment which would originally have been used to fill a thumb mark at the base.

Find ID: 2005-C-0054 Area: HAC Trench: 03 Unit: CT
Material(s): Unfired clay
Object type: Stopper
Description: 1 stopper of unfired clay, shaped like a dome.

Specialist code C-3 (Fig. II.33)
Length: 0 Breadth: 0 Thickness: 26 Diameter: 42 Weight: 55
Specialist description: Jar sealing or stopper, with dome shape. It has become heavily fired.

Find ID: 2005-C-0071 Area: HAC Trench: 03 Unit: 303
Material(s): Unfired Clay
Object type: Stopper
Description: 1 unfired clay stopper, fragile, shaped like a dome.

Specialist code C-4 (Fig. II.33)
Length: 0 Breadth: 0 Thickness: 52 Diameter: 125 Weight: 641
Specialist description: Jar seal with dome shape. Void runs right the way through it, possibly from a straw or reed.

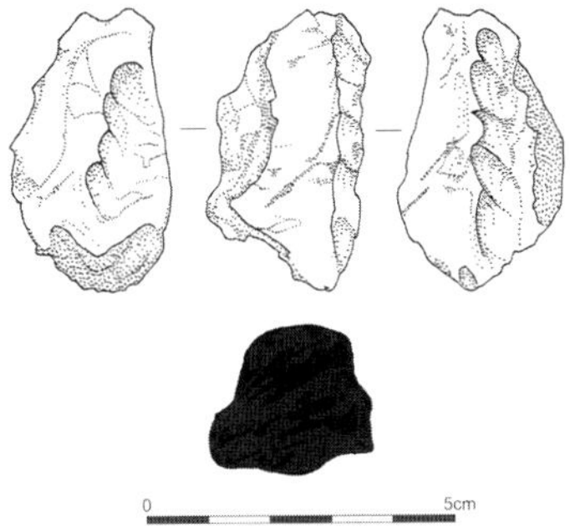

P-462

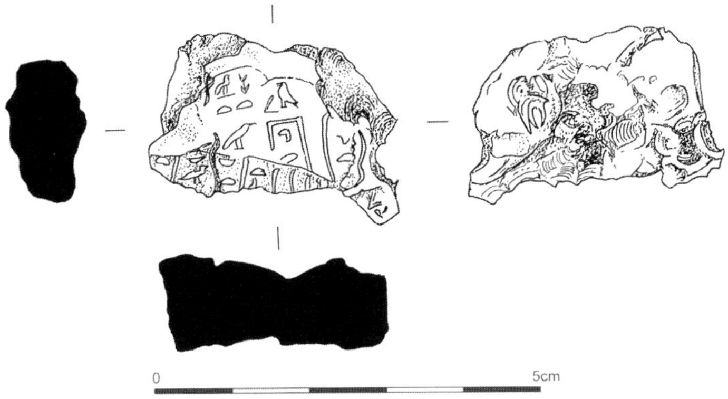

C-1

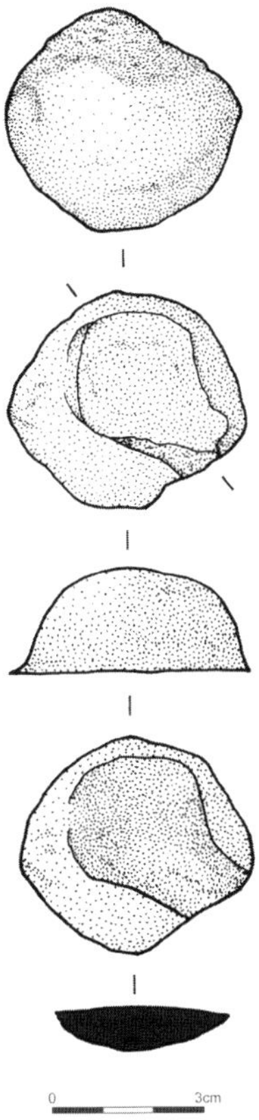

C-2

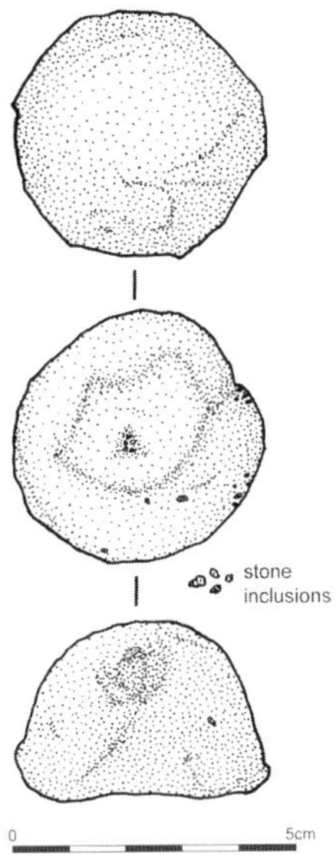

C-3

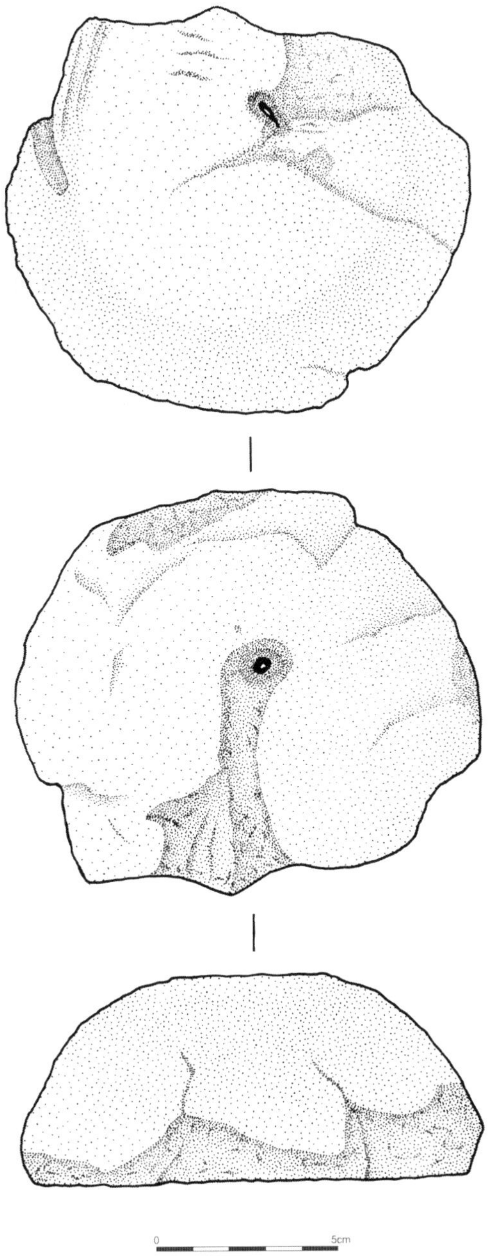

C-4

Figure. II.33

Find ID: 2005-C-0077 Area: HAC Trench: 03 Unit: 306
Material(s): Unfired Clay
Object type: Stopper
Description: 1 unfired clay stopper, dome-like, diameter c. 4 cm.

Specialist code C-5 (Fig. II.34)
Length: 0 Breadth: 0 Thickness: 18 Diameter: 42 Weight: 35
Specialist description: Dome like jar seal or stopper.

Find ID: 2005-C-0093 Area: HAC Trench: 03 Unit: 303
Material(s): Unfired Clay
Object type: Stopper
Description: 1 unfired clay seal or stopper, hemispherical in shape and 1 coprolite originally thought to be unfired clay.

Specialist code C-6 (Fig. II.34)
Length: 40 Breadth: 36 Thickness: 15 Diameter: 0 Weight: 21
Specialist description: Probably a small jar seal, somewhat oval in shape.

Specialist code C-7 (Fig. II.34)
Length: 0 Breadth: 0 Thickness: 0 Diameter: 0 Weight: 0
Specialist description: Defunct. Coprolite.

Find ID: 2005-C-0128 Area: HAC Trench: 03 Unit: 306
Material(s): Unfired Clay
Object type: Stopper
Description: 2 unfired clay stoppers, hemispherical in shape, diameters c. 4cm and 4.5cm.

Specialist code C-8 (Fig. II.38)
Length: 0 Breadth: 0 Thickness: 18 Diameter: 41 Weight: 29
Specialist description: Dome shaped jar sealing or stopper.

Specialist code C-9 (Fig. II.34)
Length: 0 Breadth: 0 Thickness: 18 Diameter: 38 Weight: 34
Specialist description: Dome shaped jar sealing or stopper.

Find ID: 2005-C-0145 Area: HAC Trench: 03 Unit: 306
Material(s): Unfired Clay
Object type: Stopper
Description: 1 unfired clay stopper, flat surfaces, diameter c. 12cm.

Specialist code C-11 (Fig. II.34)
Length: 0 Breadth: 0 Thickness: 28 Diameter: 115 Weight: 366
Specialist description: Disc of clay with chamfered edges.

Find ID: 2005-C-0178 Area: HAC Trench: 03 Unit: 307
Material(s): Unfired Clay
Object type: Stopper
Description: 1 unfired clay stopper. Diameter c. 7cm.

Specialist code C-12 (Fig. II.35)
Length: 0 Breadth: 0 Thickness: 50 Diameter: 71 Weight: 221
Specialist description: Jar sealing or stopper with tapering shape. Lower diameter 71mm, top 55mm.

Find ID: 2005-C-0184 Area: HAC Trench: 03 Unit: 309
Material(s): Unfired Clay
Object type: Stopper
Description: 1 fragment of unfired clay, possible part of stopper.

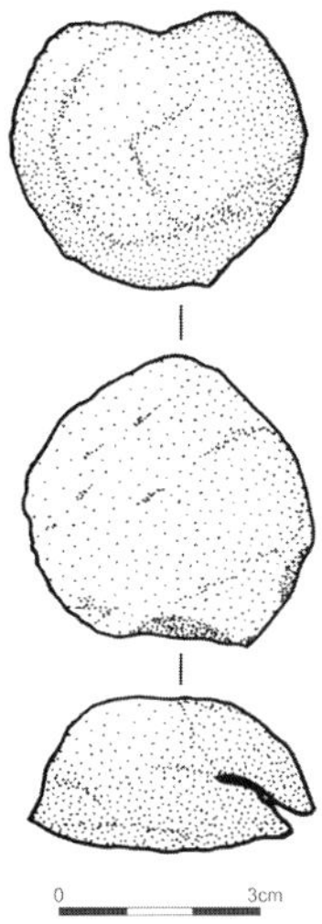

C-5

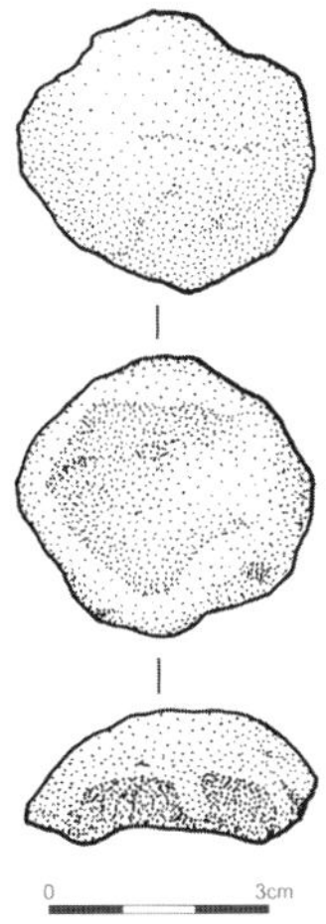

C-6

C-6 & 7

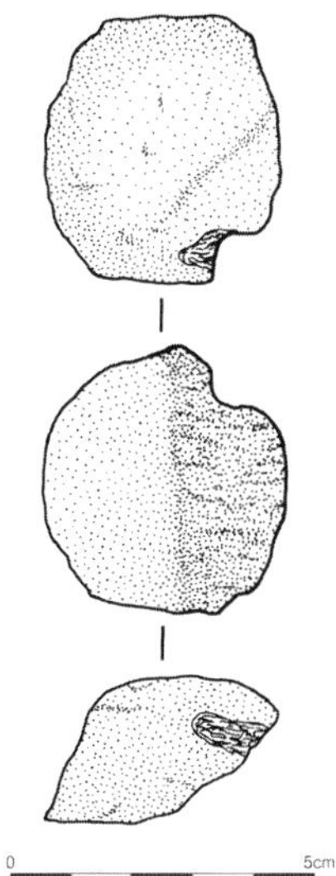

C-8

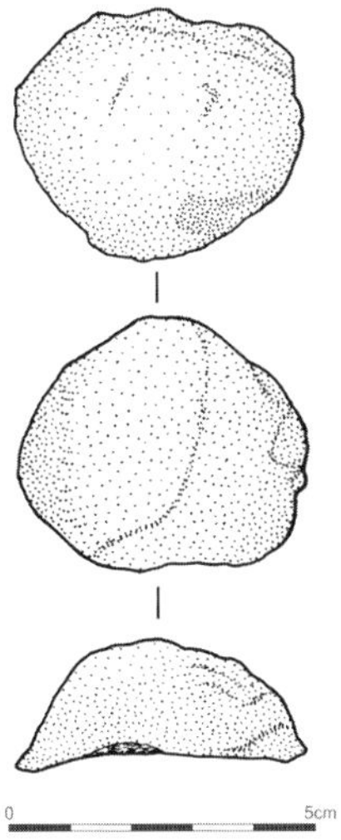

C-9

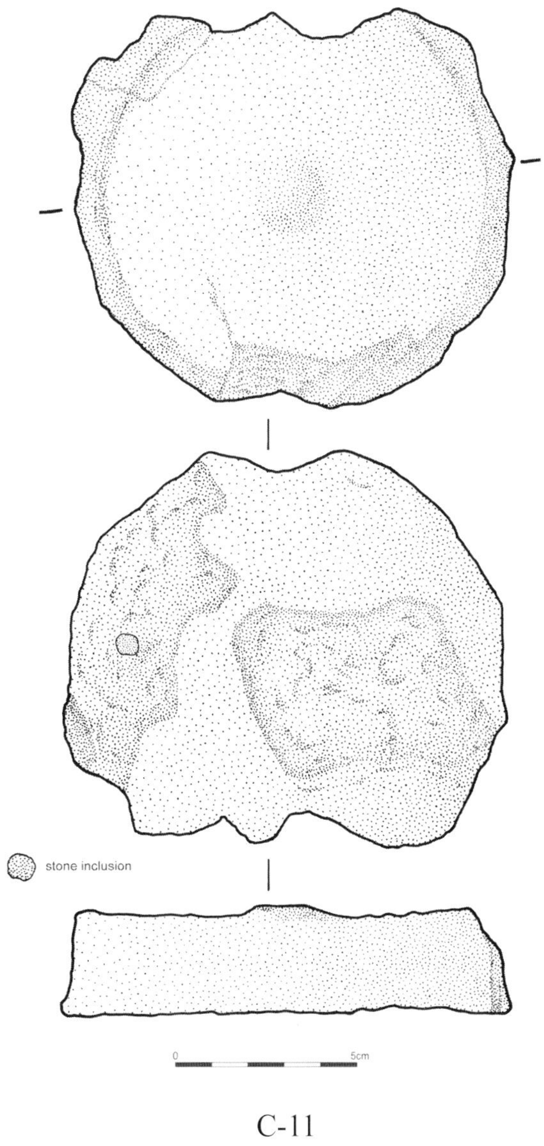

C-11

Figure. II.34

Specialist code C-13 (Fig. II.35)
Length: 0 Breadth: 0 Thickness: 35 Diameter: 120 Weight: 77
Specialist description: Edge of a jar seal with original diameter of 120mm, only 21% survives.

Find ID: 2005-C-0201 Area: HAC Trench: 03 Unit: 309
Material(s): Unfired Clay
Object type: Stopper
Description: 3 clay stoppers. All are hemispherical, diameters c.6.5, 8 and 9cm.

Specialist code C-14 (Fig. II.35)
Length: 0 Breadth: 0 Thickness: 55 Diameter: 80 Weight: 375
Specialist description: Clay stopper or jar sealing. Dome shaped.

Specialist code C-15 (Fig. II.35)
Length: 62 Breadth: 47 Thickness: 30 Diameter: 0 Weight: 73
Specialist description: Clay stopper or jar sealing. Dome shaped.

Specialist code C-16 (Fig. II.35)
Length: 75 Breadth: 70 Thickness: 52 Diameter: 0 Weight: 277
Specialist description: Clay stopper or jar sealing. Dome shaped.

Find ID: 2005-C-0202 Area: HAC Trench: 03 Unit: 309
Material(s): Unfired Clay
Object type: Stopper
Description: 1 unfired clay stopper, round shape.

Specialist code C-17 (Fig. II.36)
Length: 0 Breadth: 0 Thickness: 35 Diameter: 77 Weight: 204
Specialist description: Jar sealing or stopper, dome shaped.

Find ID: 2005-C-0216 Area: HAC Trench: 03 Unit: 311
Material(s): Unfired Clay
Object type: Stopper
Description: 5 unfired objects of which 4 are almost complete stoppers.

Specialist code C-18 (Fig. II.36)
Length: 0 Breadth: 0 Thickness: 14 Diameter: 41 Weight: 30
Specialist description: Jar seal or stopper. Circular shape with small raised central boss (resembles a bath plug).

Specialist code C-19 (Fig. II.36)
Length: 0 Breadth: 0 Thickness: 20 Diameter: 43 Weight: 33
Specialist description: Jar seal or stopper. Hemispherical.

Specialist code C-20 (Fig. II.36)
Length: 0 Breadth: 0 Thickness: 50 Diameter: 68 Weight: 127
Specialist description: Jar seal or stopper. Tapering cylindrical shape. 50% preserved.

Specialist code C-21 (Fig. II.36)
Length: 0 Breadth: 0 Thickness: 48 Diameter: 70 Weight: 247
Specialist description: Tapering jar seal. Bottom diameter 70mm, top 54mm.

Specialist code C-22 (Fig. II.36)
Length: 0 Breadth: 0 Thickness: 0 Diameter: 15 Weight: 305
Specialist description: Two fragments of jar seal or stopper, possibly from the same object. (A) diameter 15mm 12%, T.31mm, 148g. (B) 15mm 15%, T.32mm, 157g.

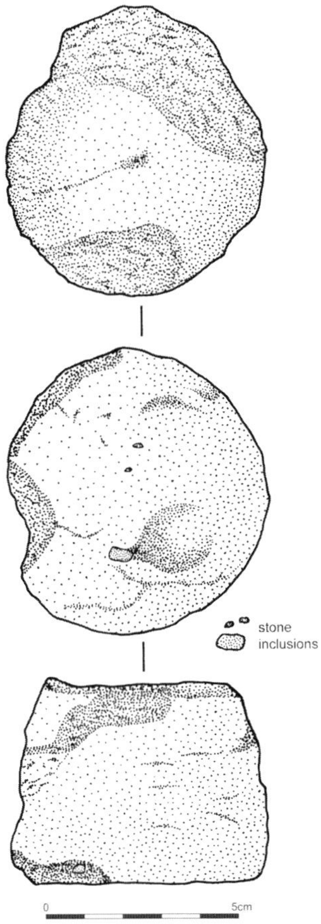

C-12

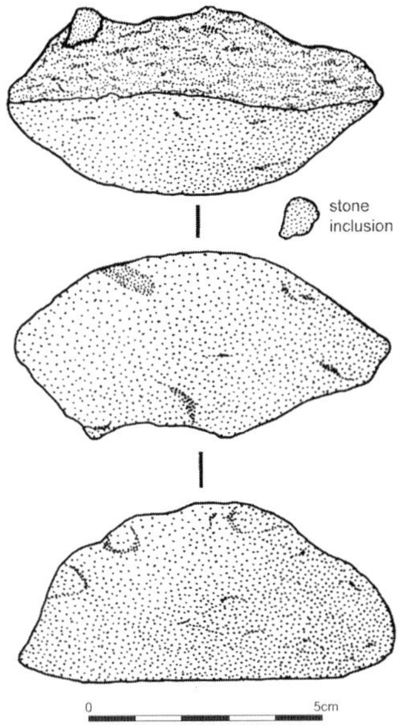

C-13

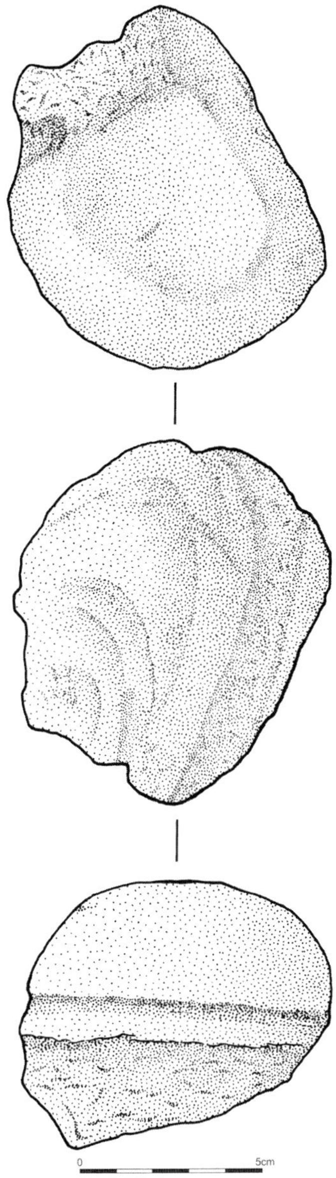

C-14

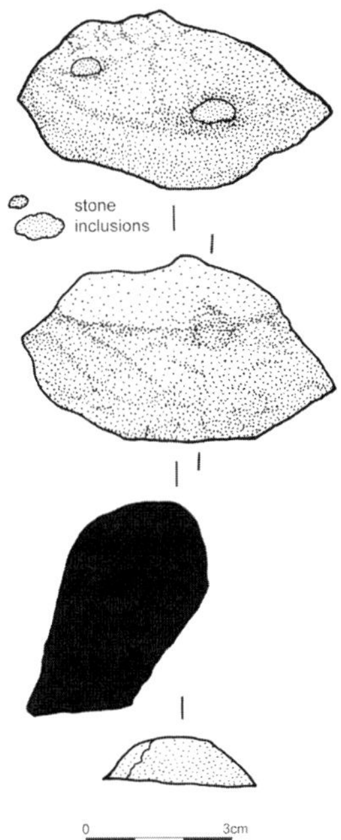

C-15

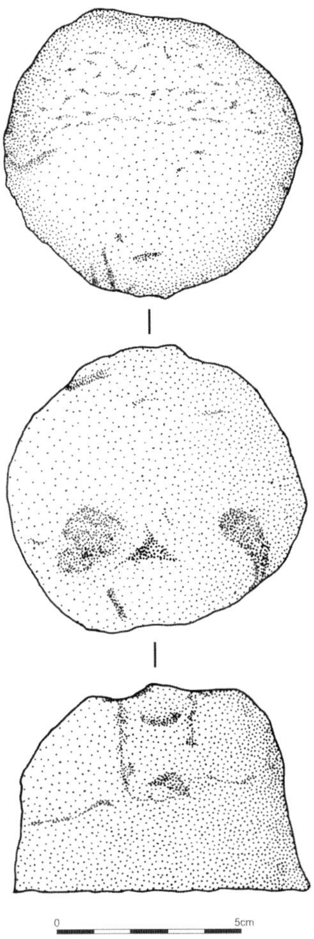

C-16

Figure. II.35

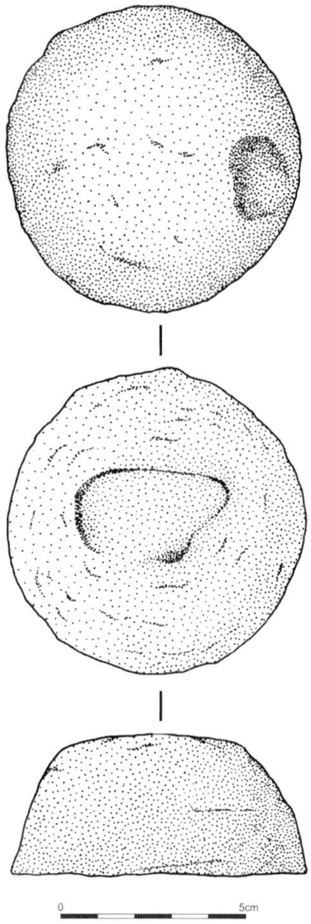

C-17

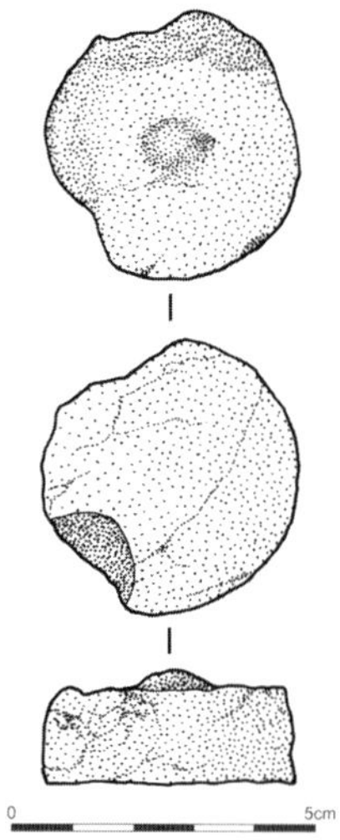

C-18

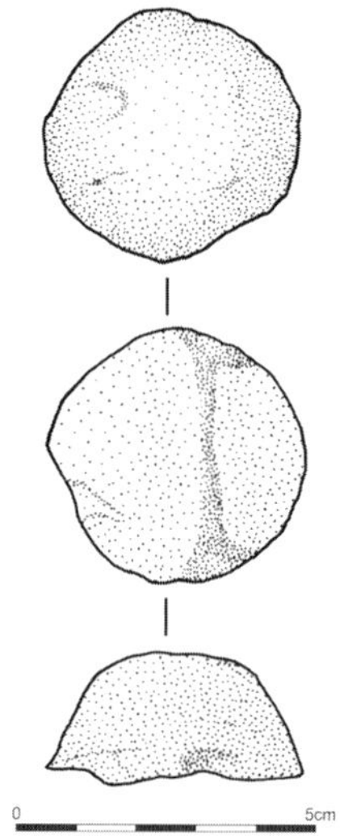

C-19

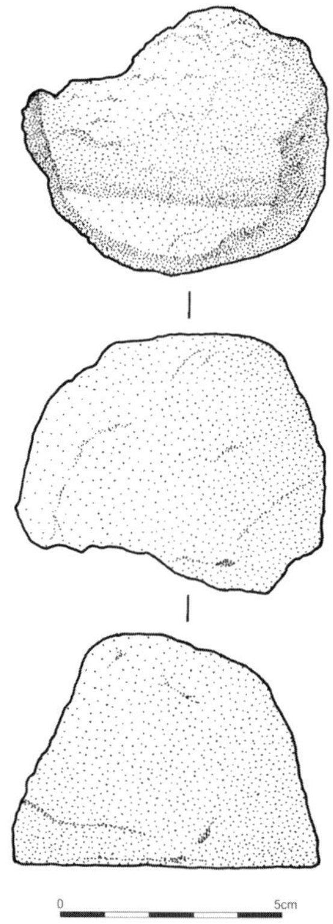

C-20

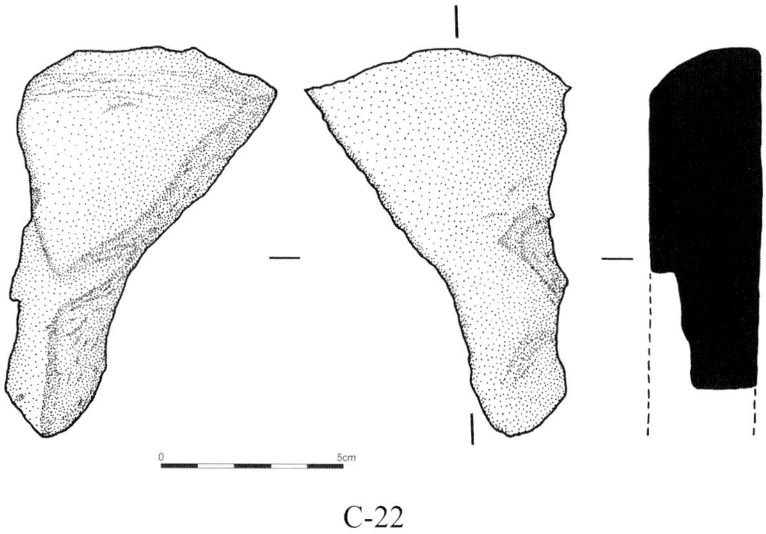

C-22

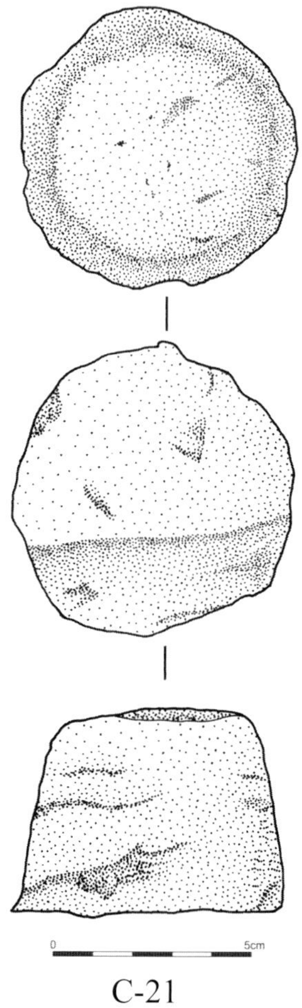

C-21

Figure. II.36

Find ID: 2005-C-0232 Area**:** HAC Trench: 03 Unit: 311
Material(s): Unfired Clay
Object type: Diverse
Description: 3 unfired clay objects: 2 'bats' and 1 stopper.

Specialist code C-23 (Fig. II.37)
Length: 0 Breadth: 0 Thickness: 27 Diameter: 140 Weight: 565
Specialist description: Disc of unfired clay ('bat') comprising two joining fragments.

Specialist code C-24 (Fig. II.37)
Length: 0 Breadth: 0 Thickness: 27 Diameter: 135 Weight: 430
Specialist description: Four joining fragments of clay disc ('bat') jar sealing.

Specialist code C-25 (Fig. II.38)
Length: 0 Breadth: 0 Thickness: 44 Diameter: 57 Weight: 168
Specialist description: Tapering jar seal. Bottom diameter 57mm, Top 46mm. String impression around side.

Find ID: 2005-C-0253 Area**:** HAC Trench: 03 Unit: 307
Material(s): Clay
Object type: Seal
Description: Clay seal from a jar.

Specialist code C-26 (Fig. II.38)
Length: 0 Breadth: 0 Thickness: 35 Diameter: 80 Weight: 204
Specialist description: Clay seal, roughly dome shaped with all the curved surfaces one. The flat under surface has a hole drilled part way through it.

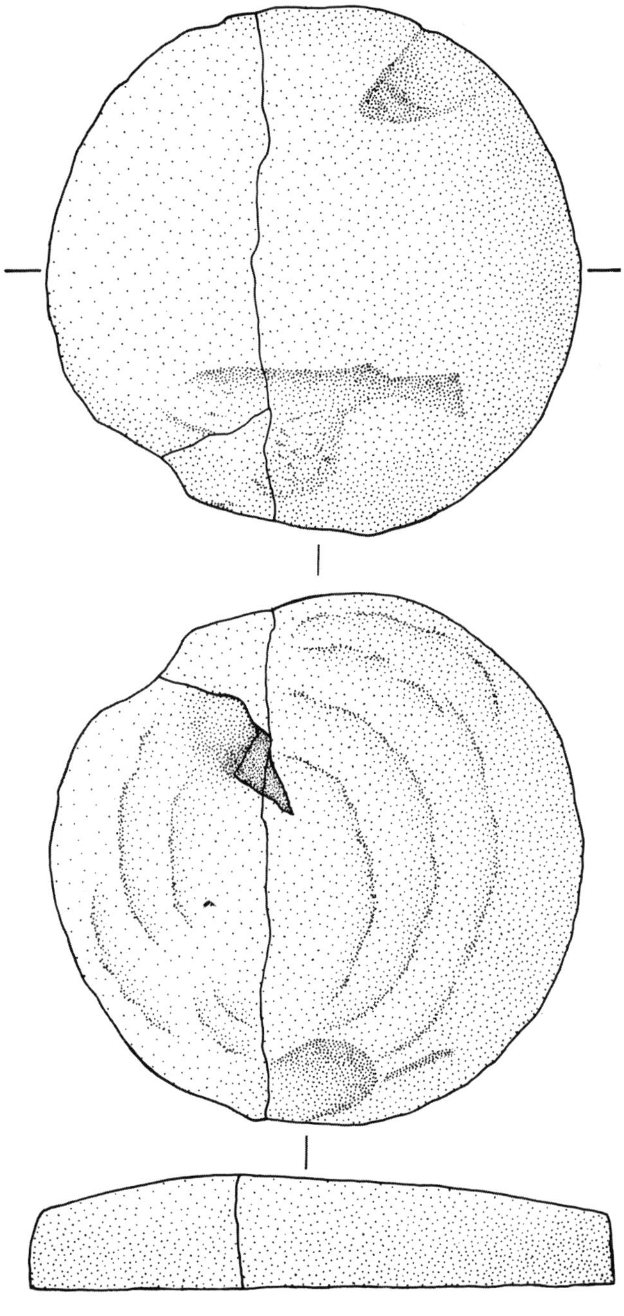

C-23

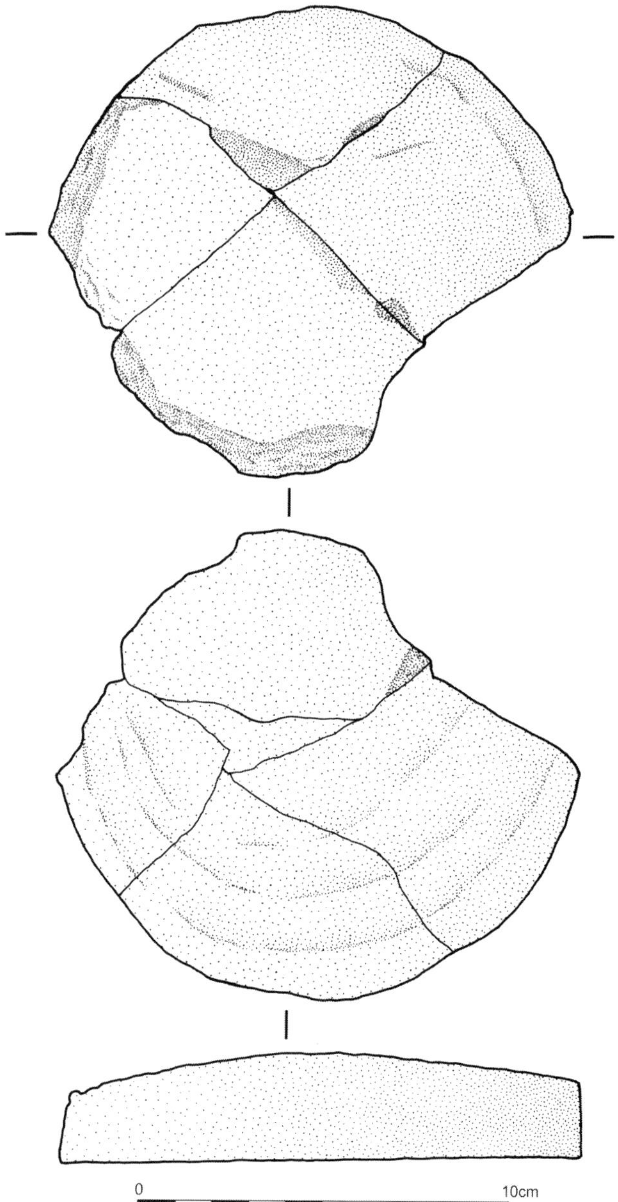

C-24

Figure. II.37

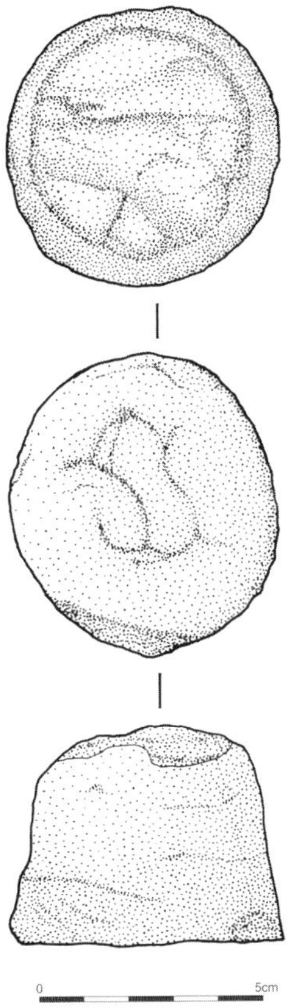

C-25

C-26

Figure. II.38

Bibliography

Abd el-Fatah, A. and Tezgör, D.K. (1998) Quelques nouveaux moules alexandrins à Kôm Giza. In A. Abd el-Fattah and P. Gallo (Eds.), **Aegyptiaca Alexandrina. Monuments pharaoniques découverts récemment à Alexandrie.** Cairo: IFAO, Études Alexandrines 1, 65 -73.

Adriani, A. (1945) L'afrodite al bagno di Rodi e l'afrodite di Doedalsas. **Annales du Service des Antiquités de l'Égypte** 44, 37-70.

Alliot, M. (1933) **Rapport sur les fouilles de Tell Edfou (1932).** Cairo: IFAO.

Andreu-Lanoe,G., Baud, M. and Sackho-Autissier, A. (2010) **Meroe: Un Empire Sur Le Nil.** Milan: Officina Libraria.

Anthes, R. (1959) **Mit Rahineh 1955.** Philadelphia: The University Museum.

Anthes, R. (1965) **Mit Rahineh 1956.** Philadelphia: The University Museum.

Arnold, D. (1981) Ägyptische Mergeltone ('Wüstentone') und die Herkunft einer Mergeltonware des Mittleren Reiches aus der Gegend von Memphis. In D.Arnold (Ed.) **Studien zur altägyptischen Keramik.** Mainz: von Zabern, 167-191.

Arnold, D. (1995) An Egyptian Bestiary. **The Metropolitan Museum of Art Bulletin** (Spring).

Ashton, S-A. (2003) **Petrie's Ptolemaic and Roman Memphis.** London: Institute of Archaeology.

Aston, D.A. (1999) **Elephantine XIX. Pottery from the Late New Kingdom to the Early Ptolemaic Period.** Deutsches Archäologisches Institut, Abteilung Kairo. Mainz: von Zabern.

Atik, N. (1995) **Die Keramik aus den Südthermen von Perge.** Tübingen: E. Wasmuth, Istanbuler Mitteilungen 40.

Aufrère, S. (1991) **L'univers minéral dans la pensée égyptienne.** Cairo: IFAO (2 Volumes).

Bachmann, H-G. (1982) **The Identification of Slags from Archaeological Sites.** London: Institute of Archaeology Occasional Publication 6.

Bailey, D.M. (1976) Pottery Lamps. In D. Strong and D. Brown (Eds.) **Roman Crafts.** London: Duckworth, 92-103.

Bailey, D.M. (1984) Review of S.I. Rotroff: 'Hellenistic Pottery'. **The Classical Review** 34 (2), 351-352.

Bailey, D.M. (1997) Roman pottery lamps. In I. Freestone and D. Gaimster (Eds.) **Pottery in the Making.** London: British Museum, 164-169.

Bailey, D.M. (2006) Terracotta and plaster figurines, sealings and a stone group. In V. Maxfield and D.P.S. Peacock (Eds.) **Mons Claudianus 3: Ceramic Vessels and Related Objects.** Cairo: IFAO, 261-288.

Bailey, D.M. (2008). **Catalogue of the Terracottas in the British Museum, 4. Ptolemaic and Roman Terracottas from Egypt**. London: The British Museum Press.

Bailey, D.M. (2009) **Catalogue of the Terracottas in the British Museum: Volume IV: Ptolemaic and Roman Terracottas from Egypt.** London: British Museum Press.

Bailey, D.M. (2011) Drinking-goblets and table-amphorae groups of Ptolemaic painted pottery. **Cahiers de la Céramique Égyptienne** 9, 71-92.

Ballet, P. (1998) Les céramiques d'Alexandrie aux périodes hellénistique et romaine. Alexandrie fouilles récentes et études nouvelles, Bulletin de la SFAC. **Revue archéologique**, 193-199.

Ballet, P. (2004) The Graeco-Roman pottery workshops of Buto. **Egyptian Archaeology** 24, 18-19.

Ballet, P. (2012) Le matériel céramique. In F. Calament, R. Eichmann and C. Vendries, **Le luth dans l'égypte byzantine. La tombe de la 'prophétesse d'Antinoé' au Musée de grenoble.** Orient-Archäologie 26, Rahden, Verlag Marie Leidorf, 32-44.

Ballet, P. and Poludnikiewicz, A. (2012) **Tebtynis V : la céramique des époques hellénistique et impériale, campagnes 1988-1993.** Cairo: IFAO.

Bass, G.F. (1987) Oldest known shipwreck reveals splendors of the Bronze Age. **National Geographic** 172 (6), 692-733.

Batchelor, R. (1994) **Henry Ford: mass production, modernism and design.** Manchester: Manchester University Press.

Bayer-Niemeier, E. (1988) **Liebieghaus Museum Alter Plastik. Bildwerke der Sammlung Kaufmann, 1.** Frankfurt-Am-Main: Griechisch-römische Terrakotten. Melsungen.

Beck, H.C. (1934) Notes on glazed stones. Part I. Glazed steatite. **Ancient Egypt and the East**, 69-82.

Bellion, M. (1987) **Catalogue des manuscripts hiéroglyphiques et hiératiques et des dessins, sur papyrus, cuir, ou tissu, publiés ou signals.** Paris: Epsilon Reproductions.

Berman, L.M. (1999) **The Cleveland Museum of Art : Catalogue of Egyptian Art.** New York: Cleveland Museum of Art, Hudson Hills Press.

Besques, S. (1992) **Catalogue raisonné des figurines et reliefs en terre-cuite grecs, étrusques et romains, 4, 2. Epoques hellénistique et romaine. Cyrénaïque, Egypte ptolémaïque et romaine, Afrique du Nord et Proche-Orient'.** Paris: Reunion des Musées nationaux.

Blackman, W.S. (1927) **The Fellahin of Upper Egypt.** London: Harrap.

Bogaert, R. (1998-1999) Les opérations des banques de l'Égypte ptolémaïque. **Ancient Society** 20, 49-145.

Bonifay, M. (2004) **Études sur la céramique romaine tardive d'Afrique.** Oxford: BAR International Series 1301.

Borchardt, L. (1932) Ein Brot. **Zeitschrift für Ägyptische Sprache und Altertumskunde** 68, 73-79.

Bourriau, J.D. (1991) Patterns of change in burial customs during the Middle Kingdom. In S. Quirke (Ed.) **Middle Kingdom Studies**. New Malden: SIA Publishing, 3-20.

Bourriau, J.D. (1996) The dolphin vase from Lisht. In R.E. Freed and P. Der Manuelian (Eds.) **Studies in Honor of William Kelly Simpson.** Boston: Boston Museum of Fine Arts, 101-116.

Bourry, E. (1911) **A Treatise on Ceramic Industries: A Complete Manual for Pottery, Tile and Brick Manufacturers.** London: Scott, Greenwood and Son.

Brandt, J. (1999) Khar-Mohre – die Entschlüsselung einer iranischen Glasurtechnik und ihre Bezüge zur Ägyptischen fayence. In R. Busz and P. Gercke (Eds.) **Türkis und Azur.** Wolfratshausen: Edition Minerva, 170-187.

Brown, D. (1976) Pottery. In D. Strong and D. Brown (Eds.) **Roman Crafts.** London: Duckworth, 74-91.

Burlington Fine Arts Club (1895) **Exhibition of the Art of Ancient Egypt.** London: Burlington Fine Arts Club.

Busz, R. and Sengle, G. (1999) Zur Kieselkeramik – Begriffe, Werkstoffe und Verfahren. In R. Busz and P. Gercke (Eds.) **Türkis und Azur.** Wolfratshausen: Edition Minerva, 192-219.

Castiglione (1969) Stele eines Kupferschmiedes. Zur Deutung der römerzeitlichen ägyptischen Grabsteine. **Mitteilungen des Deutschen Archäologischen Instituts Kairo** 24, 78-86.

Cavassa, L. (Forthcoming) La production du bleu égyptien durant l'époque hellénistique et l'Empire romain (IIIe s. av. J.-C. / Ier s. ap. J.-C.). In P. Jockey (Ed.) **Les arts de la couleur en Grèce et ailleurs.** Athens: École française d'Athènes, Bulletin de Correspondance Hellénique-Supplément.

Cervi, A. (Forthcoming) Faience vessels. In A. Boozer, **A Romano-Egyptian House in Transition: Amheida House B2.**

Charleston, R.J. (1955) **Roman Pottery.** London: Faber and Faber.

Cheshire, W.A. (1996) **Die Gipsformen aus Memphis im Roemer-Pelizaeus-Museum zu Hildesheim.** Trier: University of Trier (Thesis).

Cockle, H. (1981) Pottery manufacture in Roman Egypt: a new papyrus. **Journal of Roman Studies**, 71, 87-97.

Constandelou, L. (2004) I syllogi faientianon tou Mouseiou Benaki**. Archaiologia kai Technes (December)**, 94-101.

Cook, R.M. and Dupont, P. (1998) **East Greek Pottery.** London and New York: Routledge.

Courby, F. (1922) **Les vases grecs à reliefs.** Paris: De Boccard.

Dasen, V. (2008) La petite fille et le médecin. À propos d'une étiquette de momie d'Égypte romaine. In V. Boudon-Millot, V. Dasen and B. Maire (Eds.) **Femmes en Médecine en l'honneur de Danielle Gourevitch.** Paris: Boccard, 39-59.

Davies, N. de G. (1902) **The Rock Tombs of Deir el-Gebrawi**. London: EES.

Davoli, P. (2001) Nuovi risultati dello scavo archeologico di Bakchias (Fayyum) : 1996-1999. In M. Casini (Ed.) **Cento anni in Egitto. Percorsi dell'archeologia italiana**. Milano: Istituto italiano di cultura del Cairo, 97-105.

Dawson, W.R., Uphill, E.P. and Bierbrier, M.L. (1995) **Who Was Who In Egyptology.** London: EES.

Dayton, J. E. (1981) Faience. In G.T. Martin **The Sacred Animal Necropolis at North Saqqara.** London: EES, 135-137.

De Caro, S (2002) **I Campi Flegrei, Ischia, Vivara, Storia e archeologia**. Naples: Electa.

Del Vesco, P. (2009) A votive bed fragment in the Egyptian Museum of Florence (Italy). **Egitto e vicino Oriente** 32, 31-7.

Deonna, W. (1938) **Exploration archéologique de Délos XVIII; Le mobilier délien.** Athens: École française d'Athènes.

Desbordes, C. and Brissaud, P. (2013) Évolution de la ville de Tanis autour du temenos de la déesse Mout. **Archéothema** 27, 68-75.

Dhennin, S. (2011) Térénouthis – Kom Abou Billo: une ville et sa nécropole. **Bulletin de l'Institut Français d'Archéologie Orientale** 111, 105-127.

di Gioia, E. (2006) **La ceramica invetriata in area vesuviana**. Rome: L'Erma di Bretschneider, Studi della Soprintendenza archeologica di Pompeii, 19.

Dixneuf, D. (In press) Céramiques et lampes . In Y. Linz and M. Coudert (Eds.) **Collections égyptiennes d'Antinoé (Momies, tissus, céramiques et autres antiques). Envois de l'État et dépôts du Musée du Louvre (1895-1925).**

Downey, S. (2003) **Terracotta Figures and Plaques from Dura- Europos.** Ann Arbor: University of Michigan Press.

Drenkahn, R. (1995) Artisans and artists in Pharaonic Egypt. In J.M. Sasson (Ed.) **Civilisations of the Ancient Near East**. New York: Charles Scribner's Sons, 331-343.

Dressel, E. (1882) Vasi di pasta egizia smaltata con ornati a rilievo. **Annali dell'Instituto di corrispondenza archeologica,** 5-58.

Dunand, F. (1973) **Le Culte d'Isis dans le bassin oriental de la Méditerranée, Vol. 1: le Culte d'Isis et les Ptolémées.** Leiden: Brill.

Dunand, F. (1979) **Religion Populaire en Égypte Romaine.** Leiden: Brill.

Dunand, F. (1990) **Terres cuites gréco-romaines d'Egypte.** Paris: Musée du Louvre, Département des antiquités.

English Heritage (1991) **Management of Archaeological Projects.** London: English Heritage (2nd Edition).

Felder, E-C. (1988) **Die Ägyptischen Pilger und Neujahrsflaschen und ihre Sonderformen.** Berlin: Freie Universität Berlin (Thesis).

Fischer, J. (1994) **Griechisch-römische Terrakotten aus Ägypten. Die Sammlungen Sieglin und Schreiber.** Dresden, Leipzig, Stuttgart and Tübingen: Wasmuth.

Ford, H. (1926) Mass production. In **Encyclopedia Britannica**, Vol. 30, 821-3.

Freestone, I. (1991) Looking into glass. In S. Bowman (Ed.) **Science and the Past.** London: British Museum.

French, P. (2007) A pottery assemblage of the first half of the 6th Century B.C. **Mitteilungen des Deutschen Archäologischen Instituts, Abteilung Kairo** 63, 100-119.

French, P. (2013) **The Anubieion at Saqqara III.** London: EES.

French, P. (In preparation) **The Anubieion at Saqqara IV.** London: EES.

French, P. and Ghaly, H. (1991) Pottery chiefly of the Late Dynastic period, from excavations by the Egyptian Antiquities Organisation at Saqqara, 1987. **Cahiers de la Céramique Égyptienne** 2, 93-124.

Friedman, F.D. (Ed.) (1998) **Gifts of the Nile: Ancient Egyptian Faience.** London: Thames and Hudson with Museum of Art, Rhode Island School of Design.

Friedman, F.D. and Leveque, M. (Producers) (1998) **Gifts of the Nile** (Video). Providence, R.I.: Rhode Island School of Design/National Endowment for the Humanities.

Gabolde, M. (1988) **Les collections égyptiennes dans les musées de Saône-et-Loire.** Autun: Ville d'Autun.

Gallois, H.C. (1928) Hellenistiche, Romeinsche en Coptische Ceramiek in het Museum Scheurleer. **Babesch** 3, 9-12.

Geoplot (2001) **Version 3.0 for Windows. Instruction Manual Version 1. March 2001.** Bradford: Geoscan Research.

Ghaly, H. (1993) Pottery workshops of Saint-Jeremia (Saqqara). **Cahiers de la Céramique Égyptienne** 3, 161-171.

Gladstone Pottery Museum (n.d.). **Gladstone Working Pottery Museum: A Victorian Potbank.** Stoke-on-Trent: City of Stoke-on-Trent.

Godden, G. (1992) **Godden's Guide to English Porcelain.** London: W.H. Smith.

Goldberg, M. (1971) Packing of 14, 16, 17, and 20 circles in a circle. **Mathematics Magazine** 44, 134-139.

Golden Software (1999) **Surfer Win-32 Software.** Golden Software: Colorado.

Goldman, H. (Ed.) (1950) **Tarsus I. The Hellenistic and Roman Periods. Excavations at Gözlu Kule.** Princeton: Princeton University Press.

Grant, A. (1982) The use of tooth wear as a guide to the age of domestic ungulates. In B. Wilson, C. Grigson, and S. Payne (Eds.) **Ageing and Sexing Animal Bones from Archaeological Sites.** Oxford: BAR British Series, 91-108.

Grataloup, C. (1988) Quelques faiences égyptiennes tardives de Coptos au Musée des Beaux-Arts. **Bulletin des Musées et Monuments Lyonnais** fasc. 3, 46-50.

Greene, K. (2007) Late Hellenistic and early Roman invention and innovation: the case of lead-glazed pottery. **American Journal of Archaeology** 111, 653-71.

Grimes, W.F. (1930) Holt, Denbighshire: The Works Depot of the Twentieth Legion at Castle Lyons. **Y Cymmrodor** 41.

Grimm, G. (1972) Two early imperial vessels from Egypt. **Miscellanea Wilbouriana** 1, 71-100.

Grimm, G. (1975) **Kunst der Ptolemäer-und Römerzeit in Ägyptischen Museum Kairo.** Mainz: Deutsches Archäologisches Instituts Kairo.

Grimm, G. (1990) Paulina und Antinous. Zur Vergöttlichung der Hadriansschwester in Ägypten. In C. Börker and M. Donderer (Eds.) **Das antike Rom und der Osten: Festschrift für Klaus Parlasca zum 65. Geburtstag.** Erlangen: Universitätsbund Erlangen-Nürnberg, 33-44.

Gutch, C.C. (1899) Excavations at Naukratis. D. The Terracottas. **Annual of the British School at Athens** 5, 67-97.

Hart, G. (1986) **A Dictionary of Egyptian Gods and Goddesses**. London: Routledge.

Hartung, U., Ballet, P., Béguin, F., Bourriau, J., French, P., Herbich, T., Kopp, P., Lecuyot, G. and Schmitt, A. (2003) Tell el-Fara'in – Buto. **Mitteilungen des Deutschen Archäologischen Instituts Abteilung Kairo** 59, 199-267.

Hayes, J.W. (1997) **Handbook of Mediterranean Roman Pottery.** London: British Museum Press.

Headrick, D.R. (2009) **Technology: A World History.** Oxford: O.U.P.

Hembold, J. (2001), Ein Kleiner "Templeschatz" - das Fayence-Kästchen aus Musawarat es Sufra. **Mitteilungen der Sudanarchäologischen Gesellschaft zu Berlin** V, 11, 62-71.

Herman, G. (1968) Lapis lazuli: the early phases of its trade. **Iraq** 30, 21-57.

Hermary, A. and Nenna, M.-D. (2006) Objets divers en faïence et en verre. In S. Fourier and A. Hermary (Eds) **Amathonte VI: le sanctuaire d'Aphrodite des origines au début de l'époque impériale.** Athens: École Française d'Athènes, Études Chypriotes 17, 141-142.

H.M.S.O. (1956) **Clean Air Act 1956** London: H.M.S.O.

Herodotus. **Histories.** (Trans. A. De Selincourt). (Harmondsworth: Penguin 1954).

Higgins, R. A. (1954) **Catalogue of the Terracottas in the Department of Greek and Roman Antiquities, British Museum.Vol. I Greek: 730-330 B.C.** London: British Museum Press.

Hochuli-Gysel, A. (1977) **Kleinasiatische glasierte Reliefkeramik (50 v. Chr. Bis 50 n. Chr.) und ihre oberitalischen Nachahmungen.** Bern: Stämpfli Acta Bernensia 7.

Hochuli-Gysel, A. (2002) La céramique à glaçure plombifère d'Asie Mineure et du basin méditerranéen oriental (du 1er s. av. J.-C. au 1er s. ap. J.-C.) In F. Blondé (Ed.) **Céramiques hellénistiques et romaines : Productions et diffusion en Méditerranée orientale (Chypre, Égypte et côte syro-palestinienne), Lyon, mars 2000.** Travaux de la Maison de l'Orient et de la Méditerranée 35, 303-319.

Hodges, H. (1976) **Artifacts.** London: John Baker.

Hoffmann, B. and Tagart C. (2010) The glass and faience vessels from Saniat bin Huwaydi. In D.J. Mattingly (Ed.) **The Archaeology of Fezzan, vol. 3 : Excavations of C.M. Daniels, Tripoli**. London: Libyan Department of Antiquities and Society for Libyan Studies, 426-430.

Hogarth, D.G (1899) Excavations at Naukratis A. Site and Buildings. **Annual of the British School at Athens** 5, 26-46.

Hogarth, D.G, Lorimer, H.L. & Edgar, C.C. (1905) Naukratis 1903. **Journal of Hellenic Studies** 25, 105-136.

Hu, J.Q. and Li, H.T. (1997) The Jingdezhen egg-shaped kiln. In P.M. Rice and W.D. Kingery (Eds.) **The Prehistory and History of Ceramic Kilns.** Ohio: American Ceramic Society, 73-83.

Hull, M.R. (1963) **The Roman Potters' Kilns of Colchester.** Oxford: Reports of the Research Committee of the Society of Antiquaries of London 21.

Jeammet, V. (2005) La céramique à glaçure plombifère aux époques hellénistique et romaine. In **Faïences de l'Antiquité de l'Égypte à l'Iran, Cat. Exhibition, Musée du Louvre.** Paris, éditions du Louvre, Cinq continents, 191-197.

Jeffreys, D.G. (1985) **The Survey of Memphis I.** London: EES.

Jeffreys, D.G. (2010) **The Survey of Memphis VII: The Hekekyan papers and other sources for the survey of Memphis.** London: EES.

Johnson, A.C. (1936) **Roman Egypt to the Reign of Diocletian.** (F. Tierney (Ed.) **An Economic Survey of Ancient Rome Vol.** 2). Baltimore: Johns Hopkins Press.

Kaczmarczyk A. and Hedges, R.E.M. (1983) **Ancient Egyptian Faience.** Warminster: Aris and Phillips.

Kaczmarczyk, A. and Nenna, M.-D. (Forthcoming) Some analysis of Hellenistic and Roman imperial faience from Egypt. In J.-Y. Empereur (Ed.) **Alexandrina 4.** Alexandria: Études Alexandrines Centre d'Études Alexandrines.

Kaplony, P. (1981) **Die Rollsiegel des Alten Reiches.** Brussels: Fondation Égyptologique Reine Élisabeth.

Kaufmann, C. M. (1915) **Greco-ägyptische Koroplastik. Terrakotten der griechisch-römischen und koptischen Epoche aus der Faijûm-Oase und andren Fundstätten.** Liepzig and Cairo: Finck.

Kiefer, C. and Allibert, A. (1971) Pharaonic blue ceramics: the process of self-glazing. **Archaeology** 24, 107-117.

Kingery, W.D. (1997) Operational principles of ceramic kilns. In P.M. Rice and W.D. Kingery (Eds.) **The Prehistory and History of Ceramic Kilns.** Ohio: American Ceramic Society, 11-19.

Leach, B. (1945/1971) **A Potter's Book.** London: Faber and Faber. (2nd Edn.).

Lemonnier, P. (Ed.) (1993) **Technological Choices: Transformation in Material Cultures since the Neolithic.** London: Routledge.

Leonard, A. (1997) **Ancient Naukratis: Excavations at a Greek Emporium in Egypt. Part I: The Excavations at Kom Ge'if.** Atlanta: American School of Oriental Research.

Loeschcke, S. (1931) Die römischen Ziegelöfen im Gemeindewald von Speicher. **Trierer Zeitschrift** 6, 1-7.

Lloyd, A.B. (1983) The Late Period 664-323 B.C. In B.G. Trigger, B.J. Kemp, D. O'Connor and A.B. Lloyd **Ancient Egypt: a social history.** Cambridge: C.U.P., 279-348.

Lloyd, A.B. (2000) The Late Period 664-332 B.C. In I. Shaw (Ed.) **The Oxford History of Ancient Egypt.** Oxford: Oxford University Press, 369-394.

Lucas, A. (1962) **Ancient Egyptian Materials and Industries.** (4th Edn revised by J.R. Harris). London: Edward Arnold.

Lunsingh Scheurleer, R.A. (1979) Elephants in Faience. **Babesch** 54, 99-106.

Lunsingh Scheurleer, R.A. (1990) Misbakel in Memphis. **Medelingenblad** 48, 19-24.

Lunsingh Scheurleer, R.A. (2002) Egyptische aanwinsten uit den Haag. **Medelingenblad** 83, 5-13.

Mackensen, M. (1993) **Die Spätantiken Sigillata- und Lampentöpferein von El Mahrine (Nordtunisien).** Munich: C.H. Beck'sche.

Mackensen, M. (2009) Technology and organisation of ARS ware production-centres in Tunisia. **Journal of Roman Archaeology**, suppl.76, 17-45.

Mangone, A. De Benedetto, G.E., Fico, D., Giannossa, L.C., Laviano, R., Sabbatini, L., van der Werf, I.D. and Traini, A. (2011) A multianalytical study of archaeological faience from the Vesuvian area as a valid tool to investigate provenance and technological features. **New Journal of Chemistry** 35, 2860-2868.

Manniche, L. (1987) **Sexual Life in Ancient Egypt.** London: Routledge.

Manti, P. (2004) **Analytical Investigation and Replication Studies on the Production of Ancient Faience.** Unpublished MSc. Thesis, Oxford: Research Laboratory for Archaeology and the History of Art.

Mao, Y. (2000) Lead-alkaline glazed Egyptian faience: preliminary technical investigation of Ptolemaic period faience vessels in the collection of the Walters Art Gallery. **Journal of the American Institute for Conservation** 39, (2), 185-204.

Mao, Y. (2001) A technical examination of three Ptolemaic faience vessels. **Journal of the Walters Art Museum** 59, 17-22.

Mariette, A. (1882) **Le Sérapeum de Memphis.** Paris: F. Vieweg.

Martin, G.T. (1981) **The Sacred Animal Necropolis at North Saqqara.** London: EES.

Marucchi, H. (1891) **Monumenta papyrichea Agyptea Biblioteci Vaticani.** Rome: Ex Bibliotheca Vaticana.

McCown, D.E. and Haines, R. (1967) **Nippur I: Temple of Enlil, Scribal Quarter and Soundings**. Oriental Institute Publications 78, Chicago.

Messiha, H. and Elhitta, M. (1979) **Mallawi Antiquities Museum: A Brief Description.** Cairo: Antiquities Service.

Moorey, R.S. (1994) **Ancient Mesopotamian Materials and Industries.** Oxford: Clarendon.

Müller, H. W. (1964) **Ägyptische Kunstwerke, Kleinfunde und Glas in der Sammlung E. und M. Kofler-Truniger, Luzern.** München: Deutscher Kunstverlag, Münchner Ägyptologische Studien 5.

Musée de Marseilles (1997) **Égypte Romaine: L'autre Égypte.** Paris: R.M.N.

Muspratt, S. (1860) **Chemistry, Theoretical, Practical, and Analytical, as Applied to the Arts and Manufactures.** (2 Vols.). London: Mackenzie.

Myśliwiec, K. (1996) In the Ptolemaic workshops of Athribis. **Egyptian Archaeology**, 9, 34-36.

Nauerth, C. (1996) **Karara und El-Hibe. Die spätantiken ("koptischen") Funde aus den badischen Grabungen 1913-1914.** Heidelberg: Heidelberger Orientverlag (Studien zur Archäologie und Geschichte Altägyptens 15).

Nenna, M.-D. (2001) Éventails, boîtes à fard et candélabres en faïence. **Mélanges en l'honneur du Professeur Moustafa el-Abbadi.** Alexandrian Studies 2, Bulletin de la Société Archéologique d'Alexandrie 46, 181-192.

Nenna, M.-D., (2002) Vaisselle en faïence, en métal, en verre et en céramique: Filiations et imitations dans l'Égypte ptolémaïque. In F. Blondé (Ed.) **Céramiques hellénistiques et romaines : Productions et diffusion en Méditerranée orientale (Chypre, Égypte et côte syro-palestinienne), Lyon, mars 2000.** Lyon: Travaux de la Maison de l'Orient 35, 321-329.

Nenna, M.-D., (2003) Le mobilier non céramique et les terres cuites, secteur 2 et secteur 5 de la fouille du Pont de Gabbari. In J.-Y. Empereur and M.-D. Nenna (Eds) **Nécropolis 2.** Cairo: Études Alexandrines 7, IFAO, 279-288 and 511-532.

Nenna, M.-D., (2005a) En Égypte des Ptolémées à l'époque romaine. ***Dossiers d'archéologie*** 304, 72-79.

Nenna, M.-D., (2005b) En Égypte sous les Ptolémées. In **Faïences de l'Antiquité de l'Égypte à l'Iran, Cat. Exhibition, Musée du Louvre.** Paris, éditions du Louvre, Cinq continents, 165-173.

Nenna, M.-D., (2005c) En Égypte sous la domination romaine. In **Faïences de l'Antiquité de l'Égypte à l'Iran, Cat. Exhibition, Musée du Louvre.** Paris, éditions du Louvre, Cinq continents, 183-189.

Nenna, M.-D. (2006) Les artisanats du verre et de la faïence : tradition et renouvellement dans l'Égypte gréco-romaine. In B. Mathieu, D. Meeks and M. Wissa (Eds.) **L'apport de l'Égypte à l'histoire des techniques: Méthodes, chronologie et comparaisons.** Cairo: IFAO, 185-203.

Nenna, M.-D. (2007a) La vaisselle en faïence de l'époque ptolémaïque et du Haut Empire à Tell el-Herr. In J.-Y. Carrez-Maratray and D. Valbelle (Eds.) **Tell el-Herr à l'époque ptolémaïque et au Haut Empire.** Paris: Errance, 272-277.

Nenna, M.-D. (2007b) Le matériel en faïence. In U. Hartung and P. Ballet (Eds.) Tell el-Fara'in – Buto. **Mitteilungen des Deutschen Archäologischen Instituts Abteilung Kairo,** 63, 147-149.

Nenna, M.-D. (In press) Le mobilier en faïence (fouilles 2002-2004). In I P. Ballet (Ed.) **Recherches sur les ateliers de potiers d'époques hellénistique et romaine. Prospections et sondages (2001-2004), Buto VI, Archäologische Veröffentlichungen** 110.

Nenna, M.-D. (Forthcoming a) Le mobilier en verre et en faïence du Wadi Natrun (Beni Salama et Bir Hooker, IIIe s. av. J.-C. IIIe s. apr. J.-C.). In M.-D. Nenna (Ed.) **Les ateliers primaires de verriers du Wadi Natrun: Prospections et fouille du site de Beni Salama.**

Nenna, M.D. (Forthcoming b) **Tebtynis: mobilier en verre et en faience; l'artisanat de l'incrustation d'éléments de verre.** Cairo: IFAO.

Nenna, M.-D., Seif el-Din, M. (1994) La petite plastique en faïence du Musée gréco-romain d'Alexandrie. **Bulletin de correspondence hellénique** 118, 291-320.

Nenna, M-D. and Seif el-Din, M. (1999) Die ägyptischen Fayencewerkstätten in hellenistisch-römischer Zeit. In R. Busz and P. Gercke (Eds.) **Türkis und Azur.** Wolfratshausen: Edition Minerva, 76-83.

Nenna, M.-D. and Seif el-Din, M. (2000) **La vaisselle en faïence d'époque gréco-romaine: catalogue du Musée gréco-romain d'Alexandrie.** Cairo, IFAO, Études Alexandrines 4.

Nenna, M.-D. and Seif el-Din, M. (Forthcoming) La vaisselle en faïence d'époque gréco-romaine au Musée Gréco-Romain d'Alexandrie: compléments, typologie et bibliographie critique 2000-2012. In J.-Y. Empereur (Ed.) **Alexandrina 4.** Alexandria: Études Alexandrines Centre d'Études Alexandrines.

Nicholson, P.T. (1993) **Egyptian Faience and Glass.** Aylesbury: Shire.

Nicholson, P.T. (1998) Kiln furniture. In F.D. Friedman (Ed.) **Gifts of the Nile: Ancient Egyptian Faience.** London: Thames and Hudson with Museum of Art, Rhode Island School of Design, 255.

Nicholson, P.T. (2001) Faience production at Kom Helul, Memphis. **Egyptian Archaeology** 18, 15-17.

Nicholson, P.T. (2002a) Vitreous technology: evidence for faience production at Kom Helul, Memphis (Egypt). In M. Aldhouse-Green and P. Webster (Eds.) **Artefacts and Archaeology.** Cardiff: University of Wales Press, 90-101.

Nicholson, P.T. (2002b) A new furnace at Kom Helul, Memphis. **Egyptian Archaeology** 20, 24-25.

Nicholson, P.T. (2006) Petrie and the production of vitreous materials. In B. Mathieu, D. Meeks and M. Wissa (Eds.) **L'apport de l'Égypte à l'histoire des techniques: Méthodes, chronologie et comparaisons.** Cairo: IFAO, 207-216.

Nicholson, P.T. (2007) **Brilliant Things for Akhenaten: the production of glass, vitreous materials and pottery at Amarna site O45.1.** London: EES.

Nicholson, P.T. (2011) "I'm not the saggar maker, I'm the saggar maker's mate" saggar making and bottom knocking in Stoke-on-Trent as a guide to early saggar technology. In D. Aston, B. Bader, C. Gallorini, P. Nicholson and S. Buckingham (Eds.) **Under the Potter's Tree: studies on ancient Egypt presented to Janine Bourriau on the occasion of her 70th birthday.** Leuven: Peeters, 703-722.

Nicholson, P.T. (2012) Stone… that flows: faience and glass as man made stones in Egypt. **Journal of Glass Studies,** 54, 11-23.

Nicholson, P.T, Jackson, C.M. and Trott, K.M. (1997) The Ulu Burun glass ingots, cylindrical vessels and Egyptian glass. **Journal of Egyptian Archaeology**, 83, 143-153.

Nicholson, P.T. and Patterson, H.L. (1985) Pottery making in Upper Egypt: an ethnoarchaeological study. **World Archaeology** 17 (2), 222-239.

Nicholson, P.T. and Peltenburg, E. (2000) Egyptian faience. In P.T. Nicholson and I. Shaw (Eds.) **Ancient Egyptian Materials and Technology.** Cambridge: C.U.P., 177 -194.

Nifosi, A. (2009) **Catalogo degli amuleti di Bakchias (1994-2007).** Imola: La Mandragora.

Noble, J.V. (1988) **The Techniques of Attic Painted Pottery.** London: Thames and Hudson (Revised Edn.).

Nordström, H-Å and Bourriau, J.D. (1993) Fascicle 2: Ceramic Technology: Clays and Fabrics. In D. Arnold and J.D. Bourriau **An Introduction to Ancient Egyptian Pottery.** Mainz: von Zabern, 144-188.

OED (1989) The Oxford English Dictionary. Oxford: O.U.P. (2nd Edn.)

Olsen, F. (1983) **The Kiln Book.** London: A. & C. Black (2nd Edn.)

Oppenheim, A.L. (1973) Towards a history of glass in the ancient Near East. **Journal of the American Oriental Society** 93, 259-266.

Orton, C., Tyers, P. and Vince, A. (1993) **Pottery in Archaeology.** Cambridge: C.U.P.

Papadopoulos, J.K. (1992) ΛΑΣΑΝΑ, Tuyères, and kiln firing supports. **Hesperia** 61, 203-221.

Parlasca, Kl. (2005) Perserzeitliche Wurzeln der frühptolemaischer Zeit und "Quarzkeramik" (sogennante ägyptische Fayence). In **Ägypten, Griechenland, Rom: Abwehr und Berührung, Cat. exh. Frankfurt 2005-2006**. Frankfurt: Das Städel, 195-197, 332-333, 547, no. 111, 642-645, no. 226-231.

Parlasca, Kl. (2010) Alexandrinische Ascheurnen**. Chronique d'Égypte** 85, 278-294.

Patch, D.C. (1998) By necessity or design: faience use in ancient Egypt. In F.D. Friedman (Ed.) **Gifts of the Nile: Ancient Egyptian Faience.** London: Thames and Hudson, 32-45.

Payne, S. (1973) Kill-off patterns in sheep and goats: the mandibles from Asvan Kale. **Anatolian Studies** 23, 281-303.

Peacock, D.P.S. (1982) **Pottery in the Roman World: an ethnoarchaeological approach.** London: Longman.

Peacock, D.P.S., Bejaoui, F. and Ben Lazreg, N. (1990) Roman pottery production in central Tunisia. **Journal of Roman Archaeology** 3, 59-84.

Peltenburg, E. (1971) Some early developments of vitreous materials. **World Archaeology** 3 (1), 6-12.

Peltenburg, E. (1987) Early faience: recent studies, origins and relations with glass. In M. Bimson and I.C. Freestone (Eds.) **Early Vitreous Materials**. London: British Museum, 5-23.

Petrie, W.M.F. (1885) **Tanis 1883-1884. Part I**. London: Egypt Exploration Fund.

Petrie, W.M.F. (1886) **Naukratis I.** London: Egypt Exploration Fund.

Petrie, W.M.F. (1894) **Tell el-Amarna.** Methuen: London.

Petrie, W.M.F. (1909a) **Memphis I.** London: BSAE and Quaritch.

Petrie, W.M.F. (1909b) **The Palace of Apries (Memphis II).** London: School of Archaeology in Egypt and Quaritch.

Petrie, W.M.F. (1909c) **The Arts and Crafts of Ancient Egypt.** London: Foulis.

Petrie, W.M.F. (1909d) **Hyksos and Israelite Cities.** London: BSAE 12.

Petrie, W.M.F. (1910) **Meydum and Memphis (III).** London: School of Archaeology in Egypt and Quaritch.

Petrie, W.M.F. (1911a) The pottery kilns at Memphis. In E.B. Knobel, W.W. Midgeley, J.G. Milne, M.A. Murray and W.M.F. Petrie **Historical Studies I.** London: BSAE and Quaritch, 34-37.

Petrie, W.M.F. (1911b) **Roman Portraits and Memphis (IV).** London: BSAE and Quaritch.

Petrie, W.M.F. (1914) **Amulets.** London: British School of Archaeology in Egypt.

Petrie, W.M.F. (1931) **Seventy Years in Archaeology.** London: Sampson Low, Marston and Co. (The book bears no date but is generally cited as 1931).

Picon, M.,Vichy M. and Thirion-Merle, V. (2008) Les verres au natron et les verres aux cendres du Wadi Natrun (Égypte). **Bulletin de l' Association Française pour l'Archéologie du verre** 16, 36-41.

Pierrat-Bonnefois, G. (2010) Les objets en faïence. In M. Baud (Ed.) **Méroé : un empire sur le Nil.** Paris: Musée du Louvre and Officina Libraria, 118-123.

Pinch, G. (1983) Childbirth and female figurines at Deir el Medina and el -'Amarna. **Orientalia** 52, 405-414.

Pinch, G. (1993) **Votive Offerings to Hathor.** Oxford: Griffith Institute.

Pinch, G. (2006) **Magic in Ancient Egypt.** (2nd Edn.) London: British Museum.

Pradell, T., Salvado, N., Hatton, G.D. and Tite, M.S. (2006) Physical processes involved in production of the ancient pigment Egyptian blue. ***Journal of the American Ceramic Society*** 89 (4), 1426-1431.

Pruss, A. (2000) Patterns of distribution: how terracotta figurines were traded. **Transeuphratène** 19, 51–63.

Quibell, J.E. (1907) **Excavations at Saqqara.** Cairo: Service des Antiquités de l'Égypte.

Redford, S. (1988) Three seasons in Egypt: appendix II: the foundation deposits. **Journal of the Society for the Study of Egyptian Antiquities** 18, 49-79.

Redmount, C. A. and Friedman, R. F. (1997) Tales of a Delta site: preliminary report on the 1995 field season at Tell el-Muqdam. **Journal of the American Research Center in Egypt** 34, 57-83.

Reinsberg, C. (1980) **Studien zur hellenistischen Toreutik: Die Antiken Gipsabgüsse aus Memphis.** Gerstenberg: Hildesheimer ägyptologischer Beiträge 9.

Reisner, G.A. (1907) **Amulets: Catalogue Général des Antiquités Égyptiennes du Musée du Caire.** Cairo: IFAO.

Reisner, G.A (1924) Faience. **Harvard Excavations at Samaria 1908-1910.** Cambridge, Mass.: Harvard University Press, 326-328.

Rhodes, D. (1968) **Kilns: Design, Construction and Operation.** London: Pitman.

Riefstahl, E. (1968) **Ancient Egyptian Glass and Glazes in the Brooklyn Museum.** Brooklyn: The Brooklyn Museum.

Rodziewicz, M.D. (2005) **Early Roman Industries on Elephantine.** Deutsches Archäologisches Institut, Abteilung Kairo. Mainz: von Zabern.

Rotté, E. (2012) Egyptian plaque terracottas of standing nude women from the Late Period: Egyptian heritage or foreign influences. **Newsletter of the Coroplastic Studies Interest Group** 7, 13-16.

Rotroff, S.I. (1982) **Hellenistic Pottery. Athenian and Imported Moldmade Bowls.** Princeton, New Jersey: American School of Classical Studies at Athens, The Athenian Agora 22.

Rzeuska, T. (2006) **Saqqara II. Pottery of the Late Old Kingdom. Funerary Pottery and Burial Customs.** Warsaw: Neriton.

Sandeman, E.A. (1917) **Notes on the Manufacture of Earthenware.** London: Crosby, Lockwood and Son.

Sandeman, E.A. (1921) **Notes on the Manufacture of Earthenware.** 2nd Edition London: Crosby, Lockwood and Son.

Scarfi, B.M. (1974-1975) Vaso invetriato azzuro da Altino. **Aquileia Nostra** 45-46, 409-420.

Scheunert, V. (1999) Entries in Griechisch-Römisch section of catalogue. In R. Busz and P. Gercke (Eds.) **Türkis und Azur.** Wolfratshausen: Edition Minerva, 359-382.

Schuring, J. M. (1988) Terra Sigillata Africana from the San Sisto Vecchio in Rome. **Babesch** 63, 1-68.

Schlick-Nolte, B. and von Droste zu Hülshoff, V. (1990) **Skarabäen, Amulette und Schmuck.** Melsungen: Verlag Gutenberg.

Schmidt, S. (1997) **Katalog der ptolemaïschen und kaiserzeitlichen Objekte aus Ägypten im Akademischen Kunstmuseum Bonn.** München: Biering & Brinkmann.

Schneider, H. (1977) **Shabtis** (3 Vols.). Leiden: Rijksmuseum van Oudheden.

Seif el-Din, M. (1998) The Gayer-Anderson collection of plaster moulds in the Graeco-Roman Museum of Alexandria. In J-Y. Empereur (Ed.), **Commerce et artisanat dans l'Alexandrie hellénistique et romaine.** Athens: Ecole française d'Athènes Bulletin de correspondence hellénique Supplément 33, 165-204.

Shaw, I. (2004) Identity and occupation: how did individuals define themselves and their work in the Egyptian New Kingdom? In J.D. Bourriau and J. Phillips (Eds.) **Invention and Innovation: The Social Context of Technological Change 2.** Oxford: Oxbow, 12-24.

Shortland, A.J. and Tite, M.S. (2005) Technological study of Ptolemaic-early Roman faience from Memphis, Egypt. **Archaeometry** 47, 31-46.

Sidebotham, S. (2011) **Berenike and the Maritime Spice Route.** Berkeley: University of California Press.

Silvano, F. (2000) Alcuni frammenti di faïence egiziana al museo di Faenza. **Faenza, Bollettino del Museo internazionale delle ceramiche in Faenza** 86, 47-63.

Silvano, F. (2005) Faïence con decorazione a rilievo dal Fayum. **Egitto e Vicino Oriente** 28, 227-235.

Silver, I. A. (1969) The ageing of domestic animals. In D. Brothwell and E. S. Higgs, (Eds) **Science in Archaeology.** London: Thames and Hudson, 283-302.

Simpson, St. J. (1997) Partho-Sasanian Ceramic Industries in Mesopotamia. In I. Freestone and D. Gaimster (Eds.) **Pottery in the Making.** London: British Museum Press.

Spencer, A.J. and Schofield, L. (1997) Faience in the ancient Mediterranean world. In I. Freestone and D. Gaimster (Eds.) **Pottery in the Making.** London: British Museum Press, 104-109.

Spurr, S. (1999) Major W.J. Myers, O.E.: soldier and collector. In S. Spurr, N. Reeves and S. Quirke **Egyptian Art at Eton College.** New York: Metropolitan Museum of Art, 1-3.

Steer, J.M., Hinton-Jones, M., Valentine, J., Liu, Y., Tan, C.K., Ward, J. and Wilcox, S.J. (n.d.) **The Characterisation of the Physical and Chemical Properties of Biomass for Power Generation.** Cardiff University Institute of Energy: Unpublished Report 3161.

Stewart, H. (1995) **Egyptian Shabtis.** Aylesbury: Shire.

Swan, V.G. (1984) **The Pottery Kilns of Roman Britain.** London: RCHM Supplementary Series.

Szymańska, H. (2005) **Terre cuites a'Athribis.** Turnhout: Brepols.

Tagart, C. (1983) Roman faience from the vicinity of Germa, Wadi el Agial. **Libyan Studies** 14, 143-154.

Tait, G.A.D. (1963) The Egyptian relief chalice. **Journal of Egyptian Archaeology** 49, 93-139.

Teeter, E. (2010) **Baked Clay Figurines and Votive Beds from Medinet Habu.** Chicago: Oriental institute Publications 133.

Thomas, R. I. (2011) Terracotta figurines. In D. P. S. Peacock and L. Blue (Eds.) **Myos Hormos - Quseir al-Qadim. Roman and Islamic Ports on the Red Sea. Volume 2: Finds from 1999-2003.** Oxford: Archaeopress, BAR international Series 2286, 79-84.

Thompson, D. (1973) **Ptolemaic Oinochoai and Portraits in Faience: Aspects of the Ruler–Cult.** Oxford: Clarendon Press.

Thornton, D. (1997) Maiolica production in Renaissance Italy. In I. Freestone and D. Gaimster (Eds.) **Pottery in the Making.** London: British Museum Press, 116-121.

Times (1954) Mr. J.P. Bushe-Fox: archaeology of Roman Britain. **The Times** 19-10-1954, 11.

Tite, M.S., Bimson, M. (1986) Faience: an investigation of the microstructures associated with the different methods of glazing. **Archaeometry** 28, 69-78.

Tite, M.S. and Hatton, G. (2007) The production technology of, and trade in, Egyptian blue pigment in the Roman world. In C. Gosden, H. Hamerow, P. De Jersey and G. Lock (Eds.) **Communities and Connections: Essays in Honour of Barry Cunliffe**. Oxford: O.U.P. 75-92.

Tite, M.S. and Shortland, A. (Eds.) (2008) **Production Technology of Faience and Related Early Vitreous Materials.** Oxford: Oxford University School of Archaeology Monograph 72.

Tite, M.S. and Shortland, A.J. with Hatton, G.D. (2008) Production of Egyptian blue and green frits. In M.S. Tite and A. Shortland (Eds). **Production Technology of Faience and Related Early Vitreous Materials.** Oxford: Oxford University School of Archaeology Monograph 72, 147-185.

Tite, M.S. and Shortland, A.J with Kaczmarczyk, A. and Vandiver P.B. (2008) Faience production in Egypt. In A. Shortland and M.S. Tite (Eds). **Production Technology of Faience and Related Early Vitreous Materials.** Oxford: Oxford University School of Archaeology Monograph 72, 57-91.

Tite, M.S., Freestone, I.C. and Bimson, M. (1983) Egyptian faience: an investigation of the methods of production. **Archaeometry** 25 (1), 17-27.

Tomber, R. (2006) Egyptian Faience. In V.A. Maxfield and D.P.S. Peacock (Eds.) **Survey and excavations Mons Claudianus 1987-1993 III: Ceramic vessels and Related Objects.** Cairo: IFAO, 44-51.

Tomber, R. (2007) Faience. In D.P.S. Peacock and V.A. Maxfield (Eds.) **The Roman Imperial Quarries: Survey and excavations at Mons Porphyrites 1994-1998, vol. 2: The Excavations**. London: EES, 182.

Tomber, R. (2008) **Indo-Roman Trade.** London: Duckworth.

Török, L. (1995) **Hellenistic and Roman Terracottas from Egypt.** Rome: L'Erma di Brettschneider.

Vaelske, V. (2012) Terracottas from Tell Basta. **Egyptian Archaeology** 40: 12-13.

Vandiver, P. (1982) Technological change in Egyptian faience. In J.S. Olin and A.D. Franklin (Eds.) **Archaeological Ceramics.** Washington: Smithsonian Institution Press, 167-179.

Vandiver, P. (1983) Appendix A: The manufacture of faience. In A. Kaczmarczyk and R.E.M. Hedges **Ancient Egyptian Faience.** Warminster: Aris and Phillips, A1-A144.

Vandiver, P. (1998) A review and proposal of new criteria for production technologies of Egyptian faience. In S. Colinart, and M. Menu (Eds.) **La couleur dans la peinture et l'émaillage de l'Égypte ancienne: Actes de la table ronde, Ravello, 20 - 22 mars 1997**. Bari: Edipuglia, 121 – 139.

Vandiver, P. and Kingery, W.D. (1987a) Egyptian faience: the first high-tech ceramic. In W.D. Kingery (Ed.) **Ceramics and Civilisation** 3. Columbus, Ohio: American Ceramic Society, 19-34.

Vandiver, P. and Kingery, W.D. (1987b) Manufacture of an Eighteenth Dynasty Egyptian faience chalice. In M. Bimson and I.C. Freestone (Eds.) **Early Vitreous Materials**. London: British Museum Occasional Paper 56, 79-90.

Vergès, F.L. (1992) **Bleus Égyptiens: de la pâte auto-emaillée au pigment bleu synthétique.** Leuven: Peeters.

Vernhet, A. (1981) Un four de la Graufesenque (Aveyron): la cuisson des vases sigillés. **Gallia** 39, 25–43.

Villing, A., Bergeron, M., Bourogiannis, G., Leclère, F. and Thomas, R. (2013) **Naukratis: Greeks in Egypt.** http://www.britishmuseum.org/research/online_research_catalogues/ng/naukratis_greeks_in_egypt.aspx

Villing, A., Bergeron, M., Bourogiannis, G., Leclère, F., Masson-Berghoff, A.and Thomas, R. (Forthcoming) **Naukratis: Greeks in Egypt.** http://www.britishmuseum.org/research/online_research_catalogues/ng/naukratis_greeks_in_egypt.aspx

von den Driesch, A. (1976) **A Guide to the Measurement of Animal Bones from Archaeological Sites**. Cambridge: Harvard University Press.

Wallis, H. (1898) **Egyptian Ceramic Art, The MacGregor Collection: A contribution towards the History of Egyptian Pottery.** London: Taylor and Francis.

Walton, M.S. and Tite, M.S. (2010) Prodution technology of Roman lead-glazed pottery and its continuance into late antiquity. **Archaeometry** 52, (5), 733-759.

Waraksa, E. A. (2009) **Female Figurines from the Mut Precinct: context and ritual function.** Göttingen: Fribourg Academic Press.

Weber, W. (1914) **Die ägyptisch-griechischen Terrakotten. Königliche Museen zu Berlin, Mitteilungen aus der Ägyptischen Sammlung II.** Berlin: Curtius.

Webster, P. (1996) **Roman Samian Pottery in Britain.** York: Council for British Archaeology Practical Handbook in Archaeology 13.

Welc, F. (2011) Decorated Ptolemaic faience bowls from Athribis (Tell Atrib, Nile Delta). **Études et Travaux** 24, 244-269.

Whitcomb, D.S. and Johnson, J.H. (1979) **Quseir al Qadim 1978 Preliminary Report.** Cairo: A.R.C.E.

Wulff, H.E., Wulff, H.S. and Koch, L. (1968) Egyptian faience: a possible survival in Iran. **Archeology** 21, 98-107.

Yamani, S. (2002) New Year's bottles from Tell Marqula (Dakhla Oasis). **Bulletin de l'Institut Français d'Archéologie Orientale** 102, 425-436.

Ziegler, C. (1962) **Die Terrakotten von Warka. Ausgrabungen der Deutschen Forschungsgemeinschaft in Uruk-Warka.** Berlin: Gebruder Mann.

Internet References

www1: http://www2.stetson.edu/~efriedma/cirincir/ Accessed 17-8-2012.

www2: http://globalegyptianmuseum.org/record.aspx?id=11267/ Accessed 27-3-2013.

www3: http://www.schedia.de/Accessed 27-3-2013.

www4: http://petriecat.museums.ucl.ac.uk/ Accessed 20-6-2013.

INDEX

Excluding Catalogue

K

L

M

N

O

P

Q

R

S

T

U

V

W

Z

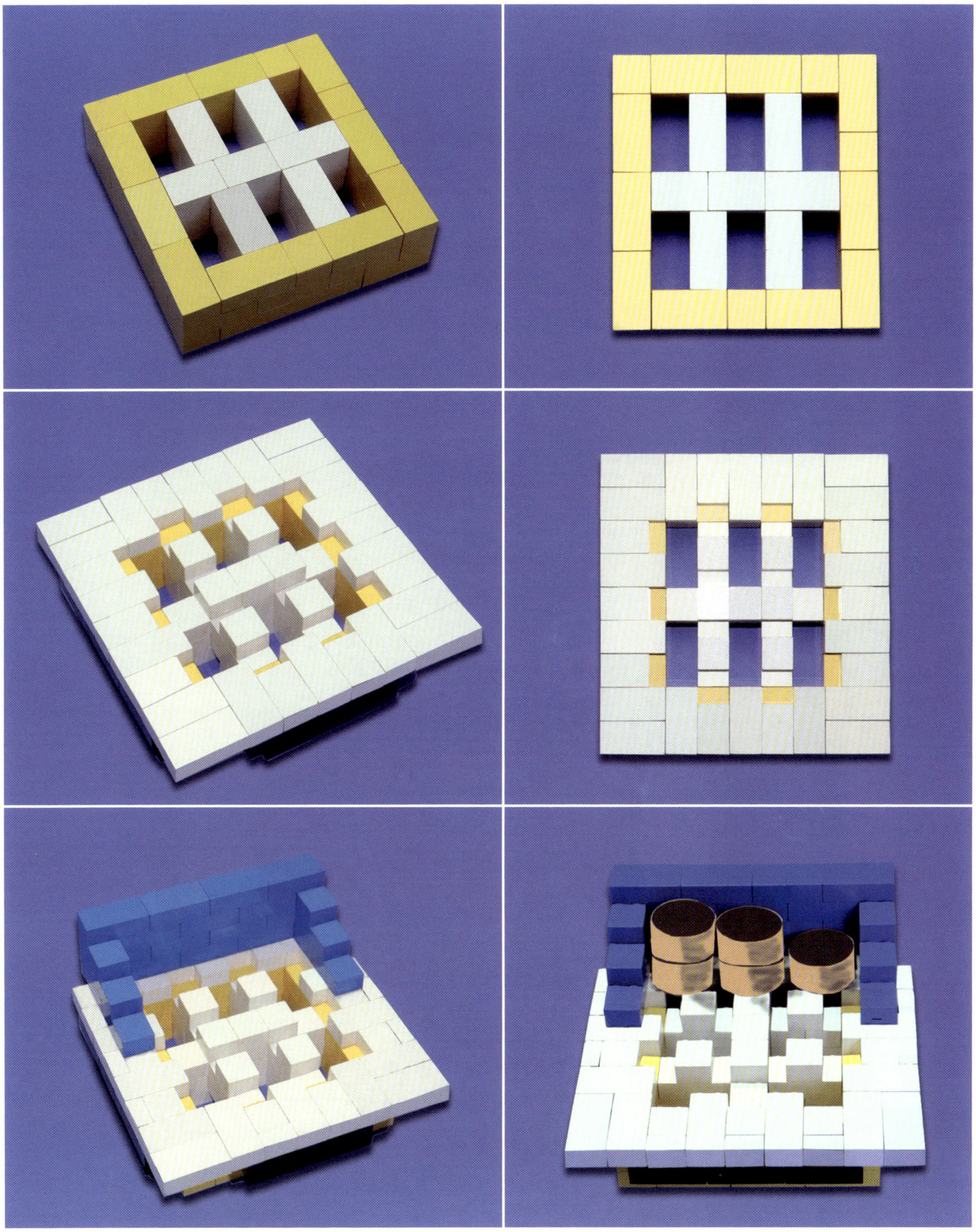

Colour Plate 1. Reconstruction of the chequer used in the HAC3 kiln showing how the actual kiln tower may have been somewhat larger than the preserved footprint of the structure. Top row: the kiln ground plan as excavated (yellow) with a simple chequer added (white). Middle Row: The chequer (white) expanded beyond the limit of the brickwork. Bottom Row: showing (L) part of the tower wall added (blue) and (R) one row of three saggars inside the kiln structure. (Reconstruction and photos: P.T. Nicholson).

Colour Plate 2. Photo-composite of the kiln and its access pit. The step down into the pit is at far left, the blocked access opening is at the centre. (Composite: J. Coyle).

Colour Plate 3. Saggar (IM-144). (Top) Exterior showing traces of the plaster coating which have become vitrified. (Bottom) Angled view showing the interior with the layer of white lime. (Photo: P.T. Nicholson).

Colour Plate 4. Saggar (IM-145). (Top) Exterior of the saggar showing vitrification. (Centre) Interior showing white lime at the bottom. Note the slightly domed profile of the base. (Bottom) Underside of the saggar with pad of clay adhering to it. This is probably a clay disc or pad perhaps such as C-24 which may be a pad rather than a jar seal. These seem to be deliberate products made for this purpose. (Photo: P.T. Nicholson).

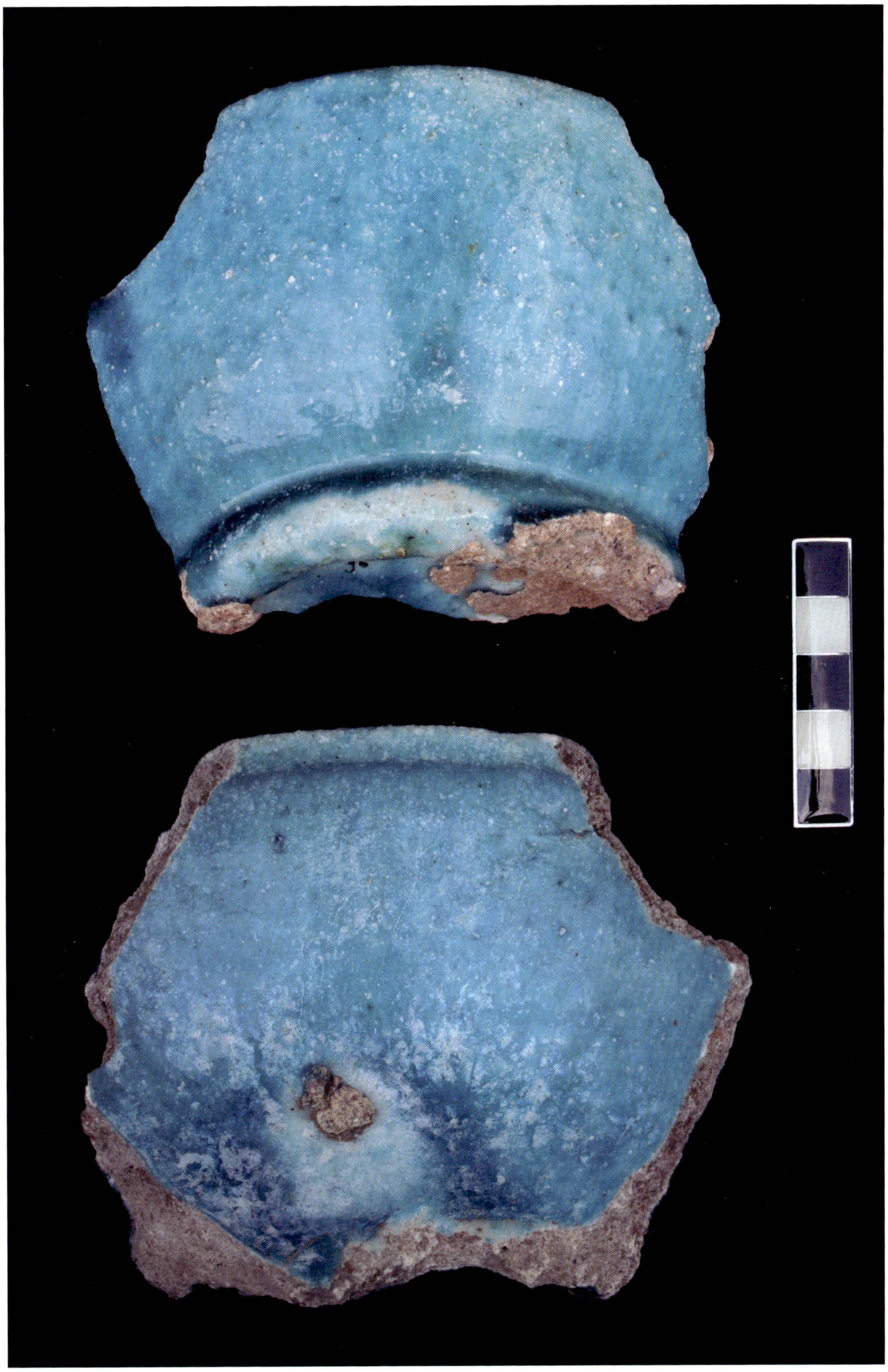

Colour Plate 5. Fragment presenting the complete profile (F-96) of a large convex bowl with inward curving rim and annular base T12.2. Traces of cones on the internal wall and the underside of the annular base can be seen. (Photo: P.T. Nicholson).

Colour Plate 6. Fragment of a hollow figurine of Serapis (F-1616) preserving only part of the head. Four waves of hair on the right temple which end in twists, on the top of the head, a circle in relief which may belong to the calathos. (Photo: P.T. Nicholson).